Navigating America:
Information Competency and Research
for the Twenty-First Century

First Edition

DAVID MOTON

GLORIA DUMLER

 **Higher Education**

Boston   Burr Ridge, IL   Dubuque, IA   New York   San Francisco   St. Louis
Bangkok   Bogotá   Caracas   Kuala Lumpur   Lisbon   London   Madrid   Mexico City
Milan   Montreal   New Delhi   Santiago   Seoul   Singapore   Sydney   Taipei   Toronto

Higher Education

Published by McGraw-Hill, an imprint of The McGraw-Hill Companies, Inc., 1221 Avenue of the Americas, New York, NY 10020. Copyright © 2010. All rights reserved. No part of this publication may be reproduced or distributed in any form or by any means, or stored in a database or retrieval system, without the prior written consent of The McGraw-Hill Companies, Inc., including, but not limited to, in any network or other electronic storage or transmission, or broadcast for distance learning.

This book is printed on acid-free paper.

5 6 7 8 9 0 QFR/QFR 1 5 4 3 2 1

ISBN: 978-0-07-338370-5
MHID: 0-07-338370-8

Editor in Chief: *Michael Ryan*
Publisher: *David Patterson*
Sponsoring Editor: *John Kindler*
Marketing Manager: *Allison Jones*
Developmental Editor: *Laura Olson*
Production Editor: *Regina Ernst*
Manuscript Editor: *Barbara Hacha*
Cover Designer: *Ashley Bedell*
Art Editor: *Sonia Brown*
Production Supervisor: *Rich Devitto*
Composition: *10/12 Times New Roman by Macmillan Publishing Solutions*
Printing: *45# New Era Matte Plus, Quad/Graphics*

Cover: Manhattan, New York: © Royalty-Free/Corbis. Hispanic male college student: Blend Images/ Andersen Ross.
Credits: The credits section for this book begins on page 731 and is considered an extension of the copyright page.

Library of Congress Cataloging-in-Publication Data
Moton, David.
  Navigating America: information competency and research for the twenty-first century/David Moton, Gloria Dumler.—1st ed.
    p. cm.
  Includes index.
  ISBN-13: 978-0-07-338370-5 (acid-free paper)
  ISBN-10: 0-07-338370-8 (acid-free paper) 1. Report writing. 2. Research. 3. College readers.
4. Information literacy. I. Dumler, Gloria. II. Title.
  LB2369.M68 2010
  001.4—dc22

                            2009000964

The Internet addresses listed in the text were accurate at the time of publication. The inclusion of a Web site does not indicate an endorsement by the authors or McGraw-Hill, and McGraw-Hill does not guarantee the accuracy of the information presented at these sites.

www.mhhe.com

DEDICATION

We dedicate this book—and any small way it helps someone figure out this world—to Henry and Avis Dumler, William "Fuzzy" Moton, and Lee Adams. These four would be the most proud of the work we've done here, and we wish they were still with us to see it.

BRIEF CONTENTS

CONTENTS

ALTERNATIVE TOC FOR SECTION 3: ANTHOLOGY OF READINGS

PREFACE FOR
INSTRUCTORS

Having taught composition and research writing for more than twenty years, we both noticed two major drawbacks when choosing textbooks to use for a course teaching freshmen how to write research papers: inadequate coverage of the skills needed for research in the world today (with its unprecedented proliferation of information), and the high cost to students of having to buy multiple texts for the class.

The first issue we wanted to address is the proliferation of information. Most texts focus on the skills needed to find academic information. There is so much more to modern-day research, however, that we were always left wanting when reading most textbooks. We wanted a text that would address how to cope with the vast amounts of information—both academic and mundane—from diverse media faced by our students, as well as the skills to uncover pertinent materials in their own research and, perhaps more importantly, to evaluate and qualify the sources they find.

The other issue we wanted to address was the cost to students of having to buy a number of textbooks to cover MLA/APA format, research tips, punctuation and grammar rules, and an anthology of readings. Aside from the cost of buying multiple texts, these books were also invariably guided by differing pedagogies and voices, and it was frustrating and time consuming trying to blend these divergent books into a cohesive whole in our classes.

We wrote *Navigating America: Information Competency and Research for the Twenty-First Century* to overcome these drawbacks and to give a focused and guided approach to the different types of materials found in the study of popular culture—and to do this in a voice that students will find friendly and accessible.

FOCUS ON INFORMATION COMPETENCY

With a constant stream of information hitting us all at every moment, learning how to find information is no longer the primary concern of college and university students in research classes. Indeed, finding information is virtually unavoidable, whether we are listening to our favorite radio stations driving to school or work, sitting in our living rooms with our remote controls, checking email and text messages on our "smart phones," or surfing the Net on our Wi-Fi laptops as we sip espresso in a neighborhood coffee shop. The real challenge is developing the ability to critically assess the information we receive in this steady barrage, and this is particularly important for today's students as they prepare to take their places in the modern world. Students must learn how to distinguish between dependable sources of information and attractive but shallow or inaccurate sources as they navigate through tangled webs of material.

The concept of information competency, also known as information literacy, is not new. Eighteenth-century mathematician and philosopher Marie Jean Antoine Nicolas Caritat, the Marquis de Condorcet, believed that every man and woman should become educated so that "they will be able to govern themselves according to their own knowledge; they will no longer be limited to a mechanical knowledge of the procedures of the arts or of professional routine; they will no longer depend for every trivial piece of business, every insignificant matter of instruction on clever men who rule over them in virtue of their necessary superiority." Condorcet believed that only through the competent mastery of information could human beings achieve a truly free and democratic society.

Two hundred years later, this idea is more important than it has ever been. Too many of us depend for our understanding of the vital issues of our day on the people who have the power to control information. Control of information can take many forms; it can mean limiting our access to certain types of information and flooding us with other types, leaving most of us in this intoxicatingly complex "Information Age" feeling rather bewildered and overwhelmed. In the nineties, author David Shenk coined the term "data smog" to describe the effect information overload can have on us, as too much and too many kinds of information come at us too quickly to be properly assimilated, creating confusion and anxiety instead of mastery and clarity. Information competency provides the way to see through this smog to the truths it obscures.

Many textbooks date themselves by neglecting to acknowledge the importance to our students of ideas gleaned from television, film, the Internet, advertising, the news media, and corporate and political advertising and propaganda. *Navigating America* is different, however. It helps train students to be competent in examining all types of information, not just traditional academic sources. (Even though television shows and films quickly fade from fashion, scholarly articles demonstrating effective modes of analysis will help students to critically evaluate the cultural impact of what is most current for them.) This emphasis on information competency is integrated throughout *Navigating America,* as the overview we provide ahead describes.

ALL-IN-ONE APPROACH

In addition to an overarching emphasis on information competency, *Navigating America* is designed to meet students' needs and budgets by serving as an all-purpose textbook for a research paper class. Typically, students in such a class have to buy a research and documentation guide, a thematic reader, and frequently a punctuation and grammar text, as well. Our book provides all three, as well as a section on identifying common logical fallacies and other errors in reasoning.

This all-in-one approach is not merely a time or cost saver, however; it is crucial to the content of this text. *Navigating America* is divided into three interconnected sections. The organization is logical but not prescriptive—we know from our own experiences that instructors assign sections of textbooks in the order that best suits their own purposes and teaching styles. We designed the sections to be as self-contained as possible and included clear references within chapters to related material in other chapters to allow teachers to use a "menu" approach when creating their own course plans. Following is a brief discussion of the goals and pedagogy of each section, as well as a snapshot of the contents in each chapter.

Section One (Chapters 1–10) covers research and writing skills, including active and critical reading; the basics of information competency (both academic and mass media); finding and narrowing paper topics; the writing process; essay structure; integrating sources into writing; forming and evaluating arguments; recognizing and avoiding plagiarism; and a guide to style, grammar, and punctuation.

- **Student Introduction.** In this, we discuss the importance of research and explain what information competency is, listing and describing its components, with an emphasis on critical thinking skills. We present arguments for the importance of critiquing popular culture, and we finish with a description of how students will use the three interconnected sections of the book.

- **Chapter 1: Finding a Topic.** We approach the problem of understanding assignments and finding a research paper topic with a number of student-friendly suggestions that break the task into manageable pieces and address different thinking and learning styles.

- **Chapter 2: Conducting Traditional Academic Research.** We offer practical examples of how to conduct traditional academic research with the technical information students will need to use libraries, as well as less-traditional sources for information, including conducting students' own field research. Our examples are chosen to help them to recognize that academic research isn't about hoops they have to jump through to please professors, but a way of finding accurate, in-depth information about issues fundamentally important to their own lives and futures.

- **Chapter 3: Conducting Other Types of Research.** We move on to an exploration of how to do research in the areas students commonly encounter in their day-to-day lives, exploring the skills needed for critically searching through mundane systems, such as the general Internet, print media, and television and radio. Although much of the material discussed in this chapter is nonscholarly and not intended for many types of academic paper, it still has a place in students' lives because this is the sort of information that they routinely consume, and they need to know how to evaluate it. (Also, some of these media may become the subjects they investigate and analyze in an academic paper.)

- **Chapter 4: Evaluating Sources and Reading Critically.** We show students how to objectively evaluate the reliability of the types of sources covered in both of the previous chapters and how to engage in ongoing evaluations through critical reading skills. Skills such as finding main ideas; questioning, outlining, and annotating sources; SASE; double-entry note taking; and writing the rhetorical précis are covered. The chapter includes samples of a student's work: an annotated article, a double-entry journal, and a rhetorical précis.

- **Chapter 5: Understanding Argument and Persuasion.** We discuss methods of evaluating arguments, elaborating on critical reading and evaluation skills that pertain specifically to argument and persuasion. This chapter shows students how to distinguish among and dissect different types of argument, as well as how they can argue logically and persuasively in their own writing, stressing the importance of keeping their audience in mind. We explain *ethos, logos,* and *pathos* and their importance for readers and writers, we demonstrate the Toulmin Method as a tool for analyzing other people's arguments and for constructing logical arguments and persuasive essays, and we also demonstrate the stages of the audience-based Rogerian Argument method. We finish with a discussion of how to identify common logical fallacies and other errors in reasoning, including suspect rhetorical devices.

- **Chapter 6: Navigating the Writing Process.** We help students to better understand their own idiosyncratic writing processes and how to figure out if they are primarily kinesthetic, auditory, or visual learners (or how they combine the different approaches). Understanding how their own brains work can help students who been frustrated because they have been trying to force themselves into writing practices that don't suit their own particular needs and strengths. We cover the elements of the writing process they most need in college: prewriting, note taking (including traditional note cards and electronic "e-cards," with samples for both types), research proposals, outlines, drafting, and revision and editing (including a discussion of the differences between the two and a checklist for each). Writing is recursive and often chaotic on the surface; our approach stresses the benefits of completing all the steps, no matter what the order, depending on individual students' needs and personal styles. The order in which we present these steps is also useful for any students who want to follow a linear approach because they enjoy a stronger sense of structure.

- **Chapter 7: Organizing the Essay.** We look at how to "build" essays, including research papers, addressing not only the organizational structure of the essay, but also issues of tone, audience, and voice. We discuss the rhetorical modes of writing and how they work in concert, and we demonstrate through graphic representations how the modes are suited to different writing situations.

- **Chapter 8: Integrating Sources into Writing.** We explain how to use information from sources within papers and the different levels of thought exhibited through summary, synthesis, and critical thought. We show how and when to write summaries and paraphrases, how to integrate quotations, and how to introduce sources to the audience, and we provide suggestions on how to integrate source information with the students' own ideas.

- **Chapter 9: Understanding and Avoiding Plagiarism.** We define and explain plagiarism, covering the different kinds (both deliberate and accidental), using a passage from George Orwell's "Politics and the English Language" to illustrate the various types of plagiarism and to demonstrate strategies for effectively and honestly using a source's words and ideas.

- **Chapter 10: Improving Style, Punctuation, and Grammar.** We avoid jargon and complicated explanations in favor of explanations and examples that fit student needs and levels of understanding (not those of professional grammarians). A punctuation pattern sheet and a numbered list identifying and explaining twenty-five common student errors, including examples and corrections, precede the guidelines and can be used by instructors as quick references in their notes on student papers. We realize that many instructors in classes at this level do not have the time nor inclination to cover basic style, punctuation, and grammar, so we have made the guidelines as "student-friendly" as possible for those students who want to review the material on their own. A web address at the end of the chapter directs them to online exercises. The website is not password protected and can be used by students who purchased used copies of the textbook.

Section Two (Chapters 11–14) thoroughly but accessibly explains and gives examples of MLA and APA format and provides sample annotated student papers in each style.

- **Chapter 11: Formatting the MLA-Style Paper.** We explain the basic format of an MLA-style paper, giving guidelines for the general appearance, titles, headers, tables, appendixes, and so on. It ends with a sample paper annotated to help the student recognize the necessary features of a properly formatted paper.

- **Chapter 12: Creating MLA-Style Parenthetical Citations.** We cover when to use in-text citations and how to create them for a variety of sources, showing a wide range of examples to address every situation a student is likely to encounter.

- **Chapter 13: Preparing the MLA List of Works Cited.** We explain how to organize lists of bibliographic entries, including lists of works cited, works consulted, and annotated bibliographies. We show how to create works-cited entries following the **2009 MLA guidelines,** which clarify the publication media of sources used for individual entries and greatly simplify the entries for Internet and database sources. The chapter begins with a directory of items to guide students to the explanations and examples they need for works-cited entries for sources ranging from books and journal articles to podcasts and YouTube clips. We realize that more and more software programs designed to format works-cited entries are being designed, but there are many variables to how citations are formed, and software will not identify and adjust to all the circumstances that influence an entry's proper format. Building these skills will help students in other areas of their lives, giving them practice in using manuals, making logical generalizations, and paying attention to detail.

- **Chapter 14: Using APA Style.** We discuss the differences between APA and MLA papers and format, cover APA-style parenthetical in-text citations and reference lists, providing numerous examples to cover traditional and nontraditional sources. The chapter ends with an annotated sample student APA paper on a topic that students cover in a psychology class.

Section Three (Chapters 15–22) is an anthology of readings tying varied topics related to popular culture to a discussion of information competency. The selections demonstrate a variety of reading levels and tones, and the topics were selected with students' needs and interests in mind. These selections encourage them to think critically about issues important in their own lives. The breadth of the selections allows instructors a variety of ways to tailor a semester, and the chapters are designed to stand alone, so their order can easily be varied. (See the sample syllabi in the online instructor's manual.) This also means that instructors can use *Navigating America* for numerous semesters without monotony.

Chapter 15: Introduction to Anthology of Readings

Chapter 16: Television

Chapter 17: Film

Chapter 18: The Internet

Chapter 19: Advertising

Chapter 20: Media Multinationals

Chapter 21: News Media

Chapter 22: Corporate America

MODEL PAPER INTEGRATION

Because all this material is presented in one book, we are able to make connections between the research methods and the actual articles themselves. To strengthen these connections, the model MLA student research paper (on a topic related to corporations and the media) is integrated throughout the entire text as we discuss writing as a comprehensive process. This integration allows students to see the entire writing process unfold before them, from prewriting to a final draft. In Section One, students learn all the steps of the writing process, from prewriting and note taking to outlining and organizing first and final drafts. Every example from each of these steps of writing comes from the sample MLA paper. Many of the articles and books cited in the model paper are included in the anthology section, so the students can get a better idea of the context of the original passages that are quoted, paraphrased, or summarized. The finished paper is annotated and presented in Chapter 11, which covers MLA formatting. Students will find the annotations helpful when formatting their own papers.

ANTHOLOGY OF READINGS

The final section of this book is an anthology of readings. Its contents focus on a popular culture theme, dealing with everything from television and film to the Internet and media ownership. However, it maintains the focus on information competency. Through the anthology section, students will learn how to better navigate the world around them and become competent not just with academic information, but with the types of information that they deal with constantly in their own lives.

The anthology of readings provides several key components to *Navigating America:*

- Chapters covering popular issues such as TV, film, the Internet (including MySpace, YouTube, and many other popular Internet topics), advertising, media ownership, news media, and corporate America.

- A thorough apparatus for each reading. The questions are flexible, so instructors can use them as presented or use some of them for in-class "quick writes," class discussions, and group work.

  - Prereading Questions: These questions are intended to be completed before the students read a given article, and they encourage an informed, focused reading of the piece. They should help students develop key components of effective reading practices—learning how to make predictions about texts and how to relate subject matter to their own ideas, experiences, and previous readings to get the most out of a selection.

  - Journal Topics: The process of reading and writing in conjunction is the best practice to improve any writer's skills. However, the constraints of strict essay prompts and students' worries about being marked wrong often hamper the creative process. The journal topics in *Navigating America* are designed as a means for students to write on topics they've just read about with no worries or penalties. They provide a chance for free writing, as they are designed to elicit "gut responses" to the readings rather than a strict dissection of content.

  - Questions for Critical Thought: These questions are intended to make students dig beneath the surfaces of the articles and to relate the information and ideas they contain to the real world. They are designed in part to encourage students to critique the strength of information and argumentation that the authors present. This is one of the best ways to generate critical thought. A key component to information competency is the ability to critically assess arguments; these questions help students practice that component. They typically include quotations and direct references to the reading to help students practice the crucial skills of evaluating specific arguments and of incorporating outside material into their own arguments. These questions are also designed to be useful in small-group discussions. Students learn best when they take an active part in learning and when they can share insights and ideas with each other.

  - Suggestions for Personal Research: After each reading selection, there are suggestions for students to conduct research in a variety of modes and settings, including the library, the Internet, television shows or movies, and their own field surveys. These questions are designed to help give students practice at following up on arguments with their own research and verifying the accuracy of information presented. They also may suggest research on specific issues and events related to themes raised in the various articles.

  - Multicultural Issues: Because many of these readings deal directly with the popular culture of the United States, these questions give students from other countries a chance to consider how these arguments apply to their own countries and backgrounds or to their new country, as well as encouraging students who grew up in the United States to look at issues from other perspectives, including those of other Americans of different backgrounds and ethnicities. Becoming competent in information and the media of the United States will be much easier if there are assignments generated with foreign students in mind.

- Vocabulary Terms: For students, a key factor in learning how to generate quality writing is expanding their vocabularies. The more challenging vocabulary terms from each article are highlighted in the lists that follow the questions. Also included in the vocabulary portion of the apparatus are occasional terms that we define for the students, titled "Terms for Clarification." These terms are often "insider" terms from certain media and disciplines, academic terms, foreign terms, and major historical figures.

- Interconnected Readings: In some chapters, there are paired readings designed to engage students in critical thought and spark class debate. These paired readings take different stands on the issues presented.

Navigating America was created to serve a research class's needs in one textbook. Its unifying focus on information competency will help students make intelligent decisions not only about what to quote, paraphrase, or summarize in a research paper, but also about how to avoid plagiarism and what ideas and evidence to trust in the world at large. *Navigating America* engages students. Every chapter and reading will get them closer to one overall objective: the ability to distinguish the different levels of reliability and relevance of the competing sources of information they consume. Students will study cultural and technological phenomena they find interesting, such as television and the Net, but in doing so, they'll learn to understand, interpret, and evaluate our information-driven world.

Students do not remain within the ivory tower their whole lives, and the ultimate test of a good text and a great course is what they carry with them when they leave the confines of the classroom. This book helps show them the research and documentation skills they need for the academic realm, but it also shows them the "real-life" relevance of information they find using traditional academic methods and how to master skills needed in the world outside of academia. Our younger students have inherited a very different world from the one most of their professors came of age in, and there are few tools out there to help them figure out how to interpret the data being hurled at them. *Navigating America* helps show them how to get to the truth behind all the information they encounter every day, no matter what the source is. At the same time, it is entertaining and provocative.

SUPPLEMENTS

For the Student

Online Learning Center: Powered by Catalyst 2.0, the Premier Online Tool for Writing and Research, the OLC offers new interactive writing tutors for different rhetorical patterns; tutorials on avoiding plagiarism and evaluating sources; more than 4,500 grammar exercises with personalized feedback for each response; Bibliomaker software for MLA, APA, Chicago, and CSE styles of documentation; and much more. Delivered in a state-of-the-art course management system featuring online peer-review utilities, a grade book, and communications tools, Catalyst 2.0 is available free with the *Navigating America* OLC. The OLC also includes additional material on plagiarism and documentation.

Navigating America **Student Website:** This website offers students additional study tips and exercises with keys on MLA and APA format and style, punctuation, and grammar, including exercises tailored to the needs of ESL and ESOL students.

For the Instructor:

Online Learning Center: The password-protected instructor version of the *Navigating America* Online Learning Center includes access to all student materials, as well as an instructor's manual and access to the instructor version of Catalyst 2.0.

Instructor's Manual: The electronic instructor's manual, available for download from the password-protected instructor OLC, guides instructors through *Navigating America* via teaching tips; sample syllabi demonstrating several ways the text can be used in both quarter and semester systems; and additional learning materials, such as exercises on MLA and APA format and style, punctuation, and grammar, including exercises tailored to the needs of ESL and ESOL students. (Exercises in the instructor's manual differ from the exercises with keys that students have online access to, so they can be assigned as homework or used as classroom exercises.)

ACKNOWLEDGEMENTS

We would like to thank several people who were indispensable in the concept, writing, proofing, and final product of *Navigating America.*

First, we would like to thank all those with the McGraw-Hill Companies who so expertly guided us through all that we did not know: Regina Ernst, Victoria Fullard, Barbara Hacha, Jesse Hassenger, and John Kindler. We also want to thank Laura Olson from Flat Irons Editing and everyone behind the scenes who made a copy, sent a fax, or otherwise had a hand in this endeavor.

Locally, our friends and colleagues shared their writing experience and other expertise, both before we started writing *Navigating America* and throughout the writing process. Though there are dozens who helped us in one way or another, we want to directly acknowledge the advice, criticism, and skill of Steven Carter, Ed Barton, Glenda Hudson, Cynthia Powell, Kim Flachmann, Michael Flachmann, David Koeth, Creighton Magers, Michael McNellis, Brad Ruff, Steve Walsh, Bill Parker, and, of course, our students who have taught us so much about learning.

To the book reviewers—you were more helpful and honest in your appraisal of our early drafts than we could have imagined. You really helped to shape this text with your feedback and guidance. Our thanks to:

Ana Arredondo, City College of Chicago

Leisa Bealleau, University of Southern Indiana

Sandra Clark, Anderson University

Deborah Coxwell-Teague, Florida State University

Holly DeGrow, Mt. Hood Community College

Larnell Dunkley, Harold Washington College

Robin Gallaher, Northwester Missouri State University

Judith Gardner, The University of Texas at San Antonio

Craig Goad, Northwest Missouri State University

Laura Halliday, Southern Illinois University

Josh Harrod, Radford University

Jane Hess, Pioneer Pacific College

Andrea Hills, Portland Community College

Tammy Jabin, Chemeketa Community College

Doug Joyce, McCook Community College

John Kivari, Erie Community College

Mary Louise Lang, Wharton County Jr. College

Jodie Marion, Mt. Hood Community College

Jody Ollenquist, Ferris State University

Cathi Parish, Mt. Hood Community College

Andrew Pegman, Cuyahoga Community College

Sydney Rice, Missouri University of Science and Technology

Kelly Ritter, Southern Connecticut State University

Linda Schmidt, Iowa Western Community College

Marti Singer, Georgia State University

Sue Spaulding, Anderson University

Nancy Taylor, Radford University

Greg Van Belle, Edmonds Community College

Carol Watt, Lane Community College

Cheryl Windham, Jones County Junior College

Melvin Wininger, Indiana University-Purdue University Indianapolis

Finally, we extend whatever exists beyond thanks to Albert Naso and Erica Fischer-Moton. This book would not exist without your love, support, patience (and squandered vacations).

STUDENT INTRODUCTION

Compare some of the following examples to events in your own life.

First, think of a time you and your friends have been sitting around chatting and have tried to think of the name of an actor from a particular film you used to love. All you can remember to say is "You know, that guy from the *Star Wars* prequels? He was in *Moulin Rouge* and *Train Spotting*? The main guy? He rode his motorcycle around the world in real life a couple of years ago?" After frustration and deliberation, you don't give up. You use your cell phone to call a friend who is a huge *Star Wars* fan. He's not home, so you log on to the Internet Movie Database (www.imdb.com) and do a quick search for *Star Wars*. You learn that his name is Ewen McGregor, and he played the young Obi Wan Kenobi. While you read his filmography, you get distracted by other details. You see Natalie Portman's name listed next to his (she, too, is in the movie), and you do a quick scan of her films. Some of her films are your favorites; many more you've never seen. You take note of one of Portman's earlier films, called *The Professional,* which one of your friends tells you is her all-time favorite, and you quickly hop over to Netflix.com and add this movie to your rental queue.

Since this is a website, of course you run into banner ads. One for a new cell phone catches your eye, so you click it and are tempted to sign a two-year contract to get the cell phone for free, but you have heard mixed reviews about the hardware. You decide to go to the website for *Consumer Reports* and see what it has to say about the phone, but when you find out you need a subscription to access the website, you simply check out the phone at Amazon.com and read some user reviews. One of the reviews leads you to a blog about phones and gadgets, so you visit this site as well to get more information, and you decide this is the phone for you. What started as a question about an actor became a quest for information, ultimately ending in an educated purchase of a new cell phone. The rabbit hole of the Internet is infinitely deep. Information washes over you in an endless stream.

Compare this scenario to what you experience in the contemporary classroom. Your business instructor assigns an upcoming research paper on the issue of the housing market in your hometown, and she says she wants two sources. Instead of doing traditional, academic library-based research, you choose to just hit Google. You do a search (housing prices + your hometown), and you get dozens (possibly hundreds) of newspaper articles, video clips from local news networks, and possibly even bigger pieces from CNN or MSNBC. You even find a blog on a MySpace page from a local real estate agent.

Information on the Net comes streaming at you so fast and furious that it's difficult to distinguish between the sources. You searched for the material, and you got hundreds of hits, but a lot of this material isn't material you should trust. Some of the news stories may seem very reliable at first glance, but they could be biased because they come from companies whose owners' primary objectives are to sell newspapers and ad space. Similarly, although you could trust a local governmental website that posts housing costs, you shouldn't trust contradicting statistics posted on the website of a real estate agent who may be distorting the information to try to sell houses. In fact, the information you get from many websites should not be trusted at all. We digest the information in good faith and believe in it—but we shouldn't.

Mainstream news is problematic, as well. Multinational media corporations own most news stations. Journalists are ultimately responsible to corporate hierarchies instead of to us, the populace. The primary goal of most news programs is to secure advertising revenue, not to inform the public. When sponsors dislike stories that may show their products, companies, favored political candidates, or industries in a bad light, they can threaten to pull millions of advertising dollars, so some important stories get altered, pulled, or postponed. This type of control of information happens with enough frequency to make us need to question our sources on a regular basis. Thus, even the news can't be trusted to provide reliable information at all times. But it's there. The news and the statistics and the polls—including "push polls"—surround us, and the flow of such information is incessant.

Quite plainly, finding information in volume is not difficult in our time. In fact, it's too easy. Even when we don't want to be pitched at or informed about products and news, it's hard to find a place where we can avoid these messages. Just one generation ago, a major skill taught in college was where to go to find information. Now, however, it finds us. The problem is value over volume. Learning how to find and evaluate reliable, unbiased, and complete information is even more crucial—and may be more difficult—than what previous generations of students had to face. Which "facts" are actually facts? Which ones are distorted, incomplete, or merely opinions? How do we know when we can trust a source?

Navigating America: Information Competency and Research for the Twenty-First Century is designed to help you answer such questions. It focuses on three areas: (1) mastering a set of skills known as "information competency" that is continually growing in importance for college classes, the workplace, and daily life, (2) writing effective essays, particularly college-level research papers, and (3) understanding the mass-media-driven, corporate-owned popular culture we all experience every day. You may, of course, be asking yourself, "Why do I need to do these things?" This introduction is a series of answers to students' frequently asked questions (FAQs). After you have read this introduction, your questions should be answered, and you will be well on your way to understanding the underlying philosophy of this text and becoming fluent in navigating the oceans of information we confront every day. Now, let's look at three frequently asked questions about writing and researching: What is **information competency** and why do I need to learn about it? Why do students have to write **research**

papers in the first place? Why should I want to study **the mass media and popular culture**?

Question 1: What Is Information Competency and Why Do I Need to Learn about It?

The ability to navigate the sea of data previously described and to come to reliable conclusions about the world is what we mean by "information competency" (also referred to as "information literacy"). This skill is growing increasingly important to everyone, and it's especially important in a college or university classroom. The originators of much of the information we are exposed to don't want us to think critically. They want us to take what they say at face value—buy their product, believe their pitch—and they are very persuasive. We have a real challenge ahead of us to analyze information thoroughly and logically.

Perhaps the most important skill you will hone by reading *Navigating America* is that of information competency. Unless you never watch TV, never go to movies, never listen to the radio, never play music, never go to plays or concerts, never log on to the Internet, and never read newspapers, magazines, or any books written more recently than a century ago, your view of the world rests largely on a foundation of information—most of which comes from popular culture. Understanding how this works requires information competency—knowing how to objectively find, view, read, and hear our popular culture in order to gain the ability to uncover, evaluate, accept, and reject information from the sources to which we are constantly exposed. Information competency has the following components:

- the ability to find, evaluate, and use information in all of its mediums and formats
- the ability to use libraries, academic research methods, and relevant technology
- the ability to recognize the ethical and legal implications of information
- the ability to apply critical thinking skills to information
- the ability to communicate information by assessing audiences and using language clearly, precisely, and unambiguously

A key term in the preceding list is **critical thinking.** Critical thinking involves the thoughtful, deliberate attempt to reason at the highest possible level: deeply, broadly, and open-mindedly. A vital component of critical thinking is developing the systematic habits of thought that favor seeking information actively and fairly. Critical thinkers are willing to accept psychological discomfort instead of instinctively rejecting new ideas that challenge their assumptions. Indeed, being a critical thinker means recognizing our own assumptions and being willing to treat them skeptically, rejecting a rigid, unchanging world view. Information competency and critical thought will help you to make the best-informed, most rational decisions in your daily life. It is also crucial to academic research and paper writing, as well as other aspects of your higher education.

Question 2: Why Do Students Have to Write Research Papers in the First Place?

If you watch a local news show on one of the major networks, one of the first things you may notice is what they call "eyewitness accounts." If there is a storm moving toward a region, a reporter is there, in the horrible weather, showing you that there is indeed a storm moving in. If there has been a shooting, the reporter will arrive on the scene and interview those who may have seen the tragic event. Conversely, you may see an interview about an important event on a national news channel that occurs back at the studio, but such interviews typically include a prominent scientist, politician, soldier, or law enforcement agent—in other words, the interview is with a nationally recognized expert in some important field. Without these accounts, the stories lose a lot of their appeal and persuasiveness.

Writing a paper presents similar demands. Unless you provide some proof, your audience will be left unconvinced and unimpressed. However, although journalists need to provide proof and a summary of events that have occurred, they are not obliged to go any further. For most journalists, their job is to report details to you and let you decide on their significance. As a writer, you're often asked to go beyond this stage. You don't just report, you interpret and come to conclusions for your audience. When you write a paper, like a reporter, you will begin with a fact-gathering phase, but a successful piece of argumentative research writing digs far deeper than this.

Many times in your college career, your instructors are going to ask for your own assessment, conclusion, or opinion in a paper. For such papers, you need to prove that you have thought critically about the topic, have paid attention to class readings and lectures, and can provide some unique insights. However, many professors are going to require that you write a paper based not on your own ideas, but on the ideas and evidence provided by genuine experts in the field. For this kind of assignment, you will need to conduct research and include the results of your research alongside your own thoughts in a paper. The purpose of this research is multifaceted. First, the appropriate use of summaries, paraphrases, and quotations lets the reader know that you yourself have become something of an expert. By displaying such research, you establish your own credibility and prove your own hard work by showing that you've read and understood some of the best scholars on your topic.

More important, however, is that research helps you to reach thoughtful, well-informed conclusions about matters of importance and to support your own arguments with logical reasoning and reliable evidence. If you make a claim in a paper that global warming is causing crops to fail in your hometown, nobody has any reason to believe you. If you can support your claim by analyzing and synthesizing the evidence and research methodology of major scientists around the world and applying this knowledge to what you find in farm reports and what you learn from local meteorologists and climatologists, your audience now has reason to believe that you may be on to something. In an academic research paper, virtually every point you make should have outside support proving that this idea is widely shared by real experts and can be supported through evidence, such as studies that can be replicated. There is strength in numbers, and this is never more evident than in research. You must use the work of other scholars in your paper—work that will help prove that your conclusions are solid.

If you've done quick or shoddy research, however, you will simply showcase your lack of preparation in your paper. Your audience will be able to tell the difference between a half-hour research session and deeper, quality research that takes days, weeks, or even months to complete. Also, if all your sources come from the same anthology, or you've used a general encyclopedia, it will prove that you haven't really explored your topic in depth. Moreover, if all your sources are strongly tilted toward one political or social agenda or one scholarly camp, it may prove that your paper hasn't been written to reach and report the truth, but simply to support the preconceived idea you had when you chose your topic. Be sure to be willing to let your research change your mind, and stay open minded during the entire process. If you set out to prove one point and ignore all other evidence in your report, it will be just as bad as providing no research at all.

Question 3: Why Should I Want to Study the Mass Media and Popular Culture?

If you grew up in New York City and met someone from Dallas on an airplane, you might not have much in common. You would go to different colleges, and you might have different majors, plan to work in different fields, and have different dreams and life aspirations. You really wouldn't have much to talk about—unless you talked about popular culture as defined by our consumption of mass media.

If you asked your fellow passenger if he or she watches your favorite television show, it could turn out that you have that in common, and you could talk about the show's characters and plot twists. You might listen to the same musical groups, both love Harry Potter, collect the same comic books, and see many of the same movies. Each of you may have a MySpace or Facebook page, a Second Life avatar, or a favorite video game. You could even discuss the brands of clothing, MP3 players, or cars that you prefer.

Somewhere in all of these and other franchises, series, sites, and brands, you can find common ground with a perfect stranger. Television shows, movies, songs, advertisements, YouTube videos, celebrity icons, and corporate mascots are all part of our own modern-day mythology. They are constantly in either the background or the forefront of our culture, yet they are seldom critically examined by most people. Most of us spend far more time watching or listening to mass electronic media than we do studying for school or reading the "canon" of great literature. In traditional education for most of the twentieth century, the kind many of your professors received, the "classics" of art, music, and literature were the only aspects of culture studied. This served as the common educational experience for entire generations. Most modern Americans have only the vaguest notions of any of these classics, however. Instead, various media create our shared experiences today.

The images and ideas disseminated by modern media are so deeply ingrained in most of us that they help to define the important themes of the day and shape our approaches to many fundamental aspects of our lives. The stories that play out on big and small screens collectively tell us how to court, date, get romantic with, marry, and even break up with a significant other. We see images of families in current TV shows and in reruns like *Malcolm in the Middle, Two and a Half Men*, and even *The Simpsons*. What we know—or think we know—about the American legal system may come from shows like *CSI* and the *Law and Order* franchise. Our ideas about doctors and hospitals are colored by shows like *Scrubs, ER,* and *House*. Graphic depictions of sexuality contribute to how many people think of sexual relationships. Traditionally, children would get the "birds and the bees speech" from either their father or their mother when they came of age. In the 1950s, teenagers would have to sneak a look at a copy of *Playboy* to see women in lingerie or female nudity (male nudity was nowhere to be found). Now, however, even children can find scantily clad models of both sexes, nudity, and suggestive acts in many facets of the media. Television ads for Victoria's Secret underwear display women moving suggestively in bras and panties—images that adult men would have had to go to "adult" bookstores and movie houses to see just a couple of generations ago. Some of the movie channels available through cable or satellite start showing what amounts to soft-core pornography after 11:00 p.m. If you visit Yahoo! for a Net search, you may have to think of how to word your search to avoid pornography more than you have to think of how to find it. Even with the best spam protection on the market, you have probably received quite a few emails purportedly from some fetching creature who wants to meet you or someone who claims to be able to tell you how to enlarge various parts of your anatomy.

For better or for worse, this is all part of what we call "popular culture." For many scholars, pop culture is the most important social, psychological, literary, and economic force in the modern era. News shows and propaganda can help to start and stop wars. A successful advertising campaign or hit music video can make us long to live certain lifestyles. Popular culture influences economics, politics, religion, and even our social or family lives. By studying the beginnings, the rapid rise and success, and the effects of the mass media and popular culture, you are studying some of the driving forces of the era in which we live. By understanding and being competent at deciphering the popular culture that we are immersed in every day, we can start to understand the powerful forces that create the world we live in.

Question 4: How Do I Use *Navigating America?*

This text is divided into three major sections that are designed to address the three key questions discussed previously. Section One is a guide for how to increase your skills as a researcher. In it, you will learn how to find academic sources, how to take effective and organized notes from sources, and how to determine what sources are worthy of use. Section One also shows how to research the world outside of the classroom. It will help illustrate how to use the Internet, television, radio, print media, and other sources of information that we are exposed to in our daily lives. You will also get a comprehensive look at plagiarism and how to avoid it. Accurately reporting where you got the information that you use and making sure that you don't represent someone else's ideas as your own are crucial to academic survival and success. This section also covers how to approach the writing process to make it easier and less daunting, how to narrow a topic to generate a strong thesis statement, how to structure an essay, how to incorporate material from sources into papers, how to avoid logical fallacies, how to understand the arguments of others, and how to improve your individual style and avoid errors in grammar and punctuation.

Section Two details the documentation styles of the Modern Language Association (MLA) and American Psychological Association (APA). When you write a formal research paper, you will probably need to follow the paper format guidelines of one of these styles, so they are presented here in detail, complete with sample research papers. This section will show you how to properly cite the sources you use in your papers and how to prepare works-cited papers for sources ranging from scholarly journals to YouTube videos.

Finally, Section Three is a reader with reading selections focusing on many of the issues driving popular culture and mass media today, such as advertising, multinational media conglomerates, corporations, television, film, and the Internet. These readings will help you practice active information competency by asking you to critically examine the types and modes of information and media that we experience every day.

If you read the selections in all three sections of this text, you will be well versed in how to conduct research for both your college classes and for your life outside college, and you will learn what makes the information machine tick. We hope this book will serve as a survival guide not just for college assignments, but for your daily, mediated lives. By the time you have finished studying *Navigating America,* you will have developed and honed skills that will serve you well in the lifelong process of maintaining mastery over information competency.

SECTION 1

Researching and Writing

1 CHAPTER

Finding a Topic

Jorge has to write a research paper, and the task seems overwhelming—he isn't even sure where to start. He has to choose a topic, and he's not sure of the best way of picking the right one. He decides to go to the college library for ideas. He passes the area where the magazines are displayed, and his eyes are drawn to a picture of a baseball player on the cover of one of them. He sees that the cover story is about steroid abuse in sports. He gets excited—he loves sports, especially baseball, and this sounds like a really great topic. He does a quick search of the library's electronic card catalog and academic databases, and he's delighted to see that there appears to be more than enough information on the topic. He gets straight to work.

A month later, Jorge has the first draft of a ten-page research paper. It discusses how widespread steroid abuse is in sports, and it explains how steroids work to improve performance and also how they hurt the bodies of the athletes who abuse them. He is proud of himself. As he heads for an appointment with his professor to go over the draft of the paper, he is full of confidence and good spirits. Twenty minutes later, when he leaves his professor's office, he is shaken and scared. His professor told him that he'll have to start over from scratch—the paper was supposed to be on the class's umbrella topic, not just on any topic a student found interesting. The final draft is due in five days.

Jorge can't imagine how he'll be able to do the research that he needs and write a paper in such a short amount of time. He is also deeply embarrassed—when he desperately told his teacher that he didn't know he was supposed to be writing a paper that had something to do with the media (the course umbrella topic), his professor pointed out with barely concealed exasperation that she'd mentioned this several times in class, that it was in the first paragraph of the research paper instructions, and that it was mentioned in the class syllabus, which she'd gone over on the very first day of the semester. She asked him if he'd bothered to read either the syllabus or the research paper handout. He had, he said—and he was telling the truth. He just hadn't read them since the first few weeks of class because he thought he'd remembered everything.

Jorge is in danger of failing his class for an all-too-common reason—he didn't double-check to make sure that he knew the exact criteria for the assigned paper. He remembers the professor discussing the research paper several times, but he somehow missed or forgot what she'd said about the umbrella topic. Sometimes, in class, it is easy for him to get distracted and think about other issues, like what he is going to do on the weekend, or his part-time job, or even what he is going to have for lunch after class. He'd written research papers before in high school. Listening to her talk about them was pretty boring, and he figured he knew what to do based on past experience. Glumly, he realizes that he may have to take the class again next semester.

Like Jorge, many students think that finding a good topic is the hardest part of the whole research paper process. It is also one of the most important parts of the process because a paper can fail simply because the student didn't understand the criteria for choosing a topic in the first place. Although some teachers will let students pick any topic that they want to write about, this is far less common in a college or university than it is in high school. Also, professors usually want students to write papers taking a particular approach, such as writing a research paper with a thesis that makes an argument that the paper will have to prove. A very good paper that is merely informative can fail—even if it is on a topic that the professor approves—because it doesn't advance and support an argument.

Although writing a paper includes many distinct steps, the first step—and for many, the hardest—is figuring out what you're going to write about. Generating the right topic is crucial because if you select an obscure topic, you may have difficulty researching the facts surrounding it, and if you pick a boring topic, you will have no personal interest in continuing the work. You must find something that can hold your interest, and this may be difficult if you don't know how to get started. If you make sure that you fully understand the writing assignment, figure out some creative ways to explore your possible topics, and manage to create a solid working thesis, you will have begun your journey as a research writer with an intriguing topic to help guide your work.

UNDERSTANDING THE ASSIGNMENT

There are several steps to take before you even start looking for your topic. First, pay close attention when your instructor talks about the criteria for your paper, and don't be afraid to ask questions in class—this could save your grade, especially if the assignment doesn't seem completely clear to you. Don't be embarrassed—countless students are afraid to ask questions because no one else is asking them, and they think everyone else "gets it." No one wants to look dumb. It could be that no one else quite gets it, either, and everyone is afraid of looking foolish by asking the professor to repeat or explain something. Also, sometimes people think they get it, but they don't. Although it isn't a bad idea to discuss assignments with classmates, don't rely on that—they may misinform you. Here are some suggestions to help you understand your assignment:

Explore the Instructions

If there is an instruction sheet—and there probably will be—make sure that you read it more than once, highlighting particularly important areas. Go over the assignment at least a couple of times—it is very easy to miss important details when you read it only once. Look for key verbs, like "evaluate," "analyze," "compare," and "contrast" (see box of important verbs, p. 4). Also, look to see if there are any technical terms, and use the dictionary if you don't know exactly what they mean. When you were younger, you were probably told to guess the meaning of words by looking at the context—this can lead you disastrously astray when you are reading material at more complex levels. Some professors give assignment sheets that break down how they will grade a paper. Go over this carefully. This may tell you exactly how many sources you need; what types of sources are required; what the minimum word count for the paper is; what documentation format your professor expects (such as MLA or APA); the sort of audience you are to imagine; and what approach you should take, such as argumentative, analytical, or informative. Your instructor may also expect you to make copies of all the sources that you use for your paper. Missing this and finding out about it after you've turned all your books back into the library can be a nightmare. Also, reread the class syllabus. You probably haven't looked at it in a while, and it may have a section that explains key points of this assignment.

IMPORTANT VERBS TO LOOK FOR IN ASSIGNMENT INSTRUCTIONS

Following is a list of key verbs to watch for when reading assignment instructions. Many students lose points on assignments unnecessarily because they failed to closely read the directions. If you decide to compare instead of define, for example, you could end up with a paper completely off topic.

Information verbs ask, "What do you know about a subject?"

- **Research:** find information from outside sources about your subject in order to establish facts and reach conclusions.
- **Summarize:** briefly state in your own words the main points of a passage, text, or argument.
- **Paraphrase:** state in your own words the entire content of a passage or argument.
- **Explain:** make an idea, situation, event, or problem clear by describing it in detail and providing relevant facts or ideas.
- **Define:** describe the meaning, nature, and scope of something.
- **Illustrate:** give clear and descriptive examples of your subject, showing how each example is connected to it.
- **Discuss:** provide a thorough and critical examination of the topic.
- **Trace:** describe how something has changed or developed from an earlier period to its current state.

Relation verbs ask, "How are events and ideas connected?"

- **Compare:** describe how two or more things are similar to each other.
- **Contrast:** describe how two or more things are different from each other.

- **Cause:** show how one or more events produce other events, phenomena, or conditions.
- **Relate:** describe the connections between two or more things.
- **Apply:** demonstrate how a theory or concept works in a given situation.

Interpretation verbs ask, "What does this material mean?"

- **Analyze:** break something down to its component parts to understand how they create or relate to the whole.
- **Support:** provide evidence and reasons to back up an assertion.
- **Evaluate:** place a value on; judge the worth of something (providing evidence and reasons).
- **Respond:** offer ideas in reply to a question, passage, text, or argument (providing evidence and reasons).
- **Argue:** provide evidence and reasons in support of or against an idea, action, or theory that is debatable (people could either agree or disagree) in order to persuade your audience that your assertions are the most logical and plausible.
- **Prove/justify:** provide evidence and reasons in support of an idea, action, or theory that is debatable in order to persuade your audience that your assertions are logical or factual.
- **Assess:** estimate the nature, abilities, qualities, or chances for success or failure of something.
- **Synthesize:** combine a number of ideas and facts from outside sources into a meaningful whole. (Don't just summarize—demonstrate interconnections in support of your paper's main purpose.)

When you are back in class, make sure that you go over important points and terms in the assignment with your professor if you are confused about any of them.

Talk to Your Instructor

Most professors like students to show an interest in the class—consider dropping by your professor's office or even asking for an appointment to take five minutes to explain what you think the assignment parameters are. This is a good way to make sure that you don't waste research and writing time because you misunderstood something. Come prepared with questions, as well, on areas the assignment sheet or lecture didn't cover or that confuse you a bit. You should not even begin your research or prewriting (see "Prewriting," p. 7) until you are quite clear about what types of information you will need, what types of sources, and how many sources. Your instructor may not want you to use certain types of sources at all, such as popular magazines or websites. During a one-on-one conversation, the professor may give you some additional information that helps you—you can even try out some preliminary topic ideas.

And remember—you may impress your professor by showing time-management and organizational skills, as well as initiative.

Organize

Keep a folder devoted just to the research paper. Keep all your handouts relating to the paper in this folder, and keep all the notes that you take in class and during appointments about the paper here, too. Take it with you when you are looking for sources and taking notes—we cannot stress enough how important it is to reread instructions regularly. It's so easy to forget an important detail or criterion during a busy quarter or semester. Also, sometimes rereading the assignment may give you an idea that you didn't have before. Make your own checklist if your instructor doesn't provide you with one. Here are questions you should ask about each topic that you consider:

1. Does the subject matter meet the class requirements? Some instructors require you to get approval of a topic before you begin research. If your instructor doesn't do this, ask for approval of your topic anyway, just to make sure it will work.

2. Is the subject one that will work well with the approach you are expected to take? Sometimes a topic that would be great for an informative paper will be difficult for you to generate an argumentative thesis about. Generally, if your instructor wants you to write an argumentative paper, for example, you'll be expected to generate a thesis that makes an assertion that reasonable people could either agree or disagree with—not just an obvious statement of fact.

3. Are enough sources of the right kinds readily available? Your instructor may enthusiastically approve a topic that meets the class criteria, but that doesn't mean that you'll be able to find enough sources. Your library may not have enough sources on this topic—or it could even be a topic that is so popular that most books that you need are constantly checked out. It isn't a bad idea to ask your instructor if your topic tends to be a very popular one—you might want to think in terms of a topic that won't have you competing with half the class for sources.

4. Are you personally interested in the topic? You will find reading about a topic a lot easier if it stimulates you. You may not have a choice, of course, but, as much as possible, try to choose a topic that you find appealing. On the other hand, it might be a good idea to stay away from a topic that you feel too passionately about—especially if the paper is supposed to be argumentative. We tend to agree with material that matches our own worldview and to disagree with material that challenges our worldview, and you can end up writing a paper that seems very logical and compelling to you, your friends, and your family, but your professor will be a lot more rigorous while grading it. The best choice is a topic that interests you about an issue where you have few or no preconceptions. You'll probably get a better grade, and you'll benefit by your new knowledge.

PREWRITING

In the quest to generate a topic you feel interested in, you will want to begin by pre-writing. Most students begin developing a research topic by completing some type of prewriting—a session of writing designed to generate ideas for you as a writer, not writing intended to present ideas to an audience. Prewriting is typically very informal, and you are the only audience it will probably ever have.

Usually, writing a paper requires you to use your imagination to think up specific details to include. In fact, the difference between an "A" paper and a "B" paper is often imaginative, even unique content that the instructor hasn't run into before. Professors read scores of papers, most of which only begin to explore the possibilities. By complet-ing some thought-provoking prewriting, you're more likely to come up with insightful ideas that go beyond the obvious. This type of creative, deep writing is the goal of any paper, and this type of thought is almost always generated by some type of prewriting.

The goal of any prewriting exercise is to generate a workable thesis. You may have some good ideas about what you plan to say in your paper, but after a session of prewriting, you'll find that you have a much more supportable idea of your thesis statement. The following types of prewriting exercises may be used by anyone, but we've noted where an exercise is particularly well suited to a kinesthetic, or an auditory, or a visual learner. Experiment with several of them to understand which ones work best for your own learning and writing style. Often the best papers are the result of a few different types of prewriting.

Also, although the assumption here is that you're writing a research paper, you may consider these prewriting techniques for essays or for brief in-class writing assignments. Even a quick essay question on a history exam will benefit from a ninety-second prewriting session. It will help to generate ideas that dig below the surface.

Subliminal Prewriting

The first true step to prewriting begins as soon as you read your essay prompt. Some quiet portion of the brain begins mulling over the topic right away. If you're assigned a paper on the topic of television, you may be at a stoplight in between songs on the radio, and your mind will drift to the topic. You'll realize that the history of television may be interesting to you, or you'll think about some of your favorite shows. The light changes, a song comes on, your brain does something else with its energies. A day later, in line at the cafeteria, you wonder what different stages there may have been in the history of televi-sion. Didn't it all start with the radio? Weren't the first TV shows the ones in the 1950s? You buy your sandwich and a bottle of juice, eat lunch, and move on with the day.

Although this isn't a formal type of prewriting that you can submit to your instruc-tor, it's important to note that some form of prewriting begins almost instantly. When you have your first breakthroughs on your paper topic, you've probably subconsciously thought of them while performing some everyday, unrelated task.

Listing

The most basic form of prewriting is to compile a simple list of ideas. Take the paper topic and make a list of everything that comes to mind—don't worry if it is not entirely on the same topic. Everything that comes to mind, no matter how small, should make this list.

Let's say your professor just gave you your first paper topic. You're asked to write a paper that explores some American corporation and the impact it has on our society. You decide to write about the companies that own the news media. To prewrite for this paper, you might decide to make a list of different aspects of the news media. A lot of ideas that come up in this prewriting will never make it to the final paper, but the key is to write as much as you can, just like the example that follows.

Note: Most of the examples of writing found in this textbook were part of the writing process for the actual sample student paper found on pages 255–262. Feel free to visit this paper to see how the prewriting in this chapter may have shaped the final product.

NEWS MEDIA

1. Television—

> Local news from my home town—I really hate how cheap local commercials are.
>
> National news stories on major networks like NBC and CBS.
>
> Cable networks—CNN, MSNBC, etc.
>
> News talk shows like *Hardball,* where they get people on to answer questions.

2. Fake News—

> *Saturday Night Live's* "Weekend Update." I've loved this since I was a kid.
>
> *The Daily Show.*
>
> *The Colbert Report.*
>
> *Real Time with Bill Maher.*
>
> *The Ironic Times* and *The Onion* (on the Net).

3. Real News on the Net—

> Yahoo and sites like that. Where do they get all those news stories from?
>
> The Associated Press.
>
> Different newspapers are found online. How does that work? Do you pay for them?
>
> Check to see if CNN and other TV stations have websites.

4. Other Technology—

> Podcasts.
>
> YouTube.
>
> Downloadable news shows on pay per view.

5. Who owns all this?

> Which corporations own all the stuff listed above?

Clustering

A cluster is a popular way to generate a list, but it has a more interesting graphic interface. You start with the central idea in the center of the page in a big circle. Each subtopic is a branch from this main topic, each in its own circle. Each subtopic may then have its own branch, and so on, leading to a very complex matrix of ideas. You could use a different color ink to circle or highlight certain ideas to rank them and keep the cluster visually engaging. An example follows:

Example:

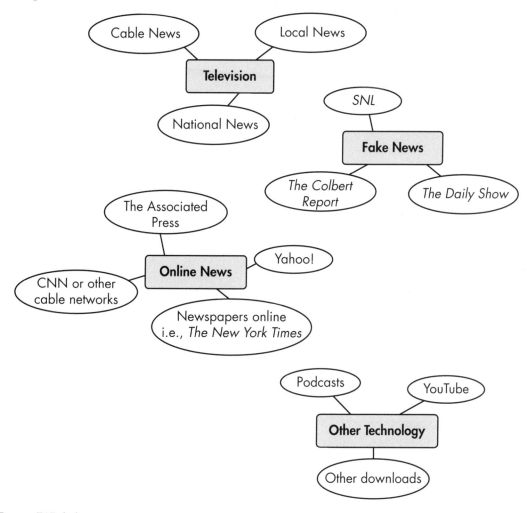

Free Writing

This is one of the most common forms of prewriting. To do it, you simply time yourself and let yourself write. A key factor in free writing is to do it in the most comfortable place possible. If you write best on your computer, sit down at your keyboard. If you're better with pen and paper in the library, go there. If you need music or total silence or the background hum of the television to get creative, make that happen before you free write. For a longer paper, you might want to give yourself ten or fifteen minutes to free write. Again, don't worry about grammar or spelling or any other technical issues. Set a timer, just start writing, and don't stop until the timer goes off. Even if you have to write "I have nothing to say" over and over for a few minutes, eventually, you'll boot your brain up and start to generate ideas. Exploring your own thoughts through this type of open-ended, private writing is very helpful.

Note that the following example starts somewhat off topic, and only gradually does the student come up with some ideas that would be appropriate for a paper:

Okay, I have to write about a corporation. I don't really care about any corporations out there. How boring. The only thing I really care about is watching TV. I guess I could write about TV. Don't corporations own all the stations and TV shows? Maybe I could look at those corporations and see what they do to impact society. I know they have a huge impact on us because everyone watches TV, but I don't know how big that influence is.

I mean, how big an influence can a diaper commercial have on the world at large?! I guess the news is pretty important, though. I watch it every so often with my parents. I know there are totally different types of news. There's the local stuff that shows weather and car wrecks and local sports scores and whatever. There's also the different national ones that come on the major television networks and the cable channels like MSNBC. I wonder who owns those channels? I wonder if they care more about advertising and making money than they do reporting important news. Sometimes it seems that all we hear about are celebrity break-ups, pop stars getting drunk or busted, and other crap about famous people's lives that I couldn't care less about.

Okay, maybe that's worth looking into. I can see who owns the news stations (and I guess newspapers and stuff while I'm at it). I can also see if they ever take bribes from corporations to not show certain news stories or do cover-ups of major abuses or crimes or anything. Probably not, but it would be an interesting paper if they did. . . . I'll talk to Dr. Carter about it during his office hours. When I had his class, he used to talk about corporate power all the time—maybe he's a good place to start . . . .

Journaling

Keeping a journal is similar to free writing, but it isn't timed, and it is ongoing. The word journal comes from the Latin word *diurnalis,* which means "daily." This is the key to keeping a journal—write daily. Whether it's for two minutes or two hours, taking time out to jot down your thoughts on paper will ensure that writing is a comfortable method of communication for you.

For journal prewriting, you keep a daily record of thoughts as you explore different ideas for your paper topic. You might have several sessions of free writing in your journal at the beginning of the paper-writing process, and you'll keep your journal updated as you continue writing. The journal is particularly helpful during longer research projects because the process of researching uncovers so many new ideas you could never have predicted. The journal is a great place to reflect on new ideas you've had and to keep streamlining your specific topic and thesis statement.

Journaling On the Go

This isn't a prewriting technique so much as a really good idea. Keeping a journal on the go is very important for longer papers. Many of you have been in line at the store or waiting while on hold with your credit card company and had a great idea for a paper, one that would finally make it all come together. However, a week later, when you sat down to write your paper, this idea had vanished. Every writer has great moments of clarity that generate ideas that are lost because they were never written down. The journal on the go is simply a small notebook you can keep in a pocket, purse, or backpack you always have with you. If you're a techie, you could even use a cell phone or similar device to take some notes; you could then email these notes to yourself as you think of them and sort them out later when you're at your computer. Also, if you know you aren't organized enough to do this type of regular note keeping, even a napkin at a restaurant or the back of a fast food receipt on your floorboard will do. When one of these ideas strikes you, make sure you write it down right away—or call yourself and leave a voicemail message. Even if you're in the shower or it's the middle of the night and you just woke up, get your idea down on paper or recorded in some way and save yourself frustration later.

Brainstorming

A brainstorm is a group-generated list. Get a few people from your class together for a cup of coffee or try this technique while waiting for class to start. The point is that you make a list with some colleagues because someone else in the group is bound to think of ideas you wouldn't have thought of on your own. On top of that, the ideas that you come up with may inspire someone else to come up with something neither of you could have thought up on your own. Brainstorming is one of the best ways to prewrite because it can often be fun working with other people, and it can help you come up with ideas you wouldn't have gotten otherwise. It may take more preparation to get people together, but this method of prewriting can be very helpful.

Journalistic Questions

Students in journalism classes are often taught the "Five Ws": Who, What, When, Where, and Why. No matter what class you are taking, if you have to write a research paper, these questions can help you with your topic. Don't look at the list as purely linear, either—some questions you ask will take you back to other, earlier types of questions and help you fine-tune your topic. Following are some journalistic questions that were asked by the student who wrote the paper reproduced in Chapter 11.

1. **Who: Who is most affected by the issue? Who has had the most impact on the issue?** Different issues have different demographic relevance (demographics are statistical data relating to particular populations and subgroups); if your paper is going to be about the mass media and corporate ownership, these issues affect almost everyone—but you could focus on television shows or even whole networks aimed at children, men, women, your own age group, ethnic minorities, or people with particular political leanings.

Example: Who owns the major television networks and print sources, such as magazines and newspapers? Who pays for the television ads? Who decides what stories air on the nightly news? Who watches certain television networks? Who is affected by media corporations owning so much of our airwaves? Who decides the laws that govern the system of media ownership?

2. **What: What problems are connected with the issue? What can be done about the problems?** With a paper topic as broad as the media, you could look at any number of issues and ask questions to generate research ideas.

   Example: What has been the impact of television on society? Do some television networks depict stereotypes about gender, age, or religious or racial groups? Do any corporations fail to cover major news stories because such coverage might offend sponsors and reduce advertising revenue? Do any news networks show biased or distorted news? What can people do to become more critical consumers of television and the news?

3. **When: When is this issue happening? Or when did it happen?** Your paper on the media could look at the evolution of the American media and explore the history of the subject you have chosen.

   Example: When did the concept of "freedom of speech" first get introduced? When has it come under attack? When did laws change to let corporations own as much of the media as they do now? When did the Internet become a key player in disseminating the news? When did the tone and approach of news programs shift from dignified and serious reporting to an emphasis in many programs and networks on entertainment and spin? In 1958, journalist Edward R. Murrow wrote that "television in the main is being used to distract, delude, amuse and insulate us." In 1961, FCC Chairman Newton Minow described American television as a "vast wasteland." Are either of these claims applicable today?

4. **Where: Where is this issue relevant?** For some topics, the first answer that comes to mind may be "everywhere," but you can narrow this by choosing particular areas. You could compare and contrast television programming in different countries. Note that in the example that follows, the questions may not start with the question word "where," but they still ask questions about locations and places.

   Example: Where else other than America are there so many media outlets? In what countries are the headquarters of the corporations that own most of the world's media outlets? How do nations like France, Germany, Italy, and the United Kingdom compare to the United States? What is their programming for children like? Does advertising dominate the programming of different countries equally? Do some governments subsidize networks? Do all the countries looked at have "public television," and how do the characteristics differ? What governmental regulations do they have when it comes to programming with violent or sexual content?

5. **Why: Why is this issue a problem? Why is it happening?** "Why" questions can be the meatiest when you are trying to generate topic ideas for argumentative papers because the answers to the questions often suggest debatable issues—or may even be debatable themselves.

Example: Why are reality shows popular (and with whom)? Why have programs gotten more graphic? Why has television programming changed over the years? Why should people take an interest in these changes? Why do many people prefer "soft" stories about celebrities over "hard" news that influences their lives? Why have so many laws about media ownership and monopolies changed? Why do some people prefer getting their news on television and others prefer the Internet, radio, or newspapers?

Secondary Prewriting

If you have the time, it may be wise to do a second set of prewriting steps after you're done with the first. Secondary prewriting can use any of the techniques of prewriting listed earlier. For example, after you have generated a list, pick two or three of the most promising items on the list and make a new list for each one of them. If you liked the idea of focusing your paper on news media, start a new list and aim for a greater degree of detail. You'll be amazed by how many more ideas you'll dream up for "News" by dedicating a new list to that topic. The same can (and should) be done for each of the types of prewriting. If you completed a ten-minute free writing session, pick an idea that really popped off the page and complete a five-minute free writing session on this more-focused idea. If you're trying to generate fresh ideas for your paper, a second wave of prewriting is a great way to do it.

Research Proposals

Another great tool to help you develop your ideas and generate a thesis statement is a formal research proposal. For more information on research proposals, see Chapter 6.

WRITING QUESTIONS

Although prewriting will help you to generate a basic idea to run with early in your writing process, for many a challenge still lies ahead. Initiating scholarly research and refining your final thesis can be very daunting tasks. Many students think about all the possible topics and consider the thousands and thousands of books and journal articles and millions of websites out there that contain information, and they start to shut down. What idea(s) should you focus on? Where do you start such a process? How do you decide the final topic with enough confidence to proceed?

A good way for many students is to generate writing questions. **Writing questions** are questions you develop that will help guide your initial research; each answer you find will get you closer to your final topic and thesis statement. You could do writing questions in two ways: 1) Exploration questions that are intended to help you shift from basic topic to specific thesis. 2) Research questions that will guide you through the research process.

Exploration Questions

Exploration questions are designed to help you go from the general (the initial thoughts you have after prewriting) to the specific (a working thesis) by exploring your own ideas, attitudes, and assumptions at the start of a project. These questions will help you understand the purpose of your writing, your audience, what is already known about the subject, even ideas you already have that can help you to develop your topic. Here are some questions you may ask yourself at this stage:

Who is my audience?

What is the purpose of my paper (to argue, inform, persuade . . .)? (See Rhetorical Modes of Writing on page 164.)

What do I already know about this subject?

What are my preconceived notions on this subject?

Do I have anything new to say about this subject?

What are the pros and cons of this subject?

Who do I already know that can help me understand this subject better?

Research Questions

After you have decided on your basic topic, you may want to do some preliminary research before you try to refine your thesis. Doing some quick Internet searches or taking a brief look at your library holdings can help to guide you by giving you an idea on the information and viewpoints available. (Note that many writers generate a list of research questions much later in the process to guide not only their early topic development but the final draft of their paper.) The research questions should be designed to give you guidance while starting either preliminary or final research for your paper. After you get started in your research, you may find that it takes on a life of its own and that such questions are no longer necessary. Having a list of them at your disposal, however, will help keep you from getting writer's block and not knowing how to proceed when you are in the library. (For more on how to research, see Chapters 2 and 3.) Here are a few sample research questions:

What is the history of this subject?

Who are the key participants and scholars on this subject?

Are there any key books/articles that have helped to define this subject so far?

What is already known about this subject?

What is yet to be discovered about this subject?

What are some key terms and jargon that may be used in this subject?

Are there opposing camps on this subject, and if so, what side will I support?

Are there any local experts (including professors) who can help me find more information?

Are there any good websites on this topic?

Is there any journalistic coverage of this topic?

DEVELOPING A WORKING THESIS

The whole point of completing a session of prewriting and generating writing questions is to help you develop a working thesis statement. You start with hundreds of topics to choose from, and prewriting helps you to focus on one issue or one set of closely related issues. Some students, however, confuse topics with thesis statements. A thesis statement is specific and makes an assertion. Your instructor will typically ask for an argumentative, or persuasive, thesis. An argumentative thesis is more than just a statement of fact—it must make an assertion that is debatable (and often expresses proof of critical thought). Also, a thesis statement is just one sentence long, and it is declarative—not a question. When you are writing your introduction, you may find it useful to introduce your thesis by asking a question, but you should not confuse the two. In fact, a thesis should always present an answer to a question, not the question itself.

Here is a simple formula to help you understand what a thesis is:

Topic + Assertion = Thesis

Here are some sample topics:

The ratio of serious news coverage to entertainment and celebrity coverage.

The depiction of young African American men.

Violent content in children's programs.

To go the next step and turn these into thesis statements, remember the following criteria:

A good thesis statement is

- An assertion, not a question
- One sentence long
- Specific

And, if your paper is supposed to be argumentative, it is

- Debatable, not just a statement of a fact

With these criteria in mind, we can generate a number of thesis statements for each topic. Here are a few:

A disproportionate amount of news coverage is devoted to entertainment stories and celebrities' antics because the media are owned by corporations that maximize profits by feeding and encouraging the public's taste for sensation.

Notice that more than one aspect of the preceding thesis is debatable. Is the coverage of entertainment and celebrities "disproportionate"? If so, by what criteria? Are decisions by corporate owners responsible? Does the public in general have a "taste for sensation" that is, as implied, as strong as or stronger than its taste for serious news? All these points would have to be addressed and supported by evidence in the research paper.

Television programs that depict young African American males tend to show them as violent, criminal, drug using, and connected to gangs.

A thesis like this invites comparison and contrast—how are young males of other races depicted? Do television programs tend to stereotype all young males in the same manner, or does race seem to play a clear role? Are young males of any other races similarly stereotyped?

The increase in the amount and severity of violent acts observed by children on television correlates with increased aggressive behavior and violence among some children.

The framer of this statement is being justifiably cautious—writers must be wary of sweeping generalizations. The claim says "correlates with," instead of "causes," and specifies "some children" without trying to claim that all children are affected in the same way.

All of the preceding thesis statements can be modified as students do more research and learn new facts. Also, each of them can be modified to suggest a course of action, as with the following example:

The increase in the amount and severity of violent acts observed by children on television correlates with increased aggressive behavior and violence among some children, so parents should monitor children's television viewing, limiting it to less than five hours a week and installing parental controls to screen out programs with violent content.

Notice that these thesis statements are fairly specific. You wouldn't be in any doubt about what the writer of any of these was going to try to prove in a paper. This is important because one of the biggest problems in student writing (related to thesis statements) is that they often do not make clear assertions about what the essay or research paper is trying to prove. The thesis is what your imagined audience needs in order to understand what position you are taking. Therefore, when you are writing your thesis, imagine the general reader. You know what your paper is about—would anyone reading just this single sentence know? It wouldn't hurt to try it out on a couple of friends to see. And don't forget that your thesis statement is what your professor will be starting with when preparing to judge just how successful you are in making your case.

You should also remember that the thesis you generate at this point is just a working thesis. You need it to help keep you focused as you do your research and because you want to make sure that your topic can generate a debatable position for you to take if that is part of the research paper requirements. Don't let your working thesis close your mind to information that challenges it. As you conduct more research, your thesis may evolve—you may even end up taking a position opposite to the one you started out with. You will be graded on your paper's strength of argument, supporting evidence, and thoroughness of research. Altering your content to fit the thesis is like "letting the tail wag the dog."

FIVE PARAGRAPH ESSAYS

You may have had high school or developmental writing classes where your instructors asked you to create an essay based on another formula, sometimes called "the five paragraph monster" by college or university instructors. This formula required an introductory paragraph, three body paragraphs, and a conclusion. This formula is basically a rubric for constructing a very simple essay; it is not a plan of action for the rest of your academic writing career. This formula has an accompanying process for constructing a thesis statement:

"_____ is _____ because [1] _____, [2] _____, and [3] _____."

It's time to lose the training wheels. There is no magic number of paragraphs for essays or research papers, and there is no magic number of premises that must be included in a thesis to shore up your assertion. You may not even be able to list all of your "becauses" in your thesis because you are writing about fairly complex issues now. Note that none of the sample thesis statements we provided fit the "A is B because 1, 2, and 3" pattern. This doesn't mean that you cannot or should not generate a thesis statement that fits the pattern, but don't limit yourself to it. It might be a good place to start; just remember that you can always refine it to make it more polished and interesting when you are finishing later drafts of your paper.

Conducting Traditional Academic Research

You're sitting in class, and your teacher asks you to write a paper on the history of television. No problem. You love TV, watch it all the time, and have plenty to say about it. She explains the details of the paper, and as you watch the clock, hoping you'll get out a few minutes early, you hear her say a few dreaded words: "I want eight outside sources on this paper." Your heart sinks. You've written very few research papers in your life, and you've never used the library where you're going to school right now. You even start to wonder if it's too late to drop the class, but because this course is a requirement for your major, you really have no choice. You're going to have to do some research. The last time you wrote a paper, you hit Google and found a lot of great articles; you quoted them and listed them correctly in parenthetical citations and on the works-cited page. However, your teacher marked you down because your sources weren't good enough. You're really not sure how to find the right sources, or even what makes one source scholarly and another one unacceptable, and you're starting to freak out just a little.

Don't panic. This reaction is typical when it comes to writing papers. In fact, one of the most fundamental steps to mastering information competency is to understand what sources you should and shouldn't trust. When writing an academic paper, you'll want to present top-notch sources so that your audience will respect your arguments. The trouble is, trustworthy sources are often hard to find, and many are not online yet. To do proper research, you'll probably have to go to an academic library and hit the stacks of books yourself.

Many instructors will insist that your paper draw exclusively on scholarly sources—work written by and for scholars. This chapter focuses on how to find such sources and use them in your paper. (Other professors will allow sources that are less traditionally academic in nature; for tips on using those sources, see Chapter 3.) To gain competency over academic information, you must work toward a couple of goals. First, you must understand the tricks to navigating an academic library, and second, you must understand the basics of the modern academic search engine.

Research Tip: Librarians

Never forget to talk to your reference librarians. They are specialists in research and search engines. If they can't find the information you are looking for, it probably doesn't exist. Most librarians also know the different instructors on your campus, and they understand their expectations. They may even be able to suggest people you could interview to learn more about your subject. Finally, most libraries offer tours to groups and individuals as well as workshops and classes dedicated to research skills. Talk to your local librarians and your instructor to see if such options exist and are right for you.

NAVIGATING THE LIBRARY

Systems of Classification

The first step in understanding how a library works is to understand the basic system it uses to classify and catalog its sources. Without a basic knowledge of this, you'll never find the book you want, even if it's sitting on a shelf waiting for you to find it.

There are two primary systems used to organize a library's holdings in the United States: the Library of Congress Classification system (LCC) and the Dewey Decimal Classification system (DDC). Both of these systems generate specific numbers and letters to identify particular books. No matter what library you visit, the identifying information assigned to a book within each system will be the same.

To locate a book within a library, you need only match up the call number you've discovered when you searched the library's catalog with the number pasted on the spine of the book on the shelves (also known as "the stacks"). A library will use one of these two systems (your school's library will probably use the Library of Congress system, and your public library will probably use the Dewey Decimal system), so being familiar with both will help you tremendously when you use different libraries. There are also classification systems used commercially, the ISBN and ISSN systems, that ensure that every book published has a unique number for cataloging and ordering purposes.

An immediate goal of doing research is simply to find the books you're interested in. You will need to log on to a library catalog search engine, which in most libraries has replaced the outdated card catalog system, and identify pertinent books and find their call numbers. However, understanding the two classification systems will help you understand the numbers the search engine gives you. (For more information on how to use the search engines, see the Library Catalog Searches section on p. 22.)

LIBRARY OF CONGRESS CLASSIFICATION

If you're researching in an American academic library at the college or university level, there's a good chance your library will use the Library of Congress Classification system. The Library of Congress is the largest library in the world, containing more than 130 million items on approximately 530 miles of bookshelves. With so many books to organize, librarians developed a system of classification that makes organization easier and more uniform. When you look up a book using this system, you'll get a call number, such as the following: **PR2894.W43 2003.** Although this may look like a stream of random numbers, the system has its own logic: it divides all fields of study into twenty-one categories, each assigned a letter based on the following list.

A: General Works

B: Philosophy, Psychology, Religion

C: Auxiliary Sciences of History

D: World History and History of Europe, Asia, Africa, Australia, New Zealand, etc.

E: History of the Americas

F: History of the Americas

G: Geography, Anthropology, Recreation

H: Social Sciences

J: Political Science

K: Law

L: Education

M: Music and Books on Music

N: Fine Arts

P: Language and Literature

Q: Science

R: Medicine

S: Agriculture

T: Technology

U: Military Science

V: Naval Science

Z: Bibliography, Library Science, Information Resources (General)

Note: For a more comprehensive look at this list and the subdivisions, visit the Library of Congress website at http://www.loc.gov/catdir/cpso/lcco/lcco.html.

These twenty-one categories are also broken down into subcategories. For example, category P is language and literature, but if you see PS, you're dealing with American Literature, and PR is the prefix for English Literature. To get even more specific, the system then gives books a series of between one and four numbers, called a "caption." Each specific area of study is assigned a caption of numbers. For example, the call number **PR2894.W43 2003** is for a book on William Shakespeare called *Shakespeare: For All Time,* written by Stanley Wells in the year 2003. A similar call number, **PR2894. D88 1989,** is for a book that is also on the topic of Shakespeare: *William Shakespeare: A Literary Life,* by Richard Dutton, published in 1989.

Notice that both call numbers start with PR for English Literature and both have the caption number 2894, which is a number for the study of Shakespeare. Thus, any book that starts with PR2894 will be on the topic of Shakespeare, no matter what library the book is found in. As you explore your major field of study more and write more research papers, you'll find yourself slowly getting familiar with the call numbers in your particular area of interest.

Research Tip: Search the Stacks

Because Library of Congress call numbers follow this logical pattern, it is a great idea to get one or two good call numbers and then head back to the shelves where the books are located. After you find one book, its neighbors are sure to be on similar topics. Pick up the books on either side of the one you found through the search engine and scan through their tables of contents and indexes. You can find some great resources by browsing through these pages.

DEWEY DECIMAL CLASSIFICATION

If you're researching at a local public library or high school library, you're likely to find the Dewey Decimal Classification system in use instead of the LCC. The Dewey Decimal system is similar to the Library of Congress system in that it assigns a code for a general category and then gets more specific by adding a decimal followed by more numbers and letters to that initial number.

The Dewey Decimal system divides all knowledge into ten major categories, each with a basic three-digit number:

- 000   Generalities
- 100   Philosophy and Psychology
- 200   Religion
- 300   Social Sciences
- 400   Language
- 500   Natural Science and Mathematics
- 600   Technology (Applied Sciences)
- 700   The Arts
- 800   Literature and Rhetoric
- 900   Geography and History

Looking at literature again, we find that any book in the 800s deals with literature or rhetoric. More specifically, any book in the 820s will be about English Literature. The book *Shakespeare: For All Time,* mentioned earlier, has a Dewey Decimal number of **822.33 W4629s.** If you looked for more books on Shakespeare using the Dewey Decimal system, you'd soon learn that the number 822.33 will always be assigned to books about Shakespeare, so finding this one book will lead to many others on the same topic.

ISBN AND ISSN SYSTEMS

Similar to the call numbers generated by the Library of Congress and the Dewey Decimal systems, there is a number known as the International Standard Book Number, or ISBN. The ISBN is ten digits long (sometimes the letter X appears with the numbers to indicate the number 10 in a single digit), and it is always separated into four hyphenated sections. This number is not generated to help organize libraries; instead, it is primarily used in international marketing to ensure that every book has a unique number for cataloging and ordering purposes. The ISBN probably won't be used in your typical academic library, but it is a great way to identify books at bookstores. If you are using a web resource such as Amazon.com or Barnesandnoble.com to find out more about a book, the ISBN can ensure that you have the proper text.

Research Tip: Professors

Always remember that the instructors on your campus are experts in various fields of study. Professors who are teaching courses you are taking now or who taught courses you took in the past usually encourage inquisitive students to visit them in their offices. Take them up on this. Even professors whose courses you haven't taken yet may be willing to be interviewed on a subject or to give advice about research. You should be ready with some good questions and preliminary research to prove to them that you are seriously interested in their areas of study.

Also, many professors keep books and resources on reserve in your library. Ask them or the library staff what materials your professors may have on reserve—these could turn out to be some of the best sources on your subject.

LIBRARY CATALOG SEARCHES

Most libraries now use a computerized search engine as a way to navigate their book and journal holdings. Although search engines differ, some basic principles apply to all your searches. Many college libraries have a separate search engine for their book holdings and then subscribe to a few database services that will help you find periodical articles. On the next page is a look at Bakersfield College's Grace Van Dyke Bird Library's book catalog page. Most library catalogs will be fairly similar to this one.

The search scrollbar shows several types of searches you can execute. You must choose the best type of search for your particular needs, or you'll leave the library frustrated, unable to find sources that are sitting on the shelves, waiting to be discovered. The screen shown is for a basic search. The tabs at the top of the page, however, show several options that allow you to conduct more advanced searches, including

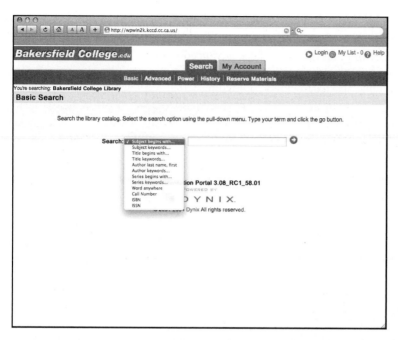

"Advanced" and "Power" searches. If you're unable to find a useful source or limit your search adequately using the basic search screen, go to an advanced search in your own library's book catalog for more options. Here is a sample of this library's "Power Search."

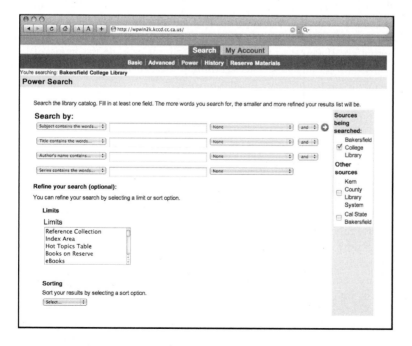

Note how many more options have come up to assist you in this Power Search. Now you can search by subject, title, author's name, keyword that is likely to be found, and any number of other options. These advanced searches may be intimidating, but play around with them and get to know their features. You can't break a search engine. (For tips on finding and narrowing a topic to research, see Chapter 1.)

Research Tip: Using Books in Research

When you have a book in hand, you are holding not only a potential source but also, figuratively, another kind of search engine. Inside a book that addresses your topic, you may find dozens of other sources you can use. Look at the source's works-cited list, footnotes, or endnotes. If you are examining a scholarly book, the author will have cited every single fact, idea, and statistic he or she has taken from other sources (unless the information is considered "common knowledge"). You can track down these sources using your library catalog.

You should also look at the table of contents and the index. A quick look at the table of contents will let you know if this book is really on the same topic as your paper. The index in the back of the book will identify pages mentioning key people, facts, concepts, and terminology that you should be looking for. If a key term related to your topic isn't listed in the index, the book may not be as helpful to you as you thought at first, and you may need to keep digging.

Types of Searches

You can perform several types of searches in most library catalogs, including searches by title, keyword, subject, author, and call number. You'll likely need each type of search eventually in your research career. Always keep in mind the type of search you're attempting. If you try to do a Title Search but provide the name of the author instead, you won't get any hits. This seemingly little mistake can cost you hours and send you packing up for home without any sources. The goal of every search is to end up with a call number so that you can find where the books are cataloged.

For each type of search described next, follow the example of the type of research done for the title search. In other words, after you find one book, let it lead you to more subjects, more titles, and more authors. You need to mine every source for as much information and as many leads to other sources as you can find.

TITLE SEARCH

If you already know the title of a book you are searching for, a **title search** is the easiest way to find its call number in your library. However, this type of search is also useful for searching for new sources. Use your imagination (and maybe a thesaurus). If you're researching a book on the subject of the history of television, for example, you can assume that books with useful information would include the words "history" and "television" in their titles. Thus, in the search box, you would enter "history television" and begin the title search. If your library has any books with these words in the title, you'll find them. This is often a great way to begin your research because authors typically include the most important concepts in the titles or subtitles of their books.

Following is an example of a title search using the words "history" and "television."

As you can see, eighteen titles in the Bakersfield College library match this search. This page typically shows you the call number (for this library, it is Library of Congress Classification), as well as whether the book is checked in. If you attend a larger university with multiple libraries, this search will also tell you at which library the book is housed. A quick look at the titles can probably rule out some of these sources right away. For example, source number one is an electronic book, source number two is a DVD, and book number three on the list is a traditional printbook called *Prime-time Television: A Concise History.* After you find a source that looks good, you can select it and look for more details about the book.

Several interesting options come up when you explore this book's entry (see page 26). Notice, for example, the list on the left side of the screen titled "Subjects." The subjects listed include "Television broadcasting—United States—History." In many search engines, these results will be hyperlinks, so if you click them, you'll be guided to all the other books written on this subject within the library. Similarly, the author's name is a hyperlink (in this case, there are three: Barbara Moore, Marvin R. Bensman, and Jim Van Dyke). You can click the name, and it will link to a list of all books in the library written by the author. Toward the bottom, you'll find which library the book is located in as well as the collection, whether it's on the shelf or checked out, when it's due back, and ultimately, the LCC call number: PN1992.3.U5 M623 2006.

Even though you started with a title search, after you get one hit, you can mine it for more and more information: subjects, authors, call numbers, and so on. This process is the same no matter which type of search you start with.

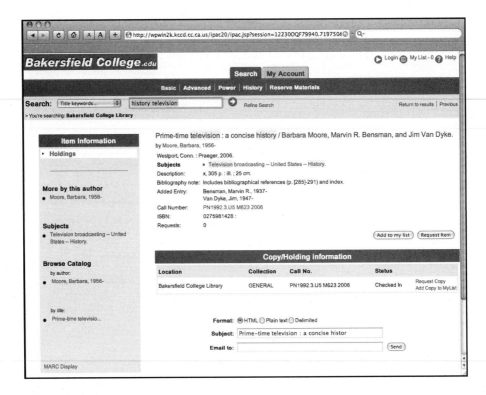

KEYWORD SEARCH

A second type of search is a **keyword search.** It may be called a "subject keyword" or some other slight variation in your particular library's database, but the function is the same. This type of search is a very broad search; it takes the word(s) you are interested in and searches for them in multiple areas—the author, title, etc. If the word(s) you identify are included anywhere in the database's entry, the book will show up in this search.

The keyword search has powerful strengths and some weaknesses. It is strong because it typically yields a great many results because it has very few parameters limiting it. This same thing, however, can be its weakness because sometimes you will get far too many results, and many of them may not be on the topic you had in mind. It is a fabulous place to start your searches, though, because it will very likely give you some books to start with.

AUTHOR SEARCH

Another type of search is the **author search,** which provides records on a specific author. Most authors become experts in one specific field of study, so if you have found one who has written a really good book on your subject, check to see if he or she has written a few more. When you conduct an author search, you'll need to consider how your college's catalog works. Some require you to list the author's last name and then the first name, whereas others allow you to use an author keyword search and will look for any author with that name.

Researchers can sometimes get confused when they look for books written about famous authors. If you are looking for books that discuss William Shakespeare or Plato, you should *not* do an author search because it will only find works written *by* these authors, not works *about* these authors. To find books about Plato, for example, you would need to do a subject or title search using "Plato" as your research parameter.

SUBJECT SEARCH

You can also conduct a **subject search,** a more advanced type of search than a title or author search. Many libraries use the Library of Congress's own system of subject headings, which have been in use since 1898 and are very well established. These headings, although very thorough, can be confusing and counterintuitive. You must be careful to specify the exact term when using these subject headings. For example, if you did a subject search using the search term "TV history" instead of "Television—History," which is the Library of Congress's term, you would find no books on your subject.

To find the proper subject terms, you need to consult the *Library of Congress Subject Headings Guides*. These are a series of large red books that are probably located very near the computers in your college's library (ask a librarian to direct you). If you look up the specific subject you're interested in, the guide will give you the headings used by the Library of Congress. They are often not what you would think they would be. For example, if you are researching the subject of date rape, you need to look under the subject heading "acquaintance rape." The *Library of Congress Subject Headings Guides* would cross-reference the term for you and point you in the right direction; however, if you jumped straight into a subject search without consulting the *Guides,* you may have missed several sources on your topic.

Following is a sample entry from the *Library of Congress Subject Heading Guides* (also called the "big red books" because they're big and red). If you looked up the term "television" in the guide, here is a brief portion of what you'd find (the entry for "television" takes up several pages in the *Guides*).

Television
    UF   Radio Vision
             TV
    BT   Artificial satellites in telecommunication
             Electronic systems
             Optoelectronic devices
             Telecommunications
    RT   Astronautics—Optical communication systems
    NT   African American women on television
             African Americans on television
             Aggressiveness on television

The abbreviations in this entry give you information about the other terms you could start searching under. UF means "used for." Any terms listed under UF (in this case "Radio Vision" and "TV") will be somewhat interchangeable with the term "television" in your searches. BT means "broader term" and indicates headings that you could use if you wanted to research subjects on a more general level than your initial search term.

For example, "Electronic systems" include dozens of technologies, of which television is only one. RT means "related term" and gives you terms for searches on topics that are similar to television.

NT means "narrower term." These terms will be more specific and give you a more focused search. In this example, "African Americans on television" comes up as just one of dozens of subfields you could explore. In this way, the *Guides* can help you to find a more narrow focus for an overly broad research topic.

Finally, the category SA, not shown in the example, means "see also." It indicates other terms you could use in your search. By learning how to navigate the entries in the *Library of Congress Subject Headings Guides,* you will have an easier time narrowing or broadening your focus, and you will be able to discover several alternative terms you can search with. Although you can find several subject headings on your own by searching your library's online catalog, you will not get as many variations as you will if you consult the big red books first.

CALL NUMBER/ISBN/ISSN SEARCH

After you find a call number using one of the search methods previously discussed, you can use a **call number** or **ISBN/ISSN search** to locate promising books on your subject. For a call number search, you would enter the call number you've found by copying and pasting the number and selecting "Call Number" in the scrollbar options. When you apply the search, the catalog should bring up a list of books by call number. As discussed earlier, the closer a book is to your initial call number, the closer it will be to your subject matter. A call number search is a great way to get a quick overview of how many holdings your particular library has on any given topic. If you use ISBN or ISSN numbers, you can search for them in the same manner.

Research Tip: Online Bookstores

To find information on a book quickly, go to an online bookstore and do a search on an author, a title, or even an ISBN you've found using any of the search methods mentioned in this chapter. This search will give you general information and perhaps an excerpt from a professional book-reviewing periodical, such as Library Journal, Kirkus Reviews, or *Publishers Weekly,* or from other reputable periodicals. This can be a handy way to quickly find information about a book or an author. Sometimes reviewers will compare and contrast the book you are looking at with others on the same subject, and you may learn about an even better book in this way. If a book you want isn't available in your local libraries or as an interlibrary loan, you may want to buy a book online at one of these sites or a site that specializes in used books. Pay attention to the ISBN, not just the title and the author, to make sure that you are getting the latest version in case there have been revisions.

Don't take too seriously the amateur reviews by people posting personal commentaries; they range from the useful (if you are lucky) to the seriously misleading. Some people give ratings to books they didn't understand—some will even rate books that they never actually read.

Boolean Logic

In the nineteenth century, a mathematician and logician named George Boole developed a system that we still use today in computer searches. This system is called **Boolean Logic.** In Boolean Logic, you use terms (and symbols) called **Boolean operators** to get more specific results when you search. Following is a list of Boolean operators. Try them in your Web and scholarly searches.

AND

If you use the AND operator, you are telling the search engine to only find results that contain both of two terms. For example, you could search for *television* AND *history*. Now your hits will include only results containing both terms; if a site mentions only one term, it will be ignored. Note: You can also use the + symbol for this operator.

NOT

If you use the NOT operator, you are specifying that you don't want a certain term in your search results. For example, if you are looking up television and keep getting hits that include an author named Shelly Stockton, whom you are trying to avoid, you can limit the search to keep her out. To do so, you would search the following: *television* NOT *Stockton*. This would eliminate any hits that contain the writer's name. Note: You can also use the − symbol for this operator.

OR

If you are trying to expand your search, you can use the OR operator. For example, if you want any results on television, but you're also interested in cable, you can search *television* AND *cable*. You'll find any source containing the word "television" as well as any source that contains the word "cable." Note: If you don't use any punctuation between the search terms, it is the same as the OR operator.

" "

If you surround your search term with quotation marks, you will do something similar to the AND operator. If you did a search for "*Television History*" it would be the same as a search for *Television* AND *History* (or *Television + History*). However, you can get more sophisticated searches by using both the quotation marks and the AND operator. You could expand your search and use the following term: "*Television History*" + "*Situation Comedies.*" Now, your search will find only results that contain both sets of phrases together. This is great technique to use if you are getting thousands of hits and don't want to sift through all of them for relevant information.

*

Although not technically a Boolean term, many search engines allow for "wild card" characters, also known as truncation or stemming characters, such as the asterisk (*). If you are searching for anything about the terms *sociology, sociologist* (singular), *sociologists* (plural), or *social,* you can add the asterisk wild card character to the end of the term like this: *soci**. This will tell the search engine to find any variation of the word, no matter what the suffix is. You should realize, however, that many engines use different wild card symbols, so look for the one specific to your database or ask your librarians for clarification.

Database or Platform	Internal Wild Card Character	End-of-Word Wild Card Character
EBSCOhost Databases	? (represents one character)	* (represents unlimited characters) Examples: *film** filmed filmgoer filmgoers films etc.
LexisNexis	* (represents one character)	! (represents unlimited characters) Examples: Film! Filmgoer Filmgoers etc. * (represents one character) Examples: Film* Films
ProQuest Databases	? (represents one character)	* (represents unlimited characters) ? (represents one character)
Gale/Cengage Databases	? (cannot use this character if default sorting is by relevance)	* (represents unlimited characters)
OVID Databases	? (represents unlimited characters) # (represents one character) $ (represents unlimited characters) $x (up to *x* number of characters)	? (represents unlimited characters) # (represents one character) $ (represents unlimited characters) $x (up to *x* number of characters)
JSTOR		+ (simple plurals; *s* or *es* only)

ONLINE PERIODICAL DATABASES

When you look for sources in periodicals, you will usually need to consult a different search engine than your library's catalog. Generally, your library home page will differentiate between the library book catalog and the periodical search engines. There are many popular search engines for periodicals, such as EBSCOhost, Gale/Cengage, and LexisNexis. These are subscriber services, which means that your campus library pays each service a fee to give students access to its databases of periodicals.

All the functions previously described in the discussion of library catalogs are likely to apply to the periodical databases available at your library. You can search by author, subject, or title to get your search results. The main difference between searching for books and periodical articles, however, is the method of retrieving the actual information. A search for books generates a list of authors, titles, publication information, and call numbers; a search for periodical articles also generates a list of authors and titles, along with dates and the issue and volume numbers for the periodicals. For many articles, especially older ones, you will need to find the physical copy of the article you've just found by locating the hard copy of the journal in the stacks of your library. You may want to make photocopies of the articles. For more recent articles, though, you'll often be able to download an electronic copy.

Here is a sample search screen from a periodical search engine, in this case the Gale/Cengage service's *Expanded Academic ASAP* database (previously known as InfoTrac).

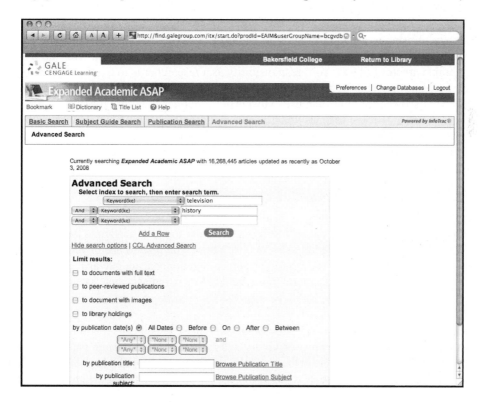

Limiting and Refining Your Searches

As in the preceding sample, most databases will allow you to limit your searches to suit your needs as a researcher. You can use the advanced search options to make sure that you get only articles that are published within a certain time frame, are full text, are refereed, or are currently held by your library. With journal databases containing thousands of articles from hundreds of journals, you'll regularly get results with thousands of hits. This is simply too much material to sift through. If this happens, you'll need to limit and refine your search to get a more manageable number. Here are five ways to limit your searches and refine your results.

ADDING TERMS

The easiest way to limit your search is to add some terms. By adding a few more details to your search, you'll find that many irrelevant results will disappear. For example, instead of just searching for *television history,* include extra terms like *cable, satellite, minorities, violence, advertising,* or other terms that may lead to more specific articles. This will eliminate many articles that don't pertain to your specific topic.

FULL TEXT

In the preceding sample page, you'll notice that you can limit the results "to documents with full text." This means that the only results you'll get are articles that include the full copy of the text in an electronic format. You can then email them to yourself, print them, or save them to your hard drive for later reference. However, if you fall into the trap of wanting all your research to be electronic, you may be missing some valuable resources. Although you will find plenty of full-text journals, you will find many more that are not full text. Your responsibility as a researcher is to track down the best materials, not the easiest, get the physical journals off the shelves, and make photocopies of the articles for your own use. Most articles published before the mid 1990s are not stored in electronic formats yet. To properly research your subject, you should not limit yourself to electronic materials. You also need to know your instructor's preferences. The requirements for your class may dictate a specific number of sources from different categories, and exclude some types of sources entirely.

PEER REVIEWED OR REFEREED

The sample search engine page also allows you to limit the results "to peer-reviewed publications." Such articles are scholarly and typically found in academic journals. This kind of limitation is a very good idea for information you plan to use in your paper. By limiting your search in this way, you'll be sure you get only academic articles that have been reviewed by a panel of experts in the field before being accepted for publication.

LIBRARY HOLDINGS

Another way to limit your search is by library holdings. This means that the search will list only those periodicals that your library subscribes to. Even if there isn't a full-text version of this article available in the database, you'll be able to find it in your library and make a copy of it for later use. If you don't select this box, the database will list every single article it contains, even though many of them may not be available in your library.

BY PUBLICATION DATE

Many periodical search engines also allow you to search by date. This option can be very useful when you need to find information about a very recent event and want to limit your search to the past few months. It is also helpful when you are searching for specific newspaper articles and you know when the story initially broke.

Research Tip: Book Reviews

When you search using a periodical database, many of the articles you will turn up are reviews of scholarly books that have just been released. These are brief reviews published in scholarly journals that are important to read when you're trying to determine whether a new book might be a good source, but you shouldn't rely on the content of these reviews for your paper. Instead of using a review as a source for your paper, locate the book the reviewer is writing about and use it. Why rely on someone's opinion of an author's research or argument when you can cite the actual work?

After you enter your search parameters, you'll get a page like the one shown next. It will show you all the sources within this database on the subject you've chosen to research. Again, we've entered the search term *television history*.

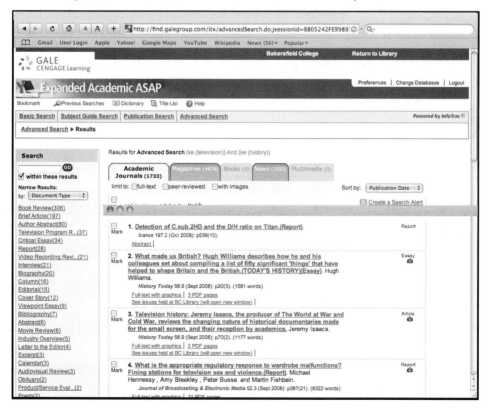

Some of these articles will seem more pertinent than others, and you'll select ones you're interested in exploring further. After you do, the engine generates specific details about the article or gives the whole article itself if the full text is available, as in the example shown in the next screen.

Notice, however, that the previous example still shows 1,733 hits just on the academic journals. This is still too large a number to try to sift through with any efficiency. Instead, you should still narrow the field.

Several important pieces of information can be found in the first few lines of the journal results. Look at some of the details from the result in the preceding screen example:

- The title and author: "What made us british? Hugh Williams describes how he and his colleagues set about compiling a list of fifty significant 'things' that have helped to shape Britain and the British," written by Hugh Williams (note that the title is not capitalized according to MLA guidelines, as it must be when you create your list of works cited)

- The name of the journal itself: *History Today*.

- The volume and issue number: volume 58, issue number 9, the date (Sept. 2008), and the page number it starts on (page 20), and the number of pages (3).

All the information listed here is vital, giving you what you would need to locate this article if the database did not contain a full-text version. Just under the abstract, however, the database indicates that the full text is available and gives copyright information, so you can email this article to yourself if you decide that the information it contains is useful.

GOVERNMENT PUBLICATIONS

The government catalogs data on many facets of our lives, and much of this data is presented in documents, publications, reports, and websites that are open to the public.

Local: The local government will have many interesting facts about your hometown and county. You can view reports from the Hall of Records, the Hall of Justice, city surveyors, often even reports by the sheriff's and police departments. If you are looking for information on taxes, land holdings, environmental impact reports, or even a local radio station's FCC license, they are all public record that you can track down. You can also check your hometown's website for reports and names and numbers of people you could contact to get this information.

State/Federal: States and the federal government spend billions of dollars. These expenditures leave long paper trails, and much of this material may be helpful in your research. Federal agencies, such as the Federal Communications Commission (FCC) and the Food and Drug Administration (FDA), have detailed websites with many published findings. There are also storehouses of public documents, such as those maintained by the Government Printing Office, found at http://www.access.gpo.gov.

THE INTERNET

The Internet is a vast ocean of information, but most of this information is far too informal and untrustworthy to include in your research papers. However, at times you will need to access the Net as part of your academic searches.

First, you should be aware that there is a major difference between the online periodical databases discussed earlier and the Internet as a whole. When you access a periodical database, such as EBSCOhost, you are technically doing research on the Internet, but you're in a scholarly database doing valid academic research. When you use a generic search engine such as Yahoo or Google, however, your search is no longer limited to scholarly sources. Many instructors will insist that you not use sources from the Internet in your papers. However, they probably mean that you should limit your use of electronic sources to the periodical databases, such as EBSCOhost and Expanded Academic ASAP, or government publications found online. A scholarly journal article is still a reputable, high-quality source even if you use the digital version, not the paper one.

You can find some scholarly information on the Net, however. Sites such as Google's scholarly database, found at http://scholar.google.com/, or Genamic's Journal Seek, at http://www.journalseek.net/, offer access to some scholarly articles. These sites are usually portals to scholarly work that was originally published elsewhere. Many such sites exist, though several of them charge a fee for you to access the material, like Questia, an online digital library of books and articles in the humanities and social sciences. Again, it will be your job as a researcher to verify the quality and authorship of the sources you find here. (For more information on how to use Internet search engines and when it is appropriate to do so, see Chapter 3.)

INTERVIEWS, SURVEYS, AND FIELD RESEARCH

All research need not be done in a library. In fact, many writers, researchers, and professors use successful research out in the field to help generate data and produce evidence. Personal research such as this can involve interviewing experts on your subject, gathering your own statistics through surveys and studies, and conducting observations and experiments. Even if you end up not being able to use any information you get from interviews in your papers, these interviews make you a much more informed researcher and can help guide you and generate questions as you continue your scholarly research.

Personal Interviews

In your community are thousands of experts in various fields who may be happy to share their expertise with you as you research. If you contact these people and set up a formal interview, you can tap their knowledge. Some people you could interview are your local sheriff or police chief, a city politician (such as the mayor or a city council member), doctors, administrators of a local veteran's hospital, or college and university professors. Contact these people and tell them you're a student, and they may be pleased at the chance to share their knowledge and opinions.

When you decide to interview someone, aim for the top. Don't just interview a cousin of yours who is in the police academy—try to get the police chief or a homicide detective. For example, if you are writing a paper on the history of television, don't just interview your boyfriend or girlfriend who just finished a class on media theory. See if you can get an interview or email response from the producer of a local news show, an editor at your local newspaper, a radio station manager, or a professor who studies the media.

Following is a list of things to consider while conducting an interview.

SCHEDULING

When you decide whom you want to interview, you should contact them first and ask permission to schedule an interview at a later date. Don't expect busy people to take time out of their day for a random and lengthy interview. Call, write, or email them to get permission and to set an appointment. They will want to know the topics that you plan to cover. It isn't a bad idea to give them a list of possible questions in advance. In fact, give them every courtesy you can think of while setting up the interview. If they are kind enough to volunteer to share their expertise and valuable time with you, you should be very gracious at every stage.

GENERATING QUESTIONS

Before your interview date arrives, you should thoroughly prepare yourself. You need to generate a written list of questions to ask. Otherwise, you could have a penetrating sequence of questions in mind, but get nervous or side-tracked and forget some of the best questions you thought of. If you have a typed list of questions, you'll stay on track, and the people you interview will understand that you've done your homework and are taking their time seriously. Think of open-ended questions that require explanations instead of simple yes/no questions. This way, you are likely to gather detailed information, and you may even learn about some issues you hadn't even thought about before the interview.

Of course, if other questions come up during the interview, jot them down and ask them before you leave, but don't go in expecting to wing it.

BEING PROFESSIONAL

Treat the people you are interviewing as the professionals they are; this means that you need to behave equally professionally. Avoid slang and swear words, and dress as if you're going on a job interview. Even if you interview a person who is not in a profession, the right attitude on your part will help elicit thoughtful, careful responses. Finally, remember to thank your subjects afterward for their time. You may not need them anymore, but they could decide to never again take the time to help a student if you don't acknowledge the time and effort they put into answering your questions. Besides, you may still need them—as you type up your notes or write the first draft of your paper, you may realize that you need to clarify one or more points. If you haven't acted in a courteous and professional manner, they will feel like dealing with you again is a waste of their time.

TAKING NOTES

Typically, people speak faster than we can write, so if you are interviewing someone in person or over the telephone, it is a good idea to both take written notes and record the session. Your notes will keep your major thoughts on paper, but the recorded interview will be an infallible source to refer back to later. Many college and university libraries have recorders you can check out as a student in case you don't have one. You can also attach microphones to many iPods and laptops. Be sure to ask for permission to take notes and record the interview in advance.

STAYING ON TOPIC

Interviews don't always go as you expect them to go. The experts you talk to may be busy, impatient, or distracted. They may want to avoid some of the issues you bring up or seem interested in only one aspect of your topic. At all times, remember that this is their time. Don't push them; just adapt. Try to steer the interview back to where you want it to go, but if you find too much resistance, don't go too far and risk upsetting them.

CLARIFYING IMPORTANT INFORMATION

Don't forget to get accurate background information from your subjects. How long have they been in this field of work? What makes them experts? Where degrees do they have, and where did they obtain them? Also, be sure you get titles and names spelled correctly and dates authenticated. You can politely interrupt and get clarification as the interview progresses, or you can jot some reminders to yourself about points that need clarification at the end. Be sure that you keep aware of the time.

Telephone and Email Interviews

You can also conduct interviews through phone or email. For example, some well-known experts are also college and university professors, and they can easily be tracked down using their institutions' websites. You can find office phone numbers, email addresses, and even office hours. You may be able to interview renowned experts on your topic. Most of the preceding guidelines are applicable to phone or email interviews. Always email or call first and ask to set up a time to call back for a phone interview or to ask for permission to send a list of questions via email. If you are doing your interviews by phone, you must make your subjects aware in advance that you would like to record them. Comply with their wishes—it isn't ethical to record subjects without their permission.

For many students, an email interview is preferable to a phone interview. Very few people have the devices needed to record a phone conversation. If you send email questions, however, you have your subject's verbatim responses.

Sample Interview Questions

Following is a list of some sample questions you could generate before conducting an interview. These questions were prepared by a student writing a paper on the subject of television news and its role in democracy. Her subjects were news anchors working at each of the three local television stations. Notice that the questions are fairly specific, so that she would be more likely to get stronger responses. Also note that for questions 6, 7, and 9, she prepared some follow-up questions in case she got a "yes" response to any of them and needed more elaboration. In practice, most interview subjects are likely to give fairly detailed answers to questions instead of simple yes or no answers, but follow-up questions are important in case a subject needs prompting—or in case a subject is very willing to talk but goes off on tangents. These questions also helped to keep her consistent with each of the three individuals she interviewed.

Date: _____

Place: _____

Interviewee: _____

Question 1: How long have you been a reporter?

Question 2: How has television news changed since you started?

Question 3: How do you think television news compares to news from other sources, like newspapers, news magazines, the Internet, and radio?

Question 4: What do you think are the strengths of television news?

Question 5: What do you think are the weaknesses of television news?

Question 6: Have you ever had pressure to not air a story?

    Follow-Up Question 1: Who tried to get the story stopped, and why?

    Follow-Up Question 2: Can you elaborate? Did the story end up getting aired?

Question 7: Have you known anyone else who had pressure to not air a story?

    Follow-Up Question 1: Who tried to get the story stopped, and why?

    Follow-Up Question 2: Did the story end up getting aired?

Question 8: Do you think television news programs in general do a good job presenting the news?

Question 9: Do you think television news is important to American democracy?
Follow-Up Question: In what ways?

Question 10: Do you think the current corporate ownership of most news outlets has hurt journalism in any way?

Question 11: What do you see as the future of television news?

Surveys and Statistical Studies

You may want to conduct your own research and get statistics about an issue. To do so, you will need to design a survey that asks questions that will help you in your research. After you give this to participants, you'll be able to come up with your own statistical information. (Don't forget to save the completed surveys; your professor may want to see your research.)

One of the most important questions to ask before you begin a survey is, "What sample size is required for a survey?" There is no definitive answer to this question; large samples with rigorous selection will give you more accurate results, but, as a student, you are limited in what you can do. Your target sample size for a survey depends on the resources available to you, the purpose of your study, and the statistical quality needed. It is best to discuss this with your professor before proceeding—you don't want to take the time and the trouble to do field research and find that days of work were lost because your professor deems your sample size too small or unrepresentative. After you decide on a sample size, don't back off. If you find yourself with only eighty percent of the number of subjects you had hoped for, keep going, even if it's taking longer than you anticipated. Trust your original assessment.

Depending on the nature of your research, there will be several places you can go to distribute the surveys. If you intend to interview only college students or faculty members, obviously your campus (or any nearby campuses) will be the best place to go. Some of your professors may even be willing to take some class time to let students voluntarily fill out questionnaires if they aren't too long. If you want a broader sampling of participants, you should go to a popular spot, such as a coffee house or shopping center. Be sure to ask permission of managers first. You can also have a simple survey that can be given over the telephone and make some cold calls to people—be sure you call at an appropriate time, though (not too early or too late, and not during dinner). Be prepared to be hung up on by people who have no interest in being questioned by you.

Following are some ideas on how to generate a successful field survey.

DON'T TRY TO DO TOO MUCH

Don't get overly ambitious and try to generate a lot of data. Design your survey with a clear idea of exactly what beliefs and attitudes you are trying to measure, and be practical. Limit the scope. You will need to be pretty specific to make sure that the results that you generate mean something, but if you try to ask too many questions, potential subjects may not want to take the time. You should be able to say, "This will only take a minute or two of your time" and really mean it. It's a good idea to rehearse your survey with a few friends—this will give you a realistic idea of how much time the survey will take, and they may even catch problems with your questions that you didn't see.

KEEP QUESTIONS CLEAR

You need to create questions that will not confuse the participants. Make sure that the language is clear and unambiguous and that you avoid technical language or jargon. Don't try to impress people with your vocabulary. If your question is worded poorly, the participants may interpret it incorrectly and skew your statistics. Use multiple choice, yes/no, and true/false questions. You'll have much more luck snagging potential participants if your survey won't take a lot of time. Few people will want to write short essays for you, but many people will fill in a couple of bubbles while they're on the go. This differs from generating interview questions, because interviews often aim for more complex, longer reactions.

AVOID BIAS AND OVERSIMPLIFICATION

Make sure your questions are straightforward, unemotional, and free from any hint of bias. It is very easy to load a question with language that makes it hard for someone not to agree with you. People tend to want to be liked, even by strangers, and sometimes they will give the answers they think that interviewers want to hear or that the people reading written survey questions want to read. If you wanted to know about subjects' feelings about abortion laws, for example, questions like "Do you feel it is ever moral to take an innocent unborn life?" or "Do you support a woman's right to control her own body?" are going to elicit very skewed results.

Also, if you are dealing with complex, nuanced issues, you should avoid questions that are too simplistic. "Are you in favor of gun control?" may seem like a straightforward, unbiased question, but it would mean very different things to different people, and your subjects will bring their own habits of thought to the question. A member of the National Rifle Association might automatically answer "No," but this same person might believe that it is perfectly reasonable not to allow people convicted of terrorist acts or people who are demonstrably psychotic to own guns. A member of the Brady Campaign to Prevent Gun Violence would answer "Yes" because this organization lobbies for gun control laws, but you still wouldn't know exactly how this person feels about the issue of individuals owning guns—some members may want private gun ownership banned altogether, but many others don't. You would get the most accurate results if you generated very specific questions, such as "Under which of the following situations should individuals be banned from owning guns?" followed by clear scenarios.

DON'T GET PERSONAL

Don't ask for any information that isn't needed for your study. You should avoid questions about race, sexual orientation, religion, political leanings, or age unless they directly pertain to the study. If any of these traits are relevant to the study, tell people in advance. Also, don't ask for data such as a phone number, social security number, student ID number, or an address; you have no business gathering that information in the first place, and your potential subjects may think you're trying to scam them. Don't even ask for names.

INCLUDE A SUMMARY

At the top of the survey, it is a good idea to summarize its purpose. Let the participants know what it is you are researching and why these questions will help you. This is especially important if you're asking for information that may seem personal (see the preceding section). It's a good idea to orally tell the participants what your survey is about before they start, but putting a summary on the survey itself will be helpful in case you are dealing with several people and don't get a chance to talk to everyone.

BE PROFESSIONAL

Always remain professional and welcoming. You are asking people to take time out of their day to help you out, so do it with a smile. Never get upset at someone for not agreeing to complete your survey (they may feel that you are "spamming" them, so if they walk away, don't hold it against them). Dress well and have clean forms, clipboards, and writing implements. If your surveys are handwritten, or if you have to ask potential subjects if they have a pencil or pen, they are likely to refuse to participate.

SAMPLE SURVEY

Following is a sample survey on the topic of television history. It is designed to assess current viewing patterns that can help prove a point about modern television. It is intended to be distributed on campus to other students.

Summary: This survey is about television viewing patterns, and the answers it generates will be used in a research paper on the history of television. It should only take a minute or two to complete this survey, and I appreciate the help you are giving me.

Your Information

Age: _____ Gender: _____

Year in School: _____

Major: _____

Questions—Circle the Most Accurate Letter:

1. How often do you watch television each day?
   A. 0 Hours
   B. 1–3 Hours
   C. 4–7 Hours
   D. 8+ Hours

2. How many televisions are in your home?
   A. None
   B. 1
   C. 2–3
   D. 4+

3. How many people live in your home?
   A. Just me.
   B. 2
   C. 3–4
   D. 5+

4. Do you have cable/satellite TV?
   A. Yes
   B. No

5. Do you have a hard disk recorder/service (like TiVo, ReplayTV, etc.)?
   A. Yes
   B. No

6. Do you ever rent episodes of television shows through services like Netflix or check them out from a library?
   A. Yes
   B. No

7. Do you own any television shows on commercially produced DVDs?

   A. Yes

   B. No

8. Please rank the following types of programming by preference, with "1" as the highest rating. Leave blank any types of programming that you do not watch.

   News   _____

   Reality shows   _____

   Comedies   _____

   Dramas   _____

   Crime dramas   _____

   Science fiction/fantasy   _____

9. Please rank the following modes of relaxation by preference, with "1" as the highest rating. Leave blank any activities you do not use for relaxation.

   Television viewing   _____

   Playing a sport/exercising   _____

   Going to a movie in a theater   _____

   Reading (books and/or periodicals)   _____

   Going to a club or bar   _____

   Playing a video or Internet game   _____

   Pursuing a hobby   _____

10. Do you have an all-time favorite TV show?

    A. Yes

    B. No

    If "yes," what is it?

    _____

Research Tip: Online Surveys

If you are part of an active online community, you may feel comfortable administering a survey through the Internet. You could post it on a blog you participate in, on a website or MySpace account you maintain, or even a chat room. There are also some websites, such as Survey Monkey (http://surveymonkey.com), which let you conduct online surveys.

You may be able to get many more people to participate in a survey conducted via the Web, and you may be able to draw people in from a much broader geographic location. Follow all the suggestions for conducting a face-to-face survey here, and you should be fine. Just be very careful about the conclusions that you attempt to draw from such surveys—you may have a broader geographical area, but in every other respect, you have a sample that is unrepresentative of the population at large because you will be reaching only people who were initially attracted to specific sites, blogs, or chat rooms.

Field Research

You may need to go into the field to conduct an observation or an experiment, especially for classes that focus on science and empirical data. Professional observations occur all the time, and they affect our daily lives. If you are on a sports team, your coach will observe tapes of your performance, looking for patterns to help improve your game. If you are in a school play, the director will observe your movements and try to correct errors in your blocking and offer suggestions on your delivery. When marketing firms and advertising agencies need to know shopping patterns, they may conduct an observation at your local mall—if customers tend to shop at the same two stores, they may develop a cross-promotion between them to lure in future shoppers. The same type of observations can be done by you when you are doing research for a paper.

Typically, experiments and observations begin with a hypothesis you plan to test. The resulting findings are included in your paper. For example, if you decided to see how popular television shows released on DVD are, you could station yourself near the counter of a DVD/video-renting store (be sure to ask permission and to not block traffic) some Friday evening from 5:30 to 6:30 to test this hypothesis: "A significant percentage of DVD rentals are for popular television shows." All you would need is a checklist with two columns: "television shows" and "movies." Of course, you would have to decide what you consider a "significant percentage" and be prepared to explain and defend this in your paper. You might also refine the observation somewhat and have three columns: "current television shows," "vintage television shows," and "movies." Other breakdowns are conceivable, but you wouldn't want too many columns or you wouldn't be able to keep up if business was brisk. With field research, you want to think your assumptions and research design through carefully before you begin.

CHAPTER 3

Conducting Other Types
of Research

You've enrolled in a film class, and your professor has just finished discussing movies that depict historic battles. In class, you've watched *Black Hawk Down, Band of Brothers,* and Frank Miller's *300,* all films based on historical wars and real people. Your instructor has assigned a paper about these films and how war is depicted in them. She wants you to cover the impression of war these films leave with the viewer, but she doesn't require research as a mandatory element. You don't know much about these wars or what actually occurred, however, so you've decided to look into the historical events behind these films to see how the fictional accounts compare to historical accounts.

Because the paper doesn't require scholarly sources, you decide to skip the library and look elsewhere. After all, you're researching for your own sake, not necessarily for academic sources to quote in your paper. There are plenty of options. You could start, of course, by searching the Web. It is a vast and endless source of information, and surely you'll find hundreds of sites on these battles. You also have other options. You could look to the print media. If you go back to the time when the films were originally released, you'd find newspaper reviews and magazine articles discussing these movies (and in the case of all three of these particular films, you can track down the books they were originally based on); in the case of *Black Hawk Down* and *Band of Brothers,* you could even find articles on the battles themselves in the times they were fought. Even the airwaves can be of help. Cable channels sometimes do research into the backgrounds of popular films like these and produce television documentaries comparing the fictionalizations to the historians' accounts and even providing interviews if there are survivors.

There are thousands of avenues that never require a person to set foot in a library to track down information. We turn to these sources on a regular basis. This type of research is perhaps the most common research ever done, and most of us consider it such a part of daily life that it doesn't "feel" like research at all. It's not something that is academic in scope, just something to ease a curiosity or inform us about the world at large.

This type of daily research is a key tool in becoming more competent at finding and evaluating information. You need to learn the skills of searching through mundane systems, such as the general Internet, print media, and television and radio. Although much of the research discussed in this chapter is nonscholarly and should not be used directly in a truly academic paper, it still has a place in college life. These sources provide starting points to begin the research process and help generate ideas. By understanding some basics of navigating the mediated world in which we live, we can come much closer to true information competency.

RESEARCH INTO POP CULTURE: NET DOMAINS

A fast way to learn something about a website is to look at its domain. The domain is the final part of the URL (short for Universal Resource Locator, the web address), and it is commonly a three-letter title that is preceded by a period (typically called a "dot"). The typical website ends in a .com domain, usually referred to as a "dotcom." This is the most common website in existence, and it's typically not scholarly, so many professors suggest that you avoid using these public websites in your papers. However, other types of websites (such as educational websites hosted by universities and professional academic organizations) are great for research. Following is a list of different types of web domains and some thoughts on when you should use them.

.com

> **Who publishes them:** Typically, individuals and corporations. These are the most populous sites on the Internet and exist for countless reasons: some to inform, some to make money—and some to misinform, so be careful.

> **When to use them:** They are great places to go for some prewriting and topic generation, but most .coms are sources you should be wary of when looking for material to use in your paper.

.gov

> **Who publishes them:** Government organizations (such as the FDA, FCC, White House, etc.)

> **When to use them:** Often such organizations publish statistics and yearly reports full of useful information. Usually, these sites contain information that is published with citations and verification of where the information came from.

.org

> **Who publishes them:** Nonprofit organizations (such as FactCheck.org, Amnesty International, Greenpeace, Doctors Without Borders, Reporters Without Borders, and various charities).

When to use them: These are useful sources for topic generation and getting some initial ideas. These sites can sometimes be used in papers because they often have their facts verified and typically provide citations showing where the information on the site is from, so you can track it down yourself. The only downside is that sometimes these sites can be one-sided on a given issue and may slight opposing viewpoints.

.edu

Who publishes them: Educational institutions such as colleges, universities, and high schools.

When to use them: These can be good sites for you to use in a paper. Many are published by the world's leading institutions of higher learning, and they often contain information that comes from scholarly sources and studies. Sometimes, however, these sites will be written by students and published as part of assignments, so you should check up on the author(s) before trusting them enough to use in a paper.

Other domain types

There are several other types of Net domains you may run into. They include .net, .tv, .biz, .info., which are often connected to businesses of various types, and various abbreviations for different countries (such as .eu for Europe and .uk for the United Kingdom).

THE WORLD WIDE WEB

The Internet is a global network of millions of computers, and the part you are probably most familiar with is called the World Wide Web. The Web is a system of hyperlinked files that we access through a **Web browser** (such as Mozilla's Firefox, Apple's Safari, or Microsoft's Internet Explorer). The Web is an endless series of sites and resources; becoming skilled in its use—which frequently means recognizing what to ignore—is a vital part of modern-day information competency.

Search Engines

After you open your Web browser and secure a connection to the Internet, you need a **search engine.** Search engines are Web resources that enable you to search the Internet for whatever information you are looking for. When you sign on to the Internet, a search engine is often part of your start-up page. You are undoubtedly familiar with at least one search engine and may even have one bookmarked or set as your home page. Google.com and Yahoo.com are probably the two biggest, but other engines such as the America Online keyword search system are also very popular.

Search engines are indiscriminate resource tools that can take you as easily to biased sites, pornography, and shady money-making schemes as they can take you to respectable information. Information and disinformation will come to you in waves, unfiltered and without reliable ranking. It is up to you, the savvy Net user, to determine what's worth reading and what is pure garbage.

Following are some images of a typical search engine. The first shows Google, the most widely used search engine on the Net. You can customize your own version of Google to contain specific elements that attract you (headlines, weather, entertainment, etc.), but the basic Google web page is a no-frills affair consisting of little more than a box to type in search terms.

After you enter your search term, you click the Google Search button to initiate your search. You will be directed to a list of all the sites that the software matched to your search query; these results are often called **hits.** An example of a search for "Television History" appears on the next page. This is a list of all the sites that Google's software found to match these two search terms. The list is a series of hyperlinks with brief descriptions next to them. You should be able to quickly scroll through the hits to find what interests you and ignore the rest.

Note that toward the top, it says the results displayed are one through ten of about 20,400,000. This means that there are over 20 million "hits" for this search term. If this were your search, you'd want to reduce this number to something more manageable. If you add a term to expand your original query from "Television History" to "Cable Television History," the results drop to 23 million, and if you change it to "Cable Television Advertising History," the results drop to 1.3 million. More than a million hits are still far too many to reliably read, though, so refining your search even more will be necessary for such a broad topic. (For more ideas, see the section on Boolean Logic in Chapter 2.)

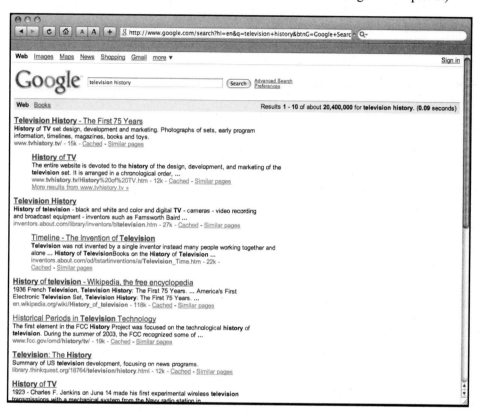

One of the unique features of Google is its I'm Feeling Lucky button. This button changes the results of your search. Instead of getting a list of all the sites you could go to, the software takes you to the first site on the list. This severely limits your results, but at times, it can be handy if you want to know the most popular site for a given search term. Note their terminology here: "I'm Feeling Lucky." This implies that you'll have to be very lucky to get what you are after on the first attempt. Web searches take time if you want to find quality material on your subject, and Google acknowledges this by suggesting that getting what you were after on the first site you find is a matter of dumb luck.

Another feature of Google and many other search engines is the Advanced Search option (see page 50). This allows you to refine your search in many ways. The next image shows that you can limit your search by a specific language, a particular type of file format, a date of publication, even domains (so you could search only in YouTube, for example). This type of refined search helps you to filter out the millions of sites that could clog your results page, and it helps you find just the information that will be useful.

Another popular search engine is Yahoo.com. Yahoo is a source for news updates, free email accounts, and searching the Web. Many people come to sites like Yahoo for their daily news and information, and many use Yahoo's search engine for every trip

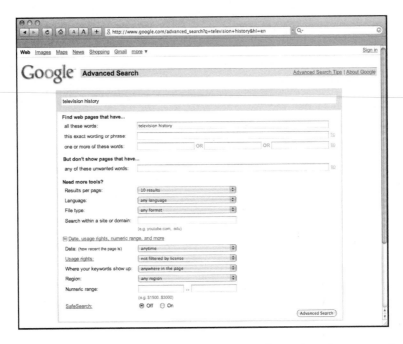

around the Web. You'll notice below that everything from shopping to weather and from news to music is all found here on Yahoo's home page. As with all search engines, you enter the term(s) you want to scour the Web for, and click the appropriate button (for Yahoo, it's the Web Search button) to get your results.

Search Types

With both the Yahoo and the basic Google images shown earlier, note that atop the search bar, you find several tabs that allow you to perform specific searches. Each type of search yields wildly different results. Explore these different types of searches and see what is most appropriate for the types of results you're hoping to find. Following is a list of some of the major types of searches you can perform.

WEB

This type of search is the most common and will scour the entire Internet for any websites containing the search terms you've used. Search engines all generate their results using different means, so you may want to scroll through the hits instead of merely clicking the first one. You may also want to search using multiple search engines or meta search engines (see pp. 52–53) to fully explore your topic.

IMAGES

If you are looking for an image of a particular historical figure, landmark, or even a celebrity, you can select to search only for images. This option typically finds the picture and loads it on your screen without actually taking you to the site it was originally found on.

VIDEO

Similar to the Image search, this search type yields only videos to view with your computer. Most videos are free to view, but many will take you to "mature" websites you may prefer to avoid.

NEWS

This is a very helpful research tool for academic work. This search option looks through only journalistic news pieces posted on the Web—all other websites are ignored. Normally, the hits will link you to the stories themselves. Some of the sites require you to be a subscriber to the original newspaper or magazine, but many will let you access the story for free or by merely registering for a free account.

MAPS

You can limit your search to maps and directions. This may have a limited place in your more formal research, but it is very handy in daily life. Popular sites include MapQuest, Google Maps, and Yahoo! Maps.

LOCAL

This search is similar to a web search, a news search, or even a map search, but it provides results for an area that you specify (typically by ZIP code). This is very handy for staying up on local events or doing academic research on issues in your hometown.

Ways to Confirm Information

Searching on the Net can yield good results, but it is not short on pitfalls. Much of the information you'll find will be woefully biased or even outright dishonest. Whether your search is for academic research or for personal information, you should get in the habit of verifying any information you come upon. For more information on how to evaluate and qualify your sources, see Chapter 4. Following, however, are a few tips for verifying information found on the Web.

- **Look for the .edu domain.** This means that a school, college, or university is responsible for publishing this on the Web. You can usually find the original author as well as contact information for the author on educational sites, and the information tends to be much more reliable because people's scholarly reputations are on the line when they publish such a site.

- **Search using multiple search engines.** Every search engine uses different parameters to determine what sites it finds and lists for you, and you'd be wise to search on a variety of engines. If you use different engines, you may be exposed to different websites. The most popular sites will all be near the top of each engine's list of hits, but you will nonetheless see a surprising amount of variety as you read further down the lists.

Meta Search Engines (Metacrawlers)

Several search engines bill themselves as "meta search engines." These engines don't actually search the Web themselves; they search the resources of multiple search engines

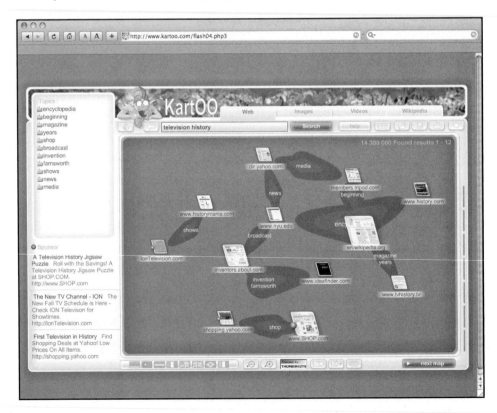

by sending a query to several search engines at once and combining the results. Your results will be more varied and come from more databases, so these are good resources when you are searching for something that's hard to find on the Web. The downside is that you may get far too many hits to be useful, or you may find that the filters used by the meta search engine are cutting out sites you'd have liked to be informed of.

Some of the more popular meta search engines are Dogpile, Excite, Vivisimo, Metacrawler, Kartoo, and Mamma. Many of the metacrawlers come up with innovative graphic organization to manage the many hits they get. On page 52 is a picture of the results for a search on "Television History" from Kartoo. Kartoo innovated a way to organize search results as a "map," and when you scroll over one particular file, the links it makes to other files all appear. Also, on the left side, a bar appears full of topics similar to your search parameter, so you can see other relevant subjects that you may not have thought of.

Research Tip: Vocabulary Check

When studying research writing, one word that comes up quite a lot is "cite." So, too, does the word "site." This can get confusing for many students. What's the difference?

Cite is the word used to describe how you give credit to any information you get from an outside source. Example: *Be sure you cite all your quotes, or you are plagiarizing.*

Site is the word used to describe a place or location, such as a website or a job site. Example: *One of my favorite sites on the Net is theonion.com.*

Sight is the word used to describe vision. Example: *She has extremely good eye sight.*

Miscellaneous Sites of Interest

Following is a list of some sites that may be of interest to you as a researcher and everyday viewer of the Web.

Allmusic (http://www.allmusic.com/). As the name implies, Allmusic is a database of music. It contains detailed listings of musicians and their music, with detailed biographies of the artists, full discographies, and references to other artists they influenced or were influenced by. Two other parts of this database are called Allgames and Allmovies. Allgames is a list of summaries of video games and their histories, and Allmovies gives detailed synopses of movies and biographies of actors; however, unlike IMDb, it lacks thorough lists of everyone involved in these projects. Sidebars tells several facts about the films, including original box office receipts and keywords and themes associated with them.

Bartleby.com: Great Books Online (http://www.bartleby.com/). Named after Herman Melville's title character in "Bartleby, the Scrivener," the site describes itself as "the most comprehensive reference publisher on the web, meeting the needs of students, educators, and the intellectually curious." Bartleby.com is known for its fully downloadable books and resources, and it lists categories under four broad subject headings: Reference, Verse, Fiction, and Nonfiction.

CIA World Factbook (https://www.cia.gov/cia/publications/factbook/). The World Fact Book is a database published online by America's Central Intelligence Agency (CIA). This database contains important information about every country on Earth, from the biggest to the smallest. It allows users to select a nation and find up-to-date census information on statistical data on issues such as capital cities, total population, ethnic percentages, major imports and exports, diseases, type of governance, and even finances, such as the Gross Domestic Product. Although this website is not written by scholars, it is funded by one of America's largest intelligence-gathering agencies, and the data presented here is thought to make up one of the most accurate such databases released to the public.

Encyclopedia of Life (http://www.eol.org). The EOL is an online encyclopedia whose lofty goal is to catalog detailed pages for each of the 1.8 million known species on Earth. Though still in its infancy, this site promises to be useful to scientists and the general public alike, stating that "It can be a handy field guide that people take with them on hikes on a personal digital assistant. It can tell you all the plants that might be found in your neighborhood" and serve "as a catalog, database, and learning tool about every organism that has ever lived on the planet. In the same way that dictionaries help literacy, the Encyclopedia can help biodiversity literacy." This site will be monitored, edited, and written by scholars, but eventually there will be a place for everyone to update the entries, like a peer-critiqued wiki. EOL's creators hope that the full encyclopedia will be completed by 2018.

FactCheck.org: Annenberg Political Fact Check (http://factcheck.org/). Fact-Check is a nonprofit, nonpartisan organization whose purpose is to reduce the inaccuracies, confusion, and deliberate deception that confront voters. It monitors statements made by "major U.S. political players" in debates, speeches, interviews, advertisements, and news releases. According to its mission statement, "Our goal is to apply the best practices of both journalism and scholarship, and to increase public knowledge and understanding." FactCheck.org is a project of the Annenberg Public Policy Center of the University of Pennsylvania.

FindLaw Academic Law Reviews and Journals (http://stu.findlaw.com/journals/). This is a law journal search engine, with journals and academic law reviews organized by topic, such as Constitutional law, criminal law, cyberspace law, military law, and tax law. It offers an introduction to legal citation and is designed for law students, but it is useful for anyone writing a paper on a topic concerning law.

History News Network (http://hnn.us/). How can history be "news"? These lines from HNN's mission statement give us some idea: "Among the many duties we assume are these: To expose politicians who misrepresent history. To point out bogus analogies. To deflate beguiling myths. To remind Americans of the irony of history. To put events in context. To remind us all of the complexity of history. Because we believe history is complicated our pages are open to people of all political persuasions. Left, right, center: all are welcome." Its several main departments include a Hot Topics page and a Students Shortcut page. The latter has links to many resources, such as live chats with professionals from the Library of Congress, comprehensive lists of reference sites, primary sources covering U.S. history, an indexed, searchable database of more than 5,000 U.S. and world history sites, guidance on how to "do" history, and a special section on 9/11.

HowStuffWorks (http://www.howstuffworks.com/). HowStuffWorks was founded in 1998 by a professor with the delightfully appropriate name of Marshall Brain. The site promises that "No topic is too big or too small for our expert editorial staff to unmask." The range of topics is huge—go straight to their home page, and you'll see their choices of a couple of dozen topics for the day, with headings like "How the Patriot Act Works," "How Pirates Work," and "How Archeology Works." The range is enormous, with articles on why our stomachs growl, along with articles on electric cars, government watch lists, and serial killers. *Time* magazine has named it one of the "25 Web Sites We Can't Live Without."

IMDb (http://www.imdb.com/). The International Movie Database is a thorough database of the film, television, and video game industry. You can search this database by title, actor, director, and producer; members of a movie's crew, such as editors, camera operators, and gaffers, are also listed here. If a person has been in a movie or voiced a game, there is a very good chance that he or she will be listed and that a brief biography may be included. IMDb even provides lists of the works of authors whose books, plays, or short stories have been adapted for movies, such as William Shakespeare or Jane Austen.

Innocence Project (http://www.innocenceproject.org/). If you want to do research on the criminal justice system, this site will give you some interesting perspectives and information. There are actually several Innocence Projects in the United States, but this site is the national organization. It was founded in 1992 by two law professors to assist prisoners who could be proven innocent through DNA testing. More than 200 people in the United States have been exonerated by DNA testing, including a number who spent years on death row. The site includes a section explaining and giving statistics on the seven most common causes of wrongful convictions, including eyewitness misidentification, unreliable or limited science, and the use of "snitches." There are also profiles of people who have been exonerated.

Library of Congress (http://www.loc.gov/index.html). The Library of Congress's website is an amazing research resource. The LOC is the world's largest library, boasting more than 130 million items and over 500 miles of shelf space. Every year, the LOC scans more and more documents and posts more and more recordings for full web access. If you are near the Washington, D.C. area, you should go to this library for one of the finest research experiences imaginable (but for the rest of us, its website will have to do).

Luminarium Anthology of English Literature (http://www.luminarium.org/). Created and maintained by Annina Jokinen, this award-winning site features works from the Medieval period up through the Restoration, along with biographies and links to critical essays and information. The site also hosts the Luminarium Encyclopedia, which has the ambition of becoming the "Who's Who and What's What in Medieval and Renaissance England."

Nieman Watchdog: Questions the Press Should Ask (http://www.niemanwatchdog. org/index.cfm). The Nieman Foundation for Journalism at Harvard University was founded in 1938 "to promote and elevate the standards of journalism in the United States." Its website states, "Great questions are a key to great journalism. But often, in the press of deadlines, the flood of raw information, manipulated news, deliberate misinformation and just plain junk, great questions are hard to develop. Reporters and editors need to know what's happening, why it happened, who's involved, who's affected and what happens next. . . ." This site suggests penetrating, critical questions a responsible press should ask about national and international issues and provides commentary, discussions, interviews, and links to articles.

OpenSecrets.org (http://opensecrets.org/about/index.php). This is the site for the Center for Responsive Politics, a nonpartisan, independent, nonprofit research group that tracks money in U.S. politics and studies its effect on elections, public policy, and citizens' lives. According to its mission statement, it "aims to create a more educated voter, an involved citizenry and a more responsive government." Its awards and honors include several Webby Awards, a National Press Club award for "Distinguished Contribution to Online Journalism," and inclusion on *Time* and *Forbes* best websites lists.

ScienceDirect (http://www.sciencedirect.com). This site promises "more than a quarter of the world's scientific, medical and technical information online." It lists categories under four broad subject headings: Physical Sciences and Engineering, Life Sciences, Health Sciences, and Social Sciences and Humanities, and it boasts more than 2,000 peer-reviewed journals. You have to register to use it, but registration is free and allows you various specialized search capabilities, and you can scan 75 million article abstracts.

Slashdot (http://slashdot.org/). Slashdot is a news website offering "News for nerds. Stuff that matters." Slashdot is a regularly updated holding of news stories from around the Web, all dealing with gadgets and technology. If you need information on games, hardware, software, computers, or networking, this is the place to go. Slashdot is famous for its active community of regular users who post on every news story. Every story on its site can also be linked here via RSS feed, and the site has an "ask Slashdot" section where users can post tech questions and get answers back quickly. (RSS stands for Really Simple Syndication. An RSS document, usually called a "feed," "web feed," or "channel," can contain a summary of content from an associated site or the full text. RSS feeds are used for frequently updated content such as news headlines.)

Snopes.com (http://www.snopes.com/). Do gang members really drive with their lights out as an initiation rite and then kill motorists who flash their headlights at them? Do iPods and cell phones really make lightning strike injuries to people more severe? Can Internet users really get cash rewards for forwarding an email to test an AOL email-tracking system? ("PLEEEEEEASE READ!!!! It was on the news!") Did Al Gore really claim that he "invented the Internet"? Snopes.com researches widely circulated rumors, urban legends, "strange news stories," gossip, "old wives' tales," and similar items. When someone emails you a claim, an alert, or a political rumor, you should check it out here before believing it or passing it along. (The answers to the four questions are #1, No; #2, Yes; #3, No; and #4, No.)

Space.com (http://space.com/). This site is a storehouse of articles, images, video, and links involving all things outer space. Topics such as science news, NASA, the International Space Station, the Hubble telescope, astronomy, technology, space flights, SETI (the search for extra terrestrial life), and the Mars rovers are all covered here. In 2003, this site was recognized by the Online News Association for its superb coverage of the space shuttle *Columbia* disaster.

SurLaLune Fairy Tale Pages (http://www.surlalunefairytales.com/). Created and maintained by Heidie Anne Heiner, this site describes itself as "A portal to the realm of fairy tale and folklore studies featuring 45 annotated fairy tales, including their histories, similar tales across cultures, and over 1,400 illustrations." This is a wonderful starting site for anyone doing folklore or fairy tale studies, especially if they are interested in cross-cultural variants. It offers more than 1,500 folktales and fairy tales from around the world. FAQ sections on children and fairy tales, women and fairy tales, and Disney and fairy tales list numerous books on these subjects.

The Pew Research Center (http://pewresearch.org/). The Pew Research Center is a nonpartisan organization that conducts public opinion polls and social science research on issues and trends affecting America and the world. The Center's work is carried out by eight projects, each with its own website accessible from the site: The Pew Research Center for the People and the Press; Project for Excellence in Journalism; Stateline.org, a news source that tracks and analyzes policy trends in the fifty states; Pew Internet and American Life Project; Pew Forum on Religion and Public Life; Pew Hispanic Center; Pew Global Attitudes Project; and Social & Demographic Trends.

The Victorian Web (http://www.victorianweb.org/). This award-winning site has been put together by scholars from several institutions and countries with an interest in the culture, politics, authors, literature, social history, religions, philosophies, science, and gender issues of the Victorian period. The site offers a wealth of information in more than 28,000 documents. It also includes material on some authors who predate the Victorian period but were influential to it, such as Jane Austen, William Wordsworth, Jonathan Swift, and Alexander Pope.

The Webby Awards (http://www.webbyawards.com). The Webby Award, established in 1996, is the "leading international award honoring excellence on the Internet." The Webbys are presented by the International Academy of Digital Arts and Sciences, a "550-member body of leading Web experts, business figures, luminaries, visionaries and creative celebrities." Browsing through the annual lists of award winners can lead you to some informative, provocative, and fun sites. In 2008, Stephen Colbert won the Webby's 2008 "Person of the Year" award for his innovative use of the web for interaction with his show's fans, "from Google bombing to make him the top search result for 'greatest living American' to challenging the 'truthiness' of Wikipedia."

VoS: Voice of the Shuttle (http://vos.ucsb.edu/). This site is excellent for research in the humanities and social sciences, with deep research links (as of this writing) in twenty-eight categories, including Art, Media Studies, Gender and Sexuality, Cyberculture, Literature, and Politics and Government. There are also links to a variety of resources, such as scholarly journals, "zines" (small press publications and alternative newsletters), conferences, listservs, newsgroups, libraries, and museums. VoS is "woven" by the University of California, Santa Barbara's Alan Liu with the help of graduate students and other contributors.

Wikipedia (http://www.wikipedia.org/). The term "wiki" means quick in Hawaiian, making it an apt name for websites that let anyone add to, edit, modify, and even delete content. Wikipedia is a wildly popular wiki encyclopedia that was started in 2001. As we write this, it boasts more than 9 million articles in more than 250 languages, with 75,000 active volunteer "wiki-pedians" working on additions and revisions, but it also warns, "Because Wikipedia is an ongoing work to which, in principle, anybody can contribute, it differs from a paper-based reference source in important ways. In particular, older articles tend to be more comprehensive and balanced, while newer articles more frequently contain significant misinformation, unencyclopedic content, or vandalism. Users need to be aware of this to obtain valid information and avoid misinformation that has been recently added and not yet removed." There is no central editor or mechanism of true peer review. Thousands of people comb through entries daily to check for errors, jokes, or bias, but there can still be errors (both massive and minor) in every entry you read. Many professors frown on its use in any academic setting, so understand that the likelihood of encountering mistakes here makes this a shoddy tool for serious research. However, in daily life, this site can be helpful because it has entries on every topic imaginable, and it can point you in the direction of scholarly research through its own citations. Just remember not to take anything here at face value.

News Websites

We've come a long way from town criers, who were the first news delivery systems. They used to walk town streets ringing bells and "crying" out official public announcements. Widespread literacy and the invention of printing presses created newspapers, broadcast technology brought us radio and television news, and now we have the Internet. With more and more people getting their news exclusively from the Net, news websites have become increasingly thorough. They have stories that are updated by the minute; they also have opinion pieces and blogs that help give different perspectives on the news. These sites are increasingly high tech, innovating podcasts and streaming videos, and many traditional newspapers and televised news shows now have their own news sites. Most news sites are free, but some will ask you to register with them to give them accurate records of their users.

Following are some of the biggest and best sources for news on the Web, including the sites of the five highest-circulating newspapers in the United States:

Yahoo News: http://news.yahoo.com/

Google News: http://news.google.com/

BBC News: http://news.bbc.co.uk/

CNN: http://www.cnn.com/

MSNBC: http://www.msnbc.msn.com/

USA Today: http://www.usatoday.com/

The Wall Street Journal: http://online.wsj.com/public/us

The New York Times: http://www.nytimes.com/

The Washington Post: http://www.washingtonpost.com/

The Los Angeles Times: http://www.latimes.com/

PRINT MEDIA AND NEWS

Although you may feel completely natural using the Internet, a vast number of people still get information about the world from print sources. Newspapers, popular magazines, and even newsletters are very common ways to get information. Make sure that in your research and your daily life, you rely on more than one medium of information; in other words, even if the Web is your comfort zone, take a look at what the print media has to offer for some more variety about the information of our world. Typically, journalists who write articles for highly regarded print news sources have strict standards and do research to verify leads before going to print. Thus, in most cases, the traditional press is viewed as more reliable than what is posted exclusively on the

Web—of course, the Web versions of print media contain much of the same information. (For more information on news media, see Chapter 18.)

Local Newspapers

Your city (or a larger city nearby) is sure to print a daily newspaper. This is a great resource for several things: 1) Local News. If there is a hot political issue in your hometown, and you need to research it, your local paper is the most logical place to turn. For your academic work, this may be the only source for local statistics, political races, and even information on crime. 2) Recent and Current Events. If something has happened recently (within the last month or two), and you want to use it in an essay or research paper, the only likely sources are going to be local newspapers (which may have online versions). 3) Entertainment and the Arts. A major reason to get a paper is to see what entertainment is happening in your town. Art shows, movie times, concerts, and many other interesting events can be reliably tracked down in your local paper.

Major Newspapers

Several major newspapers are distributed all across America, not just in their hometowns. *USA Today,* the *Wall Street Journal,* the *New York Times,* the *Washington Post,* and the *Los Angeles Times* are the nation's most widely circulated papers, and they are published from coast to coast. Similarly, you can find regional papers, such as the *San Francisco Chronicle,* which is popular for all of the Pacific Northwest, or the *Chicago Sun-Times,* which you can find throughout the Midwest.

These papers have many more resources than local papers, and they can usually afford more investigative journalists (including high-caliber reporters who win awards, such as the Pulitzer Prize, for their work) and more in-depth reporting. Just as with local papers, if there is a recently broken story, these newspapers are the only place to find information (books and scholarly journals won't be in print for a year or more after a newsworthy event takes place, but the newspaper will go to print the next morning). These national papers often break major stories that concern the entire country, such as the 2007 *Washington Post* series on the terrible conditions veterans endured at Walter Reed Army Medical Center.

The major papers are very powerful sources of news, and to maintain mastery over information competency, you must visit them from time to time. However, don't simply return over and over to news outlets and papers that spin stories in ways that fit your preferred worldview. The key to being truly well-informed is to look at a variety of sources and to see for yourself what information different sources leave out of their articles and editorials.

Popular Magazines

Many popular magazines lack the journalistic seriousness of major newspapers. Whereas a newspaper (in theory) exists primarily to disseminate news, magazines tend to focus more on entertainment and lifestyle issues. However, many serious and informative magazines do exist, including those that feature articles on news and culture alongside literature and the arts, such as the *Atlantic Monthly* and the *New Yorker.*

Wired, Scientific American, National Geographic, and *Rolling Stone* are more specialized magazines that also offer serious reporting on various issues. The *Columbia Journalism Review* and the *American Journalism Review* focus on reporting and editorials about the news media. These magazines are considered to define their respective industries. In scholarly research, your professors may not want you to use these sources because the articles are not generated using scholarly methodology, but for information about the world around us, they can't be beat.

News Magazines

Some magazines exist somewhere between the casual entertainment of the popular magazine and the rigorous journalistic standard of a major newspaper, such as *US World and News Report* and *News Weekly.* Also, the news sections of magazines like *Time, Newsweek,* and *The Economist* are as rigorously reported as those in most major newspapers. They are great sources for real world information, but you may want to verify their findings with some independent research before using them in your papers, the same as you would for stories in newspapers.

TELEVISION, RADIO, AND BROADCAST NEWS

The airwaves are another source for finding information. Though television is a much more passive medium than the options listed previously (you just sit around and watch it instead of actively tracking it down and reading through it), it can still be an effective way to gather information about our world. The obvious choice is to watch the news for facts and information, but don't underestimate the ability of some shows on cable channels or on the radio to inform us. National Public Radio is noteworthy for its in-depth news coverage and even for breaking stories through its own investigative reporters. But remember the Golden Rule of Research: consult as wide a variety of reputable sources as possible. Never rely on information presented in just one broadcast or in just one medium.

Local News

Much like local newspapers, local televised news broadcasts are very helpful when you're trying to find information about your community. Local politicians are regularly interviewed, and roving news cameras are able to capture footage of everything from city council meetings to street crime and traffic jams. If you have any reason to research local events, you should get in the habit of closely monitoring the evening news. Consider recording it and sifting through it later at a higher speed if you're serious about using the local news as an information resource. Try to record all the local news stations for different perspectives and to develop a feel for the types of information each favors or skips and for any tendencies to slant certain types of news stories.

Network and Cable News

The major television networks (ABC, NBC, CBS) produce big-budget news shows that are broadcast nationally. These shows cover events of national importance and have the budgets to send reporters around the world in search of major stories. Similar to these network news broadcasts are programs on the big cable news networks such as CNN and MSNBC. These networks have large budgets and a global reach as well, but they are easier to access because they run twenty-four hours a day and repeat major stories every hour. Again, if you're researching a breaking news story that wouldn't be in print yet, the televised news is one of the best resources for you. A VCR or DVR to record these broadcasts can be your best friend when you're trying to gather information, be it academic or personal. Be warned, though, that many cable news networks are thought by media critics to have strong political biases. (For more on the news media and possible "spin," see Chapter 21.)

Television News Magazines

News magazines are television shows that focus on the news in a longer format. Instead of focusing on breaking news stories and trying to get them to you the moment after they happen, these magazine shows take their time and produce detailed, in-depth news segments with background information and interviews designed to present differing perspectives. A typical television news story will be only a few minutes long, but the news magazine stories will last fifteen minutes to an hour or more. Really hard-hitting journalism can occur in this format. The news magazine format was born with CBS's successful *60 Minutes*. *60 Minutes* and PBS's *Frontline* are widely considered the highest quality news magazines, with the most journalistic integrity and with coverage of important stories that may be neglected by other television news shows (though *60 Minutes* also frequently airs human interest stories and profiles of celebrities, like Stephen Colbert, Bill O'Reilly, and Will Smith). *Dateline* and *20/20* are also popular news magazines. You can visit these programs' websites for videos of some of their stories, links to related information, and, in some cases, podcasts. Apple's iTunes store offers subscriptions to many news shows in podcast format for free.

Educational Television

Many cable networks focus on educational shows that give us accounts of crucial moments in history, in-depth biographies of famous people, and facts about the world in general. Networks such as The Discovery Channel, The History Channel, The Documentary Channel, The Biography Channel, and A&E thrive on this type of programming. Other networks, such as HBO and PBS, are also famous for award-winning educational documentaries. When you are interested in an issue, check the programming guide of these channels, or, better yet, visit their websites. Most will keep detailed archives of their past shows and documentaries. You may have to rent or buy the material you track down, but it can often be worth it if information is your goal. Sometimes important programs are available through video and DVD rental outlets. As with news programs, you can visit these networks' websites for videos, links to related information, and podcasts.

Radio

An old standard in mass media communication is the radio, and there are thousands of radio shows out there that do a good job of passing along information (but just as many that don't). With the tumultuous start of satellite radio, radio is a changing medium. Most radio stations focus on popular music, but they often have news segments; however, these segments are likely to focus on local news and tend to be fairly shallow. For gathering information on the radio, the daily news broadcasts and programs of National Public Radio (NPR) can be particularly helpful. NPR is an internationally acclaimed producer of noncommercial programming. Because it is an independent, nonprofit membership organization, its programming isn't dictated by advertisers and ratings. You can also visit NPR's website for transcripts of some of its stories, links to related information, recorded broadcasts, and podcasts. Apple's iTunes store offers free subscriptions to many of NPR's shows in podcast format.

Another format is "talk radio," typically found on the AM band. Talk radio is very popular with a lot of people, featuring highly opinionated hosts and citizens who call in to discuss various current events. Think of talk radio as, essentially, a collection of oral blogs. As such, these shows have the same potential weaknesses of blogs. Anybody can say anything with no ethical or editorial oversight. The news and information you find in this format is almost always unabashedly biased, usually toward the extremes of right or left, based on the personality of the hosts and the owners of the stations. If you find such shows entertaining, enjoy them—just don't consider them good sources for information or examples of critical thinking. (If you have to do an assignment for a logic class on formal and informal fallacies, they're a gold mine.)

Research Tip

With the exception of the programming produced by nonprofit organizations such as PBS and NPR, all television and radio programs exist only as long as they draw good ratings and attract and maintain advertising revenue. We aren't accusing the majority of television and radio news programs of superficiality or dishonesty, we are just noting that factors related to profits and financial risks determine what stories are reported and how they are framed. You are better off with scholarly, verifiable, peer-edited sources, as discussed in Chapter 4, especially if you plan to use them in your papers. (For a more thorough discussion of the financial issues that guide the media, see Section 3, the Anthology of Readings.)

Documentaries

Documentaries occupy a niche of their own. They sometimes air on television, but they aren't generally made by television networks. Some are made by directors such as Ken Burns and Errol Morris, who devote their careers to in-depth explorations of various subjects; others are made by people who are trying to draw the world's attention to a particular topic of importance to them. They can be good sources of information.

Be careful, though—some documentary makers are more interested in propaganda than in the truth, and with new technologies, documentary filmmaking has grown so cheap that virtually anyone can make one. Even people who are trying to be scrupulously honest cannot show you the "whole" truth; they might shoot hundreds or thousands of hours to create films that are usually less than two hours long. They exercise judgment over what to keep and what to cut, and, in the hands of people whose primary purpose is to shape your perceptions, a film can seem to prove whatever case the filmmaker wants.

You should evaluate documentaries as rigorously as any other vehicle for information. Reading multiple reviews in journals and magazines (avoiding those that are clearly politically slanted) is a good way to find out how worthwhile a documentary is. In fact, reviews can themselves be sources of information when the reviewer has a background in the subject. Documentaries may not be sources that you can use in a paper, but they can give you a feel for a topic and put a human face on issues, as well as suggest areas for research. They can also be riveting. For example, the 2001 Academy-Award-winning *Murder on a Sunday Morning* follows the story of an African American teenager picked up and arrested for the brutal murder of a white tourist in Florida. The director, Jean-Xavier de Lestrade, showed up at a courthouse one day to start work on a film on the American justice system, and he and his crew followed the case from the beginning to the end, not knowing how it would turn out. This film raises penetrating questions about eyewitness testimony, racial issues, and police and prosecutorial tactics and evidence gathering.

The other Oscar-winning documentaries of the decade (through the 2008 awards) are *One Day in September,* about a Palestinian terrorist group's taking of Israeli hostages at the 1972 Olympic games in Munich, directed by Kevin MacDonald (2000); *Bowling for Columbine,* which explores America's unique relationship with guns, directed by Michael Moore (2002); *The Fog of War: Eleven Lessons from the Life of Robert S. McNamara,* featuring interviews with the former Secretary of Defense during the Vietnam War, directed by Errol Morris (2003); *Born into Brothels: Calcutta's Red Light Kids,* about the impoverished children of Indian prostitutes, directed by Ross Kauffman and Zana Briski (2004); *March of the Penguins,* about the annual journey of Emperor penguins as they march in single file to their breeding ground, directed by Luc Jacquet (2005); *An Inconvenient Truth,* about Al Gore's campaign to raise awareness about global warming, directed by Davis Guggenheim (2006); and *Taxi to the Dark Side,* an exploration of U.S. torture practices in Afghanistan, Iraq, and Guantánamo Bay, directed by Alex Gibney (2007). Documentaries such as these offer information, entertainment, and food for thought on issues that are often highly controversial. No matter what side you take on an issue, they are fantastic sources for anyone trying to generate topics for a paper because they likely cover several major arguments on their subject matter.

Evaluating Sources and Reading Critically

After days of talking to colleagues, thumbing through your class texts, and pre-writing, you've found a topic for the research paper that is due in your American history class: you've chosen the civil rights movement. You figure that it is associated with a lot of important figures—Martin Luther King, Jr., Rosa Parks, Malcolm X, and President Kennedy—and it affected everything from politics to urban development and basic finances of the 1960s. There is plenty to research and many areas you could choose as your final focus after you've gathered your research material.

Your instructor has approved this topic, so now you need to start finding good sources for your paper. You get online and conduct a Net search, and hundreds of articles and sites come up. You read some of the online material, and you realize that a lot of it is contradictory. You go to your school library's searchable online catalog, and you see a couple of dozen books that could be relevant. A search of articles shows well over a hundred hits on various aspects of the civil rights movement—far too many to reliably read through. You were a little afraid when you started that you wouldn't be able to find enough information, but now you feel confused and overwhelmed. Ironically, you first felt that the numerous aspects you could think about when researching civil rights would make the paper easy to write, but they have, in fact, made it look harder. Where do you start? How do you narrow down all these lists? How do you know what sources are the best? A key element to becoming competent with information is to be able to evaluate sources and read critically while researching. If you master these skills, you won't be confused by an avalanche of material.

TYPES OF SOURCES

The first step in choosing sources is recognizing what a scholarly source actually is: a well-documented book or article written by one or more experts that is intended to be read by other experts and scholars in the field and by people like you who are trying to develop expertise. You also need to be able to distinguish between primary, secondary, and tertiary sources. We'll explain what primary, secondary, and tertiary sources are before moving into ways to differentiate between scholarly and nonscholarly sources and how to evaluate authors and publications.

Primary Sources

Primary sources provide original research or are original documents, not interpretations or excerpts of other research or documents. Examples include articles that record original observations or documentations, such as scientific studies, historical documents, and works of literature. When you are looking at scientific information, primary sources are especially valuable because of all the detail about the research they provide. Scientists are interested in replicability, which is the degree to which a scientific study can be repeated to see if its findings and outcomes will occur again if the study is reproduced by other investigators. Scientific reports have to provide detailed, accurate information about testing procedures, control groups, experimental groups, and so on, as well as information on possible confounding factors. (A *confounding factor,* also called a *confounding variable,* is a variable that is related to one or more of the variables defined in a study. A confounding factor may falsely demonstrate an apparent association between the study's dependent and independent variables where no true association between them exists.)

Secondary Sources

Secondary sources are one step removed from primary sources; they may take complete or partial data from primary sources and summarize, paraphrase, and interpret information. Examples include the books or articles that present a scholarly analysis of primary source material and books and articles about scientific research, historical events, and current affairs. In a study of literature, the books and articles you find that provide an examination or interpretation of the literature are secondary sources.

Tertiary Sources

Tertiary sources take information from secondary sources, though they may combine it with information taken from primary sources. Examples include various reference works, including online encyclopedias, many articles in popular magazines, and even advertisements.

Distortion of Sources

A common problem with secondary and tertiary sources is that the information they present from primary sources is an interpretation of the original material. Sometimes these interpretations can distort the primary source material, either accidentally or deliberately. Accidental distortions are likely to occur when someone who is not an expert interprets data for a popular audience, or a writer who is expert enough to understand the data inadvertently creates a misleading picture through oversimplification. Scientists are a lot less likely to try to make sweeping claims about the implications of their research than are writers for the popular market.

For example, an article in a scholarly journal reported the results of a study noting a correlation between a lower rate of heart attacks in a group of 100 men between the ages of fifty and sixty who took B-complex supplements for a year. This research became the basis of an article published in a popular magazine. The magazine article was titled "Taking B Vitamins Will Lower Your Chances of Having a Heart Attack." Whereas the original article discussed the smallness of the sample size, the short time frame of the study, the homogeneity of the group (women or younger or older men might respond differently), and the need for further research, the magazine article slighted those issues, and the title certainly didn't reflect the caution of the original researchers. After all, the publishers of the magazine want to sell magazines, and there is a ready market out there of people who want to believe that popping vitamins will protect them until they get around to losing weight, exercising, and breaking their junk food addictions.

Deliberate distortions occur when authors of books or articles or the creators of advertising campaigns have a particular agenda that they want to push, and they take information and quotations out of context to present a different picture than the one you'd find in the original work. Thus, a source may seem to be offering scientific or other types of evidence to bolster a claim, even providing documentation, but it is really just pushing propaganda. For example, in 2006 the Competitive Enterprise Institute (which is partially funded by oil companies) released its "Glaciers" TV ad. "Glaciers" shows the cover of *Science* magazine opening, and an announcer states,

> Greenland's glaciers are growing, not melting; The Antarctic ice sheet is getting thicker, not thinner. Did you see any big headlines about that? Why are they trying to scare us? Global warming alarmists claim the glaciers are melting because of carbon dioxide from the fuels we use. Let's force people to cut back, they say.
>
> But we depend on those fuels to grow our food, move our children, light up our lives. And as for carbon dioxide, it isn't smog or smoke. It's what we breathe out and plants breathe in. Carbon dioxide. They call it pollution. We call it life.

The day after this ad first aired, Brooks Hanson, a deputy editor at *Science,* stated in a news release that "The text of the CEI ad misrepresents the conclusions of the two cited *Science* papers and our current state of knowledge by selective referencing." In the same news release, Professor Curt Davis, the lead author of the study cited by the CEI, said that the CEI was engaging in "a deliberate effort to confuse and mislead the public about the global warming debate. They are selectively using only parts of my previous research to support their claims. They are not telling the entire story to the public."

Secondary and tertiary sources can provide you with good information. However, often their greatest value is to point you toward a primary source. On the other hand, a primary source may be extremely complex and too difficult for most people outside a given field to understand. Also, when dealing with the analysis of a work of literature, the scholars in the field are, by definition, creating secondary sources when they analyze different texts. Thus, research is not as simple as choosing primary sources over secondary and tertiary ones. You still need to know how to evaluate any source you look at, because secondary and tertiary sources can constitute scholarly works.

POPULAR VERSUS SCHOLARLY: HOW TO TELL THE DIFFERENCE

There are many types of sources—both scholarly and nonscholarly. Following is a list of twelve types of sources you are likely to encounter, from books to websites to wikipedias. **Periodicals** refer to magazines, newspapers, and scholarly journals because all of these are published periodically (monthly, bimonthly, or on some regular basis). You must consider the strengths and weaknesses of each type of source before using it in your paper.

Though it is hard to say for sure that one type of source is definitely better than another when it comes to researching, the following list is arranged with quality in mind. The types of sources at the beginning of the list are more academically sound, whereas the sources toward the end of the list should probably be avoided for most academic papers. Numbers one and two on the list (Scholarly Books and Scholarly Periodicals), for example, are widely considered the two best types of sources to use in your research, but books are not necessarily better than periodicals. The purpose of your research and your field of study will determine the distinctions you will make and the types of sources you will use.

Scholarly Books

These books are written by professional scholars, who rely on research, statistical data, and supporting evidence to prove their assertions and arguments. This is the type of writing that you should aspire to in your own research papers. Because scholarly books emphasize careful, detailed, thorough research and analysis, they are the most thorough, accurate, and well-documented types of sources you can use in your paper. However, these books are slow to research and write, so for research detailing events from the past year or so, you may want to look at other types of sources, such as articles from scholarly periodicals.

Articles from Scholarly Periodicals

These articles are published not to make money, but to educate and inform and to advance the reputations of the authors. They are particularly good sources because they are usually "refereed"; the article is read by several experts in its field and deemed of high academic quality before it is published. Articles are obviously shorter than scholarly books, but for current research, you can find the most recent work in scholarly journals. Scholarly articles provide a full list of citations just like scholarly books do, and they are the type of writing that you should aspire to in your own papers. Scholarly dissertations and findings from academic conferences are examples of this kind of writing, and you can also find scholarly articles in **anthologies,** books that are filled with selections written by different scholars.

Specialized Encyclopedias and Dictionaries

In the reference section of most libraries, you will find specialized encyclopedias and dictionaries. These reference works are written by experts in the field and vary widely in subject matter. You can find specialized encyclopedias or dictionaries on subjects ranging from American presidents to the Vietnam War. Because they focus on particular topics and disciplines, they are able to be more thorough than general encyclopedias. They typically have citations of outside sources, which can suggest other resources, and are often written by professors and other researchers. They also may indicate terms and keywords that you can use when searching for articles in indexes and databases.

Government Publications

Various government agencies write regular reports or professional publications. These range in purpose from securing future funding for the agencies to educating the public or informing a larger governing body, such as Congress, of their findings. Organizations such as the U.S. Census Bureau use top-notch statistical methodology, and groups like the Federal Communications Commission regularly publish their public hearings and reports. Most government publications are considered solid research material for any paper. However, do some research to find out if there have been any controversies associated with any of the material, such as accusations by government scientists that information not favorable to a given administration's political agenda was suppressed or rewritten. Sadly, this has been known to happen.

Professional Websites

Although it is often a good idea to avoid use of websites in your academic papers, some sites are very well put together and very well documented. Often government groups have websites, as do professional and academic groups. These websites are often as thorough and reliable as government publications and scholarly articles, even though they are found on the Web instead of in print. (For more on websites, see Chapter 3.)

Newspapers

Newspapers are good sources of information, especially for very current issues. If a political scandal erupted only a week ago, newspapers are probably the best place to go to find published information. The only downside to the newspaper, however, is that the daily news is not its only concern. Newspaper publishers need to make money to stay afloat, and many answer to larger corporations that now own them. It is possible that a newspaper may report only part of the story in order to keep readership up or a major sponsor happy. Ideally, quality journalism with integrity will guide the paper you read, but you can't assume this to be so, so read several newspapers to get a well-rounded idea of the news.

Industry Periodicals

Although popular magazines are far outside the realm of true academic scholarship, some periodicals are considered the best in one particular industry. The *Wall Street Journal,* for example, is the standard publication for the financial industry. On a more popular level, *Rolling Stone* is considered the best publication for music news and interviews with musical artists. Though these sources are not officially scholarly, you may find some good, exclusive content in them.

Popular Books

Even though a popular book may be a best seller, if it fails to include scholarly documentation and a professional tone, you should avoid using it as a source. The best-selling guru of the day may be a tempting source, especially if you already have his or her book on your shelf. However, such books are often full of opinion instead of fact, and some diligent time in the library will yield you a book with strong scholarly support written by a true expert in the field.

General Encyclopedias

Encyclopedias, such as *Grolier's,* Microsoft's *Encarta,* or *Encyclopedia Britannica,* are great for learning general information about a topic and generating prewriting ideas, but they are poor sources to include in your papers at the college/university level. Since they deal with an enormous number of topics, the information they provide is relatively brief and shallow.

Popular Magazines

General interest and popular magazines are fun to read and often published in their entirety on the Web (thus, they are very easy to find while researching). Although you may use these magazines to prewrite and generate initial ideas for your paper, you should avoid actually citing them in the body of your paper itself. You should avoid using popular news magazines such as *Time* and *Newsweek* and general interest magazines such as *Wired* and *O, The Oprah Magazine* as sources in a typical scholarly paper.

Popular Websites

The average website, such as those published by individuals on sites like MySpace or by corporations, may contain interesting material, but beware. You may use it, only to find later on that the authors were mistaken, joking, or just plain lying. Information on popular websites is often hearsay or simply copied from another source and pasted into the site. It is your job as a researcher to find the primary source, not rely on random websites, even ones that seem credible and look professional. Your library may also provide workshops on evaluating websites, which can help you if your instructor allows you to use material found on the Web.

Wikis

The wiki (from the Hawaiian "Wiki," meaning "quick") phenomenon exploded with the publication of Wikipedia on the web. Wikis are "open source," which means that the entries are written by anyone who logs in; people can even add or delete information in existing entries. Because of this access, people can publish false information just to get a laugh or simply because they don't realize that it is faulty. Although Wikipedia, the world's largest and most important wiki encyclopedia, claims that "scores of contributors monitor the list of contributions (particularly to important or controversial articles), and will quickly delete nonsense or obviously wrong articles, and undo baseless edits," it also concedes that "there is almost certainly inaccurate information in it, somewhere, which has not yet been discovered to be wrong." Wikis can be great sources for a quick look at a topic, but they should not be regarded as definitive. If you find a provocative piece of information on a wiki, look for the same information in a scholarly source. Quote that scholarly source, not the wiki, in your paper.

As mentioned, this list includes both popular and scholarly sources. This distinction is of vital importance to academic research. In a research paper, you want to rely primarily (perhaps exclusively) on scholarly sources. A scholarly source is usually written by a professional scholar, is well documented, and is intended to educate and inform. A nonscholarly source is usually written by a journalist or a nonacademic author, it often has no documentation, it may rely on eyewitness accounts, and it is published primarily to entertain and appeal to mass audiences, not to educate.

If you are in doubt about whether a source is scholarly or nonscholarly, there are several ways to determine the difference. How can you tell if a book, magazine, journal article, or website can be described as a scholarly source? Here are some basic guidelines:

Distinguishing Between Scholarly and Nonscholarly Sources

Scholarly Sources	Nonscholarly Sources
■ Books or articles written by scholars or experts in the field, with their institutional affiliations provided.	■ Books or articles written by people who are not scholars or experts in the field. They may or may not be professional writers.
■ Always cite their sources of information through such methods as bibliographies, in-text citations, footnotes, and end notes.	■ Rarely offer information (citations or bibliographies) about the sources of information.
■ Include information like research methods and results and specialized vocabulary.	■ Report events or opinions or summarize findings of other sources in simple language.
■ Are aimed at scholarly audiences, such as other researchers and experts.	■ Are generally published for profit and may be vehicles of opinion.
■ Are usually published in scholarly journals or by university presses or other publishing companies with reputations for scholarly works.	■ Are published in popular magazines or by popular publishing houses, sometimes those with an overt agenda (they may publish only right-wing or left-wing books, for example, or books with a particular religious bent).

EVALUATING AN AUTHOR

What are the author's credentials and educational background? Is the book or article in the area of the author's expertise? This may seem obvious, but there is nothing to stop a corporate lawyer from writing a book attacking climate change or a professor of electrical engineering from writing articles claiming that the Holocaust is a myth. Some professional authors synthesize information taken from expert sources, but they aren't experts themselves. A true scholar in the field is more trustworthy than a non-expert writing for the popular market.

What can you find out about the author's affiliations? Is he or she connected to a research institution concerned with developing greater knowledge about an issue? Or is he or she affiliated with an organization with an agenda that might suggest bias? What are its goals? The *Encyclopedia of Associations,* a standard library reference work, can give you information on more than 135,000 organizations worldwide. A database version, *Associations Unlimited,* combines data from the entire *Encyclopedia of Associations,* covering more than 456,000 organizations. Knowing about an association or organization can help you if you cannot find any information on an author. A source may seem unbiased, logical, and informative, but you should know if a sponsoring association has a political or economic agenda. If it does have one, this doesn't mean that your source can't be valuable, but it warns you to look out for a possible slant in the presentation or even the omission of relevant facts. You can also often find information online on a group or institution's own website (though some groups are self-flattering and less than candid with their descriptions of themselves and their goals).

What other works has this author written? Has this author published more than one book in this area? If he or she has published a number of books, that may indicate that he or she is a recognized expert in the field. Library references like *Contemporary Authors* and *Who's Who?* are very helpful for providing information about authors. After you access these references, some questions you should ask yourself include the following: Have you seen the author's name cited in other sources or bibliographies on your research topic?

Have other experts in the field given the book positive reviews? Don't simply trust what the blurb on the back cover says—it's there to sell the book. Information about the author's credentials and institutional affiliations is helpful, but phrases like "brilliant insights" and "leading expert" are not. Biographical information at the beginning or end of articles in periodicals should be approached in the same way. Factual information about education and affiliations is useful; flattering endorsements are suspect (authors often write their own biographies for articles). There is one way in which flattering endorsements can help you, though—look at the names of the people supplying the endorsements, and look them up. Are they verifiable experts? Do they have agendas to push or axes to grind? For in-depth information about a book, the multi-volume reference *Book Review Digest* in your college library is great, as is the *Book Review Index* on the Web. The reviews provide information about the author and the book itself, and may even compare the book to others on the subject, which can help you find other sources. If you can't find a review in one of these reference works, sometimes you can find one or more reviews by typing the author's name and the book's title and the phrase "book review" into a search engine. However, consider the source of the review—is it from a reputable source itself?

What is the author's tone? Is it serious, dignified, and respectful of dissenting opinion? Is it breezy, chatty, and informal? Is it emotional, argumentative, or even derisive? Serious experts, when they disagree, tend to do so maturely, showing professional courtesy.

Can you find any interviews with an author? Authors are often remarkably informal and frank in interviews, and when they are, you can get a feel for how they approach a topic.

HANDY EVALUATION REFERENCES IN THE LIBRARY

American Men & Women of Science
Book Review Digest
Book Review Index
Contemporary Authors
Encyclopedia of Associations
Magazines for Libraries
Who's Who?

EVALUATING A PERIODICAL

If you are using an article as a source, what kind of periodical published it? Is it in a scholarly journal, or is it in a popular magazine? You should be able to distinguish between types of periodicals. This doesn't mean that you should always avoid magazines—some have high standards. However, with a scholarly journal, much of the evaluation of a source has already been done for you. Articles in scholarly journals have been chosen and reviewed by other scholars in the same discipline. (For help in determining the type of periodical, see Distinguishing Between Scholarly Journals and Popular Magazines on the next page.) You can also consult a copy of *Magazines for Libraries*, which provides annotations and expert evaluations of approximately 7,000 periodicals, with more than 100 major subject headings. The annotations also describe the strengths and weaknesses of periodicals in relation to others within the same fields. This is a standard reference work for college libraries. Don't let the title mislead you; it deals with a range of periodical types, including scholarly journals, not simply popular magazines.

Scholarly journals often provide an **abstract** at the beginning of articles. This gives you a complete summary of the article and will help you make a decision about whether the article will be useful to you. Sometimes magazine articles begin with a brief summary or statement of purpose above or below the title. You might also check journal and magazine articles to see if they have summaries at the end. Skim the article for headings, and read the information immediately after each heading.

Distinguishing Between Scholarly Journals and Popular Magazines	
Scholarly Journals	Popular Magazines
■ Are usually published by professional organizations, associations, scholarly groups or universities and colleges.	■ Are published by corporations.
■ Generally publish only articles that are peer reviewed by other experts.	■ Do not have a peer review process.
■ Have covers and pages that tend to be plain in design, with few or no pictures or graphics; the covers tend to use black, white, and one color, and all issues look alike.	■ Use colors and images on covers and the pages. Except for the magazine name and locale, the covers tend to be very different each issue.
■ Rarely feature advertisements; if they do have advertisements, they are likely to be for scholarly books.	■ Are filled with advertisements.
■ Always name authors and provide their credentials.	■ May publish articles without bylines.
■ Often have issues that are successively numbered throughout a year, with each issue after the first beginning with the page number following the last page number of the preceding issue.	■ Usually begin each issue with a page one.
■ Have articles that are often quite lengthy.	■ Have articles in a variety of lengths, including those that are quite short, even less than a page long.
■ Are usually published only a few times a year, typically four times (though some publish as frequently as once a month or as infrequently as twice a year).	■ Are published relatively frequently, typically once a week or once a month.
■ Are usually found in libraries (or a professor's office).	■ Are available at bookstores, magazine stands, convenience stores, and supermarkets.

As noted previously, some popular magazines have high standards. Magazines like the *New Yorker, Atlantic Monthly, The Economist, Scientific Review,* and *Discover* have very good reputations—they sometimes even publish articles by authors who have published in scholarly journals but who have reason to reach a wider audience. Don't automatically abandon a source from a magazine, just be extra careful about evaluating it. However, for some research papers, you will definitely want articles only from scholarly journals. When you search an index such as Expanded Academic ASAP and some others, you can limit your search to "refereed publications." This means they are peer reviewed by scholars in the same field, so you know that all the articles your search turns up are from scholarly journals.

EVALUATING A BOOK

If you are using a book as a source, you can try to find information on the publisher. University presses or other publishing companies with reputations for scholarly works can signal that a work is likely to be scholarly. They are not automatic endorsements, of course, but they indicate a level of seriousness. See what information you can find on a publisher's own website—it can be very illuminating. In some cases, a publisher's site will indicate that it publishes only works that reflect a particular set of political, economic, social, or religious values. Knowing this can alert you to possible biases.

When was the article or book originally published? Some research paper topics are in areas of rapid development, such as the sciences, and books and articles can be out of date in less than a decade. Research in the humanities, on the other hand, has a much longer shelf life. Look for the copyright year. You can usually find this and other information on a page that follows the book's title page and precedes the table of contents. It might be immediately before the table of contents or before a dedication page. Look for a page with small print. You'll see information about the publisher, including the address, followed by information on where and when the book was first published and the date it was copyrighted. A brand new book might be a reissue of a book that is years, even decades, old. You should also look to see what edition it is. This gives you more information than just the date alone. If a book has gone through multiple editions, it might suggest that it has become a standard source. Also, later editions aren't always simply reissued books—sometimes they include added, updated material.

The next set of steps involves examining the contents of a book. Learning how to properly pull information out of different parts of your sources is one more step in your mastery of information competency.

Table of Contents/Introduction

Does the table of contents look helpful? Is an introduction provided? Sometimes a book with a title that sounds perfect turns out not to cover exactly what you thought it would. Keep your research question in mind. The table of contents and the introduction can help you to decide whether you want to keep reading. The introduction can also be helpful in other ways. If it is written by the author, you will get an idea of his or her tone and style. This can give you a hint about whether the author's approach is serious and open-minded or shallow and biased. If the introduction is written by someone else, look that person up. Sometimes, if a leading expert in a field writes an introduction for a book, that in itself serves as a very positive evaluation from a reputable source. Introductions, whether written by the author or someone else, will give you a good idea about where the author is heading with the topic.

Bibliography

The word "bibliography" (from Greek *biblion*, "book," and *graphia*, "writing") originally referred to a list of books, but now it covers all texts used in a source. Does this book provide a bibliography? How extensive is it? Do you see the names of people who are experts in the field? Is there a "Selected Bibliography," which includes sources of interest not used in the book? This can help to indicate the scope of the author's knowledge on the subject. Is there a section of end notes that points to other sources? (Sometimes these can be found at ends of chapters.)

Index

An index is an alphabetical list of terms, names, places, and subjects at the back of a book with the page numbers where they can be found. As you do your research, compile a list of important items to check for in indexes. You're not supposed to judge a book by its cover, but this handy list right before the back cover is a different matter. When you are doing research and faced with hundreds of books on dozens of subjects, the index can help you lock on to the best sources for your topic and weed out weaker ones. If key terms you're finding in your research all get several listings in the index, you've made a great find. If the index has no such terms, the book may not be useful to your research goals.

Body of the Book

Does the body give you an idea of the book's relevance and accessibility? Look for references in the index to information that would be valuable to you, and go to those sections of the book to see how extensively these areas are covered. How well are you able to follow the author's ideas? Is the language clear to you? Pick one or more chapters that look valuable in the table of contents, and go to them, reading their first and last paragraphs. This will tell you a great deal about what the chapter actually covers.

EVALUATING AN ONLINE SOURCE

Many of the preceding strategies for evaluating information are applicable to any type of resource, but the Web provides an array of challenges because anybody— even you—can put anything on the Web. Because evaluating online sources can be especially challenging, we have provided a detailed checklist of questions for you to ask:

1. *Is an author provided?* If so, does the site provide background information and credentials? As with other types of source, you should look at the relevance of an author's credentials. People naturally want to look as impressive as possible, and they will give you a full list of credentials, but they may be in areas not especially relevant to the topic being discussed. Also, see if you can use a search engine to find out more about the author—sometimes people fake credentials. The Internet is a very informal place, and anyone can put up a site saying pretty much anything.

2. *What is the domain name?* The domain tells you where the web page comes from. In the United States, the most common domains are .com (for commercial entities), .edu (for educational institutions), .gov, .mil, and .us

(for government agencies), .net (network related), and .org (for nonprofit and research organizations). Outside the United States, domains indicate countries of origin, such as .uk (for United Kingdom) and .ca (for Canada). The domain gives you some insight as to the credibility of the material, but it doesn't tell you everything. A page with an .edu domain may be an official university web page, but it could also be a page for student work.

3. *What can you find out about the site's sponsor?* Is it an individual, a company, a university, or a group or organization? Does it have an About Us section? (Other names to look for include Philosophy, Who We Are, and Background.) If so, read the information provided, but don't assume that the information is entirely candid and accurate. Use it as a starting point, and investigate other people, groups, or sites that it mentions. With serious research, you can't "one-stop shop"—you may need to get off the Net and go to the library to find out about the organizations and associations that sponsor different sites.

4. *Are there links to other sites?* What do you find when you follow a site's links? Sometimes a site that looks very reasonable is only a couple of links away to an extremist group. Even if the linked sites are not extremist in orientation, they can give you an idea of possible slants. Conversely, you may find that the links take you to reputable, solid groups, institutions, and organizations.

5. *Is there any apparent bias in the site?* (Remember that *bias* means a particular slant or disposition.) The presence of a discernible bias doesn't automatically indicate that a site is publishing false information, but it will affect the information presented and its interpretation. It is especially important to look for bias when a site presents information that corresponds to your own feelings about a subject. (Such information tends to "feel right" to us.) Look to see if the site posts links to original sources of information, or if it presents only summaries, paraphrases, or quotations. In other words, is it asking you to simply trust it, or is it giving you a chance to easily find the original source material?

6. *When was the site last updated?* Information that looks great may have been posted years ago and may no longer be accurate or relevant. If there is no date, that is a bad sign.

7. *When was the article or other material you are reading posted?* Even if the page itself has been updated recently, it doesn't necessarily mean that an article on the site is recent. Look for a date for the article itself.

8. *Does the site reproduce an article or section from another source?* Articles can easily be altered. If it does reproduce an article, does it have permission to reproduce and does it provide copyright information, as well as a link to the original source if it is online?

There are some good online directories that allow you to search by topic areas and that also provide evaluations. They include *Librarians' Internet Index, Academic.Info,* and *Infomine.*

(See Chapter 18, "The Internet," for more information).

HANDY EVALUATION REFERENCES FOR WEBSITES

- Evaluation of Information Sources (http://www.vuw.ac.nz/staff/alastair_smith/evaln/evaln.htm)
- Stanford Web Credibility Project (http://credibility.stanford.edu/)
- The Good, The Bad & The Ugly: or, Why It's a Good Idea to Evaluate Web Sources (http://lib.nmsu.edu/instruction/evalcrit.html)
- Evaluating Internet Information (http://www.library.jhu.edu/researchhelp/general/evaluating/)
- How to Evaluate Medical Information Found on the Internet (http://new.cmanet.org/publicdoc.cfm/60/0/GENER/99)
- Evaluating Foreign and International Legal Databases on the Internet (http://www.llrx.com/features/evaluating.htm)

EVALUATING CONTENT

The evaluation process isn't finished after you decide that a source looks good. You have to engage in an ongoing evaluation process as you read. Make sure you can separate facts from opinions. Facts can be checked and verified. This doesn't mean simply looking to see if your author provides citations. (We can think of at least one popular writer famous for providing citations that don't tend to stand up when traced to their sources.) Some writers are very good at making you think their opinions are facts. Be prepared to check anything that you will present as evidence in your own work. Be especially alert for sweeping generalizations that aren't backed up with statistics, but instead rely on anecdotal evidence (informal accounts of evidence and observations).

You need to carefully evaluate not just the evidence presented, but the quality of an author's argument. You should already have some idea of an author's tone. Emotive tones often go along with shaky argumentation. But a serious tone doesn't guarantee a logical or well-supported set of arguments, and sometimes an author with a question-able tone may offer logically sound arguments and solid evidence. Still, tone can be a signal that you need to be especially cautious. (See Chapter 5 for more information on evaluating arguments.)

ACTIVE READING

Whether you are looking at material you find on your own while doing the research for a paper or reading essays in an assigned textbook, you need to make sure that you are reading effectively. To do that, you need to be an active, not a passive, reader. Passive readers pick up a book or periodical and just start reading. You probably know what it feels like to read an essay or a chapter in a book and then, when you finish, you realize that you don't remember much about what you read at all. You read every single word, but the ideas just didn't stick. You may have highlighted what seemed to be important sections, but this doesn't seem to have helped. That's because you were reading passively. You need to engage with the text.

Think about lectures. Do you just sit there passively, listening to the professor, trusting that later you'll be able to remember everything he or she said? Of course not. Good students take notes, jotting down main points and important details and asking questions to clarify what they are being told. You need to be just as active—or even more so—when you read. Be prepared to take notes, the same as if you were listening to a lecture. Formulate questions as you read and then write them down. If you find that the text itself answers your questions later, add the page numbers with the answers after your questions. If you don't find answers the first time through, the questions will be ready when you reread the material. Active reading helps you to stay focused and involved and to concentrate more successfully. You'll improve your comprehension because you will be monitoring it as you go.

Additionally, be prepared to read books and articles more than once. Your professors have probably read the books they are teaching many times. Much scholarly writing is very dense and difficult to understand in just one reading. Many students think that they should understand what they've read the first time around. Don't be embarrassed or afraid to reread passages or entire works more than once to fully get their meanings.

Previewing Your Reading

Following are some preliminary steps that will help you approach a text thoughtfully:

1. *Essays/Articles/Chapters.* For essays, articles, and chapters in books, think about the title and try to predict content from that. Read the first paragraph and the last paragraph before you read the body. These paragraphs tend to emphasize the main points of the body. The first paragraph provides an overview and may provide a thesis. The conclusion probably sums up main points. If you read both of these in advance of the more fact-filled body, you will know exactly what ideas and arguments to focus on while reading. For both the introduction and conclusion, try paraphrasing the main ideas. One of the best ways to check to see whether you understand an idea is to try putting it into your own words. If you have difficulty, try reading these sections again. Also, scan to see if there are subheadings. You can find lots of clues about main ideas by looking at subheadings; terms in bold font; information in boxes; and pictorial matter, such as graphs, charts, drawings, and photographs.

2. *Whole Books.* If you are working with an entire book, follow the suggestions we just made, but also read the introduction or preface if one is provided, and look at the chapter titles in the table of contents. If the book has a section labeled "Conclusion," read that right after you read the introduction. Read it first if

there isn't an introduction. If you already know what information you need to find in the book, check to see if there is an index, and use that to go straight to what for you are the most important sections to see how thoroughly the book deals with crucial material. For example, if you're researching advertising, check the index in the back of the book. If advertising isn't listed among the major topics back there, this may not be the book for you.

3. *Audience and Purpose.* As part of your previewing process, ask yourself if you can determine the author's purpose—is it to argue, persuade, or just inform? Who is the author's intended audience? The general public? Fellow scholars in the field? People who already agree with the writer's views? People who disagree? If you can figure this out in advance, it may assist you in assessing the major ideas of the source.

FINDING AND NOTING MAIN IDEAS

After you've finished previewing your reading materials, you are ready to start looking for main ideas. Following are some tips to help you do that.

Paragraphs

As you read the body, focus on individual paragraphs, looking for the main ideas. The main idea of a reading is the central thought or message. The topic is the subject matter—the main idea is what is being expressed about the subject matter. Often the main idea of a paragraph is contained in what is called a **topic sentence,** which can be thought of as the thesis statement of the paragraph. This sentence makes an assertion about the subject of the paragraph, much the way a thesis in an essay or paper does. Where the thesis of a whole essay or paper is likely to be argumentative, however, a topic sentence supplies information, makes an evaluation, identifies a problem, adds evidence or examples to back an assertion up, and so on. Topic sentences are often the first sentences in paragraphs, but they can be found elsewhere in the paragraph—one trick is to look for the most general sentence. Sentences that have details provide evidence and discussion of the topic sentence. Ask yourself, "What general point does the author seem to make about the topic?" After you have found the topic sentence, write it down. Next, write down your own paraphrase of that sentence. If you can't, reread the whole paragraph to see if that helps. In some cases, a paragraph won't include a topic sentence at all. As an active reader, you need to decide what main idea is implied by all the sentences in the paragraph. Write that down.

Repetition

As you move through the reading's paragraphs, look for any ideas that are repeated in different ways. Repetition signals importance, and thoughts that are repeated are likely to be main ideas. Write these ideas down in your own words, too—or, if you have already written them down as topic sentences, underline or highlight them to underscore their importance. Look for transition words such as "consequently," "however," "furthermore," and "nevertheless"; these can offer clues about both importance and meaning.

Surprises

Also, you should look for information that surprises you. Do you see anything that challenges ideas that you hold? Does any of the information seem wrong or seem to contradict the notions typically held by other scholars and authors that you've found in your research? Pay careful attention to the evidence the text offers in support of this information. Look for any apparent inconsistencies or contradictions. Note these. When you reread the text, see if they are explained or resolved.

Vocabulary

Identify words you don't understand and look them up in a collegiate dictionary before proceeding. Don't assume that you can guess their meaning from the context. This doesn't always work, and if you just guess, you run the risk of misunderstanding key points. Write these words and definitions down—this will help you learn them. Write down key terms that are emphasized and repeated even if you know their meaning already—they will help you as you think about the passage. If the language is highly specialized and your dictionary doesn't contain these terms, make a note of the terms you don't understand and ask your instructor about them before or during class.

REVIEWING YOUR NOTES

After you have come to the end of an essay, article, or chapter, look at all the main ideas that you have written down in your notes. Try to determine the ones that are the most important. Next, ask yourself what facts, evidence, reasons, statistics, studies, and arguments have been offered in support. If you aren't sure, go back and reread passages until you can answer those questions, writing the answers down. It's a good idea to add page citations if you will be using the reading in an essay or research paper so that you can quickly find the material when you are writing your draft.

OUTLINING MATERIAL

It can also be useful to make an outline or a paragraph-long summary of the essay, article, or chapter. This tests your understanding of the material. If you read the material and can't effectively reproduce the main points, you need to go back and reread some more. You can also freewrite a brief response about the reading. What reactions do you have? What confuses you? What is most interesting to you?

ANNOTATING A TEXT

If you are reading a text that you own, you can annotate it as you go. This means writing your ideas in the margins. If you have a library book, consider making photocopies of the important sections and chapters so that you can annotate these. You could even scan the material into your computer and type comments alongside the original material in a different colored font. In fact, some instructors require that you turn in copies of the sources that you use with your papers, so they can track your annotations. Simply highlighting or underlining sections are passive activities, but annotating is active—it forces you to think as you go. Highlighting and underlining can (and should) be used in concert with annotating, however.

Following is a checklist to help you annotate a reading

- Look for important terms and definitions.
- Note where important information can be found with keywords or symbols.
- Write short summaries at the ends of sections.
- Write main ideas for paragraphs or sections.
- Write questions about crucial ideas next to the sections where the answers are found.
- Write questions the material raises but doesn't answer directly.
- If the author is constructing arguments, write "claim" or "conclusion" or an abbreviation, like "concl.," next to sections where the author draws conclusions about important arguments, and "premise 1," "premise 2," etc., to identify the premises. See Chapter 5 for a discussion of how to evaluate arguments and an explanation of

the Toulmin Method, which can help you to analyze the structure and strength or weakness of many arguments.

- Be alert to the author's techniques of persuasion. Aristotle described three "appeals": *ethos* (the image a speaker or writer projects), *logos* (use of logic and evidence), and *pathos* (stirring up emotions). Write these terms next to sections when pertinent. (Chapter 5 contains a detailed discussion of these appeals.)
- Be aware of the different modes of writing used in the author's rhetoric. For a full list of rhetorical modes, see page 164.
- Write "statistics" or "stats" next to sections that offer statistical evidence or where the author fails to provide statistics needed to back up evidence. (You might add a question mark for sections where statistics are missing.)

Annotated Student Reading

The following is a sample of how you can annotate your own reading as you research and gather evidence for your papers. This piece (Ben Bagdikian's "Grand Theft") can be found in Chapter 20.

The student used two highlighters while scanning this material. She highlighted phrases and words in yellow if she wanted to look into them more later on. She used a blue highlighter for terms that she needed to define.

For 25 years, a handful of large corporations that specialize in every mass medium of any consequence has dominated what the majority of people in the United States see about the world beyond their personal experience. These giant media firms, unlike any in the past, thanks to the hands-off attitude of the Federal Communications Commission (FCC) majority, are unhampered by laws and regulation. In the process, they have been major agents of change in the social values and politics of the United States.

> *I wonder how many there are?*
>
> *Specifically?*
>
> *Main Idea*
>
> *Explain*

They have, in my opinion, damaged our democracy. Given that the majority of Americans say they get their news, commentary and daily entertainment from this handful of conglomerates, the conglomerates fail the needs of democracy every day.

> *Look this up.*
>
> *What are current laws and regulations?*

Our modern democracy depends not just on laws and the Constitution, but a vision of the real nature of the United States and its people. It is only humane philosophy that holds together the country's extraordinary diversity of ethnicity, race, vastly varied geography and a wide range of cultures. There are imperfections within every individual and community. But underneath it, we expect the generality of our population to retain a basic sense of decency and kindness in real life.

> *Concl.*
>
> *Look for actual percentages.*
>
> *Look for examples.*
>
> *Pathos (A little vague.)*

We also depend on our voters to approach each election with some knowledge of the variety of ideas and proposals at stake. This variety and richness of issues and ideas were once reflected by competing newspapers whose news and editorial principles covered the entire political spectrum. Every city of any size was exposed to the early Hearst and E. W. Scripps newspapers that were the champions of working people and critics of the rich who exploited workers and used their power to evade taxes. There were middle-of-the-road papers, and a sizeable number of pro-business papers (like the old New York Sun). They were, of course, a mixed bag. Not a few tabloids screamed daily headlines of blood and guts.

> *Pathos*
>
> *Who? They must be important—I should look them up.*
>
> *Pathos*
>
> *Look up.*

With all of that, the major papers represented the needs and demands of the mass of ordinary people and kept badgering politicians who ignored them.

> *Premise 1*

Today, there is no such broad political spectrum and little or no competition among media. There is only a handful of exceptions to the rule of one daily paper per city. On radio and television, Americans see limited ideas and the largest media groups spreading ever-more extreme right-wing politics, and nightly use of violence and sex that tell parents and their children that they live in a cruel country. They have made sex a crude commodity as an inexpensive attention getter. They have made sex, of all things, boring.

> *Premise 2*
>
> *Premise 3*
>
> *I always heard that the news media was liberal. Is it mainly left-wing or right-wing? Or neither?*

Instead of newsboys earlier in the nineteenth century hawking a variety of papers to the people leaving their downtown factories and offices for home, we have cars commuting between suburbs with radio turned to news of traffic and crime. At home, TV is the major home appliance. What it displays day and night is controlled by a handful of giant media conglomerates, heavily tilted to the political right. And all of them have substantial control of every medium—newspapers, magazines, books, radio, television and movies.

> *How???*
>
> *Who are the major companies?*
>
> *Research these different companies.*

The giant conglomerates with this kind of control are Time Warner, the largest media company in the world; Rupert Murdoch's News Corporation, which owns the Fox networks, a steady source of conservative commentary; Viacom, the old CBS

> *Sounds familiar— who is he, exactly?*

Aren't they a defense contractor, too?

Ethos

Are there any left-wing talk show commentators on radio?

How many radio stations are in the US?

Ethos

Pathos

Who?

Premise 4

Find some current examples. How do they compare?

Statistics?

The main idea of this entire section seems to be that letting a few conglomerates own most of our media is hurting democracy by limiting and slanting what Americans know about important issues.

with similarly heavy holdings in all the other important media; Bertelsmann, the German company with masses of U.S. publications, book houses, and partnerships with the other giant media companies; Disney, which has come a long way from concentrating on Mickey Mouse and now, in the pattern of its fellow giants, owns 164 separate media properties from radio and TV stations to magazines and a multitude of other outlets in print and motion picture companies; and General Electric, owner of NBC and its multiple subsidiaries.

One radio firm, ClearChannel, the sponsor of Rush Limbaugh and other exclusively right-wing commentators, owns 2,400 stations, dwarfing all other radio outlets in size and audience.

In their control of most of our newspapers, the great majority of our radio and television, of our most widely distributed books, magazines and motion pictures, these conglomerates have cheapened what once was a civilized mix of programming.

We have large cadres of talented screenwriters who periodically complain that they have exciting and touching material that the networks reject in favor of repetitious junk. These writers do it for the money and could quit, as some of them have. But they once got paid for writing original dramas like those of Paddy Chayevsky and other playwrights whose work was heard in earlier days of television.

Programs appealing to the variety of our national tastes and variations in politics are so rare they approach extinction. The choices for the majority of Americans are the prime-time network shows that range from the relatively harmless petty jokes and dating games typified by "Seinfeld" to the unrelieved sex and violence of Murdoch's Fox network and "reality" shows in which "real people"—that is, non-professional amateurs—are willingly subjected to contests in sexual seduction, deceit and violation of friendships. Most TV drama is an avalanche of violence.

Here are other techniques to help you read actively and critically.

SASE

SASE stands for "summarize, analyze, synthesize, and evaluate." This method is another effective way to find main ideas and supporting information and to critically evaluate an author's arguments. It can also help you cast the material you are reading into a form that you can use in your paper—if you decide that the material is good enough.

Summarize

Start by taking a chapter, article, or even an extended passage from your source and seeing if you can recognize the main points and state them in your own words. Remember that summarizing means presenting only the author's ideas, not your opinions of them.

Analyze

Next, analyze the material by breaking it into its component parts. How does each part contribute to the whole? If there are assertions, what does the author provide to back up those assertions? Are there facts that can be checked for accuracy? Are there assumptions that are not backed up? How much of an argument depends on the author's assumption of beliefs shared by the potential audience? (When a writer makes an assertion that supports our worldview, we sometimes take it for a fact when it isn't.)

Synthesize

The third step is synthesis. Think about what else you have read about the topic. How does the information presented here compare to what you have read from other sources? (If you are just beginning your research, you may want to reread your earliest sources later on.)

Evaluate

Finally, evaluate the material. How thorough is the information? Is any important information missing? How well do the premises of arguments support their conclusions? Are there any logical fallacies? Some arguments are implicit and not always easy to recognize. Explicit arguments state their premises and conclusions clearly, but implicit arguments are more indirect; they may leave conclusions or even some premises unstated. See if you can find all the arguments in a passage that you read, including those the author just implies. (For more on understanding arguments and logical fallacies, see Chapter 5.)

DOUBLE-COLUMN NOTE TAKING

A note-taking method that encourages active and engaged reading is called *double-column note taking* or the *double-entry journal*. This is a reading journal that you use for taking notes from sources you plan to use for a research paper. You can draw a vertical line down the center of a page, or you can use facing pages in your notebook (which gives you more room to write). One column or page will be used for the notes that you take from your sources. You should be as organized as you would be with paper cards or e-cards (see Chapter 6), making sure that you write down page numbers and information for works-cited entries. The second column will be used for your reactions. As you collect ideas and evidence from your sources, you also ask questions; indicate information that confuses, surprises, or delights you; note what you believe and disbelieve; and so on. It is a lot like annotating the text itself—in fact, any ideas we discussed in the guidelines for text annotations can be employed here. Instead of annotating an entire text, however, you are annotating the notes that you take from the text. You can even simply freewrite. The following example shows some double-column notes on the same text the student annotated. At the top she put the bibliographical entry, and in the left column she put quotations and paraphrases from the source. In the right column (appropriately enough, since it is a right-brain activity), she put her own reactions.

Bagdikian, Ben. "Grand Theft: The Conglomeratization of Media and the Degradation of Culture: Twenty-five Years of Monitoring The Multinationals." Multinational Monitor 26.1-2 (Jan.-Feb. 2005): 35-7. Expanded Academic ASAP. Thomson Gale. Web. 19 Oct. 2008.

"For 25 years, a handful of large corporations that specialize in every mass medium of any consequence has dominated what the majority of people in the United States see about the world beyond their personal experience. These giant media firms, unlike any in the past, thanks to the hands-off attitude of the Federal Communications Commission (FCC) majority, are unhampered by laws and regulation."	What's a "handful"?? I wonder how many there are exactly? I wonder what mass media he excludes from "consequence"? Get more information on the FCC. What are current laws and regulations?
B. says democracy depends on "a vision of the real nature" of the US and people here.	I don't know what he means by our "real nature." This sounds pretty stirring, but it's also pretty vague—at least at this point.
He says TV and radio spread radical right-wing politics.	I always heard that the news media was liberal. Is it mainly left-wing or right-wing? Or neither? I better look for some real studies and statistics.
The "nightly use of violence and sex that tell parents and their children that they live in a cruel country."	I bet I could find studies on the effects of sex and violence on TV, especially effects on kids. Would this be relevant to my topic of media and democracy?
ClearChannel—sponsor of Rush Limbaugh & other right-wing talk show hosts owns 2,400 stations.	Limbaugh is pretty extreme—I wonder how many people actually listen to him? And how many radio stations are there in the US? What proportion is 2,400? Are there any big left-wing talk show hosts? On TV there are people like Bill Maher, Jon Stewart, and Steven Colbert. But they take pot shots at everybody. They seem more liberal than conservative, but they can be pretty merciless to liberals. They pretty much go after anybody who does or says something stupid, no matter what political party. Maybe I should compare the numbers of people who watch these TV shows with the numbers of people who listen to Limbaugh and people like him. And what are the demographics?

THE RHETORICAL PRÉCIS

In 1988, Margaret Woodworth developed a method she called the rhetorical précis, which helped students to significantly improve their reading comprehension, as well as their ability to effectively use source materials in their own writing. The rhetorical précis is very like a summary (*précis* means "concise summary"), but with a crucial difference: you evaluate the content of the work and the methods the writer employs to inform and persuade you. A rhetorical précis requires you to look at a writer's strategies as well as the work's content. Because you must be very specific and concise when you write a rhetorical précis, it is an excellent tool for building your skills at understanding the sources you read. (See Chapter 5 for more information about rhetoric.) The format is very specific:

Précis Sentence 1 includes the name of the writer, the genre and title of the work, the date of the work in parentheses, and a "rhetorically accurate verb" (one that describes what kind of action is performed), such as "asserts," "argues," "implies," "demonstrates," or "traces" followed by a "that clause" containing the work's major assertion (it can be the thesis statement). Information about the writer can be included parenthetically after the name, if you choose.

Précis Sentence 2 is an explanation of how the writer develops and supports the work's major assertion. Generally, you should summarize the author's steps in the order in which they occur in the work.

Précis Sentence 3 states your understanding of the writer's purpose, followed by an "in order" phrase. ("Her purpose is to inform readers of . . . in order to help them understand . . . .")

Précis Sentence 4 describes the intended audience and can include what you perceive to be the relationship the writer establishes with the audience.

Following is an example of a rhetorical précis on the article "Grand Theft: The Conglomeratization of Media and the Degradation of Culture" by Ben Bagdikian. The article can be found in Chapter 20. Note that this follows the requirements for the four sentences mentioned previously, and it helps to illuminate the major argument and intent of this piece:

> Ben Bagdikian, in his journal article "Grand Theft: The Conglomeratization of Media and the Degradation of Culture" (2005), argues that a handful of massive media conglomerates have harmed and undermined American democracy. The author supports his main argument by discussing specific corporations, the need for television ratings, the FCC, and public hearings that prove that American citizens aren't being heard. His purpose is to persuade his audience that corporations have grown so strong, our ability to self govern is now at risk in order to get his readers to take political action to protect and, in some cases, reinstate regulations to keep a few corporate media monopolies from controlling all U.S. news. This piece is intended for an audience of Americans who may be unaware of the condition of the American media; Bagdikian wants them to share his deep concern.

5 CHAPTER

Understanding Argument and Persuasion

You want to make sure that you get a good grade in your English class, and the biggest single part of that grade is the research paper. Your instructor warned students that they couldn't just pick any topic that they found interesting; each of you has to write a persuasive paper on a current issue that you can argue about. Your paper has to be able to back up an argumentative thesis, and that will involve reading the arguments other people make and determining how strong or weak they are. It will also mean trying to make your own arguments as airtight as possible. Your instructor warns all of you to be careful to avoid simply making emotional appeals or assuming that your audience feels the same way that you do about important issues. "You aren't preaching to the converted," she says. "Frame your arguments in such a way that you can win people over who may pick up your paper feeling the opposite of how you feel." That's a pretty daunting task.

A big part of evaluating sources and writing strong papers is the ability to evaluate other people's arguments and your own. The better you get at one skill, the better you will get at the other. Although some source material is designed only to provide information and not to persuade or advance arguments, much of what you read will contain arguments, and not all of them will be very logically developed or supported. Your own writing will be impressive if you can avoid those types of arguments. Also, as we pointed out in Chapter 4, some arguments are implicit and not easily recognized. Explicit arguments state their premises and conclusions clearly. Implicit arguments may leave conclusions or even some premises unstated. It's worth taking the time to understand how arguments are made, what to look out for, and what works best.

INDUCTIVE AND DEDUCTIVE ARGUMENTS

All **arguments** have two parts: one or more **premises** (the reasons we give in support of our claim) and the **claim** itself, which is also called the **conclusion** (even if we offer the claim before we offer any premises). If the premises adequately support the conclusion, an argument is a good one. If the premises do not adequately support the conclusion, the argument is fallacious. **Logical fallacies** can be divided into two categories: those where the form of a deductive argument is invalid (**formal fallacies**), and those where the premises of an inductive argument are inadequate to support the conclusion (**informal fallacies**).

Deductive arguments are those that assert that a conclusion follows necessarily from the premises; thus, if you have factual premises, you can prove the truth of your conclusion. This has to do with the form of the argument—if the form is such that the conclusion really does follow necessarily from the premises, the argument is considered **valid.** If you have true premises and a valid argument form, you have what is called a **sound** argument. A **categorical syllogism** is a type of deductive argument using three categorical statements (two premises and a conclusion), and we will use some as examples.

Miranda is a cat.
All cats are felines.
Therefore, Miranda is a feline.

If it is true that Miranda is a cat, and if it is true that all cats are felines, then it necessarily follows that Miranda is a feline. This is a valid form of a deductive argument. What do you think of the following argument?

Miranda is a cat.
All cats are canines.
Therefore, Miranda is a canine.

If you believe that this argument is not valid, you are wrong. It is valid because IF the premises were true, the conclusion would necessarily be true. In fact, the form of this argument is exactly the same as the form of the first argument. Validity in the narrow, specific sense of the term that is used in the study of logic makes no claims about facts—it has to do with the structure of the argument. Look at the following argument. Do you think it is valid?

Some mammals are felines.
All cats are felines.
All cats are mammals.

The preceding argument may have true premises and a true conclusion, but, even though each statement is true, this is not a valid argument because of its form—the form is not one where the conclusion follows necessarily from the premises, as can be demonstrated from the following argument with the same form but different premises:

Some girls are Americans.
All Californians are Americans.
All Californians are girls.

Deductive arguments often leave a premise unstated. We call these *enthymemes*. The premise can remain unstated because it involves an obvious or widely held assumption.

Mark is a model.
Therefore, Mark is very good looking.

The unstated premise in this argument is "All models are very good looking." Sometimes the unstated premise of an enthymeme is an incorrect assumption, an overgeneralization, or even a prejudice, so we need to be alert and be able to put into words all the unstated premises of any arguments we make or encounter.

Inductive arguments assert that the conclusion follows, not necessarily, but only probably, from the truth of the premises. For example,

> The first time Al had scallops, they made him sick. The second time Al had scallops, they made him sick. He tried scallops once again after that, and they also made him sick. Clearly, Al is allergic to scallops.

This is not an entirely bad argument—Al got the same results 100 percent of the time. However, one might argue that this is an example of reaching a conclusion with insufficient statistics. After all, he ate scallops only three times. Given the circumstances, we think it is wise that Al quit trying scallops, but there could be other explanations for why he got ill. (They could simply have been bad scallops. Or maybe he is allergic to an ingredient that was served with the scallops each time.) If the issue were more serious than what to order for dinner, however, three cases would not be enough to provide compelling evidence. If you were taking medication, you would probably be horrified if you learned that it was tested on only three people—or on only one person three times—before it was released to the public.

Most arguments are inductive, not deductive, and inductive argumentation is trickier. Deductive argumentation is more like math—a valid argument with true premises will give you a provable conclusion because there is really no new information in the conclusion: the truth is contained in the premises (think of the "Miranda the cat" example—you would know the conclusion, even if it were not stated, because it's all there in the premises). However, fallacious inductive arguments are often emotionally compelling, especially if they reinforce our own biases and worldviews. Because we tend to be unconscious of how our own biases operate, we need to know how to recognize logical fallacies and how they operate so that we can accurately evaluate the sources that we read (and so that we can write logical research papers when we synthesize our sources). An inductive argument is fallacious if it contains irrelevant premises or insufficient premises. Fallacies in inductive reasoning are called "informal" to distinguish them from fallacies in deductive reasoning, which are a matter of form. The point is to be able to recognize premises that are irrelevant or insufficient, especially if they are offered in support of a conclusion that we happen to agree with. Bad premises do not necessarily make a conclusion wrong, weak, or improbable—it is possible to give weak and otherwise insufficient reasons for supporting a conclusion that could be adequately defended with very good reasons. (Al could go to a doctor to be tested and find out definitively if he really is allergic to scallops, for instance.) However, as researchers and writers, your work will be stronger if you can recognize and avoid both formal and informal fallacies. You'll make better decisions in life, as well. It is always a good idea to ask ourselves not just what we believe about something, but why we believe it. At the end of this chapter, we include a list and examples of common informal fallacies.

APPROACHES TO ARGUMENT AND PERSUASION

The term **rhetoric** is sometimes used pejoratively. You may have heard somebody dismiss someone else's arguments as "mere rhetoric" or "empty rhetoric," as if rhetoric is by its nature insincere and superficial. Certainly, there are people who don't care much about the truth of their claims. They are interested in achieving their own ends for their own purposes, such as gaining profit or power, and they want to persuade us to buy a product, ignore a problem, see a problem where there might not really be one, vote for or against an initiative, or elect or defeat certain political candidates. But rhetoric itself is the stuff of effective writing and speaking and the art of persuasion. Arguing effectively is only superficial or unethical if used to advance goals that are superficial or unethical. Studying rhetoric can make you a better critical thinker, reader, and writer because you become better able to distinguish between form and content. You can evaluate content for what it is really worth and separate emotional appeals from logical and evidence-based appeals.

The Greek philosopher Aristotle (384–322 BCE) talked about the difference between logos (the logical content of a speech) and lexis (the style and delivery of the speaker). To a certain extent, this division is an artificial one because how we say (or write) something can also convey and even shape values. The TV or radio host who shouts opponents down or viciously ridicules them is conveying and supporting certain values simply by his or her actions, such as "people who disagree with you don't deserve respect," "the free and honest exchange of ideas isn't important," "I already know everything I need to know," and "winning an argument is more important than actually being right." Unfortunately, this disrespect for civil discourse and critical thinking doesn't simply discomfit the people who are treated poorly on the air or insulted in absentia; it encourages an acceptance of these values in the host's fan base, who may not realize another unspoken message the host's style conveys: "The people who listen to me are more likely to be swayed by emotion than logic." Form, therefore, is very important for a variety of reasons, and understanding and evaluating form can lead to a better understanding of content, including content that is not explicitly expressed.

ETHOS, LOGOS, AND *PATHOS*

In Aristotle's day, citizens got much of their information from public speeches. Aristotle taught that there were three basic persuasive appeals a speaker could use to sway an audience: *ethos, logos,* and *pathos*. These three appeals are as important in written communication as they are in oral presentations. These appeals, by the way, are not mutually exclusive; in other words, they generally work together to help form strong arguments.

Ethos doesn't translate into "ethics," despite the sound of the word (the two have the same root). Instead, it refers to the writer's or speaker's character as perceived by the audience—in other words, the person's image. Aristotle pointed out that we are more likely to accept the arguments of a person we see as honest, sensible, and knowledgeable. Image is powerful. Celebrities sell products and issues. Actors playing everything from fatherly doctors to wholesome soccer moms urge you to buy pain relievers and laxatives. Political candidates are desperate to be associated with a popular president or to distance themselves from an unpopular one. Political analysts argue about which candidates for the country's highest office would be most likely "to pull over on a highway at night and help you change a tire."

As a writer, your ethos is conveyed by your style, including word choice, and the types of arguments you mount. You need to stay conscious of your audience and your purpose. When you look at your own arguments, ask yourself the following questions:

1. What audience should I picture?
2. How do I want my audience to picture me?
3. What register (the degree of formality conveyed by word and sentence structure) is most appropriate for my writing situation?
4. What tone (emotional attitude) is most appropriate?

Generally, you should picture a diverse audience, not just people who are like you or who already agree with you. You probably want them to see you as logical, reasonable, honest, and fair. You can best do this by showing that you are capable of understanding all sides of an argument and by avoiding informal fallacies, especially ones like "arguments against the person" (attacking people instead of dealing with the merits of their arguments) and "straw person" (misrepresenting other people's arguments instead of dealing with the real ones). You also probably want them to see you as a person who has become something of an authority on the subject that you are discussing. You can help achieve this by introducing genuine authorities to your readers and establishing their credentials. Be alert to the tone your writing has; you don't want to look too casual. The tone that would work with a message to a friend is probably too informal for a research paper. Also, humor can work in some situations, but it can also be risky. Punctuation and grammar are important, too. If your sentences are awkward or obviously ungrammatical, you look less credible.

Word choice should also be a consideration. Don't fall into the trap of trying to use "big words" that you normally aren't comfortable with. You should certainly try to develop your vocabulary so that you are able to choose the most accurate and precise words, but a thesaurus or dictionary won't tell you how words will strike your audience or how they fit best into sentences. Instead of looking smarter, the "big word" strategy can backfire, sometimes comically (only the joke is on you). Enhance the credibility of your image by the evidence you can produce and the way you handle it.

When you read other people's arguments, you should ask the following questions:

1. What assumptions does the writer make about the audience?
2. What methods does he or she use to bolster the appearance of credibility?
3. What does the writer's language say about him or her?
4. What does the writer's tone convey?
5. Does the writer claim any connection, whether direct or ideological, to well-known people in order to seem more impressive? If so, how credible is the connection?

Logos means both "word" and "reason." This appeal is based on logic. A logos-based argument stresses rational thought. In everyday situations, our arguments often depend on ethos and pathos, but academic arguments require an emphasis on logos. This does not mean that you should not be conscious of your image or that you should always refrain from trying to touch your audience's emotions; you just need to present factual evidence and logical chains of reasoning to support all your claims. Recognizing the types of arguments that are employed, as well as proper identification of premises and conclusions and the logical connections between them, is a crucial aspect of logos-based writing. Some arguments are based on definitions, such as what certain terms mean or what the true nature of something is. Some arguments employ analogies or draw parallels between different situations. Many arguments assert cause-and-effect relationships. Some depend on facts and expert opinions. When you look at your own arguments, ask yourself the following questions:

1. Are all of my premises clear? Are they sound or are they simply assumptions or prejudices? If any of my premises are implicit (unspoken), would they work better if I made them explicit (clearly stated)? Do my premises clearly support my conclusions?

2. Is my language clear and precise? Have I defined all important terms that my audience might not understand?

3. Are any analogies or parallels I have used really strong? (Do the relevant similarities outweigh the dissimilarities?)

4. Have I drawn on genuine experts and accurately represented their ideas?

5. Have I provided factual data and statistics?

6. Have I avoided formal and informal fallacies?

As a participant in the scholarly community, you want to do everything you can to make your arguments stand up to careful scrutiny. This sometimes means being willing to rethink and even abandon some of your original assumptions.

When you read other people's arguments, you should ask the following questions:

1. Are all their premises clear? Are they sound or are they simply assumptions or prejudices? Are there any missing premises? Can you put them into words to determine whether they are strong or simply unwarranted assumptions, over-generalizations, or stereotypes?

2. Do we have any shared assumptions? If so, what are they?

3. Is the language clear and precise? Do any important terms need clarification? Are any important terms used inaccurately?

4. If any analogies or parallels have been used, do the relevant similarities outweigh the dissimilarities?

5. Does the writer draw on genuine experts? Are their credentials provided? Can you find sources to check whether their ideas are presented accurately?

6. What facts and statistics have been provided? Can they be verified?

7. Are there any formal and informal fallacies?

Pathos is appeal based on emotion. This isn't in itself a bad thing. In fact, there are many issues that *should* engage our emotions, but we need to be careful not to let emotions get in the way of rational thought. We can find many examples of the use of pathos in arguments in everyday life. Advertisements appeal to many of our emotional needs, such as the desire to be attractive and popular or the fear of aging or death. Politicians appeal to emotions as diverse as fear, anger, self-interest, and love of family. Emotional appeals may also hinge on people's images of themselves. Most people want to think of themselves as fair, compassionate, and intelligent, and appeals that bolster the audience's self-image can also be quite effective. Different emotional appeals can be used for different outcomes, not all of them logically legitimate. Rousing an audience's anger can be effective to motivate them to take action—especially action against an issue. Making an audience laugh at someone can encourage them to dismiss that person's ideas (the "argument against the person" fallacy). Aristotle warned his audience 2,000 years ago that playing on people's emotions to manipulate them and cause them to ignore logic and evidence corrupts judgment and harms both individuals and society. When you read other people's arguments, you should ask the following questions:

1. Is this writer trying to rouse any emotions in the audience? If so, what are they?
2. Does the issue itself tend to raise emotions? How do these emotions differ in different groups of people?
3. How do I feel about this issue? Is it one that I have trouble being open-minded about?
4. If my emotions seem to be the same as the writer's, have I allowed this to make me overlook any flaws in the arguments presented?

Recognizing how ethos, logos, and pathos all play a part in arguments can help us, no matter what type of argument model we use or that we find in the texts we read. If you consider these three appeals and how they are represented in the works you read while researching and in your own writing, you'll be one large step closer to mastering information literacy.

THE TOULMIN METHOD

Stephen Toulmin, a British philosopher, believed in what he called "practical arguments." He felt that reasoning, for the most part, didn't mean generating brand-new ideas; most of the time we encounter, test, and choose among existing ones. This is certainly true when we find sources and write research papers. Toulmin's original purpose was to come up with a way to analyze an argument that we read or hear in order to determine its strengths and weaknesses. The Toulmin Method is an effective way for a critical reader to dissect arguments to judge how well the different parts work together. This method also helps us to summarize arguments more accurately. His method was later picked up and adapted by rhetoricians—people who study the art of speaking and writing effectively and persuasively. It can be an excellent way to organize your own arguments within essays and even entire argumentative essays. Arguments written in this manner are designed to reveal their limitations as well as their strengths, so you can anticipate and handle the reservations or objections your audience may come up with. The following graph shows one way of visually representing Toulmin's Method and its six components: claim, grounds, warrant, backing, rebuttal, and qualifier.

The Toulmin Method of Argumentation

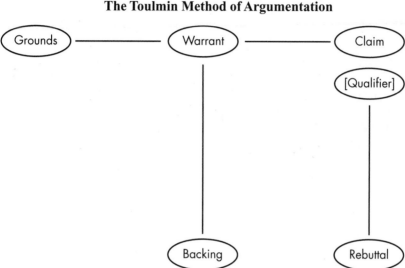

The *claim, grounds,* and *warrant* are considered the essential components of practical arguments. *Backing, rebuttal,* and *qualifier* will not be needed in some arguments.

1. Claim: the argument's conclusion.
2. Grounds: any reasons, evidence, and data used to support the claim.
3. Warrant: the principle or provision that connects the grounds to the claim. It may be simple, but it may also be a longer argument with additional sub-elements. (One way to better understand this term is to consider that the verb form of warrant means "to justify or necessitate.")
4. Backing: any needed justification or credentials that back up the warrant. This part tells the audience why the grounds support the claim.
5. Rebuttal: any exceptions or counterarguments to the claim. Counterarguments will also include a claim, grounds, and a warrant, and may also include the other three elements.
6. Qualifier: any words or phrases (like *some, many,* and *most* or *sometimes, often, almost always,* and *always*) expressing a degree of conditionality asserted. They may limit how universal the claim is.

We can better understand these components by looking at a simple argument. If you can figure out how to construct a Toulmin-style argument of your own, not only can you use this kind of argumentation in your own papers, you can more easily break down other people's arguments to find their strengths and flaws. Let's take a very simple subject: cats as pets.

To construct a **claim**, ask yourself, "What, exactly, do I want to prove?" For our sample argument, something like "cats are great" isn't a great claim. What are cats great for? Who are cats great for? Try to be specific.

Claim:

>   Cats make good pets for city dwellers.

To establish the **grounds** for the claim, try to think of all of the supporting reasoning and evidence, including data if you can find any, that can convince your audience that your claim is a strong one. Ask yourself, "Why should people, including skeptics, accept this claim?"

Grounds:

>   Cats are affectionate.
>
>   Cats don't need a lot of room.
>
>   Cats are economical.
>
>   Cats can be housebroken.
>
>   Cats don't need to be walked or taken outside for exercise.
>
>   Cats can be left on their own all day or even all weekend.

The **warrant** can be among the most important components of an argument to recognize. Warrants may include commonly accepted (but flawed) beliefs, emotional appeals, and value judgments. By making warrants explicit, you can better judge their strength. To establish the warrant for your grounds, think of it as the hook that attaches your evidence to your claim. Ask yourself, "Why should people accept my grounds as meaningful and relevant?"

Warrant:

>   People who live in cities often live in apartments and don't have yards or a lot of space. Pets that can be kept inside, can be left alone most of the day, that are economical, and are still cuddly and affectionate are good choices for city dwellers.

Having established the grounds and warrant, see if you need **backing** for anything in the warrant to make it more convincing. Ask yourself, "What information is needed to prove or explain the ideas in the warrant?"

Backing:

>   Cats are fairly economical because they don't eat a lot of food. Kitty litter is an additional expense, but many brands are quite cheap. Though cats are affectionate by nature, they are also independent enough to be left alone all day. People can buy inexpensive dry-food feeders and water dispensers for them because cats

tend to eat only what they need. If you make sure that their litter box is fresh and their feeders and water dispensers are full, you can safely leave them alone if you want to go away for the weekend.

Next, you need to consider what kind of **rebuttal** someone might make to the argument. Try to figure out any possible restrictions that may legitimately be applied to the claim. Ask yourself, "What are some other possible views on this issue?" "What exceptions could apply?"

Rebuttal:

Some people are allergic to cats, hate dealing with cat litter, don't have the patience to train them not to scratch the furniture, or they just don't like cats. Also, some people like animals that can be trained to do tricks, and cats just aren't that into that. Furthermore, some cats are fickle, jumpy, and not very friendly.

Qualifiers let you fine-tune your claim. A claim may seem to have a greater degree of force if you can make it with absolute certainty; however, that is not always possible, and making a claim with a strong sense of certainty when there are many possible exceptions will actually make it a lot less effective. It may be more reasonable to qualify it, especially in light of possible restrictions. Ask yourself, "How can I limit my claim to make it more accurate and less subject to rebuttal?" The claim "cats make good pets for city dwellers" seems pretty absolute. Can it be retooled?

Qualifiers:

Adding "can" and "many" makes the claim less sweeping and more likely to be accepted as accurate.

Revised Claim:

Cats **can** make good pets for **many** city dwellers.

The Toulmin Method is a very effective method for dissecting an argument, which makes evaluation much easier. You want to evaluate any arguments you encounter in the sources you read, but you need to evaluate your own, as well. If you can dissect your own arguments, you have a better chance at making them more foolproof. Use the Toulmin Method to examine arguments you already believe or to construct arguments in essays, starting with your claim and moving through the other stages.

THE ROGERIAN ARGUMENT

The Rogerian Argument, also called the "common ground argument," isn't a method for critically analyzing other people's arguments, but it can be used as one way of framing your own arguments. We all know people who are so convinced that they are right about an issue that they end up arguing in such a way as to bore, annoy, insult, or even enrage their audiences. Their audiences may end up being so angry that they miss any valid points that are made. They may walk away—or quit reading. Obviously, this isn't the response you want to your own work. Seeing the way people could talk (or shout) at each other without actually communicating, psychologist Carl Rogers devised a strategy he called "empathic listening." He suggested that people strive for mutual understanding and respect and hold back on making judgments until they listened carefully to other people's positions, tried to follow their reasoning, and acknowledged any points that might be valid. This is the opposite of trying to shoot other people down or to ridicule or demonize them. Rogers suggested that discussions be based on finding common ground, and good writers often think of their work as being part of an ongoing discussion. The idea is to downplay emotion and adversarial stances and highlight rational factors and common humanity. Richard E. Young, Alton L. Becker, and Kenneth L. Pike adapted Rogers's ideas for the writing process and called this process "Rogerian Argumentation." When you write a paper, you can do this when summarizing the arguments of people whose positions differ from yours and while you visualize members of your audience who might have experiences, values, and perspectives very different from your own. This approach allows you to adopt an "I win, but you do, too" approach instead of an "I'm right, you're wrong" approach.

Young, Becker, and Pike identified the following four stages for writers making a Rogerian Argument:

1. Introducing the problem to be examined and demonstrating an understanding of opponents' positions.

2. Acknowledging the contexts and situations in which opponents' positions could be valid, exploring any possible common ground between the differing positions.

3. Stating the writer's position and specifying the contexts and situations in which it is valid.

4. Stating how the opponent's position would benefit by adopting elements of the writer's position.

Let's look at a simple issue: smoking on your college or university campus. Suppose you want to argue that smoking should be totally banned on your campus. You think smoking is nasty, and you're tired of seeing cigarette butts all over the place. You think too many smokers are rude and thoughtless, and you have grown pretty sick of smokers in general.

Stage one in a Rogerian argument has two components: introducing the problem to be examined and demonstrating an understanding of opponents' positions. The first *seems* easy.

Statement of problem:

> Smoking is a filthy habit, and smoking on campus leads to litter and noxious, unhealthy fumes.

Right away, we see a problem with the phrasing of this statement—it subverts the second component. It is phrased in such a way that smokers would probably feel personally attacked. It also overgeneralizes. How can you show you understand the other side when you start like this? You really have to think about what people on the other side of your argument might feel.

Restatement of problem:

> Some nonsmokers on campus are made uncomfortable by smokers; also, some smokers contribute to campus litter.

This works better. It eliminates the overgeneralizations and it doesn't insult everyone who smokes. Now we can move on to the second component of stage one.

Understanding opponents' position:

> Smoking is very pleasurable to many people. Also, it is habit forming. Many smokers who wish they could stop have trouble doing so, and being without a cigarette for long periods of time can cause a lot of stress and discomfort to habitual smokers, making it harder to concentrate on school tasks. Smokers aren't the only people to litter. Also, it can be hard not to litter if there aren't enough outdoor ashtrays around.

Stage two involves looking at contexts and situations in which the other side's positions could be valid and looking for common ground.

Validity of other side's points and common ground:

> Breaking habits can, indeed, be very hard (you know this from personal experience). And school in particular can also be a very stressful place. As for common ground, everybody benefits when the environment is clean and attractive, and everybody benefits when stressors are reduced. (And inhaling tobacco smoke can be pretty stressful, too, for nonsmokers.)

When you move on to stage three, stating your position and specifying the contexts and situations in which it is valid, you should really consider the ideas that you have generated in stages one and two. Perhaps you should modify your objectives somewhat. You first wanted a complete ban on smoking on campus. It would certainly be healthier for everyone involved, including smokers—but smokers already know how bad for their health smoking is. Even the tobacco industry has given up trying to claim that the dangers are overstated. Sure, some smokers may be in denial, but most of them are just as smart and sensible as anyone else, so if they smoke, it must satisfy some need that is hard (or seemingly impossible) for them to give up. Smokers may be a minority, but that doesn't mean that their point of view should be ignored.

Statement of position (revised from original intent):

> Because some nonsmokers on campus are made uncomfortable by smokers, and some smokers contribute to campus litter, smoking should be restricted to certain areas on campus. These areas should be numerous enough to be convenient. Also, these areas should have enough ashtrays to meet smokers' needs.

Stage four can be the hardest—coming up with reasons for why opponents would benefit by adopting elements of your position.

Benefits for opponents:

> Even though smokers may prefer being able to smoke anywhere outside (they are already banned from smoking in any buildings), smoking in areas specifically designated will calm nonsmokers down and possibly prevent an outright ban on smoking. Also, everyone, including smokers, will benefit from a more attractive, butt-free campus.

Rogers advised trying to understand the positions of people we disagree with by listening to them with respect and seriously considering their feelings and ideas before advancing our own position. This approach can help you to write a very persuasive paper—and it may open you to divergent viewpoints, as well. The compromise suggested in the preceding sample argument may not be perfect, but it allows both sides on the smoking ban issue to receive some benefits. It is also realistic. When constructing your arguments, try to look at all sides in an issue, and demonstrate respect for people with different viewpoints. Although this may not seem possible for some issues, it is a worthy mental exercise. Trying to understand what motivates people who are very far from your views and values can help you construct better arguments, and you may even bring some people closer to your own ideas.

LOGICAL FALLACIES

The term *fallacy* is used by some philosophers and rhetoricians only for particular types of errors in deductive and inductive arguments, but others expand the term to include more categories of errors in reasoning, as well as rhetorical (persuasive) techniques that lead to untrustworthy, unsound, and improbable conclusions. We use the broader definition here because it allows us to include a greater number of common problems that students should be able to recognize in school and in life. Following is a list of some common informal fallacies and examples of faulty reasoning. This list should help you to recognize weaknesses in logic when you encounter them in other people's arguments and help you to avoid weak and fallacious reasoning in your own arguments and papers.

Accident is the fallacy of applying a general rule to a particular situation where there are circumstances that logically and ethically make the rule inapplicable.

Example: *A good soldier follows orders, so it was perfectly proper for those soldiers to obey their captain's orders to murder a village full of innocent civilians.*

An **ad hoc hypothesis** is a hypothesis that is manufactured for the sole purpose of trying to explain away facts that refute a theory, conclusion, or assertion.

Example: *Just because the last predictions I made didn't turn out to happen doesn't mean that I am not a psychic—all your negative energy is affecting my metaphysical receptors!*

The **anecdotal evidence fallacy** occurs when a person ignores or minimizes evidence arrived at by objective and systematic research or scientific testing in favor of one or more personal stories that are unrepresentative. This is also called the **confabulation fallacy.**

Example: *Smoking isn't going to hurt me—my grandpa smoked three packs a day for sixty-five years and wasn't sick a day in his life. He lived to be ninety.*

Sometimes the anecdotal evidence isn't even verified:

Example: *Of course there is a Loch Ness monster—there has to be since so many people over the years have seen it.*

Appeal to authority is the fallacy of saying that simply because an authority supports something, it must be true—or if an authority attacks something, it must be untrue. Experts can disagree. Consider what happens in a trial when one side brings in expert testimony—the other side responds by bringing in experts of their own. You should consult genuine authorities, but you should also examine how they reached their opinions and see if a consensus exists in a field. Sadly, some experts allow themselves to be bought, and they will make assertions based on what the people or corporations paying them want disseminated to the public, not what they really believe to be true. In some cases, the so-called authority isn't really an expert in the pertinent field. Some experts on logical fallacies list as a subcategory the **professor of nothing** fallacy, describing it as trying to add credibility to an argument by quoting a supposed authority who has the title of "professor" or "doctor," while omitting to mention that the discipline in which the title was earned has little or nothing to do with the subject.

Example: *Dr. Butz is a professor and a Ph.D; thus, he is obviously a highly educated man, so we should believe him when he says that the Nazis didn't deliberately exterminate millions of Jews. [Professor Butz is an associate professor of electrical engineering, not a historian.]*

Appeal to belief argues, either explicitly or implicitly, that because "most" people believe something to be true, it must therefore be true. (This fallacy is sometimes employed even when the arguer is incorrect about "most" people believing something.) It is related to the **appeal to popularity** fallacy.

Example: *According to a Harris poll, 84% of people believe in miracles, so we should assume miracles really do occur—that many people can't be wrong.*

Appeal to consequences is the fallacy that takes the form of saying we should accept conclusions that are psychologically comfortable to us and reject conclusions if they cause us psychological discomfort. We should always consider the consequences of an action, but we need to distinguish between consequences that we can prove to be logically relevant and those that might simply distress some of us.

Example: *I don't believe that human actions contribute to global warming—after all, what can I do about it? And I certainly don't want to change my lifestyle dramatically. I like the way I live!*

Appeal to ignorance argues that if you cannot prove that something is false, it must be true, or if you cannot prove that something is true, it must be false.

Example: *I believe in ghosts—no one has ever been able to prove they don't exist.*

Appeal to intuition takes the form of believing that because an idea does not match our experience of how things work or how we believe they should work, that idea is not true. Essentially, it argues that for something to be accepted as true, it must be similar to what we already believe to be true. Sometimes this fallacy is preceded with phrases like "Common sense tells us that . . ." or "My gut feeling is that . . . ."

Example: *That kid can't sit still—he has Attention Deficit Hyperactivity Disorder; giving him stimulants can't possibly help him. [In reality, stimulants are an effective method of treatment for ADHD.]*

Appeal to the moon is a whimsically named fallacy that doesn't really involve making an appeal to the moon itself. Instead, it argues that human capacities for scientific invention are so immense that sooner or later we will figure out a solution to any problems that we have—so we really don't need to worry about the problems that we are facing or creating now. After all, "If we can put a man on the moon, we must also be able to . . . ."

Example: *I don't worry about pollution. After all, if scientists can put a man on the moon, they can surely figure out how to clean up our water and air before they get too bad.*

Appeal to popularity argues that because most people have favorable emotions toward something, it must be good, or that because most people have unfavorable emotions against something, it must be bad. This fallacy has been used historically to support some pretty heinous actions, including slavery and genocide, and we still see it in operation around the world today. Think about the arguments made for and against some current controversial issues, and you'll probably be able to come up with a number of examples.

Example: *Most people think that it is fine to give up some rights and liberties if it could make us safer, so it is obviously the right course of action.*

Appeal to ridicule happens when ridicule is used instead of evidence in an argument. It often accompanies **abusive argument against the person** fallacies. Just listen to talk radio for a while—some "shock jocks" have built their careers on verbally abusing other people. Appeal to ridicule rests on making jokes about the opposition and mocking opposing viewpoints and people with different opinions instead of looking at hard facts and making careful, objective, honest analyses of arguments and information.

Example: *Of course I don't believe in evolution—except maybe in your case since you do look like a monkey.*

Appeal to tradition, also called the **traditional wisdom fallacy,** says that something must be accepted as just or good simply because it is traditional or that something must be rejected as unjust or harmful simply because it is not traditional. This resembles and sometimes accompanies **appeal to popularity,** but it draws upon the past.

Example: *I'm not voting for her—we've never had a woman mayor in this town before, so I see no reason to have one now.*

Arguments against the person, also called **ad hominem** fallacies, all involve some sort of attack or focus on the person or people making an argument, not at the real arguments. Arguments against the person often occur with the **straw person** fallacy.

Abusive ad hominem, also called **personal attack,** is when someone simply attacks someone on the other side of an argument as immoral, stupid, or something else bad.

Example: *I'm not buying that argument about sexual harassment being a problem in the workplace—it's just another femi-Nazi exaggeration.*

The **bad reasons fallacy** involves concluding that an opponent's theory or conclusion is wrong because he or she provided bad reasons. If all the possible reasons and facts used to back up a conclusion are indeed bad, then it is logical to reject the conclusion. But sometimes people who are right make poor arguments. They may even be right for the wrong reasons. But we cannot logically throw out an entire conclusion simply because one or more people who believe it provide bad reasons for believing it.

Example: *I am not going to vote in favor of that school bond plan. My neighbor was saying how she was going to vote for it because she knows the head of the group that is backing it, and he's a very nice person. That is a really stupid reason to vote for something.*

Circumstantial ad hominem arguments attack another person's argument by claiming that circumstances affecting the people making the argument render their arguments worthless. Although we should certainly pay attention to conflicts of interest, biases, and other potentially relevant factors, arguments must be judged on their own merits, not dismissed because some of the people making the argument stand to benefit or are trying to avoid negative consequences.

Example: *I don't agree with you that colleges need more money to hire more faculty to teach more classes—you are a college student, so of course you want to be able to get the classes that you need.*

Damning with faint praise attacks a position by complimenting or praising the opponent or the opponent's argument in such an unenthusiastic or distorted way that the opponent actually looks bad because of it. *Of course we should consider your suggestion of what restaurant to eat at before making up our minds—I ate there once before, and I only saw one cockroach—it was small, too.*

Poisoning the well is when a person argues that we can simply totally disregard the arguments offered by those with opposing viewpoints because they simply cannot be trusted to tell the truth. Metaphorically, such a fallacy says that "anything that comes out of that well is poisoned." In other words, anything that person says is flawed just because he or she says it, so disregard it. It is often used as an excuse to avoid arguments that the other side uses that are too strong to easily refute.

Example: *I wouldn't listen to a word he says about that proposal—he's a liar and a crook.*

The **tu quoque fallacy** ("You, also" or "You're another") occurs when someone mounts a defense against criticism by accusing the other party of being guilty of the same thing. Whether the accuser is guilty of the same or a similar wrong is irrelevant to the truth of the original charge. However, it can be very effective because the accuser is put on the defensive and frequently feels compelled to defend against the accusation, taking the heat off the opponent. This is psychologically related to the **two wrongs make a right** fallacy.

Example: *How can you accuse me of corruption when you were under investigation yourself just last year?*

Begging the question takes the conclusion of an argument and, instead of offering a genuine premise, simply rephrases the conclusion itself. No matter how strongly you feel about a subject, you should be able to see that a conclusion can't be supported with itself—it must have distinct premises that aren't rewordings of the conclusion. We tend to use circular reasoning when we are trying to defend principles that we are so emotionally sure of or have believed for so long and unquestioningly that we cannot conceive of their being false. It is also sometimes called the **vicious circle.**

Example: *Gay marriage should not be legalized because marriage should be between a man and a woman.*

Blinding with science involves misusing technical jargon to overwhelm and confuse the audience or incorrectly claiming scientific support, sometimes by using actual studies but misinterpreting and misapplying the data or leaving relevant data out. When the latter happens, the **fallacy of exclusion** is also occurring.

Example: *That study linking red meat consumption to increased risk of colon cancer is flawed because the data ignored the finiteness of the rigid cohomology of a variety over a finite field and the p-adic meromorphy of the unit root zeta function of a family of varieties over a finite field of characteristic p.*

Common practice is when you justify something wrong by claiming that a lot of people engage in the same wrong. It dismisses all other relevant factors and asks the audience to accept that something wrong is just, reasonable, or at least excusable because a lot of people engage in the activity. This is an all-too-common justification for reprehensible behavior.

Example: *I saved time by copying and pasting some paragraphs from sources I found on the Internet—lots of students do.*

Complex question is the name given the fallacy of phrasing a question in such a way that it assumes a premise that has not actually been proven.

Example: *Are you still in favor of spending taxpayers' hard-earned money on ridiculous boondoggles?*

Composition argues that because the parts of a whole have a certain property, the whole must also have the same property.

Example: *I know those people—every single one of them is a rational, intelligent person. Don't worry—that mob they have just formed will behave rationally and intelligently, too.*

Confirmation bias occurs when a person sees or accepts only the evidence that supports a desired conclusion. This is related to **tainted sample.**

Example: *I know he really, really likes me. He said my new haircut looked OK, and he took me to a nice restaurant that didn't cost me too much money, and he came over to my apartment and stayed over three hours watching the football game, and he said he'll call me sometime soon. I've found Mr. Right!*

Division argues that because the whole has a certain property, all the individual parts that comprise it must have the same property.

Example: *The United States is the richest country in the world, so all Americans are rich.*

Equivocation occurs when the same term is used with two different meanings, or a term with more than one meaning is used as if it had only one meaning. The argument depends upon an ambiguity in the meaning of a word. The following slogan is an example of equivocation because it ignores the fact that "kill" has at least two meanings. (None of us would say that arsenic can't kill us just because it cannot form the intention to do so.)

Example: *Guns don't kill people; people kill people.*

The following reasoning ignores the fact that in science, the word "theory" has a different meaning than it does in everyday conversation, where it tends to mean something that hasn't been proven or even tested. In science, a theory summarizes a hypothesis or group of hypotheses that have been supported with repeated testing. In other words, in science, a theory is as good as it gets.

Example: *I don't believe in the theory of _____; after all, it's only a theory!*

Escape to the future involves claiming that your theory or assertion will eventually be proven true because incontrovertible evidence lies in the future. This claim is often accompanied by the **Galileo gambit.**

Example: *In ten years or so, when more evidence is in, the world will know that people like me were right—they just can't see it now, but it will be clear soon. They didn't believe Galileo, either, but he turned out to be right.*

Exceptionalism is a notion held by members of some countries, religions, or classes that their groups are "exceptional" among other countries, religions, classes, etc., with special roles to play in their societies, the world, or even through human history. This notion is used to justify playing by different rules from what they expect, even demand, of members of other groups. This notion is generally accompanied by various instances of the fallacy of **special pleading.**

Example: *Adolph Hitler:* "I believe today that I am acting in the sense of the Almighty Creator. By warding off the Jews I am fighting for the Lord's work." *[Hitler believed that "Aryans," especially Germans, were a Master race who had the right to rule the world and were therefore justified to make war on "inferior" races and nations and to murder members of "undesirable" groups.]*

The **fallacy of exclusion** occurs when an arguer excludes evidence from consideration that would change the outcome of an argument. This fallacy is also called the **fallacy of suppressed evidence.** People can, in effect, lie while telling the truth if they tell you only an incomplete truth. With this fallacy, the premises offered are true—they are just seriously incomplete.

Example: *You should use this expensive new drug for your skin rash—in a study, 94% of the people who used it saw their rashes disappear within two weeks [but the argument omits the information that 94% of the subjects who used a placebo saw their rashes disappear within two weeks, too].*

False cause, also called **questionable cause,** happens when someone claims that something that follows something else or occurs with it must be caused by it. Sometimes the two are related only coincidentally, or are both caused by something not yet identified. Superstitions, selective perceptions, and selective memory lead to many examples of the **false cause** fallacy.

Example: *I know that walking under a ladder causes bad luck—I once walked under a ladder, and five weeks later, I lost my wallet. I'm never going to walk under a ladder again.*

The **Galileo gambit** is a way of trying to bolster credibility for shaky scientific theories that are rejected by the majority of experts in a given field. Although it is true that a number of brilliant visionaries were laughed at or persecuted in past times, a lot has changed since then. In earlier centuries, the scientific methods and practices that are typical today didn't exist, and people like Galileo were attacked primarily by religious establishments. Being rejected by scholarly associations and journals today isn't parallel to what Galileo, Copernicus, and others faced, and it certainly isn't evidence of superior research or reasoning. The **Galileo gambit** may be accompanied by the **escape to the future** fallacy.

Example: *The members of the scientific establishment laugh at me, but that is what establishments do—they are nearsighted, unimaginative groups of toadies who can't admit they are wrong and are afraid to face new ideas. They laughed at Galileo, too, and they persecuted him like they are persecuting me. Ultimately, he was proven to be right—like I will be.*

Glory by association and **guilt by association** are both forms of **transfer** (see page 112).

Jingoism, also called the **appeal to patriotism** fallacy, occurs when someone attempts to persuade an audience by calling on their love of country and linking what they want the audience to support to patriotism. Patriotism is laudable, but there is a problem when it is called upon in place of sound reasoning and evidence. Such arguments may also be used to attempt to refute an opposing position by calling it treasonous or unpatriotic. This is often related to the **abusive argument against the person,** where an opponent's arguments and evidence are ignored in favor of simply attacking them, and the **straw person** argument, which distorts or falsifies the other side's stands.

Example: *Of course I support the Patriot Act—it's patriotic to do so. You must not love your country if you disagree with anything in it.*

A **false dilemma** is produced when an arguer insists that there are only two possible options available, when there may be three or even more—or when the two choices are not mutually exclusive. It is also called **false dichotomy,** the **black and white fallacy,** and the **either-or fallacy.**

Example: *Either we win the war in Vietnam, or all of Asia will fall to communism.*

Hasty generalization fallacies occur when a conclusion is reached based on insufficient samples, unrepresentative samples, or a combination of these.

Example: *I'm sure I know who'll win the election—we took a poll in my English class today, and two-thirds of the students plan to vote for Candidate X.*

Imagined wrongs make a right is just a variation of the **two wrongs make a right** fallacy, which attempts to justify a wrong action by pointing to another wrong action. In these arguments, assumptions (or wishful thinking), not facts, are relied on; the wrong action used to justify another wrong action hasn't actually occurred or has occurred only in a limited number of situations, not universally, as implied.

Example: *Maybe we did let the kinds of organizations people belonged to influence who got government jobs, but this is what parties in power always do.*

Inconsistency occurs when someone asserts premises that are contradictory. This can occur in one situation, where the contradictory assertions are part of the same extended argument, but it also occurs when a person is caught making a claim or offering a premise that is inconsistent with the claims and premises the person makes before other audiences. (See also **kettle defense.**) This is not the same as changing one's mind after new evidence has been analyzed or logical reasoning followed. Not changing one's mind in these circumstances commits errors of *slothful induction, moving the goalposts,* or *invincible ignorance.*

Example: *My daughter-in-law is a terrible mother. She is way too indulgent with my grandchildren—each of them has one of those iPod things. . . . And you should see how strict she is! She makes them do way too many chores before she'll give them a penny of their allowance.*

Invincible ignorance is the fallacy of insisting on the legitimacy of a position in spite of overwhelming evidence against it. It is closely related to the **slothful induction** fallacy.

Example: *Yes, I smoke in my house and in my car with my kids around, but that can't possibly hurt them—I don't care what those doctors say.*

The **irrelevant purpose fallacy** argues against the legitimacy or efficacy of a plan, program, or an institution or of an entire organization or other body by pointing out that it has "failed to fulfill its purpose" when the ostensible failed purpose was never actually the intended one.

Example: *It is obvious that Social Security has failed—there are still poor people in the United States and the gap between the rich and the poor is growing bigger with each passing year. [The program wasn't created to eliminate gaps between the rich and the poor, but to help needy unemployed people, widows, and fatherless children.]*

The **kettle defense** is a form of the fallacy of **inconsistency** that gets its name from the following anecdote (in itself facetious, but designed to make a point): In the village court, a man has been charged by a neighbor of having returned a borrowed kettle in a damaged condition. The accused, who doesn't want to pay for a new kettle, mounts a three-part defense: 1) he returned the kettle undamaged, 2) it already had a hole in it when he borrowed it, and 3) he never borrowed it in the first place.

Example: *Oil company executive: "We don't need to worry about adding carbon dioxide to the atmosphere because 1) more carbon dioxide in the atmosphere won't increase global climate change, 2) natural sources are the cause of increased carbon dioxide that is warming the atmosphere, and 3) global warming is actually beneficial, because it will increase the growing period in some agricultural areas."*

The **lip service fallacy** gets its name from the idiom "to pay lip service" to something, meaning that someone asserts that he or she agrees with and supports an idea or plan, but this person actually intends to not do anything to help it to succeed or even wants to see it fail. This might simply seem like an example of hypocrisy, not a fallacy as such, but it is a rhetorical strategy that can be used to influence arguments and outcomes, so we are including it.

Example: *Global warming is a serious issue today, and we are committed to doing everything we can to combat it [stated by the spokesperson for a corporation lobbying against regulations to control global warming emissions].*

Misapplication or Misunderstanding of the Concept of Falsifiability

The concept of "falsifiability" is a frequently misunderstood part of the scientific method. Saying that a theory should be dismissed because it is "falsifiable" is fallacious reasoning because it ignores the actual meaning of the word as scientists and philosophers use it. Good hypotheses are always "falsifiable" in this sense, meaning that specific conditions can be stated under which the hypothesis would be overturned. There must be some way of acquiring evidence that would tend to confirm or disconfirm a hypothesis. This underscores a difference between science and dogma: with dogmatic theories, there are no circumstances or experiments under which they can decisively be proven false because they aren't testable at all. The misapplication or misunderstanding of the concept of falsifiability often occurs with fallacies like **invincible ignorance, shifting the burden of proof,** and **appeal to ignorance.**

Example: *I don't believe in the theory of _____; after all, my teacher says it's falsifiable!*

The **misuse of averages fallacy** occurs when someone argues that unacceptable conditions or situations are acceptable based on a type of average, the mean, which adds quantities and then divides the total by the number of quantities. The arguer will point out that the average value of all cases is within acceptable limits, implying that all cases are within acceptable limits. The arguer ignores the other two types of average that may actually be more appropriate (if obtaining an average is appropriate at all): the median, which denotes the value lying at the midpoint of a frequency distribution, or the mode, which denotes the value that occurs most frequently in a set of data. This fallacy is sometimes related to the fallacy of **division.**

Example: *Boris: "Pottsylvania is a country of great prosperity for everyone—the average income is two hundred thousand Pottsylrubles a year." Bullwinkle: "Yeah—but the richest 1% of the people there are averaging a billion dollars a year, and everybody else is living in poverty."*

Moving the goalposts takes the form of changing the criteria for proving an assertion. The criteria may be relaxed to make it easier for one's own side to win an argument, or they can be made stricter to refute an opponent. It can also be used to describe any situation when someone makes any goal or set of goals more difficult for someone else just as they are being met or when it looks like they will be met, whether for proving a claim or accomplishing a task. It involves changing the rules or even definitions so that one side is always right and the other side is always wrong. It is a form of **special pleading.**

Example: *Lee: "We should never have a woman president. If women were as capable as men of leading a country, why haven't we ever had a female leader before?" Pat: "The U.S. may not have had any female presidents, but Margaret Thatcher was Prime Minister of the United Kingdom, Golda Meir was Prime Minister of Israel, Indira Gandhi was Prime Minister of India, and Angela Merkel was elected Chancellor of Germany." Lee: "Well, that's in modern times. Why haven't there been any great women leaders in history?" Pat: "Hatshepsut became the female Pharaoh of Egypt around 1479 BCE, Queen Isabella I of Spain ruled jointly with her husband, Queen Catherine de Medici ruled France as her sons' regent, and Queen Elizabeth I ruled England and Ireland for over forty years." Lee: "But those women all ruled centuries ago, and they were exceptions, and besides, they weren't elected."*

No true Scotsman is the name given to a fallacy that is a way of reinterpreting evidence in order to deny the refutation of an assertion or conclusion. The source of the fallacy's name is illustrated by the following classic exchange: Mr. Y, "No true Scotsman puts sugar in his porridge." Ms. Z, "But Mr. Brodie puts sugar in his porridge, and he's a Scotsman." Mr. Y, "Well, then, he's no *true* Scotsman." In this fallacy, any facts that contradict an assertion are dismissed as untrue simply because they contradict the assertion. This fallacy combines elements of three other fallacies: **ad hoc hypothesis, begging the question,** and **invincible ignorance.**

Example: *Lee: "No computer expert would recommend that model." Pat: "Professor X teaches computer science, and she says it's a good choice." Lee: "Well, then, obviously she's no **true** computer expert."*

The **opinion entitlement fallacy** occurs when someone asserts the right to have an opinion as if it were a logical defense of that opinion. This is often a resort of people who see all the premises they use to bolster their claims get dismantled one by one. With nothing left to offer, they fall back on the assertion "I am entitled to my own opinion!" This is a fact—it is not, however, a premise that can support any argument unrelated to arguments about freedom of speech. It is also sometimes used in an attempt to rebut opponents' arguments, taking the form of "you're/they're just trying to attack my First Amendment right to freedom of speech!" Although situations occur where people try to limit other people's expressions of opinion, simply disagreeing with people—and providing strong evidence that their claims lack supporting evidence or are fallacious—isn't an instance of this. If pursued very far from the original claims and premises, this becomes a type of **red herring.** It is also related to **invincible ignorance.**

Example: *"I don't care what anyone says about this issue—I have the right to my own opinion, and no one can take that away from me."*

Quibbling happens when someone seizes on a minor point, such as a small and not very relevant factual error or a minor inconsistency, and uses this to negate the conclusion of an argument that actually has a very strong foundation.

Example: *I completely reject what she is saying about that product being unsafe. After all, she quoted Dr. Smith's study, when it was actually a study undertaken by Dr. Smythe, and furthermore, she said that 80% of the mice developed cancerous cells, and it was really only 78%.*

Red herring is the fallacy of using something irrelevant but emotional and compelling to distract the audience from the real point. The audience can be swayed because the issue may be psychologically relevant to them, so they miss the fact that it is logically irrelevant to the argument. Political debates, speeches, and press conferences are great places to look for red herrings. When a politician is asked a question he or she doesn't want to answer, a typical tactic is to try to steer the discussion in another direction. This won't work very well if the ploy is obvious and people want to stick with the original issue. But if the irrelevant issue is a "hot button" one, it may prove a big enough distraction to get the speaker off the hook—at least temporarily.

Example: *You are accusing me of changing my position on the war, but I am an expert on war—I am a decorated veteran, and I know what I am talking about, and I know what it is like to come back home to a lack of support, and I think the most important thing we can do right now is to give our troops the support they need. The recent scandals at government-run hospitals demonstrate all too clearly that we need serious reform in this area.*

Shifting the burden of proof occurs when someone defends a proposition by demanding that a contrary proposition be proven instead of being able to present arguments in defense of the original proposition. This is related to **appeal to ignorance** and **slothful induction.**

Example: *Ghosts exist. If you want to prove me wrong, then you'd better prove what else those eerie sounds that I heard in the graveyard are.*

Slippery slope arguments assert that a sequence of increasingly unacceptable events will inevitably follow from an action or event that may not itself seem undesirable or unreasonable at all, until the arguer takes us all the way to something no reasonable person would want to see occur. **False dilemma** ignores middle grounds and alternatives. Slippery slope acknowledges a middle ground, but moves you from one point at the beginning to an unpleasant extreme at the other end. *A* may be next to *B,* and *B* may be next to *C,* and so on, but that does not mean that accepting *A* will inevitably move you to *Z.*

Example: *I could let you pay your rent a day late this month without any problem, but next month you'll want to pay me two days late, and the month after that, you could ask for three, and the next thing I know, you're going to expect me to wait months for my money.*

Slothful induction is the fallacy of denying the logical conclusion of an inductive argument that presents strong evidence. This fallacy is committed when someone demands an unfairly high amount of evidence before accepting an idea. It is related to **invincible ignorance** and **shifting the burden of proof.**

Example: *I don't accept what scientists say about climate change—after all, scientific theories are always changing. You can't depend on what scientists say because it may be different next year.*

Special pleading is committed when an argument includes a double standard (a principle that is unfairly applied in different ways to different people or groups). A form of it consists of using different words to describe the same actions by different people or groups, applying positive (or at least more innocuous) terms to our actions or those of our friends and allies, and applying pejorative terms to other people's actions). This fallacy is related to the notion of **exceptionalism.**

Example: *Bill: "I can't believe she cheated on me! She even used the girls she caught me with as an excuse, but that's not fair—I'm a guy, so it isn't as serious. It doesn't mean anything when I do it."*

Straw person fallacies occur when a person attacks an exaggerated, distorted, or false version of an opponent's argument because it is easier than dealing with the real points that the opponent makes. It would be a lot easier to defeat a person made of straw in a fight than a real person—especially a strong one.

Example: *My opponent agrees with a federal vaccine advisory panel's recommendation that all girls and women between the ages of eleven and twenty-six should receive a new vaccine that prevents most cases of cervical cancer. This cancer is related to sexual activity. Encouraging girls as young as eleven to engage in sex is incredibly irresponsible; my opponent is clearly not fit for office.*

A **tainted sample** is produced when people collect evidence in such a way that they are likely to find more evidence in support of their desired conclusions than against them, despite what thorough, objective evidence-gathering would find. This is related to **confirmation bias.**

Example: *I can prove my point—I found this great website that posted dozens of articles that all show that I am right!*

The **transfer** rhetorical device has two forms, **guilt by association** and **glory by association.** Both forms work by trying to get the audience to transfer emotions (positive or negative) from one person, group, or even object to another. This is categorized as a fallacy when the actual relationship is tenuous or spurious.

Glory by association is the technique of trying to enhance the arguer's image and credibility by asserting or hinting that he or she is associated with someone or something good when the relationship is irrelevant, superficial, exaggerated, or even nonexistent. It may even refer to great people from the past. (The fallacy can also be used with objects, like alluding to a classic or luxury car model when advertising a new car model.)

Example: *As I was saying to Bill Gates the other day, I think my new gizmo will revolutionize the way we do business around the world.*

Guilt by association is the technique of trying to undermine an opponent by asserting or hinting that he or she is somehow associated with someone or something bad when the relationship is irrelevant, superficial, exaggerated, or even nonexistent. It may even refer to infamous villains from the past. (Like **glory by association,** it can be used with two objects, as well.)

Example: *I won't vote for that candidate. Change one letter of his first name, and you've got the name of the mastermind of 9–11. And his middle name is the name of the former dictator of Iraq.*

The **two wrongs make a right** fallacy attempts to justify a wrong action by pointing to another wrong action. Sometimes the arguer points to past or current actions by an opponent, and sometimes the arguer simply asserts that the other side would do the same thing if given the opportunity.

Example: *Why shouldn't we torture enemy combatants to get information out of them? They do it to our soldiers.*

Wishful thinking is when a person accepts a claim as true or rejects it as false merely because he or she strongly wishes a certain conclusion or outcome is true. It is related to **invincible ignorance** and **slothful induction.**

Example: *I cannot believe that Thomas Jefferson, one of our history's greatest men, had a slave mistress and had children by her. Some things are simply morally unimaginable and just can't be true.*

A **weak analogy** happens when an argument is based on an analogy that is so weak that the argument is too weak for the purpose to which it is put. For an argument from analogy to be effective, the things being compared should have strongly relevant similarities and no relevant dissimilarities.

Example: *Before he married Priscilla, Elvis Presley was asked what he thought about marriage, and he responded with a question: "Why buy the whole cow when you can sneak under the fence?"*

Navigating the Writing Process

Let's look at an average weekend for a couple of college students.

The first weekend is Carrie's. Carrie lives at home, commutes to college, and has a younger sister and parents who work multiple jobs in order to pay the rent. She babysits her sister all day Saturday and Sunday so her parents can work, and she goes to her job at a local pizza parlor at night. Between family duties, work, and the few hours she manages to steal away with her friends on Saturday night, she hasn't much time to think about schoolwork.

How about Antonio's weekend? Antonio works forty hours a week tending bar, has a son, and hasn't been to school in more than six years. He's decided to return to college to get his business degree, but he can't afford day care, so he watches his son by day. He works at the bar all night, and when he does get some down time, he tries to spend it with his girlfriend and son. This schedule means he typically takes courses on the weekends and online, and he seldom has time to devote himself to school because his everyday life gets in the way.

These weekends may be like yours (they may even be less stressful). Somewhere in between friends, family, children, dating, work, sports, rehearsal, and everything else, those pesky professors also expect you to complete major assignments. This is the reality of college life. When a professor assigns a paper, you may be tempted to sit on the assignment for several busy weekends before finally writing it the day before it's due. We've all done writing like this, but it's not the best way to write. In fact, it's a horrible way to write; the end product you submit for a grade will simply be a rough draft, full of mistakes and lost chances to improve.

As you will learn in this chapter, writing is a *process*. It takes time to craft a top-notch paper, and no matter how good a writer you are, understanding and following helpful steps in the process of writing will help you become a great writer. Though you'll often feel like time is against you during your college days, the steps outlined here can be accomplished in a matter of hours and can help you create a paper you can be proud of. Although ideally you should devote several days or at least several hours to each step in the process, even cramming all the steps into one evening may improve your final product.

PROCRASTINATION

We would like to offer a few words about procrastination, a subject that years of experience have made us experts on. Almost everyone procrastinates in some areas of life. Some of us even accept it as inevitable, but knowing the underlying psychological reasons behind some types of writing assignment procrastination can help us deal with the problem. Without being entirely conscious of it, some people set themselves up to procrastinate as a way of protecting their self-esteem. Consider the grade ranges below, and then look at a typical student's response to getting these grades:

> B or C: This isn't bad at all—I didn't put nearly enough time into this. In fact, it shows I'm pretty smart—I got this grade even though I really had to rush. Imagine the kind of grade I would have gotten if I'd really put all the time I should have into this! I'm a better writer than I thought!

> D or F: Wow. This is terrible. But it doesn't really reflect my real talents. I just didn't put enough time into this. I'm a lot better writer than this!

Sometimes procrastinators are perfectionists in disguise. They want everything they do to be perfect, but who can be perfect? By sabotaging themselves through procrastination, they have an excuse for not achieving perfection. Wouldn't it be better to accept that you aren't perfect, but no one else is, either, so you may as well get the very best grade that you are capable of getting with proper time management.

LEARNING STYLES

Before getting into the steps of the process every writer must go through, you should know a little something about the way your brain works. If you can come to understand how people think and learn, you'll also understand how important it is to write your paper in different steps, each separate from the others. Many of the steps of the writing process detailed next have been followed by professional writers for generations. Recent studies in psychology, sociology, neurology, and many other fields are giving scientific reasons why these steps have always worked so well.

Cognitive scientists have categorized three separate styles of learners: **kinesthetic** learners (those who learn best by touch or by doing), **auditory** learners (those who learn best by hearing), and **visual** learners (those who learn best by seeing). Every one of us utilizes a mix of the three categories, and most of us are dominant in one of the styles, using it more than the other two. However, those of us who can use all three styles equally well, will have an easier time learning in every situation.

As you read about the steps of the writing process throughout this chapter, keep these learning styles in mind. If you understand how your own brain works, what styles of learning and even what side of the brain you use most, then every step of the writing process will make more sense to you. Let's take a closer look at the styles.

Kinesthetic Learners

Kinesthetic learners process and remember information best by taking an active role in the subject matter. Many athletes are primarily kinesthetic learners because of untold hours practicing the same moves over and over. The goal of many athletes is to reach a place where there is no thought involved in the action; the body has its own kind of "memory," and this is what kinesthetic learners rely on. For example, a baseball player may get two strikes in a row because he's thinking too much—wondering what pitch is coming next, thinking about his grip on the bat, worrying about his foot placement. After he lets his body take over, he nails the ball. In karate, the same concept is called *mu shin,* which means "no mind," or "nothingness." You practice *katas* and rehearsed movements endlessly, so that eventually, your body remembers how to block and punch without your conscious mind ever coming into it.

How does all of this sports talk help us in the classroom and the writing process? It shows you a possible strength and weakness in your learning style. If you are a kinesthetic learner, you probably find yourself taking copious notes; your hand may even take notes in class while your mind is wondering what to pick up for dinner on your way home. A great way for kinesthetic learners to study is to simply rewrite their own notes a few times. A few rounds of this rewriting, and when you start your midterm, your body will almost remember the information itself once you start writing the answers for the essay question. You may find that the physical feel of drafting an essay with pencil and paper helps you more than typing at a keyboard. You may also find yourself regularly using note cards during the research process or taking notes in the margins of your books because underlining and engaging in the text helps you remember the content.

Whereas you may enjoy lectures because they give you something solid to write down, you may have trouble working in study groups because the conversational atmosphere doesn't give you any content to copy. You may get very little from overheads or information on chalk boards, but you may thrive on writing on the board and even making collages.

KINESTHETIC LEARNERS

- Learn by doing.
- Are often athletes, martial artists, dancers, or sculptors.
- Study by rewriting class notes, using note cards, and taking notes in books to stay involved in the information.
- Have as strengths in-class writing, essay drafting, note taking, sculpting, sports.

Auditory Learners

Auditory learners process and remember information best by listening to what is presented to them. Musicians, music lovers, and actors are often auditory learners because those tasks require listening. A musician's brain is trained to hear minute differences in tone or pitch and can "hear" and translate the symbols on a sheet of music into sounds that will entertain us. Even if you're simply a lover of music, you'll probably find that your ability to distinguish between the subtle differences of your favorite guitarists indicates that you are a strong auditory learner. Similarly, if you are an actor or an orator, you have to memorize long speeches and monologues, and you train yourself to listen for your cues. When another actor says, "Is someone at the door?" you know it's your time to come on to stage and say your next line.

This translates to some very helpful skill sets in the classroom setting. If you are a strong auditory learner, you'll do well to listen to lectures. Attending study groups or tutorials and talking to friends about the day's lecture will be very helpful because remembering the conversations you have will be easier than remembering the pages of a book or the contents of a classroom overhead projection. Auditory learners may have an uncanny knack for recalling details the professor says during lectures and will excel in a class based on class discussions. Tape recorders are often the best tool to help auditory learners study. Record the day's lecture and replay it the night before the test; hearing the information will help you to recall it the next day. Similarly, when you're doing research, taking notes on a tape recorder (or, preferably, a digital recorder with separate file folders to sort your notes) may be more helpful than note cards or comments written on paper.

AUDITORY LEARNERS

- Learn by listening and talking.
- Are often musicians, music lovers, actors, or orators.
- Study by attending study sessions and listening to a taped version of class lectures or taped notes during the research process.
- Have as strengths recalling lectures, talking about the subject matter.

Visual Learners

Visual learners are best able to process and remember information that they've seen. Painters grasp the fundamentals of perspective, shading, color, and painting to create abstract or representational images to create a variety of effects. Photographers can look at commonplace objects or scenes and create art through an ability to see the beauty or drama in images that other people may overlook. Architects, while relying heavily on math and geometry, have to be able to translate the lines on a blueprint into a real building that will some day exist. Fashion designers (even just people with a strong fashion sense) need to understand how every piece of clothing, every cloth type, color choice, and accessory will come together to produce a fabulous outfit.

In the classroom, a visual learner would do well with a professor who utilizes the board, overheads, and even PowerPoint presentations. You'll remember images you've seen more than notes or lectures, and you may even find yourself doodling a lot in your notebook. (Contrary to what your grammar school teachers may have said, doodling in class is actually a good thing; it proves your brain is still "on"). When you read a textbook, you may find that you visually recall a certain photo or graphic on a page, and only then do you remember what the words on the page said. To study for this type of visualization, skim over the chapter several times after you've read it; this will make you familiar with the book and remind you of materials in association with pictures and obvious visuals in the book. While taking a test, you may find yourself closing your eyes to remember what your page of notes looked like in order to dig up that memory. Often, your notes will simply be a graphic representation of exactly what the professor put on the board, and you may study by using a lot of different colored highlighters and pens to visually separate different bits of information.

VISUAL LEARNERS

- Learn by seeing.
- Are often painters, photographers, architects, or fashion designers.
- Study by using various colors of ink and highlighters to give notes distinct visual presences; skim over chapters/notes to become familiar with visuals.
- Have as strengths remembering what's on the board, recalling books, benefiting from highlighters.

Left- and Right-Brain Thinking

Aside from the three modes of learning previously discussed, another major distinction between learning styles (and a major factor in the steps of the writing process) comes from the biology of the brain. The human brain has two hemispheres, a left one and a right one. Recent research suggests that each hemisphere of the brain is responsible for different types of thought. Thus, each side of the brain is responsible for different steps of the writing process. People are generally more dominant in one hemisphere of the brain than in the other. The closer you are to a fifty-fifty "brain mix" (or an "orbital" brain function), the better off you'll be. Read the different brain functions described next and try to figure out which side of the brain you may favor.

First, let's look at the left side of the brain. This lobe of the brain is said to be responsible for logical functions. It keeps track of time, and it views the world very much like a computer, separating everything you perceive into parts and bits of data (it may see an eyeball, a nose, black hair, and a mouth, but it may not put it all together as belonging to a face). This side of the brain controls all functions that require systems and organization, such as logic, mathematics, geometry, chemistry formulas, grammar, spelling, and all the formulaic rules of writing.

If you are left-brain dominant, you may find that you excel at math, and complicated formulae that baffle your friends make sense to you. Blueprints and schematics may be easy for you to understand, as well as logic, Boolean logic, and computer languages. In writing, this side of the brain controls all the mechanical issues: grammar, spelling, MLA and APA documentation rules, outlining, structure, and so on. If you ever turn in papers and have your teacher tell you that your grammar is strong, but you need better content, you may be left-brain dominant.

The right side of the brain controls the opposite functions. Whereas the left controls logic, the right controls emotion. The saying "Time flies when you're having fun" reflects this side of the brain; it controls pleasure, and it has no concept of time. On a basic level, while the left side of the brain assembles the parts of the world, the right side puts them together into a comprehensive whole (all those features I'm seeing are actually a face . . . my mom's face!). If you are right-brain dominant, you may excel at the humanities. Art, music, theater, literature, even aspects of philosophy or the imagination to truly understand history all come from this side of the brain.

In writing, your ability to generate imaginative and innovative content as well as the sense that something just *sounds good* is linked to the right side of the brain. Similarly, if you've written a paper, and your instructor says that it flows well and your arguments are creative, but you need help with grammar and punctuation, the right side of the brain was probably taking over.

The distinctions between left- and right-brain thinking are perhaps the most important reason for the separate stages of the writing process. Each step of the process requires that a different side of the brain take over. Think about starting a car in the winter. You can turn on the ignition, but if you drive right away, your car will not be very efficient—no heat, poor visibility due to frosted windows, and you may even keep stalling out. If you let it run for a few minutes, however, you'll find a smoothly running, efficient engine. This is how your brain works, as well. If the proper side of the brain isn't given time to warm up before being used, you will be inefficient in your thought processes.

If you complete a right-brain task, then switch to a left and back again, neither side of the brain ever gets a chance to fully warm up. This means both types of thought process will be slow and foggy. If you separate the steps of the process, however, you'll find that each one will get all the brain power it deserves. For a good example of how one side of the brain gets fired up and takes over whatever task you're doing, think of a time you've been enjoying a hobby (playing or listening to music, painting, playing video games, writing, even gossiping on the phone) and completely lost track of time. This "lost time" is because the right side of your brain took over and the left side "powered down." Let each step of the writing process fire up the appropriate portion of your brain before proceeding.

LEFT BRAIN	RIGHT BRAIN
Logic	Emotion
Time	No Time
Parts	Whole Picture
Systems/Math	Art/Beauty
Grammar	Content
Spelling	Poetics

THE WRITING PROCESS

There are several steps to the process of writing a research paper: prewriting, research and note taking, generating a research proposal, outlining, drafting, and revising/editing. The steps are listed next in an order that many students find logical and natural. If you have never written a research paper and are intimidated by all the work that lies ahead, you may want to follow the steps in the linear order they are described here. However, you may find that you perform these steps in a different order—you may even perform some of them simultaneously, such as generating a rough outline as you generate your research proposal to see if your topic is workable before you have to commit yourself. Writing tends to be a very organic, messy, and recursive activity. ("Recursive" means that you move back and forth from earlier to later stages.) You may feel like you are going in circles at times, bouncing back and forth between these steps in order to write. That doesn't mean that you aren't making progress—writing a paper can be a lot like painting a portrait. Artists don't start at the top of the canvas and move down. They do some quick sketches to stimulate ideas. After they are happy with a basic idea of organization, they sketch on the canvas itself. Then they start applying the brushstrokes of paint, working on different sections of the canvas that seem to need their attention the most, then moving on to other sections. They often come back to areas that have already been painted to add some extra touches. They may even paint over sections of the canvas if they don't like an area or get a better idea.

The point is to learn what type of writing style best suits you. Just don't slight any of the steps that you need simply to save time. We know that your time as a college or university student is limited and valuable, and some of these steps may seem unnecessary and time consuming, but even briefly focusing on each step will help you create a stronger paper.

PREWRITING

Prewriting is a means to help generate your actual topic and refine a working thesis statement for your paper-writing process. It is a crucial first step of anyone's writing process. For more information and examples, prewriting is fully discussed in detail in Chapter 1.

RESEARCHING AND NOTE TAKING

After you have done some prewriting to generate ideas, the next step in the process is gathering information on the topic you've chosen to write about. Every argument you make in support of your thesis in your research papers needs to have a substantial fact or piece of evidence to help prove your point. This step in the prewriting process is the point when you gather those bits of information. Think of the notes you take at this stage as little time capsules for your future self, who will be busy writing the paper and won't have time to do any more research or dig through disorganized stacks of information. Always have your thesis in mind while taking notes. When you sit down to write your paper, it will be easier if most of your notes relate directly to your thesis.

The process of research, if done properly, typically takes more time than it will take to write the actual paper. You may find yourself spending several entire weekends at the library to generate research for a paper that you can draft in one evening. Researching is a painstaking process, and many writers make mistakes early on that hinder their progress. Some of these errors include the following:

1. You lose data. While researching, you may find a perfect passage to quote in a book, but a week later when you start writing your paper, this passage is impossible to find. Similarly, you may find a great source on a database, but when it's time to collect that source in the library, your limited notes prevent you from

getting your hands on the actual book or journal. Even the most simple fact, quotation, or bit of information is easy to forget when you're under a deadline and trying to write a good paper quickly. Trust us on that.

2. You lose citation information. Often, in a rush to get out of the library or speed up the research process, students cut corners when taking notes on the bibliographic and citation information for sources. This loss is often disastrous. You may find yourself using materials from a book to prove some major arguments in your paper, only to realize at the end that you have to take these ideas out of the paper because you can't properly attribute their sources with in-text citations and on your works-cited page—and you don't want to get a failing grade because of plagiarism.

3. You don't have regular access to a source. Some of the best sources in a library are found in the reference section (they typically have the code "REF" before the call numbers). These sources cannot be checked out of the library; they are meant to be accessible to any student at any time. Because you can't take these books home with you, good note taking is essential. Also, the typical academic library lets you borrow a source only for a very limited number of days. You'll need the information longer than that, so you need to master the skills of taking notes thorough enough so that you can complete your paper without having the actual book in hand.

These research perils, however, are very easy to overcome if you develop a good system of note taking. The system detailed below is just one way to organize your notes. Try it out, and then experiment with variations and differences as your college career continues. Modify your note-taking system to suit your needs and your own learning style. The key to any note-taking system you develop, however, is consistency. Don't use one system for taking notes and saving bibliographic information for one source and another system for another source. That type of variation will cause you to miss key information and lead to more work (and headaches) for you later.

Electronic or Paper Research "Cards"

In research writing, the traditional way to take notes on your sources is to use paper note cards. In fact, many professors require you to use note cards and submit them with your final paper to show how you gathered your data; others may have you submit them throughout the term to make sure that you are making progress in your research. Note cards are very handy because you can easily store them for use later in the class. They're small and easy to transport, and they're relatively durable, so they don't get wrinkled and ripped while you're transporting them from library to home and back again.

Alternatively, you may choose to create electronic "cards" on your computer. Many students have access to computers or even laptops they can take right into the library while doing research, and, of course, they can access library databases on their home computers. Electronic "cards," which can also be called source sets, information sets, or e-notes, have certain advantages over paper cards—for example, the information stored on your computer is easily integrated into your paper when you are at the drafting stage. Your professor may accept these sets submitted electronically, or you can print out the appropriate sections and paste them onto cards, enabling you to meet your professor's requirements and still have all your notes stored on your computer (and, we hope, a backup flash drive).

Paper cards have their own advantages. They are more portable, they force you to be more concise (you may have only one main idea or quotation to a card), and they can enable you to spread cards out in front of you on a table and move ideas around like puzzle pieces. This can be a lot easier than cutting and pasting information in a computer document. Arranging physical cards on a table can let you see the "big picture." You may even decide to combine the two types of note taking to suit your own purposes. Even though you may end up not using physical paper cards at all, we are going to refer to the source information sets as card sets for simplicity's sake.

A typical set contains two types: bibliography (works cited) cards and note cards. Your instructor may also require other types, such as evaluations that you have created using reference sources like *Book Review Digest, Contemporary Authors,* and *Magazines for Libraries.* (For a more complete discussion of evaluating sources, see Chapter 4.)

Bibliography Cards

The bibliography (work cited) card should be the first card you fill out whenever you find a source you plan to use. It needs to be thorough and accurate—don't cut corners to save a few minutes. The following bibliography card is an example.

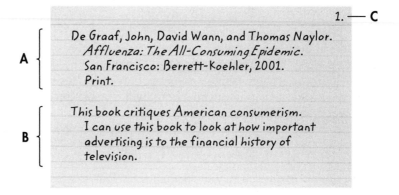

Note the following key elements to this card:

A is the full bibliographic entry for the source in either proper MLA or APA format. This entry should be done *exactly* how it will be reprinted in the works-cited page of your paper. It is a bit time consuming to do it this way, but it will save you a lot of time during your paper draft, and it virtually eliminates any mistakes you'd make while compiling the works-cited list at a later date.

B is an annotation (brief explanation) of the source. On larger papers, you'll read so many sources that it will be hard to tell the difference between them later on. You will probably end up reading more sources than you actually use. Later on, when you are preparing to write your paper, the annotation should help you recall exactly what source you're dealing with. It could include a brief description of the major arguments you're drawing on and what made the source good enough for you to use. If you are a visual learner, you may even want to include a physical description, like "the blue book with all the good graphs in the back."

C is a source number. Every source you pick up should have its own number assigned to it. The first book you pick up is number 1. Finish the bibliography card and start taking notes from this source. The next source is number 2. Finish that bibliography card and take all the notes out of that source next. This seems very simple at this stage, but the source numbers become a life saver when we get to the note cards.

In Chapter 4, we discussed a variety of techniques for evaluating sources and reading critically, such as annotating texts, the SASE (Summarize, Analyze, Synthesize, and Evaluate) method, and writing a rhetorical précis. If you used any or all of these techniques, they are fertile ground for your research paper notes.

Note Cards

Note cards contain the actual notes themselves. Every bit of information you have from a source needs to be documented. As a general rule, with paper cards, you should make only one note per card, and you should try whenever possible to keep the entire note on the front side of the card. Don't forget to cite the source's page numbers. There are several sizes of note cards to choose from. The 3 × 5-inch note cards are small—it can be hard to squeeze a lot of information on one card, so you may prefer to use a larger card for your notes. The 4 × 6-inch note cards are fairly standard. If you're a visual learner, you may even want different colored note cards to help you make an association between colors and content. If your cards are electronic, try to think in terms of how much information you could get on a physical note card (especially useful if you will be pasting your typed notes on regular cards). Even if you don't have to turn physical cards in, you want to make sure that your e-notes are distinct and concise. It will make organizing your information a lot easier later on when you are writing your paper.

Types of Notes

DIRECT QUOTATIONS

You should use direct quotations sparingly. In fact, a general rule is to keep direct quotations to ten percent or less of your total paper (check with your instructor). When you find a quotation that you think you may use in your paper, it should do two things for you. First, it should contain information that is critical to the argument you are making. If the content of the quotation does not help you support your own thesis in some way, you shouldn't use it. Second, a direct quotation should express an idea in an especially lively, arresting, or otherwise interesting way. The content is important, obviously, but you could always paraphrase the information, so the quality of the prose is a key to deciding whether to use a direct quotation. Try to quote only passages that sound better than anything you could have phrased yourself. Of course, sometimes you have to use direct quotations instead of paraphrasing, because the information may be very technical and impossible to paraphrase.

When you copy a quotation onto a note card, you'll need to be careful to copy it verbatim (word for word). You can also photocopy a passage and glue it to the note card if you use physical cards. Students often copy passages too quickly or sloppily and later inadvertently misquote their sources without even realizing it. Although it is possible to use too many quotations in your paper, it is not possible to have too many quotations in your note cards when you start your paper. You will be better off deciding which quotations to keep, paraphrase, or cut while you are drafting than trying to find more information at the last minute. Make your notes accurate, and you'll be saving yourself time when it comes to write your first draft.

SUMMARIES AND PARAPHRASES

Most often, when you find good information that you want to use in your paper, it's better just to say it in your own words instead of using a direct quotation. When you do this, you are either summarizing or paraphrasing. Summarizing is when you take only the main points of a passage and put them into your own words. Paraphrasing is when you restate all the ideas of the original passage in your own words, which means the paraphrase will be roughly the same length as the original. (For a more complete discussion of summarizing and paraphrasing, see Chapter 8.) Why not just use direct quotations instead? Perhaps the original source material is very formal and wordy, full of vocabulary that is more formal—or informal—than the language you're using in your paper. In the sciences, for example, your source could be highly technical and full of jargon. You may want to keep the content but make it more "reader friendly." Also, you don't want to have a greater percentage of direct quotations than what your instructor specifies.

Remember, these notes are for your own use as your write the paper. If you have a hard time understanding something, take the notes in a way that will be easier for you to digest later as you write. When you put a summary or paraphrase on a note card, keep in mind that you'll still need to include a page number for the source material. You should be just as careful with these types of notes as with direct quotation notes.

It is a good idea to keep a photocopy (or electronic copy, when possible) of the original passages that you quote or paraphrase. Why? So that later, as you polish your paper, you don't accidentally "improve" your own writing back to the original wording without even realizing it.

STATISTIC/DATE/HISTORICAL FACT

Many times you will find a simple fact, date, or statistic in a source that you will want to use. The language is not beautiful or provocative enough for a direct quotation, and the information is too brief to bother trying to paraphrase. Nevertheless, such facts and details will help bolster your arguments (and prove to your professor that you did your research). If you were writing a paper on the singer Kurt Cobain for a course on the history of rock and roll, for example, you may need to cite a statistic (one album sold three million copies in less than three months), a specific date (he committed suicide on April 8, 1994), or a biographical fact about him (he was born in Hoquiam, Washington).

For note-taking purposes, quickly summarizing these types of facts is just fine for your note card or e-card. As suggested earlier, it is wise to keep a copy of a summarized passage to refer back to. As always, include the page number(s) where you originally found any of these facts when you use print sources.

PERSONAL THOUGHTS AND IDEAS

Finally, some of the sources you're reading may bring up memories from past classes or give you a new insight. Always make time to take these notes, as well. If a source led you to some conclusion of your own, be sure that you write it down right away. It's a good idea to jot down your idea in either paper note card or e-card format because consistency is important—keep your own ideas cataloged using the same format you use for all note taking. You might misplace the insight unless you preserve it and know where to look for it. Also, you may want to mention the original source material that led you to this conclusion, so citing that source alongside your own thoughts might not be a bad idea.

Sample Paper Cards and E-Cards

Take a look at the following sample quotation note card:

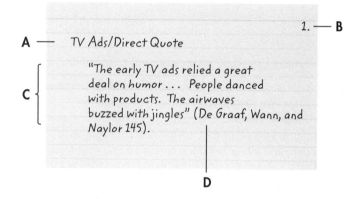

Note the following elements on this note card:

A is the topic heading for the note card. The topic heading lets you know at a glance exactly what type of information is on this card. Here it says, "TV Ads/Direct Quote" to let you know the type of information on the card and whether the card contains a quotation, paraphrase, or summary. The topic heading should ultimately correspond to specific points on your outline. Your card could even have a topic heading, such as "II.B.2 TV History/Direct Quote." The "II.B.2" tells you that this will ultimately be used in that specific point of the outline (see the outlining section of this chapter for more details).

B is the source number. This number corresponds to the source number of the bib card for the source the note comes from. By using this simple system of source numbers, you'll never have to write any bibliographic information on your note cards. If you see the number 7 in that corner, just flip to the bib card with a number 7 on it for the corresponding bibliographic information. This system will save you hours of copying the same bib notes repeatedly.

C is the note itself. This is the most important part of the note-taking process, obviously. You will need to take different types of notes: direct quotes, paraphrases, statistics, dates/historical facts, and personal thoughts. (For more on types of notes, see pages 123–125.)

D is the citation information, in proper MLA or APA format. Note that you've included the author's last name (or an abbreviation of the title if no name is given), just as you would in the body of your paper. Following proper documentation format at this stage will make citing sources easier when you write your paper. The most important detail on this part of the note card is the page number. Get in the habit of always including page numbers in your note cards. Note cards will probably become your primary method of taking notes while researching, so if the page number isn't part of your note, you will not be able to provide an accurate in-text citation.

Tips for Electronic Note Taking

The key to electronic note taking, as with paper note cards, is to remain as organized as possible. If you have dozens of saved word files sprawled around your desktop or on several thumb drives, these notes will be difficult to access when it comes time to draft your paper.

Consider the following tips while taking notes on a computer:

1. *Organize:* You must decide how you want to organize your e-notes before you begin taking them. We recommend a single, separate word-processing document for each source you use. For example, if you take ten notes out of one book you're using, save all of that as one file, complete with the work-cited entry, annotation, and any other information you recorded, such as a source evaluation. Later, you simply open that book's note file, and you'll find all the information you thought to copy down. Make sure your document names are clear, like "Set 1, *Affluenza*." (Beginning each document name with the same word, like "set," "card," or "e-card," will help you to keep them organized in your computer files.) Later, when you are writing your paper, you can start blending all the e-card sections you choose to use into one document.

   On the opposite page is an example of the first section of a single-document e-card set. This is the sort of set a professor might ask a student to turn in, so all the elements are in MLA format. If you are keeping electronic cards for your own purposes only, you don't need to double-space or have your name and course identification information in the upper-left corner. In fact, you might even choose to use the last name of the author of your source in the upper-right header.

2. *Track the Original Location:* The author and page number (when available) of every note you take must be tracked during your note taking. (If there is no author, use the first important word or words of the title; also, nonprint sources will not have page numbers unless they are PDF files.) You could use MLA or APA style parenthetical citations to track the author and page number, or you could use a system more akin to the note cards mentioned previously.

Dianne Jeffries

Professor Rupert Giles

English 1A: 12:30 MW

17 October 2009

Research Information Set #7

Work-Cited

McChesney, Robert W. *Corporate Media and the Threat to Democracy.* Ed. Greg
     Ruggiero and Stuart Sahulka. New York: Seven Stories, 1997. Print. Open Media
     Pamphlet Series.

Annotation

This book examines the media conglomerate corporations that own the majority of the
public airwaves throughout America (and the world). One of the book's main arguments
is that corporate control of mass media is a threat to self-governance and democracy.
McChesney's research should be helpful to my paper because he provides many examples
of corporate media control and a lot of historical facts about the media and journalism.

Author Evaluation

McChesney is a well known author, research professor, and the president and co-founder
of The Free Press, an organization which informs the public about corporate controlled
media. According to *Contemporary Authors*, McChesney "has devoted his professional
career to understanding the media, educating others about his findings, and working to
reform it."

Note #1

Historical Journalism. Paraphrase: The 1820s and 1830s were a golden age of journalism
when newspapers existed simply to inform the masses and get them involved in the political process. In the 1840s, many newspapers changed their format when they realized they
could make a profit from their work (McChesney 12).

Note #2

Political Journalism. Quotation: "The press was closely linked to the political culture of
the day; any given city might have several newspapers providing very different interpretations of public issues. Some modern scholars term this era the 'Dark Ages of American
Journalism'" (11).

3. *Bibliographic Information:* Just as note cards start with detailed work-cited cards, your electronic notes must begin with electronic bibliographic information. Every bit of information you may need for a works-cited page should be copied down during note taking. The way you take down this information depends on how you took your e-notes: A) If you decided to take all your notes in one large file, you could use the bibliographic information as a way to organize your notes visually. Each time you start a new source in this large file, you begin that section with a full works-cited entry for that source. B) If every note is its own saved file, you could organize them all in one "folder" along with a separate saved file that contains nothing but the bibliographic information. This way, each folder contains all the notes and works-cited information you'll need. C) If you opt to make each source its own file, the top of that document should contain the bibliographic information.

4. *Backups:* Make backup copies of all your notes. Data loss and computer crashes are very commonplace events, and a fried hard drive would be catastrophic if it cost you all of your notes. Email the notes to yourself, so they're sitting on a server somewhere, and don't delete them until after the end of the term. Put them on separate thumb drives. You can even store them on a friend's computer until the paper is finished. You are never too paranoid when it comes to protecting electronic data.

Copies and Printouts

Another way to keep track of your sources is to make full copies. Virtually every library will give you access to a photocopier, so you can make copies of the sources you're using. This is especially important for print versions of journal articles and reference books, which can't be checked out. You'll still want to keep good notes using one of the methods previously discussed, but having the source on hand can be very important during the writing process. Many databases now allow you to email yourself whole articles and files, so you can save on print costs (and trees) by keeping electronic versions of the sources you're using.

After your note cards or e-cards are all completed, you'll need to organize them in some fashion. The most logical way to do this is to create an outline (see "Outline," p. 131). After your outline is complete, go through your cards. Set aside paper cards that you don't think you'll need and put all the rest in the order you'll probably end up using in the paper. Paste e-cards you think you'll use into a document that can become your first draft. Remember, this type of logical organization is a left-brain activity, whereas writing the draft of your paper is a right-brain activity. If all the organizing is done in advance, you'll be free to write without distraction, pulling information from cards in the order that you need it.

Another type of note taking that can be useful is called "double-column note taking" or the "double-entry journal." See page 85 for an explanation and example.

RESEARCH PROPOSAL

At some point in the writing process, you may be asked to propose your ideas to your instructor, so she can give you feedback and guidance on what you plan to include. The research proposal has many applications later in life as well: in your jobs you may be asked to submit such proposals to secure funding for a project or to get a cash grant; in graduate school you will be asked to write a prospectus of your thesis or dissertation before you start working on it. The proposal you write should let the audience know exactly what you plan to research and write about. You may want to submit a proposal after you've done some preliminary research (so you know what you are talking about), but before you fully commit to your ideas and gather your final sources. Even if nobody assigns a research proposal, you may wish to complete one anyway. The action of putting your plans down on paper will help to clarify your process and what actions you need to take to complete your paper. Consider writing yourself a proposal using the steps detailed next, just to explore your own ideas and assumptions.

There are two types of proposal you can write. The first is an informal proposal that is brief and to the point. The second is a formal prospectus that goes into much greater detail. Your instructor should clarify which type of proposal she is interested in.

Informal Proposal

The informal proposal is typically brief (often only a paragraph long) and gives a quick overview of your thoughts and plans for this project. Within this paragraph, you should include the following elements and any others you think important:

- The purpose of the paper (to inform, persuade, critique, etc.).
- The audience of the paper (a general audience, your peers, instructor, professionals in the field, etc.).
- The topic you have chosen (and possibly why you chose this topic).
- Your working thesis statement.
- Major arguments you plan to include.
- Any other key challenges that are ahead of you, your original research question(s), your title, a timeline, or reactions you hope to get from the audience.

Following is an example of a research proposal for Dianne Jeffries's sample paper found in Chapter 11. This does not contain the final thesis she used in the actual paper; this was a much rougher working thesis that was refined as her writing process continued. Finally, notice that she uses the term "in this paper, I plan to . . . ." This statement is perfectly acceptable in a proposal—after all, the whole point is to tell the instructor what you plan to do. However, it should generally be avoided in the actual paper itself because many instructors find such phrases redundant and tedious.

Freedom of speech is not just something that lets us sit in a coffee shop and talk bad about the government. Instead, it is a fundamental right to accurate and free information that is important to our world and safety. With the current system of corporate media ownership, however, there is no free speech. As media companies own more and more of the airwaves and websites we rely upon for information, information starts to cost us money and get distorted. In this paper, I plan to inform an audience of my peers about the nature of modern-day media cartels and then convince them that these corporations are hurting the values we need to keep America strong. Major arguments will include a look at how free speech is crucial for democracy as well as opinions from several media experts who think this system is harmful to our society. My working thesis will be this: American media corporations are hurting free speech and the very nature of democracy.

Formal Prospectus

A formal prospectus is a much longer endeavor than the informal proposal. It is still designed to help you decide how to proceed in the writing of your paper, but it is a much more thorough piece of work. It is often several pages long and could include many of the following elements. Often, the nature of your paper and research will determine which elements you will ultimately include in your prospectus, but before starting, you should find out from your instructor exactly which elements she may prefer.

TITLE PAGE

This would be an MLA or APA style title page that gives the planned title of your project.

INTRODUCTION

Because this is a longer project, you will need an introduction, just as you would with a short paper. This introduction should include your preliminary thesis statement as well as a quick rationale of why you have chosen this topic. If you started with an informal proposal like the preceding one, you could adapt that paragraph as the introduction of your prospectus.

ABSTRACT

An abstract is a brief summary of your overall plan. It should encapsulate all the major arguments and research you plan to include and should neatly sum up your entire paper in 50–150 words. An abstract is very popular in the sciences and in papers written in APA format.

REVIEW OF LITERATURE

Here you briefly review the major sources, documents, and research that exists on this subject (also called the "literature" of a subject). You should discuss the major sources you found in your early research and tell the audience about the major arguments and scholarly camps that exist in this field of study.

BIBLIOGRAPHY (OR ANNOTATED BIBLIOGRAPHY)

This is a working bibliography of all sources. It could easily be merged with the Review of Literature to get an Annotated Bibliography, or it can be a standalone list of bibliographic entries in your documentation style (MLA, APA, etc.) to serve as a quick reference list for you and your audience.

RESEARCH METHODS

Here you discuss the overall plan for your research. Research encompasses many types of information gathering, so for this portion of the prospectus, you will determine the nature of the research you will be conducting. Here are some questions you may ask: What types of sources will you be using, and will you need help from colleagues, professors, or library staff to gather them? Will you be using traditional library research, or will you need to conduct surveys and experiments to support your final thesis? Will you need funding and, if so, where will you secure it? What is your timeline for the research?

OUTLINE

The next step in the paper-writing process is crucial, whether you're writing an extended research project, a personal narrative, or even an in-class essay. It's the outline. This is the step that most students skip and consider a waste of time, whereas, ironically, it is the biggest time saver and tool for quality assurance in writing. Many writers find that while facing an immediate due date, the simple act of scrawling several major points they intend to cover and in what order they intend to cover them makes a significant difference in the quality of the final paper and actually makes writing it faster.

Think of your outline as the blueprint for your paper. Just as an architect would never turn the construction of a house over to the contractors without perfect blueprints detailing every aspect of construction, you should never start your draft until you have a blueprint of your own. Similar to note taking, your outline is a message to your future self. You're doing this work now so you don't have to do even more work later. Consider when you're six pages into writing the draft of a ten-page paper, and you have just run out of things to say. You can either panic and spend another hour pouring over note cards and wondering what you originally had in mind, or—if you've done some planning—you can look at a well-developed outline. That outline will tell you exactly what point you should make next and exactly what quotation or paraphrase to use, and you can keep writing without interruption. It's a very secure feeling knowing that you have that blueprint to fall back on.

Next we show several ways to construct an outline.

Casual/Scratch Outline

The first type of outline, a **casual or scratch outline,** is simply a brief sketch of what you'd like to put in your paper. If an instructor asks you for a formal outline (see the section "Formal Outline"), a casual outline might even be your first step in constructing that type of outline. Creating a casual outline is a great way to plan for quick in-class writing for short essay answers on tests. A casual outline may consist of a quick list or a series of keywords, but it seldom consists of complete sentences (or even complete thoughts).

Casual outlines are commonly used before or during the research process. You might want a quick overview of your major ideas, so you know what to start researching. Similarly, this type of outline may be the result of a solid afternoon at a library. Outside sources may have given you these ideas in the first place, so you draft a quick outline to help you continue your research and your thought-generation process. Following is an example of a casual outline. (This outline was used in researching the sample MLA format research paper beginning on page 255.)

RESEARCH PAPER: CORPORATE MASS MEDIA OWNERSHIP

- History of American corporations
- Early American corporations
- Modern American corporate mergers
- Federal Communications Commission
- Mergers of communications corporations
- Freedom of speech
- Examples of faulty news reporting

Informal Outline

An **informal outline** is the intermediate step between the casual and formal outlines. It has far more detail and structure than a casual outline, but it's still largely intended to be seen only by the writer. The informal outline is still a sketch at times, leaving out some of the minor points that will be in the paper and focusing instead on the major arguments you intend to make. You might use a series of numbers to delineate your points, and you might even include some major quotations or your initial thesis statement. This is a good choice when you don't have to turn an outline in, but you still need those blueprints to base your draft on. You may still have questions about your topic, specific arguments, and thesis at the outlining stage. Don't worry, the answers will come when you write the draft. Informal outlines are likely to change significantly during the writing process. Ultimately, they can provide either the final outline you use for a brief paper or the early draft of a formal outline that will come together later in the writing process.

Following is an example of an informal outline. Note that, like a casual outline, an informal outline doesn't require complete sentences or correct grammar: fragments and incomplete thoughts are fine, as long as you'll understand them later. This is still a somewhat vague outline at times, but it's plenty to sink your teeth into while you're still doing research or preparing a very rough draft. (This outline was used early in the writing process of the sample MLA format research paper found on page 255.)

INFORMAL OUTLINE

Thesis: Today, modern corporations' power over the media has damaged democracy by limiting public exposure to a diverse and comprehensive range of information, perspectives, and analyses, even resulting in lies and misinformation in the news media.

- Introduction with thesis
  - Quote from Madison
  - Brief overview of issues
- History of American corporations
  - Early American Corporations
  - Corporations becoming legal "people"

- Modern corporations
- Mergers of communication corporations
- Federal Communications Commission
  - Define the FCC
  - Commissioners' statements
- Effects of mergers
  - Harm to freedom of speech
  - Harm to diverse viewpoints
  - Harm to trustworthy news and information
- Examples of faulty news reporting
  - Mass media that promotes corporate agendas
  - Celebrity scandals instead of real news
- Conclusion
  - Reiteration of thesis and major arguments
  - Remind reader of opening quote

Formal Outline

The **formal outline** has a rigid structure; it is incredibly detailed, and it includes every single point that will make its way into the paper. This level of formality is often reserved for outlines that are part of an assignment; they are typically intended for an audience of some sort (even if it's only your professor, a tutor/proofreader, or partners in a class peer group) who need to get a strong sense of your paper before they even read it. Formal outlines are the ultimate writing blueprints because every single argument and fact from your paper, no matter how minor, shows up in it. They take time and dedication, but they definitely pay off in the end.

Below is the typical form for a formal outline. The following series of heading and subheadings, letters, and numerals is used at almost every college and university. The major headings are listed with Roman numerals. Here are the first twenty Roman numerals: I, II, III, IV, V, VI, VII, VIII, IX, X, XI, XII, XIII, XIV, XV, XVI, XVII, XVIII, XIX, XX.

 I. First Major Heading
  A. First Sub-heading (level 1)
   1. First Sub-heading (level 2)
   2. Second Sub-heading (level 2)
    a. First Sub-heading (level 3)
    b. Second Sub-heading (level 3)
     (1) First Sub-heading (level 4)
     (2) Second Sub-heading (level 4)
      (a) First Sub-heading (level 5)
      (b) Second Sub-heading (level 5)
  B. Second Sub-heading (level 1)
 II. Second Major Heading

A variation on the formal outline is listed below. It is often used in the sciences, business, and even computer studies, and it's based on decimals instead of the Roman numeral structure shown previously.

1. First Major Heading
   1.1 First Sub-heading (level 1)
      1.1.1 First Sub-heading (level 2)
      1.1.2 Second Sub-heading (level 2)
         1.1.1.1 First Sub-heading (level 3)
         1.1.1.2 Second Sub-heading (level 3)
   1.2 Second Sub-heading (level 1)
      1.2.1 First Sub-heading (level 2)
      1.2.2 Second Sub-heading (level 2)
2. Second Major Heading

Topic Outlines and Full-Sentence Outlines

There are two options for formal outlines: the topic outline and the full-sentence outline. The topic outline lists all the major topics as you will include them in your paper, but as phrases instead of as complete sentences. The full-sentence outline, however, uses only complete sentences. You should aim for parallel structure in both types of outlines: don't phrase some sentences as assertions and others as questions, and don't switch back and forth between passive and active voice (active voice is preferable).

TOPIC OUTLINE

Although a **topic outline** shows the general structure of the paper, it is possible for gaps or flaws in the argument to go undetected because it is still rather skeletal and just a brief sketch of the final paper. The main points will be clear, however, and the outline will be a great help as you draft. Following is an example of a topic outline. (This is the outline that was used while the student wrote the sample MLA format research paper beginning on page 255.)

FORMAL TOPIC OUTLINE

Thesis: Today, modern corporations' power over the media has damaged democracy by limiting public exposure to a diverse and comprehensive range of information, perspectives, and analyses, even resulting in lies and misinformation in the news media.

  I. Introduction
    A. Quote from Madison—reader "hook"
    B. Importance of communication on democracy
    C. Thesis statement
  II. History of American corporations
    A. Early American Corporations
    B. Boston Tea Party
      a. Quote from Lasn
      b. Critical discussion of Lasn's quote

      C. Corporations becoming legal "people"

III. Modern Corporations
     A. Recession of the 1980s
     B. Branding
         a. Quote Klein
         b. Critical discussion of Klein's quote
     C. Mergers of communication corporations
         a. Quote Bagdikian
         b. Critical discussion of Bagdikian's quotes
     D. The threat to democracy
         a. Quote McChesney
         b. Critical discussion of McChesney's quote

IV. Federal Communications Commission
     A. Define the FCC
     B. Commissioner Adalstein's statements
     C. Commissioner Copps's statements

V. Effects of mergers

VI. Examples of faulty news reporting
     A. *Project Censored*
     B. Sunny Lewis article
         1. Quote Lewis article
         2. Critical discussion of Lewis's quote
     C. Bovine Growth Hormone news story
         1. Background of news story
         2. Quote from *Project Censored*
         3. Critical discussion of quote
     D. Celebrity Scandals
         1. Information from Halpern's *Fame Junkies*
         2. Critical discussion of Halpern's information
         3. Pew Research Center's study
         4. Real News replaced by celebrity scandals
            a. For ratings
            b. Low cost

VII. Conclusion
     A. Reiteration of thesis and major arguments
     B. Remind reader of Madison's quote

FULL-SENTENCE OUTLINE

A **full-sentence** outline takes considerably more time to create than any of the other options, but preparing one is a major step toward completing your first draft. This type of outline is likely to reveal any problems in your argument. If you are not spending enough time developing one specific point, or if a flaw exists in the logical organization of your paper, you'll probably see the problem with this full-sentence outline. Similarly, with a little editing, many of the sentences you use in the outline can serve as topic sentences in your body paragraphs and transitional statements helping to wrap up major arguments. Cut and paste these sentences from outline to draft as you write.

Also, although the example that follows does not do so, many writers type or cut and paste all their quotes and paraphrases directly into their full-sentence outline. Again, this step will be time consuming up front, but when you're actually drafting your paper, a simple cut and paste will keep your writing flow going, in contrast to fishing for quotations and typing in someone else's words and then having to recover your writing flow. The following is a formal, full-sentence outline. (This is the outline that was used while the student wrote the sample MLA format research paper beginning on page 255.)

FULL-SENTENCE FORMAL OUTLINE

I. Introduce the paper by discussing key notions of democracy as connected to free communications.
   A. Madison proves that reliable information is a key component to a true self-governing democracy.
   B. The growth and power of the modern corporation limits the ability of Americans to receive quality information.
   C. Thesis Statement: Today, modern corporations' power over the media has damaged democracy by limiting public exposure to a diverse and comprehensive range of information, perspectives, and analyses, even resulting in lies and misinformation in the news media.

II. The history of the American corporation provides a background for the discussion of media control.
   A. Corporate corruption in the early colonies leads to the Boston Tea Party.
   B. The spirit of the American Revolution kept corporations small for years.
   C. The Santa Clara legal decision gives corporations the same rights as an individual person.

III. The modern corporation grows in stature and power, eventually dominating the American airwaves.
   A. The recession of the 1980s forces corporations to develop new models of business to keep operating.
   B. Marketing and slick "branding" techniques give corporations more wealth and power than before.
   C. Mergers of communication corporations create six major media conglomerates that own the bulk of all means of mass communication.
   D. These media conglomerates care about profit more than anything else, and this harms several key components to American democracy.

IV. The Federal Communications Commission's primary function is to manage and safeguard the American airwaves, ensuring that they are still owned and run by citizens and that free speech is strong and viable.
   A. Chairman Adalstein thinks the airwaves should promote an "uninhibited marketplace of ideas," but they fail to.

   B. Commissioner Copps believes that though the public airwaves belong to the citizenry, they are entirely dominated by corporate interests bent on gaining advertising revenue, not serving the needs of the people.

 V. In spite of this corporate stranglehold on information, however, watchdog groups can still provide us with reliable information.

VI. Several examples of faulty news reporting exist that will show the misinformation caused by corporate media ownership.

   A. Every year, *Project Censored* creates a list of twenty-five significant news stories that have not properly been reported.

      1. Sunny Lewis's article shows mass pollution in American water that is never reported in the mainstream media.
      2. Fox News cuts a story on Bovine Growth Hormone being found in American milk.

   B. Corporate news media is increasingly looking more like entertainment than news.

      1. The book *Fame Junkies* shows that celebrity news was more important than major stories like the genocide in Darfur or the war in Iraq.
      2. The *Pew Research Center* study shows that the people are tired of watching the same tired stories about celebrities in trouble, but it dominates the airwaves because these stories are cheap, easy, and help fill the need for 24 hours of information being broadcast on cable networks.

VII. Conclude by discussing the truth in Madison's quote about American democracy merely being a farce or a tragedy.

Outlining is an inherently left-brain activity. It requires logic, sequential order, and a focus on the system you'll use to convince your audience of your thesis. This is perhaps the most important time in all of the writing process to separate left- and right-brain functions. If you attempt to skip this step and move straight to writing your paper, you're really hampering your own creativity. For most writers, every time their left brain gets warmed up, and they are thinking of their next logical step in the paper (figuring out what comes next), they have to switch gears and start getting creative. By the time their right brain is hot, and they're starting to lose themselves in the writing, they run out of things to say and have to toggle back to left-brain, sequential thought. However, you need to realize that your individual writing process will be unique. For example, you might discover that your organization is not working and decide to reorganize while you are in the middle of drafting your paper. There is nothing wrong with that, even though drafting is a right-brain activity and organizing is a left-brain one. Learn to become conscious of what works best for you.

Do yourself a favor and prepare your outline ahead of time in one shot. This will let your left brain do its thing and then allow your right brain to really cook when you have to get creative in the next step of the process. Even a brief sketch outline on the back of a paper napkin will help you keep your mental states separate. Finally, keep in mind that most word processing programs have an outline feature built in to them. However, you should experiment with this option in the software before starting your outlines.

Many people find the software's automatic formatting in this type of outlining to be confusing and hard to control.

DRAFTING

As you can see by now, there are several steps to the process of writing a good paper that should be completed before you begin your first draft. Many students simply write a draft, run a spell check, and call it a paper. This method may get you a passing grade, but starting with the drafting step and ignoring the others will seriously diminish the quality of your paper. Professional writers of all types—reporters, novelists, screenwriters, even bloggers—complete all the steps of the writing process and often double back and redo them. These writers realize that they can't produce a top-quality final product that they can be satisfied with by taking one stab at a draft and then submitting it for publication.

When you write your first draft, remember that it's a *rough* draft. It doesn't need to be perfect. In fact, it doesn't even need to be grammatically correct at this point. You should turn off your spell check and grammar check while you're drafting. Don't second guess yourself or correct things as you go. Writing is a right-brain process, and worrying about spelling and rules will take you away from your right brain and give control to the left. You need to stay creative, let your imagination flow, and just write. All mistakes can be corrected in the edits you do later. Rely on the outline at all times. Every time you have to worry about what comes next, you're hurting your creativity. Focus on creativity, and when you're not sure what comes next, look at your outline, refer to your well-documented note cards or e-cards, and keep writing.

If you're having writer's block and struggling to get started, try skipping the introduction. You already have an idea of the thesis by now, and you have an outline waiting to be fleshed out, so just start with the first part of your body. Often the opening of a paper is the most difficult part to write; however, by starting with the body and then coming back later, you'll discover that the introduction may seem to write itself. After all, how can you effectively introduce something that doesn't exist yet? The introduction is the first thing that your audience will read, but there is no reason that it should be the first section that you write. In fact, if you still have writer's block while trying to begin the body of your paper, try writing several paragraphs on the part of your paper that you personally find most interesting and the easiest to write about. Because you are probably using a word processor, it doesn't really matter where you start. Your outline will be your blueprint when you finally put all the parts together.

REVISING AND EDITING

As you complete the process of crafting the perfect paper, you will need to do a series of edits and revisions. Notice that we say a *series* of edits and revisions, not simply one edit and revision. Yet again, recognizing how our left and right brain hemispheres function is valuable here. **Revising** (which is rereading for content, personal style, and "flow") is mainly a right-brain activity. **Editing** (correcting style, mechanics, punctuation, grammar, and spelling) is mainly a left-brain activity. Another word for editing that you are probably familiar with is "proofreading." Keep these processes separate. Think of revision as a continual process of writing and rewriting, with editing focusing more on style, punctuation, grammar, word choice, and spelling after you have produced a draft with evidence, organization, and ideas that you are happy with. (See Chapter 10 for guidelines.)

Revision

Revision is global. Look at your entire essay or research paper and pay attention to your organization, the integration of your sources, your overall argument, supporting arguments, the logical flow of your ideas, and the quality of your evidence. Ask yourself how well you are using rhetorical appeals (see *Ethos, Logos,* and *Pathos* in Chapter 5). Be prepared to ruthlessly cut out any sentences or even paragraphs that you wrote that don't add to the overall impact of your paper, and ask yourself what you may need to add to bolster any weak sections. Be prepared to cut and paste and rearrange. Revise anything larger than a paragraph on a hard copy of your work before you do any major rearranging. If you do everything on the computer screen, you can have difficulty seeing the "big picture" of your paper.

Visualize the audience you are trying to reach. Try to look at your work as if you are a member of the audience and you have never seen the paper before. Another way to look at it is in the persona of an editor who is reading a paper that has been submitted to your periodical for publication. You have high standards, and you accept only top-notch work.

Following is a checklist of questions to ask yourself when you are revising. These questions are designed for the typical college essay or research paper, so we assume a certain level of formality.

REVISION CHECKLIST

- Does my introduction include a thesis statement that clearly states, in one sentence, the assertion that my paper will prove? Is it a debatable point, not merely a statement of fact?

- Do all my body paragraphs support my thesis in some way? Do they create a unified effect? Are they presented in the most logical order?

- Have I kept in mind a broad audience of people representing a spectrum of ages, cultural backgrounds, sexual preferences, religious choices (including no religion), political viewpoints, economic and social classes, and places of national origin?

- Have I put myself in the shoes of my audience and asked myself what my readers will need to know to understand the points that I am making?

- Have I been fair to my subject and audience? Have I avoided logical fallacies or other instances of shaky reasoning? Have I anticipated any arguments that people who might disagree with me could raise, and have I answered them?

- Have I avoided unnecessary references to myself and my feelings? (Are my personal emotional reactions relevant to my audience?)

- Does my conclusion provide a sense of closure, highlighting the key points that I have made and showing how they have supported my thesis?

- Do I have in-text citations for ideas from every source I used, whether paraphrased, summarized, or quoted? Have I introduced my sources to my audience, letting my readers know why they are credible? Do I have works-cited entries for each source? Do I have the correct number of sources that my instructor requires?

Editing

After you have revised to your satisfaction—which should take several rereadings—you can engage a different part of your brain and go over your paper at the "micro" level, looking for problems in style, punctuation, and grammar. Chapter 10's "Twenty-Five Common Punctuation and Grammar Errors to Avoid" and the "Commonly Confused Words and Phrases" can help you with this part of the process.

EDITING CHECKLIST

- Have I checked my paper for errors in format (MLA, APA, etc.)? Have I made sure my identification information is in the correct order and placed on the first page? Are all titles formatted correctly by type of source (article titles enclosed in quotation marks, periodical and book titles italicized or underlined, etc.)?
- Have I avoided dry, formulaic sentences like "This essay will prove . . . ," "This paper will be about . . . ," and "I will discuss . . ." in my introduction and "In conclusion . . . ," "To sum up all of my main points . . . ," and "As this paper has proved . . . " in my conclusion?
- Have I been clear, effective, and concise in my word choice?
- Is the tone of my writing appropriate for my situation? Have I avoided slang and idioms?
- Have I avoided sexist or exclusionary language of any kind? (Changing singulars to plurals is a graceful way to avoid problems.)
- Have I used pronouns appropriate for formal writing, avoiding second person ("you" and "your") completely, avoiding first person ("I," "me") unless it is absolutely necessary, and avoiding using plural pronouns ("they," "their") with singular nouns?
- Have I eliminated any fused sentences and sentence fragments?
- Do my sentences vary in structure, rhythm, and length?
- Have I looked for typical grammar problems? Have I used a consistent verb tense? Do my subjects and verbs agree? Do my pronouns and antecedents agree?
- Have I looked for typical punctuation problems, such as comma splices?
- Have I used—but not solely relied on—a spelling and grammar check?
- Have I checked my own error portfolio? (See page 141.)

OTHER TIPS FOR REVISING AND EDITING

Get a Second Opinion

A second pair of eyes can catch errors that you won't notice. You may know exactly what you mean in a sentence that doesn't come out the way you think it does. Sometimes a sentence that makes perfect sense to the writer is totally confusing to the audience. Another reader can also catch spelling errors that spell-check programs don't. (For example, you wrote "there" when you meant to write the pronoun "their"; when you read your own draft, your brain saw what you meant to write, not the error, and the spell checker can't tell the difference.) When at all possible, get your paper done early, and see if your instructor will look at it with you to give you some overall notes about the strength of your essay's logic, content, critical thought, and so on. Your school should have a tutoring center, as well; tutors are hired to read essays, and they'll be able to point out at least some of your errors and show you how to correct them on future drafts. Don't stop there, though: teaching assistants, friends, relatives, roommates, classmates, and even professors from previous terms can all help you. Every reader can give you some type of feedback you can use.

Read Aloud

Another way to identify errors and improve your writing is to read your own paper aloud. You can read your paper aloud to someone else and get their feedback, but reading it aloud to yourself is still a very helpful practice. We are all much better at speaking and listening than writing (we speak and listen approximately sixteen hours a day, but we may write only sixteen or so hours a semester). Reading a paper aloud will reveal flaws in syntax and sentence structure. If you can't get through a sentence as you're trying to read it aloud, you should highlight it and keep reading. Go back later and revise the sentences you got snagged on—they probably have serious problems.

Read Backwards

As mentioned earlier, your brain often sees what you meant to write instead of what you actually did write. Reading your paper backwards, sentence by sentence, interrupts the flow of your thoughts and makes it easier to catch errors, especially sentence fragments.

Keep an Error Portfolio

Keep track of errors from earlier papers in a portfolio from the current and even recent semesters. (Don't keep them too long, or you'll be looking for error types you've already mastered.) Watch for these recurring errors specifically during your revisions. It is also helpful to keep a list of words you know you regularly misspell. This way, you already know what to look for (and can even program your spell checker to autocorrect them for you). The error portfolio takes dedication on your part, but it will make you a much better writer as time goes on.

Edit Multiple Times for Multiple Error Types

Another great way to edit is to hunt down specific errors in a single edit. If you keep an error portfolio, this step is particularly helpful because you'll know exactly what to look for. If you know, for example, that you always make mistakes with comma usage, mark each comma in your paper with a yellow highlighter, then check later to make sure each is used correctly. Next, if you have your list of commonly misspelled words, go through with a blue highlighter, looking for those errors. If you have trouble with your parenthetical citations, highlight those with an orange highlighter. Later, you can rewrite to correct these problems, and the use of different colored highlighters will help you in your organization. This is a great way to edit your paper because you can search for one type of sentence error and then look up the rules for correcting that error specifically. You won't get bogged down with every error type under the sun.

KNOW THYSELF

The processes that we have discussed in this chapter are useful for most writers in most situations. This discussion has been one that addresses different learning styles, writing approaches, and typical difficulties. However, understanding your own unique thought processes is infinitely more important. As you think about the writing process, consider your own process. Discover what type of learner you are (kinesthetic, auditory, or visual), and figure out what hemisphere of the brain is dominant for you. More specifically, you need to understand what makes you become creative. What will help you ignore distractions and focus on the writing task before you?

Start by reflecting on some previous writing sessions. Was there something that distracted you constantly and kept you from writing? Many students claim that for some reason, whenever they write, they have to do so in a completely clean house. The cleanliness of the house probably isn't really the issue. What's happening is that the house cleaning has somehow become part of their writing process. The hour or more they spend picking up clothes, magazines, and other belongings and putting them away (probably listening to music and being alone the whole time) may be just what they need to collect themselves and get ready to write. In fact, they often find that they have unconsciously begun drafting sections of the paper—they seem to flow almost automatically after they sit down at the keyboard.

If you're trying to write and you keep thinking about a cup of coffee, get it. If you're longing for a candy bar or an ice cream cone or some peanuts, go get them. The distraction will only get worse, and in the meantime your body may be telling you it needs certain proteins, sugar, or caffeine before it feels like writing. Those little nagging distractions may be your brain telling you it needs another few minutes before it starts writing, or that it's hungry for some specific fuel it needs before getting creative.

Also, although all the steps outlined previously are good for most people, be prepared to adapt them. Your instructor will probably want a certain set of prewriting steps submitted for part of your grade, so obviously you need to follow those instructions. If you need to take note cards in a different manner than the one outlined earlier, or if you have a very innovative way to outline your paper on your computer, do it your way. If you are a new writer, you'd be wise to try out the exact techniques listed previously. However, as time goes by, and you've written more frequently, stick with what works. Above all else, "to thine own self be true."

CHAPTER 7

Organizing the Essay

The number one student complaint when faced with writing a paper is, "I don't know how to get started!" You've probably made this complaint a couple of times in your own academic career, and if you haven't, you will. There's an old Chinese adage that says the hardest part of any journey is taking the first step. This is especially true with writing papers.

No matter how much prewriting and research a student does, no matter how strong the outline, the actual task of launching the paper is almost always a tough one. Every step until the first keystroke on the keyboard or the first ink scrawl on the page is preparation. Your paper is still in the theoretical stage. But when you sit down to begin drafting that introduction, it's all too real. If you've never written a research paper or documented essay before (and plenty of incoming college students have not), starting the first draft can often seem so frightening that it produces writer's block (a mental state which temporarily "blocks" people from being able to write).

However, if you know some tips and tricks about what to include in introductions and how to structure them to have maximum impact, this knowledge will make your paper-writing process much less daunting. The same is true about drafting your body paragraphs and conclusions: the more you know about how to structure an essay, including research papers, the more you can reduce the stress associated with writing your first draft. The first part of the equation is a solid thesis statement (see Chapter 1 for more details on what a thesis statement is and isn't, as well as tips for generating a working thesis). The second part is a strong introduction designed to showcase your thesis statement and to let your audience know what to expect from your paper. The third part is a well-developed body that supports your thesis statement, and the last part is your conclusion, which reminds your audience of how you have supported your thesis. If you look at the process of generating a first draft as a matter of completing manageable individual steps, getting started will be easier.

We begin our discussion of the writing process with the introduction because that is the first part of your work that your audience will read, but we don't recommend trying to write a fully developed introduction as your first step. How well could you introduce a person you'd barely met to an audience eager for meaningful information? Introductions to papers work much the same way. You need to know your paper well before you can introduce it well, so you will only frustrate yourself (and make your writer's block more severe) if you try to complete the entire introduction first.

INTRODUCTIONS

In many ways, your **introduction** is the most important part of the entire paper. In just a few sentences, you suggest the topic and scope of your paper, set your tone, demonstrate your writing style, and provide your thesis; you may even set up some of the major arguments the audience will encounter. (Even though your literal audience is your instructor, imagine yourself as a professional who is writing for a wider, general audience.) If you write a flat, generic introduction, the audience is already expecting an uninspired paper. However, if you present your readers with an introduction that's full of insight, strong development, and even wit, they will already be pleased with their decision to read the upcoming paper, and they will want to continue reading what you have to say.

Before getting into the elements that make an introduction effective, let's take a look at the introduction to an actual paper. This paper's broad topic is the media, but as you can see by the end of the introduction, the student has gotten specific and focuses on the negative aspects of corporate media ownership. Using this eleven-sentence example, let's look at the key ingredients and functions of an introduction. (This is the introduction to the sample student paper found in Chapter 11 on page 255.)

1) James Madison once said that a "popular government without popular information, or the means to acquiring it, is but a prologue to a farce or a tragedy, or perhaps both" (qtd. in McChesney 6). 2) With this, Madison—America's fourth president, often called the father of the Constitution—establishes an important aspect of democracy. 3) The people must be informed about world events in order to be able to make informed decisions during any democratic election. 4) If people are misinformed, their votes for or against candidates, bills, and propositions are based on false information. 5) In nondemocratic countries, history shows a pattern of misinformation and media manipulation emphasizing propaganda, suppression of the truth, and even mass brainwashing. 6) The ideal of American journalism and freedom of speech is supposed to protect us from governmental influences over the mass media, ensuring us reliable news and information. 7) However, with the recent and steady rise in power of the modern corporation, the media is no longer as free as many would think. 8) Instead of the kinds of governmental intrusions on the news media that nondemocratic countries endure, we face a system of corporate ownership, which dominates news media instead. 9) As corporations have grown over the last one hundred years, they slowly acquired more and more aspects of the "mediascape," and now a few corporations own the majority of television stations, movie studios, publishing houses, and newspaper and magazine printing presses. 10) Over time, the American corporation has transformed from being just a business model to the nation's most powerful force. 11) Today, modern corporations' power over the media has damaged democracy by limiting public exposure to a diverse and comprehensive range of information, perspectives, and analyses, even resulting in lies and misinformation in the news media.

Gradual Buildup

Notice that this introduction doesn't start right away with dates, data, or a thesis. Introductions that start that way fail in their basic function: to introduce. An effective introduction should gradually "walk" a reader into the topic. The audience has no idea what is coming up in a paper when they first pick it up. Their minds could be on anything from what to eat for dinner to what time the party starts. Only through the introduction does the reader finally understand what the topic is. To just start your introduction "cold" and pack the opening sentence with a lot of information and facts is like waking people up by throwing cold water on their faces. It's harsh.

A successful introduction will take into consideration the fact that your readers have no idea what's coming just yet. (The only clue your audience has about the topic is what they've gleaned from the paper's title.) Thus, your introduction will gradually provide information, bit by bit, and by the time the thesis statement is revealed, your readers will have anticipated it and will be prepared to consider the often complex concepts you're presenting.

The preceding sample introduction begins with a quotation from James Madison (sentence 1). A quotation such as this one is a great way to begin an introduction. First, it is a good hook for the audience (see "Hooks" later in the chapter). Second, it begins to introduce the topic gradually. Readers now have a hint about the content of the paper: it will be about information, or government, or James Madison himself. As the introduction builds, the topic moves away from Madison, though. Sentences 2–5 use Madison's quote as a sounding board to open up a broader discussion of the media and democracy. By sentences 6 and 7, readers know they are reading a paper about corporate media and democracy. Starting with sentence 8, the writer gives readers some specific details they are likely to find in the paper, and by the final sentence—the thesis statement—the audience is fully aware of all the major ideas to be presented in the body of the paper.

PAPER TITLES

The title of your paper is an important part of introducing your audience to the specifics of your paper. Don't give your paper bland or vague titles like "Research Paper Number One," "Television," or even "Television History." Instead, give some specific details about your topic and argument. A title such as "Television History and the Evolution of Information Control" provides some key phrases and ideas. The reader now knows to look for history, the evolution of the technology, and the concept of information control.

You can even make your title a catchy phrase followed by a subtitle containing the important details, such as "The Boob Tube: A History of the Evolution of the Most Important Communications Device on Earth."

Hooks

Not only does a good introduction need to gradually build up to the major points you'll make, it also needs to make an audience interested in reading the paper. Consider our sample introduction again. What if the opening line of the paper was actually the thesis? Would you want to read a paper that began with the following sentence?

> The rapid spread of advertising that penetrates most aspects of public life is both desensitizing and angering to the American population, so we need to consider legislation to limit the amount and frequency of advertisements that we are exposed to on television, following the model of European Union countries that limit product placement in programs and allow commercials to interrupt shows only at designated intervals.

To most people, that introduction would sound dull, and they'd anticipate a dull paper. That is not a good way to start your relationship with your audience. After you've hooked the audience with an interesting introduction, it is easy for the readers to stay on track even through less interesting parts of the writing. The techniques that follow will help you hook your audience and make them want to read your paper instead of considering it a chore.

QUOTATIONS

You can always open a paper with an interesting **quotation.** Many papers written for literature classes open this way, but it is a technique that you can use in many other disciplines. You should stick with quotations that have some substance. Here are some suggestions to consider while picking an opening quotation:

a. Consider using a famous quotation. Reference works like *Bartlett's Familiar Quotations* and the *Oxford Dictionary of Quotations* are great resources available in most libraries and bookstores, and the Literature Network provides selections from *Bartlett's Familiar Quotations* online in a free, searchable database (http://www.online-literature.com/). Interesting and pertinent quotations are also very easy to find with a quick Web search, but there are dangers associated with this searching method. You can't always trust the site you're getting the quotation from (there could be typos, missing words, false information, or false attribution), and you can't always find reliable citation information for later inclusion in your works-cited page through these online sources. You are better off with reference works like the ones mentioned.

b. Consider quoting someone famous. Whether you turn to the classics or more modern sources, even if the quotation itself isn't familiar, the fact that it came from a well-known person will help "sell" the quotation. Consider the quotation in our sample introduction. Madison was one of the founding fathers and was largely credited as one of the authors of the Constitution. If he has something to say about democracy or government, an audience will trust that he knows what he's talking about. If you were writing a paper about quantum physics, you could turn to a prominent physicist like Stephen Hawking. Some students even have success finding quotes from famous films or television shows, especially when writing on popular culture.

c. Look for observations that are beautifully or powerfully stated. You may find a perfect quotation from someone who is not particularly famous. It could be from a scholar, a poet, or even a songwriter, but if the wording will grab your audience and make them think about your topic and your slant on it, it can be just as effective as a famous saying from a famous person.

Make sure that you properly attribute any quotation that you use. Many quotations are famous enough to be public information—for example, a quotation from the Declaration of Independence or from a famous speech, such as John F. Kennedy's "Ask not what your country can do for you, but what you can do for your country." These meet common knowledge guidelines (because the quotes are very well known to almost everyone, they don't need to be cited) and do not need entries on works-cited pages; however, you should clearly identify the sources in your paper—never assume your audience knows where even very well-known quotations come from. Many of Shakespeare's most famous lines, for example, are often mistakenly attributed to the Bible. Most quotations do not meet common knowledge guidelines and will need full citations on your works-cited page, as well as identifying information in the paper itself.

BACKGROUND INFORMATION OR INTERESTING FACT

Another effective way to hook your audience is to provide them with some background on your topic. Often you will need to provide a great deal of explanation to set up your thesis statement. This technique also shows the audience right away that you've done enough research to become an expert on the subject you've chosen to discuss, so it helps to establish your authority. If you are writing about a certain television show, for example, you could open with some interesting facts about the stars of the show, the director, or how long it was on the air. If you are writing a paper about local businesses, you could start with a brief sketch about the history of the major businesses in your hometown.

Similarly, you can start with interesting theories or facts about your subject. If you have found assertions that surprised you when you first read them, consider opening with them. Your audience is also likely to be surprised by these ideas and then be intrigued to see what your take on this information is as they continue to read your paper.

In the example that follows, we've replaced the Madison quotation from the earlier introduction with the suggestion that the news media have possibly contributed to the conditions that led to some of the world's worst atrocities. The writer may consider this information to be too insignificant for the body of the paper, but it may be such an unfamiliar idea that it will grab a reader's attention right away. The highlighted portions are the new hook and are just as effective at drawing the attention of the audience as the Madison quote they've replaced.

1) Many people wonder how the horrors of the Second World War came to pass and how the atrocities of Hitler and Stalin were ever tolerated. 2) Some people think it was due to the lack of perspectives and the one-sided nature of their news media (McChesney 11). 3) With only one side of every argument being aired, entire schools of thought and whole truths were buried under lies and propaganda; shockingly, this type of information control could some day happen in America. 4) The people must

be informed about world events in order to be able to make informed decisions during any democratic election. 5) If people are misinformed, their votes for or against candidates, bills, and propositions are based on false information. 6) In nondemocratic countries, history shows a pattern of misinformation and media manipulation emphasizing propaganda, suppression of the truth, and even mass brainwashing. 7) The ideal of American journalism and freedom of speech is supposed to protect us from governmental influences over the mass media, ensuring us reliable news and information. 8) However, with the recent and steady rise in power of the modern corporation, the media is no longer as free as many would think. 9) Instead of the kinds of governmental intrusions on the news media that nondemocratic countries endure, we face a system of corporate ownership, which dominates news media instead. 10) As corporations have grown over the last one hundred years, they slowly acquired more and more aspects of the "mediascape," and now a few corporations own the majority of television stations, movie studios, publishing houses, and newspaper and magazine printing presses. 11) Over time, the American corporation has transformed from being just a business model to the nation's most powerful force. 12) Today, modern corporations' power over the media has damaged democracy by limiting public exposure to a diverse and comprehensive range of information, perspectives, and analyses, even resulting in lies and misinformation in the news media.

The notion that the media may be partially to blame for the horrors of the war should grab people's attention, especially when compared to our own media. The author here didn't provide a direct quote because it wasn't a *great* quote; the facts were very interesting, but the wording of the original didn't merit inclusion in the paper. The author simply wanted to include this information right away and didn't think this data was suited for the body of the paper. Any material that needs to be part of your argument should come later as support for your thesis. The introduction is a good place for information that will pique the audience's interest and make them want to learn more.

RHETORICAL QUESTIONS

Another great way to hook an audience, a **rhetorical question** is asked not to prompt an actual response but to inspire thought, conversation, or an argument. It makes the reader think for a moment about an issue for which there may be no final answer, but instead an ongoing debate. Such a device is good to use for an introduction. If you can get your audience to think about a pressing question right away, you've interested them in your subject matter.

Here's a warning, though: too many rhetorical questions in the body of a paper can leave your readers with a sense that you haven't done enough research. Questions don't have much of a place in a paper after the thesis has been revealed. The body of your paper is supposed to provide answers to questions, not raise more questions. The introduction, however, is a great place to ask questions that your thesis, body, and conclusion will set out to prove or disprove.

The following example shows how to open with a rhetorical question.

1) How do podcasts of nightly news anchor Katie Couric ensure that we have a healthy, working democracy? 2) Why would Benjamin Franklin sleep better at night watching a politician squirm and try to defend herself while Jon Stewart makes fun of her on *The Daily Show?* 3) These questions may seem frivolous, but they actually help establish important aspects of democracy. 4) The people must be informed about world events in order to be able to make informed decisions during any democratic election. 5) If people are misinformed, their votes for or against candidates, bills, and propositions are based on false information. 6) In nondemocratic countries, history shows a pattern of misinformation and media manipulation emphasizing propaganda, suppression of the truth, and even mass brainwashing. 7) The ideal of American journalism and freedom of speech is supposed to protect us from governmental influences over the mass media, ensuring us reliable news and information. 8) However, with the recent and steady rise in power of the modern corporation, the media is no longer as free as many would think. 9) Instead of the kinds of governmental intrusions on the news media that nondemocratic countries endure, we face a system of corporate ownership, which dominates news media instead. 10) As corporations have grown over the last one hundred years, they slowly acquired more and more aspects of the "mediascape," and now a few corporations own the majority of television stations, movie studios, publishing houses, and newspaper and magazine printing presses. 11) Over time, the American corporation has transformed from being just a business model to the nation's most powerful force. 12) Today, modern corporations' power over the media has damaged democracy by limiting public exposure to a diverse and comprehensive range of information, perspectives, and analyses, even resulting in lies and misinformation in the news media.

Notice that the questions really do get you thinking. References to TV personalities and podcasts may at first seem silly and irrelevant, but in the context of the rest of the introduction, they make sense. They also add a bit of humor, which can be a way to get your audience interested, as well (see "Humor" on page 151). Such questions are too casual and speculative to include in your paper's formal body, but they work nicely as an introductory hook.

PERSONAL ANECDOTE

Another great way to hook a reader is to tell a **personal anecdote.** An anecdote is simply a brief, amusing, or interesting personal story. Everyone has stories to tell, and often these stories pertain directly to essays you may be writing. Using a personal story is often a great way to hook the reader. Such a narrative may let the audience know that there's more to this paper than just clinical facts—there's a personal angle as well.

Caution: Personal anecdotes should be used carefully because they can lead to problems with your paper if not used properly. Many college professors insist that you not use "I" in your writing because statements such as "I think" or "I feel" or even "I agree" downgrade your writing from a discussion of facts to an airing of personal opinion. They are also usually redundant because readers fully understand that the views in a paper are yours. Solid research papers are based on empirical evidence and facts, and including too many personal opinions hurts your argument.

Personal anecdotes are inevitably "I" pieces of writing, and in a true research paper, they have very little place. Thesis statements in such essays should be supported by research and data, not emotional appeals and personal stories. However, using a personal narrative to open a piece of academic writing can be a clever way to introduce a topic, as long as you don't overdo it. Eventually, your introduction will end up with a focus on the thesis, and you will avoid using stories as evidence in the body of your paper.

If we opened our sample introduction with an anecdote instead of Madison's quote, it would look something like this:

1) When I was still in my junior high government class, I remember we studied freedom of speech. 2) We spent weeks studying the importance of information to our government, and I remember being bored to tears and not understanding how the ability to simply talk and listen actually equaled democracy. 3) Recently, however, I noticed how trivial and repetitive televised news is, and I started to wonder if communication and free speech do indeed have an impact on our lives as the founding fathers seemed to have thought. 4) I realized that in a true democracy, the people must be informed about world events in order to be able to make informed decisions during any democratic election. 5) If people are misinformed, their votes for or against candidates, bills, and propositions are based on false information. 6) In nondemocratic countries, history shows a pattern of misinformation and media manipulation emphasizing propaganda, suppression of the truth, and even mass brainwashing. 7) The ideal of American journalism and freedom of speech is supposed to protect us from governmental influences over the mass media, ensuring us reliable news and information. 8) However, with the recent and steady rise in power of the modern corporation, the media is no longer as free as many would think. 9) Instead of the kinds of governmental intrusions on the news media that nondemocratic countries endure, we face a system of corporate ownership, which dominates news media instead. 10) As corporations have grown over the last one hundred years, they slowly acquired more and more aspects of the "mediascape," and now a few corporations own the majority of television stations, movie studios, publishing houses, and newspaper and magazine printing presses. 11) Over time, the American corporation has transformed from being just a business model to the nation's most powerful force. 12) Today, modern corporations' power over the media has damaged democracy by limiting public exposure to a diverse and comprehensive range of information, perspectives, and analyses, even resulting in lies and misinformation in the news media.

This personal story about the author's experiences in junior high ties directly to the concept of how important communication and information are to democracy. This simple story will make others think about what the author is pausing to think about. Everyone has heard the term "freedom of speech" thrown about, but how many people have really pondered its importance? This narrative successfully hooks readers. Notice how the introduction gets more professional and scholarly in tone, though, as it moves toward the thesis. This story is not referred to in the body of the paper. It's purely a means of appealing to the audience and drawing them in.

HUMOR

Like the personal anecdote, **humor** should usually be avoided in academic writing, especially in the body of your paper, where you need to maintain an academic tone. However, striking a witty or quirky note in the opening lines of an introduction may be a good way to grab your audience's attention.

The previous rhetorical question example uses a bit of humor to lure in the reader; the question is strange and unexpected, somehow linking podcasts, Katie Couric, and Jon Stewart to Benjamin Franklin having a good night's sleep. This simple bit of humor lets the audience smile a bit before getting into the more scholarly tone of the rest of the introduction and the paper that follows it. The humor here isn't always laugh-out-loud funny, but it's witty and quirky enough to lighten the mood or bring a smile to the reader's face.

Additional Tips on Writing the Introduction

THESIS PLACEMENT

Remember that an introduction should introduce your topic to your audience as interestingly as possible, give the topic a sense of context, and clearly state your thesis—the point about your topic that you support with arguments in the body of your paper. Unless your instructor specifically asks for you to put the thesis first (this may happen in science classes—in fact, you may be asked to open your paper with a brief abstract), you should always consider placing the thesis toward the end of the introduction. In fact, the very last sentence is ideal. It makes a strong impact there; it serves as a marker that the introduction is done and the body is about to begin, and your audience will know what to look for as they continue reading your paper. You don't want readers to wonder what you are trying to prove. You want them to leave the introduction with a clear idea of your purpose. However, always check with your instructor for his or her personal preference. (For more detail on the thesis statement, see Chapter 1.)

KNOW YOUR AUDIENCE

When choosing the information you need to include in a paper and when constructing your arguments, you should imagine a general audience of intelligent people who may not be the experts that you are on a particular topic. Don't forget that you have a reader who is not imaginary—the person who will be grading your work. Before choosing an introduction hook, find out your instructor's requirements, which will help you determine the proper tone for your paper. Don't try to guess—ask.

One professor may have an active sense of humor and love to crack jokes during lectures, so a humor hook could be great, but it could also fall flat if he or she wants students' papers to have a strictly academic tone. Another professor may strike everyone as a consummate professional and scientist, but this person may actually enjoy an introduction that begins with a funny story. Still another professor may cultivate a daring, edgy persona in the classroom but expect a traditional style of writing, so attempting a daring, edgy gimmick in your introduction could backfire. If your professor doesn't explicitly address tone and level of formality when talking about an assigned paper, you should assume that your paper should be written in a formal, academic tone (or you should raise your hand and ask). Use a hook that is appropriate for your overall writing purpose and your audience.

LENGTH

Introductions can—and should—be different lengths for different papers. Many writers think that the introduction must be one paragraph long, period. If you're writing a three-page paper, the introduction should be about a paragraph long, but this is not an established rule of academic prose. Longer papers require longer introductions. You may find that in a ten-page paper, your introduction may be two paragraphs long or even a full page long (or longer). Let your argument, and what you need to say in order to prove it, determine how many paragraphs you need to introduce your topic.

CONTRACT WITH YOUR AUDIENCE

One way to think of your introduction is as a contract between you and your audience. The introduction tells the audience exactly what to expect from the upcoming paper, in form and content as well as style. Go back and review the first example introduction for this section (page 147) one last time.

Did you notice the essay structure that this introduction suggests? Sentences 9–11 show major ideas we now expect to see in the paper (corporate domination of the media, media saturation, and so on). If any of these main points of your argument are missing from the body of the paper, you have broken your contract with the reader. In fact, even if you present your points in a different order than the order you presented them in the introduction, you've already started to break your contract. Always read your introduction again after you've finished your paper. Writers often end up cutting a section or adding a new argument, and these changes need to be reflected in your introduction and your thesis. It's silly to go back and change your whole paper to reflect your introduction; change a sentence or two in your introduction to reflect a new element in your paper instead.

Also, if you use sophisticated vocabulary and sentence structure in your introduction, your readers will expect that style for the entire paper. In our sample introduction, notice the use of terms like "flippant," "proliferation," "antagonisms," and "psychological." If the paper stops using this level of diction, the audience will notice a shift in your style—another violation of the contract.

FIRST IMPRESSIONS

Remember that your introduction is your audience's first impression of you and your ideas. If your introduction is full of typographical errors, punctuation mistakes, and weak sentence construction, the audience will expect that your entire paper will be full of the same types of errors. Your readers will need several well-crafted pages to forget what they noticed in the introduction, be it good or bad. Think about how strong first impressions are when you are introduced to someone. At a party you can meet a very bright, witty person who is having a bad day, and you will walk away from that person feeling unimpressed, with no idea of how intellectually stimulating he or she actually can be. In fact, you may want to avoid having to listen to that person ever again. A poor introduction to a paper can have the same effect. Make your introduction count!

Starting an introduction can be very difficult. Perhaps you've got so many ideas and information that even with your outline, you truly don't know where to begin. Those first few words can be the hardest of your entire paper. You think you'd be fine if you could just start with the body of your paper—then go ahead! If you're having trouble starting, skip the introduction for now and proceed with the

INTRODUCTIONS FOR SCIENTIFIC DISCIPLINES

Writing a scientific paper is significantly different from writing a report or an argumentative paper in the humanities. You typically have an audience of experts in scientific writing, and you will be more concerned with providing data and interpreting it than compiling a research-based argument. One of your major goals in this type of writing is to present the information clearly but concisely so that your experiments are easy to interpret and possible to duplicate. Introductions in this scientific format are far more structured, data driven, and formal. Following is a list of some of the elements your professor may expect in an introduction to this type of paper:

Hypothesis

Your entire scientific paper will revolve around a hypothesis, a working assumption that you plan to prove or disprove through your study. You will clearly identify your hypothesis here and let the readers know whether your hypothesis was proved or disproved in your paper (both results are equally valid and desirable in scientific writing).

Abstract

Here you provide a brief discussion/summary of your entire paper. You will probably include the primary reason for writing this paper and conducting this research. It will include a brief discussion of the results and conclusions you've drawn.

Methods

Your introduction may include a discussion of the methods you've used to support your hypothesis and how you conducted your study. It will include a discussion of the data collection and statistical analysis portion of the paper as well as how you designed the experiments you conducted.

Results

For this portion, you tell the reader what you found in your study. Summarize your data here, using tables, charts, and graphs as well as text if necessary. Do not try to interpret the meaning of the data or extrapolate on how they support your hypothesis in this portion; simply report on the basic findings.

first paragraph of the paper's body. Start with facts and move on from there. The introduction is often the last section that experienced writers will write. Having the entire body and the conclusion finished can liberate you when writing your introduction. If you already know exactly what's coming up in the paper itself, introducing it can be easier. Give this method a try if you're stuck; it might just break your writer's block.

THE BODY OF THE ESSAY

Normally, students have the easiest time writing the body. It's based upon research you've already spent a considerable amount of time on, so by this stage of the writing process, you know your material fairly well. You've also completed an outline, so you know the order and logic of your arguments. It's just a matter of writing them down. However, to successfully support your thesis, the body of a well-crafted research paper should do much more than state a lot of facts, give a lot of quotes, and list a lot of dates. The outside evidence you've compiled and your own ideas and conclusions need to come together as an integrated whole.

You, as the writer, need to do more than state facts; you need to interpret the facts and use them to support your paper. You also need to prove to the audience that you've critically examined your sources and that you fully understand the ramifications they have for your thesis statement and your own arguments. (For more on how to integrate source material, see Chapter 8.) Following is a sample body paragraph from the student essay found on page 255. It is a body paragraph in support of the sample introduction used previously.

1) Instead of making money by selling a quality product, corporations started to practice "branding." 2) Branding is when a corporation makes the identity of a certain brand name (such as Coke, Nike, or the Gap) become synonymous with high quality, luxury, or just "being cool." 3) This branding worked better than anyone could have ever hoped and seemed to end the financial woes that the recession brought to corporate America. 4) Naomi Klein, media activist and author of the influential book on advertising, *No Logo*, discusses this corporate success story:

> The astronomical growth in the wealth and cultural influence of multinational corporations over the last fifteen years can arguably be traced back to a single, seemingly innocuous idea developed by management theorists in the mid-1980s: that successful corporations must primarily produce brands, as opposed to products. (1) Until that time . . . the primary concern of every manufacturer was the production of goods.

5) When corporations focused on enhancing their brands instead of manufacturing products, as Klein suggests, they started making record earnings and grew in power and stature. 6) Making a high-quality burger that tasted good did not sell nearly as well as selling the notion of "cool" or by convincing the audience that they are indeed "loving it," as McDonald's suggests in their highly successful ad campaign. 7) Brand loyalty proved far more successful for the corporation than high-quality products seemed to, and the corporation was able to grow in wealth and stature as a result.

Topic Sentence

The first element to note in this sample body paragraph is the **topic sentence,** which tells the reader what the paragraph is about. Some instructors prefer that you begin every paragraph in your body with a topic sentence, which can work especially well when the final sentence in the previous paragraph is used as part of a transition. Many writers prefer to embed the topic sentence somewhere in the paragraph. For example, they may introduce ideas that build up to the topic sentence, then give the topic sentence, and follow it with extra examples or supporting ideas. Some writers' topic sentences may be implicit (not directly stated), but this can be risky in student writing, so we don't recommend it. Being able to clearly state your topic sentences helps to keep you on track. It's a great idea to come up with them before you even begin the paper—they can serve as the main points in the outline you create. Wherever you place each topic sentence, you should consider it a miniature thesis statement. Where the thesis is in effect the controlling argument for the whole of the paper, the topic sentence is the controlling argument or idea for the individual paragraph. Often, you may use one topic sentence to set up a few paragraphs if they are all closely related, but make sure that you have a topic sentence before every argument.

Here is the sample topic sentence for the sample body paragraph:

> Instead of making money by selling a quality product, corporations started to practice "branding."

This topic sentence tells the reader that the focus for the upcoming paragraph is the notion of branding. As you read through the rest of the paragraph, every sentence, including the quotation, supports this assertion.

In your own writing, when you reread a paragraph and notice that one of the sentences does not directly support the topic sentence, you should either cut or revise it. Otherwise, you risk wandering off topic and losing the paragraph's **coherence,** the quality of writing in which all of the elements relate to one another and to a central idea. Similarly, after you've finished your rough draft, if you find any topic sentences that fail to support the thesis directly, you should cut or revise them (and their corresponding paragraphs) as well.

Support

The body paragraph should introduce, provide, and examine evidence to support the point made in your topic sentence. This support can be a logical argument you generate yourself or evidence drawn from sources such as a quotation, paraphrase, statistic, or fact. Notice that in the sample body paragraph on page 154, sentences 2 and 3 gradually set up the evidence the author later presents us with. Sentence 4 directly introduces the source, complete with the author's names and background and the title of the book. Sentence 4 contains the actual quotation, and sentences 5 through 7 discuss the importance and meaning of the quotation. We learn here that the writer thinks this quotation is accurate, and she provides more examples to give further support to her thesis.

Transitions

When you have made one point, whether it is one paragraph or one page long, you always need to provide a logical **transition** to your next main point. A **transition sentence** helps readers move from one paragraph to the next. One of the goals of great writing is to make the reading of your words an effortless task. When you leave out transitions, your readers don't know they need to shift mental gears from Point A to Point B. They finish with one point and get several sentences into the next one before they realize there's been a shift. This makes following the details of your individual arguments difficult, and it forces your readers to have to continually reread sections of your paper to stay on track. Transitions help readers stay on track by announcing shifts in advance. A transition should subtly tell readers, "I'm done with Point A and moving on to Point B now." Transition words such as *although, finally, however, in conclusion, moreover, nevertheless, on the one hand, therefore,* and *though* let your readers know how one idea relates to another within a paragraph.

Transitions also give your essay continuity. When you use transitions to connect paragraphs, the audience knows that your essay is written according to a logical plan and that it all works together seamlessly. If you're writing a longer paper, and you have points going on for several paragraphs or even several pages, don't feel that you need a transition at the end of each paragraph. You should make sure they happen at the end of every point you make. If you have a longer or shorter point, you should adjust the placement and frequency of your transitions accordingly.

Here is another excerpt found in the sample student paper. Look at the bottom of this paragraph to see the transition:

1) In fact, in his book (appropriately titled *Corporate Media and the Threat to Democracy*), McChesney suggests that

> the commercial basis of U.S. media has negative implications for the exercise of political democracy: it encourages a weak political culture that makes depoliticization, apathy and selfishness rational choices for the citizenry, and it permits the business and commercial interests that actually rule U.S. society to have inordinate influence over media content . . . for those committed to democracy, it is imperative to reform the media system. (7)

2) In this quotation, McChesney not only shows the negative impact of the media conglomerates, he even posits that someone who is truly dedicated to democracy and free speech must explore ways to change things. 3) One government body is indeed doing some fact finding to try to find a way to change things in favor of the citizens, and that is the Federal Communications Commission.

In this paragraph, the first two sentences introduce, provide, and discuss a bit of evidence. Sentence 3 shows us a solid transition. It begins by addressing the issues of this paragraph—someone needs to look for a way to change the current media system—but it ends up introducing the Federal Communications Commission. The next paragraph is entirely about the FCC, and this transition sentence serves to not only wrap up the current point, but let the reader know what the next point will be about. This transition sentence does a great job of leading the audience from one topic to the next.

Thesis Reminders

Your readers are never as familiar with your topic or your specific arguments as you are, so you should make a conscious effort to remind them of your original thesis statement at various points throughout your paper. You don't want to simply cut and paste the same sentence over and over, but you need to keep nudging the audience back toward your controlling argument. These reminders may seem redundant, but because your goal is to make your readers understand what you write and agree with your points, reminding them about your specific thesis is always a good idea.

More practically, your professor is your true audience, and he or she will be reading a *lot* of papers before and after yours. Suppose everyone in the class is writing about television. The instructor will be reading arguments about television for hours, and your individual voice might easily be drowned out. With solid reminders of your thesis throughout the body of your paper, however, your instructor (or any reader) will always remember exactly where your paper started and exactly what your paper is constructed to prove. Often, it can be part of a transition or some other part of the body of your essay. Like a transition, you don't need to add a thesis reminder after every paragraph in a longer argument. In fact, you don't need them in every point you make. It's possible to add too many. There is no rule for how many to provide, or how often to provide them, but think about including one after every page or two. If you have rather complex points with a lot of facts or tangents, you will need to remind your audience of your thesis a bit more often.

Remember the thesis from the sample introduction:

Today, modern corporations' power over the media has damaged democracy by limiting public exposure to a diverse and comprehensive range of information, perspectives, and analyses, even resulting in lies and misinformation in the news media.

Consider the following paragraph from the student essay and how it supports this thesis. The last sentence of the paragraph (highlighted in yellow) serves not only to wrap up the current argument, but to remind the audience of the specifics of the thesis sentence:

Indeed, in 2003, these five corporations were controlled by just five men: Richard Parsons, head of Time Warner; Michael Eisner, head of Disney; Sumner Redstone, head of Viacom; Rupert Murdoch, head of News Corps (and current owner of the Wall Street Journal); and Reinhard Mohn, a man who had deceived the public about his company's Nazi history (Bagdikian, New 27–28). These conglomerates have merged and bought out every type of information technology possible—magazines, newspapers, websites, cable networks, even Internet service providers and the physical infrastructure of satellite systems and phone lines. If there is a way to get information about our world, odds are these conglomerates own it, and that is where free speech—and its corollary, free, accurate, and uncensored information—becomes limited for citizens.

Additional Tips on Writing the Body of Your Paper

PARAGRAPH LENGTH

Just like the introduction and the conclusion, there is no standard length for the body of your essay. More to the point, there is no set length for a body paragraph. You should play around with the size of your paragraphs, but understand that paragraphs are constructed to contain distinct units of information. If you have a lot to say, you can easily spread one point (thus one transition and one topic sentence) over two or three separate paragraphs, making one larger point. The first paragraph could introduce the point, the second could provide concrete supporting examples, and the third could offer a conclusion. Conversely, some points may be briefer, with all these elements occurring in one paragraph. Instead of thinking about your paragraphs in terms of word count, think about the clearest way of presenting your information and ideas.

THESIS

While you revise your paper, always keep your thesis in mind. If you read a paragraph during revision, and you decide it has no bearing on the thesis, cut that paragraph or revise it to apply directly to your thesis.

MINI-PAPERS

Often, the thought of writing a ten- or fifteen-page paper is enough to make a student drop a class. Don't panic! The best way to think of longer papers is simply as a collection of smaller papers strung together. Instead of obsessing about writing a fifteen-page paper, divide your points up into major sections. Perhaps you're making four distinct points in your paper, and each one will be three pages long. You'll start with a topic sentence (instead of a thesis), then give the evidence/argument (which is like the body), and end with a transitional or closing statement (like a micro conclusion). If you break the writing up into several two- to four-page mini papers, in no time, you'll find that you've just written a fifteen-page paper, and you have done it by breaking the process into smaller, more manageable tasks. After these shorter papers are complete, all you'll have left to do is to write a full introduction and conclusion and tie the papers together with thesis reminders and transitions.

YOUR IDEAS MATTER

In a research paper, your ideas are important. If you provide only facts and quotations, you haven't written a research paper—you've strung together other people's ideas and information. For this reason, you should usually avoid opening and closing a body paragraph with a quotation. If you open with a quotation that will be a major part of a point you're making, then you fail to introduce the source, and you fail to provide a topic sentence to help guide that paragraph. You need that topic sentence to give a sense of transition. Similarly, you typically don't want to end on a quotation or paraphrase; the paper is supposed to be your own interpretation of outside evidence, so you need to end with your ideas, not those of other scholars. End your body paragraphs with a critical look at how the quotations or paraphrases you've presented apply to your thesis.

CONCLUSIONS

The final part of any paper is, of course, the **conclusion.** Traditionally, this is the place for an author to make his or her final statements about all the evidence he or she has just presented. It is the final chance to shore up the argument so that the thesis is fully developed and proven. The conclusion serves several other functions as well, though. Much as the introduction eases readers into the paper's topic, the conclusion should ease the readers back out, leaving them with a clear sense that the paper is finished.

Here is the conclusion to the sample paper from which the sample introduction and body paragraph from earlier in this chapter were taken:

1) Serving the needs of the people should be of paramount importance to every citizen in our mediated world, however, not simply the financial bottom line of corporate America. 2) Corporations used to be manageable and closely monitored by the people and the government. 3) The current corporate dominance of the airwaves, though, undermines our ability to stay well informed, feel a sense of community, and therefore fully participate in our own democratic government. 4) We cannot let corporations control and limit what we know about our own country and the rest of the world. 5) As President Madison, one of the fathers of this democracy, said, "popular government without popular information, or the means to acquiring it, is but a prologue to a farce or a tragedy, or perhaps both" (qtd. in McChesney 6). 6) If the corporations become the ultimate gatekeepers of the powers of mass communication, our own ability to engage in true free speech and to have complete access to the information we need to make truly informed decisions about everything from our health to the leaders we elect will be only a farce or a tragedy as Madison predicted.

Thesis Finality

If there is any place in your paper where your audience needs to be fully reminded of your thesis statement, it is in the conclusion. You've said all you have to say—all the citations and evidence and all the points you've made—but remember that the audience has just digested a lot of information. After you've presented your research and findings, the audience may make its own interpretations and come to its own conclusions about the evidence. Your final words need to clarify your conclusion. Don't make the mistake of assuming that the reader will necessarily understand what all of your evidence just proved. This is your job as a writer.

Often, the first sentence or two of a conclusion are a concise attempt to remind the audience of exactly what your thesis was and how you just proved it, as sentences 2 and 3 do in the previous example. They sum up the thesis (which is less boring if it is worded differently from the original). They also manage to briefly encapsulate all the major points made in this paper. Opening your conclusion this way gives your readers a reminder of all the pertinent details from your paper as well as a solid topic sentence for the concluding paragraph.

You may have a much longer conclusion than the one shown earlier. It could even be several paragraphs long, and you may go over several of the key points of your paper in more detail. A more detailed conclusion is useful for a longer project or a paper filled with scientific or mathematical findings.

Conclusion Structure

There is no set pattern for writing a conclusion; just remember the main goal is to give readers a sense of finality about your thesis and your essay. Naturally, some writers end up with a conclusion that mirrors their introduction. When you remind the reader of the thesis in your first sentence, you've already mirrored your introduction to some extent, of course. You open the conclusion with the thesis, just as you closed the introduction with it.

In your introduction, your second step is to gradually walk the reader into your topic; alternatively, in the conclusion, your second step is to gradually walk the reader away from your topic and back out of your paper. Finally, your introduction probably started with a fairly general statement and some kind of hook; true to its mirror form, your conclusion will end with a general statement or hook.

In this sample conclusion, notice that sentences 4, 5, and 6 all depart from the specifics of the thesis and end up with more general ideas about Madison's opening quote and what we have learned about it since the paper started.

Hooks

Just as the introduction needs a hook to entice readers to *want* to read a paper, you need to end your paper with a hook that will make them remember it. It is often effective to end your paper with the same hook you opened with. The reader will remember how you hooked him or her in the beginning of this paper; ending with the same hook creates a good sense of closure.

A concluding hook needs to engage the readers. It needs to let them ponder the future or think of ways to confront issues in the present. Try to make an impact with your closing statement.

Different Hooks

QUOTATIONS

If you opened with a quotation, you can end with the same quotation, or at least a continuation of it. You can revisit the quotation and reaffirm it in light of the evidence you've presented, or discuss how it doesn't hold up to what you've actually revealed in your paper. You can remind the audience of your opening quotation and then reflect on it to show how you (therefore, they) have changed in the course of your research. In the sample conclusion, the author ends by reminding the audience of the Madison quotation and by hoping the sentiments expressed in that quotation haven't come true in modern America.

BACKGROUND INFORMATION/INTERESTING FACT

Discussing the background of a topic in your introduction always gives you a great opportunity to discuss the future of the same topic in your conclusion. Take the ideas you opened with and project them into the future; the audience will enjoy the ride.

Here is a final conclusion-closing hook for the preceding conclusion example. The final sentence is revised to reflect the essay's original introduction hook. Revisit the

"Background Information" sample introduction on page 147 to see how it all comes full circle.

1) Serving the needs of the people should be of paramount importance to every citizen in our mediated world, however, not simply the financial bottom line of corporate America. 2) Corporations used to be manageable and closely monitored by the people and the government. 3) The current corporate dominance of the airwaves, though, undermines our ability to stay well informed, feel a sense of community, and therefore fully participate in our own democratic government. 4) We cannot let corporations control and limit what we know about our own country and the rest of the world. 5) Stalin and Hitler were infinitely worse than the modern corporation, but they did manage to control all information and thus their people. 6) Although the tragedies visited upon the world under their rule will hopefully never occur again, we cannot let a different set of tragedies come to pass in our modern age through corporate manipulation of the media.

RHETORICAL QUESTION

A writer who opens with a rhetorical question owes it to the audience to give a final reflection on the opening question by the end of the paper. This doesn't need to be an actual answer to the question (there may not even be such a thing), but the readers will need to be taken past this original question. You could also end with deeper questions; good research often leads to the need for more research. Let your audience know that you aren't finished with your quest for answers, and let them know they shouldn't be done with their own quest, either.

Here is a closing hook for the sample conclusion. It poses even deeper questions— ones that couldn't be answered in the limited number of pages of this research paper.

1) As advertising continues to grow and spread, then, and as consumers continue to grow either deadened or angry at the constant onslaught, something must be done. 2) There must be a call for more legislation against spam, bulk mailing, and telemarketing; similarly, we as consumers must let the corporations themselves know that we want ads to be limited. 3) Though this message could be sent through activism or boycotts, the corporations must be sent a message or they will not change, and this message could be as simple as purchasing goods and services only from corporations whose business methods you support. 4) After all, most corporations aren't trying to annoy us; they simply want to make money and satisfy customers and shareholders. 5) If these corporations are made aware that the populace is tired of advertising, they may willingly change just to keep customers happy. 6) If legislation and activism fail to work, how can we change American advertising? 7) What can we do to make sure future generations can see a blue sky at a park instead of miles of billboards hawking beer, sex, and cologne?

1) Serving the needs of the people should be of paramount importance to every citizen in our mediated world, however, not simply the financial bottom line of corporate America. 2) Corporations used to be manageable and closely monitored by the people and the government. 3) The current corporate dominance of the airwaves, though, undermines our ability to stay well informed, feel a sense of community, and therefore fully participate in our own democratic government. 4) We cannot let corporations control and limit what we

know about our own country and the rest of the world. 5) But if we do nothing to stop the mergers and power of the modern media corporations, how much of the truth will they eventually own? 6) Will we one day reach a point where all information is owned and traded like commodities? 7) Or will we simply reach a day where, like the novel 1984, the truth becomes indistinguishable from the lies?

PERSONAL ANECDOTE

If you opened with a personal anecdote, you can also use this same anecdote to close your paper. Follow it through to its conclusion. If the story in your introduction brought up a problem, make sure you present a solution or at least a resolution of some kind (even if it means revealing a deeper problem) in your conclusion. You could even tell an alternative version of the tale where events happened differently, and the hypothetical outcome was better.

Here is the sample intro with the final sentences revised to reflect on the opening anecdote found in the introduction on page 149.

1) When I was still in my junior high government class, I remember we studied freedom of speech. 2) We spent weeks studying the importance of information on our government, and I remember being bored to tears and not understanding how the ability to simply talk and listen actually equaled democracy. 3) Recently, however, I noticed how trivial and repetitive televised news is, and I started to wonder if communication and free speech do indeed have an impact on our lives as the founding fathers seemed to have thought. 4) I realized that in a true democracy, the people must be informed about world events in order to be able to make informed decisions during any democratic election.

1) Serving the needs of the people should be of paramount importance to every citizen in our mediated world, however, not simply the financial bottom line of corporate America. 2) Corporations used to be manageable and closely monitored by the people and the government. 3) The current corporate dominance of the airwaves, though, undermines our ability to stay well informed, feel a sense of community, and therefore fully participate in our own democratic government. 4) We cannot let corporations control and limit what we know about our own country and the rest of the world. 5) When I think back on my apathy toward freedom of speech when I was still in junior high, it makes me wonder if anyone else even cares about the media and free speech. 6) Perhaps the disinterest I felt back then is what has allowed corporations to grow as much as they have. 7) Perhaps if enough of us realize that communication and information are the true cornerstones of a democracy, more people will start to concern themselves with who owns our airwaves.

Additional Tips on Writing the Conclusion

LENGTH

Like the introduction and the body of a paper, there is no set length for a conclusion. Let the requirements of the assignment and your writing situation dictate the length of your conclusion. If you've written a fifteen-page paper, your conclusion may very well be a page or more in length. Similarly, if you have written a shorter paper full of dense facts and data, you may need to summarize these in your concluding paragraph before you sum up your own arguments or revisit your thesis statement.

NEW EVIDENCE AND POINTS

Your conclusion is not the place to introduce new material. If you find that you're using your conclusion to squeeze in new information or one last fact, you haven't really finished writing the body of your paper yet. A conclusion should sum up the main points you have developed in the body of your paper to support your thesis, not make a few more points. Any new material you present in the conclusion will distract your readers and weaken the impact of your paper, so fold all such information into your body paragraphs instead.

VISUAL PAPER STRUCTURE

One way to imagine your paper as a graphic image is to picture a martini glass. At the top is an upside-down pyramid, at the bottom is a smaller pyramid (normal side up), and in the middle is a solid line. This image doesn't represent the size or even the importance of the different sections of your paper—your body contains your arguments and your evidence—but it does show how your audience moves through your paper.

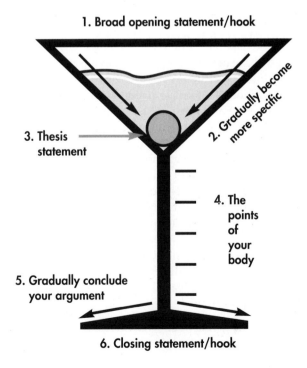

An introduction is intended to move your audience from the general to the specific (as found in your thesis). Because you need to walk your audience into the topic gradually, you begin with a generic statement or a hook—nothing too specific. As the introduction continues, you slowly close in on your thesis, revealing more and more details to your audience. As the inverted pyramid narrows, it focuses on a sharp point: your final thesis statement.

Next is the body. The body is a column, a straight line of points, one after the other, all in an orderly, organized row. In architecture, a column can support a great deal of weight, and this column of evidence here will support and ultimately prove your thesis.

Finally, you arrive at the conclusion, which is almost the mirror image of the introduction. You start with a reminder of your thesis statement to help readers recall what you've just accomplished. You then walk readers away from your specific topic and thesis, just as you brought them gradually into your paper in your introduction. You end the paper with a broad statement that lets readers "out" of the paper and returns them to the world around them (you may want to bring your readers full circle by reemphasizing the hook in your introduction).

You may even try drawing this shape on a piece of paper before you prepare your outline. You could sketch key ideas and points next to or inside this glass. It's a great way for visual learners to see their outline and a great way for kinesthetic learners to get to interact with the form of their paper. For more help on essay structure, you can also look at our discussion of the Toulmin Method on pages 94–97 in Chapter 5. First designed as a model for dissecting arguments that we read or hear, it also shows an effective way to structure our own arguments and argumentative papers.

RHETORICAL MODES OF WRITING

The organization that we have been talking about up to this point covers the chronological presentation of the different sections in essays and research papers. Writing also has different types of organization of information relating to different purposes for writing. We refer to the categories that differ by purpose as the "modes of writing." Rhetorical modes are patterns of organization aimed at achieving a particular effect in the reader. The following four are usually categorized as the basic modes: description (describing a person, place, or event so that the audience can "see" it), narration (telling a nonfiction or fiction story), exposition (providing information), and argument/persuasion (asserting and supporting an opinion). These modes can be further subdivided into the following nine rhetorical modes, which are the ones generally taught in English classes: **exemplification, extended definition, comparison/contrast, description, narration, cause/effect, classification/division, process analysis,** and **argument.** You may be asked to read or write essays that exemplify individual modes, but most writing relies on creating effective combinations of different modes. Thus, the content of your essays and research papers must also be organized with an eye toward your overall purpose and the purposes of different sections.

> **Exemplification** is "the giving of an example." The purpose of an exemplification is to give an extended example or a series of shorter examples to

illustrate a main idea, which can be an abstraction. An essay in this mode typically draws on the modes of *extended definition* and *comparison/contrast*.

Extended definition consists of defining a subject at length (rather than briefly, like a dictionary). An essay in this mode typically starts with a term to be defined, may follow with a dictionary definition, and then elaborates. An essay in this mode typically draws on the modes of *exemplification* and *comparison/contrast*.

Comparison/contrast essays show how two or more subjects are alike and/or different. This mode can be applied to any number of subjects, including people, organizations, values, and viewpoints. The writer can take different points and alternate between comparing and contrasting the subjects on these points, or have one section listing all the similarities and another that lists all the differences. An essay in this mode typically draws on the modes of *exemplification* and *description*.

Description is also sometimes called "illustration," and one definition of "illustrate" is "to describe with pictures." A description essay can take a person or object to describe in great detail, including details that involve other senses besides sight. Most writers choose specific organizational plans. An essay that describes how a person looks could start from the feet and work up, or start at the head and work down, for instance (direction is less important than consistency).

Narration provides the details of an event. Like a description, it should have an organizational plan, and chronological order is logical and the most common. It is like a list of events written in paragraph form. Newspaper articles are often narrations, and narration is often used in *cause/effect* essays.

Cause/effect essays start with a subject, such as an event, and then show the causes (reasons) for it or the effects (results) of it. These could involve a simple single cause, a single effect relationship, or an entire chain of events leading up to a particular outcome or even series of outcomes. Cause and effect essays often employ *narration*.

Classification/division essays divide a whole into parts or sort related items into categories. Classification places items into different groups according to specific criteria, and division breaks one item into parts and then examines the parts in relationship to the whole. This is especially helpful with broad and complicated subjects because they make the subjects more manageable. An essay in this mode typically draws on the modes of *exemplification* and *description*.

Process analysis explores how to do something or how something works. (This could cover the range from how to change a light bulb to how Arctic ice melts.) An essay in this mode typically draws on the modes of *exemplification* and *description*.

Argumentation is also called "persuasion" because arguments are often about persuading people to believe something or to take some action. The writer offers a debatable opinion (not a simple fact) and then provides support through evidence and logic. The best argumentative essays also provide opposing viewpoints to explain and rebut. Argumentation papers typically draw on most, even all, of the other modes. Important terms must be defined, examples should be given, cause and effect relationships may need to be explained, and so on.

Sometimes essays can use one pattern of organization to support a larger purpose. The following table shows the main rhetorical modes. Any one of them can be the main point of a piece of writing, but, with an argumentative paper, all the other modes are likely to be drawn upon in service of making the main point that you are trying to prove clear to your audience. Most college research papers are supposed to be argumentative.

Exemplification	Extended Definition	Description
Narration	**Argumentation**	Process Analysis
Comparison/ Contrast	Classification/ Division	Cause/Effect

The table shows the centrality of argument in a research paper, but it does not indicate the proportions of other modes represented in the paper. The proportions will be determined by need. In different types of writing, this can also be dictated by situation.

Suppose you decide that you want to write a letter to the editor about some issue you feel strongly about. Your main point is to support an argument so that you can persuade your audience—other people in your community—to see the issue the way you do or even to act upon it. You sit down and type furiously, and in just half an hour you have come up with a terrific letter. You have named the problem, given examples, talked about the effects that will occur if something isn't done, and identified and rebutted arguments made by people on the other side of the issue. You proofread the letter, make some organizational changes, make your opening sentence a stronger "hook" to grab people's attention, and then you go to the paper's website and look at the guidelines for submitting letters to the opinion page. They tell you that letters must be 250 words or fewer. You do a quick word count. You have 598!

In this situation, you have to make some hard choices about your own writing. You have to get rid of a lot of sentences you really love. What do you get rid of, and what do you keep? You realize that you need to focus on the argument, and you start to think about what examples, definitions, and other sections of your letter you can cut out without ruining your points. You realize that lots of examples and information in your paper are common knowledge to people who have been following the issue that you are addressing, and that helps you. You finally get your letter down to exactly 250 words. As far as the modes of writing are concerned, the ratio looks like what you see in the following pie chart:

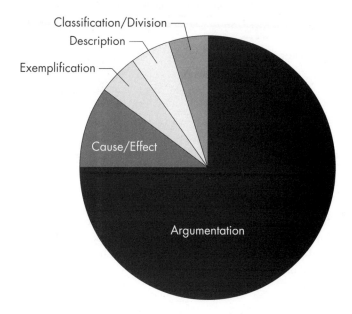

Classification/Division
Description
Exemplification
Cause/Effect
Argumentation

You submit your letter and contact information and mention that you are a student at the local college. A couple of days later, you are contacted by the editor of the opinion page. She liked your letter, and she wants to know if you would consider writing an extended version for the Community Voices section, which is used to give people in the community the chance to have editorial-length pieces published. She likes the idea of presenting a college student's perspective on the subject. She wants to know if you can expand your letter to between 750 and 1,000 words. You agree, and you go back to your original letter (it's a good thing you saved the original version before you started revising it to a much shorter length). Now you need to think of what to add to make your arguments stronger and your letter more compelling. After all, you can't convince anyone unless they are willing to read your opinion piece all the way through.

You decide that you can begin with a couple of examples that are really vivid, and in your conclusion you warn about what could be coming in the future if there aren't any changes. If you were to create a pie chart that showed the modes of writing you employed in this longer letter, it might look like the following:

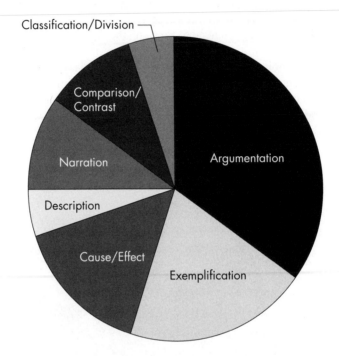

When you write essays and research papers for classes, the proportions of the modes that you draw on should shift with your needs. Keep these modes in mind along with your audience and purpose as you write to make sure that you don't spend too much time in some modes and too little in others.

CHAPTER 8

Integrating Sources into Writing

If you watch the evening news, you should be familiar with what journalists call "eyewitness accounts." If a storm is moving into a region, a reporter is there "live," in the horrible weather, showing you that there is indeed a storm moving in. If a shooting occurred, a reporter arrives on the scene and interviews those who may have seen the tragic event. Conversely, you may see a news interview that occurs back at the studio, but such interviews typically include a prominent scientist, politician, soldier, or law enforcement agent—in other words, the interview is with a recognized expert in some important field. Without these accounts, the stories would lose a lot of validity. A reporter simply telling you about the incoming storm lacks the impact—the proof—that a reporter in the field provides.

Writing papers is very similar. Unless you provide some proof—an expert testimonial or evidence that you've found (the academic equivalent of an eyewitness account)—your audience will be left unconvinced. However, although journalists need to provide proof and a summary of events that have occurred, they are morally obliged to go no further. Ideally, their job is to report the facts to you and let you decide on their significance. As a writer, you're often asked to go beyond this stage. You don't just report; you interpret and come to conclusions for the audience.

Many times in your college career, your instructors are going to ask for your assessment, conclusion, and opinion in a paper. For such papers, you need to prove you've thought critically about the topic, have paid attention to class readings and lectures, and can provide some unique insights on the topic. Mostly, such papers are all about *you*. However, many more professors are going to require that you write a paper based not on your own ideas, but the ideas of the experts in the field. For this type of project, you need to master the processes of researching and interpreting your findings.

But why do students need to research at all when writing papers? The purpose of research is multifaceted. First, including summaries, quotations, and paraphrases from respected sources on your topic lets readers know that you yourself have become more of an expert. By displaying such research, you establish your own credibility and demonstrate your hard work by showing that you've read and understood some of the best scholars on your topic.

More important, however, is that research helps you to support your own arguments. If you simply state in a paper that global warming is threatening polar bears with extinction, skeptics who think global climate change is exaggerated have no reason to believe you. However, if you can present information that you found in an article published by scientists in a refereed scholarly journal that analyzes twenty years of data showing that polar bears' hunting seasons are growing shorter and shorter, and that, as a consequence, their health is declining from less access to food, your audience now has reason to believe that you may be on to something. In an academic research paper, virtually every point you make should have outside support proving that the ideas presented in your thesis are widely shared and can be supported. There is strength in numbers. You must present the work of other scholars in your paper, people who will "stand with you" and help prove that your conclusions are valid.

If you've done quick or shoddy research, you will showcase your lack of preparation in your paper. Your audience will be able to tell the difference between a half-hour research session or a Web search from your laptop versus deeper research that takes days, weeks, or even months. If all your sources come from the same anthology or you've used a general encyclopedia, it will prove that you haven't fully explored your topic. Moreover, if all your sources are strongly tilted toward one agenda or scholarly camp, it may prove that you were less interested in finding facts than you were in proving your argument. Be sure to let your research change your opinions, and stay open-minded during the entire process. Your audience will dismiss your argument if you don't acknowledge and address opposing viewpoints in your paper.

SUMMARY, SYNTHESIS, AND CRITICAL THOUGHT

In any writing task, there are three levels of thought you could demonstrate: **summary, synthesis,** and **critical thought.** For some brief writing assignments, a professor may simply ask for a summary or synthesis as the goal for a paper. However, if you are asked to complete a successful piece of argumentative research writing, you will need to show the third and most difficult level: critical thought.

Summary

The first level of thought is what the reporters mentioned in the preceding example do. It is simple summary. In a summary, you research, you compile data and evidence, and you report it to your audience exactly as you found it in the first place. Unlike television reporters, however, you're not providing video clips and interviews with people on the street. You're providing well-documented and thorough research—a paper trail that other scholars can follow if they need to find the same data or verify a claim. Your findings will range from statistical facts and historical dates to illuminated ideas and conclusions of some of the best scholars working today. This type of information is crucial to any good research paper; however, it is not the ultimate goal of many writers.

A paper that does nothing but regurgitate facts and data is not very intellectually stimulating. In fact, it can be quite boring. Readers could simply read your works-cited page or bibliography and go straight to the sources themselves. If you don't critique or assess your sources, readers will wonder what is the relevance of your paper. Your paper will be a sea of statistics that never supports a thesis or comes to a particular conclusion. To create a meaningful research paper, you need to think critically about your sources.

Synthesis

Synthesis is a more advanced level of writing than summary, and it is an important skill to master. In a summary, you present material to your audience exactly as reported in the first place; in a synthesis, you bring several sources together to make one larger point. After you've provided outside materials, you need to prove to the reader that you've not only understood this information, but you've mastered it. You need to prove that you've read through several sources and have presented the best of the information gathered for your paper.

If you're writing a paper about the history of television, you won't just present every source in a simple summary. Instead, you'll present them in an order (perhaps chronologically for the purposes of your paper) and select only the information that will directly support the theme or thesis of your paper. You'll also present material from multiple sources here, whereas in a summary, you discuss only one source. In a good synthesis, your paper reports important facts to the audience, but includes no grand conclusions or intricate argument. This type of paper is good for a basic history report or an overview of general policies or facts.

For example, for the paper you are writing about television history, you find a source that discusses modern-day advertisers on television. Here is what the source says: "Moreover, to appease advertisers, media firms are increasingly giving them greater identification with and control over the programming. Proctor and Gamble, one of the world's largest advertisers, has signed major production deals with both Sony's Columbia TriStar Television and with Viacom's Paramount to coproduce television programs" (McChesney 41).

While you read this quotation, it reminded you of an article you took some notes from as you researched. You paraphrased the argument in the article, and you include this paraphrase in your paper, as well. The article explained that soap operas are called "soaps" because they were directly sponsored and funded by soap companies. There would be ads in the middle of the show, acted out by the same people on the stage for a soap opera scene. You report this fact next to the quotation, but all you do is report the facts here.

When writing a paper using synthesis as the highest level of thought, all you do is report the facts you've found in these sources. You are including this type of material for many sources, so you're not simply compiling a summary. However, because you never provide an interpretation, argument, or critical exploration of the material, you still aren't at the highest level of cognition—critical thought.

Source: McChesney, Robert. *Rich Media, Poor Democracy: Communications Politics in Dubious Times*. New York: New, 1999. Print.

A **Socratic Dialog** is a dialectical method of inquiry—that is, it involves an exchange of propositions and counter-propositions to reach a correct conclusion. Socrates would ask probing questions to cause people to reveal—and thus be compelled to examine—their methods of reasoning and underlying assumptions in order to test the logic and accuracy of their arguments. The goal of asking such questions was to strip away bias, misinformation, and logical fallacies to ultimately reach the truth.

Critical Thought

Critical thought is the highest level of thought that can occur in academic writing. It is based upon a strong, argumentative thesis, which you support by not only summarizing and synthesizing sources, but by critically examining and scrutinizing the sources, as well. Critical thought tends to be question-based, just like a Socratic Dialog. By asking yourself several important questions (or applying these questions to the sources you're considering for your paper), you start to generate new thoughts and angles to approach in your argument. In fact, your thesis sentence is often an answer to a question you've generated earlier in the writing process.

To perform critical thought in your paper, your thesis may be designed to state a problem, create a solution, or take a stance or position for or against something. These levels of thought are not possible with the basic nature of a summary or the fact-finding synthesis. Instead of simply presenting the facts you've found, you both state them and then critique them. Whereas a synthesis is ultimately about the sources themselves, a paper full of critical thought is a mix of the scholars' ideas and your own.

What the experts say is always crucial in any research endeavor. However, good critical thinking goes beyond paraphrasing the opinions of experts. You must present a mixture of their thoughts and facts and your own conclusions. For example, you won't just provide a quotation and then leave it as it is. Instead, you critically interpret this outside material. You tell the audience how this information ties in to your own thesis. You ask questions of the experts, and you discuss their findings actively and critically.

Critical thought is often question based. In your paper, you should generate answers for several key questions about the source material:

- Is the author of the source a true scholar and worthy of your attention?
- Were the statistics gathered using a true empirical, scientific method, or are they in some way flawed or skewed?
- Could the author's integrity be compromised by his or her sources of funding?
- Do the conclusions line up with what other scholars say about the same topic?
- Are the source's conclusions logically valid, or do they use fallacies and jump to inaccurate conclusions?
- How do these ideas line up with your own arguments and conclusions?
- If experts disagree, can you present both sides and explain whose arguments are strongest, and why?

Mastering critical thought is a difficult process, but it yields the highest quality and most interesting and successful papers.

PRESENTING INFORMATION: SUMMARIES, PARAPHRASES, AND DIRECT QUOTATIONS

There are three ways to present material in your papers: **summarizing, paraphrasing,** and **directly quoting.** Each of them should be used at different times for different rhetorical purposes, so mastering all three is crucial. (Guidelines for creating parenthetical in-text citations for MLA papers are given in Chapter 12, and guidelines for creating parenthetical in-text citations for APA papers are given in Chapter 14.) Following is a brief description of these ways to present information and some suggestions as to when you should use each one.

Summaries

When you take longer source material and state it briefly in your own words, you are summarizing. The key to summarizing is to provide your readers with only the main points found in the original passage. Often, you may summarize an entire argument or source in just a few sentences for the purposes of supporting your thesis. To summarize, you ignore the original style and length of the piece and present a concise version of it in your own words.

When summarizing, do not use quotation marks—you should not copy the exact language of the source material. Also, specific details and minor arguments are not typically included in a summary, simply the major facts and arguments. Keep in mind that even though you may be summarizing several pages of a source into a few sentences, you still need to provide a citation in the appropriate documentation style (MLA, APA, etc.) and must list the source in your works-cited page.

Following is an example of some original material from Mike Davis's *Ecology of Fear: Los Angeles and the Imagination of Disaster.* Pay attention to key details and then look at the summary of it that follows.

Once or twice each decade, Hawaii sends Los Angeles a big, wet kiss. Sweeping far south of its usual path, the westerly jet stream hijacks warm water-laden air from the Hawaiian archipelago and hurls it toward the Southern California coast. This "Kona" storm system—dubbed the "Pineapple Express" by television weather reporters—often carries several cubic kilometers of water, or the equivalent of half of Los Angeles's annual precipitation. And when the billowing, dark turbulence of the storm front collides with the high mountain wall surrounding the Los Angeles Basin, it sometimes produces rainfall of a ferocity unrivaled anywhere on earth, even in the tropical monsoon belts.

Source: Davis, Mike. *Ecology of Fear: Los Angeles and the Imagination of Disaster.* New York: Vintage, 1999. Print.

HERE IS A GOOD SUMMARY OF THIS PASSAGE

A couple of times a decade, a Kona storm system from Hawaii brings half of Los Angeles's annual rain in one single storm system (Davis 1).

Note how many details are left out of this summary—the fact that the storm comes from a different place than most California storms, the fact that the storm is called the Pineapple Express, the fact that this storm produces worse rain than at any other place on Earth. This summary really just tells the reader that there is a storm from Hawaii, it's called a Kona system, and it produces a lot of rain for Los Angeles. Your paper's thesis may not have needed any of this extra information, so you cut it out, paring down the information to just things you need for your own argument. Also, note that the entire tone and language of the passage has changed in your summary. The idiosyncratic style of the original language (wording such as the "big wet kiss" of the storm) is now gone, and, instead, we have one or two simple facts in a much more straightforward, academic tone.

HERE IS A WEAK SUMMARY OF THAT SAME PASSAGE

A few times a decade, a Kona storm system from the Hawaiian jet stream hijacks warm water-laden air and brings half of Los Angeles's annual rain in one single storm system (Davis 1).

Note that the language "jet stream hijacks warm water-laden air" is taken word-for-word from the original material. If you're using any verbatim language like this, you need to skip the summary and go for a direct quotation instead, or your paper could receive an "F" for plagiarizing the passage.

WHEN TO SUMMARIZE

Following are several legitimate reasons to summarize. Never use summarizing as an excuse to take one bit of information out of context to make it seem that a passage supports your thesis if in reality it does not.

1. The original passage is too long. Often, you read a wonderful passage that includes information you deem helpful, but is rather long. A summary is a great way to distill information into manageable size. You may very well be boiling down an entire chapter or source to one sentence in order for it to fit your paper's needs. Often stating things simply and quickly is the best way to convey information.

2. The original language isn't appropriate. Many sources are written to be entertaining instead of educational. If you find such a source, you may still want to use the information, but you want to clean up the tone of the passage. In the previous example, the "wet kiss" language is not particularly scholarly in tone, so avoiding such rhetorical flourishes and stating things in more professional language will have a greater impact in your paper.

3. You need only one piece of information. Sometimes the source material contains many facts and statistics in a section, but you need only one bit of that data. In such cases, summarize only one part of the original material in your paper. There is no need to quote or paraphrase a passage that contains information that does not directly support your thesis statement. Select only information that is relevant and important for inclusion in your writing. Summarizing is often the best way to ensure this.

4. You have too many statistics and data. You may find a great scientific source full of statistics and data, but you don't want your own paper to be flooded with graphs and mathematics. Instead of quoting statistic after statistic, you may just summarize them into shorter units of information that are easier to take in.

Paraphrasing

Sometimes you need to restate source material in your own words, while still including all the points it makes. When you do this, it is called a paraphrase. A paraphrase conveys all the ideas in a passage, unlike a summary, but like a summary, you put all the ideas into your own words. A paraphrase should ideally be the same length as or even slightly longer than the original passage. If you paraphrase a single sentence from a source, your version should be a single sentence. If you are using a full paragraph from the source, your paraphrase should be a full paragraph as well. You will not alter the length of the original material as significantly as you will in a summary.

One danger of paraphrasing is that you may use language that too closely resembles the original. The paraphrase cannot contain direct phrases or wording from the original. If it does, you should quote the source instead or put quotation marks around phrases that you just cannot put into your own words. One of the major reasons to paraphrase is to keep the length and content of source material fairly similar while changing the wording to be consistent with the style of the rest of your paper. If you use the same words as the original, you fail to maintain consistency, and, even worse, you risk plagiarizing the source. Remember that even though you are rewording the original material, you are still using someone else's facts. Thus, you must provide an in-text citation and include the source in your works-cited page. Following is a piece of original source material from T. Colin Campbell and Thomas M. Campbell's *The China Study*.

It was widely thought that much of the childhood malnutrition in the world was caused by a lack of protein, especially from animal-based foods. Universities and governments around the world were working to alleviate a perceived "protein gap" in the developing world. In this project, however, I uncovered a dark secret. *Children who ate the highest protein diets were the ones most likely to get liver cancer!* They were the children of the wealthiest families.

Source: Campbell, T. Colin, and Thomas M. Campbell II. *The China Study: The Most Comprehensive Study of Nutrition Ever Conducted and the Startling Implications for Diet, Weight Loss and Long-term Health.* Dallas: Benbella, 2005. Print.

HERE IS A STRONG PARAPHRASE OF THE ORIGINAL MATERIAL

Many nutritionists have traditionally held that worldwide childhood malnutrition was caused by a deficiency in protein from animal sources. Research institutions and government groups worldwide thought there was a "protein gap" between wealthy and developing nations. In a twenty-year study of nutrition and health, however, Dr. T. Colin Campbell discovered something rather shocking. Children from the wealthiest families who ate the most protein were the ones who had the highest percentages of liver cancer (Campbell and Campbell 1).

Notice that the wording in the paraphrase is significantly different from the original (aside from use of the term "protein gap"). The dramatic flair of the italicized sentence with the exclamation point has been replaced by a sentence that doesn't use such emphasis. This rewording is more consistent with the tone of the student's paper. Also notice that this paraphrase needed some rewording in the third sentence. Instead of the use of the original "I," the scientist's name was supplied, acknowledging the source material on which this paragraph is based. Finally, note that the idea of a "dark secret" is supplanted by "something rather shocking."

HERE IS A WEAK PARAPHRASE OF THE ORIGINAL MATERIAL

Many experts in the world thought that global childhood malnutrition was caused by a lack of protein, especially from animal-based foods. Research institution and government groups worldwide thought there was a protein gap between wealth and developing nations. In the study found here, however, I uncovered something shocking. Children from the wealthiest families who ate the most protein were the ones who had the highest percentages of liver cancer (Campbell and Campbell 1).

This paraphrase has a few major problems. First, the opening sentence uses wording too close to the original source. The author should have used a different term than "animal-based foods." Similarly, the phrase "protein gap" is used without use of quotation marks, and you can never use an exact phrase without using quotation marks. Also, the third sentence is confusing because it retains the original use of the word "I." This makes the sentence hard to follow—does "I" refer to the author of the original work or the author of the paraphrase? This should be revised for clarity.

WHEN TO PARAPHRASE

There are three primary circumstances that call for paraphrasing:

1. The original language is not academic in tone. Like the preceding summary example, you may find that the original source material uses slang or is a bit too casual for your tastes. You may want to paraphrase the information, keeping the same length and content, but writing in an academic voice.

2. The original language may be difficult for your audience to understand. Perhaps the original is a scientific paper full of technical jargon and language the average reader will not understand. You may want to reword it to make the content easier for your audience to read. Instead of using a direct quote that may be confusing and hard to digest, a paraphrase will make the content easier to comprehend.

3. The original language sounds outdated. You may have reason to use a source that is decades old or even older. The source may use language that is outdated, even archaic sounding, and just doesn't fit with the rest of your paper. By paraphrasing it, you retain all the original content, but you can update the style and make it easier for your audience to read.

Remember that you must always be honest when you paraphrase. Don't succumb to the temptation to alter or slant information to support your thesis.

Direct Quotations

When you find language in an outside source that is so perfect and informative you need to use it exactly as it is, you use a **direct quotation.** When you use a direct quotation, one of the most important things to remember is that you must—with the exception of the following circumstances—reproduce the exact quotation, using every word and every punctuation mark in the original. If you find yourself unhappy with how the original author worded something, you should paraphrase the source.

You can make minor alterations to the body of a quotation, such as adding information to clarify it or cutting out unnecessary wordiness, by using brackets to distinguish your additions or changes from the original quotation. You should do this only if you are in no way changing the meaning of the original passage. However, if you see an obvious typographical error, you can fix it; for example, change "teh" to "the." (For more information on this and on the technical details of using quotation marks, adherence to MLA or APA style, how to make changes within a quotation, how to include a long quotation, etc., see Chapters 9–14.)

WHEN TO DIRECTLY QUOTE

1. The original wording is compelling. Often, you'll find quotations that say exactly what you're thinking, but they say it far more eloquently and gracefully than you could have put it. In this case, you should quote the material. Many published authors write for a living, so make use of their years of experience at crafting sentences. When you read a passage during research and think, "Wow, I wish I could say it that way," you may want to include it as a direct quotation.

2. The quotation will help establish credibility. Many scholars from the past and present have become famous and have set the standards in their field of study. Use of their thoughts and their exact words will give your paper even more credibility than simply paraphrasing them. Well-known thinkers, such as Martin Luther King, Jr., Albert Einstein, and Noam Chomsky, carry a lot of weight and can impress your audience.

HOW TO INCORPORATE SOURCES INTO YOUR PAPERS

Every time you include material from an outside source (be it a summary, paraphrase, or direct quotation), you need to remember that the audience may be encountering this material for the first time. They have no idea where this material came from; they have no idea who the author is; they don't even understand the connections between this material and your thesis. It is up to you to tell the audience all these things. Information with no introduction or exploration can actually make a paper harder to read. Unless you introduce and then critically examine every quotation, summary, and paraphrase that you provide, the audience won't understand how your source information helps further your thesis. A bit of information used improperly in your paper will weaken its impact and could even result in inadvertent plagiarism. (See Chapter 9 for more advice about recognizing and avoiding plagiarism.)

INTRODUCING YOUR SOURCES

To begin the process of critically exploring your sources, you need to get in the habit of introducing your experts to your audience. You've read several books and articles on your topic by the time you conclude your paper. Ideally, you've become a bit of an expert on the subject—but remember that your audience may not be nearly as informed as you have become. To educate the reader on the quality of the authors you've chosen, you need to provide an introduction to your sources before you use them. (Note that this process of introduction is different from writing the introduction of your entire paper, and it's even different from the topic sentence of your paragraphs.) These introductions typically come after the topic sentence but before use of the source material.

Why Introduce Your Sources?

1. It is important to distinguish between the source and you. One of the biggest reasons to always introduce outside information is to let the audience know where the source starts and you stop. When you paraphrase and summarize, if you fail to provide a brief introduction about where the information came from, your readers will be confused. It is very easy to paraphrase something poorly and have the readers believe that the entire thought was your own, when it was not. By introducing the material before you give it, you clue your readers in; you tell them "This is someone else's information, and I'm just borrowing it."

When you quote, it is going to be more obvious which thoughts are yours and which ones come from outside sources because of your use of quotation marks. However, you'll still need to introduce the information for the following reasons listed.

2. You should establish the credibility of the author. With the rapid spread of information and computer databases full of journal articles, dissertations, and scientific reports, even the most learned scholars will not have read everything on their subject. You may cite a source that even an expert has never heard of. However, a quick introduction lets the reader know something about the author. What do you know about his or her field? Background? Experience? Credentials? Giving your readers additional information about the author of your source lends credibility to the ideas you use. Even if your audience is unfamiliar with the author, this extra information goes a long way to establishing his or her credibility as a scholar and an author.

How to Introduce Your Sources

The trick with introducing your sources is to figure out how to provide a maximum of information about the source and its author in a minimum amount of space. After all, although introducing your sources is important, the bulk of your paper needs to focus on the information you've gathered and your interpretation of it. Typically, you want to provide two elements in these brief introductions: the authors' names and why they are experts worth considering.

Following are some examples of the types of introductions you might use in your paper. Keep in mind that these are not the entire body paragraphs. You would still include a topic sentence before these citations and a thorough discussion of them afterward within your body paragraph (see p. 154).

INTRODUCTION OF A SOURCE WITH ONE AUTHOR

This basic source introduction includes mention of the author's full name and important background information that bolsters his or her credibility in the field. When you introduce the author, specifying degrees held by the author (Ph.D., M.A., M.D., etc.) doesn't really tell your readers much—hundreds of thousands of people have degrees, but that alone doesn't mean that all of them are credible experts.

Example: According to award-winning inventor Ray Kurzweil, the man described in 2005 by Bill Gates as the person best able to predict the future direction of artificial intelligence, "nanotechnology will enable the design of nanobots: robots designed at the molecular level, measured in microns (millionths of a meter) such as respirocytes (mechanical red-blood cells)" (28).

Source: Kurzweil, Ray. *The Singularity Is Near: When Humans Transcend Biology.* New York: Viking, 2005. Print.

This source's introduction quickly lets the reader know the author's full name and that he is well regarded by other experts, and then it proceeds with the quotation itself. Note that the example begins the sentence with "According to," but here are some other variations you may consider. Don't feel limited here; use different language to give the reader some variety.

Example: Artificial intelligence expert Ray Kurzweil, winner of the Lemelson-MIT Prize and the National Medal of Technology, says that "nanotechnology will enable the design of nanobots: robots designed at the molecular level, measured in microns (millionths of a meter) such as respirocytes (mechanical red-blood cells)" (28).

Some other phrases you could use to introduce the quotation include these:

> According to Kurzweil . . .
>
> One argument Kurzweil makes is that . . .
>
> Kurzweil argues . . .
>
> Kurzweil asserts . . .
>
> Kurzweil maintains . . .
>
> Kurzweil contends . . .
>
> Kurzweil suggests . . .

INTRODUCTION OF SOURCE WHEN CITED REPEATEDLY

Often, you will use one source repeatedly within your paper. You may cite a passage and need a paragraph or two to critically discuss its meaning. After you're done, you may have more evidence you need to cite. You should introduce this source thoroughly the first time, but every time thereafter you need not repeat the title or the author's first name.

Example: Kurzweil also says that "nanobots will have myriad roles within the human body, including reversing human aging" (28).

INTRODUCTION OF A SOURCE WRITTEN BY MULTIPLE AUTHORS

Many sources are collaborative efforts, so you need to introduce all authors as well as the source. The first time you introduce them you should use the full first and last name of each author.

Example: Ray Kurzweil, winner of the Lemelson-MIT Prize and the National Medal of Technology, and Terry Grossman, who is the founder and medical director of Frontier Medical Institute, claim that as we "peer even further into the 21st century, nanotechnology will enable us to rebuild and extend our bodies and brains and create virtually any product from mere information, resulting in remarkable gains in prosperity" (5).

Note: Your citation requires no information other than the page number because you have mentioned both authors in your text, and so your readers will look for an entry indicating both Kurzweil and Grossman as authors on your works-cited page, not just the entry indicating the book authored only by Kurzweil.

If you have already introduced both authors, you can simply use their last names.

Example: Kurzweil and Grossman further claim that as we "peer even further into the 21st century, nanotechnology will enable us to rebuild and extend our bodies and brains and create virtually any product from mere information, resulting in remarkable gains in prosperity" (5).

Source: Kurzweil, Ray, and Terry Grossman. *Fantastic Voyage: Live Long Enough to Live Forever.* New York: Rodale, 2004. Print.

INTRODUCTION OF A SOURCE WITH NO AUTHOR INFORMATION

Some source material may have no author listed. In such cases, you still need to introduce the source before you quote it.

Example: One source on nanotechnology, *Nanotech and the Next Big Wave,* asserts that "nanotechnology will make us smarter by increasing the number of neurons that can fire in our brains" (128).

INTRODUCTION OF A PARAPHRASE

Whether you use a direct quotation or a paraphrase, you must still indicate where the information came from. In fact, it's even more important to introduce a paraphrase because the lack of quotation marks makes it difficult for a reader to understand which arguments are yours and which belong to outside sources. Following is an example of a paraphrase without an introduction. It is virtually impossible to tell which ideas are original and which are borrowed from a source. The only clue we have is the parenthetical citation at the end.

Weak example: In the future, nanotechnolgoy will lead to use of nanobots which are robots which are built at the molecular level. Things this small are measured in microns which are one millionth of a meter, and they include artificial red-blood cells known as respirocytes (Kurzweil 28).

Following is the same paraphrase, but notice how the introduction makes it clear that this is not the student writer's ideas and gives credit to the appropriate source.

Strong example: According to Ray Kurzweil, nanotechnology will lead to use of nanobots, which are robots that are built at the molecular level. Machines this small are measured in microns, which are one millionth of a meter, and they include artificial red-blood cells known as respirocytes (28).

INTRODUCTION OF A SUMMARY

Much like the introduction of a paraphrase, summaries need introductions because readers will not be able to tell the difference between a quick summary of a source or your own idea.

Example: According to Ray Kurzweil, in the future, microscopic nanobots will be possible (28).

Do not "emote." When you introduce a source, don't gush about its quality in your introduction. You should avoid saying things like "In this groundbreaking book" or "his insightful research." Let the source material, the qualifications of the original author, and your critical thought of the source prove the quality.

When Not to Introduce a Source

SIMPLE DATES OR STATISTICS

Sometimes you may want to include a simple fact or date without going through all the effort of an introduction. In such cases, this information will be small side notes in your argument, but will help establish some minor facts. You will still provide a full citation for all such information, and you'll include it in your works-cited page; however, for brevity, you'll skip the introduction.

Example: In 1997, children between the age of four and twelve spent $24 billion, and these purchases were directly influenced by advertisements they saw on television (McChesney 45).

AFTER THE MATERIAL

Always introduce the material *before* the quotation, paraphrase, or summary. To properly introduce a source, you have to give the information right away. If you quote or paraphrase and then tell the audience where the information came from later, you will cause confusion.

ANALYZING AND INTERPRETING INFORMATION FROM SOURCES

Although informing the audience where information comes from is an important step in your research project, the true key to good research writing is what you do with the information after you present it. You can provide a brilliant quotation in your paper, but if you fail to examine it and present your own critical interpretation of this quotation, you might as well not present research at all. Only by exploring the importance of information do you begin the highest level of paper writing—prose that demonstrates critical thinking skills.

How to Discuss Information

The following three tasks will help you discuss your outside sources. If you perform at least one of these three tasks after you present information, you've started to incorporate your source material successfully into your paper. Ideally, however, you'll perform more than one.

TASK 1: INFORMATION COMPETENCY

You will probably provide in your paper several statistics or interesting conclusions a scholar has reached. If your audience reads the quick quotation or the paraphrase you've provided, they may very well ask themselves, "so what?" With information so readily available, your readers can find the material you quoted rather easily and read the scholars' works themselves instead of your short "snapshot" of the ideas.

What your paper should do to stand out, though, is provide unique insights and interpretations of this material. What do *you* think about these ideas? How do *you* interpret their statistical data? Your handling of this information is really what information competency is all about. Any of your readers can find what you find if they dig hard enough. What they can't find without reading your paper is what you think about it.

Similarly, your discussion of complex material will let your instructor understand that you fully comprehend the material in question. Often research material is difficult to understand and interpret. By commenting on the information's importance and using and interpreting complex passages to support your own argument, you prove that you're competent in handling even the most difficult information.

TASK 2: CONNECTION OF SOURCE MATERIAL TO YOUR OWN THESIS AND ARGUMENTS

When you insert the information you have found in your research into your paper, it will do nothing to prove your arguments or support your thesis until you make the connections yourself. Do not leave it to the audience to connect the dots, or they may never be able to—they may even try to do so and come up with a different picture than the one you intended because they don't understand the material as well as you now do. When you discuss how the outside information supports your arguments, however, you will make all these connections clear to your audience. If you don't let the reader know *how* specific information supports your thesis, your thesis has not actually been supported at all.

TASK 3: EXPLORATION OF HOW YOUR SOURCE MATERIAL TIES IN TO OTHER IDEAS IN THIS BODY OF SCHOLARSHIP

You should have compiled a great deal of research by the time you print your final paper and submit it. In essence, you've become an expert on your topic while researching. You may have used a combination of scholarly books and articles that nobody else has synthesized in the same way. You need to take advantage of that information—use the unique perspective that is your own individual mind working with the specific sources you've read.

Surely your professor has read many of the sources you've chosen to incorporate into your paper, but probably not all of them. And if she has, she probably hasn't ever joined these specific facts together in the same way that you yourself may have. Not only are you showing off your information competency by explaining and analyzing the information, you're showing off your grasp of at least a portion of the scholarly body of work on this subject.

Understanding and Avoiding Plagiarism

It's Sunday morning, and Sandy's research paper is due Monday. She has been staring at her computer screen for almost an hour. She's checked her email and hit her MySpace page for a while, but she can't think of a way to get started on her paper. Sandy's starting to feel a bit shocked that the last few weeks went by so fast. She has several fantastic library books sitting on her desk, as well as some articles she found in the college library database. She's read parts of most of the articles and scanned sections of the books, but she hasn't had a lot of time—she's taking an overload, she's on the volleyball team, and she has an active social life—and she has to admit to herself that she really hasn't understood most of what she has read during her research. Besides, she finds it pretty boring.

Finally, Sandy turns to the Internet for some ideas just to help her get started. Her topic is Reality TV, and she enters that term into a search engine along with "research" and "paper," and pretty soon she stumbles across an article on a site called GradeSaver posted by "Anonymous" and dated July 3, 2006. It is all about the movie *The Truman Show* and how it satirizes reality TV. She reads the first paragraph and gets excited. It sounds great:

> Peter Weir's *The Truman Show* is a film of great satirical intellect and poignancy. However, beneath the facade, this "comedy" conveys important social messages that provide a warning for the future. It mocks human beings' automatic acceptance of what they are presented with and shows how manipulative and addictive the media can be. On a deeper level, the film also cautions against accepting absolute authority, the interminable hunt for Utopia, and the evils inspired by the desire for wealth. Whether *The Truman Show* is a satire, a comedy, a documentary, a fable, or even a hoax is debatable, but what is impossible to question is the need to consider its themes and digest its principal lessons.

She's saved! Wow, she thinks, the name "GradeSaver" sure applies. The research paper is worth thirty-five percent of the course grade. Her panic vanishes. She'll be able to turn her paper in the next day after all. She doesn't plan on just copying the paper—that would be totally cheating—but she can copy and paste it, go through and paraphrase it, and add some of her own thoughts and sources. Besides, she isn't even an English major; she's majoring in agriculture, and it's not like she's going to have to write research papers when she leaves college. This is just one of those classes she has to take and pass to get her college degree. And her schedule is so busy that she doesn't have time to do everything expected of her. Each professor seems to think that theirs is the only class students are taking.

She pastes the article into her Word document and starts to type. Pretty soon (with the help of a thesaurus) she has her first paragraph:

The Truman Show by Peter Weir is a deeply emotional, moving, satirical, intellectual movie. Nevertheless, beneath the surface, this so-called comedy transmits crucial social messages that give us a warning for the future. It makes fun of people's automatic acceptance of things they are presented with and shows that the media can be manipulative and addictive. The movie also cautions against accepting authority that is absolute, the unending search for Utopia, and the evils caused by wanting wealth. We can debate whether The Truman Show is a satire, a comedy, factual, or even a hoax, but we cannot question the need to look at its themes and contemplate its principal lessons.

By the end of the day, she has taken the GradeSaver essay, altered its wording and the order of some of its paragraphs, added information about Reality TV from her books and articles (at least one factoid from each), and, for good measure, thrown in some more paraphrases from other articles she finds on the Net. After she has finished her works-cited page (which does not, of course, mention GradeSaver) and printed the whole thing out, she has a sense of satisfaction—she's finished the assignment, and she even feels like she's really learned something about the subject. Besides, she now has time to study for a test she has in her math class Tuesday.

A week later, Sandy is flabbergasted when her professor gravely hands the research paper back to her with an "F" for plagiarism and a note telling her that she will receive an "F" for the entire course and a mark on her permanent record for violating her college's policy on academic honesty. He has stapled a copy of the GradeSaver paper to the back of her assignment as well, so she abandons all thought of trying to convince him that she didn't cheat. That night—angry, frightened, and humiliated—she cries herself to sleep.

There are lots of reasons students find themselves tempted to cheat. Often, those who do so rationalize that it isn't even wrong—or at least not "seriously" wrong. They have lots of pressures, not a lot of time, and, besides, "everybody does it," including people in the "real world." Also, the Internet has made stealing other people's work much easier than it was in the past. A 2003 study of 18,000 students enrolled in twenty-three colleges in the United States found that nearly forty percent of them admitted to using the Internet to plagiarize. So, you might ask, "Why is it such a big deal?"

The first and most obvious answer is that plagiarism—the unattributed use of other people's ideas or words—is unethical. It is both a form of lying and a form of theft. When you plagiarize, you are lying to your professor about the work you have done (or not done), and you are stealing another person's ideas and benefiting undeservedly from that person's hard work. You might rationalize that you aren't stealing from someone else if the paper has been posted on the Net to use or if you have actually paid money to a friend or a term-paper mill, but it is intellectual theft, nonetheless—and you are undisputedly lying to your professor.

A second answer is that if you plagiarize, you are not only robbing someone else, you are robbing yourself: you are depriving yourself of developing skills that would make you a better scholar while in school and a better critical thinker and intelligent consumer of information after you graduate.

A third answer—and the one that may be the most compelling to students who are seriously tempted to cheat—is that you can get caught and flunk not only the assignment, but an entire class. Depending on your institution, you could even be placed on academic probation or expelled. Sure, lots of students manage to get away with plagiarizing—at least for a while—but lots of students get caught, too. Your professors have been reading in their disciplines a lot longer than you have, and they may recognize works they have read before. They have also been reading students' papers for a long time, and students have their own distinctive writing styles. When a student displays newly sophisticated diction and sentence structure and suddenly drops idiosyncratic writing habits, a professor will see the change in style as a pretty strong clue that the student has copied or only slightly modified all or part of someone else's work. Furthermore, though this seems to come as a surprise to many students, most of your professors are at least as adept at searching the Internet as you are. Think about it—if you can find an article on the Net, so can anyone else. Also, students aren't the only people who lead busy lives, and more and more professors are turning to professional services such as Turnitin, Plagiarism.org, Integriguard, and MyDropBox to quickly and efficiently identify plagiarized papers.

Some types of plagiarism are not as obvious as Sandy's. In fact, some students plagiarize without even realizing that they are doing so, either through misunderstanding how to properly use and document sources or because of other mistakes. This chapter will help you to avoid any kind of plagiarism by discussing common problems and by telling you when to document the sources that you use. (See Chapters 12, 13, and 14 for detailed information on parenthetical in-text citations and works-cited pages in MLA and APA styles).

TYPES OF PLAGIARISM

We can divide plagiarism into five main categories: total plagiarism, substantial plagiarism, incidental/occasional plagiarism, "buddy"/tutor plagiarism, and accidental plagiarism.

Total plagiarism occurs when students turn in other people's work as their own. It is intentional and the most blatant and offensive form of academic dishonesty, and it can meet with very harsh punishments. Total plagiarism might involve an entire paper copied or purchased off the Internet or written by another student, or a "patchwork quilt" of a paper stitched together from a series of other works. Such papers may have language changed and may even have citations from sources the student has found and inserted in order to disguise the paper's true origins.

Substantial plagiarism occurs when students do most of the writing in their own papers but frequently (1) borrow ideas and rephrase them without giving credit to the original source, (2) borrow exact phrases and sentences without enclosing them in quotation marks and without giving credit to the original source, (3) or borrow exact phrases and sentences without enclosing them in quotation marks even though credit is given to the original source. These acts of plagiarism are also deliberate and blatant.

Incidental/occasional plagiarism occurs when students write their own papers, but there are sections that will not withstand strict scrutiny because of one or more passages where exact quotations of sentences and phrases are not enclosed in quotation marks even though they are attributed to their sources, or there are one or more passages where paraphrased ideas are not attributed to their sources. Sometimes examples of plagiarism in this category may be accidental.

"Buddy"/tutor plagiarism occurs when students get too much help from friends or tutors. It is certainly a good idea to have someone else look at your paper, but don't allow or ask them to help you rewrite it. Use another person's input to help you find technical errors or to alert you to areas that aren't clear, but do the rewriting yourself. Remember, tutors are there to show you your mistakes and to teach you how to correct them; they are not supposed to correct your paper and fix all the problems for you.

Accidental plagiarism occurs when students don't realize that using other people's ideas and paraphrasing them is plagiarism if the source is not clearly identified. It can also occur when people haven't been careful while taking notes and forget to put quotation marks around direct quotations, or they polish the paraphrased language of an attributed source and inadvertently rephrase it into the original language of the source without adding quotation marks (for tips on how to avoid these problems while note taking, see Chapter 6). This is perhaps the most common form of plagiarism and can be corrected with proper citations and documentation format.

AVOIDING PLAGIARISM

There are three rules for avoiding plagiarism, the first of which is pretty obvious:

1. Be honest. Don't buy, borrow, or steal anybody else's words or ideas.

2. Cite *all* material that you take from a nonfiction source, whether you quote, paraphrase, or summarize, unless it is common knowledge (we'll discuss that in greater length later). You should also cite any graphical material that you copy, such as charts and illustrations. If you are writing an essay about a single work of literature, the convention is to cite page numbers only for direct quotations from the work of literature, and not when you summarize any sections, but you still must cite all information you take from critical sources concerning the work of literature if you use any outside sources.

3. Use language and sentence structures that are essentially your own—simply changing or rearranging a few words here and there isn't enough to avoid charges of stealing.

ORIGINAL PARAGRAPH WRITTEN BY GEORGE ORWELL IN HIS ESSAY "POLITICS AND THE ENGLISH LANGUAGE"

Most people who bother with the matter at all would admit that the English language is in a bad way, but it is generally assumed that we cannot by conscious action do anything about it. Our civilization is decadent, and our language—so the argument runs—must inevitably share in the general collapse. It follows that any struggle against the abuse of language is a sentimental archaism, like preferring candles to electric light or hansom cabs to aeroplanes. Underneath this lies the half-conscious belief that language is a natural growth and not an instrument which we shape for our own purposes.

PLAGIARIZED PARAGRAPH, WITH PLAGIARIZED WORDS AND PHRASES HIGHLIGHTED

Many individuals who bother with the issue would admit that the English language is in terrible shape; however, we generally assumed we cannot alter this by conscious action. Our society is decadent, so our language, it is argued, shares in the problem. Some people might argue that trying to stop the abuse of language is old-fashioned and useless because they half-consciously think language is natural instead of something we shape as we please.

The student who wrote the paragraph above is guilty of plagiarism for three reasons: 1) phrases are copied verbatim from the original but are not enclosed in quotation marks, 2) the original author is not given, and 3) there is no citation indicating the page number the material was taken from. The effect of the plagiarized material is to indicate that all the words and ideas are the student's own.

PLAGIARIZED PARAGRAPH, WITH PLAGIARIZED WORDS AND PHRASES HIGHLIGHTED

Many individuals who bother with the issue would admit that the English language is in terrible shape; however, we generally assumed we cannot alter this by conscious action. Our society is decadent, so our language, it is argued, shares in the problem. Some people might argue that trying to stop the abuse of language is old-fashioned and useless because they half-consciously think language is natural instead of something we shape as we please (Orwell 12).

The paragraph above is still plagiarized because even though the author and page number appear in a parenthetical citation at the end of the sentence, phrases are copied verbatim from the original but are not enclosed in quotation marks. The effect of the plagiarized material is to indicate that although the ideas are Orwell's, all the words are the student's paraphrase of the original passage, which is clearly not the case.

PLAGIARIZED PARAGRAPH

Many individuals who ponder the condition of the English language are likely to conclude that it is in terrible shape, but they probably take for granted that we cannot think of any solutions. Some people might argue that society is in a moral and cultural decline; therefore, it follows that our discourse must also decline and that to try to fight this shows an inability to deal realistically with the times. This attitude suggests an unexamined assumption that language is something that evolves on its own, as opposed to a tool we utilize for our own purposes.

Though the paragraph above is an effective paraphrase (we don't worry about the words "English language" not being enclosed in quotation marks because there is no other logical way to name it), the student has still clearly plagiarized because 1) the author is not given, and 2) there is no citation indicating the page number the material was taken from. The effect of the plagiarized material is to indicate that all the ideas are the student's own.

UNPLAGIARIZED PARAGRAPH

Many individuals who ponder the condition of the English language are likely to conclude that it is in terrible shape, but they probably take for granted that we cannot think of any solutions. This attitude suggests an unexamined assumption that language is something that evolves on its own, as opposed to a tool we utilize for our own purposes. "Our civilization is decadent, and our language—so the argument runs—must inevitably share in the general collapse" (Orwell 12).

This example is *not* plagiarized. Most of the paragraph is put into the student's own words, and the passage ends with both a direct quotation and an MLA-style parenthetical citation.

UNPLAGIARIZED PARAGRAPH

As George Orwell points out about the English of his time—and his observations hold true today—many individuals who ponder the condition of the English language are likely to conclude that it is in terrible shape, but they probably take for granted that we cannot think of any solutions. Some people might argue that society is in a moral and cultural decline; therefore, it follows that our discourse must also decline and that to try to fight this shows an inability to deal realistically with the times. This attitude suggests an unexamined assumption that language is something that evolves on its own, as opposed to a tool we utilize for our own purposes (12).

This paragraph also avoids plagiarizing. It is the same paraphrase from the previous example, but it begins by attributing the ideas to their originator, George Orwell, and there is a parenthetical citation at the end to let the reader know the page number of the original material (the last name is not needed within the parentheses in this case because Orwell is mentioned before the paraphrase).

UNPLAGIARIZED PARAGRAPH

Many individuals who ponder the condition of the English language are likely to conclude that it is in terrible shape, but they probably take for granted that we cannot think of any solutions. Some people might argue that society is in a moral and cultural decline; therefore, it follows that our discourse must also decline and that to try to fight this shows an inability to deal realistically with the times. This attitude suggests an unexamined assumption that language is something that evolves on its own, as opposed to a tool we utilize for our own purposes (Orwell 12).

This example contains no verbatim word use, and it has a proper citation, so this student has also avoided plagiarism.

COMMON KNOWLEDGE EXCEPTIONS

Common knowledge exceptions refer to generally known facts. Here are examples of different types of common knowledge exceptions:

1. Information known by the average person (for example, President Abraham Lincoln was assassinated by John Wilkes Booth in 1865; U.S. and British forces invaded Iraq in 2003).

2. Information known by the average scholar in a particular discipline (for example, William Shakespeare died in 1616 at the age of 52; Milton Friedman won the Nobel Prize for Economics in 1976).

3. Information that is repeated in many different sources (for example, thalidomide is known to cause birth defects; the Great Fire of London happened in 1666). "Many" is an ambiguous term, and there is no universal agreement on exactly how many sources it takes to make something "common knowledge," but the standard assumption in academia is that facts are common knowledge if you can find the same information reported in at least five different sources (it isn't a bad idea to ask your own professor for guidance).

To be safe, if you aren't sure if an idea is "common knowledge," assume that it isn't, and cite the source of your information. After all, it is a lot less hazardous to have a citation that you don't need than it is to risk a charge of plagiarism.

Frequently, students get nervous and worry that they have "too many" citations. Think about it: you are writing research papers, which means that you are presenting research—you are supposed to have a lot of in-text citations. Citations let your reader know what sources you used, the page numbers of information found in print sources, and where to look for complete publication information on your works-cited page. (For graceful introduction of sources and how to discuss their relevance and show that you have thought critically about their assertions, see Chapter 8.)

WRITING TIP

If you quote someone, don't set up the quotation by saying that person "quoted" something, as in *Neil Postman quoted, "Anyone who has studied the history of technology knows that technological change is always a Faustian bargain."* Neil Postman didn't quote that sentence, he wrote it—you are the person doing the quoting, not him. Instead, you would say, *Neil Postman stated, "Anyone who has studied the history of technology knows that technological change is always a Faustian bargain."*

CHAPTER 10

Improving Style, Punctuation, and Grammar

DIRECTORY OF GUIDELINES AND RULES

We don't know how much of this chapter your instructor will cover in class—or if it will even get covered during class time at all. Many instructors figure that you have had enough instruction in the rules of style, punctuation, and grammar in earlier English classes, and they may not have the time to address these issues at this level. This is especially true in the quarter system, where so much material has to be covered in so little time. This chapter is designed to make it as easy as possible for you to brush up on style, grammar, and punctuation skills on your own.

For many students, English classes are the scariest courses. Lots of students put English classes off as long as possible. Why? In part because the rules of writing mystify them. Trying to figure out where to put commas and apostrophes can be a frustrating experience. And semicolons? Forget it. Furthermore, having problems with writing seems to be more embarrassing for most people than having problems in a math or science class. After all, no one expects math or science to come naturally, but English is the language we use every day.

One problem contributing to this mystification is the jargon (the specialized terminology used by a particular profession or group) found in so many style manuals and punctuation and grammar guides. Jargon can be difficult to understand for people who are not experts in a field. A student trying to understand rules for writing may, when confronted with terms like *faulty predication, gerund,* and *intransitive,* feel hopeless. Trying to understand what is meant by "good style" may seem equally elusive, especially because what is considered good style in one writing situation may not be in another, depending on purpose and audience. As for vocabulary, most of us are comfortable with and use a relatively small number of words—around 1,200 to 2,000—when we speak, and many of these are slang. We're pretty used to hearing and saying expressions that aren't technically correct—like "that's real good" instead of that's "really good" or using *they* when talking about one person. And when did you last—if ever—use the word *whom* when talking? Most of us can't depend on our ears to tell us if language is being correctly used because we've been conditioned by all sorts of casual expressions, verbal shortcuts, and nonstandard usages. Use of typical email and text message language also serves to weaken our mastery of standard English. Many people use "u" instead of "you" or "L8r" instead of "later" just to save time.

Learning how to write correctly and gracefully doesn't have to be difficult or agonizing. This chapter is designed to demystify the process for you and help you to develop your skills and confidence. And, because we realize that most people don't find grammar and punctuation as fascinating as we do, we're cutting to the chase and beginning with a visual guide to correctly punctuated sentences, which we follow with a list and examples of twenty-five of the most common errors that plague writers.

The sections that follow in the rest of the chapter will give you a deeper understanding of the components of sentences, the rules covering punctuation, and grammar issues, such as subject-verb agreement and pronoun use.

PUNCTUATION PATTERN SHEET

Here is a quick and simple visual guide to help you remember how to use commas, periods, semicolons, and colons in common sentence types.

An independent clause has a subject and a verb and can stand alone as a sentence.

1. *Independent clause. Independent clause.*
2. *Independent clause,* for *independent clause.*
   - and
   - nor
   - but
   - or
   - yet
   - so
3. *Independent clause*; *independent clause.*
4. *Independent clause*; therefore, *independent clause.*
   - however,
   - consequently,

Nonrestrictive (nonessential) elements can be removed from sentences without changing the meaning of the sentence and are set off with commas.

5. *Independent,* of course, *clause.*
   - on the other hand,
   - who is,
6. *Independent clause,* which is . . . .
   - of course . . . .
   - on the other hand . . . .

A subordinating conjunction in front of an independent clause turns it into a dependent clause. (Phrases lack subjects or verbs or both; treat them like dependent clauses when you punctuate sentences.)

7. If *dependent clause, independent clause.*
   - Because . . . ,
   - Since . . . ,
   - Even though . . . ,
8. *Independent clause* if *dependent clause.*
   - because
   - since
   - even though
9. *Independent clause:* a, b, and c.
10. *Independent clause:* a, nonrestrictive element; b, nonrestrictive element; and c, nonrestrictive element.

TWENTY-FIVE COMMON PUNCTUATION AND GRAMMAR ERRORS TO AVOID

1. COMMAS OMITTED AFTER INTRODUCTORY ELEMENTS

When you have an introductory element (such as a dependent clause or a phrase) in front of an independent clause, don't forget to use a comma.

INCORRECT:

When I tripped Bobby Jo giggled.

Omitting the necessary comma in the sentence above makes it very confusing. Did Jo giggle when I made Bobby trip? Or is Bobby Jo one person who giggled when I tripped? The following sentence clarifies the situation.

CORRECT:

When I tripped, Bobby Jo giggled.

INCORRECT:

Embarrassed I blushed.

CORRECT:

Embarrassed, I blushed.

If a phrase is very short and there is no possibility of confusion, you can omit the comma if you choose—but it is never incorrect to have it.

2. COMMAS ADDED AFTER DEPENDENT CLAUSES OR PHRASES THAT FOLLOW INDEPENDENT CLAUSES (UNLESS THE SECOND CLAUSE OR THE PHRASE IS NONRESTRICTIVE)

INCORRECT:

Do not use a comma, when you don't have a situation requiring one.

CORRECT:

Do not use a comma when you don't have a situation requiring one.

3. COMMAS OMITTED WHEN LINKING TWO INDEPENDENT CLAUSES WITH A COORDINATING CONJUNCTION

Using a coordinating conjunction without a comma between two independent clauses is an error called the *run-on sentence*.

INCORRECT:

Global climate change is a very hot topic and many people passionately disagree about its causes.

CORRECT:

Global climate change is a very hot topic, and many people passionately disagree about its causes.

(You could also substitute either a period or a semicolon for the comma and the coordinating conjunction.)

4. COMMAS USED BETWEEN TWO INDEPENDENT CLAUSES WITHOUT A COORDINATING CONJUNCTION

This error is so common that it has its own name: the comma splice. A comma alone is not sufficient between two independent clauses—you need something stronger, like a period or a semicolon, or you can add a coordinating conjunction after the comma.

INCORRECT:

Octavia Butler was an African American author, she became the first science fiction writer to receive the MacArthur Foundation "Genius" Grant.

CORRECT:

Octavia Butler was an African American author; she became the first science fiction writer to receive the MacArthur Foundation "Genius" Grant.

Octavia Butler was an African American author. She became the first science fiction writer to receive the MacArthur Foundation "Genius" Grant.

Octavia Butler was an African American author, and she became the first science fiction writer to receive the MacArthur Foundation "Genius" Grant.

5. INDEPENDENT CLAUSES JOINED WITH NO PUNCTUATION OR LINKING WORDS BETWEEN THEM

Fused sentences, which are also called run-on sentences, can be fixed the same way you fix comma splices. Add a period, a semicolon, or a comma and a coordinating conjunction.

INCORRECT:

Joe Lewis knew he had to beat Max Schmeling he dropped him in the first round.

CORRECT:

Joe Lewis knew he had to beat Max Schmeling. He dropped him in the first round.

Joe Lewis knew he had to beat Max Schmeling; he dropped him in the first round.

Joe Lewis knew he had to beat Max Schmeling, and he dropped him in the first round.

6. SUBJECTS AND VERBS SEPARATED WITH COMMAS OR OTHER PUNCTUATION MARKS

Do not use a comma—or any other punctuation mark—between a subject and its verb unless additional information requiring commas, such as a nonrestrictive element, is also inserted between the subject and the verb.

INCORRECT:

Big, expensive movies with lots of special effects, are not always successful at the box office.

"Big, expensive movies with lots of special effects" is the subject of the sentence, and "are" is the verb.

CORRECT:

Big, expensive movies with lots of special effects are not always successful at the box office.

7. COMMAS OMITTED WITH NONRESTRICTIVE ELEMENTS

When the nonrestrictive element is completely inside a clause, it needs commas on both sides. If it ends a sentence, the terminal punctuation mark takes the place of the second comma.

INCORRECT:

Kareema the person with the most speed and stamina won the marathon.

Kareema, the person with the most speed and stamina won the marathon.

Kareema the person with the most speed and stamina, won the marathon.

CORRECT:

Kareema, the person with the most speed and stamina, won the marathon.

INCORRECT:

Kareema won the marathon which delighted her friends and family.

CORRECT:

Kareema won the marathon, which delighted her friends and family.

8. COMMAS USED TO SET OFF RESTRICTIVE ELEMENTS

Using commas with restrictive elements can change the meaning of your sentence to something that you don't intend. The comma tells your readers that the information within them isn't necessary, so try reading the sentence to yourself without the element to see if the meaning agrees with your intentions.

INCORRECT:

All the people in my class, who wanted smoking banned on campus, signed the petition.

If we take out the element set off with commas, we have "All the people in my class signed the petition," which may not be true.

CORRECT:

All the people in my class who wanted smoking banned on campus signed the petition.

INCORRECT:

Jane Austen's novel, *Pride and Prejudice,* is one of my favorites.

Jane Austen wrote more than one novel.

CORRECT:

Jane Austen's novel *Pride and Prejudice* is one of my favorites.

9. COMMAS OMITTED IN A SERIES

MLA format requires that three or more items in a series be separated with commas, including a comma in front of the coordinating conjunction that sets off the last element in the series. (An exception is when the items themselves have commas, in which case you use the semicolon. See page 215 for examples.)

INCORRECT:

Next semester I am taking French, History 1A and English 2.

CORRECT:

Next semester I am taking French, History 1A, and English 2.

Also, two or more words that are the same parts of speech in a series, such as adjectives or adverbs, should be separated from each other (but not the terms they modify).

INCORRECT:

The turbulent threatening sea intimidated the novice sailors.

CORRECT:

The turbulent, threatening sea intimidated the novice sailors.

10. SENTENCE FRAGMENTS

Don't use a terminal punctuation mark (such as a period, an exclamation point, or a question mark) unless you have at least one independent clause. An independent clause needs both a subject and a verb and doesn't begin with a subordinating conjunction. Phrases and dependent clauses cannot stand alone.

INCORRECT:

People have become more distrustful of corporations over the years. Especially since the Enron scandal.

CORRECT:

People have become more distrustful of corporations over the years, especially since the Enron scandal.

11. COLONS USED TO SET OFF ELEMENTS NOT INTRODUCED BY INDEPENDENT CLAUSES

INCORRECT:

I checked out books on: corporations, news media, and the Internet.

CORRECT:

I checked out books on the following topics: corporations, news media, and the Internet.

I checked out books on corporations, news media, and the Internet.

12. MISUSED SEMICOLONS

Don't use semicolons unless you are separating two independent clauses that don't have a coordinating conjunction between them or unless you are separating items in a series that have commas themselves. Do not confuse the colon with the semicolon; they have different uses.

INCORRECT:

I just read Toni Morrison's *Beloved;* and I think it is one of the best novels I have ever read.

CORRECT:

I just read Toni Morrison's *Beloved;* I think it is one of the best novels I have ever read.

I just read Toni Morrison's *Beloved,* and I think it is one of the best novels I have ever read.

INCORRECT:

Russell recommended the following books; *Fight Club, Geek Love,* and *Wicked.*

CORRECT:

Russell recommended the following books: *Fight Club, Geek Love,* and *Wicked.*

13. MISSING OR INAPPROPRIATE APOSTROPHES

Use apostrophes to make nouns possessive, but not pronouns—they have possessive forms, like *its, whose, theirs,* and *yours.* (*It's* is the contraction for *it is.*) A noun needs an apostrophe or an apostrophe followed by an *s* to be possessive. Don't use apostrophes if the noun is plural, not possessive. To test whether a noun is possessive and needs an apostrophe, see if you can rephrase a sentence and use *of* with the noun.

INCORRECT:

All three dancer's performances were beautifully choreographed; each dancers' routine was technically demanding, as well.

CORRECT:

All three dancers' performances were beautifully choreographed; each dancer's routine was technically demanding, as well.

INCORRECT:

The newspaper increased it's circulation.

CORRECT:

The newspaper increased its circulation.

INCORRECT:

The newspapers circulation increased.

CORRECT:

The newspaper's circulation increased.

(The circulation of the newspaper increased.)

INCORRECT:

I want to watch a few movie's this weekend.

CORRECT:

I want to watch a few movies this weekend.

INCORRECT:

She was a friend of Emily's.

(She was a friend of Emily's *what?*)

CORRECT:

She was a friend of Emily.

She was Emily's friend.

Apostrophes are also used to form contractions. (See page 216 for more information and examples.)

14. QUESTION MARKS USED WITH INDIRECT QUESTIONS

Indirect questions report that a question was asked. They aren't really questions.

INCORRECT:

He asked if the play was any good?

CORRECT:

He asked if the play was any good.

He asked, "Is the play any good?"

15. MISSING OR INCORRECT PLACEMENT OF PUNCTUATION MARKS BEFORE AND AFTER DIRECT QUOTATIONS

Use commas before direct quotations when they are introduced with introductory words such as *says, suggests, writes,* and *asserts.* When words like *that* precede a quotation, the quotation should be treated as part of the flow of the sentence.

INCORRECT:

Vendler writes "The odes of John Keats belong to that group of works in which the English language finds an ultimate embodiment" (3).

CORRECT:

Vendler writes, "The odes of John Keats belong to that group of works in which the English language finds an ultimate embodiment" (3).

INCORRECT:

Vendler writes that, "The odes of John Keats belong to that group of works in which the English language finds an ultimate embodiment" (3).

CORRECT:

Vendler writes that "The odes of John Keats belong to that group of works in which the English language finds an ultimate embodiment" (3).

16. MISSING OR INCORRECT VERB ENDINGS

It is typical for many of us not to fully pronounce verb endings, like *ed* and *s,* when we speak, so it can be easy to forget to include them in our writing. Try saying some of these phrases aloud to see what we mean: "She was supposed to," "I advised him to wait," and "he stereotyped them." Regular verbs need *-ed* or *-d* at the end for the past tense or past participles forms. (See pages 225–228 for more information and examples.)

17. INCORRECT TENSE OR VERB FORM

Verbs should be in the correct tense; they should clearly indicate when an action is, was, or will be completed. Verbs should also be in the correct form, which means not confusing the forms of irregular verbs like the forms of *be* and *go.*

INCORRECT:

I sung in the school choir for two years.

CORRECT:

I sang in the school choir for two years.

INCORRECT:

I been late twice this week.

CORRECT:

I have been late twice this week.

INCORRECT:

I seen you yesterday.

CORRECT:

I saw you yesterday.

INCORRECT:

We was there.

CORRECT:

We were there.

18. LACK OF AGREEMENT BETWEEN SUBJECTS AND VERBS

A singular subject takes a singular verb, and a plural subject takes a plural verb. Pronouns with *one* and *body* in them are singular, as are the words *each, either,* and *neither.*

INCORRECT:

Neither of us are in a hurry to get home.

CORRECT:

Neither of us is in a hurry to get home.

INCORRECT:

Every one of those kittens look like they want to go to war.

CORRECT:

Every one of those kittens looks like it wants to go to war.

19. CONFUSING SHIFTS IN VERB TENSE

Verb tenses indicate when actions take place. Avoid confusing shifts in tense, such as presenting an event as happening in the present at one point in your sentence as happening in the past or future at another point.

INCORRECT:

I was turning the corner on my bike when suddenly this car comes at me on the wrong side of the street.

CORRECT:

I was turning the corner on my bike when suddenly this car came at me on the wrong side of the street.

20. LACK OF AGREEMENT BETWEEN PRONOUNS AND ANTECEDENTS

Pronouns stand in for nouns. The nouns they stand in for are called their *antecedents*. Pronouns and their nouns should agree in number and gender.

Number:

INCORRECT:

Each of our entries did well in their category.

CORRECT:

Each of our entries did well in its category.

With antecedents joined by *or* or *nor,* the pronoun should agree with the noun that is nearer the pronoun.

INCORRECT:

Neither Ethan nor Matthew believed that they had gotten the raise that they deserved.

CORRECT:

Neither Ethan nor Matthew believed that he had gotten the raise that he deserved.

INCORRECT:

Either Colette or the twins will get her choice of the movies tonight.

CORRECT:

Either Colette or the twins will get their choice of the movies tonight.

Gender:

INCORRECT:

A person should make sure that he carries a flashlight and spare batteries when exploring a cavern.

CORRECT:

A person should make sure that he or she carries a flashlight and spare batteries when exploring a cavern.

People should make sure that they carry a flashlight and spare batteries when exploring a cavern.

Person:

INCORRECT:

When I went into the cavern, it was so dark that you couldn't see your hand in front of your face.

CORRECT:

When I went into the cavern, it was so dark that I couldn't see my hand in front of my face.

Missing antecedent:

INCORRECT:

The party was great, but they should have had more food.

CORRECT:

The party was great, but the hosts should have had more food.

21. CONFUSING PRONOUN SHIFTS

Pronouns standing for the same elements in a sentence should agree in number (plural or singular), gender (male or female), and person (first, second, or third.) Confusing shifts in pronoun use between person usually involve imprecise use of second person (*you, your*).

INCORRECT:

When I went into the cavern, it was so dark that you couldn't see your hand in front of your face.

CORRECT:

When I went into the cavern, it was so dark that I couldn't see my hand in front of my face.

In formal academic writing, your teacher may prefer that you not use second person.

22. MISSING OR INCORRECT PREPOSITIONS

Mastering preposition use can be difficult, especially for people whose original language isn't English. Even native speakers can have trouble because some prepositions are similar sounding ("in," "on"). Here are some common prepositions and their meanings, with examples:

At: "The location of something; indicating a point in space."

You need to stop at the supermarket.

In: "Contained or surrounded by something."

San Francisco is in California.

You are in big trouble.

On: "Physically supported by the surface of."

There is dust on my keyboard.

You need to get on top of this project.

"Having something as a medium for storing or transmitting ideas or data."

You should back up all your work on a flash drive.

"In the course of a journey."

She's on her way home now.

"Having something as a topic."

I just saw a great documentary on corporations.

To: "In the direction of."

The last time I saw him, he was headed to work.

"Approaching and reaching."

Are you going to school today?

With: "Accompanied by."

We vacationed with our families.

"Possessing as a feature."

I want a laptop with a lot of memory.

"Indicating the item used to perform an action."

I got the splinter out with my tweezers.

"In a relationship."

I think she's with Jan these days.

"In agreement on."

Are you with me?

"In opposition to."

Please don't fight with each other.

23. MISPLACED, DANGLING, AND SQUINTING MODIFIERS

Misplaced modifiers are words or phrases that are in the wrong place in your sentence. When they are at the beginning of sentences and not followed by the part that they are intended to modify, they seem to modify the part of the sentence that they precede.

INCORRECT:

Seizing its favorite food, the cheese was eaten by the mouse.

CORRECT:

Seizing its favorite food, the mouse ate the cheese.

Dangling modifiers lack words or phrases to logically modify.

INCORRECT:

Staring out the window at the rain, the afternoon passed dismally.

CORRECT:

Staring out the window at the rain, she passed the afternoon dismally.

A squinting modifier is placed between two elements that it could modify, causing confusion as to which one it really belongs to.

INCORRECT:

Students who skip assignments often fail their courses.

CORRECT:

Students who often skip assignments fail their courses.

or, depending on meaning

Students who skip assignments fail their courses often.

24. FAULTY PARALLELISM

Sentence elements, such as paired independent clauses or items in a series, should match grammatically, meaning that expressions of similar content and function should use the same pattern of words.

INCORRECT:

Barack Obama was the first African American to run for president, and the election was won by him.

CORRECT:

Barack Obama was the first African American to run for president, and he won the election.

INCORRECT:

Gabriela's goals include earning her college degree, a good job, and she wants to raise her children to be good citizens.

CORRECT:

Gabriela's goals include earning her college degree, getting a good job, and raising her children to be good citizens.

25. INCORRECT USE OF WORDS AND PHRASES

Writers often mix up words that sound similar (such as *your* and *you're*) or misuse or misspell phrases they have heard spoken but never seen in print (like writing "for all intensive purposes" instead of "for all intents and purposes." Also, sometimes student writers try to sound more sophisticated by using dictionaries or thesauri to look up fancier-sounding words. This can backfire. The appendix "Commonly Confused Words and Phrases" at the end of this book is a helpful reference.

Grammar and Punctuation Rules and Guidelines Explained

Many English textbooks make punctuation rules seem overly complicated by requiring students to master too much unnecessary jargon and long lists of rules. (In practice, you can collapse a lot of these rules into simpler rules by skipping distinctions between types of phrase and other sentence elements that are relevant only to grammarians.) We've tried to simplify the rules for you to make them easier to understand and remember.

Here are some questions that will help you to diagnose how much you know (and how much you need to know) about punctuation and grammar:

1. Can you distinguish between strings of words that can stand alone as sentences and strings of words that can't stand alone as sentences?

2. Can you distinguish between strings of words that can be taken out of a sentence without changing the meaning of that sentence and strings of words that alter the meaning of the sentence if they are removed?

3. Can you distinguish between terms that are singular (referring to only one) and terms that are plural (meaning more than one)?

4. Can you tell when a noun is in possession of something?

5. Can you recognize when a pronoun is possessive (like *hers, his,* and *its*)?

RECOGNIZING INDEPENDENT CLAUSES

An **independent clause** (also called a main clause) has a **subject** and a **predicate** and can stand alone as a sentence because it expresses a complete thought.

Subjects: The subject tells us whom or what the sentence or clause is about. The subject is the person, animal, place, abstraction, or object that acts, is acted on, or is described in the sentence. The **simple subject** is the main word or word group that tells us this. The **complete subject** includes words that modify the subject. There are also **compound subjects,** which are made of two or more subjects joined by a conjunction.

To determine the subject of a sentence, first isolate the verb and then make a question by placing "who?" or "what?" before it: the answer is the subject.

For example, take the sentence "Susan and Tim became the committee co-chairs." The verb is *became,* and when we turn the sentence into a question, we get "Who became the committee co-chairs?" The answer, *Susan and Tim,* is the subject.

Simple Subject	Compound Subject	Complete Subject
Susan	Susan and Tim	Susan and Tim, the committee co-chairs
Birds	birds and bats	many varieties of birds and bats
civil rights	civil rights and justice	The protection of civil rights and justice

Predicates: The predicate must contain a verb or verb phrase. A **simple predicate** is the verb or verb phrase (the verb plus helping verbs, also called auxiliary verbs). A **complete predicate** includes the verb and all the words that describe the verb and complete its meaning. There are also **compound predicates,** which are two or more predicates that say something about the same subject. In the sentence "Susan and Tim talk about projects and schedule meetings," the verb *talk* marks the beginning of the complete predicate: *talk about projects and schedule meetings.*

Simple Predicate	Compound Predicate	Complete Predicate
talk	talk about projects	Talk about projects and schedule meetings
fly	fly hundreds of miles	fly hundreds of miles, hunt for food, and look for shelter
obtain	obtain civil rights and justice	obtain civil rights and justice for all people in the United States

Verbs are often described as "action words," but they can also convey the idea of existence, such as *is* and *be,* or they might simply help the main verb in the sentence. There are three types of verbs: action verbs, linking verbs, and helping (also called auxiliary) verbs.

Action verbs describe what a subject does, such as *love, read, swim, type,* and *shout.* For example, "Nathaniel and Isabel love movies."

Linking verbs give the idea of a state of being, such as *is* and *be.* For example, "Albert is an artist."

Modal helping verbs, like *may* and *will,* have no real meaning on their own—they "help" the main verb, as in "Albert will paint a picture." They are necessary for the grammatical structure of a sentence. Primary helping verbs can function as either main or helping verbs.

Modal Helping Verbs (They Can Never Function as Main Verbs)			
may	can	will	shall
might	could	would	should
must			

Primary Helping Verbs (They Can Also Function as Main Verbs)		
be	**do**	**have**
being	does	has
been	did	had
am		
are		
is		
was		
were		

Unless you plan to teach English or another language some day, you don't really have to worry about the different names for different kinds of verbs—as long as you recognize them as verbs.

If you can recognize all of these concepts and tell subjects and predicates apart no matter how many words each has, it doesn't really matter whether you remember the terminology—you'll still be able to understand the rules of when you should or should not use commas and other punctuation marks.

PUNCTUATING INDEPENDENT CLAUSES

Remember that you can recognize an independent clause by these traits: it has a subject, it has a predicate, and it expresses a complete thought. It can stand alone as a sentence. There are three primary ways to punctuate consecutive independent clauses: with a period, with a comma in front of a coordinating conjunction, or with a semicolon. When you use a semicolon, it is usually inappropriate to follow it with a coordinating conjunction; however, you may want to use a conjunctive adverb (*however, therefore, thus*, etc.) as a transitional device. (For a complete list of coordinating conjunctions, conjunctive adverbs, and other transitional words, see page 209.)

1. Separate consecutive independent clauses with a period.

   Artificial intelligence is the branch of computer science concerned with creating computers that can "think" like humans. The term was first used by John McCarthy in 1956.

2. Separate consecutive independent clauses with a comma in front of a coordinating conjunction.

Artificial intelligence is the branch of computer science concerned with creating computers that can "think" like humans, but no computers have been created that display full artificial intelligence.

3. Separate consecutive independent clauses with a semicolon.

Many science fiction authors have written stories and novels about artificial intelligence; two pioneers in this genre are Arthur C. Clark and Isaac Asimov.

Note: We generally reserve the semicolon for situations where we have two closely related independent clauses of roughly equal "weight" (importance and length).

If you use a conjunctive adverb as a transitional device, separate it from the clause it is in with commas. If it is at the very beginning or end of an independent clause, a semicolon or period can take the place of a comma.

Artificial intelligence is the branch of computer science concerned with creating computers that can "think" like humans; however, no computers have been created that display full artificial intelligence.

Artificial intelligence is the branch of computer science concerned with creating computers that can "think" like humans; no computers, however, have been created that display full artificial intelligence.

COMMON CONJUNCTIONS

Coordinating Conjunctions (used in compound sentences to link independent clauses):

  for, and, nor, but, or, yet, so

Common Conjunctive Adverbs (used in compound sentences to indicate transitions and relationships):

  accordingly, also, anyhow, besides, certainly, consequently, conversely, finally, furthermore, hence, henceforth, however, indeed, instead, likewise, meanwhile, moreover, nevertheless, next, nonetheless, otherwise, similarly, still, subsequently, then, therefore, thus

Correlative Conjunctions (used in compound sentences to indicate relationships):

  both . . . and, either . . . or, neither . . . nor, not only . . . but (also), whether . . . or

Common Subordinating Conjunctions (these precede dependent clauses and are used in complex sentences to connect dependent clauses with independent clauses):

  after, although, as, as if, as long as, as though, because, before, even if, even though, how, if, in order that, once, provided that, rather than, since, so, so that, than, that, though, unless, until, when, whenever, where, wherever, whether, while

RECOGNIZING AND PUNCTUATING DEPENDENT CLAUSES AND PHRASES

Like an independent clause, a dependent clause (also called a subordinate clause because it is subordinate to the independent, or main, clause) has a subject and a predicate, but it cannot stand alone as a sentence because it does not express a complete thought. It loses its independence because it begins with a subordinating word (like **subordinating conjunctions** or relative pronouns). Dependent clauses must join with independent clauses in order to form complete sentences. How we punctuate them depends on whether they precede or follow an independent clause. (For another look at ways to separate clauses, see "Sentence Combining" on page 211.)

Phrases cannot stand alone as sentences because they lack a subject, a verb, or both. Generally, we punctuate them the same way we punctuate dependent clauses; however, if an introductory phrase is very short (two or three words), and there is no possibility of confusion if we omit the comma, the comma is optional.

1. When a dependent clause precedes an independent clause, separate the two with a comma.

   When we get ready to write a research paper, we take our computers for granted.

2. When a phrase precedes an independent clause, separate them with a comma.

   Preparing to write a paper, we take our computers for granted.

   Because they make revising papers so much easier, I love computers.

   When the phrase is very short, and there is no possibility of confusion, the comma is optional but never incorrect.

   Every fall students return to classes.

   Every fall, students return to classes.

3. When an introductory word precedes an independent clause, separate the two with a comma. Such words are usually conjunctive adverbs used as transitions, and they can also be considered nonrestrictive elements—that is, you can remove them without changing the sentence's meaning, so you set them off with commas anywhere inside the sentence. At the beginning of the sentence, the period or other mark that ends the previous sentence takes the place of one of the commas.

   However, some students decide not to stay.

4. Generally, no comma or other punctuation is needed when an independent clause precedes a dependent clause or phrase.

   We take our computers for granted when we get ready to write a research paper.

   I love computers because they make revising papers so much easier.

   Sometimes, however, a dependent clause that follows an independent clause is also nonrestrictive, in which case a comma is appropriate. Think about the intent of the clauses. The following sentences demonstrate how to approach this:

The library has extended its hours. I'm glad, because I've been working extra hours and haven't had as much time in the library as I need.

The first sentence makes the meaning of the second clear. This person isn't glad *because* she has been working a lot and hasn't had needed library time; she's glad because now that the hours have been extended, she will have the time she needs. The dependent clause is serving as a nonrestrictive element. Without the comma indicating this, the meaning of the sentence would be that not having enough time makes her glad.

SENTENCE COMBINING

Sentence combining is a way to construct sentences of varied length and with different types of internal relationships between sentence components. Think of it as the prose equivalent of working with Legos, and you'll do just fine. If you're still making basic sentence-level errors, understanding sentence combining will help you to recognize and correct them. If you're more advanced, the different levels of subordination and coordination you learn through sentence combining will help you make increasingly effective choices.

Simple Sentences

The first type of sentence is the **simple sentence.** The simple sentence is our most basic sentence form. It is a single independent clause followed by a terminal punctuation mark (also called an end punctuation mark): a period, a question mark, or an exclamation point. Often simple sentences are fairly short, like the first example that follows; they can get more sophisticated, however, as the other examples show. The shortness of a simple sentence can give it a strong impact, but too many in a row can sound unsophisticated, even childish. Here are some examples:

- The monkey typed.
- The tireless monkey typed randomly throughout infinity.
- The monkey reproduced the complete collected works of William Shakespeare.

Compound Sentences

The **compound sentence** consists of two or more independent clauses with no dependent clauses. Remember that you must correctly separate independent clauses from each other. For many college writers, this is the most error-prone sentence type because of the comma rules involved. See the punctuation rules on pages 208–209 for the three primary methods of separating independent clauses: (1) a comma in front of a coordinating conjunction, (2) a semicolon (with or without a conjunctive adverb), or (3) a period. What you choose will depend on what you are saying and the impact that you want to give. Semicolons tend to feel more formal than using a comma and a coordinating conjunction. Also, semicolons express a close logical relationship. Choose a semicolon only when the two independent clauses are closely connected in meaning and when the ideas contained within them are of equivalent weight. Here are some examples:

- The professor explained the "infinite monkey theorem," and a student asked if the number of monkeys was infinite.
- The professor explained the "infinite monkey theorem"; however, she pointed out that the monkey is simply a metaphor.
- The professor explained the "infinite monkey theorem"; it states that a monkey randomly hitting typewriter keys throughout infinity would almost surely type a particular text.

Complex Sentences

A **complex sentence** consists of one independent clause combined with one or more dependent clauses. The process of adding a dependent clause to an independent clause is called *subordination*. You are making one thought subordinate to (or dependent on) another thought. The clauses are connected through the subordinating word that begins a dependent clause. A dependent clause may be the first or second clause in the sentence. Review the punctuation guidelines because the order will determine whether you use a comma. Here are some examples:

- The monkey reproduced *Othello* after he typed for a few million years.
- After he typed for a few million years, the monkey reproduced *Othello*.

Compound-Complex Sentences

A **compound-complex sentence** consists of at least one dependent clause and two or more independent clauses. In other words, to make a compound-complex sentence, you join a compound sentence with a complex sentence using any of the preceding methods. Here are some examples:

- The monkey kept typing; he still had poems and more plays to finish after he completed *Othello*.
- After he had typed for a few million years, the monkey took a short break, so he felt refreshed.
- The monkey rested after he typed *Othello,* and then he went back to work.

PUNCTUATING RESTRICTIVE AND NONRESTRICTIVE ELEMENTS

Restrictive material is grammatically essential to the sentence it is within. That may sound like jargon, so we'll put it another way: if you remove the material, you will change the meaning of the sentence. You will not alter the meaning of the sentence by removing nonrestrictive material even though this material may contain important ideas that a writer wants to convey in an essay or research paper.

Here is an example of restrictive information in a sentence:

All students <u>who plagiarize</u> will automatically receive failing grades.

If we take the restrictive element out, we have the following:

All students will automatically receive failing grades.

The meaning has clearly changed—the altered sentence does not convey the actual intent of the original sentence.

1. Do not set restrictive elements off with any punctuation marks. If you look at the examples, you'll see that the restrictive elements are actually part of the complete subjects.

    Students <u>who get As on all their earlier exams</u> don't have to take the final.
    Wild mushrooms <u>that aren't poisonous</u> are great additions to many recipes.

2. Set nonrestrictive elements off with commas.

    Portobello mushrooms, <u>which are actually just large crimini mushrooms,</u> are great for stuffing or grilling.
    Many classic science fiction authors, <u>including Arthur C. Clark, Isaac Asimov, and Philip K. Dick,</u> wrote stories and novels about artificial intelligence.
    Many classic science fiction authors wrote stories and novels about artificial intelligence, <u>including Arthur C. Clark, Isaac Asimov, and Philip K. Dick.</u>

Now that we've approached some basic punctuation guidelines within the context of how sentences are put together, we can move on to summarize some of the rules we've mentioned and to introduce some new ones.

USING COMMAS

The comma is probably the most misused punctuation mark. There is no rule that says that you must use a comma every time you pause. We pause for lots of reasons, and a lot of them have nothing to do with grammar. Also, there is no "word-to-comma" ratio. Sometimes people write a longish sentence and figure there needs to be a comma in there someplace, so they guess and stick one in. Other times, people don't add commas they need because they think they already have too many commas and more commas will "look funny." There is no comma rule based on visual esthetics, either. Use a comma if there is a rule saying you need one at a particular point, and don't use a comma if there is no rule requiring one. It's that simple. Don't guess. The following rules and the previous discussion of phrases, different types of clauses, and restrictive and nonrestrictive elements should help you master the confusing task of comma use.

1. Use a comma before a coordinating conjunction (*for, and, nor, but, or, yet, so*—think "fanboys") between two independent clauses.

   I want to use commas correctly, so I am going to study the rules.

2. Use a comma after a dependent clause or an introductory phrase or word that precedes an independent clause.

   When I know the rules, I feel more comfortable.

   Looking at the rules, I realize that they aren't that hard to understand.

   Fortunately, I have a good memory.

3. Use commas to separate three or more items in a series (as long as the items themselves don't have commas), including a comma before an *and* joining the last item to the list. You may have been told by some instructors to leave the comma before *and* out; however, MLA, the most commonly used style in English classes, requires this comma. Other styles, particularly journalistic style, do not include it.

   I'm taking history, English, chemistry, and geography this semester.

Two or more words that are the same parts of speech in a series, such as adjectives or adverbs, should be separated from each other (but not the terms they modify).

   The sky was a deep, clear, beautiful blue.

4. Use a comma after introductory words—such as *said, says, asserts, suggests, writes,* and *claims*—when they come before direct quotations.

   Helen Vendler states, "The history of Keats criticism is a complicated one."

5. Use a comma after and before quoted material that you interrupt with a phrase of your own within a sentence.

   "The history of Keats criticism," states Vendler, "is a complicated one."

6. Use a comma before a contrasting element.

   I wanted the vegetarian pizza, not the pepperoni one.

   He started to jump into the unheated swimming pool, but balked.

7. Use a comma to set off *or* and a word or phrase when they are being offered as a synonym or definition of a word preceding these.

   He wanted chick peas, or garbanzos, as we call them.

8. Use commas to set cities off from states and regions, states and regions off from countries, days off from months when the months precede them, years off from months and days, degree abbreviations for degrees, and *junior* and *senior* when they follow names.

   Maria Suarez, Ph.D., was born on January 10, 1983, in Los Angeles, California.

   Lincoln Williams, Jr., will graduate in June, 2009, and celebrate by spending three weeks in Paris, France.

USING SEMICOLONS

1. Use a semicolon to set off two closely related independent clauses when they don't have a coordinating conjunction between them.

    She loved studying history; she hoped to teach it one day.

    He enjoyed studying French; however, he had little chance to practice it.

If a period wouldn't work to replace it, don't use a semicolon at all, except for the following exception:

2. Use semicolons to set off items in a series of three or more when one or more of those items has a comma.

    Her tour included visits to Florence, Italy; Paris, France; and London, England.

    They read poetry by William Blake, who was an artist as well as a poet; William Wordsworth; and Samuel Taylor Coleridge.

Note: Sometimes students get confused and reverse the semicolon and commas. Here's a hint to help you remember which goes where: Remember that in situations like those above, the commas are serving as connectors—they connect an explanation, description, or some other piece of information about an item to that item—and the semicolons are functioning as separators between different items. Which looks bigger and stronger, the comma [,] or the semicolon [;]? Make sure you understand where each item begins and leaves off, and put the semicolons where you are separating the items.

    Her tour included visits to [1] Florence, Italy; [2] Paris, France; and [3] London, England.

If you are wondering why we have a semicolon in front of the *and,* remember that in MLA format, we put a comma in front of *and* when it sets off the last item in a series of three or more. However, when our items themselves have commas, we need to turn all the "separating" commas that we would ordinarily have in a series into semicolons, including the one preceding *and*.

USING COLONS

1. Colons are used to introduce sentence elements, but only after independent clauses. Use them when your independent clause is designed to create a feeling of anticipation for the information that is to follow. They can introduce a series, direct quotations, or even other independent clauses if the second clause interprets, explains, or amplifies the first.

    She refused only one pizza topping: anchovies.

    The pianist played works by three composers: Chopin, Liszt, and Beethoven.

    Classic science fiction writers who tackled the theme of artificial intelligence include the following: Arthur C. Clark, Isaac Asimov, and Philip K. Dick.

He offered this advice: "Neither a borrower, nor a lender be."

Their enmity could be explained by one simple fact: they were competing for the same job.

Do not use a colon if the element being introduced does not follow an independent clause.

Classic science fiction writers who tackled the theme of artificial intelligence include Arthur C. Clark, Isaac Asimov, and Philip K. Dick.

2. Colons are used between titles and subtitles.

Our class read Maria Tatar's *The Classic Fairy Tales: Texts, Criticism*.

USING APOSTROPHES

The apostrophe has three uses: forming contractions and making nouns possessive.

1. Use the apostrophe to form contractions by inserting it in place of missing letters or numbers.

It's is the contraction of *it is* (it is not the possessive form of *it*).
Don't is the contraction of *do not*.

2. Use the apostrophe to make nouns—not pronouns—possessive. Where or whether an "s" is added depends on whether a word is singular or plural and on its spelling.
When words do not end with an *s*, make them possessive by adding an apostrophe and then an *s*.

the child's bicycle
the children's toys

When words do end with an *s*, make them possessive by adding only an apostrophe when no extra *s* sound is pronounced.

two cats' kittens
both houses' roofs

When words end with an *s* or an *s* sound, and an extra *s* sound is added when the word is made possessive, add an apostrophe and an *s* after it.

her house's roof

USING QUOTATION MARKS

Quotation marks are used when you use someone else's exact phrasing (unless the quotation is over four lines in your paper, in which case you indent two tabs from the left margin instead) and to indicate the titles of works such as stories, essays, articles, songs, and poems.

Miranda said, "I love the novels and short stories of Angela Carter."

"The Courtship of Mr. Lyon" and "The Tiger's Bride" are both based on the fairy tale "Beauty and the Beast."

For quotations or titles of such works inside a quotation, use single quotation marks (also called "inverted commas") inside the quotation.

> Miranda said, "My favorite story is 'The Tiger's Bride' by Angela Carter."

Although you have probably seen examples of periods and commas outside of closing quotation marks, this is not correct in MLA, APA, or other standard American formats. The only time you will have a sentence's period outside a closing quotation mark is when the sentence is followed by an in-text citation, in which case the period follows the citation (see Chapters 12, 13, and 14 on MLA and APA documentation styles), unless you have a lengthy, indented quotation. If you have a situation where you need a colon or a semicolon after material in quotation marks, the colon or semicolon will follow the closing quotation mark.

> Her essay analyzed a standard fairy tale motif in "The Tiger's Bride": transformation.
>
> She briefly mentioned "The Courtship of Mr. Lyon"; it is another Angela Carter story based on "Beauty and the Beast."

If you directly quote a question or if a question mark is part of a title, the question mark goes inside the closing quotation mark. Also, only one end punctuation mark is used with quotation marks, so you don't follow a quotation with a period if you have a quotation mark inside.

> "He asked, "What was the name of that story we read by Joyce Carol Oates?"
>
> The name of the story is "Where Are You Going, Where Have You Been?"

If you ask a question about material enclosed within quotation marks, the question mark goes outside the closing quotation mark.

> Did you read Raymond Carver's stories "The Bath" and "A Small, Good Thing"?

USING DASHES

Dashes can be used as substitutes for other punctuation marks, such as commas and semicolons. They are used to indicate a shift in tone; they can emphasize a point or set off an explanatory comment.

> She was known for her quick wit—but she could be rather mean sometimes.

They can also be used to avoid confusion when you want to set off a nonrestrictive phrase with numerous commas.

> He was good at numerous sports—swimming, tennis, rugby, and soccer, to name a few—and won many trophies.

Dashes are relatively informal, so don't overuse them. When you use a word processor, type a dash as two hyphens with no spaces on either side, and the program will turn the hyphens into a real dash for you.

USING END PUNCTUATION

Periods, question marks, and exclamation points are called terminal punctuation marks because they can all terminate sentences.

Using Periods

1. Use periods to end sentences that are not direct questions, rhetorical questions, or actual exclamations. If a sentence makes a reference to a question without asking a question, use a period.

   Note: The MLA recommends using only one space after periods and other punctuation marks that conclude sentences.
   They were very upset by the fire.
   We asked when the research paper was due.

2. Use a period for certain abbreviations.

B.A.	Ms.	etc.	A.M. (or a.m.)
M.A.	Mrs.	i.e.	P.M. (p.m.)
M.S.	Mr.	e.g.	
Ph.D.	Dr.		

   Note: Some abbreviations can be written with or without periods.
   C.E. or CE for Common Era, which is increasingly being used around the world in place of A.D. or AD (for *Anno Domini,* in the year of our Lord).
   B.C.E. or BCE for Before Common Era, which is increasingly being used in place of B.C. or BC (before Christ).

   Acronyms (words formed from the initial letters of a series of words) or very well-known abbreviations do not require periods.

FBI	UNESCO	NOW
CIA	NATO	MADD
IRS	NAACP	PETA

Using Question Marks

1. Use question marks at the end of sentences that ask questions, including rhetorical questions and requests made in the form of questions.

   What topic did you choose for your paper?
   Are you crazy?
   Would you please pass me the cayenne pepper?

   Remember that placement of question marks in relation to quotation marks is important. If you are quoting a question, put the closing quotation mark after the question mark.

   The professor asked, "Who wants to earn extra credit?"

If you are asking a question about quoted material, place the question mark after the closing quotation mark.

> Did you really mean it when you said, "I quit"?

Using Exclamation Points

Exclamation points are used to express strong emotion. In general, you should avoid them—they do not make the points you assert in an essay sound stronger; they are the written equivalent of raising your voice or shouting. They can give your work an amateurish and immature feel. Look at the difference in the following two statements. Which one looks more serious and mature?

> The scientists presented very compelling data.

> The scientists presented very compelling data!

If your ideas do not have force, following them with an exclamation point won't make them seem stronger. However, exclamation points may be appropriate in creative writing or when transcribing excited utterances.

> "Fire!" she screamed.

USING HYPHENS

Hyphens have several uses, but you need to be careful not to use them when they are not called for. They are used to join two or more words when they are functioning as an adjective directly in front of the noun that they are modifying.

> Nineteenth-century writers studied in the course include William Wordsworth and Mary Shelley.

> John disparaged what he called typical middle-class values.

> They have three-year-old twins.

Don't hyphenate adjectives or adverbs when they do not precede the words they are modifying.

> Their twins are three years old.

Hyphens are also used to join the parts of some compound words. There are relatively few compound nouns that need hyphens; these include words that begin with *self,* like *self-esteem.* If you are not sure if a term is a compound word, look it up in a dictionary.

> Enrique loved his mother-in-law.

> They were loyal comrades-in-arms.

Most compound nouns should not be hyphenated.

> The attorney general was besieged with questions.

> Azar was a notary public.

> What high school did you attend?

Hyphens are used to join the parts of compound numbers from twenty-one through ninety-nine. (In MLA format, use numerals for 100 and greater.)

> Javier won nineteen chess games in a row last month, but his record was twenty-nine games in a row.

Hyphens are used with all fractions that are spelled out.

> One-half of the prize money is mine.

Most of the time, prefixes and suffixes are connected to root words without a hyphen. However, hyphens are used with prefixes when they come before proper nouns.

> She accused her critics of being un-American.

Hyphens are used with prefixes ending in *a* or *i* when the root word begins with an *a* or *i*.

> Samuel was a semi-invalid for a while after the accident.

Hyphens are used with the prefix *ex*.

> Savannah stayed friends with her ex-boyfriend.

Use the hyphen with the prefix *re* only when it means *again* and if omitting the hyphen would cause confusion.

> It was less expensive to re-cover the old sofa than to buy a new one.

> I had scarcely recovered from the first surprise when I got a new one.

Words with double *e*'s and double *o*'s are usually made into one word with no hyphen, but you should use a dictionary if you are not sure.

> They tried hard to cooperate.

> The funds for the party were co-opted for other purposes.

USING ELLIPSIS MARKS

Ellipsis marks (together a set is referred to as an *ellipsis*) are indicated by three periods. An ellipsis can appear next to other punctuation, including an end-of-sentence period (resulting in four periods). Use four only when the words on either side of the ellipsis make full sentences. Most style manuals and house styles prefer the periods to be spaced. They are used to indicate a sentence that is allowed to deliberately trail off.

> Gillian was assured that the used car she was thinking of buying was very reliable, but . . .

Ellipses are also used to indicate the omission of quoted material. The current convention is to put brackets around ellipses that you insert into direct quotations to make it clear that the ellipses aren't part of the original passage.

> "In our time, political speech and writing are largely the defense of the indefensible [. . . .] Thus political language has to consist largely of euphemism."
> —George Orwell, "Politics and the English Language."

In the preceding example, the brackets indicate that the writer quoting Orwell added the ellipses, not Orwell himself.

USING PARENTHESES AND BRACKETS

Technically, brackets include parentheses, or round brackets ( ); square brackets, or box brackets [ ]; curly brackets, or braces { }; and angle brackets < >. Most commonly—at least in American usage—the term *bracket* is used to mean square brackets, and parentheses usually aren't called brackets. (We don't use curly brackets in sentences, so they won't be discussed.)

Using Parentheses

1. Use parentheses to set off a part of your sentence that is not part of the main thought. They indicate an *aside* or an exception to a point. However, be careful not to overuse them in this way. The question you should ask yourself is this: "If it isn't part of my main thought, why do I want it in my sentence?"

    Marie Antoinette (infamous for a statement she never actually made, "let them eat cake") was the subject of two recent movies.

2. Use parentheses to add clarifying information, such as definitions.

    Nanobots would be measured in microns (millionths of a meter) and be invisible without powerful microscopes.

3. Use parentheses to enclose numerals or letters indicating the items of a list.

    Marie Antoinette is most well known today for (1) a cavalier comment she never actually made and (2) being guillotined.

4. Use parentheses for in-text citations.

    At the end of Kate Chopin's "The Story of an Hour," Mrs. Mallard drops dead upon learning that her husband is alive. In the final irony of the story, doctors report that she has died of a "joy that kills" (25).

    Women across the social spectrum shared and modified fairy tales (Smith 172, Warner 316–17).

Using Brackets

We use square brackets, usually referred to simply as *brackets,* when we insert material into, delete, or change material within quotations in order to make our additions or changes clearly distinct from the actual quoted material.

1. Use brackets to add explanatory information:

    William Gibson recounted that "My colleague Bruce Sterling [considered another one of the founders of cyperpunk in science fiction] and I were invited to Washington a couple of years ago to address the National Academy of Sciences special meeting on the computerization of American public schools."

2. Use brackets when you change an uppercase letter to a lowercase letter or a lowercase letter to an uppercase letter. Here are some lines from Theodore Roethke's poem "The Waking":

> Great Nature has another thing to do
> To you and me, so take the lively air,
> And, lovely, learn by going where to go.

If you wanted to incorporate these lines into a sentence of your own and still follow conventional capitalization guidelines for sentences, you could write,

> I feel, like Roethke, that "Great Nature has another thing to do / [to] you and me, so take the lively air, / [a]nd, lovely, learn by going where to go."

Note: The slash is used to indicate a division between lines of poetry in the original version, but it does not need to be enclosed in brackets.

3. Use brackets when you change a word in a quotation. Take, for example, the following lines from a poem by Stevie Smith:

> I was much further out than you thought
> And not waving but drowning.

This could be altered to

> Like Smith's character, he "was much further out than [we] thought / [a]nd not waving but drowning."

4. Use brackets around the term *sic* (Latin for "thus") to indicate errors or unusual spelling variations that are "thus in the original":

> Jonson told Drummond that "Skakspeer [*sic*] wanted art."

Sic is Latin, and MLA format suggests italicizing foreign words.

5. Use brackets around ellipses [. . .] when following MLA style to indicate that material has been deleted (do so only if you are in no way altering the meaning of the original passage).

> William Gibson recounted that "My colleague Bruce Sterling and I were invited to [. . .] address the National Academy of Sciences special meeting on the computerization of American public schools."

Note: The use of brackets around ellipses is a relatively new MLA guideline, so you've probably seen more ellipses without brackets than with them. APA guidelines don't require brackets with ellipses.

6. Angle brackets can be used to enclose URLs in works-cited entries. Current MLA guidelines recommend omitting URLs unless your readers wouldn't be able to locate a source otherwise. If you do include the URL, it should be enclosed in angle brackets and followed by a period.

"Oochigeaska, the Rough-Faced Girl." English 1A: Expository Composition. Gloria Dumler's home page. English Department. Bakersfield College. 8 May 2008. Web. 11 Jan. 2009 <http://www2.bc.cc.ca.us/gdumler/ English%201A% 20FolderMisc%20Documents/oochigeaska.htm>.

USING THE SLASH

The slash is also called the slant line, the oblique stroke, the bar, and the virgule. Use it to indicate a separation between lines of poetry or lines in a play written in poetic verse if you are not retaining the original verse form in your sentence. (Put a space before and after the slash.)

> King Richard laments, "I shall despair. / There is no creature loves me; / And if I die, no soul shall pity me: / Nay, wherefore should they, since that I myself / Find in myself no pity to myself?"

Avoid using the slash in formal, academic writing as a shortcut. We often see people writing and/or, she/he, and him/her, the latter two proliferating as we try to avoid sexist language. But people don't talk that way, and good writing sounds good when spoken aloud. When was the last time you heard someone referring to a "him/her" or a "he/she"? It is better to write "him or her" or "he and she" and even better to make your nouns plural so that you can correctly use the plural pronouns *they* and *them*. That way you can avoid sentences that get bogged down with too many pronouns.

MAKING SUBJECTS AND VERBS AGREE

The rule is simple: a singular subject takes a singular verb, and a plural subject takes a plural verb. The tricky part is figuring out whether subjects are singular or plural, especially with subjects separated from the verb and with compound subjects.

If a subject is composed of two or more nouns or pronouns connected by *and,* we treat it as a plural, so use a plural verb.

> Moya and Cynthia are coming to dinner.

If two or more singular nouns or pronouns are connected by *or* or *nor,* use a singular verb.

> Either Cynthia or Moya is bringing dessert.

If the subject contains both a singular and a plural noun or pronoun joined by *or* or *nor,* the verb should agree with the part of the subject that is nearer the verb.

> The cats or the dog gets to sleep inside the house, depending on whose turn it is.
>
> The dog or the cats get to sleep inside the house, depending on whose turn it is.

If a phrase comes between the subject and the verb, the verb must agree with the subject, not with a noun or pronoun in the phrase that comes before the verb.

The person who mismanaged all the accounts is not working here anymore.

The most interesting chapters of that book are near the end.

If you use the relative pronouns *who, which,* or *that,* use verbs that agree with the word the pronoun refers to.

The cars that were most popular at the show were the ones with the best fuel economy.

The car that was the most popular of all got 60 mpg in town and 51 mpg on the highway.

One and *body* are singular, so the pronouns *anybody, anyone, nobody, somebody, someone, no one, each one, everyone*, and *everybody* are also singular, as are the words *each, either,* and *neither*. They all require singular verbs.

Everybody loves cake.

Each of these cakes is delicious.

Either ice cream or cake is fine.

Neither of us is hungry anymore.

Some nouns that end with an "s" are treated as singular, such as *news, civics,* and *mathematics. Dollars* is singular if you are talking about an amount of money, but it is plural if you are talking about actual dollars.

Mathematics is a difficult subject for many people.

The news is good.

A hundred and fifty dollars is a lot of money for a textbook.

How many dollars can I get for twenty Euros?

Nouns for certain items that have two parts, such as scissors, tweezers, and trousers, require plural verbs.

I think your trousers need mending.

Where are the scissors?

Collective nouns, like *family, class, organization, team,* and *committee,* indicate groups of individuals, and in the United States they are usually treated as singular.

My family wants to go camping.

The committee has to reach a solution to the problem.

When expressions such as *with, including,* and *in addition to* are used, pay attention to the subject. If the subject is singular, so is the verb, and if the subject is plural, the verb is, too.

Jaden, along with all the finalists, is going to the competition.

All of the finalists, including Jaden, are going to the competition.

USING CORRECT VERB TENSES

Verb tenses indicate the time of an action in relation to the time that we speak or write about the action. English has three "simple" tenses—past, present, and future—and three "perfect" tenses. All six of these have what are called *progressive forms*.

We use the **simple present tense** to describe what we are currently doing, actions that are repeated or usual, and future actions that begin at a specific time. We also use the simple present tense to express general principles, to describe the ongoing events in the plot of a literary work, and when quoting, paraphrasing, or summarizing sources in essays and research papers. There are two basic forms for the simple present tense; one ends with *s* and the other doesn't.

I hear you.	Jim hears you, too.
I run every day.	Sophia runs every day.
I start my new job tomorrow.	My new job starts tomorrow.
Cats chase mice.	My cat chases mice.
Hamlet and Laertes fight.	Hamlet stabs Polonius.
The authors write, . . .	Moyers points out that . . .

We use the **simple past tense** to describe actions completed in the past.

I ran one mile yesterday.	They ran four miles.

We use the **simple future tense** to describe actions that will occur or that we can predict will occur.

I will run two miles tomorrow.	I will be healthier if I exercise more.

Here are more examples of simple tenses, using the regular verb *explain* and the irregular verbs *write* and *be*.

SIMPLE VERB TENSES

Simple Present

Singular		Plural	
I	explain, write, am	we	explain, write, are
you	explain, write, are	you	explain, write, are
she/he/it	explains, writes, is	they	explain, write, are

Simple Past

Singular		Plural	
I	explained, wrote, was	we	explained, wrote, were
you	explained, wrote, were	you	explained, wrote, were
she/he/it	explained, wrote, was	they	explained, wrote, were

Simple Future

I, you, she/he/it, we, they	will explain, will write, will be

Perfect tenses describe more complex relations in time. They consist of a form of *have* and the past participle form of the verb, which usually ends in *-ed*.

We use the **present perfect tense** to describe an action that began in the past but is still occurring or an action that began in the past and is finished at the time of writing.

> Elizabeth has run in the annual marathon for years.

> The dog has chased the cat up a tree.

We use the **past perfect tense** to describe an action that has already occurred by the time another past action has occurred or to describe an action that has been completed at a specific time in the past.

> By the time Sara got to the library, all the parking spaces had been taken.

> By 2:00 in the afternoon yesterday, I had finished my first draft.

We use the **future perfect tense** to describe an action that will have been completed by or before a specific time in the future.

> I will have finished my paper by the time you start yours.

PERFECT TENSES

Present Perfect

I, you, we, they	have explained, have written, have been
she/he/it	has explained, has written, has been

Past Perfect

I, you, she/he/it, we, they	had explained, had written, had been

Future Perfect

I, you, she/he/it, we, they	will have explained, will have written, will have been

The simple and perfect tenses also have **progressive forms.** These forms describe actions that are in progress, actions that were in progress at a particular point in the past, or actions that will be in progress at a particular time to come. Some verbs, such as many expressing a state of being or mental activity, are not usually used with progressive forms. Some examples are *appear, believe, know,* and *want.*

The **present progressive form** is used to describe actions currently occurring or actions that will occur in the future at a specific time.

> My kitten is at war with a ball of yarn.
>
> I am starting my new job next Monday.

The **past progressive form** is used to describe past actions that are in progress.

> My dad was busy cooking dinner last night.

The **future progressive form** is used to describe future action in progress.

> I will be going to a new school in the fall.

PROGRESSIVE FORMS

Present Progressive

I	am explaining, am writing, am being
she/he/it	is explaining, is writing, is being
you, we, they	are explaining, are writing, are being

Past Progressive

I, she/he/it	was explaining, was writing, was being
you, we, they	were explaining, were writing, were being

Future Progressive

I, you, she/he/it, we, they	will be explaining, will be writing, will be being

The **perfect progressive forms** describe the length of time an action is, was, or will be occurring.

The **present perfect progressive** indicates the length of time an action currently occurring has been going on.

> I have been going to the gym for three years.

The **past perfect progressive** indicates the length of time an action was performed in the past.

I had been working out regularly for two years until I pulled a muscle.

The **future perfect progressive** indicates the length of time an action will have been performed at a point in the future.

On July 15, 2013, Michael and Judy will have been married for forty years.

PERFECT PROGRESSIVE FORMS

Present Perfect Progressive

I, you, we, they	have been explaining, have been writing, have been being
she/he/it	has been explaining, has been writing, has been being

Past Perfect Progressive

I, you, she/he/it, we, they	had been explaining, had been writing, had been being

Future Perfect Progressive

I, you, she/he/it, we, they	will have been explaining, will have been writing, will have been being

UNDERSTANDING PRONOUNS

Pronoun **case** expresses the relationship of a pronoun to other words in the sentence. There are only three pronoun cases.

Subjective case: pronouns used as subject.

Objective case: pronouns used as direct or indirect objects of verbs or prepositions.

Possessive case: pronouns used to express ownership.

Singular	Objective	Possessive
I	me	mine
you	you	yours
she, he, it	her, him, it	his, hers, its
we	us	ours
they	them	theirs
who	whom	whose

The relative pronouns *this, that, these, those,* and *which* do not change form.

(If you are wondering where *my, your, her, our,* and *their* are, they are possessive adjectives—they describe nouns, they do not stand in for them (*his* and *whose* are both adjectives and pronouns).

Compound subjects and objects make pronoun choice confusing. Sometimes the simplest way to figure out what form to use is to drop one of the words from the compound as a test.

> You would not write, "The new standards benefit I."
>
> You should not write, "The new standards benefit Luz and I."
>
> You should write, "The new standards benefit Luz and me."

> We would not write, "Me went to the store."
>
> We should not write, "Barbara and me went to the store."
>
> We should write, "Barbara and I went to the store."

> We would not write, "Barbara likes I."
>
> We should not write, "Barbara likes both Hal and I."
>
> We should write, "Barbara likes both Hal and me."

Sometimes a descriptive noun phrase follows a personal pronoun.

> We would not write, "Us want lower tuition."
>
> We would write, "We want lower tuition."
>
> We should write, "We students want lower tuition."

Who and *whom* correspond to *they* and *them,* and so on. *Who* is the subjective form, and we use it when an action is being performed. *Whom* is the objective form, and we use it when a person is the recipient of an action or if the action is being performed for him or her. It is helpful to remember that while not all pronouns in the objective case end with the letter *m,* the only pronouns that end in *m* are in objective case. A quick and easy way to figure out whether you should use *whom* in your writing (it has fallen into disuse in most spoken English) instead of *who* is to see if *them* or *him* would work in its place if you reworded the sentence to answer a question.

Whom do you love?	You love him.
Who loves you?	They love you.
To whom should I address the letter?	Address it to him.
Who ate the last cookie?	She ate the last cookie.

Pronouns used in comparisons can be tricky. Comparisons usually follow *than* or *as.* Comparisons usually omit words because they are clearly implied and we don't really miss them. If you complete the comparisons in your head, you can choose the correct case for the pronouns. You can also think about how the pronouns sound if you were not making comparisons.

Correct sentence with implied words: "Jacob is faster than I [am fast]."

You would not write, "Me am fast."

You should not write, "Jacob is faster than me."

You should write, "Jacob is faster than I."

Correct sentence with implied words: "The new standards benefit you as much as [they benefit] me."

You would not write, "The new standards benefit I."

You should not write, "The new standards benefit you as much as I."

You should write, "The new standards benefit you as much as me."

Correct sentence with implied words: " Chloe is as happy as I [am happy]."

You would not write, "Me am happy" or "Me is happy."

You should not write, "Chloe is as happy as me."

You should write, "Chloe is as happy as I."

Pronoun **agreement** is important in writing. Pronouns should clearly agree with specific **antecedents** (the nouns that they stand in for) and with each other (when referring to the same antecedents) in **number** (plural or singular), **gender** (male or female), and **person** (first, second, or third).

As we mentioned when discussing subject and verb agreement, the pronouns *anybody, anyone, nobody, somebody, someone, no one, each one, everyone,* and *everybody* are singular, as are the words *each, either,* and *neither.* Gender disagreement issues can pop up when you refer to everyone in a group as either male or female (unless you happen to know for sure that only one gender is represented in the specific group). "He and she" can sound awkward when repeated, so a simple solution is to make both the nouns and pronouns plural.

Agreement in number and gender:

When a person speeds, he or she can get pulled over by the police.

When people speed, they can get pulled over by the police.

Everyone should turn his or her essay in on time.

All students should turn their essays in on time.

Neither of the men gave up his position.

Either of the women could have guessed the correct answer.

Agreement in person:

I need to be careful when I plan my schedule.

If you want to do well, you should not procrastinate.

When we manage our time, we do better in our classes.

Sometimes using the noun again instead of a pronoun is the best solution if a sentence doesn't make clear what noun a pronoun refers to.

Confusing: The cases have sturdy lids, but they may still need to be replaced eventually.

Clear: The cases have sturdy lids, but the lids may still need to be replaced eventually.

Clear: The cases have sturdy lids, but the cases may still need to be replaced eventually.

SUGGESTIONS FOR IMPROVING WRITING STYLE

The word **style** has a few meanings, including "the manner of doing something" and "elegance and sophistication." When we talk about writing style, we mean both. Part of the problem with understanding style in any area—music, fashion, art, and writing—is that it's subjective. Readers have different ideas about what constitutes good writing style—we can see that easily enough by looking at an article in *People* (a magazine focusing on celebrity gossip and human interest stories) and comparing it to one in the *New Yorker* (a magazine focusing on culture, politics, current events, literature, and reviews). Different instructors and different academic departments have differing ideas about style, too. So how do we define "good" style? If style is so subjective, aren't all styles equal? Not really. Good style involves (1) correctly understanding your audience and the level and type of diction that is appropriate and (2) avoiding sentences that are clumsy and unclear. Here are some general guidelines to make your own style the best it can be—and to help you figure out what those notes your professors keep scrawling on your papers mean.

Write with a Clear Sense of Your Purpose

Most of the time, when your instructor gives you a writing assignment, she will tell you what the purpose of your paper is. It could be to inform readers, to analyze a text, to persuade a community to believe your conclusions about a controversial issue, to call people to action of some kind, or simply to explore your own feelings about a topic. Clarifying your purpose will determine the tone you take (serious, somber, impassioned, playful) and the audience that you should imagine. Typically, you will announce your purpose with a clear, well-placed thesis statement. The last sentence of the introduction is a good location for your thesis because that position draws the reader's attention.

Write with a Clear Sense of Your Audience

Ask your instructor what kind of people you should imagine as your **audience.** Many instructors want you to imagine a larger community outside the classroom. After all, what is the purpose of learning how to write just for instructors and the other people in class with you? That isn't going to help you when you leave school. Some instructors will ask that you write essays or papers with a knowledgeable audience in mind. In a literature class, you might be asked to write an analysis of a novel, and your instructor may tell you to imagine someone who is familiar with the book. But another instructor may want you to write an essay that anyone would understand, including people unfamiliar with the work. Obviously, for that audience, you are going to have to include more summary and details. A science teacher may ask you to imagine an audience of scientists when you write and not require you to provide definitions of scientific terms. However, if you choose a scientific topic such as global climate change for an argumentative research paper in your English class, your instructor may want you to imagine an audience of laypeople and may expect you to clearly define all scientific terms and to not assume that your audience knows anything about the topic you are discussing. Here is a series of questions to help you imagine your audience:

How well informed are your readers about your topic?

How well informed are your readers about your discipline?

What do you want your readers to learn about your topic?

What do you want your readers to do about your topic?

Unless you are told otherwise, you should imagine an audience that is diverse, just like the larger community. Don't assume that everyone reading your paper shares your gender, age group, ethnicity, race, sexual preference, physical abilities, or political and religious beliefs. You can alienate readers if your comments and arguments indicate that you have excluded them from your audience.

Maintain a Consistent and Appropriate Tone

Tone refers to the attitude of a writer revealed in the choice of vocabulary and other elements of style. Tone comes out in spoken language, as well. Think of the way you talk when you are with your closest friends, the way you talk when you are in the classroom, the way that you talk with your family, and the way you talk when you are at work. There are likely to be subtle differences at least, and some differences are pretty extreme. We need to remember that we convey tone with the choices we make when we write. Most of us wouldn't dream of using exactly the same language in class or at a job that we use with our friends. Consider the following:

Formal:

> Television producers understand that commercial advertising generally portrays women who represent an impossible ideal of beauty. They also know that girls see these advertisements and start to compare their own bodies to the perfect bodies seen on the screen. This, in turn, creates a false sense of beauty, one that a normal human being cannot possibly live up to. Advertisers and television executives are complicit in undermining girls' sense of self, even leading to eating disorders and unnecessary cosmetic surgery.

Informal:

> TV producers know that ads mostly show women who are totally babelicious and that real women can't ever look this good. They also know kids see these ads on the tube and compare their own bods to the babes they see on the screen. This makes girls

green with envy. Advertisers and TV bigwigs help make girls unhappy with themselves; the girls end up starving themselves or barfing up their food and even getting boob jobs.

Most of your instructors probably prefer a serious, objective, reasonable-sounding, "academic" tone. There are writing situations where other types of tone are appropriate; for example, when you brainstorm for ideas, you shouldn't worry about tone or style. Some instructors may ask you to keep journals and encourage you to feel creative and informal. But your essays and research papers should be written in a different "register" (level of formality). What you don't want to do is to start writing without thinking about your tone. Don't let it just "happen." If you write with no clear sense of tone in mind, your tone may shift around with your moods. Your thinking may appear chaotic if you are casual in one paragraph and formal in another, objective in part of your paper, and passionate and personal in the next. Determine the tone best suited to your purpose, and stick with it. Because we focus on writing the research paper in this book, much of our advice assumes that your tone should be objective and scholarly.

Avoid Slang and Idiomatic Language

Slang consists of nonstandard words or phrases that tend to originate in subcultures within a society. Subcultures can consist of groups unified by age range, ethnicity, race, hobbies, and so on. **Idiomatic language** (also called **idioms**) consists of words or phrases whose meaning is different from their literal meanings but that are understood by speakers of the same language or dialect, such as "kick the bucket." There is a lot of overlap, so we are combining them here. Whether an expression is slang, idiomatic, or both, you should avoid it because it is too informal for academic writing and because some members of your audience might not understand it. *Awesome, sick, sweet, bad, cool,* and *wicked* may all mean something great to you, but they may not be understood in the same way by readers of all ages and backgrounds. Even words like *guys* and *kids,* though understood by everyone, are too informal for scholarly writing. You may also consider avoiding contractions (such as saying *don't* instead of *do not*). They aren't really slang, and there is nothing inherently wrong with them—we use contractions ourselves—but they are relatively informal, and many instructors prefer that you don't use contractions in your papers.

Avoid Pompous Phrasing and Jargon

At the other end of the spectrum from slang and idiomatic language is pompous language. Trying to be so formal that you reach for difficult and obscure words in an effort to show off to your audience is just as bad as being too informal—maybe even worse. Good writing is clear writing; it doesn't scream, "Behold my ostentatious erudition and ersatz profundity exacerbated by the plethora of sesquipedalian terminologies that bespeak my jejuneness!" (Translation: "Look at my pretentious show of learning and my fake depth of insight made worse by my choice of overly long words that demonstrate my superficiality!") Your readers should be able to move through your prose with such ease that your ideas take center stage. The more you make your audience struggle, the less successful you will be as a writer. One piece of advice is never to write a sentence that you'd feel silly saying aloud.

Depending on the topic you research, you may also encounter quite a bit of specialized terminology, also called *jargon*. If you have picked a topic you are pretty familiar with, you may already know the terminology you find. Or you may have to look it up as you do more research. Keep in mind that—unless your professor tells you otherwise—you should be picturing a general audience of ordinary people as you write. Avoid jargon when you can, but, if some jargon is necessary, make sure that you define it in plain language for your readers.

You don't want your writing to be too informally conversational in style, but you don't want to sound pretentious or ridiculous, either. We don't want to discourage you from developing your vocabulary to the fullest—your instructors will be impressed by precise, accurate language. But showing off tends to backfire, especially when you reach for "fancy" words you may not understand very well. (*Simplistic,* for example, isn't a more-sophisticated version of *simple;* they have very different meanings. See our list titled "Commonly Confused Words and Phrases.") When you were much younger, your teachers probably encouraged you to develop your vocabulary by trying to guess what words meant based on their context and their sound. Think of those two techniques as "training wheels." You should be well beyond that stage now. College-level vocabulary is more complex and nuanced, so don't take the lazy way out—reach for your dictionary. You may find that a lot of words don't mean what you think they do. Taking the extra effort to use a dictionary can save you some embarrassment in the future, not to mention helping you to write better papers and get better grades.

POMPOUS AND JARGONISTIC:
The obtuseness of his verbiage was impenetrable.

STRAIGHTFORWARD AND CLEAR:
He was impossible to understand.

Avoid Clichés

Clichés are sayings that are overused and betray a lack of original thinking. Some examples of common clichés include:

in a nutshell

against the grain

can't see the forest for the trees

from feast to famine

from the ground up

gut reaction

level playing field

If you find yourself using a cliché in your writing, try to express the cliché in plain words.

CLICHÉD:

Creative individuals tend to think outside the box.

FRESH:

Creative individuals tend to approach problems in new ways.

Avoid "Ready-Made Phrases"

Ready-made phrases (the term comes from George Orwell in his essay "Politics and the English Language") are those that are overused and come to us because we hear them used so much they seem "right." Like clichés, they indicate a lack of original thought.

READY-MADE PHRASE	ACTUAL MEANING
on a daily basis	daily
with reference to	about
at this point in time	now
the fact of the matter is that	(an unnecessary filler)
as a matter of fact	(an unnecessary filler)
poses a threat to	threatens
in the event that	if
for the purpose of	to

Avoid Redundant Words and Phrases

Many ready-made phrases are also redundant. Terms that are **redundant** are superfluous—not needed because of a useless repetition in meaning. As you can see from the examples that follow, sometimes all you need to do is strip away extra words—or the entire phrase.

REDUNDANT	CHANGE TO
true fact	fact
square (or round, or triangular, etc.) in shape	square, (or round, or triangular, etc.)
up until	until
end result	result
the reason was because	The reason was
alleged suspect	suspect [or alleged criminal]
very unique	unique
cooperate together	cooperate
completely eliminated	eliminated
totally devastated	devastated
in close proximity	in proximity
unexpected surprise	surprise

Avoid Wordiness, Including "Filler" Words

Using more words than necessary to say what you mean will bog down your writing. There are different reasons students are too wordy. Sometimes they do it on purpose to pad an assignment that has a minimum word count. Trust us—that doesn't work. When instructors ask for thoroughly developed papers, they are talking about your ideas, not the literal number of words. Sometimes students are wordy because they don't edit carefully—and ruthlessly—enough. Often whole sentences and even whole paragraphs can be removed because they add nothing new to the paper or may even be off the topic. It's human nature to go off on tangents, especially when we are writing to generate ideas. It's good to let yourself use the writing process to stimulate thought, and you shouldn't worry about being on topic when you are brainstorming. But a crucial component of writing is revising, and you need to learn to let some of what you have written go. Think about cooking disasters—wouldn't it be great if, when you added too much salt to the stew, you could take it out again? We can't repair that kind of mistake when we are cooking, but we can fix problems of wordiness in our writing.

When we talk, we often use a lot of "filler" words that don't add to the meaning of our sentences. Sometimes we bring these filler words into our papers. Beginning sentences with "well" is an example. Other examples of wordiness include redundant words and phrases, as explained earlier, and overused qualifiers, such as *very, often, hopefully, basically, really, mostly,* and *practically.*

WORDY SENTENCE:

Well, I really think we as American citizens should investigate alternative sources of energy so we can reduce greenhouse gas emissions, hopefully.

STREAMLINED SENTENCE:

Americans should investigate alternative sources of energy to reduce greenhouse gas emissions.

Avoid Emotional Language and Language That "Gushes"

Emotional language is usually out of place in scholarly writing because, from a reader's point of view, your emotions aren't relevant to most topics. You don't need to say that you love or hate something or that something is "sad" or "terrible." "Gushing" about something means unrestrainedly praising it. Sometimes students, trying to think of something interesting to say about a person or subject, say that it is "very interesting" or "great," or "wonderful," and so on. These are empty adjectives—they don't tell your reader anything concrete, and they may keep you from saying anything meaningful because you may be under the illusion that you just did. They are also value judgments. Avoid these adjectives or any other kind of effusiveness in favor of words and phrases that convey specific ideas.

MEANINGLESS:

Samantha Powers' book *A Problem From Hell: America and the Age of Genocide* is a very sad book. It is very interesting.

MEANINGFUL:

Samantha Powers' book *A Problem From Hell: America and the Age of Genocide* is an indictment of American indifference to genocide in other countries. It is painstakingly researched and carefully documented.

Use Pronouns Appropriate for the Situation

As we have already indicated, don't use plural pronouns such as *they* and *them* with singular nouns; almost everyone speaks this way, but, technically, it is not yet standard formal written English. Because overuse of "he and she" and "him and her" can become awkward, the simplest solution is to make both the nouns and pronouns plural. (As we stated earlier, never write "he/she" or "him/her"; we don't speak that way, and it is very awkward—choose one pronoun instead.)

INCORRECT:

When a reporter is covering a story, they should check facts carefully.

CORRECT BUT POTENTIALLY AWKWARD:

When a reporter is covering a story, he or she should check facts carefully.

CORRECT AND RECOMMENDED:

When reporters are covering stories, they should check facts carefully.

Most instructors would prefer that you avoid using **second person** (*you, your*). It is informal and sometimes technically incorrect. It is correct when you are directly addressing your readers—as we are addressing you in this book—but this is usually not the situation in academic writing. All too often, people use second person when they should be using **third person** (*they, them, she, her, he,* and *him*). Consider the following sentence from a student essay:

When you fabricate stories like Stephen Glass and Jayson Blair did, you run a very real risk of getting caught and ruining your career.

Who is the audience for that statement? Literally, they would appear to be journalists who have been making up stories to publish. A revised sentence using third person makes more sense:

When journalists fabricate stories like Stephen Glass and Jayson Blair did, they run a very real risk of getting caught and ruining their careers.

Most instructors would also prefer that you avoid **first person** (*I, me*). Sometimes first person is appropriate, as when you have been asked to write about a personal experience. However, first person is rare in formal academic writing, and your instructor may prefer that you adopt a scholarly tone. You might find yourself with a personal anecdote that would fit well into an essay or research paper. What should you do? The safest thing is to ask your instructor if that is appropriate. Using first person isn't bad writing. Instructors tend to discourage it partly because of its informality, and because they don't want you dragging feelings into your writing or adding unnecessary words. Let's look at variations of the sentence about dishonest reporters.

> I think that when reporters are covering stories, they should check facts carefully.
>
> I feel that when reporters are covering stories, they should check facts carefully.
>
> I believe that when reporters are covering stories, they should check facts carefully.
>
> When reporters are covering stories, they should check facts carefully.

The first three examples begin with useless phrases. Your readers know what you think, feel, and believe because you wouldn't be writing these ideas otherwise. Here is a short passage using another sentence we looked at earlier.

> I was really surprised when I found out that reporters have been caught making up stories. I think that's terrible. When journalists fabricate stories like Stephen Glass and Jayson Blair did, they run a very real risk of getting caught and ruining their careers.

Do the first two sentences add anything that your readers are likely to find relevant? No. They want to be informed—they don't care about your personal feelings.

Avoid Exclusionary Language

Today, all major writing style guides advise writers to employ **inclusive language,** including **gender-neutral** language. Some people sneer at such advice by saying it is "political correctness" gone too far, but it is actually a matter of accuracy and even simple courtesy, as well as clarity. Consider the rather poetic, but ambiguous, statement, "Only Man has wings for Art." What does the writer mean? Does he mean that only human beings are capable of creating true art? There have been articles about chimpanzees, gorillas, and even elephants who are "artists." Or does the writer mean that only *male* human beings are capable of creating true art?

Your writing will be clearer if you avoid *he, him, man,* or *men* when you mean *human being(s), humankind,* or *people.* As noted earlier, you can use plural nouns and pronouns. This is generally preferable because it is never awkward. You can also replace pronouns with articles.

INACCURATE IN MOST SITUATIONS:

Each student should consider audience and tone when writing his research paper.

ACCURATE IN MOST SITUATIONS:

Each student should consider audience and tone when writing the research paper.

Students should consider audience and tone when writing their research papers.

Your language will be clear, accurate, and inoffensive if you remove ambiguities and avoid assumptions of gender roles. Gender-neutral terms allow you to avoid reinforcing stereotypes.

WORDS AND PHRASES TO AVOID	ALTERNATIVES
man, mankind	humans, humankind, women and men, man and woman
manned flight	piloted flight
chairman, chairwoman	chair, chairperson
layman	layperson
man in the street	ordinary people, average person
manpower	workforce, staff, employees, human resources
manning	staffing
man hours	hours worked
primitive man	primitive people
businessman, businesswoman	businesspeople
fireman	firefighter
manmade	synthetic, artificial, manufactured
mailman	letter carrier, postal worker
policeman, policewoman/policemen	officer/police
spokesman, spokeswoman	spokesperson, representative
foreman	supervisor
Congressman, Congresswoman	member of Congress, representative, legislator, senator
girl, young girl (unless under eighteen),	young woman, woman
lady	woman (except when used in conjunction with gentleman)

Write in Active Voice (Most of the Time)

When you write in active voice, the subject of the sentence acts:

The chicken crossed the road to get to the other side.

That is, the subject of the verb (the chicken, in this case) performs the action.

A sentence in **passive voice** shows the subject being acted upon; the writer is making the object of an action into the subject of a sentence.

The road was crossed by the chicken.

In passive voice, the agent of the action is often left unspecified.

> The road was crossed.

Proponents of writing in active voice believe that it has a more direct and vigorous feel. However, that doesn't mean all professors reject passive voice or that passive voice is automatically an indicator of poor style. Compare the following two sentences:

> Most humanities professors prefer active voice. (Active voice)
>
> Passive voice is often acceptable to professors in business and science classes. (Passive voice)

Both are perfectly fine sentences. Given the general preference, you are probably safest sticking with active voice, but you should ask if your instructor has a preference. The bottom line is that sometimes passive voice can lead to problems with clarity—and a problem with clarity is always bad style, no matter what form it takes.

Use Parallel Structure

The principle of parallel structure, or parallelism, requires that expressions of similar content and function should be similar in form, using the same pattern of words. This can happen at the word, phrase, or clause level. Why do professors like parallel structure? Parallel structure creates clarity in your writing. Compare the following sentences, and see which one you think sounds the best:

> I love to read novels, watching movies, and music is good to listen to.
>
> I love reading novels, watching movies, and listening to music.

The first example doesn't exhibit parallel structure, whereas the second one does because all of the verb forms have *-ing* endings. Here are some additional tips on creating parallelism in your writing at the word, phrase, and clause levels:

1. WORD AND PHRASE LEVEL

With **gerunds** (verb forms ending in *-ing* that function as nouns):

> I love reading novels, watching movies, and listening to music.

With **infinitive phrases** (the *to* form of verbs):

> I love to read novels, to watch movies, and to listen to music.
>
> I love to read novels, watch movies, and listen to music.

With **adverbs:**

> I cleaned house slowly, thoroughly, and unenthusiastically.

With **phrases:**

> She got a good grade on her paper because she evaluated her sources rigorously, wrote her first drafts carefully, and revised her final draft thoroughly.

2. CLAUSE LEVEL

With **dependent clauses** (clauses that begin with subordinating words or relative pronouns):

> The babysitter told the children when they should have lunch, when they should take a nap, and when they should get up.

With **independent clauses** (clauses that can stand alone because they express complete thoughts):

> I wanted to go to New York, and I also wanted to go to London.

With a series of items following a colon:

> She loved the following activities: swimming, hiking, and rock climbing.

> (*Note:* Remember to use colons only when you have an independent clause before the sentence element you introduce.)

Avoid Unclear Modification

Modifiers are words and phrases that say something about other words or phrases. They need to be placed correctly in the sentence to clearly modify the correct part of the sentence. There are three types of problem modifiers: **misplaced, squinting,** and **dangling.**

MISPLACED MODIFIERS

Misplaced modifiers are words, phrases, or clauses that are in the wrong place in the sentence.

CONFUSING:

Stinking and moldy, she threw the four-week-old chili down the drain and turned on the garbage disposal.

In the preceding example, the opening phrase is meant to describe the old chili, but its position means that it erroneously describes the woman. The following sentences convey the intended meaning correctly and clearly.

CLEAR:

She threw the stinking, moldy, four-week-old chili down the drain and turned on the garbage disposal.

She threw the four-week-old chili, which was stinking and moldy, down the drain and turned on the garbage disposal.

CONFUSING:

Wagging his little tail, the man watched his poodle, Spike, eat the dog biscuits.

In the preceding example, the literal meaning of the sentence is that the man has a little tail that he is wagging, which was not the writer's intention.

CLEAR:

Wagging his little tail, his poodle, Spike, ate the dog biscuits while the man watched.

The man watched his poodle, Spike, wagging his little tail as he ate the dog biscuits.

In the revised sentences, it is clear that the poodle was the one with a wagging tail.

SQUINTING MODIFIERS

Squinting modifiers are those modifiers that are confusingly placed between two words or phrases so that it is unclear what is being modified.

CONFUSING:

The woman who was mumbling distractedly summoned help.

In the preceding example, it is not clear whether the woman is distractedly mumbling or distractedly asking for help.

CLEAR:

The woman who was mumbling summoned help distractedly.

In this revision, the woman is distracted as she summons help.

or

The distractedly mumbling woman summoned help.

In this revision, the woman is mumbling distractedly as she summons help.

CONFUSING:

A man who was dancing clumsily made a pass at his partner.

In the preceding sentence, it is not clear whether the man's dancing was clumsy or whether the pass he made was clumsy.

CLEAR:

A clumsily dancing man made a pass at his partner.

In this revision, the man's dancing was clumsy.

or

A dancing man clumsily made a pass at his partner.

A dancing man made a clumsy pass at his partner.

In these revisions, the pass the man made was clumsy.

DANGLING MODIFIERS

Dangling modifiers have no words in the sentence to logically modify.

CONFUSING:

Working on the problem, the solution seemed impossible.

This is confusing and illogical because it literally means that the solution is working on the problem of itself.

CLEAR:

Working on the problem, she thought the solution seemed impossible.

This sentence adds a subject to work on the problem.

CONFUSING:

Staring out the window, the day was rainy and dismal.

This is confusing and illogical because it literally means that the day is staring out the window.

CLEAR:

Staring out the window, he saw that the day was rainy and dismal.

This sentence adds a subject who is staring out the window.

Avoid Mixed Constructions

In grammar, a **construction** is the arrangement of words following grammatical rules. Mixed constructions occur when a writer begins a sentence with one type of construction and finishes the sentence with another. Following are typical problems to avoid.

1. Don't turn a prepositional phrase into the subject of the sentence.

INCORRECT:

For news consumers who want to be well informed and avoid biased accounts should get their news from a variety of media.

CORRECT:

For news consumers who want to be well informed and avoid biased accounts, a variety of media should be used to get their news.

News consumers who want to be well informed and avoid biased accounts should get their news from a variety of media.

2. Don't turn a dependent clause into the subject of the sentence.

INCORRECT:

Because junk food has so many calories and trans fats is why we should avoid it.

CORRECT:

Because junk food has so many calories and trans fats, we should avoid it.

Junk food has so many calories and trans fats that we should avoid it.

3. Do not begin with a dependent clause and end with a clause that assumes the initial clause was independent.

INCORRECT:

Because we were terribly late; therefore, we missed the whole first act.

CORRECT:

Because we were terribly late, we missed the whole first act.

We were terribly late; therefore, we missed the whole first act.

4. Don't shift from **indirect questions** to **direct questions** or vice versa. (A direct question asks a question, whereas an indirect question reports a question without asking it.)

INCORRECT:

I wonder if I will get a good grade on my paper, and will I get a good grade in the class?

CORRECT:

I wonder if I will get a good grade on my paper and if I will get a good grade in the class.

Will I get a good grade on my paper? Will I get a good grade in the class?

5. Avoid constructions with the phrases *is where, is when,* and *the reason . . . is because.*

INCORRECT:

Acupuncture is where thin needles are inserted through the skin to control pain and other symptoms.

CORRECT:

Acupuncture is a procedure in which thin needles are inserted through the skin to control pain and other symptoms.

Acupuncture involves inserting thin needles through the skin to control pain and other symptoms.

INCORRECT:

Bipolar disorder is when there is a medical illness that causes shifts in a person's mood and ability to function.

CORRECT:

Bipolar disorder is a medical illness that causes shifts in a person's mood and ability to function.

INCORRECT:

The reason I was late turning in my paper is because the cat ate my computer mouse.

CORRECT:

The reason I was late turning in my paper is that the cat ate my computer mouse.

I was late turning in my paper because the cat ate my computer mouse.

Avoid Unnecessary Shifts in Person

We've already mentioned that most professors prefer that you write in third person, but sometimes second or first person can be acceptable. It is never acceptable, however, to **shift** (switch back and forth between) person confusingly.

INCORRECT:

We used to go to restaurants and bars and have to endure cigar and cigarette smoke. Now when you go out, the air in these places is a lot cleaner and healthier. People are used to this now, and most of them appreciate it.

CORRECT:

People used to go to restaurants and bars and have to endure cigar and cigarette smoke. Now when they go out, the air in these places is a lot cleaner and healthier. They are used to this now, and most of them appreciate it.

We used to go to restaurants and bars and have to endure cigar and cigarette smoke. Now when we go out, the air in these places is a lot cleaner and healthier. We are used to this now, and most of us appreciate it.

Avoid Unnecessary Shifts in Verb Tense

Do not shift from one verb tense to another when the time frame for each action or state is the same. Generally, you should use **past tense** to narrate events that have already happened and use **present tense** to state facts, to describe habitual actions, to discuss ideas expressed by an author in a particular work, and to describe action in a fictional narrative.

INCORRECT:

Hannibal was a Punic military commander, and during the Second Punic War, he marches soldiers and elephants over the Pyrenees and the Alps.

CORRECT:

Hannibal was a Punic military commander, and during the Second Punic War, he marched soldiers and elephants over the Pyrenees and the Alps.

INCORRECT:

Hannibal is ranked as one of the greatest military tacticians in history, and his life was also the basis for a number of movies.

CORRECT:

Hannibal is ranked as one of the greatest military tacticians in history, and his life is also the basis for a number of movies.

INCORRECT:

Hamlet heard someone behind the curtain, and he stabs him, thinking he was killing Claudius.

CORRECT:

Hamlet hears someone behind the curtain, and he stabs him, thinking he is killing Claudius.

For electronic exercises to improve your style, punctuation, and grammar skills, go to the website for this book at www.mhhe.com/moton1.

SECTION 2

Handbook for Documentation

Formatting the MLA-Style Paper

You've just finished all the stages of the writing process for your research paper. You've done your prewriting and generated a solid thesis. You hit the library and the online databases and found plenty of sources and organized your ideas into notes. You wrote an outline, generated a rough draft, and revised that draft. But you aren't done yet. You need to make sure that your paper is in the proper format. That can lead you to dozens of questions. For example, when you use a quotation, how do you let the reader know where it comes from? Do you use footnotes or put page numbers in parentheses? When do you italicize or underline the titles of works, and when do you put them in quotation marks, instead? Where do your page numbers go? Where do you put your name and the title of your paper? How big should you make the margins?

These questions are all matters of paper formatting, and there are systems developed to help you format papers properly. A properly formatted paper looks professional, and it also reinforces your credibility when you take care to attribute information that is not common knowledge to your sources, a practice that protects you from charges of plagiarism (see Chapter 9 for a discussion on plagiarism).

Modern Language Association (MLA) style is one of the most commonly used styles for college and university papers because it is the standard for courses in liberal arts and the humanities. It provides guidelines for formatting manuscripts and properly referencing sources through in-text parenthetical citations (see Chapter 8 for more on integrating your sources into your papers) and Works Cited and Works Consulted pages, all of which will be described in this chapter. MLA is a very comprehensive system of paper formatting. It covers everything from the general appearance of your paper to the in-text citations within it and the list of sources used at the end. The Modern Language Association does not publish its documentation guidelines on the Web. For an authoritative explanation of MLA style, see the *MLA Handbook for Writers of Research Papers* (for high school and undergraduate college students) and the *MLA Style Manual and Guide to Scholarly Publishing* (for graduate students, scholars, and professional writers). The MLA website at http://www.mla.org also includes a helpful list of frequently asked questions about the style.

This chapter shows you the basic important elements of MLA style and helps prepare you to write properly formatted essays and research papers. (For the format of papers written using American Psychological Association, APA or style, see Chapter 14.) It closes with a sample student paper in correct MLA format.

MLA DOCUMENT GUIDELINES

General Appearance

MLA style requires that the general appearance and basic physical layout of your paper conform to certain guidelines. These guidelines are as follows:

- *Paper Size:* Whether you use a computer or a typewriter, your paper should be printed on one side only of eight-and-a-half-by eleven-inch white paper with one-inch margins on all sides. (The default margin for Microsoft Word is typically 1.25 on the left and right, so you will need to change this.)

- *Alignment:* Justification is the term used to explain how the type is aligned on your paper. If you are using a computer, justify the lines of your paper at the left margin; don't right-justify, center, or full-justify them.

- *Font Size: Font* is the style of typeface you use in your writing. No matter how tempted you may be by the variety of fonts available, choose a simple, legible font such as Times New Roman, 12 point. (If your instructor has given you a page count instead of a word count, don't try to achieve the desired number of pages by using an extra-large font.)

- *Indentations:* Indent the opening lines of paragraphs one-half inch (five spaces) from the left margin. Block quotations (quotations that take up more than four lines in a paper) are indented one inch (ten spaces) from the left margin but not indented on the right. In works cited entries, every line of an entry after the first is indented one-half inch from the left margin.

- *Sentence Spacing:* MLA style recommends using only one space after terminal punctuation marks (periods, question marks, and exclamation points), but your instructor may prefer two spaces, so ask.

- *Line Spacing:* The entire paper (with the exception of content footnotes, if you have them) should be double-spaced, including your heading; indented quotations (any quotations that are longer than four lines should be indented); any endnotes, tables and appendixes; and the works-cited page or any other source lists. Don't add extra spaces above or below titles or in between the works-cited entries.

- *Fastening:* Most instructors prefer that you fasten the pages with a single staple in the upper-left corner. Also, most instructors prefer that you do not use folders and report covers because they must be removed prior to reading when they grade your papers. It may not look as fancy, but a plain paper with a simple staple is typically what your instructor wants.

Many of these format elements will be easier for you to incorporate into your paper if you use a computer. In fact, some instructors will insist that you use a computer for your papers, not only because it is more efficient to do so, but also because computer literacy is a requirement for college and university students. Even if you do not own a computer, your school undoubtedly provides computers for student use.

Here is an image of a typical MLA paper's headers and first page. Use it as a reference for all general formatting details mentioned here.

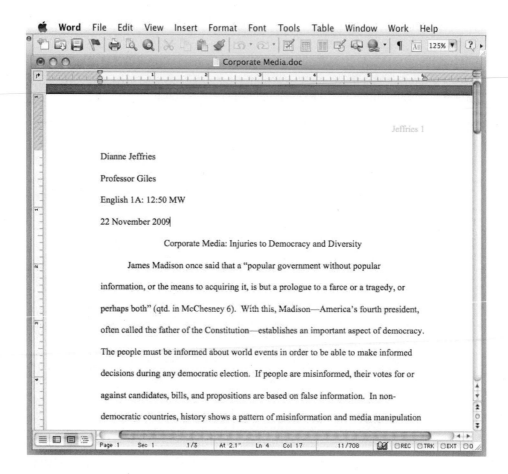

First Page

Title pages are no longer standard for research papers and other essays in MLA style. Instead, you will usually use a simple **personal and class identification heading** on the first page of your paper (see the image above), a **header,** and a **title** above the body of your paper.

Personal and Class Identification Heading

The heading should contain the following information, and, just like the rest of the document, it should be entirely double-spaced.

1. **Your full name.**
2. **Your professor's name.** The title "Professor" should precede his or her last name; don't use a first name.
3. **The name of the course.** Some professors who teach more than one section of the same course also want students to follow the course name with a colon

and the starting time and days abbreviated to the first letters, for example, English 1A: 10:30 MTW.

4. **The date the paper is due.** MLA has a specific format for listing the date. The day should precede the month, which should not be abbreviated.

For example: 8 September 2009

Header

In the upper-right corner of each page of your paper, you should provide a header that consists of your last name, a space, and the page number positioned one-half inch below the top of the page. This upper-right header must appear on every page of your paper. You should not try to create this header by simply typing it in what you judge to be the upper-right corner of each page, because if you add or delete any information, the header will no longer appear in the right place. Instead, you should learn how your particular word processing software handles headers. In virtually every word processor, there is a way to set your last name and auto-number the pages.

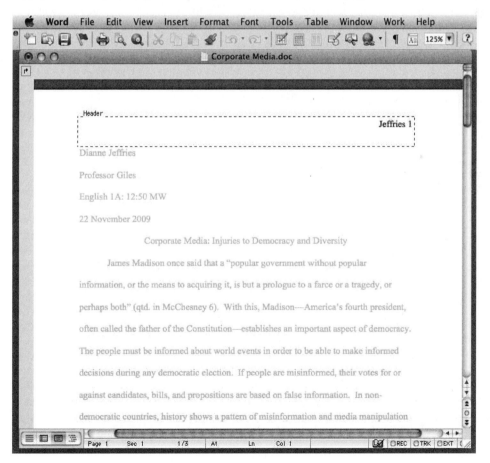

Title

The title of your essay should be carefully thought out and should indicate the topic and scope of your paper. Avoid, for example, titling your paper "Research Paper Number One." Your title should be double-spaced below the heading and centered (remember not to add an extra line—the distance between the last line of your heading and the title should be the same as the distance between each line of the heading and each line of the rest of the paper). Use the Center Alignment icon in your toolbar to properly center the title; do not simply hit the space bar until it looks like the title may be centered. The title should not be followed by a period, but you can end it with a question mark or an exclamation point. Don't italicize or underline your title or put it in bold type or within quotation marks. (However, if you use part of a work's title within your own title, it should be formatted properly.)

In MLA format, titles of books and journals are italicized or underlined, for instance, and titles of essays and poems are enclosed in quotation marks. MLA recommends italics over underlining. (Check with your instructor, though—many don't like students to use italics and would prefer the use of underlining instead because it can be clearer.) Capitalize all words except the following (unless they are the first words of a title or subtitle): articles (*a, an,* and *the*), prepositions, coordinating conjunctions, and the *to* in infinitives (as in "How to Capitalize Titles"). If your title is lengthy enough to go to two or more lines, use an inverted pyramid. Here is an example:

Gender Roles and Television: Changing Attitudes in the

United States, Great Britain, and Germany

Tables, Illustrations, and Appendixes

You may want to include photos, illustrations, tables, or graphs in your research paper. Generally, you should place tables and illustrations as close as possible to the sections of your paper that they augment, unless they are lengthy and would interrupt the flow of the paper. In that case, you can gather them together in one or more appendixes.

TABLES

For the heading of a table, follow the word *Table* with the appropriate Arabic numeral aligned at the left margin above the table, and add an explanatory caption on the next line, also aligned at the left margin, and capitalized the way you would a title (see the preceding section). As with all else in the paper, double-space the headings and the contents of the table. Follow the table with its source and any notes you add. Use dividing lines as necessary for clarity to set the table off from the caption and source information and any headings inside it from the figures that follow. Following is an example of an MLA-style table based on data collected from the sample student survey found in Chapter 2.

TABLE 1 Summary of Television Viewing Patterns Survey [a]

Question	Response
Hours of TV per day	4–7 Hours
TVs in Home	2–3
Persons in Home	3–4
Cable/Satellite Subscriptions	178
DVR Service Subscriptions	47
TV show DVD Rentals	111
Own TV shows on DVD	52

Source: Summary of Television Viewing Patterns Survey. Personal Survey. 18 October 2009.

[a] This graph represents a 250-person survey conducted over the course of one week on the campus of Bakersfield College. These numbers are the averages for the questions asked.

Fig. 1: "Light Classical" by Al Naso

ILLUSTRATIONS

Illustrations include drawings, maps, photographs, and other visuals and are referred to in your paper as Figures (abbreviated to Fig.). The label Fig. is followed by the appropriate Arabic numeral and an explanatory caption, and it appears below the illustration, as shown above. Source material and notes follow the caption.

APPENDIXES

"To append" means to add something as a supplement, and extra material added after the conclusion of the paper is placed inside *appendixes*. If you have numerous tables, illustrations, or other material, such as samples of questionnaires and their results or lists of interview questions, it is best to include them at the end of the paper. Each appendix should begin on a new page. Label each page with the word *Appendix* centered at the top, followed by the capital letter *A* for the first appendix, *B* for the second appendix, and so on. The appendix title should be treated just like the title of your paper: double-space the title above the appendix, and don't italicize or underline it or put it in bold type or within quotation marks. Don't include extra lines between the heading and the text of the appendix. The appendix itself should be double-spaced, just like the rest of the paper. Your table, illustration, or other material should appear below the heading, formatted just the way it would be if you had placed it within the body of your paper.

Footnotes and Endnotes

Parenthetical citations (see Chapter 7 on integrating sources into your writing) are used to identify the sources that you use in your paper and to direct your readers to the proper entries in your list of works cited, but you can use notes—either footnotes or endnotes—to provide additional information about your topic that you consider important or simply interesting, but that doesn't really fit anywhere in the body of your paper. Although such information may be worthwhile to your readers, it shouldn't interrupt the flow or logical organization of your paper. For example, if you're writing a paper about racial stereotyping in the early years of television, and you quote a source who uses the term "Uncle Tom," you could include a footnote that discusses the origin of the term in *Uncle Tom's Cabin,* an antislavery novel written by Harriet Beecher Stowe and published in book form in 1852. This information may not be directly relevant to your paragraph, but it is still interesting and informative. You can use either endnotes or footnotes to provide supplementary information or observations in MLA style. Ask if your instructor has a preference; if not, go with the endnotes, which are easier to format.

Footnotes and endnotes are numbered consecutively throughout a paper. Add the numbers in superscript. To do this, add the number at the end of the sentence you want to follow with a note, and highlight it. In the Format menu, click Font, and then click the Font tab. Select the Superscript check box. Your footnote or endnote will begin with the same number in superscript preceding it. Endnotes go on a page headed *Notes,* with the heading treated like any other title, and the page double-spaced. Indent each note a half-inch from the left margin, and begin it with the proper number in superscript. This page should follow the body of the paper and precede the works-cited page. Footnotes go at the bottom of pages within the paper, beginning two double spaces (four lines) below the text. They are the only items in your paper that should be single spaced, but if you have more than one footnote on a page, add an extra space between them. In the example that follows, note that the name James Madison in the first line has a raised number 1 next to it; this points to footnote 1 at the bottom of the page.

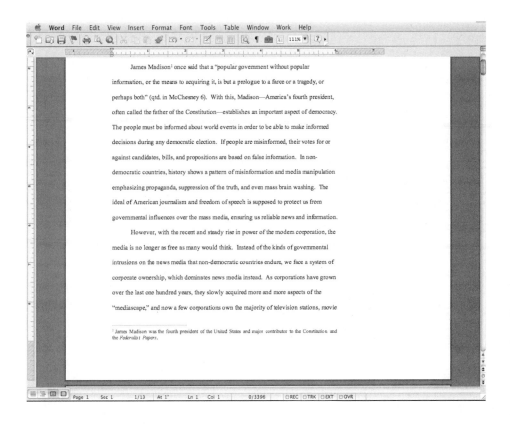

Corrections and Insertions

Sometimes you find a mistake in a paper after you have printed it out and typed it—at times, right before you are about to submit it. Ask your professor if brief corrections are allowed—many will say they are not. If so, write the corrections neatly in ink with a blue or black pen directly above the faulty word or words, using a caret (^) to indicate where the correction belongs. In the case of missing punctuation marks, add the mark where it belongs instead of adding it above the line with a caret. Even if your professor says that inserted corrections are acceptable, use them only for infrequent or minor corrections. If you have to make quite a few corrections, or if any of the corrections are large and detailed, retype the pages involved.

ANNOTATED SAMPLE MLA PAPER

We are closing this chapter with an annotated sample paper written by a student utilizing some of the sources that you'll find in this book. This sample paper will show you the correct format for an MLA-style paper, as well as showing how a student supports an argumentative thesis with documentation from credible sources, correctly attributed through in-text citations and a works cited page.

Jeffries   1

Dianne Jeffries

Professor Rupert Giles

English 1A: 12:50 MW

22 November 2009

Corporate Media: Injuries to Democracy and Diversity

James Madison once said that a "popular government

without popular information, or the means to acquiring it, is

but a prologue to a farce or a tragedy, or perhaps both" (qtd. in

McChesney 6). With this, Madison—America's fourth presi-

dent, often called the father of the Constitution—establishes an

important aspect of democracy. The people must be informed

about world events in order to be able to make informed deci-

sions during any democratic election. If people are misinformed,

their votes for or against candidates, bills, and propositions are

based on false information. In non-democratic countries, history

shows a pattern of misinformation and media manipulation

emphasizing propaganda, suppression of the truth, and even

mass brain washing. The ideal of American journalism and

freedom of speech is supposed to protect us from governmental

influences over the mass media, ensuring us reliable news and

information. However, with the recent and steady rise in power

of the modern corporation, the media is no longer as free as

Annotations (left margin):

The student's last name and page number appear as a header one-half inch from the top in the right corner of every page in the paper. Use the header function in your word processing program.

The paper's top, bottom, and left and right margins should be one inch.

The student's name, the professor's name, class name, and the date of submission appear in the upper-left corner. The day precedes the month in MLA format.

The title is centered and double-spaced. Colons set off subtitles. Do not add extra spaces above or below titles.

Opening the paper with a quotation helps to "hook" the reader and generate interest in the subject matter.

Use "qtd. in" for people quoted by your sources.

Dianne's introduction starts with broad statements that gradually reveal the paper's topic by getting more specific as we near the thesis.

many would think. Instead of the kinds of governmental intru-

sions on the news media that non-democratic countries endure,

we face a system of corporate ownership, which dominates

news media instead. As corporations have grown over the last

one hundred years, they slowly acquired more and more aspects

of the "mediascape," and now a few corporations own the

majority of television stations, movie studios, publishing houses,

and newspaper and magazine printing presses. Over time, the

American corporation has transformed from being just a busi-

ness model to the nation's most powerful force. Today, modern

corporations' power over the media has damaged democracy by

limiting public exposure to a diverse and comprehensive range

of information, perspectives, and analyses, even resulting in lies

and misinformation in the news media.

>   To begin an effective discussion of the corporate dam-

age to American democracy, a look at the evolution of the

corporate entity would be logical. Kalle Lasn, filmmaker and

creator and editor of the magazine *Adbusters,* a nonprofit

anti-consumerism organization, discusses the history of the

American corporation. He suggests that all of American his-

tory has been filled with oversized corporations, dating all

the way back to the Boston Tea Party and the dumping of the

Dianne's introduction is now getting very specific as the thesis nears.

The first paragraph ends with the paper's thesis state-ment, which clearly states the assertation that the paper aims to prove.

The second paragraph's topic sentence follows a transition sentence.

Dianne establishes this author's credentials here before paraphrasing him. Because this is the first men-tion of the author, she uses his whole name.

Jeffries   3

Citations don't need authors' last names if the name is in the sentence.

East India Tea Company's leaves into Boston Harbor (66). The events of the Tea Party made early Americans wary of corporate power, but as time went on, Americans forgot the lessons of the early colonies. Indeed, Lasn later discusses a change in this apprehension that came with the court case *Santa Clara County v. Southern Pacific Railroad* (a legal battle over a railroad route), in which the final outcome was "that a private corporation was a 'natural person' under the U.S. Constitution and therefore entitled to protection under the Bill of Rights" (68). This landmark ruling empowered the corporation, affording them all the legal rights of a human being, and it led to the modern era.

Because Lasn was already fully introduced above, Dianne only needed to use his last name at this point.

During this modern era of the corporation, these companies gained increasing wealth, power, and influence. Lasn argues that corporations "merged, consolidated, restructured and metamorphosed into ever larger and more complex units of resource extraction, production, distribution and marketing, to the point where many of them became economically more powerful than many countries" (69). Here, Lasn suggests that now corporations not only share the same rights as any American citizen, but the largest and most powerful have greater wealth than many smaller nations. The court

Discussion of the quotation helps give the readers a critical context for the material.

Jeffries   4

ruling in *Santa Clara County v. Southern Pacific Railroad*
is what slowly let these once small businesses grow to be
modern-day financial powerhouses. However, the recession
of the 1980s slowed down corporate growth.

Indeed, in the 1980s, the financial recession caused a
slump in production and purchases for the American public.
Naomi Klein, media activist and author of the influential
book on advertising, *No Logo,* suggests that in the 1980s,

> A consensus emerged that corporations were bloated,
>
> oversized; they owned too much, employed too many
>
> people, and were weighted down by *too many things.*
>
> The very process of producing—running one's own
>
> factories, being responsible for tens of thousands
>
> of full-time, permanent employees—began to look
>
> less like the route to success and more like a clunky
>
> liability. (4)

Thus, in order to avoid this "clunky liability," corporations
needed to change how they made money.

Instead of making money by selling a quality product,
corporations started to practice "branding." Branding is
when a corporation makes the identity of a certain brand

Transitional sentences at the end of paragraphs introduce topic sentences in the following paragraphs.

Because this quotation was over four lines long, Dianne followed MLA guidelines by indenting the quotation one inch from the left margin and omitting the quotation marks.

name (such as Coke, Nike, or The Gap) become synony-

mous with high quality, luxury, or just "being cool." This

branding worked better than anyone could have ever hoped

and seemed to end the financial woes that the recession

brought to corporate America. Klein discusses this corporate

success story:

> The astronomical growth in the wealth and cultural influ-
>
> ence of multinational corporations over the last fifteen
>
> years can arguably be traced back to a single, seemingly
>
> innocuous idea developed by management theorists in
>
> the mid-1980s: that successful corporations must prima-
>
> rily produce brands, as opposed to products. (1)

When corporations focused on enhancing their brands

instead of manufacturing products, as Klein suggests, they

started making record earnings and grew in power and

stature. Making a high-quality burger that tasted good did

not sell nearly as well as selling the notion of "cool" or by

convincing the audience that they are indeed "loving it," as

McDonald's suggests in their highly successful ad campaign.

Brand loyalty proved far more successful for the corporation

than high-quality products seemed to.

Dianne takes time to discuss her own interpretations of this outside material to help prove her current argument.

Jeffries   6

With cunning marketing that makes citizens loyal to a
brand, and with artifical entities having the same rights as a
real human being, corporations have grown enough to dominate everything from what we eat to what we watch and read
and even think. Several corporations have gotten so large
that they've been able to buy an almost endless number of
smaller corporations, helping to secure their financial might
and cultural influence. Ben Bagdikian, author of several
books about the modern media system, discusses many of
the major corporations, which he calls media conglomerates.
In his 1983 book *The Media Monopoly,* he showed that at the
time only fifty corporations controlled a huge majority of all
American news media. By 2003 (and his completely revised
and updated edition of this book, called *The New Media
Monopoly*) just five of these corporations—Time Warner,
Disney, Viacom/CBS, News Corp, and Bertelsmann—
controlled most of the media in the United States.

Indeed, in 2003, these five corporations were controlled
by just five men: Richard Parsons, head of Time Warner;
Michael Eisner, head of Disney; Sumner Redstone, head of
Viacom; Rupert Murdoch, head of News Corps (and current
owner of the *Wall Street Journal*); and Reinhard Mohn, a

> Use colons to introduce sen-
> tence elements only if they fol-
> low independent clauses.

man who had deceived the public about his company's Nazi history (Bagdikian, *New* 27–28). These conglomerates have merged and bought out every type of information technology possible—magazines, newspapers, websites, cable networks, even Internet service providers and the physical infrastructure of satellite systems and phone lines. If there is a way to get information about our world, odds are these conglomerates own it, and that is where free speech—and its corollary, free, accurate, and uncensored information—becomes limited for citizens.

This is the format for a citation for two or more works by the same author. The author's last name is followed by a comma and the first important word or words of the title of the work.

Also, while discussing the media conglomerates, Bagdikian argues that they have dealt a blow to our democracy. He states that since the "majority of Americans say they get their news, commentary and daily entertainment from this handful of conglomerates, the conglomerates fail the needs of democracy every day. Our modern democracy depends not just on laws and the Constitution, but a vision of the real nature of the United States and its people" ("Grand" par. 1–2). Here, Bagdikian shows that a free flow of information is essential to running a true democracy, but the conglomerates don't really want us to have access to a free flow of information because a completely informed population might be less

In a citation for a second source by the same author, the first important word of the article title enclosed in quotations is sufficient since the author's name is in the sentence. Numbers indicate the paragraph of an electronic source.

Jeffries   8

likely to buy the same products or sit by in ignorance while corporate lobbyists get politicians to push through laws that benefit corporations but hurt consumers. Most major media are owned by corporations, with the biggest ones absorbing smaller competitors, giving tremendous power to a few companies with holdings in a variety of industries, so conflicts of interest interfere with investigative journalism and accurate, fearless reporting. Clearly, as these conglomerates are allowed to grow, our access to information continually shrinks, but Bagdikian is not the only scholar to think so.

> Reminder of thesis statement.

Another scholar of the media is Robert McChesney. McChesney, author of eight books and over 200 articles on media ownership, was perhaps the first to worry about the threat to democracy due to media ownership. McChesney argues that three different areas are crucial to a healthy participatory self-government.

- Lack of extreme gaps between the rich and poor of a nation
- Feeling of kinship on the part of citizens to their communities
- Reliable and honest systems of political communication through the mass media (5).

> Often bullets, charts, illustrations, or other visual elements help to make information easier to digest.

Of these three areas, McChesney seems to argue that the third category—an effective system of political communication—is the most important and most at risk in our culture. Quite simply, without a reliable method of public communication, free speech is severely hampered.

In fact, in his book (appropriately titled *Corporate Media and the Threat to Democracy*), McChesney suggests that

> the commercial basis of U.S. media has negative implications for the exercise of political democracy: it encourages a weak political culture that makes depoliticization, apathy and selfishness rational choices for the citizenry, and it permits the business and commercial interests that actually rule U.S. society to have inordinate influence over media content . . . for those committed to democracy, it is imperative to reform the media system. (7)

In this quotation, McChesney not only shows the negative impact of the media conglomerates, he even posits that someone who is truly dedicated to democracy and free speech must explore ways to change things. One government body is indeed doing some fact finding to try to find a way to change

Dianne continues to discuss her quotations and tie them back in to her own arguments.

Jeffries   10

things in favor of the citizens, and that is the Federal Commu-

nications Commission.

The FCC's primary function is to manage and safeguard

the American airwaves (and net connections), ensuring that the

public airwaves are still owned and run by and for the people

and ensuring that free speech is not only possible, but strong

and viable. In the fall of 2006, the FCC held a public hear-

ing at the University of Southern California on the topic of

regulations in corporate media ownership. They held an open

discussion with the public to get feedback on what the people

felt about the media conglomerates. In his opening statement

at these proceedings, one of the five FCC commissioners,

Jonathan Adelstein, claimed that "there should be no disagree-

ment that our media ownership proceeding is, fundamentally,

about one thing: *our democracy*" (par. 2). Adelstein also says

that "central to our American democracy is the 'uninhibited

marketplace of ideas,' where everyone is able to exchange and

share music, news, information and entertainment program-

ming over the public airwaves" (par. 2). However, with a few

major corporations owning so many media outlets, everyone

is not able to participate in the "marketplace of ideas" and

share music, news, or information that is important to them.

> When electronic sources number the paragraphs, provide the abbreviation for "paragraph" followed by the number.

Instead, we are all forced to watch, listen to, and read very few corporate-generated ideas such as an endless regurgitation of similar reality shows, rehashes of the same tired situation comedies, and shallow or biased news reports. This lack of media diversity harms McChesney's second key to democracy, an important connection to community. Many minority voices are never heard in this corporate media environment, so the sense of "community" may not be strong enough.

> The paragraph ends with a sentence that serves to tie this argument back to the earlier argument about McChesney.

Another FCC commissioner is also concerned with how the lack of unique voices can break down a community. In his own opening statements to the 2006 public hearing, Commissioner Michael J. Copps asks if he and others actually have access to the public airwaves—can regular citizens actually get a show or advertisement aired, or will we be priced out of the market by multi-billion dollar corporations? (par. 7) After asking this question, Copps emphasized a very important point—that the airwaves are *public* airwaves. "They belong to you and me and every other person in this country, not to any corporation or conglomerate. We allow broadcasters to use the airwaves—for free—in return for offering programs that serve the public interest" (par. 7). Copps indicates here that there is a dichotomy. Though the

Jeffries   12

public airwaves belong to the citizenry, they are entirely

dominated by corporate interests bent on gaining advertising

revenue, not serving the needs of the people. Thus, the cor-

porations own the capability to communicate and speak to

the masses, and our own power of free speech and diversity

are severely limited.

In spite of this corporate stranglehold on information,

however, there is one way that we can still get important

news stories on a variety of issues. We can look at "watchdog

groups," which monitor the media. Project Censored is a na-

tional research effort begun in 1976 in the Communications

Studies Department at Sonoma State University. It compares

the news published in independent media with the news

covered by the mainstream, corporate-owned media. Every

year, Project Censored creates a list of twenty-five significant

news stories "that have been overlooked, under-reported or

self-censored by the country's major national news media"

(*Project Censored*). They publish the stories in a yearbook

and on the Internet at their website.

Stories that the project spotlighted as important news

ignored by corporate media include "Factories, Cities Across

USA Exceed Water Pollution Limits" by Sunny Lewis of the

Dianne provides a citation for a web page because the site didn't have individual article titles.

Jeffries   13

Environment News Service. This story revealed that between July 2003 and December 2004, "More than 62 percent of industrial and municipal facilities across the country discharged more pollution into U.S. waterways than their Clean Water Act permits, and "The average facility discharged pollution in excess of its permit limit by more than 275 percent, or almost four times the legal limit" (qtd. in *Project Censored*). This discrepancy between fact and reported news shows that the corporations that own the media do not want the public to get too upset about corporate poisoning of drinking water.

A particularly disturbing 2003 story that Project Censored highlighted and that was perhaps understandably ignored by mainstream media is one that revealed that a Florida court ruled that media can legally lie. Two investigators were hired by Fox News at WTVT in Florida for a story on bovine growth hormone (BGH), which is manufactured by Monsanto Corporation. According to Project Censored, the "couple produced a four-part series revealing that there were many health risks related to BGH and that Florida supermarket chains did little to avoid selling milk from cows treated with the hormone, despite assuring customers otherwise"

> Though this source was written by Lewis, the citation is for Project Censored because Project Censored is the source found in the works-cited page.

Jeffries   14

(*Project Censored*). Monsanto pressured Fox to revise the
story and include false statements as facts; Fox told the reporters to change the story to fit Monsanto's demands. They
were fired when they refused. When the reporters sued Fox
for being wrongfully fired,

> FOX asserted that there are no written rules against
>
> distorting news in the media. They argued that, under
>
> the First Amendment, broadcasters have the right to lie
>
> or deliberately distort news reports on public airwaves.
>
> Fox attorneys did not dispute Akre's claim that they
>
> pressured her to broadcast a false story, they simply
>
> maintained that it was their right to do so. (*Project*
>
> *Censored*)

This Florida case shows that major broadcasters are not
only capable of telling lies to the public through their own
airwaves, but they are actually lying. Though a Florida
jury ruled in favor of one of the reporters, an appeals court
overturned the ruling, and Fox won the legal battle. This is
not a story that Fox itself or any other corporate media outlet
showcased; such a story might shake the public's belief that
they are being correctly served by big media.

Dianne connects her example
to her thesis statement.

There are other problems with corporations' priorities for the public. Corporate news media is increasingly looking more like entertainment than news. Jake Halpern authored a book called *Fame Junkies,* which is about Americans' supposed obsession with celebrities. In an article in the *Wall Street Journal* (which has since been bought by Rupert Murdoch's News Corporation), Halpern provided statistics that included the fact that in 2004, the three major news networks gave Martha Stewart five times more news coverage than they gave the genocide in Darfur, and that CNN's coverage of Britney Spears when she lost custody of her children was three times greater than its coverage of the war in Iraq (Halpern). Ironically, Halpern was scheduled to appear on CNN that day to discuss his book, but when he arrived, he was told that his interview had been cancelled. When he inquired about what had happened, he was asked, "Didn't you hear, Britney Spears just lost custody of her kids?" (Halpern). An author being bumped for a celebrity may not be very disturbing, but the amount of time the public is being fed stories about Britney Spears, Martha Stewart, Lindsay Lohan, and Paris Hilton is disturbing.

Jeffries   16

One might ask, why is this disturbing if this is what

people want to hear? One answer would be that it takes

time away from genuine news. For every Paris Hilton story,

one can only imagine what stories get cut from the air. The

question this raises is, are we getting a constant stream of

stories about celebrity scandals because it really is what

the American public wants to hear? A 2007 study by the

Pew Research Center for People and the Press says no. This

study looked at 165 separate national surveys and found that

celebrity scandal ranks lowest among all news preferences

("Two Decades"). This statistic helps to prove that the people

are tired of watching the same tired stories about celebri-

ties in trouble, but it dominates the airwaves because it is

cheap, easy, and helps fill the need for twenty-four hours of

information being broadcast on cable networks. However,

when critical news about things as important as genocide get

less air time than a story about Martha Stewart, the corpo-

rate control of the media truly fails to serve the needs of the

American public.

Serving the needs of the people should be of paramount

importance to every citizen in our mediated world, however,

not simply the financial bottom line of corporate America.

> Rhetorical questions can serve as effective transition sentences.

Jeffries   17

A conclusion should clearly remind the readers of the paper's thesis statement and the arguments that support it.

Corporations used to be manageable and closely monitored by the people and the government. The current corporate dominance of the airwaves, though, undermines our ability to stay well informed, feel a sense of community, and therefore fully participate in our own democratic government. We cannot let corporations control and limit what we know about our own country and the rest of the world. As President Madison, one of the fathers of this democracy, said, "popular government without popular information, or the means to acquiring it, is but a prologue to a farce or a tragedy, or perhaps both" (qtd. in McChesney 6). If the corporations become the ultimate gatekeepers of the powers of mass communication, our own ability to engage in true free speech and to have complete access to the information we need to make truly informed decisions about everything from our health to the leaders we elect will be only a farce or a tragedy as Madison predicted.

Ending the paper with the same quotation it opened with helps Dianne to provide a stronger sense of closure by coming "full circle."

Jeffries   18

Works Cited

Adelstein, Jonathan S. Statement. Broadcast Media Ownership Public Hearing, University of Southern California. 3 Oct. 2006. Print.

All entries on the works-cited page are in alphabetical order, and everything is double-spaced.

In each entry, every line after the first line is indented.

Bagdikian, Ben. "Grand Theft: The Conglomeratization of

Media and the Degradation of Culture: Twenty-Five Years

of Monitoring the Multinationals." *Multinational Monitor*

26. 1–2 (Jan.–Feb. 2005): 35–7. *Expanded Academic ASAP*.

Thomson Gale. Web. 19 Oct. 2008.

---. *The New Media Monopoly*. Boston: Beacon, 2004. Print.

Copps, Michael, J. Broadcast Media Ownership Public

Hearing, University of Southern California. 3 Oct. 2006.

Remarks.

Halpern, Jake. "Britney Spears, 'Breaking News.'" *Wall Street

Journal Online*. 4 Oct. 2007. Web. 18 Oct. 2009.

Klein, Naomi. *No Logo: Taking Aim at the Brand Bullies*. New

York: Picador, 1999. Print.

Lasn, Kalle. *Culture Jam: The Uncooling of America*. New York:

Eagle Brook, 1999. Print.

McChesney, Robert W. *Corporate Media and the Threat to

Democracy*. The Open Media Pamphlet Series. New York:

Seven Stories, 1997. Print.

Project Censored. Sonoma State University. Web. 2 Nov. 2009.

"Two Decades of American News Preferences." Pew Center

Publications. 22 Aug. 2007. Web. 2 Nov. 2009.

Here, Dianne uses three hyphens to indicate that this is the second source written by Bagdikian and used in this paper.

Shorten the names of publishers to the first important word or words, omitting words like *Publishers* and *Press*. (See separate guidelines for university presses.)

When there is no author, alphabetize an entry by the first important word of the title.

Creating MLA-Style Parenthetical Citations

WHEN YOU SHOULD USE PARENTHETICAL CITATIONS

Whether you are writing a paper in MLA or APA format, you need to indicate the sources that you use each time you take information from any of them and, in the case of most print sources, the page numbers the information comes from. MLA- and APA-style papers use **parenthetical in-text citations** rather than footnotes or endnotes for publication information. You must cite all the nonfiction sources used within research papers and other essays, whether paraphrased, summarized, or directly quoted, unless the material cited is considered "common knowledge." In-text citations are also used in MLA-style papers discussing literary works to identify the page numbers for direct quotations from these works of literature. (If you are writing about literature, you need in-text citations only for direct quotations from the work, not for summaries of the plot, character descriptions, and other comments about what takes place in the fictional world.)

In-text citations don't stand alone, of course. The first word in a parenthetical citation, usually the last name of an author or the first important word or words of a work without an author listed, must correspond to the first words that begin the entries on your lists of sources used at the end of the paper. This way, your readers can easily locate the full publication and other relevant information for each source that you used in your paper. MLA-style papers usually call these lists Works Cited if you include citations only for material you used or Works Consulted if you also include citations for material you read for background but didn't actually incorporate into your paper (see Chapter 13). APA papers usually call these lists References (see Chapter 14).

Remember that you must document *all* ideas you take from nonfiction sources and use in your research papers, not just direct quotations. If you fail to do so, you are plagiarizing. (For more information on how to recognize and avoid plagiarism, see Chapter 9.)

PLACEMENT OF PARENTHETICAL CITATIONS

Place a citation as close to the quoted, paraphrased, or summarized material as possible without disrupting the sentence. When material from one source and the same page numbers is used throughout a paragraph, use one citation at the end of the paragraph rather than a citation at the end of each sentence. However, if you have added your own thoughts inside the paragraph, you need multiple citations to distinguish between your source's ideas and your own.

In most cases, a parenthetical citation includes the author's last name and the specific page number for the information cited, or just the page number if the author is clearly identified elsewhere in the sentence, but there are also many instances when you need to include additional information in your citation. The following section gives you the guidelines for MLA in-text citations, including use of authors' names, placement of citations, and treatment of electronic sources. (For APA guidelines on in-text citations, see Chapter 14.)

1. Author's Name Given in Your Sentence

2. Author's Name Not Given in Your Sentence

3. More Than One Work by the Same Author

4. Two Authors with the Same Last Name

5. Two or Three Authors

6. Four or More Authors

7. No Author Provided

8. Sacred Texts and Commonly Studied Literature

9. Sources Quoting Other Works

10. Indented Quotations

11. Quotations Within Quotations

12. Information from More Than One Source

13. Work in an Anthology

14. Online and Other Electronic Sources

15. Other Nonprint Sources

1. AUTHOR'S NAME GIVEN IN YOUR SENTENCE

Often in writing, you will introduce the author before giving the actual quotation, summary, or paraphrase. In such cases, you need include only the page numbers in your parenthetical citation. The reader will be able to find the author's name in your sentence and on the works-cited page because you have given it in your text. In the parentheses, do not use the abbreviation "p" or "page" before the number; simply give the number by itself. In the following examples, the author is citing an author with the last name of Zipes. Because the author is mentioned in the text of this paper, his name does not need to appear in the parentheses with the page numbers. Notice that the sentences' periods follow the citations; they do not directly follow the sentences themselves. When you are quoting directly, the closing quotation mark should precede the citation. See the following examples.

Paraphrased material:

> Zipes argues that we really cannot absolutely separate the oral, folkloric fairy tale from the literary fairy tale because we cannot trace stories to their origins (222).

Quoted material:

> Zipes states that "This is an impossible task because there are very few if any records with the exception of paintings, drawings, etchings, inscriptions and other cultural artifacts that reveal how tales were told and received thousands of years ago" (222).

You may want to quote the same source more than once in a single paragraph in your paper. As long as you do not include any quotations from other sources in between, you can use one parenthetical citation after the last quotation.

> "Austen's irony is both worldly and unworldly, finding nothing to be surprised at in human immorality, but nothing to be cynically indulged about it either." Her irony is subtle and put to the task of defending the cultural and moral status quo. "One should not be misled by Austen's good-natured irony into imagining that she is, in the modern sense of the word, a liberal" (Eagleton 107, 108).

2. AUTHOR'S NAME NOT GIVEN IN YOUR SENTENCE

If you choose not to provide the name of the author in your own sentence, you will need to provide the name in your parenthetical citation. Without this information, your audience will not be able to identify the correct entry for the source on your works-cited page. In this case, provide the name and a space and then the page number.

Paraphrased material:

> Following the Thomas-Hill hearings, sexual harassment became an issue of greater importance to the American public (Mayer and Abramson 352).

Quoted material:

> "But it may have been inside the Senate itself that the hearings left their most lasting impression" (Mayer and Abramson 352–53).

3. MORE THAN ONE WORK BY THE SAME AUTHOR

If you are citing more than one work by an individual author, include the first important word or words (don't use *a, an,* and *the*) of the title of the work you are citing in addition to the author's name and relevant page number(s). Remember to underline or use quotation marks around the title as appropriate. Separate the author's name—if you need it in the citation—and the title with a comma:

> "The term 'neoliberalism' suggests a system of principles that is both new and based on classical liberal ideas: Adam Smith is revered as the patron saint" (Chomsky, *Profit* 19).

4. TWO AUTHORS WITH THE SAME LAST NAME

If the document uses two sources by authors with the same last name, include each author's first name in the text or the parenthetical citation. In the following example, Martin Amis is talking about his father, novelist Kingsley Amis, whose works are also included in the paper:

> "In retrospect I can see that these questions would have played on my father's deepest fears" (Amis, Martin 3).

5. TWO OR THREE AUTHORS

If the work you are citing has two or three authors, use all their last names, even if two or more of them share a last name. If you are citing three authors, be sure you separate each name with a comma and use *and* before the last name in the list. Always keep the authors in the order in which they are listed in their book.

> "It would be a mistake to underestimate the significance of *Frankenstein*'s title page, with its allusive subtitle" (Gilbert and Gubar 224).

> "Even the most casual assessment of the daily flow of news reveals a complex tapestry of issues and events" (Neuman, Just, and Crigler 39).

6. FOUR OR MORE AUTHORS

If a source has four or more authors, there are two ways you can write the citation. First, you can include the first author's last name followed by *et al.* (an abbreviation of the Latin phrase *et alli,* meaning "and others") either in the text or in the parenthetical citation:

> "And some essayists are not out to change the world at all: some are completely indifferent to immediate circumstances or practical ends" (Scholes et al.3).

> Scholes et al. point out that "some essayists are not out to change the world at all: some are completely indifferent to immediate circumstances or practical ends" (3).

You can also name all the authors:

> "And some essayists are not out to change the world at all: some are completely indifferent to immediate circumstances or practical ends" (Scholes, Klaus, Comley, and Silverman 3).

> Scholes, Klaus, Comley, and Silverman point out that "some essayists are not out to change the world at all: some are completely indifferent to immediate circumstances or practical ends" (3).

7. NO AUTHOR PROVIDED

If a source does not include an author's name, substitute for the author's name the title or a shortened form of the title in the text or a parenthetical citation. You can use the first important word or more; the idea is to give as short a form of the title as you can without risking it being confused with a similar title beginning an entry on your works-cited page. Format the title words the same way they are formatted on the works-cited page; if the title is in quotation marks on that page, it must be treated the same way in the citation, and so on.

> The term *annus horribilis* means "horrible year," and it was brought into somewhat popular use after Queen Elizabeth II publicly used it to describe the year that her sons' respective marriages foundered and Windsor Castle caught fire (*Latin* 13).

8. SACRED TEXTS AND COMMONLY STUDIED LITERATURE

Commonly studied works of literature and sacred texts are reprinted in many editions, so you can help your readers by providing more information than the page number from your edition. With prose works of literature, such as novels, novellas, and plays, giving a chapter number or an act number will make it possible for your audience to easily find a quotation even if they have a different edition of the work than you do. Start with the author's last name unless it is clearly indicated before the quotation, follow with the page number (with no comma between them), and then add a semicolon and the supplemental information. Use the abbreviations *pt.* for part, *ch.* for chapter, *bk.* for book, *sec.* for section. If your source doesn't have page numbers, this information is especially important.

> Jude and Sue are shocked and horrified when they discover the hanged bodies of their three children. Grief-stricken, they realize that the eldest child killed his siblings and then himself, leaving a note which reads, "Done because we are too menny" (Hardy 331; pt. 6, sec. 2).

Commonly studied poems and verse plays don't need page numbers in citations. Instead, give the numbers of the works' divisions—such as books, parts, cantos, acts, and scenes—followed by the numbers of the lines, separated by a period. If you are using a line number, precede it by *line*. Use arabic numerals unless your instructor requests Roman numerals (some professors prefer Roman numerals for the acts and scenes in plays).

> Hamlet's disgust manifests itself once again when, in a speech to Rosencrantz and Guildenstern, he describes the sky as "A foul and pestilent congregation of vapors" (2.2.311).

> In Eliot's "The Love Song of J. Alfred Prufrock," the narrator exclaims, "No! I am not Prince Hamlet, nor was meant to be" (line 111).

With sacred texts, just as with other works, you need to clearly indicate in your paper how your readers can find the appropriate entry on your works-cited page. Indicate the word that begins the entry on the works-cited list, either in the parenthetical citation or in your paper. This could be the last name of the editor of a critical edition, the first important word of the title of the section you use, or the important first word or words of the entire text.

> "[Amos] is unique in opening with a motto, a short, general thematic statement that is meant to (re)focus how the book should be understood" (Berlin and Brettler 1177).

> "In the beginning / The Universe was the Self, / Pure Consciousness, alone" (Upanishads 211).

9. SOURCES QUOTING OTHER WORKS

If your source quotes someone else, indicate that person's name in your sentence, and put your source's name inside the citation preceded by the abbreviation for "quoted in."

> Janet Smith pointed out that "the Grimms did not refrain from changing stories when it suited their purposes" (qtd. in Tatar 321).

10. LONG QUOTATIONS

When you use a direct quotation in your paper that is four full lines or longer (in your paper, not the original source you're reading), you need to set off the quotation and indent it. The following list gives the proper format for a long quotation.

- Indent the entire quotation one inch or ten spaces, roughly the length of two standard tabs. This will be twice the indentation of your typical paragraphs.
- Double-space the quotation, just like the rest of the paper.
- Do not change fonts or type sizes for a long quotation.
- Do not use quotation marks. The indentation, instead of quotation marks, will indicate that this is a quotation.
- The end punctuation precedes the parenthetical citation instead of following it.

Following is an example. (Note that the sentence that introduces the quotation is the beginning of a new paragraph, so it is already indented one-half inch. The quotation is indented a full inch to indicate it is a long quotation.) As in a shorter quotation, because Jack Zipes is named in the sentence, his name need not appear within the citation. The sentence that introduces the quotation ends with a colon.

> Jack Zipes disputes the approach used by many folklore scholars:
>
> > For the past three hundred years or more scholars and critics have sought to define and classify the oral folk tale and the literary fairy tale, as though they could be clearly distinguished from one another, and as though we could trace their origins to some primeval source. This is an impossible task because there are very few if any records with the exception of paintings, drawings, etchings, inscriptions and other cultural artifacts that reveal how tales were told and received thousands of years ago. (222)

11. QUOTATIONS WITHIN QUOTATIONS

Enclose quoted material (or titles that require quotation marks) that is within other quoted material within single quotation marks (use the apostrophe key) unless the material takes up more than four lines in your paper. Because you omit quotation marks when you indent lengthy quotations, you can use regular double quotation marks for quotations inside longer quotations because they won't cause confusion about where the larger quotation ends.

> According to David Riggs, "During that same summer of 1592, Robert Greene famously attacked Shakespeare as an 'upstart Crow, beautified with our feathers,' much as Nashe had attacked Kyd three years previously" (282).

12. INFORMATION FROM MORE THAN ONE SOURCE

If you have information that comes from different sources, indicate them all.

> Women across the social spectrum shared and modified fairy tales (Smith 172, Warner 316–17).

13. WORK IN AN ANTHOLOGY

For quotations or other information taken from works you get from an anthology (a collection of works, usually by different authors), make sure that you list the last name of the author of the work, not the editor of the anthology. The author's name will come before the editor's name in the works-cited page. For example, an essay by Edwin C. Baker, called "Implications of Rival Visions of Electoral Campaigns," is in a book titled *Mediated Politics: Communication in the Future of Democracy,* which is edited by Lance W. Bennett and Robert M. Entman. If you used information from this essay, you would provide Baker's name in your citation, followed by the page number.

> "Both our electoral process and our media coverage of elections are a disgrace" (Baker 342).

If you used Baker's name in your sentence, all you would need is the page number.

14. ONLINE AND OTHER ELECTRONIC SOURCES

In-text citations for online and other electronic sources, such as email, are treated much as those for print texts are; you need to provide the authors' last names if you have them and the important words of titles if you do not. The only real difference occurs because electronic texts do not usually have page numbers. If you try to assign page numbers for an online article that you print out yourself, you cannot be sure that the page numbers would be the same if someone else printed out the same article from a different browser and using a different printer. In general, you should give page numbers only when you have found an article or other work that is reprinted in PDF format, because the page numbers provided will be the same as the print version of the source.

Sometimes numbered paragraphs appear in an electronic source. In such cases, you may use the paragraph numbers. The paragraph number should appear in your citation. After the author's name, you should include a comma and the abbreviation *par.*

If you give the name of the author in your sentence, you can actually omit an in-text citation when you have no numbers to put in the parentheses; your audience can find all the publication information on the works-cited page by locating the author's name at the beginning of the bibliographic entry.

> "The CIA's Publications Review Board has expressly forbidden Valerie Plame to reveal details of her past at the Agency in her upcoming memoir, saying that she can't even say she worked for them" (Douglas).

> "The CIA's Publications Review Board has expressly forbidden Valerie Plame to reveal details of her past at the Agency in her upcoming memoir, saying that she can't even say she worked for them" (Douglas, par. 6)

Nick Douglas reports that "The CIA's Publications Review Board has expressly forbidden Valerie Plame to reveal details of her past at the Agency in her upcoming memoir, saying that she can't even say she worked for them."

15. OTHER NONPRINT SOURCES

As with online and other electronic sources, use an author's name if one is available or the title of the work if one is not—the point to remember is that you must give the information that your readers need to find the proper entry in the alphabetized list of works cited. If you have used a director's name as the first word in an entry about a film, that name is what you must use in your citation. If you use the title of the film as your first word, that title is what you should use. If you have taken information from a lecture or speech, include the name of the lecturer or speaker.

"Toto, I've got a feeling we're not in Kansas anymore" (Fleming).

"Toto, I've got a feeling we're not in Kansas anymore" (*Wizard*).

L. Frank Baum's *The Wizard of Oz* has been regarded as an American fairy tale, and the 1939 film version, directed by Victor Fleming, has become iconic (Powell).

Preparing the MLA List
of Works Cited

A bibliography is a list of sources that you compile while researching a paper. MLA-style papers usually call these lists Works Cited if you include citations only for material you used or Works Consulted if you also include citations for material you read for background but didn't actually incorporate into your paper (see Chapter 13). APA papers usually call these lists References (see Chapter 14). There are also Annotated Bibliographies, which include annotations (brief summaries that may also include evaluations) after each entry on a list of sources. (See the explanation and examples at the end of this chapter.) For simplicity's sake, we will refer to all bibliographical citations as works-cited entries—the format is the same, no matter what you call the list itself. Following is the directory of the different examples of works-cited entries in this chapter.

DIRECTORY OF SAMPLE WORKS-CITED ENTRIES

ARRANGEMENT OF ENTRIES ON THE WORKS-CITED PAGE

MLA guidelines require that you arrange all the entries on your works-cited page alphabetically, no matter what type of source you are using. Begin with the author's name, inverting the first and last names. If a source has more than one author, invert only the name of the first author because that is the only name relevant to alphabetizing the entry. You should treat authors' names exactly as they appear on the title page of the source you're citing; do not use their initials unless that is how their names appear on the title page. Do not include titles and degrees, such as Dr. or PhD, when you name the authors on the works-cited page.

Often you will have to look at more than one example to create a citation. For instance, you may be creating a works-cited page and realize that you not only have two essays by the same author, but both essays also have translators. Also, the essays appeared in periodicals, not books. You aren't going to find a single example with each of those factors here—and you probably wouldn't find it in any other stylebook or text, either. No one can give you every possible combination, so you have to look at instructions in different categories and at more than one example. In the fourth and seventh categories in the section on books, we show you what to do when you have more than one work by an author and when you have a translated work. You would need to take information from both of those categories and also from the section on periodicals to create the correct citations.

WORKS-CITED ENTRIES FOR BOOKS, WORKS IN BOOKS, AND PLAYS

The basic book entry is probably the most common type of entry you will ever include in a works-cited list. Basic entries for published plays look just the same. All the information you need to complete this type of works-cited entry is provided on the title page of the book or on its copyright page, which generally follows the title page (see sample on next page). Typically, the title page provides the title and subtitle of the book, the author(s), and even the city and publishing house. On the copyright page, you'll find the full publication information: the address of the publishing company, ISBN number, Library of Congress Subject Headings, copyright dates, and most recent year of publication. Learn to mine these opening pages for all your works-cited information.

The following list indicates most possible components for a basic book entry:

1. **Author:** Begin with the author's name (first and last names reversed), followed by a period. If there is a middle name or initial, it should follow the first name. In the case of pseudonyms, you may add an author's real name in brackets in between the pen name and the period (for example, Genêt [Janet Flanner]). You can also follow initials with the full name in brackets for clarification (for example, Eliot, T[homas] S[terns]), but this is generally not considered necessary. If there is more than one author, put *and* before the last author's name, and a comma after the preceding author even if there are only two authors. Only reverse the first and last names of the first author listed.

2. **Title:** Next, you'll give the title, italicized or underlined. If a question mark or exclamation point is part of the title, italicize or underline it with the rest of the title, but do not italicize or underline the period after the title. If there is a subtitle, it should be set off from the title with a colon. End with a period unless a question mark or exclamation point is part of the title.

3. **Translator:** If the book has been translated, use the abbreviation "Trans." after the title, followed by the name of the translator. (If other information is relevant, such as the editor of a critical edition, an introduction by another author, or an illustrator, present the names in the order given on the book's title page).

4. **Edition:** Indicate the edition after the title, abbreviated, but *only* if the book is not a first edition or it is a critical or revised edition.

5. **City of Publication:** Give the city in which the book was published next (the first one listed if more than one city is named on the title page). Do not give the state, province, or country unless the city is not well known or could be confused with another city with the same name (for example, "Paris, TX"). Follow the city's name with a colon.

6. **Publisher:** Provide the name of the publisher, shortened to the most important word if it is not a university press. For example, Alfred A. Knopf, Inc., would be shortened to Knopf; Free Press would be shortened to Free; and Simon and Schuster, Inc., would be shortened to Simon. For university presses, abbreviate university to *U* and Press to *P.* For example, University of South Carolina Press would become U of South Carolina P, and Oxford University Press would become Oxford UP (note that periods do not follow *U* or *P* and the letters *U* and *P* are not separated by spaces when they are together). Follow the publisher's name with a comma to set it off from the year of publication. You do not need a publisher if the book was published before 1900; in such cases, give the city, followed by a comma, followed by the year.

7. **Year:** Look for the most recent year of publication given. If no publication date is provided, use the most recent copyright date. If you cannot find any dates, use *n. d.* End with a period.

   When you have a book that was originally published many years earlier than the edition that you have, the convention is to also include the original year of publication after the book's title, preceded and followed by periods. This way, your readers will have a more accurate idea of the age of the source than they would if you merely provided the date of publication of the edition that you are using.

8. **Medium of Publication:** With the increasing availability of sources, including books, in electronic form, the most current MLA guidelines require the medium of publication following the year of publication, so follow the year of publication with the word *print,* capitalized and followed by a period.

9. **Pertinent Supplementary Information:** Sometimes additional information is helpful to readers who want more information about your sources, such as the complete number of volumes of a multivolume set.

Here is an example of a basic book entry:

Diamond, Jared. *Guns, Germs, and Steel: The Fates of Human Societies.* New

   York: Norton, 1999. Print.

To cite a work within a book when you are using only one selection from the book, you need to combine information about the individual work and the publication information about the book itself. (See #18, Multiple Selections from an Anthology, on p. 290, for additional information.)

These basic types of entries are very simple. However, you will soon encounter dozens of variations as you write your college papers. The basics will always remain the same, but you will need to provide extra information if you are using a book with, for example, more than one author, just one part of a book, a book in a series, a multivolume work, a book with a translator, and so on.

Sample MLA Works-Cited Entries

Following is a directory of sample works-cited entries.

1. BOOK OR PLAY BY A SINGLE AUTHOR

Cave, Nick. *And the Ass Saw the Angel.* New York: Penguin, 1990. Print.

Ishay, Micheline R. *The History of Human Rights: From Ancient Times to the Globalization Era.* Berkeley: U of California P, 2004. Print.

Stoppard, Tom. *Rosencrantz and Guildenstern Are Dead.* New York: Grove, 1967. Print.

Set titles off from subtitles with colons. If you are unsure whether a phrase below a title on the cover of a book or in its title page is a subtitle or just a descriptive phrase, check the Library of Congress cataloging-in-publication data, which can be found on the copyright page of the book.

2. BOOK BY TWO OR THREE AUTHORS

Always give the authors' names in the order that they are presented in your source. Note in the following example that only the first author's first and last names are reversed.

Gallagher, Catherine, and Stephen Greenblatt. *Practicing New Historicism.* Chicago: U of Chicago P, 2000. Print.

3. BOOK BY MORE THAN THREE AUTHORS

When you are citing a book with four or more authors or editors, you may use *et al.* (Latin for *et alii,* which means "and others"), followed by a period, in place of the names of the authors after the first one. (You can name all of the authors if you choose to, however. Just be consistent and use either all their last names or et al. after the first author's last name in your in-text citations.)

Bennett, Jeffrey, et al. *The Cosmic Perspective: Media Update.* New York: Addison, 2004. Print.

4. TWO OR MORE WORKS BY THE SAME AUTHOR(S)

Note that the entries are alphabetized according to the first important words of the titles. *9* is treated as *nine.* When you use more than one work by the same author or authors, use their names in the first entry only, and use three hyphens for the works by the same authors that follow. If the individuals named are editors, compilers, or translators, follow the three hyphens with a comma and the correct abbreviation: *ed., comp.,* or *trans.* Insert an *s* before the period of the abbreviation if more than one individual is listed. If the order of the names of works with multiple authors is changed, do not use the hyphens. Order is important; it indicates the lead author of a work. If an author of a single work that you use is a co-author of other works that you cite in your paper, do not hyphenate his or her name. You should never combine the three hyphens with other authors' names.

Chomsky, Noam. *9-11.* New York: Seven Stories, 2001. Print.

- - -. *Profit over People: Neoliberalism and Global Order.* New York: Seven
     Stories, 1999. Print.

Herman, Edward S., and Noam Chomsky. *Manufacturing Consent: The Politi-*
     cal Economy of the Mass Media. New York: Pantheon, 1988. Print.

Rampton, Sheldon, and John Stauber. *Trust Us, We're Experts! How Industry*
     Manipulates Science and Gambles with Your Future. New York: Tarcher,
     2002. Print.

Stauber, John, and Sheldon Rampton. *Toxic Sludge Is Good For You: Lies,*
     Damn Lies and the Public Relations Industry. Monroe, ME: Common
     Courage, 1995. Print.

Gilbert, Sandra M., and Susan Gubar, eds. *Feminist Literary Theory and*
     Criticism: A Norton Reader. New York: Norton, 2007. Print.

- - -. *The Madwoman in the Attic: The Woman Writer and the Nineteenth-*
     Century Imagination. New Haven: Yale UP, 2000. Print.

5. AN ILLUSTRATED BOOK OR GRAPHIC NOVEL

When illustrations are a significant part of a book, begin with the author and the title, as usual, and follow the title with the abbreviation of "illustrated by," *Illus.,* and the illustrator's name. If the illustrator's work is your focus, begin with that name, and follow the title of the book with "By" and the author's name.

Carroll, Lewis. *The Story of Sylvie and Bruno.* Illus. Harry Furniss. 1904. New
     York: Mayflower, 1980. A facsimile of the 1926 edition. Print.

Gorey, Edward, illus. *Old Possum's Book of Practical Cats.* By T. S. Eliot. New
     York: Harcourt, 1982. Print.

In a graphic novel, the text and illustrations are equally important. If the text's author is also its illustrator, the entry will be the same as with any other novel.

> Gibbons, Dave. *The Originals*. Vertigo, 2006. Print.

When different people collaborate, begin with the person whose contributions you focus on, and include the other contributor or contributors after the title, using the appropriate abbreviations for their functions.

> Gaiman, Neil. *Preludes and Nocturnes*. Illus. Sam Kieth, Mike Dingenberg,
>
>   and Malcolm Jones, III. Introd. Karen Berger. New York: DC Comics,
>
>   1991. Print. Vol. 1 of *The Sandman*. 10 vols. Print.

> Harris, Joe, and Stuart Moore, adapt. *The Nightmare Factory*. By Thomas
>
>   Ligotti. Illus. Colleen Doran and Ben Templesmith. New York: Harper,
>
>   2007. Print.

6. BOOK WITH AN AUTHOR NOT LISTED

When a source does not have a listed author, you should alphabetize by the first important word of the title, ignoring (but not moving) *a, an,* and *the* (these parts of speech are called *articles*).

> *Beowulf*. Trans. Burton Raffel. New York: Signet, 1999. Print.

7. TRANSLATIONS

If the work was written in another language and translated, include the translator's name if provided, preceded by the abbreviation *Trans*.

> Ellul, Jacques. *Propaganda: The Formation of Men's Attitudes*. Trans. Konrad
>
>   Kelle and Jean Lerner. New York: Knopf, 1965. Print.

For books that are much older than their publication date would indicate, the convention is to put the original year of publication after the book's title.

> Machiavelli, Niccolò. *The Prince*. 1513. Trans. and ed. Robert M. Adams.
>
>   2nd ed. A Norton Critical ed. New York: 1991. Print.

8. BOOK THAT IS PART OF A MULTIVOLUME WORK

If the book has more than one volume and you use only one volume, list the volume you have used, followed by number of the volume used if you are using part of a multivolume work.

> Casanova, Jacques. *The Memoirs of Jacques Casanova de Seingalt*. Trans.
>
> Arthur Machen. Vol. 2. New York: Putnam, 1945. Print.

You may add the total number of volumes in the work, if you choose, as supplementary information at the end of the entry, but this is not a requirement. If the work appeared in print over a number of years, you may provide the inclusive years, as well.

> Casanova, Jacques. *The Memoirs of Jacques Casanova de Seingalt*. Trans.
>
> Arthur Machen. New York: Putnam, 1945. Print. 6 vols.

9. EDITION (OTHER THAN FIRST)

> Cirlot, J. E. *A Dictionary of Symbols*. Trans. Jack Sage. 2nd ed. New York:
>
> Barnes, 1995. Print.

> Pratkanis, Anthony, and Elliot Aronson. *Age of Propaganda: The Everyday Use
>
> and Abuse of Persuasion*. Rev. ed. New York: Freeman, 2001. Print.

10. WORK IN A COLLECTION OF AN AUTHOR'S WORK

> Carter, Angela. "The Snow Child." *The Bloody Chamber and Other Stories*.
>
> New York: Penguin, 1979. 91–92. Print.

11. BOOK WITH THE TITLE OF A BOOK OR A PLAY IN ITS TITLE

If a title contains another title that would ordinarily be italicized or underlined, do not italicize or underline it.

> Ward, Candace, ed. Everyman *and Other Miracle and Morality Plays*. New
>
> York: Dover, 1995. Print.

12. SACRED TEXT

Sacred texts, unlike other books, are neither underlined nor italicized unless they are unique and distinct in some way from other versions, such as critical editions. With critical editions, which add commentary on the sacred writings, you may begin with the editors of the text. Books not in English often have variant spellings. Use the spelling found on the book. If acronyms are used, retain all the capital letters.

> Ali, Maulana Muhammed. *The Holy Qur'an with English Translation and
>
> Commentary*. Columbus: Ahmadiyya Anjuman Ishaat, 1991. Print.

> Felder, Cain Hope, ed. *The Original African Heritage Study Bible*. Valley Forge:
>
> Judson, 2007. Print.

Holy Bible. King James Version. Philadelphia: National, 1978. Print.

Berlin, Adele, and Marc Zvi Brettler, eds. *The Jewish Study Bible.* Jewish Publi-

cation Society TANAKH Translation. Oxford: Oxford UP, 2004. Print.

The Upanishads. Trans. Eknath Easwaran. Tomales, CA: Nilgiri, 2007. Print.

13. ANTHOLOGY

To cite an anthology, provide the name(s) of the editor or compiler of the book if it is an anthology, followed by the correct abbreviations (*ed.* or *comp.,* with an *s* before the period if there is more than one individual).

Bennett, W. Lance, and Robert M. Entman, eds. *Mediated Politics: Communica-*

tion in the Future of Democracy. New York: Cambridge UP, 2004. Print.

14. ARTICLE, ESSAY, POEM, SHORT STORY, OR OTHER SHORT WORK FROM AN ANTHOLOGY

Use this format when you are using only a single work from an anthology; if you take more than one work from an anthology, use the cross-referencing method described on page 290. If you are taking a chapter, essay, article, short story, or other work from a book or anthology, begin with the author of this work. If you are citing one specific part of the book, such as a chapter or article, include the title of the part of the book, enclosed in quotation marks. End with a period within the closing quotation mark unless a question mark or exclamation point is part of the title; if it is, it should also be within the closing quotation mark.

1. **Author:** Begin with the author's name (first and last names reversed), followed by a period. (Follow the same guidelines listed previously if there is more than one author.)
2. **Title of the Selection:** The title of the selection will usually be given in quotation marks following the name of the author of the selection. End with a period within the closing quotation mark, followed by the title of the book.
3. **Translator:** Provide the name of a translator if there is one, preceded by *Trans.*
4. **Title of the Book:** Next, you'll give the title and subtitle of the book, italicized or underlined, followed by a period (unless the title has its own end punctuation mark, like a question mark).
5. **Editor's Name:** The name of the editor of the anthology or other type of book in which the selection appears follows the title of the book; it is not inverted but is preceded by the abbreviation *Ed.* It is followed by the name of the city of publication.

6. **Edition:** Indicate the edition after the title if the book is not a first edition or it is a critical or revised edition.

7. **City, Publisher, and Year:** Follow with the city of publication, a colon, the shortened name of the publisher, a comma, the year, and a period, according to the guidelines listed earlier.

8. **Page Numbers:** Follow the publication information with the first and last page numbers of the selection. Give the complete numbers for any numbers between one and ninety-nine, but with higher numbers you should shorten the final page number if it falls within the same range (100–99, 1100–200, 1125–35). End with a period.

9. **Medium of Publication**: Follow publication information with the word *print,* capitalized and followed by a period.

10. **Pertinent Supplementary Information**: Although not a requirement and usually not necessary, you may end with any extra information that may be important for the readers to know.

> Holland, Peter. "Farce." *The Cambridge Companion to English Restoration*
>
> *Theatre.* Ed. Deborah Payne Fisk. Cambridge: Cambridge UP, 2005.
>
> 107–26. Print.

> Lacan, Jacques. "The Symbolic Order." Trans. Alan Sheridan. *Literary*
>
> *Theory: An Anthology.* Ed. Julie Rivkin and Michael Ryan. Rev. ed.
>
> Oxford: Blackwell, 1998. 184–89. Print.

15. ARTICLE, ESSAY, POEM, SHORT STORY, OR OTHER WORK WITHOUT AN AUTHOR

When a selection does not have an author, begin with the title. Remember to alphabet-ize the entry on your works-cited page by the first important word (not the articles *a, an,* or *the*) of the title.

> "The King of the Cats." *"The King of the Cats" and Other Feline Fairy Tales.*
>
> Ed. John Richard Stephens. Boston: Faber, 1993. 24–25. Print.

16. UNTITLED INTRODUCTION, PREFACE, FOREWORD, OR CONCLUSION

If your source is an untitled introduction, preface, foreword, afterword, or conclu-sion, provide the appropriate designation but do not enclose it in quotation marks.

> Ishay, Micheline R. Introduction. *The History of Human Rights: From Ancient*
>
> *Times to the Globalization Era.* Berkeley: U of California P, 2004. 2–14.
>
> Print.

17. BOOK, PLAY, OR NOVEL IN AN ANTHOLOGY

Books, plays, and novels that are included in anthologies are treated the same way that shorter works, such as articles and essays, are treated; however, you should italicize or underline the titles, not enclose them in quotation marks.

> Kyd, Thomas. *The Spanish Tragedy*. 1592. *Four Revenge Tragedies*. Ed. Katherine
>
> Eisaman Maus. Oxford: Oxford UP, 1995. 1–91. Print.

18. MULTIPLE SELECTIONS FROM AN ANTHOLOGY (CROSS-REFERENCING)

When you need to cite more than one selection from an anthology, it is time consuming and unnecessary to type the publication information for the anthology for every selection you are listing. Instead, MLA allows you to cross-reference multiple works to an anthology by using the editor's last name in front of the work's page numbers. Your readers can find the rest of the publication information in the entry for the anthology, which you provide only once. Each cross-reference should include the following information: (1) author, (2) title of work, (3) editor's last name (note that this information is not followed by a period or comma), and (4) inclusive page numbers for the work. If a work has a translator, the translator's name follows the title of the work.

> Baker, C. Edwin. "Implications of Rival Visions of Electoral Campaigns."
>
> Bennett and Entman 342–61.

In the following example of a list of sources, W. Lance Bennett and Robert M. Entman are the editors of an anthology called *Mediated Politics: Communication in the Future of Democracy*. Note that the entry for the anthology does not contain any information about any of the individual works. Note as well that all entries are arranged alphabetically. Do not begin with an anthology unless its editors' last names would put it at the top of the list. Note that each entry begins flush with the left margin.

Works Cited

> Baker, C. Edwin. "Implications of Rival Visions of Electoral Campaigns."
>
> Bennett and Entman 342–61.
>
> Bennett, W. Lance, and Robert M. Entman, eds. *Mediated Politics: Communica-*
>
> *tion in the Future of Democracy*. New York: Cambridge UP, 2004.
>
> Carpini, Michael X. Delli, and Bruce A. Williams. "Let Us Infotain You." Bennett and Entman 160–81.
>
> Underwood, Doug. "Reporting and the Push for Market-Oriented Journalism:
>
> Media Organizations and Business." Bennett and Entman 99–116.

Sometimes editors of anthologies include their own articles. You must still give their last names after their article's title so that your readers know what anthology the selection is taken from. In the following example, the entry for the article by Bennett and Entman precedes the entry for the anthology because the *C* of the article title comes before the *M* of the anthology title.

Bennett, W. Lance, and Robert M. Entman. "Communication in the Future of

Democracy: A Conclusion." Bennett and Entman 468–80.

- - -, eds. *Mediated Politics: Communication in the Future of Democracy.* New

York: Cambridge UP, 2004.

19. REPRINTED WORK

For a reprinted work, give the original publication information found for the work, followed by the abbreviation for reprinted (*Rpt.*), the word *in,* and the publication information for the anthology. Following are some variations you may encounter.

A work taken from a collection by the author:

Merriam, Eve. "Tryst." *The Nixon Poems.* New York: Atheneum, 1970. Rpt. in

No More Masks: An Anthology of Poems by Women. Ed. Florence Howe

and Ellen Bass. Garden City: Anchor, 1973. Print.

An article from a weekly magazine reprinted in an anthology when the anthology does not provide the page numbers of the article:

Said, Edward R. "The Clash of Ignorance." *The Nation* 3 Oct. 2001. Rpt. in *A*

Just Response: The Nation *on Terrorism, Democracy, and September 11,*

2001. Ed. Katrina Vanden Heuvel. New York: Thunder's Mouth, 2002.

233–39. Print.

Because *The Nation* is the title of a magazine, it should not be underlined or italicized in the book's title as it would be when it is not part of the title; not underlining or italicizing it sets it off from the rest of the title of the book.

An article from a scholarly journal reprinted in an anthology:

Yolen, Jane. "America's Cinderella." *Children's Literature in Education* 8

(1977): 21–29. Rpt. in *Cinderella: A Casebook.* Ed. Alan Dundes. Madi-

son: U of Wisconsin P, 1988. Print.

An article from a scholarly journal reprinted in a critical edition of a work:

Gurr, Andrew. "*The Tempest's* Tempest at Blackfriars." *Shakespeare Survey*

41 (1989): 91–102. Rpt. in The Tempest: *Sources and Contexts, Criticism,*

Rewritings and Appropriations. By William Shakespeare. Ed. Peter Hulme
and William H. Sherman. Norton Critical ed. New York: Norton, 2004.
250–65. Print.

An untitled excerpt of a chapter from a book reprinted in a critical edition:

Greenaway, Peter. ["Prospero's Books."] Prospero's Books: *A Film of Shakespeare's The Tempest*. London: Chatto and Windus, 1991. 20–25. Rpt.
in The Tempest: *Sources and Contexts, Criticism, Rewritings and Appropriations*. By William Shakespeare. Ed. Peter Hulme and William H.
Sherman. Norton Critical ed. New York: Norton, 2004. 325–31. Print.

A chapter from a book reprinted in a critical edition:

Marcus, Leah. "The Blue-Eyed Witch." London: Routledge, 1996. 5–17. Rpt.
in The Tempest: *Sources and Contexts, Criticism, Rewritings and Appropriations*. By William Shakespeare. Ed. Peter Hulme and William H.
Sherman. Norton Critical ed. New York: Norton, 2004. 286–98. Print.

Remember that when you have the title of a book, film, or play in the title of a work
that is italicized or underlined, as in the preceding examples, you set it off by refraining
from italicizing or underlining it.

PERIODICAL PRINT PUBLICATIONS

You typically need six main elements in a works-cited entry for a periodical: author
(when provided), title of work, title of the medium the work appears in, and publication information for that medium, page numbers, and medium of publication. You can
find the first five elements on the cover or contents page of the periodical and on the
opening page of the article you are citing.

In works-cited entries for works from periodicals, list the following elements in order:

1. **Author:** Begin with the author's name, when provided, last name first, followed
   by a period. If there is more than one author, follow the same guidelines as for
   books.
2. **Title of Article:** The title of the article, in quotation marks, followed by a
   period within the final quotation mark comes next.
3. **Title of Periodical:** Next you will need to provide the title of the periodical,
   underlined or italicized, and not followed by a period.
4. **Volume and Issue:** In the past, MLA format required only the volume number
   for scholarly journals that were continuously paginated throughout the volume
   year, while it required the volume number followed by a decimal and the issue

number if each issue began with page one (such as 19.3). When there was only one number, readers would assume that it was the volume number, and when there was a number, a decimal point, and another number, they would assume that the first number was the volume number and the second was the issue number. The newest guidelines recognize that issue numbers can be valuable even when a journal is continuously paginated, so always include them. If a journal has issues only and no volume numbers, then you will have only one number with no decimal point.

5. **Date:** When citing journals, list the date of publication in parentheses. Often, the journal will be published by seasons; in this case, you need only list the year. For all other periodicals, list the date (day, month, and year for a weekly magazine, and just the month and year for a monthly) followed by a colon. Do not enclose the year in parentheses the way you would a journal. Abbreviate the names of months except for May, June, and July.

6. **Page Numbers:** After the colon, you list the first and last page numbers of the entire article. Give the complete numbers for any numbers between one and ninety-nine, but with higher numbers you should shorten the final page number for numbers higher than one hundred if it falls within the same range, just as you would with articles found in anthologies. If an article does not appear on consecutive pages, give the number of the first page followed by a plus sign, such as 19+. To cite newspaper articles, you'll need to provide both section numbers and page numbers. When an article does not appear on consecutive pages, give the section letter if there is one and the number of the article's first page followed by a plus sign, such as A2+.

7. **Medium of Publication:** Follow the page numbers with the word *print,* capitalized and followed by a period.

8. **Pertinent Supplementary Information:** If you have any supplementary information to add, such as an article being part of a series, place it at the very end of the entry.

Sample Entries for Print Periodicals

20. ARTICLE FROM A JOURNAL WITH CONTINUOUS PAGINATION

Marks, Elise. "*Othello/me*": Racial Drag and the Pleasures of Boundary-

Crossing with *Othello.*" *Comparative Drama* 35.1 (2001): 101–24. Print.

21. ARTICLE FROM A JOURNAL THAT BEGINS EACH ISSUE ON PAGE ONE

Sadoff, Ira. "Olena Kalytiak Davis and the Retro-New." *American Poetry*

Review 35.4 (2006): 11–15. Print.

22. SPECIAL ISSUE OF SCHOLARLY JOURNAL

If you are citing more than one source from a scholarly journal that has published a special issue with a title, treat the issue itself like an anthology. Begin with the special issue's editor, followed by the name of the special issue. Add *Spec. issue of* before the name of the journal. Format the rest of the entry like a regular journal, but end with the inclusive page numbers of the entire journal. For articles in the special issue, cross-reference them to the edition the way you would multiple articles from an anthology (see #18).

> Haase, Donald, ed. *Jack Zipes and the Sociohistorical Study of Fairy Tales.*
>
> Spec. issue of *Marvels and Tales: Journal of Fairy-Tale Studies* 16.2
>
> (2002): 1–274. Print.

> Jones, Jane. "Jack Zipes and German Folklore." Haase 27–41.

If you are citing only one article from a special issue, use the following form:

> Jones, Jane. "Jack Zipes and German Folklore." *Jack Zipes and the Sociohis-*
>
> *torical Study of Fairy Tales.* Spec. issue of *Marvels and Tales: Journal of*
>
> *Fairy-Tale Studies* 16.2 (2002): 27–41. Print.

23. ARTICLE FROM A WEEKLY OR BIWEEKLY MAGAZINE

You can tell whether a magazine is weekly or biweekly (published every other week) by looking at the date on the cover. If the day is supplied as well as the month, it is weekly or biweekly. Don't give volume and issue numbers for magazines.

> Kumin, Maxine. "Looking Back in My Eighty-First Year." *New Yorker* 1 Dec.
>
> 2006: 64. Print.

Occasionally a magazine that is normally published on a weekly basis will publish one issue a year that spans two weeks (as in the holiday season) and give two dates on its cover. When this happens, use both dates.

> Erdrich, Louise. "Demolition." *New Yorker* 25 Dec. 2006/1 Jan. 2007: 70–81.
>
> Print.

24. ARTICLE FROM A MONTHLY OR BIMONTHLY MAGAZINE

To cite monthly or bimonthly magazines, you need only provide months and years. For example:

> Douthat, Ross. "The Truth about Harvard." *Atlantic* Mar. 2005: 95–99. Print.

> Robbins, Alexandra. "Powerful Secrets." *Vanity Fair* July 2004: 119+. Print.

If a magazine that typically publishes once a month publishes an issue that spans two months, provide both months.

> Fallows, James. "Success without Victory." *Atlantic* Jan./Feb. 2005: 80–90.
>
> Print.

> Note: Monday through Saturday, the *New York Times* is usually divided into lettered sections, just like most other newspapers. However, sometimes the Saturday edition is continuously paginated from the first page to the last with no section numbers. Just use the page numbers of an article after the edition.
>
> The Sunday *New York Times* contains numbered sections. After the edition, give the section number preceded by the abbreviation *sec.*

25. NEWSPAPER ARTICLE

> Walters, Dan. "$400 Million a Big Deal? Not Really." *Sacramento Bee* 23 Oct.
>
> 2006, metro final ed.: A3. Print.

26. A SERIALIZED ARTICLE OR SERIES OF RELATED ARTICLES

Sometimes lengthy articles are serialized across more than one issue of a magazine or newspaper. If each installment of such an article has the same author and title (or just title, if there is no author), create a single entry. For journals, after the usual publication information, including page numbers, add a semicolon, and then follow with the same information for subsequent issues. For magazines and newspapers, use the appropriate dates (and section numbers, if applicable). End with medium of publication. If the different installments have individual titles, you'll need to create an entry for each. You may add supplementary information after the medium of publication to indicate that each article is part of the same series.

> "Gay Marriage Controversy Comes to Kern County." *Bakersfield Observer*
>
> 16 June 2008, A1;17 June 2008, A1–2. Print.

> Liptak, Adam. "Inmate Count in U.S. Dwarfs Other Nations." *New York Times*
>
> 23 Apr. 2008, late ed.: A1+. Print. Pt. 1 of a series, American Exception,
>
> begun 17 Oct. 2007.

> - - -. "Lifers as Teenagers, Now Seeking Second Chance." *New York Times*
>
> 17 Oct. 2007, late ed.: A1+. Print. Pt.1 of a series, American Exception,
>
> begun 17 Oct. 2007.

27. EDITORIAL OR OPINION PIECE

Editorials, both signed and unsigned, must be indicated as such to distinguish them from straight reporting and other types of articles in newspapers. This information follows the title of the piece. Use *editorial* if no authors are given, but refer to a signed editorial as an *opinion piece* because it is written by an individual columnist or guest contributor, not the paper's editorial board. (In your entry, do not underline, italicize, or enclose these terms in quotation marks.)

> Henderson, Noris. "Give Defense Reform a Chance." *Times-Picayune*. Opinion
>
> piece. 14 Oct. 2006, metro ed.: 7. Print.

28. REVIEW

Give the title of the review, followed by a period (if the review does not have a title, just put *Rev. of* and the title of the work being reviewed followed by a period). Write *Rev. of* and the title of the book, a comma, and its author (preceded by *by*); or the title of the film, a comma, and its director (preceded by *dir.*); or the title of the series, a comma, and its network. End with the medium of publication.

> Oates, Joyce Carol. "Dangling Men." Rev. of *Indecision,* by Benjamin Kunkel.
>
> *New York Review of Books* 3 Nov. 2005: 36–40. Print.

> Travers, Peter. "American Idols." Rev. of *Dreamgirls,* dir. Bill Condon. *Rolling*
>
> *Stone* 14 Dec. 2006: 132. Print.

> Friend, Tad. "The Paper Chase." Rev. of *The Office,* NBC. *New Yorker* 1 Dec.
>
> 2006: 94–100. Print.

29. CARTOON OR COMIC STRIP

Give the name of the cartoonist followed by the title of the cartoon if it has one, or the name of the cartoon strip if it is part of a series. Otherwise, write *Cartoon* or *Comic Strip*. Then give the publication information for its source. End with the medium of publication.

> Rees, David. "Get Your War On." *Rolling Stone*. 31 May 2007. 10. Print.

30. ADVERTISEMENT

Give the name of the product or company being advertised, followed by the word *Advertisement*. Follow with the publication information for the advertisement's source.

> Hypnôse by Lancôme. Advertisement. *Playbill* May 2007: 42–43. Print.

WORKS-CITED ENTRIES FOR WORKS FROM REFERENCE DATABASES

In works-cited entries for articles you find in online databases, your entries should begin exactly as they would if you were working with an article from the print publication; however, you also need to include additional information about the online location of the electronic version you found. Provide information about the subscription database in the order listed next. If only the starting page number of an article is given, give the number followed by a hyphen, a space, and a period; if the database gives the total number of pages, as in 53(4), which means that the article begins on page 53 and is four pages long, you need to calculate the number of the article's last page (in this case you would list it as pages 53–57). If pagination is not available, use *n. pag.*

1. **Original Publication Information for the Article:** Follow the guidelines for the original print versions of journal, newspaper, and magazine, etc., articles.

2. **Name of Database:** Name of database (for example, LexisNexis), italicized or underlined, followed by a period.

3. **Medium of Publication:** The MLA previously recommended providing the URL of electronic sources, but its 2009 guidelines recommend omitting them. URLs are often unreliable because they may change over time or even according to different users and Internet sessions. Simply use the term *Web*.

4. **Date of Access:** Day, month, and year, not separated by commas, followed by a period.

Suppose you are planning on writing a paper about television, and you decide to look for articles on television history. You use your home computer to go to your library's online pages and look at the list of searchable archives and gateways to databases. You choose EBSCOHost, which gives you access to numerous online databases, such as *Academic Search Elite, Business Source Premier, EBSCO Animals, ERIC, GreenFILE, Health Source: Nursing/Academic Edition, Newspaper Source, MEDLINE, Psychology & Behavioral Sciences Collection, Religion and Philosophy Collection,* and various health- and business-related databases. You use "television" and "history" as your search terms in *Academic Search Premier,* limiting publication type to periodicals, and one of the articles you find looks interesting. It is called "What's Wrong with Television History?" and it is from the periodical *History Today.*

You decide to use this article. To do the citation, you start by reviewing how to do a work-cited entry for a periodical article. You start with the author, located near the top of the screen, under the article title, and then follow with the title, then the name of the periodical, not adding a period.

Stearn, Tom. "What's Wrong with Television History?" *History Today*

There is quite a bit of information following the name of the periodical, including date, volume, and issue. Because your paper will be in MLA format, you realize you need to know if this is a magazine or a journal. The library has this article in

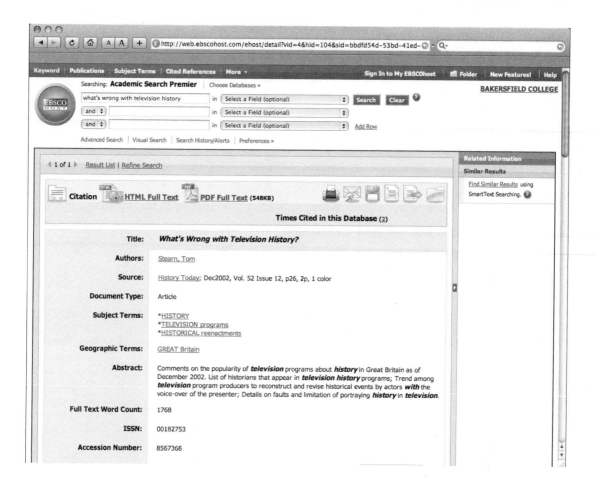

the database, but no physical copy of *History Today*. You choose to download it in a Portable Document Format (PDF) file, and you see that the article begins with a brightly colored illustration of actors staging a Saxon battle. This type of illustration is typical of a magazine, not a journal. You decide to do a Net search for more information, and you type in "history today periodical." Your first hit takes you to an online bookstore that describes it as a magazine and shows a copy of a cover, which is also brightly illustrated and standard magazine size. You now know how to proceed, and you know that you need the date of publication, but not the volume or issue number. Because the article is from a magazine, you don't enclose the date with parentheses. You need to follow with the page numbers. You see "p26, 2p," at the end of the publication information, so you know that the article was on pages 26 to 27.

Stearn, Tom. "What's Wrong with Television History?" *History Today*

Dec. 2002: 26–27.

Now that you have the entry you'd have if you actually had the magazine, you need to complete it with all the information for the database. You give the database, underlined or italicized and followed by a period, and the name of the subscription service that provides access to the database, not italicized or underlined, followed by a period.

Stearn, Tom. "What's Wrong with Television History?" *History Today*

Dec. 2002: 26–27. *Academic Search Premier*.

Now all you need to do is add the term *Web,* followed by a period and then your day, month, and year of access, finishing the entry with the usual period.

Stearn, Tom. "What's Wrong with Television History?" *History Today*

Dec. 2002: 26–27. *Academic Search Premier*. Web. 30 Nov. 2008.

Following are more examples.

31. ARTICLE FROM A NEWSPAPER IN NEWSPAPER SOURCE

Goldman, Tim. "Expecting U.S. Help, Sent to Guantánamo." *New York Times*

15 Oct. 2006: sec. 1:26. *Newspaper Source*. Web. 9 Oct. 2008.

32. ARTICLE FROM A JOURNAL WITH CONTINUOUS PAGINATION, EXPANDED ACADEMIC ASAP

Goldstein, Gary B. "Did Queen Elizabeth Use the Theater for Social and

Political Propaganda?" *Oxfordian* 7.1 (2004): 153 – . *Expanded Academic*

ASAP. Web. 18 Jan. 2009.

33. ARTICLE FROM A JOURNAL THAT BEGINS EACH ISSUE ON PAGE ONE, ACADEMIC SEARCH PREMIER

Susman, Jeff. "Harry and Louise Redux." *Journal of Family Practice* 55.4

(2006): 276. *Psychology and Behavioral Sciences Collection*. Web.

21 Sep. 2008.

34. ARTICLE FROM A MAGAZINE, LEXISNEXIS

"All on the Mind; Cognitive Enhancement." *Economist* 24 May 2008,

U.S. ed.: n. pag. *LexisNexis*. Web. 20 Jan. 2009.

WORKS-CITED ENTRIES FOR INTERNET SOURCES

To cite online sources, list each of these elements, when provided, in this order:

1. **Author:** The work's or Web page's author's name if there is one, followed by a period.

2. **Title:** The title of the work, underlined or italicized, if the work stands alone, or enclosed in quotation marks if it is part of a series of pages on a site, followed by a period. Untitled works should be identified by a descriptive label, such as *Online posting* or *Home page,* and neither italicized, underlined, nor enclosed in quotation marks.

3. **Publication Information:** Original print publication information, if the work is reprinted and this information is provided (book titles are followed by periods, periodical titles are not).

4. **Site Title:** The name of the site on which the work is posted (unless the work stands alone), underlined or italicized, followed by a period.

5. **Publisher, editor, site sponsor, or Web Master:** This information is followed by a period. If not available, use the abbreviation *n. p.*

6. **Publication Date:** Provide the day, month and year, if available. If not available, use the abbreviation *n. d.*

7. **Medium of Publication:** As noted earlier, MLA no longer recommends providing the URL of the online source because URLs are often unreliable. Searching for Internet content using authors and titles is frequently more efficient than trying to use URLS, which may be obsolete. The MLA now recommends simply using the term *Web.*

8. **Date of Access:** The day, month, and year that you visited the site, not separated by commas, and followed by a period.

9. **Supplementary Information:** Include a URL only if your readers wouldn't be able to locate a source otherwise or if your instructor requests it; if in doubt, ask. If you do provide the URL, it should follow your date of access and a period and be enclosed in angle brackets. Sometimes you may need other information, such as naming a specific service, such as iTunes, if necessary to find a podcast. End the entry with a period.

35. NEWSPAPER ARTICLE PUBLISHED ONLINE

> Murphy, Kim. "British Accuse Ex-KGB Agent in Poisoning Death." *Los Angeles Times* 22 May 2007. Web. 22 May 2009.

36. AUTHORLESS ARTICLE ON AN ORGANIZATION'S WEBSITE

> "China: Google Hints at China U-turn." Amnesty.org.uk. 8 June 2006. Web. 11 June 2008.

37. ESSAY REPRINTED ON A WEBSITE

> Orwell, George. "Politics and the English Language." *Shooting an Elephant and Other Essays*. London: Secker and Warburg, 1950. N. pag. George Orwell's Library. 24 July 2004. Web. 19 Apr. 2009.

38. ARTICLE FROM AN INDIVIDUAL'S TITLED WEBSITE

> Shah, Anup. "War, Propaganda and the Media." *Global Issues That Affect Everyone*. Anup Shah. 31 Mar. 2005. Web. 11 Feb. 2009.

39. ARTICLE FROM AN ONLINE JOURNAL

> Hollis, Erin. "Gorgonzola Sandwiches and Yellow Crayons: James Joyce, *Buffy the Vampire Slayer,* and the Aesthetic of Minutiae." *Slayage: The Online International Journal of Buffy Studies* 22 (2006): 11 pages. Web. 15 Mar. 2009.

(Pages are supplied for the preceding article because it is downloadable in PDF format.)

40. MATERIAL FROM PROFESSORS' WEBSITES

Cite material found on a professor's website in the same way you would cite other online sources. Include the course number and name (if available) and the name of the department and school at which the professor teaches. As with other website entries, only include the URL as supplementary information at the end of the entry if that is the only way your readers can find the source.

> Hastings, Waller. "Motifs and Tale Types." *Fairy Tales*. Waller Hastings' home page.
>
> English Department. Northern State University. N. d. Web. 11 Nov. 2008.

41. CARTOON PUBLISHED ONLINE

> Marlette, Doug. "New York State of Mind." *Slate.com*. 2007. Web. 1 June 2007.

42. BLOG

Blogs (from "web log") are everywhere on the Web, and most are as worthless to researchers as someone else's daily diary or even a commentary scrawled on a bathroom wall. Nevertheless, blogging by mainstream journalists, scientists, educators, and others has been increasing over the years, and many important newsletters feature distinguished bloggers on their websites. Often these are people whose credentials you can evaluate, and they may provide useful perspectives. Just be careful—anyone can publish a blog, and rampant biases voiced with no editorial oversight are quite common. If you use a blog as a source, provide the pertinent information for the blog entry, such as the individual writing the blog, the title of the entry if there is one, the name of the blog, and *Blog*. Next, give the title of the blog itself, the title of the sponsoring organization if there is one, the date the material was uploaded (even if the actual time is provided, you don't need to include this unless it is necessary to locate the entry, as when someone has several entries on a given day but no titles), followed by a period, followed by *Web,* followed by your date of access.

> Shachtman, Noah. "Nation's Spies: Climate Change Could Spark War." *Danger Room*. Blog. *Wired Blog Network*. 23 June 2008. Web. Oct. 29 2008.

> Sullivan, Andrew. " 'Disgrace,' Ctd." *Andrew Sullivan: The Daily Dish*. Blog. *The Atlantic.com*. 19 June 2008. Web. 20 Nov. 2009.

43. PODCAST

Podcasts are an increasingly popular method for disseminating information on the Net and include a variety of sources, such as radio programs and college and university lectures. If you use a podcast as a source, provide the pertinent information for the type of material being podcast, such as the individual doing the podcast, the title if there is one, and *Podcast* followed by a period following the title of the work (or taking the place of the title if there is none). End with the usual information required in an online entry: the date the material was uploaded, followed by a period, followed by *Web,* followed by your date of access.

Podcast from a site's home page:

> Fisher, Ian. "The Rome Bureau Chief on the Attack on the U.S. Embassy in Athens." Interview. Podcast. *New York Times: Backstory*. 12 Jan. 2007. Web. 13 Jan. 2007.

> "Sexual Orientation Legislation." Podcast. *Today*. BBC Radio 4. Web. 1 Jan. 2007. Web. 12 Jan. 2007.

Podcast from an outside service:

Podcasts available exclusively through services such as Apple's iTunes Store present a different problem since they cannot be found through a unique URL or through a simple Web search. Instead, you must download the iTunes software to gain access.

> "The Long Hard Winter." Podcast. *Nightline*. ABC News. 1 Jan. 2007. iTunes Store. Web. 13 Jan. 2007.

44. YOUTUBE OR OTHER ONLINE VIDEO CLIP

The YouTube video-sharing website where users can upload, view, and share video clips is immensely popular, and it is where some viewers first see any number of clips, from moments on news and entertainment programs to commercials and personal video. Other Internet sites also offer clips. To cite a clip from the Internet, you will need to give the original broadcast information and the YouTube information, including the date of uploading and the posted user name of the uploader. Include your date of access before the URL.

1. **Title:** Begin with the title of the clip if there is one, and a descriptive label if there is not. Titles should be enclosed in quotation marks, but labels should not. Follow with *Video clip,* not italicized or underlined.

2. **Original Broadcast Information:** If the clip wasn't created by the uploader, provide the original broadcast information following the format for such entries.

3. **Site:** Indicate the site the video is uploaded to, underlined or italicized.

4. **Upload Information:** Provide the name or pseudonym of the person uploading the material if provided and the date of the upload if provided. Use *n. d.* if there is no date.

5. **Medium of Publication:** Use Web.

6. **Date of Access:** End with the day, month, and year that you accessed the clip.

> "Stephen Colbert on *The O'Reilly Factor*." *The O'Reilly Factor*. Fox News
>
> Channel. 18 Jan. 2007. *YouTube*. Rackjite1. 19 Jan. 2007. Web.
>
> 22 May 2007.

If you want to emphasize an individual in the clip, you may begin with that person's name.

> Pausch, Randy. "Dying Professor's Final Farewell." Multimedia Producer: Reda
>
> Charafeddine. Reporter: Jeff Zaslow. *The Wall Street Journal* Digital
>
> Network. Network. N. d. *YouTube*. Web. 10 June 2007.

WORKS-CITED ENTRIES FOR OTHER SOURCES

45. FILM, VIDEOCASSETTE, OR DVD

1. **Title:** The typical entry for a movie begins with the title, underlined or italicized.

2. **Director:** Cite the director (preceded by *Dir.*) after the film title.

3. **Pertinent Supplementary Information:** After the title, you may cite the producer, preceded by "Produced by" (not in quotation marks); screenwriter, preceded by "Screenplay by" (also not included in quotation marks), and the lead actors (preceded by *Perf.*) or narrator (preceded by *Narr.*).

4. **Distributor and Date:** Add the name of the distributor and the year of the work's release.

5. **Medium:** Indicate Film, Videocassette, DVD, or Laser disc. If you are citing any of the last three, you may also include the film's original release date before you give the information on its subsequent release in another medium.

> *Borat: Cultural Learnings of America for Make Benefit Glorious Nation of*
>
> *Kazakhstan*. Dir. Larry Charles. Perf. Sacha Baron Cohen. 20th Cen-
>
> tury Fox, 2006. Film.

> *High Fidelity*. Dir. Stephen Frears. Perf. John Cusack and Iben Hjejle. 2000.
>
> Walt Disney Video, 2001. Videocassette.

After the title of the film and its director and performers, the amount of information that you give in an entry for a film depends on its relevance. If the film is based on or suggested by a literary or nonfiction work of the same name, you can indicate this before the distributor. If the film and the literary work have the same title, simply write "Based on the [novel, short story, novella] by [name of author]."

> *Syriana*. Dir. Steven Gaghan. Perf. George Clooney, Matt Damon, and
>
> Amanda Peet. Suggested by *See No Evil* by Robert Baer. Warner Bros.,
>
> 2005. Film.

If the work of the screenwriter, director, or an actor is the primary focus of your paper, you may begin with this person's name, followed by his or her role, followed by the title of the film.

> Jordan, Neil, dir. *The Company of Wolves*. Perf. Angela Lansbury, David
>
> Warner, and Graham Crowden. Based on the story by Angela Carter. Pal-
>
> ace Productions, 1984. Film.

46. RADIO OR TELEVISION PROGRAM
Provide the information for these programs in the following order:

1. **Title:** Begin with the title of the episode or segment, enclosed in quotation marks.
2. **Program or Series:** Follow with the title of the program, underlined or italicized.
3. **Name of the Network:** Provide the name of the network, if there is one.
4. **Call Letters and City:** Provide the call letters of the local station if available and the local city, separated by commas and with a comma following.
5. **Broadcast Date:** Provide the day, month, and year the segment was broadcast, not separated by commas. End with a period.
6. **Medium of Broadcast:** Indicate whether the program was on the radio or television.

7. **Pertinent Supplementary Information:** Although not required, you can end with supplementary information if you believe it will help your readers.

> "Ghosts of Rwanda." *Frontline*. PBS. WGBH, Boston, 1 Apr. 2004. Television.

If you are focusing on the contributions of an individual, put that person's name before the title.

> Sedaris, David. "It's Catching." *Fresh Air*. Natl. Public Radio. WHYY, Philadel-
>
> phia, 9 June 2008. Radio. Excerpt from *When You Are Engulfed in Flames*.

47. SOUND RECORDING

1. **Primary Artist:** Begin the name of the person you want to emphasize, such as the composer, performer, or conductor, or the name of a group or ensemble.
2. **Title:** For a short work, use quotation marks. For a long work, use italics or underlining. **Other Artists:** Follow if appropriate with the names of other relevant individuals, such as singers, musicians, and orchestras and conductors.
3. **Manufacturer and Date:** Provide the manufacturer and release date. (Often only the year is available.) If no date is available, use *n. d.*
4. **Medium:** Indicate whether the recording is on a compact disc (CD), Long-playing record (LP), an audiocassette, or an audiotape.

> Waits, Tom, comp. *The Black Rider*. Perf. Tom Waits and Williams
>
> Burroughs. Island, 2 Nov. 1993. CD.

> LuPone, Patti, perf. "The Worst Pies in London." *Sweeney Todd: The Demon*
>
> *Barber of Fleet Street*. 2005 Broadway Revival Cast. Comp. Stephen
>
> Sondheim. Nonesuch, 31 Jan. 2006. CD.

48. INTERVIEWS

Use any of the elements that are pertinent in the following order.

1. **Person Interviewed:** Begin with the name of the person interviewed, followed by a period.
2. **Interview Title:** If the interview is part of a publication or program and has a title, add the title, enclosed in quotation marks, followed by a period. If it does not have a title or if you conducted the interview yourself, just write *Interview, Personal interview, Telephone interview,* or *Email interview.*
3. **Interviewer:** The interviewer's name may be added after *Interview with,* following either the title of the interview or the interviewed person's name if known and pertinent. You do not need to include your own name if you conducted the interview.

4. **Publication Information:** Include pertinent publication information, following the format for the type of source. If you conducted the interview, end with the date(s).

5. **Medium of Broadcast:** If the interview was broadcast on the radio or television, indicate this at the end.

Following are examples of interviews published in the online version of a newspaper, conducted through email, and conducted on a radio program.

> Jablonski, Nina G. "Always Revealing, Human Skin Is an Anthropologist's
>
> Map." Interview with Claudia Dreifus. *New York Times* 9 Jan. 2007. Web.
>
> 11 Jan. 2007.
>
> Olson, Laura. Email interview. 11 Jan. 2007.
>
> Whedon, Joss. Interview with Terry Gross. *Fresh Air*. Natl. Public Radio.
>
> WHYY, Philadelphia. 9 May 2000. Radio.

49. ORAL PRESENTATIONS

If you cite lectures, speeches, addresses, or readings, use any of the elements that are pertinent in the following order.

1. **Speaker's Name:** No prefix or title is necessary.

2. **Title:** Enclose the title in quotation marks; if there is no title, the descriptive label at the end of the entry will suffice.

3. **Meeting and Sponsoring Organization:** Provide what information you have about the occasion of the presentation and the sponsor.

4. **Location and Date:** Provide the name of the institution or building, followed by the city and the date.

5. **Form of Delivery:** End with a label that describes the mode of delivery.

> O'Hare, Denis. "Beyond Lies the Wub" by Philip K. Dick. Selected Shorts.
>
> Symphony Space, New York. 21 Oct. 2006. Reading.
>
> Moton, David. English 1A: Expository Composition. Bakersfield College.
>
> Bakersfield, CA. 22 May 2007. Lecture.

50. LIVE PERFORMANCE

1. **Title:** Live performances, comedy shows, concerts, plays, ballets, or operas, are treated much like films. Typically, begin with the title of the work. If there is no title, use a descriptive label.

2. **Author or Composer:** Follow with the name of the author or composer, preceded by the word *By.*

3. **Pertinent Supplementary Information:** Follow the author or composer with relevant information about the performance, such as the major performers (*Perf.*); the director (*Dir.*), the composer (*Comp.*); the choreographer (*Chor.*), and the conductor (*Cond.*).

4. **Production Information:** Next, give the company if provided, the theater, the city, and the date of the performance.

5. **Medium:** End with the medium—*Performance.*

> *Frost/Nixon.* By Peter Morgan. Dir. Michael Grandage. Perf. Michael Sheen and Frank Langella. Bernard B. Jacobs Theater, New York. 22 May 2007. Performance.

> *Edward Scissorhands.* Dir. and Chor. Matthew Bourne. Comp. Terry David and Danny Elfman. Perf. Sam Archer and Richard Winsor. New Adventures. Ahmanson Theater, Los Angeles. 31 Dec. 2006. Performance.

If your focus is a particular individual, you may begin the entry with that name.

> Poundstone, Paula. Stand-up comedy. Moore Theater, Seattle. 15 Nov. 2008. Performance.

51. PAINTING, SCULPTURE, PHOTOGRAPH, OR OTHER WORK OF VISUAL ART

1. **Artist:** Begin with the artist, if known.

2. **Title:** Italicize or underline the title of the work if provided. Otherwise, use a descriptive label, not underlined or italicized.

3. **Date:** List the year of composition; if unknown, use *n. d.* If an approximate date or range is known, follow by a question mark.

4. **Medium of Composition:** Specify the medium; be precise, for example, write "oil on canvas" rather than just "painting."

5. **Exhibition Title:** If the work is part of a temporary exhibition, add the name of the exhibition after the medium, followed by the exhibition dates.

6. **Location:** Name the museum, gallery, or other institution the work is housed in; if it is in a private collection, use "Collection of" (not in quotation marks) followed by the person's name or "Private collection" (not in quotation marks) if that information is not available or if the owner prefers anonymity.

Mapplethorpe, Robert. Untitled (self-portrait). 1972. Polaroid photograph.
  Polaroids: Mapplethorpe. 3 May 2008–7 Sep. 2008. Whitney Museum,
  New York.

Naso, Albert. *Rainstorm in the Amazon*. 2000–2001? India ink on paper.
  Private collection.

Picasso, Pablo. *Gertrude Stein*. 1906. Oil on canvas. Metropolitan Museum
  of Art, New York.

ANNOTATED BIBLIOGRAPHIES

What Is an Annotated Bibliography?

An annotated bibliography follows each works-cited entry with notes about the source. You annotate each entry with a few sentences that summarize what each source contains. You may also include evaluative information. A bibliography can contain more works than you actually use in your paper. Although *annotated bibliography* is the generally used term, some instructors may ask you to make an Annotated List of Works Cited instead; in this, you include only the sources that appear in your paper. You may also be asked to provide an Annotated List of Works Consulted, which includes sources that you looked at that may have helped you with background and context, but that you did not actually use in your paper. No matter what heading you use (based on what your instructor asks you to include), the principle for all of these lists is the same: give citations providing publication information so that your readers can find each source themselves if they choose, then follow each with a brief, informative annotation that may also include comments about what is useful in the source or how it stacks up against other materials out there.

Why Should I Write an Annotated Bibliography?

1. The most common reason, of course, is simply that it has been assigned by your instructor. However, this isn't just "busy work"; an annotated bibliography can help you write a stronger research paper. You read a source carefully and critically when you have to prepare an annotation, so it is a good idea to write the annotations as you read your sources and not wait until your instructor asks you to submit the assignment. Also, think of these annotations as works in progress—as you read more sources, you become more informed, and you become part of the ongoing conversation about your topic. You learn what experts see as the most important issues, what people are arguing about, and how they support and defend their own theories. Your growing knowledge can be reflected in your annotations. Many instructors want something slightly different when it comes to an annotated bibliography, so be sure to get details from your instructor before proceeding.

2. Organization. Even if it is not a formal assignment, many researchers and students choose to complete an annotated bibliography anyway. Think of it as a tool for organizing and arranging your own material as you research. It helps make sure you capture all the pertinent information for your final works-cited page, and it helps remind you exactly which source is which. When doing a lengthy research project, you will go through dozens of sources on the same topic. It can get hard to remember which source is which, so these annotations will help distinguish your sources from one another.

3. Context. As noted earlier, you can put more than just a quick summary in your annotated bibliography. You can start the annotation with the summary of the material being covered, but then move on to evaluative comments, as well. Was anything unique about this source? What makes you want to use it in your paper? How does it compare with other research material you have found? Answering questions like these can help give your sources a better context.

Caution: Make sure that you find out what your instructor wants included in your final paper. Some instructors may ask you to turn in an annotated bibliography separately, but want the works-cited pages in your paper to be free of annotations.

How Do I Write My Annotated Bibliography?

1. You will begin your entry with a full MLA-style works-cited entry.

2. Begin the annotation on a new line, but do not indent any lines. Typically, you will include two to four sentences summarizing the source. For a book, you could either summarize the entire work or simply summarize the single chapter or article that you have chosen (but always check with your instructor for a preference here).

3. If you choose and your instructor approves, follow the summary with a brief evaluation of the source and discuss how it fits in with your research. If you prepare your annotations throughout the research process, this information can be used when you are writing the first draft of your paper.

4. Do not number or label your sources (such as source A or B). List them all in alphabetical order exactly as you would on an unannotated works-cited page. Also, do not place the works-cited information in bold or use a different type or color of font—there is no need to set if off in any way.

5. Skip a space between entries.

Below are two examples of annotated bibliography entries for a paper written by student Dianne Jeffries; it ties to the sample paper found on page 256.

Bagdikian, Ben. "Grand Theft: The Conglomeratization of Media and the

Degradation of Culture: 25 Years of Monitoring the Multinationals.

Multinational Monitor 26.1–2 (Jan–Feb 2005): 35–7. *Expanded Academic ASAP*. Thomson Gale. Web. 19 Oct. 2008.

A small group of media conglomerates owns the majority of communication venues, such as television networks, billboards, and radio stations. According to Bagdikian, this lack of competition and unique voices undermines a key element to true democracy—well-informed citizens. American citizens are supposed to own the airwaves in this country, but the lack of regulation from the FCC and the size and power of these corporations make that an impossibility. This article expresses the opinion of a well-informed scholar more than it does hard facts, but it is still very useful. He lists several of the conglomerates and major players by name, so it gives me something more to research later on.

Lasn, Kalle. *Culture Jam: The Uncooling of America*. New York: Eagle Brook, 1999. Print.

Lasn's call-to-action book argues that corporations have grown in might and have become more powerful than countries or religious institutions. His basic premise is that we are all somewhat brainwashed by the corporations and that they utterly dominate our entire culture. He proposes the solution of "culture jamming," doing small things on a daily basis to rebel against corporate culture and to try to win back individuals' hearts, minds, and freedoms. This book is very useful for statistics and the detailed history and dates used throughout. Its language is far more casual than that in Bagdikian's article, so I may have to paraphrase all the information I use in order to keep up the academic tone I need.

Using APA Style

You feel really good about everything you've learned in your English class, so you are confident that you are going to do well on the paper you just turned in to your psychology professor. There's only one problem—you turned the paper in using MLA format, and your instructor expects APA format. You remember hearing something about that format, but what's the big deal? They're both just ways to do the same thing, aren't they? How different can they be? The answer—a lot. When you are preparing a paper for a course, it is crucial that you adhere to the format required by the discipline being studied, or your great paper may earn a less-than-great grade.

American Psychological Association (APA) style is the most commonly used style after MLA style. It is used not only for courses in psychology, but for other disciplines, such as sociology, nursing, and criminology. Like the MLA, the APA provides guidelines for formatting manuscripts and properly referencing sources through in-text parenthetical citations and lists of sources used. (For the most detailed explanation of APA style, consult the latest edition of the *Publication Manual of the American Psychological Association*. The association's website *APA Style.org* at http://www .apastyle.org/ is also helpful, particularly its "Specific Questions" section in its "Style Tips" pages at http://www.apastyle.org/previoustips.html.) Though there are similarities between MLA and APA styles, there are also some major differences, so it is important to know which style your instructor wants you to use. Carefully adhering to APA guidelines will help you to produce a credible, professional-looking paper, and protect you against charges of plagiarism. This chapter will discuss the proper format for your paper's appearance, for the list of sources consulted, and for parenthetical citations.

DIRECTORY OF REFERENCES ENTRIES

FORMATTING THE APA-STYLE PAPER

General Appearance

APA style requires that the general appearance and basic physical layout of your paper conform to certain guidelines. These guidelines are as follows:

- *Paper Size:* Your paper should be typed on one side only of eight-and-a-half-by eleven-inch white paper with one-inch margins on all sides. (The default margins in Microsoft Word are 1.25 on the left and right sides, so you should go to the Document section in the Format menu to modify this.)

- *Alignment:* If you are using a computer, justify the lines of your paper at the left margin (don't right-justify or full-justify).

- *Font Size:* Choose a simple, legible font, such as Times New Roman, 12 point.

- *Sentence Spacing:* APA style recommends using only one space after terminal punctuation marks (periods, question marks, and exclamation points), but your instructor may prefer two spaces, so ask.

■ *Line Spacing:* The entire paper (with the exception of content footnotes, if you have them) should be double spaced, including your title page; indented quotations; any endnotes, tables and appendixes; and the references page or any other source lists. Don't add extra spaces above or below titles or in between the works-cited entries.

Title Page

APA style requires a title page, which should contain four elements: a **header,** a **running head** for publication, a **title,** and a **byline** with your name and institutional affiliation (your school).

Header

The header goes in the upper-right corner one-half inch below the top of the page of each page of your paper, so you should use the "header" function in Word (see p. 313 in the MLA chapter if you don't know how to do this). Because articles for publication sometimes receive "blind" reviews, APA requires that the first two or three words of the title be used in the header instead of the author's last name. Next, type five spaces and add the page number by clicking the page number icon in the Header and Footer floating menu.

Running Head

The running head is a shortened version of the title that appears on every page of a published article. It should not exceed fifty characters and spaces. Type it after the phrase "Running head" and a colon in all capital letters at the top of the paper flush with the left margin (it will appear below the header when it is printed).

Title and Byline

The title and byline are centered and go together midway between the top and bottom of the page. The title itself should be concise but also fully explanatory. Avoid abbreviations and redundant words and phrases, like *method, results, a study of,* and *an experiment.* An example of a title that clearly states the paper's content and avoids unnecessary words is "Gender and Social Contact Effects on Attitudes Toward Lesbians and Gay Men" (from the sample student APA paper later in this chapter). A shortened form of this title for the header would be "Gender and Social," and the running head would be "Gender and Social Contact Effects on Attitudes." Don't italicize or underline your title or put it in bold font or within quotation marks. If your title is lengthy enough to go to two or more lines, use a pyramid shape.

Your name, including your middle initial, goes below the title. If the paper is a group effort, the convention is to give the names in the order of the authors' importance in contributing to the paper. The name of your school goes below your name.

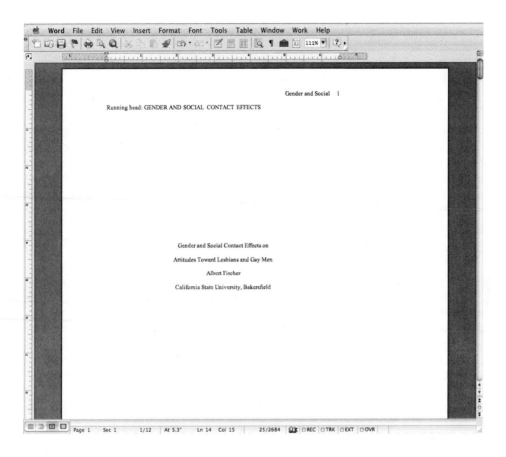

Abstract

Professors in different disciplines have different expectations and requirements for student papers. Many professors in the sciences may ask you to include an **abstract** in your paper. An abstract is a concise summary of your paper that clearly reflects its content and purpose. The abstract should be on a separate page following the title page. It should include the running head and the title *Abstract* centered above the text. (Note: Neither *Abstract* nor any other headings should be italicized, underlined, in bold font, or enclosed in quotation marks.) The text of the abstract should be brief enough to fit on one page. Begin with the most important information, such as your thesis or the results and conclusions of a study or experiment. Include the first initials and last names of authors you cite in your text, as well as the publication dates. If your paper is about an empirical study or an experiment that you conducted, state the problem you investigated; the pertinent characteristics of participants or subjects (number, species, age, gender, etc.); the experimental method, such as apparatus and data-gathering procedure; the results, including statistical significance levels; and your conclusions. If your paper is about a case study, describe the subject's pertinent characteristics, such as age, gender, or anything else relevant to the study; the problem illustrated by the example; and the questions your paper raises for additional research. If your paper is methodological, describe the general class of method, your method's essential features, its range of application, and its behavior, including power and robustness. An abstract for a theoretical paper should include your topic, thesis, scope, sources, and conclusions.

First Page of the Body

On the first page only, your title should be double-spaced above your body text and centered (remember not to add an extra space). Use the Center icon, not the space bar, to properly place the title. The title should not be followed by a period. The body of your paper should begin with an introduction that describes the problem that you are studying and your research strategy if you are presenting your original research, such as an experiment or case study. Discuss the literature on your topic, state your paper's purpose, define your variables, and state your hypotheses, clearly developing your rationales.

Sections and Subsections

If you are describing your own research, you will divide your paper into sections. They should not begin on new pages. The **Method** section begins with *Method* centered above it and may be divided into subsections, such as **Participants** or **Subjects, Apparatus** or **Materials,** and **Procedure.** The Method section describes in detail how you performed the study so that someone else would be able to replicate it. Each subsection should have an italicized heading flush with the left margin.

Follow your Method section with a **Results** section, centering the title *Results* above the text. In the Results section, briefly state your main findings before going into detail and providing your statistical analysis. You may choose to include tables and figures in your Results section; however, if they are lengthy, they may be better off as appendixes. (See "Tables, Illustrations, and Appendixes" in the chapter on MLA format, page 252.) End with a **Discussion** section that you use to evaluate your results and to interpret their implications.

Should you use the term *Subjects* or the term *Participants* for your heading?

The heading **Subjects** or **Participants** depends on whether animals or humans are used in your study. If animals are used, call them *subjects,* and if humans are used, call them *participants.* Indicate who participated in the study, the number, and how you selected them. With human participants, explain how you complied with guidelines on informed consent—your instructor will be able to provide you with the list of APA guidelines, and you can also find them on the APA website's section on "Ethical Principles of Psychologists and Code of Conduct" at http://www.apa.org/ethics/code2002.html#8_02. Include any details that are relevant to the study. For animals, include gender, age, species, and weight. For humans, include gender, age, race/ethnicity, and, if relevant, information such as socioeconomic status, level of education, religion, and sexual orientation. You should also indicate what type of reward or motivation was used to gain their participation.

Include an **Apparatus** or **Materials** section to describe the materials you used and how they functioned in the study, including any equipment you used and the model numbers and manufacturers. (Remember that you must give enough detail so that anyone could read your paper and re-create your study exactly.)

You may want to include a **Design** section, where you identify your independent and dependent variables, indicate what the levels of the independent variables were, and whether factors were repeated, matched, or independent. *Variables* are the characteristics or properties of an event, object, animal, or person that can take on different values or amounts. *Independent variables* are those that are manipulated by an experimenter in order to see effects on the dependent variables. The *dependent variables* are those that the experimenter is trying to explain in terms of the independent variables. For example, if you decided to conduct a study on whether positive or negative movie reviews affected individual moviegoers' ratings of a film, the two kinds of reviews would be the independent variables, and the subjects' ratings would be the dependent variables. Also, describe how subjects were assigned to groups and what your control procedures were. (Do not describe procedures in this section. A helpful trick is to avoid using action verbs in this part of the paper.)

In the **Procedure** section, summarize each step in the execution of the study, indicating what a typical test, trial, or session involved and describing the phases of the study and any instructions that were given to your subjects. Give your groups descriptive names, such as "tutored group" and "untutored group," instead of just "group 1" and "group 2."

Footnotes

In APA style, the term *footnote* is used both for notes that appear at the foot of the page and for those that follow the body of the paper (called *endnotes* in MLA-style papers). Use them sparingly, if at all, and only for information that strengthens the discussion of your topic. Follow the procedures for footnoting in the MLA style section (page 254) for notes placed at the bottom of the page. If you add the note at the end of the paper, center the word *footnotes* at the top of a separate page. The first line of each note should be one-half inch from the left margin and begin with the number in superscript that corresponds to the numbers placed in your paper. This page should follow the body of the paper and precede the references page.

Tables and Figures

Tables and figures should be simple, clear, and provide only necessary information that is not duplicated in the body of the paper. Tables generally feature two to three horizontal lines: the first line comes below the italicized title, which should briefly but clearly explain the table's contents; the second comes below column headings, if there are any, and above the information in the table; and the third comes below the table. Notes can be added below this line if necessary. Use zeroes before decimal points when numbers are less than one. Figures are used for illustrations or to convey patterns of results that would be less clear in a table. As with tables, use them only if they are needed to provide necessary information that augments instead of duplicates information in the body. Figures should be identified by number in the text of the paper, and the figures follow any tables at the end of the paper.

References Page

The body of your paper should be followed with a list of the sources that you used. In a research-based paper, this is a vital step. It shows the readers all the details of the research you've compiled, so that they can track down these sources themselves. This list should begin on the page following the last page of the paper itself and should include the word *References* centered at the top.

SAMPLE APA REFERENCES ENTRIES

General Guidelines

- APA style divides types of reference into two groups: periodicals and nonperiodicals. Periodicals include scholarly journals, magazines, newsletters, and any other item published on a regular basis. Nonperiodicals include books, reports, manuals, and audiovisual media. The first line of every entry on a references page is flush with the left margin, and every other line is indented half an inch.

- All of the entries on your references page should be arranged alphabetically by either the last name of the first author in an entry or the first important word of the title if there is no author. Unlike with MLA format, however, you generally use only last names of authors followed by initials. When two authors' names are identical, use the first important words of the titles of their works to determine order. When two or more entries with coauthors begin with the same name but have different people listed after, alphabetize by the last name of the second author listed. If the first two coauthors are the same, alphabetize by the third author, and so on. If you use more than one work by the same author, use his or her full name for each entry, but arrange them by year of publication, with the earliest year first. If the works are published in the same year, alphabetize them by the initial letter of the title (ignoring *a, an,* and *the*). When there is no author, you should alphabetize by the first important word of the title, ignoring (but not moving) *a, an,* and *the*.

- List all authors up to and including a sixth author. If you have more than six, use *et al* (Latin for *et alii,* which means "and others"), followed by a period, for every name following the sixth. Always leave the authors' names in the order that they are presented. Set the name of the last author off with an ampersand (&), not the word *and*. When you have two authors or editors in an entry, use a comma before the ampersand (&) separating their names. When authors are listed following the word *with,* include them in the entry, but enclose them in parentheses after the other authors.

Format for Periodicals

Entries for periodicals will include the following information in the following order:

1. **Author:** Begin with the author's last name followed by first initials; if you have two or more authors, separate their names with commas and set the last author off with an ampersand (&), not *and*.

2. **Date:** The date of publication is especially important to the disciplines that require APA style, where up-to-date research in the sciences is crucial, which is why the date is provided earlier in the entry than it is in MLA format. In parentheses, add the year of publication for journals and the exact date for other types of periodical (the year followed by a comma and the month, not abbreviated and the day, if a day is provided); type (*n.d.*) if there is no date provided; follow with a period.

3. **Title of Article:** Provide the title of the article, not enclosed in quotation marks, capitalizing only proper nouns and the first letter of a title and the first letter of the subtitle if there is one, followed by a period.

4. **Title of Periodical:** Add the title of the periodical, underlined or italicized (APA recommends italics, but you should ask whether your instructor has a preference), capitalizing all words except for *a, an, the, and, but,* and prepositions, followed by a comma.

5. **Volume and Issue:** Give the volume number, also underlined or italicized, for a periodical that is continuously paginated through a volume. If each page of a periodical begins on page one, follow the volume number with the issue number in parentheses (not underlined or italicized); follow with a comma.

6. **Page Numbers:** End with the page numbers of the article (give the full number of the last page), preceded with *pp.* only if the periodical is a newspaper, followed by a period.

Sample Entries for Periodicals

1. ARTICLE FROM A JOURNAL WITH CONTINUOUS PAGINATION

Herek, G. M., Capitanio, J. P., & Widaman, K. F. (2003). Stigma, social risk, and health policy: Public attitudes toward HIV surveillance policies and the social construction of illness. *Health Psychology, 22,* 533–540.

2. ARTICLE FROM A JOURNAL OR MAGAZINE THAT BEGINS EACH ISSUE ON PAGE ONE

Silverstein, M. (2006). "A word by which you will be revealed": The problem of language in Will Eno's monologues. *American Drama, 15*(2), 61–91.

3. ARTICLE FROM A WEEKLY OR BIWEEKLY MAGAZINE (NO VOLUME OR ISSUE GIVEN)

Lemann, N. (2006, November 27). The weekly warrior. *New Yorker,* 126–133.

4. ARTICLE FROM A NEWSPAPER

> Proctor, C. (2007, January 8.) An educational alternative is winning students
>
> over. *Los Angeles Times,* p. 83.

5. REVIEW OF A BOOK OR MOTION PICTURE

Reviews are treated like other articles, but you follow the article title with the type of medium being reviewed and its name in brackets. If the article is untitled, use the material inside the brackets as the title, retaining the brackets to make clear that this is a description, not an actual title.

> Schudson, M. (2007). Owning up: A new book stops short of deepening the
>
> discourse on media concentration [Review of the book *Fighting for air:*
>
> *The battle to control America's media*]. *Columbia Journalism Review,*
>
> *54*(5), 56–58.

6. CARTOON

Give the name of the cartoonist, followed by the date of publication and title of the cartoon if it has one or the name of the cartoon strip if it is part of a series. Write *Cartoon* in brackets. Then give the publication information for the cartoon's source, the same way you would for any other material from a periodical.

> Rees, D. (2007, May 31). Get your war on [Cartoon]. *Rolling Stone,* 10.

7. ADVERTISEMENT

Give the name of the product or company being advertised, followed by the date of publication, followed by the word *Advertisement* in brackets. Follow with the publication information for the advertisement's source, the same way you would for any other material from a periodical.

> Hypnôse by Lancôme. (2007, May). [Advertisement.] *Playbill,* 42–43.

Format for Electronic Sources

Electronic sources follow the same guidelines for printed articles, followed by the word *Retrieved* and the month, day, and year (in that order) followed by the word *from* (not set off with a comma) and the URL (not enclosed in angle brackets), followed with a period or the name of the database followed by a period.

8. INTERNET ARTICLE ORIGINALLY PUBLISHED IN PRINT FORM

The *Publication Manual of the American Psychological Association,* 5th ed., advises using the same guidelines that you would use for the print version, but adding

Electronic version in brackets after the article title, unless the article has been changed in some way—for instance, if page numbers aren't indicated or additional information has been added to the online version. In those cases, follow the same guidelines for printed articles, followed by the word *Retrieved* and the month, day, and year (in that order) followed by the word *from* (not set off with a comma) and the URL (not enclosed in angle brackets), followed by a period.

Herek, G. M., Capitanio, J. P., & Widaman, K. F. (2003). Stigma, social risk, and health policy: Public attitudes toward HIV surveillance policies and the social construction of illness [Electronic version]. *Health Psychology, 22,* 533–540.

Hart, A. J., & Morry, M. M. (1997). Trait inferences based on racial and behavioral cues. *Basic and Applied Social Psychology, 19,* 33–49. Retrieved January 29, 2007, from http://www.questia.com/ PM.qst?a=o&d=76988465.

9. ARTICLE IN AN INTERNET-ONLY JOURNAL

Hollis, E. (2006, November). Gorgonzola sandwiches and yellow crayons: James Joyce, Buffy the Vampire Slayer, and the aesthetic of minutiae. *Slayage: The Online International Journal of Buffy Studies, 22.* Retrieved March 7, 2007 from http://www.slayageonline.com/Numbers/slayage_ 22.htm.

10. ARTICLE IN AN INTERNET-ONLY NEWSLETTER

APA responds to Tom Cruise's anti-psychiatry remarks. (2005, June 28). Retrieved February 2, 2007, from http://www.medicalnewstoday.com/medicalnews .php?newsid=26719.

11. ARTICLE FROM A UNIVERSITY PROGRAM OR DEPARTMENT WEB SITE

Black, J. B., McClintock, R., & Hill, C. (1994). Assessing student understanding and learning in constructivist study environments. Retrieved May 11, 2007, from Columbia University, Institute for Learning Technologies Web site: http://www.ilt.columbia.edu/publications/asulcse.html.

12. WORK FROM AN ONLINE INDEX

Susman, J. (2006, April). Harry and Louise redux. *Journal of Family Practice,*
  55(4), 276. Retrieved June 18, 2007, from Psychology and Behavioral
  Sciences Collection EBSCOhost database.

Format for Nonperiodicals

Entries for nonperiodicals, such as books, pamphlets, reports, and any other material that is not published periodically, will include the following information in this order:

1. **Author:** Start with the name of the book's author(s) or the author(s) of a chapter, essay, article, story, or other work from a book or anthology if that is your source. End with a period. Provide authors' last names followed by first initials; if you have two or more authors, separate their names with commas and set the last author off with an ampersand (&), not *and.*

2. **Year of Publication and Other Identifying Information:** In parentheses, enclose the year of publication and any other information necessary to help identify the item, such as edition, volume number, or report number.

3. **Portion Title:** If you are citing one specific portion of an item, such as a chapter or article, you will include the title of this, not italicized, underlined, or enclosed in quotation marks, capitalizing only proper nouns and the first letter of a title and the first letter of the subtitle if there is one, followed by a period.

4. **Editor:** If you are using an article or other work from an edited book, type *In* and follow with the editor's first initials followed by his or her last name and the abbreviation *Ed.* or *Eds.* in parentheses (if the book has no editor or is an encyclopedia, put *In* before the title), followed by a comma.

5. **Book or Other Nonperiodical Title:** List the title and subtitle of the item, underlined or italicized, capitalizing only proper nouns and the first letter of a title and the first letter of the subtitle if there is one. If your source is a portion of the item, enclose the inclusive page numbers, preceded by *pp.,* in parentheses after the title (if the work is an encyclopedia, write *Vol.* and the volume number followed by a comma before *pp.*); end this part of the entry with a period.

6. **City of Publication:** Give the city in which the item was published (the first one listed if more than one city is named). If the city is not well known, provide the state's abbreviation (if the publisher is a university and the state is part of the name, do not give the state's abbreviation after the city).

7. **Publisher:** Give a brief form of the publisher's name, omitting words and abbreviations such as *Publisher, Co.,* and *Inc.* but keeping *Books* or *Press;* finish the entry with a period.

Books

13. BOOK WITH ONE AUTHOR

Felsen, R. B. (2002). *Violence and gender reexamined*. Washington, DC:

American Psychological Association.

14. BOOK WITH THREE AUTHORS

Bush, S. S., Connell, M., & Denney, R. L. (2006). *Ethical practice in forensic*

psychology: A systematic model for decision making. Washington, DC:

American Psychological Association.

15. TRANSLATIONS

Ellul, J. (1965). *Propaganda: The formation of men's attitudes* (K. Kelle &

J. Lerner, Trans.). New York: Knopf.

16. ARTICLE OR CHAPTER FROM AN ANTHOLOGY

Ford, J. G. (2002). Healing homosexuals: A psychologist's journey through the

ex-gay movement and the pseudo-science of regenerative therapy. In

A. Shidlo, M. Schroeder, & J. Drescher (Eds.), *Sexual conversion therapy:*

Ethical, clinical, and research perspectives (pp. 69–86). New York:

Haworth Medical Press.

Other Types of Sources

17. MOTION PICTURE, VIDEOCASSETTE, OR DVD

Begin with the names of the director, the producer, and/or writer, following them with their roles in parentheses. Follow with the year in parentheses, followed by a period. Next is the title, underlined or italicized, capitalizing only the first word, followed by *Motion picture* in brackets, followed by a period. Provide the primary country of origin and movie studio, followed by a period, or, if the film is of limited circulation, the distributor's name and address enclosed in parentheses.

Del Toro, G. (Producer, Writer, & Director). (2006). *Pan's labyrinth* [Motion

picture]. United Kingdom: Picturehouse.

18. TELEVISION OR RADIO BROADCAST OR RADIO PROGRAM

Begin with the name of the director, the producer, or both, following them with their roles in parentheses. Follow with the date in parentheses, followed by a period. Next comes the title of the broadcast, series, or episode title, followed in brackets by what the work is. If it is a series episode, do not italicize or underline it, and follow with the name of the series, italicized or underlined, followed by a period. Place the producer of the series after the series title, preceded by *In*. End with the city and the network or radio call letters.

> Whedon, J. (Writer & Director). (1999, December 14). Hush [Television series episode]. In J. Whedon (Producer), *Buffy the Vampire Slayer*. Los Angeles: WB.

> Gross, T., & Miller, D. (Producers) & Sorrock, R. (Director). *Fresh air* [Radio program]. Philadelphia: WHYY-FM.

19. PODCAST

> Diamond, M. (Professor). (2006, fall). Organization of the body. *1B 131: General human anatomy* [Podcast]. Berkeley: University of California, Berkeley. Retrieved February 2, 2007, from http://www. apple.com/ itunes/store/podcasts.html.

PERSONAL COMMUNICATIONS AND LIVE LECTURES AND PERFORMANCES

Personal communications—conversations, meetings, email, letters, instant messages, text messages, and telephone conversations—and public performances and lectures differ from published references because they are not "recoverable" by your readers. They should not be included on your references page, but you should cite them in your paper if you use any information obtained through such communications or from performances.

For personal communications, provide the individual's last name, first initial(s), the phrase *personal communication,* and a date: (J. Doe, personal communication, August 13, 2009). This can be added as a parenthetical citation, integrated into your text, or presented as a combination of the two.

For public performances and lectures, provide the individual's last name, first initial(s), the title in quotation marks if the event has one, a short word or short phrase to identify the format (such as *lecture, comedy routine,* or *campaign speech*), and the location and date. If the event is part of a course, conference, or lecture series, you can add that after the performance title, if there is one, or the descriptive phrase if there is no title. This can also be added as a parenthetical citation, integrated into your text, or presented as a combination of the two.

For plays, concerts, or any other live productions with groups of people, what you list first depends on your paper's focus.

Sexual orientation legislation. (2007, January 1). *Today on BBC Radio 4*

[Podcast]. Retrieved January 12, 2007, from http://downloads.bbc.co.uk/

rmhttp/downloadtrial/radio4/today/today_20070109-0800_40_pc.mp3.

20. YOUTUBE CLIP

Stephen Colbert on the O'Reilly Factor. (2007, January 18.) [YouTube.]

Retrieved May 22, 2007, from ≤http://www.youtube.com/

watch?v=DJvY_RftA4I>.

APA IN-TEXT PARENTHETICAL CITATIONS

You must include citations within your paper to direct your readers to the correct entries on the references page. MLA format and APA format treat in-text citations differently. APA style requires the author-date method of citation. Only the author's last name is used in the document and within parenthetical citations. Also, APA uses the ampersand (&) instead of the word *and*. The following section will give you the guidelines for APA in-text citations, including use of authors' names, placement of citations, and treatment of electronic sources.

1. Author's Name Given in Your Sentence
2. Author's Name Not Given in Your Sentence
3. Two Authors with the Same Last Name
4. Works with Multiple Authors
5. Two or More Sources Within the Same Citation
6. Six or More Authors
7. No Author Provided
8. Works by Associations, Corporations, Government Agencies, etc.

1. AUTHOR'S NAME GIVEN IN YOUR SENTENCE

Generally, an author's last name (do not include first name or initials) appears in your paper followed by the year of publication in parentheses.

> Chilcoat (2004) asserts that a "defining feature of cyberpunk cinema is the fantasy of detachment of the human mind from the mortal body so it can live on indefinitely in cyberspace."

2. AUTHOR'S NAME NOT GIVEN IN YOUR SENTENCE

If you do not mention the author of the material you are quoting or paraphrasing within the text of your paper, follow the author's last name with a comma and the year of publication in parentheses.

> When it comes to gender roles, cyberpunk cinema is actually conservative (Chilcoat, 2004).

3. TWO AUTHORS WITH THE SAME LAST NAME

If your paper has two authors with the same last name, include the first and middle initials of each author in all citations.

> R. A. Smith (2002) and C. R. Smith (2000) have both looked at issues of gender and diversity in the work environment.

> Inventories distributed to three groups—male officer trainees, male conscientious objectors, and a group of women of comparable ages—indicated that the "strongest determinator of moral approval of aggression was the choice of refusal to engage in military service" (Lagerspetz; Björkqvist, K.; Björkqvist, H.; & Lundman, 1988).

4. WORKS WITH MULTIPLE AUTHORS

When a work has two authors, cite both names every time the reference occurs in the text. In parenthetical material, join the names with an ampersand (&).

> Data collected in Minnesota indicated that negative responses to the GLBT population on the part of police, such as inadequate help or outright victimization, outnumbered positive responses (Wolff & Cokely, 2007).

In the text itself, join the names with the word *and*.

> Wolff and Cokely (2007) studied data collected across ten years by a GLBT group in Minnesota.

When a work has three to five authors, cite all authors the first time the reference occurs.

> Lagerspetz; Björkqvist, K.; Björkqvist, H.; & Lundman (1988) distributed attitude and personality inventories to three groups: male officer trainees, male conscientious objectors, and a group of women of comparable ages.

In all subsequent citations in the same paragraph, include only the surname of the first author followed by *et al.* and the year of publication.

> The inventories indicated that the "strongest determinator of moral approval of aggression was the choice of refusal to engage in military service" (Lagerspetz et al., 1988).

5. TWO OR MORE SOURCES WITHIN THE SAME CITATION

When citing two or more sources by different authors within the same citation, place the authors' names in parentheses in alphabetical order, followed by the year of publication and separated by a semicolon:

> Homophobia, particularly in men, has shown to correlate with increased aggression (Bernat, Calhoun, Adams, & Zeichner, 2001; Whitley, 2001).

6. SIX OR MORE AUTHORS

If a work has six or more authors, cite the last name of the first author followed by *et al.* in all citations:

> Smith et al. (2005) studied nonfatal work-related injuries among American adults.

> "The prominence of occupational injuries among injuries to working-age adults reinforces the need to examine workplace conditions in efforts to reduce the societal impact of injuries" (Smith et al. 2005).

7. NO AUTHOR PROVIDED

If a source does not include an author's name, substitute for the author's name the title or a shortened form of the title in the text or a parenthetical citation. You can use the first important word or more; the idea is to give as short a form of the title as you can without risking it being confused with a similar title beginning an entry on your works-cited page. Format the title words the same way they are formatted on the works-cited page; if the title is in quotation marks on that page, it must be treated the same way in the citation, and so on.

> The government's Uniform Crime Reports indicate that the overall homicide rate remained stable in recent years ("Social Statistics").

8. WORKS BY ASSOCIATIONS, CORPORATIONS, GOVERNMENT AGENCIES, ETC.

Corporate authors can be written out each time they appear in the text or a citation.

> According to Doctors without Borders, "Since 1998, civilians in the North Kivu province of the eastern Democratic Republic of Congo have been caught in the middle of a battle for control between local and foreign militias, the Congolese army, and UN forces" (2007).

> "Since 1998, civilians in the North Kivu province of the eastern Democratic Republic of Congo have been caught in the middle of a battle for control between local and foreign militias, the Congolese army, and UN forces" (Doctors without Borders, 2007).

If organizations have well-known abbreviations, the names of corporate authors can be written out in the first reference and abbreviated in subsequent citations as long as enough information is given for a reader to easily locate its source in the list of references.

> The Federal Bureau of Investigation (FBI, 2007) posts the following on its website: "If you have any information about a crime or an act of terrorism that has happened or may happen, please go straightaway to our tip line and give us the facts."
>
> "In the early morning hours of this past September 11, an Arizona man logged into our website, went to our electronic tips page, and reported what he had just seen on the Internet. And we are so glad he did" (FBI, 2007).

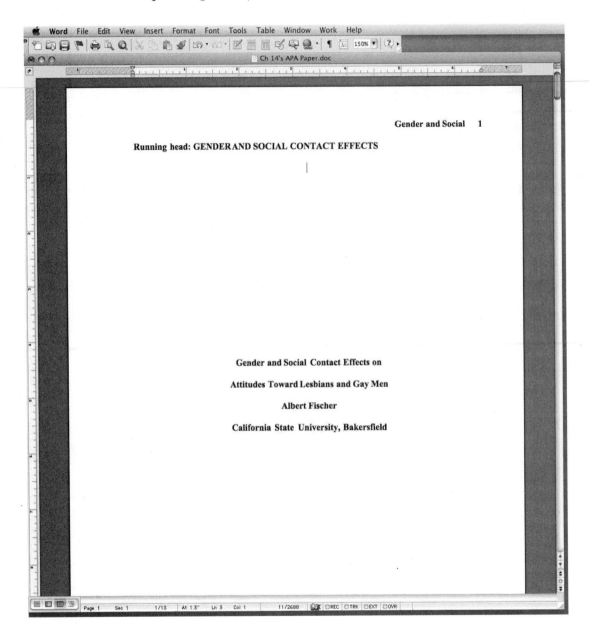

SAMPLE ANNOTATED APA-STYLE PAPER

Following is a sample student paper that shows you the correct format for an APA-style paper.

Gender and Social   2

Abstract

Understanding homophobia and reducing its influence may improve the lives of people of all sexual orientations. The effects of the gender of the respondent, gender of the gay person, and social contact with gay individuals (no socializing vs. socializing at least once every 6 months) on attitudes toward lesbians and gay men were examined. Participants were 108 heterosexual university undergraduates (42% male and 32% nonwhite) with an average age of 24.40 years ($SD = 6.73$ years). A three-way mixed-design analysis of variance revealed main effects for respondent gender ($p < .05$, $O^2 = .05$) and social contact ($p < .0001$, $O^2 = .14$) and a two-way interaction between gender of the respondent and gender of the gay person ($p < .0001$, $O^2 = .32$). Heterosexual women and those who have social contacts with gay people were more accepting of lesbians and gay men than heterosexual men and those who do not have social contacts with gay individuals, and each gender was less accepting of gay people of their own gender.

The abstract should be on a separate page following the title page. It should include the running head and the title *Abstract* centered above the text.

Albert keeps the abstract short, in keeping with APA guidelines. He begins with the most important information: the main point that the paper will prove and a description of the results and conclusions of his study.

Gender and Social Contact Effects on

Attitudes Toward Lesbians and Gay Men

Lesbians and gay men have long been targets of hostility and victims of various forms of legal and de facto discrimination. Negative views of same-sex attraction and prejudiced attitudes against gay men and lesbians occur in diverse groups, including teachers, students, and the public in general (Herek, 2000; Yang, 1997). Even law enforcement officials are apparently prone to homophobic responses; for example, an analysis of 1,896 incident reports spanning 1990 to 2000 that were collected by a Gay/Lesbian/Bisexual/Transgender (GLBT) advocacy group in Minnesota indicated that negative responses and behaviors on the part of police, such as inadequate help or outright victimization, outnumbered positive responses (Wolff & Cokely, 2007). Many heterosexual people feel an intolerance of gay men and lesbians that can range from mild disdain to hatred and disgust, and this can even result in violence. Homophobia, particularly in men, has shown to correlate with increased aggression (Bernat, Calhoun, Adams, & Zeichner, 2001; Whitley, 2001). This fear and intolerance, whatever the degree, is most often referred to as homophobia. However, heterosexuals' attitudes

---

Marginal notes:

Albert's title is double-spaced above his first paragraph and centered.

His introduction begins by describing the problem that he studied.

APA format requires the last names of the authors of the two studies that Albert used for this information, followed by the years the articles were published.

With two or more authors of one study, use the ampersand instead of "and" before the last name given.

This underscores the seriousness of the issues addressed by the paper.

toward lesbians and gay men are not universally negative, and research suggests that one factor is relationships, with individuals having at least one homosexual friend, relative, or acquaintance more likely to have positive attitudes (Eldridge, Mack, & Swank, 2006; Lance, 1987; Wills & Crawford, 2000).

Reducing homophobia would obviously benefit lesbians and gay men, who suffer the consequences of others' prejudices. "Closeted" individuals fear that disclosure of their orientation might threaten relationships with friends and family, jeopardize employment opportunities, and invite verbal and physical harassment; and those who are "out of the closet" often have to deal with these problems.

Reducing homophobia might also benefit heterosexuals. Homophobia may be an integral part of the American male's ideal of heterosexual masculinity, meeting basic psychological needs that are nonetheless hazardous to physical and psychological health (Herek, 1986). Homophobia may cause some men to have difficulty expressing their feelings, demonstrating emotional vulnerability, and feeling intimacy with other men, which can cause harmful stress (Monroe, Baker, & Roll, 1997). With disdain toward lesbians and gay

> The tone of an APA paper is usually different from what students write in English classes. APA papers tend to be drier and avoid rhetorical flourishes designed to "hook" readers.

> Suggesting homophobia has negative effects on heterosexuals makes the appeal of the paper broader.

> Albert backs up his assertions throughout the paper with references to research that supports them.

men being so widespread, some heterosexuals may be afraid of being falsely labeled as gay.

Gender and feelings about gender roles, age, religiosity, and fear of AIDS are all factors that appear to affect attitudes towards lesbians and gay men; in particular, women tend to be more tolerant than men (Burn, 2000; Eldridge, Mack, & Swank, 2006; Whitley, 2001).

Some research has found that both heterosexual men and women are more homophobic toward gay persons of their own gender (Gentry, 1987; Whitley, 1988) and that this effect is stronger in men than in women (Herek, 1984, 1989). Acquaintance with lesbians and gay men generally results in more tolerance and more favorable attitudes (Furnham & Taylor, 1990; Herek, 1986; Wills & Crawford, 2000). Based on the literature review, it was hypothesized that heterosexual participants would display more homophobia toward gay individuals of their own gender, that women would be less homophobic than men, and that heterosexuals who socialize with gay people would show more acceptance than those who don't have social contacts with them.

Race can also be a factor, and African Americans are believed by some researchers to have significantly less tolerance of homosexuality than White Americans. This may result in greater stigmatization among African Americans, with African American homosexuals feeling intense pressure to hide their homosexuality within their own communities. Attitudes toward homosexuals and homosexuality on the part of African Americans should not be looked at simplistically, however, and they may be complex, even seemingly paradoxical in some respects. A study comparing the opinions of approximately 7,000 African Americans and 43,000 Whites on lesbian and gay relationships, employment rights, and civil liberties found more homophobia among African Americans, but it also found more support for civil liberties for lesbians and gay men and more opposition to employment discrimination (Lewis, 2003). Also, among African Americans, women may feel less negatively toward homosexuals than men (Battle & Lemelle, 2002).

Based on the literature review, it was hypothesized that heterosexual participants would display more homophobia toward gay individuals of their own gender, that women would be less homophobic than men, and that heterosexuals who socialize with gay people would show more acceptance than those who don't have social contacts with them.

> Hypotheses should be informed ones. Albert drew on the research conducted by experts in the field.

Since Albert conducted his own research, which he will describe, he divides his paper into sections, beginning with the Method section.

Since his study involved humans, this section is called Participants, not Subjects.

Sometimes it is necessary to omit participants; indicate how many and why they were omitted.

Sometimes information about participants may be missing, but if the information is not relevant to traits being measured, the participants need not be eliminated.

This section describes the materials Albert used and how they functioned in his study.

Method

Participants

Questionnaires were distributed to 135 undergraduates in six classes at a California university: History of Film, Management Information Systems, Islam, African-American Issues, and two sections of Logical Reasoning. Of the 135 participants who were given the questionnaire, three were omitted from the data analyses because they indicated on their questionnaires that they did not want to participate, two were omitted because they failed to complete the questionnaire, and two were omitted because they did not identify their gender. Twenty individuals were eliminated from the data analyses in order to be sure that only heterosexuals were analyzed: 14 who did not identify their sexual orientation, 3 who identified themselves as gay male or lesbian, and 3 who identified themselves as bisexual. Of the remaining 108 participants, 45 were male and 70 were white, and they had an average age of 24.40 years ($SD = 6.73$ years). Five participants failed to indicate their ethnicity.

Apparatus

The two-page questionnaire collected demographic and attitude information. The demographic information included age, gender, and sexual orientation. Sexual orientation was measured on a scale similar to the 7-point Kinsey scale (Kinsey, Pomeroy, & Martin, 1948), but which measured attraction rather than actual behavior and ranged from (0) "attracted to others of the opposite sex" to (6) "attracted to others of the same sex." Respondents were also asked to report the frequency of socializing with one or more lesbians or gay men.

Acceptance of gay men and lesbians was assessed by a series of 18 six-point Likert-scale questions, nine referring to gay men and nine parallel questions referring to lesbians (e.g., "I would feel at ease talking to a gay woman at a party" and "I would feel at ease talking to a gay man at a party"). Questions from the questionnaire are provided in Table 1. Scales measuring acceptance of gay men and lesbians were created by averaging responses to the questions on each subscale.

> The table is an appendix at the end of the paper after the References page.

Procedure

Data were collected by one male and two female researchers who went into classrooms in a pair or individually to distribute the survey. Data collectors used the same script in each classroom, telling students that they were conducting research for a psychology class project, that

> This section summarizes each step in the execution of the study.

participation was voluntary, that all information would be kept confidential, and that the results of the survey would be posted outside the faculty sponsor's office at the end of the quarter. After the questionnaires were collected, the participants were given a brief statement about the hypotheses of the study.

Ethical standards require that participants be informed of the aims of a study, but not until after they have answered the questionnaires, or the information would taint the study.

This section was written to clearly state the results and the statistics used.

Results

The average acceptance score was 3.62 ($SD = 1.26$); the Likert scale categories were defined as 3 = "moderately disagree" and 4 = "moderately agree." Scores on negatively phrased items were reversed.

Subjects were divided into two groups based on the reported frequency of social contact with one or more gay people. Subjects indicating that they never socialize ($n = 19$) or that they don't know how frequently they socialize with gay people ($n = 57$) were placed in one group, and subjects indicating any socializing were placed in a second group ($n = 29$). The second group included 2 subjects who reported socializing with gay people at least once a month, 4 subjects who reported socializing with gay people at least once every three months, and 3 who reported socializing with gay people at least once every 6 months.

A three-way mixed-design analysis of variance was used to examine the effect of respondent gender, amount of socializing (no socializing vs. socializing at least once every 6 months), and the gender of the gay person on acceptance. A corrected eta-squared statistic (Tabachnick & Fidell, 1983) was calculated for each significant result as a measure of its strength. There was a significant main effect for respondent gender, $F(1, 100) = 5.76$, $p < .05$, $\odot^2 = .05$. Female respondents averaged 3.90 ($SD = 1.20$), and male respondents averaged 3.23 ($SD = 1.23$). There was also a significant main effect for social contact, $F(1, 100) = 16.31$, $p < .0001$, $\odot^2 = 140$. Subjects who indicated socializing with gay people averaged 4.38 ($SD = 1.10$), and subjects who did not indicate socializing with gay people averaged 3.32 ($SD = 1.19$). In addition, there was a significant interaction between respondent gender and the gay person's gender, $F(1, 100) = 46.14$, $p < .0001$, $\odot^2 = .32$. Female subjects showed more acceptance toward gay men ($M = 4.13$, $SD = 1.25$) than toward lesbians ($M = 3.68$, $SD = 1.26$), and male subjects showed more acceptance toward lesbians ($M = 3.58$, $SD = 1.22$) than toward gay men ($M = 2.87$, $SD = 1.35$).

Discussion

The respondents averaged 3.62 on their acceptance of homo-

sexuality, suggesting, on average, neutral attitudes.

It was hypothesized that heterosexual respondents would

display more homophobia toward gay people of their own

gender, that women would be less homophobic than men, and

that heterosexuals who socialize with gay people would show

more acceptance than those who do not have social contacts

with them. Results supported all three hypotheses and were

consistent with previous research (Eldridge, Mack & Swank,

2006; Furnham & Taylor, 1990; Gentry, 1987; Herek, 1984,

1986, 1989, 2000; Lance, 1987; Wills & Crawford, 2000).

As with any study, this one had limitations. The sample

was small and consisted only of undergraduates at a small

university, which may call into question its generalizability.

The confusion that some respondents seemed to experience

with the questionnaire suggests that it may have been vague in

some areas. Also, the attitudes measured were self-reported;

actual discomfort was not measured, nor was behavior

toward homosexuals. There may be a discrepancy between

what people say they feel and how they really behave. Though

one implication of this study is that exposure to gay men and

---

This section presents Albert's findings and clearly relates them to the points he raised in his introduction.

A paper should indicate when a study is consistent with other research on the issues examined. This adds strength and credibility.

It is important to note any possible problems with a study.

Gender and Social   12

lesbians is associated with increased acceptance, it does not

answer the question of whether respondents who had more

exposure were more comfortable because of it, or whether

they had more exposure because they were already relatively

comfortable with lesbians and gay men. Future research could

explore these possibilities.

> Albert provides suggestions for relevant future research related to the issues he discusses in his paper.

Future research should also attempt to determine why

heterosexuals are more homophobic toward gay people

of their own gender. Possible explanations include fear of

sexual advances or fear of latent or actual attraction to gay

people, which might threaten the heterosexual's self-concept.

However, it should not be taken for granted that women and

men are same-gender homophobic for the same reasons.

The question of whether men are really more homophobic

than women—and, if so, why—should be more fully ex-

plored. Women may feel fewer social pressures to be homo-

phobic. Another possible explanation could be a combination

of two factors: for males, the heterosexual's discomfort with

gay people of the same gender could be exacerbated by the

higher standard for "normality" and gender-role conform-

ity expected of men in our culture. Also, the AIDS epidemic

has been viewed by many people as a gay male disease,

and this has served as a focusing point of hostility for some Americans (Herek, 1989).

Research that will shed light on dissimilarities between the causes of homophobia in heterosexual women and men will be valuable because the "cures" may turn out to be different (Burn, 2000). If homophobia is indeed part of the American heterosexual male role, simple exposure to lesbians and gay men may be less effective in reducing homophobia in men than in women.

References

Battle, J., & Lemelle, A. J. (2002). Gender differences in African American attitudes toward gay males. *Western Journal of Black Studies, 26*(3), 134–139.

Bernat, J. A., Calhoun, K. S., Adams, H. E., & Zeichner, A. (2001). Homophobia and physical aggression toward homosexual and heterosexual individuals. *Journal of Abnormal Psychology, 110*(1), 179–187.

Burn, S. M. (2000). Heterosexuals' use of "fag" and "queer" to deride one another: A contributor to heterosexism and stigma. *Journal of Homosexuality, 40*(2), 1–12.

Eldridge, V. L., Mack, L., & Swank, E. (2006). Explaining comfort with homosexuality in rural America. *Journal of Homosexuality, 51*(2), 39–56.

Gentry, C. S. (1987). Social distance regarding male and female individuals. *Journal of Social Psychology, 127*(2), 199–208.

Furnham, A., & Taylor, L. (1990). Lay theories of homosexuality: Aetiology, behaviors and "cures." *British Journal of Social Psychology, 29,* 135–147.

The paper ends with the equivalent of an MLA-format Works Cited page. In APA format, the word References is used instead.

All the sources are listed in alphabetical order.

IN APA format, authors' last names precede their initials even when they are not the first name in an entry.

Capitalize only proper nouns and the first letter in the first words of titles and subtitles.

The journal, volume, and issue are italicized but the issue number and parentheses are not.

Initials are used, not first and middle names.

Most or all of the sources in an APA style paper will be scholarly journals.

Hansen, G. (1982). Measuring prejudice against homosexuality (homosexism) among college students: A new scale. *Journal of Social Psychology, 117,* 233–236.

Herek, G. M. (1984). Beyond "homophobia": A social psychological perspective an attitudes toward lesbians and gay men. *Journal of Homosexuality, 10*(1–2), 69–81.

Herek, G. M. (1986). On heterosexual masculinity. *American Behavioral Scientist, 29,* 563–577.

Herek, G. M. (1989). Heterosexuals' attitudes toward lesbians and gay men: Correlates and gender differences. *Journal of Sex Research, 25,* 451–475.

Herek, G. M. (2000). The psychology of sexual prejudice. *Current Directions in Psychological Science, 9,* 19–22.

Kinsey, A. C., Pomeroy, W. B., & Martin, C. E. (1948). *Sexual behavior in the human male.* Philadelphia: Saunders.

Lance, L. M. (1987). The effects of interaction with gay persons on attitudes toward homosexuality. *Human Relations, 40,* 329–336.

Lewis, G. B. (2003). Black-White differences in attitudes

toward homosexuality and gay rights. *Public Opinion*

Quarterly, 67, 59–78.

Monroe, Mi., Baker, R. C., & Roll, S. (1997). The relation-

ship of homophobia to intimacy in heterosexual men.

Journal of Homosexuality, 33(2), 23–37.

Tabachnick, B. G., & Fidell, L. S. (1983). *Using multivariate*

statistics. New York: Harper & Row.

Whitley, B. E. (1988). Sex differences in heterosexuals'

attitudes toward homosexuals: It depends upon what you

ask. *Journal of Sex Research, 24,* 287–291.

Wills, G., & Crawford, R. (2000). Attitudes toward homosex-

uality in Shreveport-Bossier City, Louisiana. *Journal of*

Homosexuality, 38(3), 97–116.

Wolff, K. B., & Cokely, C. L. (2007). To protect and to

serve?: An exploration of police conduct in relation to

the gay, lesbian, bisexual, and transgender community.

Sexuality & Culture, 11(2), 1–23.

Yang, A. S. (1997). The polls—trends: Attitudes toward

homosexuality. *Public Opinion Quarterly, 61,*

477–507.

City and state are capitalized because they are proper
nouns.

Tables and any other appendixes follow the References page.

Table 1

Questions Used in the Questionnaire

1. Having a gay (male/female) friend could be an enriching experience.

2. I would avoid a (man/woman) if I knew (he/she) was homosexual.

3. Gay (men/women) should be allowed to be (Boy/Girl) Scout leaders.

4. I would feel nervous being in a group of gay (men/women).

5. The average gay (man/woman) is as mentally healthy as the average heterosexual (man/woman).

6. I would not feel comfortable working with a gay (man/woman).

7. I would feel at ease talking to a gay (man/woman) at a party.

8. Society as a whole would benefit if gay (men/women) did not feel that they needed to hide their sexual preference.

9. If I found out that one of my best (male/female) friends

was a homosexual, it would severely damage our

friendship.

SECTION 3

Anthology of Readings

15 CHAPTER

Introduction to Anthology of Readings

Whereas the first sections of this book are meant to focus primarily on your ability to research and to learn to master information competency for academic purposes, the following section is designed to show you how to master different types of information disseminated through what is commonly called "popular culture." Popular culture is a relatively new field of scholarly study. Traditionally, cultural studies in colleges and universities focused on what was referred to as "high culture," such as historic art, classical music, traditional theater, and literary classics. The idea of studying television, popular movies, advertising, and comic books would have seemed insignificant and strange to professors fifty or sixty years ago.

Now, though, the popular "low culture" that we all experience every day is arguably one of the most powerful forces on Earth, and the most important part of our current popular culture is the mass media. The mass media includes television, film, radio, music, the Internet, magazines, advertising campaigns, and any number of other forms of media designed to reach the masses (you and me). Many scholars recently have argued that popular culture generated through this mass media is perhaps the most important subject we should be studying. More to the point, understanding the influence and power of popular culture is a key to modern-day information competency.

Why is popular culture so important for information competency? Take the example of Howard Dean. In the 2004 presidential election, Howard Dean was the frontrunner to become the Democratic nominee for president—he stood a decent chance of becoming among the most powerful men on earth. In one speech given to rally supporters who were disheartened by his third-place position in the Iowa caucuses, he named states he was going to win, and then ended by shouting, "And then we're going to Washington, D.C., to take back the White House! Yeeaarrgghh!"

The news media picked up on this clip and aired it relentlessly. Bloggers sampled the scream and added dance beats. It was satirized over and over on late-night comedy shows. Dean was parodied as a giddy, excitable man unworthy of the presidency, and his numbers in the polls immediately dropped. Ultimately, the Democratic Party gave the nomination to John Kerry, instead. One brief moment aired repeatedly on TV and the Net derailed a top candidate's chance at the presidency. If Abraham Lincoln had made that strange noise on his campaign trail, nobody outside of his immediate audience would have heard it (or probably even heard about it). Now, however, anyone of any importance lives under the constant scrutiny of paparazzi and news media hungry for material to fill their twenty-four-hour news machines. One exclamation or one ill-considered—or even misinterpreted—statement can ruin someone's career and shift mighty political trends. A force powerful enough to topple a presidential hopeful in one day—especially since he ultimately did nothing wrong—is surely a force worthy of study.

To become a master of information, you will need to understand the power that the mass media have. They influence your choices and shape your perceptions. They determine what is considered important and what is not. They tell you what's in and what's out. They can frame a public figure as a hero, an authority, a scoundrel, or a buffoon. The readings in this section are designed to help you peel back the surface of our mass-mediated culture and examine it critically. After reading and thinking about the selections in this section, you may start to question the credibility of some of your favorite news programs, question what is really going on in advertisements, and distinguish between information worth considering and sensational sound bites meant to drum up ratings.

Following is a list of the seven chapters in this section:

Television

K aren is a natural athlete, and she would rather be outdoors playing a sport than doing anything else. Karen's thirteen-year-old sister, Tiffany, is a self-proclaimed "couch potato." She loves TV and spends a few hours of every day in front of the set. She loves Reality TV shows, *American Idol,* and a number of

comedies and crime shows. Tiffany is also a bit of a know-it-all, which gets on Karen's nerves, especially because everything she is so sure about comes from some TV show or another. Karen tries to tell Tiffany that she is wasting too much of her time in front of the TV set, but Tiffany doesn't listen, and her parents think that the TV is harmless. When Karen's English professor assigns a paper on some aspect of the media, Karen decides to research television to see if she can make a case for "less is more" when it comes to the family's TV viewing habits.

In completing this research, Karen found that television has become the primary conduit of information for most American households, replacing print news and books for information about the world at large. She also discovered that it is the major source of entertainment for most Americans. According to the A.C. Nielsen Company, the average American watches more than four hours of TV each day, the equivalent of two full months of nonstop viewing a year. Let's put that into even greater perspective. If you are lucky enough to get eight hours of sleep every night (something many college students only wish for), that would be the equivalent of four full months of nonstop sleeping. If you meet the national average of TV watching and are also used to a good night's sleep, you have what amounts to six months out of every year when you aren't watching television or unconscious. Averages, of course, don't tell us what individuals are doing—you may watch less than four hours of TV a week, for instance, or you may watch even more than four hours a day. No doubt about it, though—Americans, in general, are dependent on their television sets.

But what are we getting when we turn on the TV? What is the content of that "average" four hours? There is no simple answer to that question, as there are now hundreds of channels for people to choose from. Your TV may not be your neighbors', parents', professors', coworkers', or classmates' TV. The American television audience is vast, but we have so much to choose from that the survival of individual programs and even networks is precarious. As broadcast and cable networks struggle for viewers, programming grows increasingly specialized. In the early days of television, with just three major national networks and no cable or satellite, most Americans would not have imagined that the future would hold entire networks devoted to cooking, interior decorating, travel, animals, history, women, men, and individual ethnic groups. Indeed, some people who study television say that networks aren't so much "broadcasting" as "narrowcasting," aiming their programming at specific niche audiences in order to survive.

If you get most of your news from TV, what you know—or think to be true—about the country and the world will depend entirely on what networks and shows you like to watch. Although the best way to form an accurate idea about news is to read, watch, and listen to as varied an amount of media as possible, statistics show that most people don't do this—even though modern technology makes this more possible than it ever has been. (See Chapter 21 for more on the news media.) Our ideas about the world aren't shaped just by the news media, however. We are being "taught" something about the world by every story we read or program we watch or listen to, whether we are fans of sitcoms or crime shows—or even science fiction and fantasy. All these programs presume a certain worldview and disseminate information. They may not be trying to teach anyone anything—some, obviously, do want to do so—but we're still getting information, misinformation, opinions, and attitudes, and we're filing them away in memory, consciously or unconsciously. Information competency requires an aware-ness of how the narratives we get from TV may shape our worldview.

As an example, consider what you know about criminal law. There is a very good chance that most of what you believe is what you have gotten from shows such as the *Law and Order* franchise, *Cold Case, CSI, The Shield,* and even *24*. When we watch these shows, we realize we are watching the works of writers' imaginations, and, if asked, most of us would say that we realize these shows do not paint a completely ac-curate, realistic view of what goes on in criminal investigations, courtrooms, or anti-terrorist units. But what other in-depth "information" do most of us ever get?

What do you think about the insanity pleas in court cases? According to several polls, most Americans believe that it provides a loophole that murderers can use to squirm out of convictions just by "acting crazy." After all, they've seen this happen dozens of times—on TV. In reality, a defense by reason of insanity is difficult to argue and almost never successful. Because of this, defense lawyers rarely use it. The insanity plea is used in less than 1% of all criminal cases in the United States, and it is successful in only one out of four of those cases. Jeffrey Dahmer killed at least thirteen people, preserving the heads and genitals of some of them and keeping these and other remains in his apart-ment. He cooked and ate the flesh of many of his victims because consuming them made him feel closer to them and less lonely. In court, his attorneys attempted to plead Dahmer not guilty by reason of insanity, and the jury didn't buy it. Andrea Yates killed all five of her children. Before she did this, she had been treated for depression and diagnosed by her psychiatrist as psychotic. The jury didn't accept an insanity defense in that case, either. People who are mentally ill do not fit the legal definition of insanity if they are aware that their actions are considered wrong by society—even if they believe they are getting their instructions from aliens, dead people, or talking animals. Yet most of us have a very inaccurate idea about this and other aspects of the law because we have seen countless shows that show us quite different scenarios in the service of their plots.

Whatever the subject—crime, justice, medicine, national security, terrorism, cli-mate change, race relations, war, family, romance, or sex—you name it, and most peo-ple's general impressions and many specific ideas have been shaped as much or more by fiction than by objective research.

Nothing comes value free or information neutral. What we watch shapes us in subtle (or not so subtle) ways, and what we demand in entertainment shapes what networks give us. They get advertising revenue only if we tune in, and so a symbiotic relation-ship is formed—the networks try to give us what we want, and what we want is shaped by what we are used to getting. The cycle goes on and on. Did you ever wonder why so many TV shows seem like barely disguised clones of other shows? It is because the networks don't like taking chances—when a show is successful, executives put out orders to make others as much like it as possible.

TECHNOLOGICAL ADVANCES

Most scholars of television studies focus on program content more than technology, but technology is vitally important, and technological advances may end up shaping the type of programming we see as much as concerns about content. Television now provides images in amazingly clear resolution, and it connects to other technologies, such as video game consoles and DVDs. Understanding these technological advances is crucial in understanding the future of the medium, the means through which future entertainment will be funded, and the transmission of information about the world around us.

HDTV

High Definition Television has been around for several years, but FCC regulations required all TV stations to broadcast only in HDTV by 2009. To get broadcast television, every television in these households has to be HDTV ready, or their owners need to buy receiver boxes to pick up the Digital UHF signals that replaced the UHF and VHF frequencies formerly in use.

The biggest upside of the change may very well be the surge of content. Digital technology allows broadcasters to offer more channels. This may lead to a revolution of free, high-quality digital programming that can change the face of the television market. Everyone will be able to get free HD shows over the air, and, with the expanding lineup of channels, cable will no longer be needed by a great many people. This will change the way television is marketed and lead to a paradigm shift similar to the shift from UHF to cable in the 1980s.

DVR

The **Digital Video Recorder,** or **DVR,** is another innovation that will drastically change the way the television industry works. A DVR is a mix between a VCR and a computer hard drive. One feature this technology allows is the ability to pause and rewind "live TV" as you watch it. If you missed an important play in a sports broadcast or a crucial line of dialogue in a drama, you can just "rewind" as if you were watching the show on tape. The system also scans the program guide and records whatever you want it to record. You can use the keypad on your remote to search for all the shows scheduled for the next week and a half starring a favorite actor. You can search for shows based on headings such as genre or title. Current systems hold hundreds of hours of television at a time, and capacities will inevitably expand even more.

The reason this will lead to a paradigm shift in television is that it easily leaves advertisers in the dust. Most people with DVR systems abandon live television. They record everything or pause the live show and wait a few minutes before playing it, so they can fast forward through the commercials. Advertising agencies are trying hard to catch up. If most viewers can soon skip past all advertisements, corporations will have to find other ways to market their products to us. One way is by placing the products into the programs themselves. Corporations now rely on product placement and any number of other means to advertise to us (see Chapter 19 for advertising). Shows that are sponsored by soft drink companies require that their brands be displayed prominently onscreen, for instance, and the cars that the popular character Jack Bauer drives in *24* are all provided by one company. As active observers of information, we should watch what these trends and new technology will do to the landscape of the American media.

Video Games

Another technology that is tied into television is video gaming. Whereas games used to exist only in arcades and on computers, the current generation of games exists on advanced console systems that you play on your television. The holiday season of 2006/2007 showed a surprising turn of events for video games. The "next generation" of gaming consoles was released with much fanfare and heated competition. Microsoft's high-end Xbox 360 sold very well, capturing the bulk of the video game market for this generation of gaming. Sony's Playstation 3 launched with very slow sales and a disappointing release of games. The big winner, however, was Nintendo's latest console, the Wii. The Wii is a computational midget compared to the high-end graphics and sound capabilities of the 360 and the PS3; however, its innovations made it the hottest gift of the holiday season when it debuted (and again a year later for the 2007/2008 season).

Instead of a standard joystick, the system uses a "wii-mote," which is a sign of things to come in gaming. In it is a sensor that detects the motions and position of the device, so it truly exists in a 3D environment. You steer with it just like you would a steering wheel in racing games, you swing it like a golf club or a baseball bat, and it even has a force feedback "rumble" feature to stimulate your hand.

The video game industry has made more money than all of Hollywood's movies combined for the last several years in a row, and some of the games themselves are described by fans as mature, story-driven works of art as well as a new mode of storytelling. As such, the importance of video games in today's popular culture should not be undervalued. Just as studying film and television once seemed frivolous and unimportant to much of academics, video games may one day see mainstream scholarship and academic consideration. To fully understand our media-driven culture, we must now understand the ubiquitous video game.

DVD

There is nothing new about DVD technology. Most film studios quit putting movies on VCR tapes around the year 2001, and DVD technology is so cheap that virtually everyone can afford a DVD player. Many things are changing about DVDs, however, and they will lead to some major changes in the future of television viewing. First, there are now hundreds of **DVD box sets.** These are collections of favorite film and television series all in one place, usually an entire season at a time. Many people watch television shows by renting, borrowing from a library, or buying entire seasons of a show. Instead of waiting impatiently from week to week and enduring endless advertisements on top of the delay, people opt to watch the shows on their own terms through DVDs. (A miniseries that takes place over six hours and three nights can be rented and watched over, for instance, two nights and takes only five hours—that's an hour of commercials you don't have to watch, and if you feel like watching the whole series in one night, that's your choice, too.) Manufacturers make DVDs, especially the collectors' boxed sets, even more attractive by adding a host of features—you may be offered audio commentary, featurettes about the making of a show, cast and director biographies and filmographies, and music videos. This is slowly changing the mindsets of many television viewers who demand their viewing on their own schedules and not at the whims of networks, who may put a show on a brief hiatus midseason, shift its time or day, or indulge in too many cliffhangers. Again, this spells bad news for advertisers who are missing out on a prime chance to air commercials.

Online DVD rental services, such as Netflix, are now changing the face of renting. Instead of driving to a video store to rent films and shows, people can register online, set up a queue of titles, and receive movies in the mail. On top of that, there are no late fees. These services also carry tens of thousands of titles (Netflix boasts a library of more than 90,000, which grows daily), so you've always got access to whatever film you're looking for. As more and more classic movies and vintage television series get transferred to DVD, the choices increase. Another very attractive feature is the ability to search a service's database online by genre, subgenre, actor, and director, as well as by title. In a mood for "Britcoms" (imported British situation comedies)? The service will obligingly produce a list of titles to browse through. Do you have a sudden thirst for vampire movies? You can get everything from campy horror kitsch from the 1960s to the latest in special-effects-created gore. Are you a fan of documentaries or *Masterpiece Theater*? You could keep yourself supplied for years. This is shifting the economy of renting, forcing many local video stores to close and forcing many video rental companies to change their policies.

High Definition DVDs are another innovation we'll be seeing more of in the immediate future. As more households get used to high-definition television programming, the low-definition DVD player will seem archaic. Thus, high-definition films are now being released in the more advanced Blu-ray format. Blu-ray disks hold more data and can deliver high-definition signals to utilize the incredible resolution of HDTVs. Bluray hasn't quite become a mainstream technology yet because players are very pricey, and the library of films is limited, but most analysts agree that this could be the format of choice for future movie enthusiasts.

Downloadable Content

DVRs and DVDs even have competition. Many customers choose instead to download entertainment and skip the need for a disk or a broadcast. Whether through a podcast, a website, or an on-demand pay-per-view service, there are several means to download such content. Services such as Vongo allow you to download entire films as "rentals" and watch them for a small fee. Netflix has introduced this service for its customers, and Amazon.com now has a downloadable "unbox" that lets you purchase digital entertainment. Apple's iTunes allows dozens of television and film downloads for a price, and you can watch them on your iPod or computer, or send them to your TV with Apple TV. The typical pay-per-view feature of cable broadcasting has been updated to include on-demand viewing that can be paid for and downloaded. All these options truly allow people to customize what they watch. Perhaps most Americans will soon feel that there will be no need for traditional television channels at all, needing only access to downloaded content.

IN THIS CHAPTER

Television and the technologies that accompany it provide a vast electronic space that reflects our fantasies, fears, values, hopes, and preoccupations. This chapter focuses on broadcast entertainment television, including situation comedies, Reality TV, and how television has changed since 9-11. As you read, you should consider the following questions:

- How does the content of the shows that we watch shape our perceptions of the real world?

- What effects do depictions of extreme violence have on viewers?

- How accurately does television reflect the diverse country and world that we live in?

- Do the creators of television shows have any ethical responsibilities related to their programming?

- How will the content of TV shows change as technologies change in the very near future?

- How will advertisers continue to reach an audience who can buy shows on DVD or download them commercial free?

- How has the transition from having three major networks (NBC, ABC, and CBS) to having hundreds affected our culture?

The Triumph of Popular Culture: Situation Comedy, Postmodernism, and *The Simpsons*

Matthew Henry

Prereading Questions

1. What sitcoms (see "Terms for Clarification" at the end of this chapter) do you watch, and what do you enjoy about them?

2. Do you see your own life in any sitcoms? Is your family in any way like any families that you see in sitcoms?

3. If you don't like sitcoms, why do you think they fail to amuse you? Is the problem with the genre itself, or the way sitcoms are written and directed today?

Good art that reaches thirty million people and makes them feel connected may have more to offer us now than great art that reaches three thousand and makes them feel more or less alone. In our time the standards for art have changed, expanded. The future belongs to Bart Simpson.

—*Tad Friend, 1993*

Ars Pro Multis

Art is currently in a conceptual crisis, and its status is now one of the most contentiously debated issues in academe. This is a debate inclusive of all disciplines (painting, sculpture, architecture, photography, film, music, and literature); a debate embodied by discussions of the difference (or loss of difference, to paraphrase Leslie Fiedler) between traditionally high and low art forms; and a debate haunted by the imprecision of the concept of postmodernism in relation to modernism, both artistically and historically. The modernists' insistence upon the separateness of the artist and the autonomous nature of art as a closed "object" yielded a concept of art that has had dominion for much of the twentieth century. The implication of Tad Friend's statement above is that this "great" art, the canonized art of high culture, has less meaning for us now: it is an art of isolation, for it maintains a distance between object and viewer, and an art accessible only to the elite.

However, the popular art of mass culture, or "good" art, has great significance for us now: it is art that questions the need for critical distance; it is art that, instead of making people feel isolated, makes them feel connected to society. Many of the traditional art forms are not capable of this contemporarily, but many of the predominant new art forms are, especially film and television. Television, in particular, offers strong societal connections: it has created a new form of tribalism, for it is a "shared cultural experience" in which important issues are addressed and through which the viewer is engaged.[1]

Friend is then correct in asserting that the standards for art have "changed, expanded."[2] A radical alteration has been, and still is, taking place. Art is not dead in our age, as some critics have been hasty to assert; it has simply been transformed.

A slightly different version of this chapter was originally published in *Studies in Popular Culture* 17, no. 1 (1994): 85–100. It has been reprinted here by permission of the publisher.

Nevertheless, Friend's bold statement that the "future belongs to Bart Simpson" poses some difficult questions for the academic: how, exactly, does the future belong to Bart Simpson? why should it belong to him? and if so, what are the social and political implications of such dominance? I hope to answer these questions by examining *The Simpsons* in numerous contexts, but I am most interested in viewing this show with regard to postmodernism. Linda Hutcheon asserts postmodernism is a phenomenon "unavoidably political"[3]; it is critical of power and domination but also involved in it, unable to "escape implication in that which it nevertheless still wants to analyze and maybe even undermine."[4] This is true of *The Simpsons,* which incorporates into the sitcom format many of the techniques of postmodernism with the result of paradoxically both critiquing and creating American popular culture. In short, *The Simpsons* is involved in the production of the very "culture" it satirizes: it is at once a hilarious situation comedy, a biting social commentary, and a monumental merchandising phenomenon. Hence the primary foci of my discussion: the primacy of the family sitcom today, its manifestation in *The Simpsons,* and the methods by which this show influences and is influenced by contemporary American culture.

The Rise of the Sitcom

Situation comedies have become the preferred mode of television; they are "our most pervasive, powerful and cherished form of media output."[5] And a look at the statistics affirms this: in terms of viewership, of the ten top-rated television shows in 1952, shortly after the introduction of television, only one was a sitcom; by 1972, three of the top ten were sitcoms; and in 1992 an incredible seven of the ten most watched shows were sitcoms.[6] What is the appeal of sitcoms? Foremost, being simultaneously more ridiculous and more realistic than the viewer imagines his own life to be, sitcoms imbue the banal with "potent allegorical force.[7] They offer viewers the myth that all problems can be resolved with wit and humor within a short period of time. More significantly, the rise in popularity of the sitcom has coincided with the rise of television shows based on blue-collar families, a tradition begun in the 1950s with *The Honeymooners,* continued with great success in the 1970s with *All in the Family,* and continuing into the 1990s with popularity in shows like *Roseanne* and *Married . . . with Children.*[8]

The Simpsons was, therefore, inevitable, the next logical step in the blue-collar tradition; its enormous success, however, was quite unexpected. Less than a year after its premier in December 1989, the show was "a breakaway ratings hit, industry trendsetter, cultural template, and a viewing experience verging on the religious for its most fanatical followers."[9] The appeal of *The Simpsons* lies in the fact that it is a cartoon and blue-collar sitcom all in one. Though it has strong appeal for (and is thus quite successfully marketed to) a youth audience, *The Simpsons* is also a show for adults, baby boomer adults in particular: it plays upon their sense of nostalgia for similar shows, especially *The Flintstones* and *The Jetsons,* tapping into a desire for lost youth, the childlike enjoyment of watching cartoons, and the comedic surrogate family. But *The Simpsons* is also packed with witty jokes, sophisticated satire, and numerous references, both obvious and obscure, drawn from both "high" and "low" culture. This latter quality signals the intertextuality of *The Simpsons,* which works on one level as a form of postmodern pastiche, a collage of (seemingly) unrelated surfaces. In this sense the show operates like a "mobile game of trivia" for its adult fans,[10] and trivia, as David Marc has noted, is "the most salient form of sitcom appreciation.[11]

Secondarily, *The Simpsons* functions at a level similar to other sitcoms based on the working class, such as *Roseanne,* in that it allows an identification with characters who are somewhat more "real" and whose lives more closely resemble those of its viewers. Thus, all members of the audience can identify with the Simpsons on some level: with the Simpsons' struggle to make ends meet, with Homer's difficulties as both provider and role model, with Marge's attempts to be "supermom," with Lisa's desire to find a place where her intelligence will be "an asset instead of a liability," or with Bart's anti-establishment, bad-boy posture. Though the members of the Simpson family are far from the media-constructed norm represented on television by shows like *Leave It to Beaver, Father Knows Best,* or even *The Flintstones,* they are perhaps closer to the actual norm. This distinction was well displayed in the debate over "family values" during the 1992 presidential election, during which George Bush made his infamous call for "a nation closer to the Waltons than *The Simpsons.*"[12] Bush's comment was a lament for the loss of an idealized past and concept of family. What Bush failed to see is that these were only *images* of self and family, only media-constructed identities intended to further a capital-istic philosophy: in short, advertisers and the media gave the masses the life they desired. Thus, Bush's call for the past was a call for a return to falsity, to unreality. *The Simpsons* are more akin to what we are today, more representative of the American family and more attuned to the realities of contemporary life. They live in a society "loosed from its moorings," full of corruption, voracious consumerism, and moral decay.[13] Their America is our America. They are as dedicated to family values as the Waltons ever were but, in such a society, find it increasingly hard to live up to them.

Working Against the Tradition

Television's tradition for the family sitcom was defined by the middle-class lifestyle represented on shows like *The Adventures of Ozzie and Harriet* (1952–66), *Father Knows Best* (1954–62), *Leave It to Beaver* (1957–63) and *Dick Van Dyke* (1961–66). Foremost, these sitcoms offered visions of intact nuclear families, which have been "the fundamental unit of organization in urban industrial America."[14] Atop the nuclear family was posited a patriarchy in which the father was portrayed as knowing, correct, and superior to his wife and children, a structure that worked to reinforce the preva-lent sexual stereotypes. Primarily concerned with the high jinks of one or more of its characters (plots usually centered on some form of miscommunication or misunder-standing), these shows also posited a sheltered environment dissociated from the "real world": economic or social problems did not penetrate the fictional world and impact upon the characters. Moreover, traditional family sitcoms established and perpetuated the myth of the happy family. No matter the conflict, resolution and a return to happi-ness were guaranteed: each week the narrative would return the characters to the same situation and frame of mind with which they began—they would learn nothing new, and would neither change nor grow.[15] With the exception of the working-class sitcom *The Honeymooners* (a ratings bomb that ran only one season, from 1955–56), such middle-class family sitcoms dominated the airwaves in the 1950s and 1960s; after *The Flintstones* left the air in 1966, no other working-class family series appeared on television until *All in the Family* in January 1971.[16]

However, after the success of *All in the Family* (1971–83), working-class family sitcoms began to emerge and rapidly supplant the traditional middle-class family sitcom. The decade of the 1970s was thus a highpoint for working-class sitcoms. One reason for this stands clear: the sitcom needed to add to its "mimetic agenda" the complex social and political issues of the day in order to retain its credibility as "chronicler and salesman of the American family."[17] Nevertheless, during the 1980s there was a strong shift back towards the genre's conventional family center and its hermetic, middle-class lifestyle, a movement that coincided with the conservative zeitgeist of the Reagan years. Although its heyday was past, the myth-tradition was largely carried on in a number of sitcoms during this period: *Family Ties* (1982–89), *Growing Pains* (1985–92), and the wildly successful *Cosby Show* (1984–92) all offered a return to the secure ground of middle-class suburbia and the stable nuclear family.

The 1990s saw a return to shows based in the working class, and these types of sitcoms became predominant. Both critically and economically, the most popular sitcoms of the decade were *Roseanne, Married . . . with Children,* and *The Simpsons.* What set these three sitcoms apart from their predecessors most distinctly is that they incorporated real-world problems into their stories, thereby problematizing the traditionally hermetic nature of family sitcoms. Moreover, these shows are a revolt against the idealized images of domestic life portrayed by sitcoms like *Leave It to Beaver* or *Father Knows Best.* But, unlike many of their contemporaries, they did not attempt to reflect the changing family structure in America. Instead, *Roseanne, Married . . . with Children,* and *The Simpsons* each revived the domestic sitcom, using the traditional nuclear family construct (mom, dad, kids, dog and a house in the suburbs) in order to skewer its conventions. In these shows, the patriarchy is shattered, the universal authority and correctness of both the mother and the father are undermined, and the dominant values systems are rigorously questioned. Thus, by including contemporary realities and subverting the myth-traditions of the family sitcom, these three shows significantly changed the face and nature of the television sitcom.[18]

Complicitous Comedy

Like all forms of popular media in a postindustrial economy, sitcoms are vital modes of image production, and *The Simpsons* is a premier example. Above all, the sitcom is a corporate product. It is a mass consumption commodity and an expression of the underlying assumptions of the corporate culture that has come to dominate American society.[19] It is a vehicle for bringing consumers to advertisers in the marketplace. Demographically, sitcoms appeal to the largest buying audience—teenagers and young working adults with disposable income. *The Simpsons* succeeds as a business because it bridges the gap between these groups and an older, established audience with even more spending power: it has multigenerational appeal, attracting "boomers" and "busters" alike. Thus, *The Simpsons* is an industry that, by capitalizing upon the immaterial, upon the image, is able to sell phenomenal amounts of merchandise—both its advertisers' and its own.

The initial success of *The Simpsons* was due to the willful manipulation of the image of Bart Simpson, which capitalized upon the archetype of the adolescent rebel. The sitcom also skyrocketed to fame on the commodification of language: Bart's instantly reproducible phrases "Don't have a cow, man," "Eat my shorts," and "Ay, caramba!" were decontextualized, packaged, and sold to the public en masse. Bart's image and words appeared on T-shirts, bumper stickers, baseball caps, beach towels, coffee mugs, and dozens of other items. The ubiquity of Bart's image has had great influence on consumers, to the delight of merchandisers to be sure. But, more significantly, Bart's ubiquity has also had profound societal ramifications: school officials in a number of states (Ohio and California were the first) quickly condemned the cartoon show and singled out Bart Simpson as a poor role model for school children, going so far as to ban the wearing of a T-shirt bearing Bart's image and the slogan "Underachiever and Proud of It!"[20]

An episode of *The Simpsons* speaks tellingly of both the rampant commodification and the postmodern qualities of the show. In "Bart Gets Famous" (February 3, 1994), Bart, already a commodity in our world, becomes a commodity in the alternate "real" world of the television show when he appears as a fill-in on the variety show of his hero, Krusty the Clown. Frightened by the scrutiny of the audience, Bart is unable to speak his single line and accidentally destroys the set. His instant reply, "I didn't do it," is merely a conditioned response, an excuse derived from years of delinquent behavior. But it is accepted as part of the act, deemed hilarious, and instantly reproduced. Thus, Bart inadvertently becomes a pop culture icon. His commodification is compounded by the rapid production of a cheap biography, a recording contract and hit song, a Bart-Chat hotline, and a Bart Simpson doll.

The irony of this episode is that quite similar things happened in the exterior, "real" world after the initial success of *The Simpsons:* in addition to the aforementioned capitalization upon Bartspeak and the distribution of his image, *The Simpsons* has given us a newsletter, an "uncensored" family album, four separate comic book series, and a hit record, *The Simpsons Sing the Blues*. The show's producers are obviously aware of the strong parallels between the commodification of Bart's image in the fictional world of the television show and the real world of its viewers, and they self-consciously, blatantly play upon this. They know that the irony in *The Simpsons* depends upon a certain degree of cynicism on the part of the audience regarding commercial television and its mission of providing advertisers with a market. The episode cited here thus ends on a tellingly self-reflexive note. Having found himself suddenly unpopular, Bart is gathered at home with his family taking consolation. His sister Lisa says, "Now you can go back to being you instead of a one-dimensional character with a silly catch-phrase," which, in one sense, is what he is. We then get a rundown of the major characters' own catchphrases. Lisa however, refuses to cooperate: with a look of disdain for those identified by surface and image, willing to participate in their own commodification, Lisa says, "I'll be in my room." Homer then asks, "What kind of a catchphrase is that?" Thus, we can see that *The Simpsons* is simultaneously complicitous in and critical of its role in the production of popular culture.

Patricia Waugh states that postmodern texts "flaunt their implication in and complicity with Late Capitalism by deliberately incorporating aspects of mass culture."[21] Such complicity is evident in *The Simpsons'* intertextuality: the show includes material from all aspects of the cultural terrain, from film, television, literature, science fiction, and other comics, to name a few. Such intertextual incorporations, blatant transgressions of real-world boundaries, problematize the ontological status of the cartoon's fictional world by acknowledging its artifice. This self-conscious blurring of boundaries is, in fact, one of the ways in which *The Simpsons* most effectively comments upon itself and the culture of which it is a part, and I will speak more in the next section on the use of these as a means of critiquing American culture. Let me point out here that the use of other forms and "texts" in *The Simpsons* underscores both its complicity in popular culture and its intertextual nature, and these characteristics further distinguish it as a postmodern sitcom. I have also argued here for the status of *The Simpsons* as a producer of popular culture. Fredric Jameson notes, in defining pastiche, that with the collapse of "the high-modernist ideology of style . . . the producers of culture have nowhere to turn but to the past."[22] The pastiche or, as Jameson says, the "cannibalizing" of the past is a primary practice of post-modernism, and this is eminently displayed in *The Simpsons*. However, as I will argue next, the "neutral practice" of pastiche is merely one aspect of this cartoon's agenda, and it is inextricably bound with the more active practice of parody. As a postmodern text, *The Simpsons* does indeed have an "ulterior motive": to critique contemporary American society, using the past as well as the present with a strong satirical impulse.

Critical Comedy

According to Linda Hutcheon, "most television, in its unproblematized reliance on re-alist narrative and transparent representational conventions, is pure commodified com-plicity, without the critique needed to define the postmodern paradox."[23] This critique is crucial to the definition of postmodernism. It is also what sets *The Simpsons* apart from the sitcoms defined by the myth-tradition. Those who have criticized *The Simpsons* have missed the point. Above all else, the show is a satire, one fundamentally involved with a critique of American society. Foremost, *The Simpsons* is a satire upon the idealized images of family life depicted in the mythic traditional sitcom; but it is also a knowing and sharp satire upon the excessive, complex, hypocritical, and often idiotic state of contemporary American culture.

As noted earlier, *The Simpsons* works against the tradition of the family sitcom by deconstructing the myth of the happy family. *The Simpsons* highlights the superficiality of the myth (exposing the falseness of tension-free relationships), decenters its author-ity (radically removing it from the traditional realm of the father), and undermines its conventions (subverting concepts such as the "moral" and the "happy ending"). *The Simpsons* refuses to be complicitous in the perpetuation of the myth-tradition; its refu-tation is founded upon a more pragmatic, realistic approach to representations of the family today, as Victoria Rebeck has accurately stated: "Rather than engage in the pre-tentious misrepresentation of family life that one finds in the 'model family' shows (from *The Donna Reed Show* to *The Cosby Show*), [*The Simpsons*] admits that most parents aren't perfect. They haven't worked out their own childhood confusion, and they don't have the answers to all their children's problems."[24]

It is important to point out here Rebeck's deceptively casual use of *The Cosby Show* as an example of the "model family." As noted previously, *The Cosby Show* embodies the myth-tradition of the sitcom in numerous ways; in short, it sums up a great deal of television sitcom history. In the media-hyped showdown between *The Simpsons* and *The Cosby Show,* when Fox moved *The Simpsons* to Thursday nights, the weaknesses of the traditional family sitcom were made abundantly clear. It was a stroke of genius for Fox to put the cartoon up against what Jerry Herron calls "NBCs 2-D paterfamilias," for it exposed *Cosby*'s "informational nullity" and forced a visual showdown that demonstrated "the impoverishment of historically constituted forms."[25] The ratings triumph of *The Simpsons* (and subsequent cancellation of *Cosby*) underscored the fact that the family sitcom in its traditional structure and conventional trappings was null and void.

Although *The Simpsons* is critical of the myth of the happy family, it nevertheless utilizes some of its conceits in order to strengthen its position as a viable family sitcom: the genius of *The Simpsons* is that it "leaves what is real and valuable about the myth unscathed."[26] That is, in the Simpson family, behind all the confusion and bickering, there is always an underlying sense of commitment and caring that does not appear artificial or prefabricated; ultimately, the affection here is sincere, all the more so for the problems that confound it and complicated manner in which it is finally exposed. The traditional sitcoms were less problematic regarding familial affection—it was a given at the onset of each episode, exemplified by the plot, and reinforced by the conventional happy ending.

It was stated previously that one of the most pervasive conventions of the myth of the happy family was the assurance that in each episode resolution was guaranteed, and that each week the narrative would return the characters to the same situation and frame of mind with which they began. This is not to say that in countering the tradition *The Simpsons* offers characters who learn from their mistakes and, as a result, change or grow. Instead, *The Simpsons* satirizes this convention by self-consciously acknowledging it as such.

The finest example of this comes from the episode "Homer Loves Flanders" (March 17, 1994). Homer and Ned Flanders, Homer's fundamental Christian neighbor, become close friends when Ned does Homer a kindly deed. Within the context of the show, this is surprising, for Ned has been Homer's object of both ridicule and indifference for the eight years they have been neighbors. When Bart expresses concern over the continuation of this friendship, Lisa assures him that "every week something odd happens to *The Simpsons* . . . [but] by next week we'll be back to where we started from, ready for another wacky adventure." When Ned tires of Homer's irritating presence and coldly shuns him, it appears this is the case; but there is a subsequent reunion, and it now appears the episode will end with them still friends, thereby undermining the convention that would return the characters to an original blank status. This worries Bart; he says to his sister: "I don't get it. You said everything would be back to normal, but Homer and Flanders are still friends." She sadly replies: "Yeah, maybe this means the end of our wacky adventures." Cut to: the Simpson living room and the caption "The Following Thursday, 8:00 P.M." As Homer is pitching the concept of *The Simpsons'* latest "wacky adventure" (aptly, a stay at a haunted house), Ned stops by. "Get lost, Flanders," Homer shouts. Bart and Lisa look at one another and heave a sigh of relief, happy that the convention has been maintained. Thus, the convention is exposed for what it is: an artificial structure superimposed upon the sitcom to appease the audience with the myth of easy resolution and a circulation back to happiness.

The Simpsons also uses techniques associated with postmodernism in order to subvert and critique traditional sitcom notions such as the "warm moment," wherein everyone embraces, all problems are (re)solved and we learn a valuable moral lesson. This is most emphatically displayed in the episode titled "Blood Feud," in which Bart donates blood to save the life of Homer's boss, Mr. Burns. Hoping to ingratiate himself, and thereby receive a generous reward, Homer forces Bart to donate. When the family receives nothing more than a "thank you," Homer dashes off a sarcastic note, thus reaping the ire of Mr. Burns, who immediately decides to have Homer killed. But Burns has a change of heart and decides to give *The Simpsons* a gift after all: a stone head, an ancient Olmec Indian carving so large it completely fills their living room. With *The Simpsons* gathered round the head, staring at it, eating dinner on trays, this episode denies us closure and any sense of a lesson by self-consciously ending with a debate on the moral of the show:

> MARGE. The moral of this story is "A good deed is its own reward."
>
> BART. Hey, we got a reward. The head is cool!
>
> MARGE. Well, then, I guess the moral is "No good deed goes unrewarded."
>
> HOMER. Wait a minute. If I hadn't written that nasty letter, we wouldn't have gotten anything.
>
> MARGE. Well, I guess the moral is "The squeaky wheel gets the grease."
>
> LISA. Perhaps there is no moral to this story.
>
> HOMER. Exactly. It's just a bunch of stuff that happened.

Such self-consciousness is abundant on *The Simpsons*. In addition to being a means for exposing its intertextual nature, as outlined in the previous section, it is a method by which the show highlights its refusal to take either the myth-tradition or itself seriously and through which the show calls attention to itself as artifice. Within the scope of this paper, it would be impossible to do justice to the self-reflexive quality of *The Simpsons,* for there are innumerable examples. I will offer only a few, beginning at the beginning. In the aforementioned title sequence of the show, three distinct features are self-consciously altered each week. First, Bart's chalkboard missives almost invariably begin "I will not . . . ," but they are changed for each episode to accommodate his most recent misbehavior (e.g., "I will not teach others to fly," "I will not make flatulent noises in class," "I will not yell 'she's dead' during roll call"). Second, Lisa's saxophone solo, with which she disrupts her band practice, is noticeably different each week. But the feature that plays most upon this conceit is the sequence's final moment, when the family gathers in the living room. Two particular episodes of *The Simpsons* speak most tellingly of its self-conscious stance: in one, *The Simpsons* arrive to confront themselves already seated on the couch—confused glances all around; in the other, as *The Simpsons* dash into the room from one side, they dash out of the frame on the other (filmic frames are drawn to acknowledge this), turn momentarily in empty white space, and then dash back into the living room again.

Marguerite Alexander states that among the prerequisites for postmodernism is a "shattering of the fictional illusion."[27] As is obvious from the examples just cited concerning the opening sequence of the show, *The Simpsons* accomplishes a shattering of the fictional illusion, self-consciously and confrontationally flaunting its status as artifice. This accomplishment is facilitated by the fact that *The Simpsons* is a cartoon, which allows the show to also revel in the realm of the absurd, and this further sets it apart from its predecessors and its contemporaries. Instead of dealing with probabilities, *The Simpsons* often deals with improbabilities. *The Honeymooners,* for example, dealt with the former: Ralph was always trying to rise above the level of the exploited working class through a series of get-rich-quick schemes. *The Simpsons,* however, deals in the latter: Homer easily rises (and as easily falls) to any social and/or economic level—witness the episode in which Homer becomes a Colonel Tom-like manager of a country-western singer or the episode in which Homer becomes an astronaut. Such a self-conscious pose is one of the key methods for conveying satire on *The Simpsons.* To effect this, the members of the Simpson family, as well as the entire cast of the show, are continually put into unlikely and/or absurd situations—witness the episode in which *The Simpsons* are kidnapped by aliens or the one in which Homer and friends form a wildly successful pop music group, The B-Sharps. However, the satire on *The Simpsons* is most effective when it is rooted in contemporary realities. Among other things, *The Simpsons* mercilessly exposes the hypocrisy and ineptitude of pop psychology, modern child-rearing, commercialism, consumerism, fundamental religion, environmental abuse, corporate greed, and the deceits of American education. Considering its great success, both commercially and critically, David Berkman rightly forces us to question whether it is only in the cartoon, the "visually unreal," that we can accept the harsh realities that satire shows us.[28] Perhaps this is so. Since the satire of *The Simpsons* is so pervasive and its targets so widespread, it would be impossible to discuss it in total within this paper. We have already seen numerous examples, both direct and implied. For the sake of brevity, then, let me deal with only one already mentioned instrument of the show's satire: *The Itchy and Scratchy Show.*

The Itchy and Scratchy Show details the exploits of a cat and mouse comedy team modeled on Tom and Jerry. But this cartoon goes its model one better: we are shown every gruesome detail of the ways in which this cat and mouse team seek to destroy each other. They are forever being sliced, diced, disemboweled, de-skinned, beheaded, impaled, and exploded, all with gratuitous amounts of blood. Of the violence in cartoons and live-action shows, Matt Groening has said: "My problem . . . is that there's an anticipation of cruelty which I find really repugnant."[29]

Groening satirizes America's desire for cruelty by offering it up in spades: *The Itchy and Scratchy Show* takes the violence associated with contemporary cartoons to the extreme, thus confrontationally exposing the powerful appeal of violence, its ubiquity today, the crass manner in which it is marketed to children, and the blasé attitude towards it that parents adopt.

The Itchy and Scratchy Show appears on *The Simpsons* with great regularity, offering up its doses of extremely violent and bloody images for the sheer entertainment of its viewers, meaning both the Simpson children and us, the viewers of *The Simpsons.* These images were always shown without any overt commentary at the sitcom's diegetic level the satire was allowed to speak for itself. But in one episode, the show finally addressed its own complicity in the controversial issue of cartoon violence, likely in response to the controversy over censorship raging at that time in the media. In "Itchy and Scratchy and Marge," Marge is disturbed by the amount of time her children spend indoors watching television, especially *Itchy and Scratchy,* and the amount of violence to which they are thus exposed. She organizes a moral watchdog group that campaigns to ban the *Itchy and Scratchy* cartoon. They win the case, and the kids lose their show. We are then given a scene wherein the children emerge from their homes into the sun-filled outdoors to the sounds of Beethoven's Pastoral Symphony. It appears to be the first time their stunted existences have been freed of consumer society's traps. But this traditional happy ending is quickly subverted; it is an ironic and mock-glorious ending, for a new problem arises: Marge's watchdog group now wants to ban the appearance of Michelangelo's *David*. Marge is opposed to this idea and thus realizes that if "great art" is to be protected from censorship, popular art must be as well. At the end of the episode, Bart and Lisa are again watching *The Itchy and Scratchy Show,* and Marge helplessly looks on, wondering if she has done the right thing. Gerard Jones states that the effectiveness of the point about censorship is "undercut by the deep, queasy ambivalence it evokes about the value of television, the impoverishment of life, and the effectiveness of social action."[30] I find no such ambivalence. *Itchy and Scratchy* is back on the Simpsons' television, and *The Simpsons* is still on ours: It is the triumph of popular culture.

NOTES

1. Stuart M. Kaminski, *American Television Genres* (Chicago: Nelson Hall, 1985), 8.

2. Tad Friend, "Sitcoms, Seriously," *Esquire,* Mar. 1993, 124.

3. Linda Hutcheon, *The Politics of Postmodernism* (New York: Routledge, 1989), 1.

4. Ibid., 4.

5. Friend, "Sitcoms, Seriously," 114.

6. Ibid., 115.

7. David Marc, *Comic Visions: Television Comedy and American Culture* (Boston: Unwin Hyman, 1989), 161.

8. Harry Waters, "Family Feuds," *Newsweek*, Apr. 23, 1990, 60.

9. Ibid., 58.

10. Lawrence Grossberg, "The In-Difference of Television," *Screen* 28, no. 2 (1987): 30.

11. David Marc, *Demographic Vistas: Television in American Culture* (Philadelphia: Univ. of Pennsylvania Press, 1984), 12.

12. Harry Stein, "Our Times," *TV Guide,* May 23–29, 1992, 31.

13. Ibid.

14. Darrell Y. Hamamoto, *Nervous Laughter: Television Situation Comedy and Liberal Democratic Ideology* (New York: Praeger, 1989), 17.

15. John Ellis, *Visible Fictions Cinema: Television: Video* (London: Routledge and Kegan Paul, 1982), 125.

16. Richard Butsch, "Class and Gender in Four Decades of Television Comedy. Plus ça Change . . ." *Critical Studies in Mass Communications* 9 (1992), 392.

17. Marc, *Demographic Vistas,* 13.

18. David Berkman, "Sitcom Reality," *Television Quarterly* 26, no. 4 (1993): 64.

19. Gerard Jones, *Honey, I'm Home! Sitcoms: Selling the American Dream* (New York: Grove, 1992), 4.

20. Victoria A. Rebeck, "Recognizing Ourselves in the Simpsons," *The Christian Century,* Jun. 27, 1990, 622.

21. Patricia Waugh, ed., *Postmodernism: A Reader* (London: Edward Arnold, 1992), 191.

22. Frederic Jameson, "Postmodernism, or, The Logic of Late Capitalism," *New Left Review,* 146 (1984): 65.

23. Hutcheon, *Politics of Postmodernism,* 10.

24. Rebeck, "Recognizing Ourselves," 622.

25. Jerry Herron, "Homer Simpson's Eyes and the Culture of Late Nostalgia," *Representations* 43 (1993): 18.

26. Frank McConnell, "'Real' Cartoon Characters," *Commonweal,* Jun. 15, 1990, 390.

27. Marguerite Alexander, *Flights from Realism* (London: Edward Arnold, 1990), 4.

28. Berkman, "Sitcom Reality," 69.

29. Sean Elder, "Is TV the Coolest Invention Ever Invented?" *Mother Jones,* Dec. 1989, 30.

30. Jones, *Honey, I'm Home!* 268.

Journal Topics

1. Henry says that sitcoms appeal to us because they are "simultaneously more ridiculous and more realistic than the viewer imagines his own life to be. . . . They offer the viewer the myth that all problems can be resolved with wit and humor over a short period of time." Do you enjoy situation comedies? Do they primarily offer you an entertaining escape from reality, or do they amuse you while reinforcing your values and view of the world? What do you think your tastes in sitcoms say about you?

2. Think about the three plot points found in a sitcom. How accurately does this describe the typical sitcom? Does this repeated format make sitcoms become dull and predictable, or does it make it a trustworthy pattern we enjoy and come to expect?

3. Can you come up with your own criteria for what make a great sitcom? In your opinion, what is the best sitcom ever made? How does it meet your criteria?

4. If you don't like sitcoms at all, what kind of comedy programs do you like, and what do you like about them? What do you think your tastes in these shows say about you?

Question for Critical Thought

1. "Postmodernism" is a controversial and wide-ranging term that is applied to a variety of disciplines, including the studies of art, film, television, and literature. The defining characteristics of postmodernism are not universally agreed upon, but the following attributes are commonly named: denial of the existence of any ultimate governing principles; skepticism toward explanations or interpretations that claim validity for all groups of people; the uselessness of divisions between "high" and "low" art and culture; the precedence of concrete experience over abstract principles; the ambiguous, unstable, contradictory, inconclusive,

indeterminate, fragmented, unfinished nature of human experience; and a celebration of pastiche and the parody of multiple styles. How does the author use the term when discussing *The Simpsons*? How well do you think it fits? Can you think of any other television series the term could be applied to?

Suggestions for Personal Research

1. Some prominent people, such as the first President Bush, and William Bennett, whose books include *The Book of Virtues: A Treasury of Great Moral Stories* and *The Children's Book of Virtues,* have publicly criticized *The Simpsons* as being anti-authority and subversive of family values, in large part to the anti-authority attitude of Bart Simpson and the inadequacy of Homer Simpson as a role model. Rent or check out of your public library a season of the series. What different types of authority are represented? Does an anti-authority stance always pay off? Are there situations where rejecting the dictates of authority figures is the best thing to do? Does *The Simpsons* really carry a subversive message? Are there plot lines and characters that convey alternative messages? For example, Homer's boss, Mr. Burns, is portrayed as comically evil—for him, profit is more important than loyalty, personal relationships, or even human life. Storylines for individual episodes frequently use him to expose members of the Simpson family to various temptations, and Bart's and Homer's greed is often exploited to great comic effect; nevertheless, at episode conclusions, greed doesn't carry the day.

2. Reverend Lovejoy is the minister at the church the Simpsons attend. He is presented as judgmental, simplistic, and pompous. Ned Flanders, the Simpson's evangelical Christian neighbor, is shown as naïve, moralistic, and boring. However, he is also presented as genuinely compassionate, sincere, and helpful to others, as well as being a loving family man. What could the TV show be saying about both religion and religiosity? As with the preceding question, you'll need to watch multiple episodes to draw meaningful conclusions.

3. Rent or check out of the library some episodes of one or more of the earlier, more traditional family sitcoms mentioned in the article. Compare and contrast these with *The Simpsons* in terms of humor, gender roles, depiction of family, and apparent underlying family values.

4. Research what psychologists and media and culture critics have had to say about *The Simpsons* and what it says about American life and values.

5. Go on the Web and find half a dozen or more definitions of postmodernism, and see if you can synthesize a succinct and clear explanation of what is generally meant by the term.

Multicultural Issues

1. If you are from a different country, are there any sitcoms about families equivalent to any of the shows appearing on American television? If so, how do they compare to sitcoms here? Is *The Simpsons* TV series popular in your country?

Does it seem reflective of universally humorous situations, or does it seem quintessentially American?

2. *The Simpsons* is a very "white" show. Even though people from other nationalities are represented, most of them are white, like the Scottish groundskeeper, Willie. Apu, the Indian owner of a convenience store, is a notable exception. Does this character seem to be just a reflection of stereotypes about Indian immigrants? Or is Apu used to satirize stereotypes? Or is he just one more funny character?

Vocabulary Terms

contentious	patriarchy
postmodernism	mimetic
autonomous	hermetic
allegory	zeitgeist
intertextuality	ubiquitous
pastiche	diegetic
salient	satire
nuclear family	

Terms for Clarification

Sitcom   An abbreviation for "situation comedy." A sitcom is usually a thirty-minute comedy (typically with a live audience and shot with three cameras in only one or two takes). There are recurring characters, and the humor derives from the funny situations these characters find themselves in. The plot for most sitcoms usually comes in three acts, each act usually punctuated with a commercial break. These acts (1) present a problem the characters have to face, (2) make the problem worse, and (3) solve the problem to provide a strong sense of resolution for the characters and to return their lives to "normal."

High and Low Culture   "High" culture is a term that referred historically to the types of culture consumed by aristocratic and wealthy or well-to-do classes, like fine art, ballet, drama, and opera. "Low culture" was a term applied to entertainment enjoyed by the lower classes, such as popular music and dance and melodrama, and, today, popular television shows and movies (except for what are called "art movies").

Late Capitalism   The capitalism of the second half of the twentieth century.

Leslie Aaron Fiedler   (March 8, 1917–January 29, 2003.) An influential American literary critic. He championed genre fiction, utilizing psychological theories and helping to introduce questions of sexuality, gender, and race to American literature.

Linda Hutcheon   (1947–   .) Professor of English and Comparative Literature at the University of Toronto and a prominent theorist on postmodernism and feminism.

Real or Not, It Doesn't Matter

Richard M. Huff

Prereading Questions

1. Have you ever wanted to be on a reality TV show? How do you imagine it would feel to have a camera crew following you around most of the time?

2. Why do you think reality shows appeal to so many people? What kinds of people do they appeal to?

3. How many reality shows have you watched (if any)? What did you like or dislike about what you watched? How "real" do you think these shows are? And does it matter?

When *Survivor* hit the airwaves in the summer of 2000, part of the appeal was the notion that the people were real, regular folks from the street, and that everything that happened on screen was as it really happened before the cameras. These weren't actors. They were people. They were everyday people from all walks of life who were willing to do seemingly anything to win $1 million, even agreeing to be stranded on a small island without basic necessities.

In that first reality show outing most viewers were willing to ignore the facts that the people were on the island for 39 days and just an hour of footage aired every week, suggesting that lots more happened than was shown. "Real" would be seeing every hour, even the extremely boring ones the contestants spent on the island. And, viewers also overlooked the fact that the contestants, "castaways" as they were called on the show and by the media, were not alone but surrounded by camera crews, medical teams, and producers.

It was real, or so everyone thought. What viewers learned later on, and by 2006 seemed to accept just fine, was that reality programming isn't real. In many cases, it's not even close. Such talk when *Survivor* launched would have been blasphemous. The notion that everything was real was largely driven by the media, which pumped up—and played into CBS's media campaign—the idea of real people struggling for food on an island. It was sexy. It sold papers and magazines. If only it was real.

Incidentally, it was *Survivor* that gave viewers their first notion that the reality was unreal. That's because a number of the players coming off the game mentioned what got on the air wasn't exactly who they were. Through editing characters were created or, more realistically, enhanced. A producer can't make a bitchy character out of someone who is sweet all of the time. But those cantankerous players who gave producers enough similar footage to piece together saw the editing booth results of reality.

And in reality, viewers should have realized it wasn't all real early on when *Survivor* producer Mark Burnett was the first to admit that *Survivor* was a contrived drama and referred to it as an "unscripted drama," rather than using the term "reality" for the genre. "This new type of television, which is not so really reality, it's more like an unscripted, nonacted drama," Burnett said on NBC's *Today* show. "I mean, that's what I do, at least. A reality show is more like *Cops,* I think."

Cops, of course, was one of the first programs built completely on footage of real peo-ple. The Fox staple follows police officers as they deal with everyday crimes. *Survivor* was different, though. The crimes and scenarios are real; camera crews simply capture the mo-ments. It's shot more like a documentary, with producers getting the action as it happens. The difference is that shows such as *Survivor, The Biggest Loser, American Candidate,* and *The Next Action Star* are built around people being put into various situations and cameras filming them.

As it turns out, Burnett was also part of the first reality show pseudo-scandal when in 2001 it was revealed that Burnett staged or reenacted some scenes of *Survivor* so he would have better camera angles. For one scene, Burnett hired stand-in actors to duplicate a scene of contestants swimming across a river. The reason for the stand-ins was to reshoot a scene from overhead without capturing images of the ground-level film team used during the actual competition. "I'm not embarrassed about it," Burnett told a panel at the Museum of Television & Radio. He added that the footage "didn't change the outcome of the race."

The scenes were shot from high over head looking down at a group of people swim-ming. No faces were clearly visible, and if Burnett hadn't mentioned the reshoots, no one would have ever noticed or cared. To that end, no one ever questioned the fact that the shots of alligators, bugs, and other critters that inhabit the areas where *Survivor* was set weren't actually in the same place as the contestants at the time.

What Burnett's admission did that May 2001 night, though, was change the way people viewed reality television in general, and specifically with the media. Until then, Burnett had always stressed that what happened on the show was real. Yet, apparently not all of it was. At the time, CBS issued a statement saying: "What Mark is talking about is nothing more than window dressing. It doesn't involve the contestants and doesn't in any way influence the outcome of any challenge, tribal council, or change the view of reality as it occurred. The series is exactly what it appears to be—16 people battling the elements and each other."

Likewise, first-season contestant Stacey Stillman sued Burnett and CBS, claiming Burnett met with two contestants during the filming to influence their decision and get her rather than Rudy Boesch voted off the show. "And I'm saying a product was sold to the American public as a reality show, in order to lure viewers in, in order to raise ad rates, and that what was sold to them as being pure reality was not pure reality," Still-man said on MSNBC after filing the suit. CBS and Burnett denied the charges, as did other contestants who were said to have been involved in the scheme.

"It was real as it could possibly be—for such an unreal situation of putting people on an island," Sean Kenniff, one of the original contestants told the *New York Daily News* at the time.

Dragged into the discussion over what was real in *Survivor* was the issue of whether it was a game show, which would require certain things to occur by law (specifically, producers not altering the outcome) or if it was an unscripted drama, not covered by those laws. Eventually, the flap died down, however, and the show moved on.

Nevertheless, the suit raised questions about what was "real" in reality. Yet, at the same time, it also opened up people to the realization that it wasn't real. "I remem-ber the journalists were absolutely breathless in their outrage," said Professor Robert

Thompson, who heads up Syracuse University's Center for Popular Television. "But consistently, when you talked to viewers, there was a sense, in many ways, that viewers understood the esthetics of reality TV long before the professionals."

Some of the problems, perhaps confusion, stemmed from the use of the term *reality* as a way to describe the new form of programming Burnett brought to viewers with *Survivor*. Television writers and network executives could easily describe sitcoms and dramas, but this new form of television had no clear-cut description. Despite repeated claims from Burnett that *Survivor* was unscripted drama rather than reality, the reality moniker stuck.

The not-so-real reality of reality programming actually began in the days of MTV's *The Real World,* the first reality show of note. For starters, the people were brought together to live in a specially wired apartment with camera crews living in another room. That wasn't real simply because those people were there for the show and not because they came together on their own. Also, despite the impression left by the show—an impression that continues to this day—the housemates are not confined to being together or even spending all their time in the house. They leave. Some go home from time to time during filming.

One of the staples of reality shows, the confessional segments, may be one of the most tweaked segments in all of reality. The segments are usually brief interviews with the contestants talking about some aspect of the show viewers either saw or will see unfold. Oftentimes, the segments appear too clean, too perfect. That's because producers will ask for reshoots if the speaking wasn't right the first time.

NBC's *The Apprentice* has a couple of scenarios in each episode that stretch the meaning of reality. Every episode ends with a scene of the "fired" player heading out of Trump Tower and into a waiting cab. Those cab shots are shot at the beginning of the season, long before anyone knows when they'll be kicked off the show. When players are summoned to the boardroom to meet star Donald Trump, they're only allowed to bring in one carry-on bag. After they're booted from the show they return for the rest of their belongings.

ABC's *Wife Swap* is built on the notion that the program unfolds over a two-week period. Filming, however, often is done in less time, a fact never reflected on-screen.

Moreover, as reality programming has become a launching pad for future actors—and out-of-work actors—then the idea that anything that happens on the screen is real is up for question. Many of them have had acting jobs before landing on the reality shows, yet they're described on-screen as being in some other business. Ytossie Patterson and Taheed Watson from Fox's first edition of *Temptation Island* said afterward that producers knew they were actors, yet they were identified as an executive administrator and a production assistant, respectively. On Fox's *Joe Millionaire,* the bachelorettes were culled from acting and modeling agencies. Zora Andrich and Sarah Kozar, the final two bachelorettes who were vying for Evan Marriott's affection at the end of the show, had acted professionally, albeit on a small scale, before landing the reality show job. Neither, of course, was identified as an actress. Mandy Lauderdale, who appeared on the first *Temptation Island,* in postshow interviews said she was an actress, yet appeared in *Road Trip* as an extra a year before *Temptation island.* Lauderdale was described as a singer-waitress in Fox's bio.

And Andrea Langi, who appeared in two editions of NBC's *For Love or Money,* was in a film and an episode of *Law & Order: Special Victims Unit* before landing on the reality show. When she appeared on *For Love or Money,* Langi was billed as "party planner from New Jersey." "The reality of my life, is, yes, I am somewhat of a struggling actor," Langi said.

Being an actor actually comes in handy on reality shows when it comes to the contestants. After the first *Survivor* contestants realized they could launch acting careers on reality shows, the genre became a haven for wannabe actors who might have had trouble going the traditional route. Beyond straight acting, the appearances also led to endorsement contracts and speaking engagements, oftentimes putting the players on a path of an entertainment career that may have not been considered before the show. Those cases were rare, though. Most players going on reality shows in this era are looking for something more than just a shot at a prize.

The influence of *Survivor* and MTV's *The Real World* much earlier on how much was real in reality was profound. Before either show, no one knew what to expect from the programs or the genre. But after one cycle of each, future contestants saw how to play the game or gain air time. Now, virtually every show has an outspoken female, who gets labeled a bitch. There's often an African-American player standing up for equality. Frequently, there's a gay player, modeled after Richard Hatch's brilliant performance in the first *Survivor*. Players now go into reality shows with agents, and knowing that the loudest, brashest contestant gets the most air time. Oftentimes they'll alter their performance on the shows just to gain air time.

"People that go to MTV talent searches are essentially going to try out for certain roles," said Thompson. "Everyone who comes on is absolutely savvy to how they work. You don't have to tell the obnoxious woman, or whatever, to be obnoxious, because she knows. They're completely aware of how it works and in most cases it doesn't matter."

To that end, really bad singers show up for *American Idol* auditions just so they can get air time, and, maybe, a shot at fame for being terrible.

Victoria Fuller, who with her husband Jonathan Baker appeared on CBS's *The Amazing Race,* said they went in knowing they would play the role of the villain. "We always thought we would be the team people loved to hate, but not really hate," Fuller said. "All of our favorite characters were villains—Richard Hatch, Omarosa, Johnny Fairplay," Fuller said. "Once everything is said and done, you don't remember what they've done, but you remember them."

Just having cameras on all the time can lead to a change in the way a person behaves. "With any reality show that's a real challenge," said Tony DiSanto, the producer of MTV's *Laguna Beach* and *Run's House*. "It's always a concern when you go into a reality show; are people going to put a wall up, is reality going to be altered? Yes, reality is altered. Our job as producers is to reduce the alteration of reality." In the first couple of days on any shoot, the alteration is dramatic, according to DiSanto. Over time some of that diminishes. But not always.

During the first edition of *The Simple Life,* a show that had rich girls Paris Hilton and Nicole Richie live with an Arkansas family, Hilton generated laughs when she asked the family what Wal-Mart was. The line played right into the fish-out-of-water aspect of the show the producers wanted. Hilton, however, admitted later she added some flavor to her ditzy blonde attitude because she was on a television show. "I'm doing a TV show," Hilton told reporters before the launch of *The Simple Life 2*. "Obviously I wouldn't act like that in real life. The things I do on the show, I know I'm being filmed. But I don't really mind [looking dumb or spoiled]. I know it's a funny show. It makes people laugh. That's all I care about. I'm just entertaining people." She and Richie also admitted they messed up on the jobs they were given on the farm to enhance the humor in the show. If they didn't, they said, the show would be boring.

"On reality shows you're made more of a persona, a personality," said Tara Scotti, who, with her brother Charles, appeared on an episode of *Fear Factor*. Scotti said at one point a producer prodded her to be a little more competitive and aggressive toward other contestants. "I was loving everyone," she said. "The way they say it, is, 'So and so is talking smack about you' in a way to get you pissed off."

"Pissed off" can lead to controversy, and conflict, which anyone who has watched two minutes of a reality show knows is part of the mix. "There are so many things you said, they edit it," she said. "They clip it in a way to make you look different than you are."

Editing, heavy editing, is also part of the process that drains some of the real out of reality. Many players complain about the editing of reality shows, though they know going in they're susceptible to what may happen in the editing bay with what they said along the way. A report in *Radar* magazine, citing five veteran production staffers of reality shows, said editors routinely clip together bits of dialog to have people saying something on air they never said. It's a process that's been dubbed "frankenbyting" by people in the business.

"I think on *The Bachelorette,* everything was real," said Bob Guiney, who appeared on *The Bachelorette* and later *The Bachelor*. "Those are exactly how I remember them. From *The Bachelor* I really wanted to have fun. They sort of edited, and packaged it, and I was a little bummed that there were some funny moments that ended up on the cutting room floor."

Guiney said during a rose ceremony on *The Bachelor* in which he selected the women who would continue on in the show, he accidentally knocked the rose off the stem. So, when a woman walked up, rather than say, "Debby, will you take this rose?" he said, "Debby, will you take this stem?"

"They actually shot around it," Guiney recalled.

Victoria Fuller, who with her husband Jonathan Baker, made waves on *Amazing Race* when Baker shoved Fuller and seemed to dominate and berate his wife, said the show was edited so to only show the bad stuff between the couple. "I felt that, really, out of 500 hours, they only really use an hour of footage, six to eight, tops," Fuller said. "And they're taking the most sensational, most raw moments." In the end, Fuller said, "It's not really an accurate portrayal of your real self; it's you on a heightened level. In my real life I'm never running around with a back pack, or never washing my hair."

Having appeared on two editions of *The Bachelor,* Jen Schefft is well aware of how the show can be altered in the editing bays after the filming has stopped, yet she understands the process well enough to understand why and how it happens. "It's very realistic," she said. "They can't make people say something they didn't say. We were there for five weeks pretty much filming the show every single day, all day. You can't show everything that happens. You're just seeing the highlights. It's true, but it's condensed." Everyone has more sides to them, but not all of that makes it on the air, Schefft said, adding she didn't feel misrepresented during her run on *The Bachelor* and *The Bachelorette*.

Following her win on *The Swan,* DeLisa Stiles felt her portrayal was fairly balanced with the exception of how her ex-husband was portrayed on the show. During the show viewers saw the moment when she was served divorce papers from him. "He's not so bad a guy," she said. "He has a lot of good qualities. But the show is so limited in its scope."

Beyond editing, the entire idea of reality or unscripted programming—especially in 2006—is up for debate. Hollywood writers have frequently challenged the notion that reality shows are unscripted. The hosts, they argue, don't just whip off their introductions and instructions without some writing help. Challenges, which are choreographed, tested, and directed, also have some written instructions. Others have suggested there were larger shooting scripts that outlined the show step by step. "We have to take all the little bits and give it a clear story arc, give it structure, out of what in reality might be a big mess. That, to me, is writing," Todd Sharp, a Hollywood writer who worked on several reality shows told the *New York Times*.

"In a show like *The Bachelor* there probably is a little more scripting than *Survivor* or *Amazing Race,*" Guiney said.

Scripting in reality may actually be a misnomer. There are shooting scripts, which tell producers where to be and when, and all involved in the genre admit some situations are staged for maximum drama. Producers will stick a contestant with a height fear on a top bunk or send them on an airplane ride to stir their emotions. They'll also pair unlikely partners in bunk situations, hoping the emotions will bubble up while the cameras are on.

"We create situations," *Survivor*'s Burnett told the *Hollywood Reporter* in May 2004. "This is clearly contrived situations creating genuine emotions. Because, were I to wait for 16 people to happen to be shipwrecked, I'd be waiting a long time to do a show."

Laguna Beach's DiSanto said that producers go in with a plan based on the events going on in the subject's lives, though that plan often changes along the way. For instance, on *Run's House,* which followed Run DMC's Rev. Run (Joseph Simmons), the producers knew Simmons's daughter was going to graduate from high school and that there would be a party, so an episode storyline, per se, was set up to plot an episode around that event. "They'd ask me what's going on, what we're going to do, and we'd say such and such, and that's how the show would get named," Simmons said.

Producers will frequently reshoot moments if they've missed the dialog or want the subjects to say something more clearly, or more directly, or to get a better angle. "There was a little bit, but it was only if they didn't catch it," said Elaine Bramhall, who appeared on ABC's *Wife Swap*.

"They really try to capture the essence of what you may have said before," Stiles said of her experience on *The Swan*. "They may say, 'In this interview we need to get this in a concise statement.' They try to take what you were feeling."

"None of the dialog is scripted," DiSanto said. "But just like any reality show, you may miss something. You may ask them to do it again."

On a larger scale, just like throwing a group of people together who might not normally be together just to film a show, producers tend to steer the situations for the best dramatic effect. On a show like *Survivor* or *The Amazing Race,* those situations come in challenges. On *The Real World,* those situations develop by having hot tubs and lots of alcohol available, which could lead to sexual shenanigans before the cameras. Likewise, *Real World* contestants usually have a job or a project to work on, which, of course, leads to the creation of tension for the cameras.

On a more exaggerated scale, sending Hilton Hotel heiress Hilton and her friend into the Midwest to live with a farm family creates an entirely contrived situation for the benefit of the cameras. "It's not their lives," executive producer Jonathan Murray told reporters before the launch of *The Simple Life 2.* "But it's taking them as real people and throwing them into situations where they're out of their element. . . . And out of that comes humor."

Those are all scenarios that would be unlikely if the people were thrown together and left to their own devices, but for a reality show the situations are there to make good television. "When you're on *Survivor,* when you're on *Amazing Race,* they put you in situations where you're not yourself," Fuller said.

"They didn't direct us, but they certainly arranged for situations that they thought might lead the story where it would go," said Bramhall. In Bramhall's case, the most direct involvement came midway through the taping of her edition of *Wife Swap.* On the show, Bramhall, a highly organized married mother from New Jersey, was sent to the home of a single mother with unruly kids and a messy house. Under the guidelines for *Wife Swap,* during the first half of the swap, the visiting wives are to live by the existing rules in the house. After that period, which is supposedly a week, the visiting wives create a new set of rules for the home, which are usually marked by dramatic changes that go totally against what the wife who lives there demands. In some episodes, where kids were denied television, the visiting wife equipped the home with televisions. In more than one, unhelpful husbands were called on to clean the house and handle some chores. In others, if the kids were not allowed junk food, the visiting wives ordered junk food for the second week of filming.

Early on in her stay at the new home, Bramhall had difficulty meshing with the host family. So much so, when it came time to create new rules, she soft-pedaled them, figuring it would be better to ease them into new situations rather than make dramatic demands. However, dramatic demands are what make for good drama.

"They consult you for the rule changes," Bramhall said. "The production crew has to make arrangements, arranging for [the other woman's job]. They also wanted me to come down much harder than I would have. I said, 'Let's see if we can make some improvements.' They said, 'no, no you've got to change all the rules.' What happened, I was not surprised. I said they're all going to walk out."

And, when it came time for the show to air, the rules Bramhall read were not the ones she originally conceived. Instead, they were juiced for her to create tension in the home. "I just didn't think it would be effective," she said. "If we went a little softer we could meet half way."

DiSanto said the involvement of the producers may redirect locations based on the ability of the producers to actually shoot the show. If, for instance, the group of young men and women on *Laguna Beach* say they're heading out for dinner and the restaurant they've chosen will not allow his camera crews in, he'll suggest they go to a different location where they can film.

How much altering happens, either through editing, reshoots, or adding elements after the fact, has a lot to do with the program in question. By all accounts, lower-quality shows tend to have the most alterations. "I think it depends on the show," Murray, the producer of *The Real World* and *The Simple Life,* told reporters. "In the case of *The Real World,* we had an episode about [housemate] Frankie [in 2004], who cuts herself. . . . That was played very straight and just as it happened. With Paris and Nicole, we might put a funny sound effect, we might have some fun with it. I think the audience doesn't have a problem because of the context of that show."

Ultimately, more than five years after *Survivor* opened the door for reality or unscripted programming to become a full-fledged staple of the prime-time landscape, and covering topics from hair salons to teens dating (the N network's *Best Friend's Date*), issues about what's real or not have fallen to the background. No longer does it matter if the shows are all real or not; rather it's whether they're good and entertaining. "This is not *CBS Reports,*" Thompson said of the reality genre in general. "People are not watching it for the same sort of accuracy."

Journal Topic

1. Some people think that reality shows are reducing TV viewers' imaginations because there is no story, plot, or critical thought involved in watching them. What do you think? Is "reality" TV worse for us than scripted television? Does it lead to the "dumbing down" of the audience?

Questions for Critical Thought

1. Huff's article points out how in reality shows situations are set up and participants are often guided in certain directions for more dramatic filming. People auditioning for these shows sometimes create a character to play because they know that producers are looking for certain types of people, and many participants are actors even though they are presented as working other jobs. Also, footage is edited down to relatively few hours of viewing, and producers can to a large extent choose how viewers will respond to participants by emphasizing certain characteristics. How well does the designation "reality show" really fit?

2. Given all of the manipulation that goes on during the making of shows that are presented as "reality," are there any ethical issues involved in using the designation, or is it enough that many producers point out that their shows are "unscripted drama"? How "unscripted" are they?

3. *Schadenfreude* is a German word that means pleasure derived from someone else's misfortune. This word has entered the English language, and it is often applied to such situations as the enjoyment of someone else's public humiliation. Could this pleasure account for much of the popularity of reality shows?

Suggestions for Personal Research

1. Some people have asserted that reality shows provide insights into human behavior. Others argue that the fabricated situations and the participants desire to perform for the camera undercut any possibility of genuine insights into real behavior. Research arguments on both sides of this issue to see who makes the most compelling case.

2. Researchers from a variety of fields, including psychology, sociology, political science, and communications, have investigated reality TV's impact on and insights into issues like self-esteem, cultural identity, decision-making strategies, and even office politics. Look at the variety of topics generated by the study of reality TV and what it says about human nature and American culture.

3. Look for stories, reviews, and scholarly articles that examine reality TV shows from other countries. How do they compare with ours? What cultural differences do they suggest?

Multicultural Issues

1. If you are not from America and your native country also had reality shows, how do they compare to American shows of the genre (assuming you have watched these shows)? If you didn't have reality shows and had never seen any before, what did you think when you first saw American versions? Did you think they reflected anything "real" about Americans?

Vocabulary Terms

contrived	susceptible
tweaked	misnomer
brash	genre

The Fast-Forward, On-Demand, Network-Smashing Future of Television

Frank Rose

Prereading Question

1. What kind of impact do TV ads have on you? Can you think of an ad that actually made you interested in a specific product? If so, why was it effective?

It all started with the VCR. In 1975, when Sony introduced the notion of "time shift," as cofounder Akio Morita dubbed it, television was a staid and profitable business controlled by three national broadcast networks. *All in the Family,* the number-one show, was watched in 30 percent of American homes. Cable was something you got for better reception. The big question facing the industry was whether *Happy Days* would propel ABC to the top. (It did.)

This year's top series, *CSI,* was on in just 16 percent of households. The three broadcast networks are now six, most of them struggling to make a profit. More than 300 additional channels are available through digital cable and satellite. And time-shifting has progressed to the point that millions of viewers rely not on a VCR but on a digital video recorder, which makes it easy to find anything on those hundreds of channels and watch it anytime while fast-forwarding through the ads. The revolution that started in analog is now exploding in digital, and suddenly everything about television is up for grabs—the way we watch it and the ads that pay for it, the kinds of programs we get and the future of the networks that carry them.

The DVR, pioneered in the late '90s by TiVo, is the linchpin. It's taking hold at the same time that digital compression—which multiplies tenfold the number of signals a slice of bandwidth can carry—is enabling cable and satellite providers to pump out channels targeted to narrowly defined audiences. Throw in electronic programming guides—search functions that essentially let you Google your TV—and the implications for Hollywood are, as one exec puts it, "cataclysmic." Technology is empowering the couch potato. The fundamental premise of traditional broadcasting is its ability to control the viewer—to deliver tens of millions of eyeballs to advertisers and to direct those eyeballs from prime time all the way to late night. That control has been eroding ever since the advent of the VCR, but now it's being blasted away entirely.

As is usually the case, the revolution has not proceeded as forecast. Digital broadcasting is still stalled, and high-definition TV along with it. Although TiVo engendered panic in the industry after it appeared, it's proved a hard sell with consumers as a stand-alone device. Forrester discovered last year that 70 percent of consumers didn't even know what a DVR was.

Around the same time, satellite companies started building DVRs into their set-top boxes—and sales finally started to take off. In the growing competition between cable and satellite, DVRs have become bait to lure subscribers. When cable providers started pushing video-on-demand, satellite companies—unable to deliver on-demand service—countered with DVRs.

They've become so popular that cable operators like Time Warner and Comcast are now offering the systems as well. In the past year, the number of DVR-equipped households has more than doubled to 4 million. Forrester projects that in three years, 27 percent of US homes will have DVRs and one-third will have video-on-demand. Either way, control shifts from the networks to the viewer.

Television is run by people who make their living telling other people what to watch and when, while cramming in more and more ads to pay for it all. Plug in a device that short-circuits the system and they're in trouble. Network execs don't get paid millions to admit their best years are behind them. But late at night, when they're sitting in their Dolby surround-sound home theaters flipping past Letterman and Leno and *Nightline* to channels 252 and 286 and beyond, or checking their TiVos to see what they missed during dinner, they know.

"This business is not broken in such a way that it's going to implode next week or next year," declares Alec Gerster, CEO of Initiative Worldwide, an agency that purchases $21 billion in ads annually on behalf of such clients as Bayer, BellSouth, and Coors. "But it is going to be increasingly difficult to do the same thing each year as if we were back in 1980. There is a freight train coming at us, and the only thing holding it back is the time it takes for consumers to bend this technology to the ways they want to use it."

"It's all about the consumer," says Jed Petrick, president of the WB network. "The question is, how does the business model find a way to maintain itself or adapt to the new consumer model?"

To some of the savvier people in advertising, the real problem isn't the DVR. The problem is the 30-second spot itself—the "30," in industry parlance. "We are dealing with a world-class disconnect between the way we're trying to communicate and the way the consumer wants us to communicate," says Gerster. All DVRs have done is force the ad business to admit the obvious—that most people will avoid commercials whenever possible. And it isn't just the spots themselves, it's their ubiquity. The networks are now squeezing 16 to 17 minutes of ads and promos into each hour of programming, up from 14 minutes a decade ago. "Technology gives you the ability to skip commercials, and clutter gives you the reason," says Andrew Green, an executive at rival buying agency OMD, which handles clients like Pepsi and McDonald's. "We are driving this thing into the ground."

So far, the networks have been able to get more and more money for fewer and fewer top-rated shows because advertisers are desperate to pile into the handful of vehicles that are left. At last spring's up-front market, where ad buyers sign up for airtime on the upcoming fall season, they dumped $9.3 billion on the six broadcast networks, well over the record $8.1 billion they'd spent the year before. But this won't go on forever. A recent Forrester survey showed that if 30 million households had DVRs—a milestone we've projected to reach in early 2007—three-quarters of the national advertisers would cut their spending on TV. And just because advertisers are buying today doesn't mean they're happy about it. "Most clients are losing faith that they're going to put the money out there and get results," says Gerster. "So how do I get my message out in a way that people will at worst tolerate it, and at best be engaged by it?"

That's the challenge. The most obvious alternative is product placement—product integration, to use the current buzzword. But ad agencies operate on commission, a percentage of the price of the ads they buy. They never bothered with product placement until their clients started pressuring them to come up with something new. Now they're faced with questions like, how do you value a Coke can that appears for 15 seconds on *Friends*? Is it worth more if Jennifer Aniston drinks from it than if it just sits on the kitchen counter? How much more?

A New York marketing entrepreneur named Frank Zazza claims to have the answer. Zazza has come up with a scheme that grades placements by 10 levels of impact, from having the product in the background to naming an entire episode after it. Mix this in with his carefully calibrated "awareness scale" plus a couple of other factors, and you get the dollar value of a placement. For $300,000 you could buy, say, 3 seconds of "verbal" (talk about the product) or 90 seconds of background. "This has the ability to completely change the dynamic of television and the way it's bought," says Peter Gardiner, chief media officer of Deutsch, one of New York's hottest ad agencies.

Zazza has his eye on an even bigger prize. He's working with a company that inserts virtual billboards into sports broadcasts to apply the same technology to product integration. Instead of having an actual Coke can on the set of *Friends*, the producers could digitally insert it before the show airs. If Pepsi offered more for the DVD version of the series, they could replace the Coke with a Pepsi. It's product integration without the product. What this means for the networks is unclear; the important thing, Zazza says, is to keep the advertisers happy: "Unilever, Procter & Gamble—they're going to be around a long time after *CSI* is kicking up daisies."

But product integration, virtual or otherwise, isn't enough. Big brands want impact— the kind you get from having your identity tied to a hit show. In the '50s, when advertisers routinely produced their own shows, that meant programs with names like *Ford Theatre* and *Ford Star Jubilee*. Today it means Ford everywhere you look on *American Idol* and *24*.

At first, Ford tried to develop a show itself. It had been a while since anyone in Hollywood got a pitch from a carmaker, so it was news three years ago when Ford and its ad agency, J. Walter Thompson, teamed up with Lions Gate Entertainment to make a trekking-through-the-wilderness reality series. Based on a hit format from Norway, the show was titled *No Boundaries*, after the tagline for the company's SUV campaign. The WB finally aired it a year and a half later, only to drop it after six episodes. "We were very proud of *No Boundaries*," says Rich Stoddart, a marketing manager at Ford. "But you can make the most wonderful content in the world, and without a commitment from a distribution outlet, you have an audience of one."

Since then, Ford has stuck to shows that a network has already committed to. It's had the *American Idol* contestants sing car songs: "Mustang Sally," "Fun, Fun, Fun ('til her daddy takes the T-Bird away)." It's gotten *The Tonight Show* to park a Mustang in the studio audience: "The best seats in the house," Leno quipped. And this October, for the second straight year, it's introducing the season premiere of *24*, the Fox series starring Kiefer Sutherland as a rogue CIA agent. Ford is presenting the first episode without commercial interruption, bookending it with 3-minute ads. As part of the deal, Sutherland drives an Expedition, and other models are woven into the story. "Basically, we own the show," says Rob Donnell, who heads a four-person team in JWT's Detroit office that looks for innovative ways to promote the brand on TV. It seems to work: The ad-rating service IAG reported that the pair of 3-minute commercials that introduced *24* last season, though never rebroadcast, were among the most-remembered ads of the year. No other automotive spots even placed.

Meanwhile, network execs are trying desperately to hang on to elements of the past. In August, NBC announced a scheme to sandwich minimovies between its 30-second spots in an attempt to keep viewers glued to their sets—as if there wasn't enough clutter already. But ad people are moving on. Instead of one product—the 30—Madison Avenue is developing an entire arsenal, from 3-minute "advertainment" sequences like Ford's to 5-second spots too short to skip.

The irony is that, as networks and ad agencies scramble, the ultimate advertising innovation may be brewing at TiVo: spots that lure viewers into handing over their contact info for a follow-up. The project, known as the TiVo Showcase, relies on the firm's ability to feed special programming directly to its subscribers' DVRs. This summer, for example, the company partnered with Chrysler to present video clips featuring its new Crossfire sports coupe.

DVRs may seem like an unlikely friend to advertisers, but TiVo's new president, Marty Yudkovitz, likes to talk about his company's ability to "target the viewer and take him deeper inside the message." And while TiVo makes a point of saying it doesn't collect data on individual subscribers, viewers who want to know more about the showcase product can "opt in" by requesting a CD-ROM, landing them in a database of possible customers. Ultimately, Yudkovitz argues, DVRs could let television fulfill the promise Web advertising made in the boom years: ads targeted not just by demographic, not just by zip code, but by household, based on what the people who live there watch and want. "Television has always been great at brand awareness," he says, "but that's it. Measurability, targeting, the marriage of brand awareness and direct marketing—that is the holy grail." There's only one catch: TiVo—not a network—gets the revenue from these ads.

What ads look like, how to figure their worth, who gets paid for them—"every part of the model is under threat," says OMD's Andrew Green. "Which is wonderful, really, because it makes for an exciting life."

For television executives, ads are only half the equation—the half that pays the bills, but not the only half that matters. DVRs, in tandem with the explosion of channels in digital cable and satellite, will disrupt programming as ruthlessly as they have advertising. Successful programming is why NBC can claim to have "Must See TV" on Thursday nights, and why it can charge top dollar for its ad time as well. If time slots become irrelevant, scheduling does, too.

Marty Yudkovitz argues that DVRs—make that TiVo—can help television programmers as well as advertisers. "Programmers want to know not only who's watching, but where they came from and where they're going," he says. TiVo can tell them what the patterns are. It can also program a message to appear touting, say, next week's guest star on *Will & Grace* while you're watching an earlier episode. "It's a very powerful place to be," he maintains.

But it will take more than this to make the future work, particularly for programmers at the four biggest broadcasting networks—ABC, CBS, NBC, and Fox. To people in the industry, these four are what it's all about: They get the biggest audiences, the most money, and the most buzz. Yet broadcast television is almost an anachronism—some 85 percent of US households now get TV via cable or satellite—and the giant broadcast networks, with their common-denominator programming, are increasingly outdated as well. "Mass audiences, mass media—a lot of people are clinging to those old models," says Tim Hanlon, a vice president at Starcom MediaVest, a global marketing consultancy that counts TiVo among its clients. "But it's not really that way anymore."

Instead of chasing the same 18-to-49 demographic, the big broadcast networks should just admit that the time when the whole family gathered round the tube is over. Advertisers are now buying into new-style networks that deliver precisely targeted, highly desirable consumers. Take the WB, which like cable channels is known for a specific style of show: Viewers go there for relationship dramas with Gen-Y appeal and a lot of stuff about coming of age. It caters to a niche audience of 12- to 34-year-olds, especially females, and it charges advertisers a premium to reach this hard-to-get demographic. This gives the WB a brand identity the big four networks can't match.

"I watch my kids when they watch their TiVo," says Jordan Levin, the WB's programming chief, who at 35 has the soothing presence of a model suburban dad. "They have 300 channels, but they gravitate to the ones that satisfy their expectations—Nickelodeon, Disney, the Cartoon Channel, the WB. It takes a huge hit that the kids are all talking about at school to get them to try something new."

But just one show won't make them stick around. "There are going to be thousands of brands," Levin continues, "and the ones that stand for something are going to make the transition to the new playing field that digital technology is creating. The broader-based brands that don't stand for anything will go the way of *The Saturday Evening Post*."

Even the brands that stand for something will be challenged in the next phase of television. A few years from now, the 300-plus channels we have now will evolve into one: MyTV, the channel you program yourself. The increasingly sophisticated electronic programming guides that make this feasible, known as EPGs, won't be the simple onscreen listings most cable and satellite systems carry today, but interactive services with advanced search and sort functions. TiVo lets you search listings a week or two ahead and record shows when they air. Time Warner Cable is working on a system that will let you search backward in time and record shows that have already aired. (Essentially a form of video-on-demand, it works by storing programs at cable headends after they've been broadcast.) Eventually, TV listings will be marked with metatags—embedded keywords that pop up during a search, just as they do on the Web. When that happens, the amount of information your EPG picks up won't be limited to the eight or ten words most guides have now; it could include every name in the cast and a dozen other keywords as well. Want to record anything in which John Travolta had even a bit part? No problem. "Navigation is almost the crux of the future of television," says consultant Hanlon. "Not everyone has figured it out yet, but they will."

In a DVR-enabled, viewer-programmable world, with EPGs trawling the schedules to find anything you want to see, you have to wonder about the value of even a niche brand. If people end up using only the search function to assemble the programming they want to watch, the branding of networks and cable channels might not matter—and television would devolve into little more than a digitally distributed home-video business. Established brands might still have some draw, just as they do on the Internet: Google can take you anywhere on the Web, yet twice as many people head for ESPN.com as any other sports site. "But it's going to be harder and harder for any network to stand out," says Hanlon.

Right now, though, network execs have more immediate worries, like what's going to pay the overhead if the ad pie starts shrinking. "That's our biggest concern," says the WB's Levin. All that new stuff Madison Avenue is trying might work for advertisers, but there's no guarantee it will ever be the jackpot for television that 30-second spots have been. What do they do then? Try to charge subscription fees like HBO? Cut prime time from three hours to two? Put their shows on DVD and hawk them on street corners? Nobody really knows. But the freight train that used to seem such a long way off is getting closer and closer, and it won't be long before they have to decide which way to jump.

Journal Topics

1. What do you think about new advertising techniques, such as product placement, inserted in the television shows themselves? Are they more distracting than traditional advertisements?

2. Can you think of any ads that you have liked, regardless of what they were trying to sell you, simply because they were entertaining or stimulating in some way?

Questions for Critical Thought

1. With the popularity of subscription services like HBO and Showtime and new technology like DVRs, advertisers are having to develop new strategies to reach television viewers, such as product placements and "logo bugs" that appear near the bottom of the screen while a program is being broadcast. How effective do you think such forms of advertisement are? Could they fail by being too subtle or, conversely, too intrusive?

2. Looking at the ideas raised in the article, can you think of any forms of advertising that might emerge in the future that you think would be especially effective?

Suggestions for Personal Research

1. One way that advertisers have tried to get their ads watched is by trying to make them so interesting that people will want to watch them—even seek them out. For example, BMW created a series shown on the Internet called *The Hire* with short adventure/suspense films starring Clive Owen as "The Driver" and with other notable actors in supporting roles. Each short film has a well-known mainstream director. Other companies try to create events that will get news coverage, as when Adidas suspended two soccer players by bungee cords high above the streets of Tokyo, kicking a ball tethered between them. Volkswagen commissioned a life-sized ice sculpture of its Polo Twist model and parked

it outside a gallery in London. Research the increasing use of nontraditional advertising strategies that are being developed in response to the changes in people's TV viewing habits. Are these new strategies proving as effective as more traditional forms? Could they be even more effective? How do experts picture the future of advertising in a rapidly changing world?

2. Advertisers want people to take a second look and remember their products. To do this, some ads employ a variety of visual tricks, like optical illusions, to grab viewers' attention. Investigate the varieties of techniques advertisers use to get people to pay attention and remember their products. Are these new techniques proving as effective as more traditional forms? Could they be even more effective? As with the preceding question, research how experts picture the future of advertising in a rapidly changing world.

Multicultural Issues

1. If you aren't from the United States, how do you compare the kinds of TV ads you were exposed to in your own country with those that you see on American TV? Are there any obvious (or even subtle) differences that underscore differences between the cultures?

Vocabulary Terms

linchpin
buzzword

demographic
revenue

Entertainment Wars:
Television Culture After 9/11

Lynn Spigel

Prereading Questions

1. Looking at the title, what can you predict about the issues raised in the article? What do you think "television culture" means?

2. The September 11, 2001 attacks on the United States by al-Qaeda changed America and Americans in dramatic ways. Can you generate a list of the ways you think that the United States has been altered by these attacks?

3. How old were you on September 11, 2001? Can you remember how you felt in the days and weeks that followed? Did the attacks affect your sleep or give you nightmares?

4. In what ways do you think that 9/11 has shaped your views about the world you live in? Has 9/11 helped to shape your values in any way?

After the attacks of September 11, traditional forms of entertainment had to reinvent their place in U.S. life and culture. The de rigueur violence of mass media—both news and fiction—no longer seemed business as usual. While Hollywood usually defends its mass-destruction ethos with claims to "free speech," constitutional rights, and industry-wide discretion (a la ratings systems), in the weeks following September 11 the industry exhibited (whether for sincere or cynical reasons) a new will toward "tastefulness," as potentially trauma-inducing films like Warner's *Collateral Damage* were pulled from release. On television, violent movies also came under network scrutiny. USA cancelled its primetime run of *The Siege* (which deals with Arab terrorists who plot to bomb New York). At TBS, violence-packed films like *Lethal Weapon* were replaced with family fare like *Look Who's Talking*. TNT replaced its 1970s retro lineup of *Superman, King Kong,* and *Carrie* with *Close Encounters of the Third Kind, Grease,* and *Jaws* (although exactly why the blood-sucking shark in *Jaws* seemed less disturbing than the menstruating teen in *Carrie* already begs questions about exactly what constitutes "terror" in the minds of Hollywood executives).[1]

But it wasn't just the "hard" realities of violence that came under self-imposed censorship. Light entertainment and "diversions" of all kinds also didn't feel right. Humorists Dave Letterman, Jay Leno, Craig Kilborn, Conan O'Brien, and Jon Stewart met the late-night audience with dead seriousness. While *Saturday Night Live* did return to humor, its jokes were officially sanctioned by an opening act that included a somber performance by Paul Simon, members of the New York City Fire Department, and Mayor Rudolph Giuliani himself. When producer Lorne Michaels asked the mayor if it was okay to be funny, Giuliani joked, "Why start now?" (implicitly informing viewers that it was, in fact, okay to laugh). In the midst of the new sincerity, numerous critics summarily declared that the attacks on the Pentagon and World Trade Center had brought about the "end of irony."[2]

Despite such bombastic declarations, however, many industry leaders were actually in a profound state of confusion about just what it was the public wanted. Even while industry leaders were eager to censor out trauma-inducing images of any kind, video outlets reported that when left to their own discretion consumers were eagerly purchasing terrifying flicks like *The Siege* and *The Towering Inferno*. One video retailer noted an "uneasy" feeling about consumer desire for films like *The Towering Inferno,* and one store owner even "moved such videos so they were arranged with only the spines showing, "obscuring the covers."[3] Meanwhile, Internet companies worried about the hundreds of vulgar domain names for which people applied in the hopes of setting up web sites. One major domain name reseller halted auctions for several names it considered tasteless, including "NewYorkCarnage.com."[4] As these cases suggest, the media industries had to balance their own public image as discriminating custodians of culture with the vagaries of public taste.

Given its historical status as a regulated private industry ideally meant to operate in the "public interest," television was the most hard hit by this conflict between maintaining the image of "public servant" and the need to cater to the public taste (or at least to what advertisers think the public likes). Getting back to the normal balance between their public service and entertainment/commercial functions posed problems for broadcasters and cablers alike.[5] In the midst of the turmoil, the Television Academy of Arts and Sciences and CBS postponed the Emmy Awards ceremonies twice.

To be sure, television executives' nervous confusion was rooted in the broader havoc that 9/11 wreaked on television, not just as an industry, but also as "a whole way of life."[6] Most fundamental, on September 11, the everydayness of television itself was suddenly disrupted by news of something completely "alien" to the usual patterns of domestic TV viewing.[7] The nonstop commercial-free coverage, which lasted on major broadcast networks and cable news networks for a full week, contributed to a sense of estrangement from ordinary life, not simply because of the unexpected nature of the attack itself, but also because television's normal routines—its everyday schedule and ritualized flow—had been disordered. As Mary Ann Doane has argued about television catastrophes more generally, not only television's temporal flow, but also television's central narrational agency breaks down in moments of catastrophe.[8] We are in a world where narrative comes undone and where the "real" seems to have no sense of meaning beyond repetition of the horrifying event itself. This, she claims, in turn threatens to expose the underlying catastrophe of all TV catastrophes—the breakdown of capitalism, the end of the cash flow, the end of the logic of consumption on which U.S. television is predicated.

By the weekend of September 15, television news anchors began to tell us that it was their national duty to return to the "normal" everyday schedule of television entertainment, a return meant to coincide with Washington's call for a return to normalcy (and, hopefully, normal levels of consumerism). Of course, for the television industry, resuming the normal TV schedule also meant a return to commercial breaks and, therefore, TV's very sustenance. Already besieged by declining ad revenues before the attacks, the television industry lost an estimated $320 million in advertising revenue in the week following the attacks.[9] So, even while the media industries initially positioned entertainment and commercials as being "in bad taste," just one week after the attacks the television networks discursively realigned commercial entertainment with the patriotic goals of the nation.[10] In short—and most paradoxically—entertainment and commercialism were rearticulated as television's "public service."

By September 27, Jack Valenti, president and CEO of the Motion Picture Association of America, gave this "commercialism as patriotism" ethos an official stamp of approval. In a column for *Variety,* he wrote, "Here in Hollywood we must continue making our movies and our TV programs. For a time, during this mourning period, we need to be sensitive to how we tell a story. But in time—and that time will surely come—life will go on, must go on. We in Hollywood have to get on with doing our creative work. . . . The country needs what we create."[11] Valenti's message was part of a much older myth of show business—a myth that ran through countless Depression Era and World War II musicals—a myth of transcendence in which showbiz folks put aside their petty differences and join together in patriotic song. If in the 1940s this myth of transcendence emboldened audiences for wartime sacrifice, now, in the twenty-first century, this transcendent myth of show business is oddly conjoined with national mandates for a return to "normal" consumer pleasures. In a bizarrely Baudrillardian moment, President Bush addressed the nation, begging us to return to normal life by getting on planes and taking our families to Disneyland.[12]

In fact, despite the initial tremors, American consumer culture and television in particular did return to normal (or at least a semblance of it) in a remarkably short span of time. Yet, while many people have noted this, the process by which this happened and the extent to which it was achieved beg further consideration. Media scholarship on 9/11 and the U.S. attacks in Afghanistan has focused primarily on print and television news coverage. This important scholarship focuses on the narrative and mythic "framing" of the events; the nationalist jingoism (for example, the use of flag graphics on news shows); the relative paucity of alternative views in mainstream venues—at least in the immediate weeks following the attacks; the role of alternative news platforms—especially the Internet; competing global news outlets—particularly Al Jazeera; and the institutional and commercial pressure that have led to "infotainment."[13] Despite its significant achievements, however, the scholarly focus on news underestimates (indeed, it barely considers) the way the "reality" of 9/11 was communicated across the flow of television's genres, including its so-called entertainment genres.[14] The almost singular focus on news fails to capture the way television worked to process fear (even fear trumped up by the media) and return the public to "ordinary" life (including routine ways of watching TV). The return to normal has to be seen from this wider view, for it was enacted not just through the narrative frames of news stories, but through the repositioning of audiences back into television's fictive time and places—its familiar series, well-known stars, favorite characters, and ritualized annual events (such as the Emmy Awards).

In the following pages, I explore how an assortment of television genres—dramatic series, talk shows, documentaries, special "event" TV, and even cartoons—channeled the nation back to normalcy, or at least to the normal flows of television and consumer culture. I am particularly interested in how these genres relied on nationalist myths of the American past and the enemy/"Orient." But I also question the degree to which nationalist myths can sustain the "narrowcast" logic of today's multichannel television systems (and the more general movement of audiences across multiple media plat-forms). In other words, I want to interrogate the limits of nationalist myths in the post-network, multichannel, and increasingly global media systems.

Admittedly, the fate of nationalism in contemporary media systems is a huge ques-tion that requires perspectives from more than one field of inquiry. (For example, we would need to explore the impact of deregulation and media conglomeration; the dis-persal of audiences across media platforms; competition among global media news/entertainment outlets; relations between local and global media flows; audience and interpretive reception contexts; and larger issues of national identity and subjectivity.) My goal here is not to provide exhaustive answers to all of these questions (no one essay could do so), but rather to open up some points of interrogation by looking at post-9/11 media industry strategies, the discourses of the entertainment trade journals, and especially the textual and narrative logic of television programs that channeled the nation back to commercial TV "as usual."

History Lessons After 9/11

Numerous critics have commented on the way that the attacks of 9/11 were perceived as an event completely outside of and alien to any other horror that ever happened anywhere. As James Der Derian notes, as a consequence of this rhetoric of American exceptionalism, "9/11 quickly took on an *exceptional ahistoricity,*" as even many of the most astute critics refused to place the events in a political or social context from which they might be understood. Der Derian argues that when history was evoked in nonstop news coverage of destruction and loss, it appeared as nostalgia and analog, "mainly in the sepia tones of the Second World War—to prepare America for the sacrifice and suf-fering that lay ahead."[15] But, at least after the initial news coverage of which Der Derian speaks, history was actually marshaled in a much more contradictory field of statements and images that filled the airwaves and ushered audiences back—not just toward nostal-gic memories of World War II sacrifice—but also toward the mandates of contemporary consumer culture. On television these "contradictory" statements and images revolved around the paradox of the medium's twin roles as advertiser and public servant.

In the week following 9/11, television's transition back to normal consumer enter-tainment was enacted largely through recourse to historical pedagogy that ran through a number of television genres, from news to documentaries to daytime talk shows to primetime drama. The histories evoked were both familiar and familiarizing tales of the "American experience," as newscasters provided a stream of references to class-room histories, including, for example, the history of U.S. immigration, Pearl Harbor, and Vietnam.[16] They mixed these analogies to historical events with allusions to the history of popular culture, recalling scenes from disaster film blockbusters, science fiction movies, and war films, and even referencing previous media events, from JFK to Princess Diana. Following 24/7 "real time" news strategies that CNN developed in 1991's Gulf War, major news networks provided a host of "infotainment" techniques that have over the past decade become common to war reporting (i.e., fast-paced "MTV" editing, computerized/game-style images, slick graphics, digitized sound-effects, banter among "experts," and catchy slogans).[17] On September 12, CNN titled its coverage, "The Day After" (which was also the title of the well-known 1980s made-for-TV nuclear disaster movie). Fox sported the slogan, "America Strikes Back"—based, of course on the *Stars Wars* trilogy. Meanwhile, the FBI enlisted the television show *America's Most Wanted* to help in the hunt for terrorists.[18] As we searched for familiar scripts, the difference between real wars and "made-for-TV" wars hardly mattered. History had become, to use Michel de Certeau's formulation, a heterology of science and fiction.[19]

But what did this turn to familiar historical narratives provide? Why the sudden appeal of history? Numerous scholars, from Roland Barthes to Marita Sturken, have analyzed the ways in which history and memory serve to produce narratives of the nation. This work has shown how media (from advertising to film to television to music) play a central role in conjuring up a sense of national belonging and community.[20] Certainly, after 9/11, the media's will to remember was connected to the resuscitation of national culture in a country heretofore divided by culture wars and extreme political partisanship. However, for the culture industries, the turn to history was not only connected to the resuscitation of nationalism; history was also connected to the parallel urge to restore the business routines and marketing practices of contemporary consumer media culture.

At the most basic level, for television executives who were nervous about offending audiences, history was a solution to a programming dilemma. History, after all, occupies that most sought-after realm of "good taste." It is the stuff of PBS, the Discovery Channel, the History Channel—it signifies a "habitus" of educated populations, of "quality" TV, of public service generally. History's "quality" appeal was especially important in the context of numerous critical attacks on television's lack of integrity that ran through industry trade journals and the popular press after 9/11. For example, Louis Chunovic, a reporter for the trade journal *Television Week,* wrote, "In the wake of the terrorist attack on the United States, it's hard to believe Americans once cared who would win *Big Brother 2* or whether Anne Heche is crazy. And it's hard to believe that as recently as two weeks ago, that's exactly the kind of pabulum, along with the latest celebrity/politician sex/murder/kidnapping scandal, that dominated television news." Chunovic therefore argued, "We cannot afford to return to the way things were."[21] Ironically, however, the industry's post 9/11 upgrade to quality genres—especially historical documentaries—actually facilitated the return to the way things were. Historical documentaries served a strategic role in the patriotic transition back to "normalcy"—that is, to commercial entertainment and consumer culture.

Let's take, for example, ABC's programming strategy on Saturday, September 15. On that day, ABC became the first major network to return to a semblance of normal televisual flow. Newscaster Peter Jennings presented a children's forum, which was followed by an afternoon lineup of historical documentaries about great moments of the twentieth century. The lineup included episodes on Charles Lindbergh, the Apollo crew and the moon landing, and a documentary on the U.S. press in Hitler's Europe. Interestingly, given the breakdown in surveillance, aviation, and communication technologies that enabled the attacks, all of the chosen histories were about great achievements of great men using great technologies—especially transportation and communications technologies.[22]

Meanwhile, from an economic point of view, these historical documentaries were first and foremost part of the contemporary network business strategy that industry people refer to as "repur-posing." The documentaries were reruns repackaged from a previous ABC series narrated by Jennings and now "repurposed" for patriotism. This is not to say that Jennings or anyone else at ABC was intentionally trying to profit from disaster. Certainly, Jennings's forum for children provided a public service. But, as anyone who studies the history of U.S. television knows, the logic of capitalism always means that public service and public relations are flip sides of the same coin. In this case, the public service gesture of running historical documentaries also served to transition audiences from TV news discourse and live reportage back into prerecorded narrative series. Similarly, with an even more bizarre resonance, on the evening of September 15 NBC ran a special news report on *Dateline* followed by a rerun of the made-for-TV movie *Growing Up Brady.*

More generally, history was integral to the transition back to entertainment series programs. On October 3, 2001, NBC's *The West Wing,* one of television's premiere quality series, preempted its scheduled season premier to provide a quickly drafted episode titled "Isaac and Ishmael." On the one hand, the episode (which teaches audiences about the situation in the Middle East) was clearly an earnest attempt by the cast and creator–executive producer Aaron Sorkin (who wrote the script) to use television as a form of political and historical pedagogy.[23] On the other hand, the episode was also entirely consistent with contemporary business promotional strategies. Like the ABC strategy of repurposing, the NBC network followed the business strategy of "stunting"—or creating a stand-alone episode that attracts viewers by straying from the series architecture (the live episode of *ER* is a classic example of the technique). In this case, *The West Wing* was in a particularly difficult position—for perhaps more than any other network series its "quality" appeal lies in its "timely relevance" and deep, if melodramatic, realism. (The series presents itself as a kind of parallel White House universe that runs simultaneously with the real-life goings-on in Washington.)[24]

The credit sequence begins with successive headshots of cast members speaking to the audience in direct address (and in their celebrity personae). Martin Sheen welcomes viewers and announces that this episode is not the previously scheduled season premiere. In a subsequent headshot, another cast member even refers to the episode as "a story-telling aberration," signaling its utter discontinuity from the now routinely serialized/cumulative narrative structure of contemporary primetime "quality" genres. Meanwhile, other cast members variously thank the New York Fire and Police Departments, while still others direct our attention to a phone number at the bottom of the screen that viewers can call to donate money to disaster relief and victim funds. In this sense, the episode immediately asks audiences to imagine themselves foremost as citizens engaged in an interactive public/media sphere. Nevertheless, this "public service" ethos is embroiled in the televisual logic of publicity. The opening credit sequence ends with cast members promoting the new fall season by telling audiences what kinds of plots to expect on upcoming episodes. The final "teaser" comes from a female cast member (Janel Moloney) who hypes the fall season by promising that her character will have a love interest in future shows.

After this promise of titillating White House sex, the episode transitions back to its public service discourse. Essentially structured as a teach-in, the script follows a group of high school students touring the White House and caught in the west wing after a terrorist bomb threat. Attempting to calm the nerves of the students, various cast members lecture this imaginary high school class about the history of U.S.-Middle East relations. In an early segment, Josh Lyman, a White House "spin doctor," lectures the frightened students on terrorism and Middle East animosity toward the West. After a wide-eyed female student asks, "Why is everyone trying to kill us?" Josh moves to the blackboard, where he begins his history lesson. While he admits that the United States is somewhat to blame (he mentions economic sanctions, occupation of Arab lands, and the U.S. abandonment of Afghanistan), he says all of this at such rapid-fire speed that there is no in-depth consideration of the issues. Instead, the scene derails itself from its "teaching" mission by resorting to the colonialist rhetoric of "curiosities." The scene ends with Josh telling the students of his outrage over the cultural customs of Islamic extremism. The familiar list of horrors—from the fact that women are made to wear a veil to the fact that men can't cheer freely at soccer games—redirect the episode away from ethics toward an ethnocentric celebration of American cultural superiority.[25] Josh ends by reminding the students that, unlike Islamic extremists, Americans are free to cheer anything they like at football games, and American women can even be astronauts.

In this regard, the episode uses historical pedagogy to solidify American national unity *against* the "enemy" rather than to encourage any real engagement with Islam, the ethics of U.S. international policy, or the consequences of the then impending U.S. bomb strikes. Moreover, because the episode's teach-in lectures are encompassed within a more overarching melodramatic rescue narrative (the terrorist bomb threat in the White House), all of the lessons the students (and by proxy, the audience) learn are contained within a narrative about U.S. public safety. In other words, according to the logic of this rescue narrative, we learn about the "other" only for instrumental reasons—our own national security.

In all of these ways, *The West Wing* performs some of the fundamental precepts of contemporary Orientalism. First, as Edward Said suggests, in the United States—and in particular after World War II—Orientalism retains the racist histories of "othering" from the earlier European context, but becomes increasingly less philological and more concerned with social scientific policy and administration that is formulated in federal agencies, think tanks, and universities that want to "know" and thus police the Middle East. In this configuration, the production of knowledge about the Middle East is aimed at national security and the maintenance of U.S. hegemony. And as Said suggests, this kind of social scientific knowledge orientalizes the Middle Eastern subject and demonizes the Arab as "other"—as the antithesis of Western progress and humanity.[26] Indeed, when Josh details the cultural wasteland of Islamic extremism, he enacts one of the central rhetorical principles of Orientalism. For as Said argues, the "net effect" of contemporary Orientalism is to erase any American awareness of the Arab world's culture and humanity (its poets, its novelists, its means of self-representation), replacing these with a dehumanizing social-scientific index of "attitudes, trends, statistics."[27]

The fictional schoolroom on *The West Wing* performs this kind of social scientific Orientalism in the name of liberal humanism. And it does so through a pedagogical form of enunciation that places viewers in the position of high school students—and particularly naïve ones at that. The program speaks to viewers as if they were children, or at best, the innocent objects of historical events beyond their control. The "why does everyone want to kill us?" mantra espoused by *The West Wing*'s fictional students becomes, to use Lauren Berlant's phrase, a form of "infantile citizenship"[28] that allows adult viewers comfortably to confront the horrors and guilt of war by donning the cloak of childhood innocence (epitomized, of course, by the wide-eyed figure of President Bush himself who, in his first televised speech to Congress after the attacks, asked, "Why do they hate us?").

In the days following the attacks, the Bush administration spoke often of the eternal and "essential goodness" of the American people, creating a through-line for the American past that flattered a despairing public by making them the moral victims of a pure outside evil.[29] In a similar instance of denial, commentators spoke of "the end of innocence"[30] that the attacks ushered in, as if America had been completely without knowledge and guilt before this day.[31] Not surprisingly, in this respect, the histories mobilized by the media after 9/11 were radically selective and simplified versions of the past that produced a kind of moral battlefield for "why we fight." As Justin Lewis shows in his survey of four leading U.S. newspapers, print journalists writing about 9/11 tended to evoke World War II and Nazi Germany while "other histories were, regardless of relevance, distinctly less prominent." Lewis claims that "the more significant absences [were] those histories that signify the West's disregard for democracy and human rights [such as] the U.S. government's support for the Saudi, Arabian Theocracy."[32] He argues that the history of World War II and Nazi Germany was mobilized because of its compelling narrative dimensions—especially its good vs. evil binary. While this creation of heroes and villains was also a primary aspect of television coverage, it seems likely that many viewers weren't really looking for "objective truth" so much as narrative itself. In the face of shock and uncertainty that seemed to make time stand still, these narratives offered people a sense of historical continuity with a shared—and above all, moral—past.[33]

The need to make American audiences feel that they were in the correct moral position ran through a number of television's "reality" genres. One of the central ways that this moral position was promoted was through the depiction of women victims. In her analysis of news coverage of 9/11, Jayne Rodgers argues that the news tended to frame stories in "myths of gender," and, she claims, one of the central trajectories of these myths was a reversal of the gendered nature of heroism and victimization. Rodgers points out that even while "male deaths from the attacks outnumbered female deaths by a ratio of three to one," news narratives tended to portray men as heroes (firemen, policemen, Giuliani) and women as victims (suffering and often pregnant widows). Despite the fact that there were thirty-three women firefighters and rescue workers on duty on September 11, the media portraits of heroism were mainly of men, which, as Rodgers aptly argues, worked to "restore gender, as well as social and political order."[34]

On television, these myths of gender were often connected to age-old Western fantasies of the East in which "Oriental" men assault (and even rape) Western women—and more symbolically, the West itself. (Cecille B. DeMille's *The Cheat* [1915] or Rudolph Valentino in *The Sheik* [1921] demonstrate the longevity of this Orientalized "rape" fantasy.) In the case of 9/11, the United States took its figural place as innocent victim in stories that interwove myths of gender and the Orient. Both daytime talk shows and nighttime news were filled with melodramatic tales of women's suffering that depicted women as the moral victims of Islamic extremism. And "women" here meant both the women of Afghanistan who live under Taliban rule and American survivors (the widows) who lost their husbands during the attack. While, of course, these women are at one level real women who really suffered, on television they were fictionally rendered through melodramatic conventions that tended to elide the complexity of historical causes for the tragic circumstances the women faced.

For example, in the weeks following the attacks, *Oprah* included episodes featuring pregnant survivors who had lost their husbands. These episodes intertwined personal memories (via home videos of the deceased) with therapy sessions featuring the traumatized women. In these episodes, the "talking cure" narrative logic of the talk show format was itself strangely derailed by the magnitude of events; the female guest was so traumatized that she was literally unable to speak. In one episode, for example, a young pregnant woman sits rigidly on stage while popular therapist Dr. Phil tells her about the twelve steps of trauma (and Oprah interjects with inspirational wisdom). The episode presents this woman as having lost not only her husband, but also her voice, and with that her ability to narrate her own story. In the process, the program implicitly asks viewers to identify with this woman as the moral and innocent victim of *chance*. In other words, any causal agent (or any sense that her suffering is actually the result of complex political histories) is reduced to the "twist of fate" narrative fortunes of the daytime soap.

Writing about the history of American melodramas, Linda Williams argues that this theme of the "suffering" moral victim (particularly women and African Americans) can be traced through cinematic and televisual media representations (including depictions of American historical events). Williams claims that victim characters elicit our identification through sentiment (not only with them but, allegorically, with historical injustices they face). Following Lauren Berlant and Ann Douglas, she cautions that sentiment and vicarious identification with suffering—in both media texts and politics more generally—are often stand-ins for actual social justice, but that, importantly, sentiment is not the same as justice. By offering audiences a structure of feeling (the identification with a victim, their revealed goodness, and their pain), melodrama compensates for tragic injustices and human sacrifice. Or as she puts it, "Melodramatic climaxes that end in the death of a good person—Uncle Tom, Princess Charlotte, Jack Dawson (in *Titanic*)— offer paroxysms of pathos and recognitions of virtue compensating for the loss of life."[35] In political melodramas (like the stories told of 9/11's female victims), pathos and virtue can often be an end in itself; the spectator emerges feeling a sense of righteousness even while justice has not been achieved in reality, and even while many people feel completely alienated from and overwhelmed by the actual political sphere.

Addressing the public with this same kind of sentimental/compensatory citizenship, President Bush used the image of female suffering in his first televised address before Congress after the attacks. Harking back to Cold War paranoia films like Warner

Brother's *Red Nightmare* (which was made with the Defense Department and showed what a typical American town would look like if it were taken over by "commies"), President Bush painted a picture of the threat that terrorism posed to our freedom. "In Afghanistan," he claimed, "we see Al Qaeda's vision of the world," after which he listed a string of daily oppressions people might be forced to face should Al Qaeda's vision prevail. First on his list was the fact that "Women are not allowed to go to school." The rhetorical construction here is important because by suggesting that Al Qaeda had a vision for the world, President Bush asked TV audiences literally to imagine themselves taken over by Al Qaeda and in the women's place—the place of suffering. Having thereby stirred up viewers' moral indignation and pathos, he then went on to justify his own plan for aggression, giving the Taliban a series of ultimatums. Whatever one thinks about Bush's speech, it is clear that the image of suffering female victims was a powerful emotional ploy through which he connected his own war plan to a sense of moral righteousness and virtue (and it is also clear that we had never heard him speak of these women in Afghanistan before that day).

A more complicated example is CNN's airing of the documentary *Beneath the Veil*, which depicts the abuses that women of Afghanistan suffered under the Taliban. Originally made in the spring of 2001 for Britain's Channel 4, *Beneath the Veil* was produced "under-cover" by Saira Shah (who grew up in Britain but whose father is from Afghanistan), and with considerable risk to the filmmaker (photography was outlawed by the Taliban, and the fact that Shah is a woman made the whole process doubly dangerous). *Beneath the Veil* not only outlines the Taliban's oppression and cruelty, but also global neglect and responsibility, as well as the need for immediate political action. Shah is careful to reflect on her own Western assumptions about women, feminism, and Islam. She avoids—as much as possible—the narcissism inherent in her documentary and aims to rescue these women by showing that it was the Afghan women themselves—a group known as the Revolutionary Association of the Women of Afghanistan (RAWA)—who were the first to fight against the Taliban.

Beneath the Veil opens with footage shot (via hidden cameras) by RAWA. There are images of women huddled in a pick-up truck and being brought to a football field turned public execution arena. They are killed for alleged adultery. Interspersed throughout the film are images of and dialogues about the women's oppression, RAWA's own efforts to liberate women, and Shah's documentary witnessing of the events. An accompanying web site (still up) provides numerous links to information and zones of action and participation. The program and its web site constitute an important political use of electronic media. While there are images of female suffering, the pathos elicited by the pictures is organized around the desire for action (which Williams reminds us can also be part of melodrama) rather than just sentiment as an end in itself.

However, when rerun and repurposed by CNN in the context of the post-9/11 news coverage, the politics of *Beneath the Veil* were significantly altered. In the two months following the attacks, CNN reran *Beneath the Veil* so many times that it became a kind of daily documentary ritual. Although it was certainly important for audiences to learn about this human rights disaster, we should nevertheless wonder why Western eyes were willing to look at this documentary with such fascination after 9/11 (as opposed to, say, on September 10). First, it should be noted that in the wake of 9/11 documentaries of all sorts (but especially ones about terrorism) were, according to *Variety,* a "hot property" in the television industry.[36] Second, whatever the original achievements of the program, in this new context audiences were led to make easy equivocations between the kind of oppressions the women of Afghanistan faced and the loss of innocent life on American soil on September 11. In the context of CNN's programming flow we saw *Beneath the Veil* adjacent to news footage depicting Ground Zero, stories of American victims and heroes, anthrax attacks, public safety warnings, mug shots of the FBI's most wanted terrorists, and war footage depicting a bizarre mix of bombs and humanitarian aid being dropped on Afghanistan.[37] In this programming context, *Beneath the Veil* could easily be read as a cautionary tale (like *Red Nightmare*) and a justification for the U.S. bombings in Afghanistan. In other words, it might well have conjured up national unity for war as a moral position.

In the midst of the U.S. bombings, Shah produced a follow-up film, *The Unholy War,* which aired on CNN in mid-November 2001. This film documented the lives of women (especially three young Afghan girls) in the midst of the U.S. war against the Taliban. The film showed the destruction caused by bombings, the problems entailed in building a post-Taliban regime, and Shah's own failures in trying to save the lives of the three girls (she attempts to get them an education) whose father rejected her humanitarian efforts. *The Unholy War* disrupted the "flow" of CNN's rotation of *Beneath the Veil.* It also punctured President Bush's melodramatic rescue/war narrative, and questioned (the usually unquestionable) ideologies of "humanitarianism" that legitimated the U.S. bombings. As Shah said in an interview with Salon.com:

> I couldn't believe that we couldn't help them and that money wouldn't solve their problems. . . . That was a real revelation for me. I rather arrogantly, in a very Western way, assumed that I could solve their problems because I had good will and money. It taught me that their problems are more complex. It also taught me a lot about what's needed in Afghanistan, and how frustrating it is rebuilding a country that's been destroyed to the extent that Afghanistan has.[38]

Event TV and Celebrity Citizenship

While Shah's *Unholy War* suggests that there were indeed counternarratives and anti-war messages to be found on the airwaves and on web sites like Salon.com, the news images of unfathomable destruction that aired on 9/11 resulted in industry attempts to match that spectacle with reparative images on a scale as great as the falling towers. In this respect, "Event TV" (or television programs designed to take on the status and audience shares of media events) flourished after 9/11, and with this another staging of national unity after the attacks.

The first of these was the celebrity telethon, *America: A Tribute to Heroes.* Telecast live from New York, Los Angeles, and London on September 21, 2001, at 9 PM, the 120-minute program was simulcast on more than 320 national broadcast stations and cable networks. According to the Nielsen ratings, the program garnered a 65 share of U.S. households, making it one of the most-watched programs of the year, behind only the Super Bowl.[39]

America: A Tribute to Heroes featured an overwhelming community of stars recounting the stories of those who died or risked their lives in the struggle. These eulogies were interspersed with musical performances of popular hits from the baby boom to post-boomer past (the assumed generations of donors). Like all televised funerals, this one deployed television's aesthetics of liveness to stave off the fear of death. In other words, not only the "live" feed, but also the sense of unrehearsed spontaneity and intimate revelations, gave viewers a way to feel that life will go on in the present. The ritualistic and funereal atmosphere resurrected the recently dead for the living, restoring faith not only in spiritual terms but also in terms of the medium itself. (In other words, it was that most "degraded" of media—television—that brought us this powerful sense of healing and community.)[40]

While certainly designed to be a global media event, this was a deliberately "understated" spectacle, achieved through a deliberate display of "star capital" minus the visual glitz and ego. Staged with "zero degree" style (just candles burning on an otherwise unadorned set), the program appealed to a desire to see Hollywood stars, singers, and sports heroes reduced to "real" people, unadorned, unrehearsed (or at least underrehearsed), and literally unnamed and unannounced (there was no variety "host" presiding over the entertainment, no identification of the stars, and no studio audience). This absence of style signified the "authenticity" of the staged event, thereby giving stars the authority to speak for the dead. So, too, the actual mix of stars (for example, Mohammad Ali, Clint Eastwood, Paul Simon, Julia Roberts, Enrique Iglesias, Bruce Springsteen, Celine Dion, Chris Rock, Sylvester Stallone) combined what might otherwise have been a battle of stars semiotics (given their often at-odds personae and historical associations) into a compelling—and for many people, moving—site of mourning. The program's "interactive" aspect further strengthened the telethon's aura of community as on-demand celebrity phone operators, from Goldie Hawn to Jack Nicholson, promised to reach out and touch us. In all of these ways, *America: A Tribute to Heroes* is a stunning example of how post-9/11 television has created not a public sphere per se, but rather a self-referential Hollywood public sphere of celebrities who stand in for real citizens, and who somehow make us feel connected to a wider social fabric.

The 53rd Annual Emmy Awards ceremony—which was twice delayed because of the attacks—is another example. Jack Valenti's "show must go on" ethos was everywhere in the publicity leading up to and culminating in this yearly television event. Somehow the industry was convinced that the airing of the Emmys was so important to America that any sign of celebrity resistance to gather (whether for fear of being attacked or fear of looking crassly self-absorbed) would somehow be tantamount to "letting the terrorists win." As the Academy of Television Arts and Sciences chairman Bryce Zabel told viewers, canceling the Emmys "would have been an admission of defeat. Like baseball and Broadway, we are an American tradition."[41]

It seems just as probable, however, that the Academy and CBS were also worrying about their own commercial viability in the post-9/11 climate. In other words, canceling the Emmys would not just be an admission of the defeat of the nation; it would also be an admission that the consumer logics of TV—its annual ceremonies and self-congratulations—had been defeated. In this regard, in the wake of 9/11, the Emmys also came to signify the degree to which the televisual and marketing scene could be revitalized. The broadcast, which took place on November 4 at Los Angeles's Shubert Theatre (almost two months after the originally scheduled broadcast), was carefully orchestrated in this regard. Although there were more "no-shows" than usual, and while the area outside the theater was reportedly a "surreal" scene of rooftop sharpshooters, the Emmy producers encouraged the stars to perform their roles in the usual fashion. Before the broadcast, executive producer Gary Smith coached the stars, "Don't be afraid to be excited. . . . That's what people are looking for."[42]

The Emmy Awards program was another self-referential celebrity public sphere, this time constructed through appeals to television and Hollywood history. The opening sequence begins with Christian trumpet player/singer Phil Driscoll doing a bluesy rendition of "America the Beautiful" with a backup choir of students from different colleges across the country. The national unity theme is underscored by a large-screen display of video images (everything from the flag and the Statue of Liberty to historical footage of Charles Lindbergh's lift-off and civil rights protests to landscapes of prairies and cities, all spliced together in a seamless quilt of meaning). This is followed by a female voice-over that announces, "Tonight television speaks to a global audience as we show the world images of an annual celebration. Our presence here tonight does more than honor an industry, it honors those cherished freedoms that set us apart as a nation and a people." After this, the scene cuts to veteran newscaster Walter Cronkite, who appears via satellite from Toronto. Cronkite directly addresses the camera and narrates a history of television's importance to American politics and culture. Evoking the words of the World War II broadcaster Edward R. Murrow, Cronkite says, "Television, the great common denominator, has lifted our common vision as never before, and television also reminds us that entertainment can help us heal."

The Driscoll performance, the video-backdrop, the female voice-over, and finally the widely respected Cronkite provide a prelude to what will be the night's apologetic theme: the ritualistic honoring of stars is not narcissistic commercialized self-indulgence, but instead a public service to America and its image in the world.[43] The opening sequence then transitions to host Ellen DeGeneres, who delivers her monologue as the cameras cut back and forth to a bevy of Hollywood stars seated in the audience. Significantly, among those singled out are stars associated with Hollywood liberalism—including the cast of *The West Wing* and Bill Maher (who had already been in trouble with his sponsors for what they perceived to be unpatriotic comments). In other words, as with the telethon, the Emmy ceremony was not simply "right-wing" in its approach to patriotism; it presented well-known Hollywood liberals (including a grand finale by Barbra Streisand and, of course, DeGeneres herself) as part of a national community who leave their identity politics at home to join together and defend the larger American cause. Drawing attention to the patriotic mission of this liberal constituency, DeGeneres humorously asks the audience, "What would bug the Taliban more than seeing a gay woman in a suit surrounded by Jews?"

While the opening act establishes television as its own historical reference and television stars as their own public, a sequence near the end of the broadcast is even more blatant in its self-referential memories of Hollywood nationalism and celebrity citizenship. And while the first act uses network era "hard" newsman Cronkite (who is in Toronto and far removed from the pomp and pageantry), this later segment features the ultimate postnetwork celebrity journalist, Larry King (who is dressed in a tuxedo and is obviously part of the Hollywood community). King introduces a montage of vintage footage portraying Hollywood's efforts in wartime (e.g., the Andrews Sisters; Betty Grable's legs; Bugs Bunny; Bob Hope and the USO; Marilyn Monroe posing for the boys and kissing a wounded GI; Frank Sinatra signing an autograph; Harpo Marx clowning on stage; Hope and a bevy of sexy starlets in Vietnam; Hope, Steve Martin, and Jay Leno in the Gulf interspersed with Vietnam footage of Hope and Phyllis Diller as well as black-and-white images of Nat King Cole and Milton Berle performing for the troops). The rapid, decontextualized series of star fetish icons, the musical accompaniment (from the Andrews Sisters's World War II hit "Boogie Woogie Bugle Boy" to a standard rock riff to Lee Greenwood singing "I'm Proud to be an American") establish a "commonsense" and highly sentimental history of Hollywood patriotism (or as Larry King put it while introducing the montage, "Over the years the beat of the music changes, but the heart beneath it never waivers"). This nostalgic display of stars with its thesis of unchanging Hollywood sentiment obscures the different historical contexts in which World War II, Korea, Vietnam, and the Gulf War were fought (and obviously also the very different levels of popular support these wars had).

The montage sequence ends with an overhead traveling shot picturing a vast audience of GIs applauding Bob Hope during the Gulf War. The sequence then dissolves back to an overhead traveling shot of the celebrity audience applauding in the Shubert Theatre. This dissolve from the GIs to the Emmy audience—and the fact that the shots are perfectly matched—establishes a visual rhetoric that asks viewers to imagine that soldiers and celebrities are contiguous publics, and perhaps even comparable public servants. Immediately after the dissolve, the show cuts back to Larry King (live) on stage where he speaks into the camera: "Once again we're in a time when America's armed forces are being sent to defend our freedom, and once again the entertainment industry is giving what it can." The entire segment legitimates future wars through a sentimental journey down Hollywood's wartime past.

The segment is capped off by yet another invocation of Hollywood's self-referential public sphere. Larry King speaks directly into the camera but not, as is usually the case, in order to address the home audience. Instead, he addresses an ailing Bob Hope at home: "We know that Bob Hope is watching at home tonight. And you should know, dear Robert, that we are thinking of you. . . . From all of us here, thanks for the memories." King's direct address to Hope—intercut with stars applauding in the studio audience—creates a completely enclosed universe of citizen celebrities, orchestrating a set of complex relays between popular memories of vintage Hollywood, military history since World War II, and the present-day meanings of nationalism and war. In this televised display of celebrity patriotism, public service and publicity find their ideal meeting ground.

Osama bin Laden Meets the South Park Kids

In the introductory pages to his essay "The Uncanny," Sigmund Freud discusses the intellectual uncertainty he faces during World War I when he finds it impossible to keep up with the flow of international publications.[44] In today's world of electronic "instant" histories, these problems of intellectual uncertainty are compounded in ways that Freud could never have imagined. The "uncanny" seems an especially appropriate trope for the current situation, as nothing seems to be what it was and everything is what it wasn't just minutes before it happened. In this context, the literate pursuit of history writing seems slow to the point of uselessness. This is, of course, compounded by the fact that the publishing industry is painfully behind the speed of both war and electronic media. So rather than partake in either historical "conclusions" or future "predictions," I want to open up some questions about television and nationalism vis á vis the changing economies of industrially produced culture.

Given the political divisions that have resurfaced since 2001, it seems likely that the grand narratives of national unity that sprang up after 9/11 were for most people more performative than sincere. In other words, it is likely that most viewers really did know that all the newfound patriotism was really just a public performance of belief in national myths of unity. And if you didn't perform this role, then somehow you were a bad American. In this respect, no matter what they thought of the situation, in the wake of 9/11 stars had to perform the role of "love it or leave it" citizen to remain popular (a lesson that Bill Maher learned with a vengeance when his TV show *Politically Incorrect* was cancelled).[45]

But did the performance really work? Just days after the attacks, the limits of performative nationalism were revealed in *America: A Tribute to Heroes* when, in the final sequence, everyone gathered 'round Willie Nelson to sing "America the Beautiful." Now, this was certainly a bad performance. Most of the celebrities were either too embarrassed to sing, or else they just didn't know the words to this show tune turned national anthem.[46] Some stars were visibly squinting at tele-prompters with consternation—hoping to sing a verse. Yet, because the telethon was foremost aimed at baby boom and post-baby boom generations, most audiences would have known the popular ballads that were directly aimed at these niche generations. Clearly, pop songs like John Lennon's "Imagine" (sung by Neil Young), Bob Marley's "Redemption Song" (sung by Wyclef Jean), or Paul Simon's "Bridge Over Troubled Waters" have more historical meaning to these taste publics than any national anthem does.

More generally, I think the post-9/11 performance of nationalism will fail because it really does not fit with the economic and cultural practices of twenty-first-century U.S. media society. The fact that there is no longer a three-network broadcast system means that citizens are not collected as aggregate audiences for national culture. As we all know, what we watch on TV no longer really is what other people watch—unless they happen to be in our demographic taste culture. The postnetwork system is precisely about fragmentation and narrowcasting. While the new multichannel cable systems may not provide true diversity in the sense of political or cultural pluralism, the post-network system does assume a culture that is deeply divided by taste—not one that is unified through national narratives.[47] In a multinational consumer culture it becomes difficult for media to do business without addressing the niche politics of style, taste, and especially youth subcultures that have become central to global capitalism. In the end, the new media environment does not lend itself to unifying narratives of patriotism, if only because these older forms of nationalism have nothing to with the "return to normalcy" and normal levels of consumption. While nationalist popular culture does, of course, exist (and obviously rose in popularity after 9/11), it appears more as another niche market (those people who hang flags off their cars), than as a unifying cultural dominant.[48]

The actual cultural styles in these new narrowcast media markets are increasingly based on irony, parody, skepticism, and "TV literate" critical reading protocols. For people who grew up watching *The Simpsons*'s hilarious parodies of mass culture and national politics, for people who fell asleep to Dave Letterman or Conan O'Brien, and for viewers who regularly watched *Saturday Night Live, In Living Color, The Daily Show,* and *Mad TV*'s political/news parodies—a sudden return to blind patriotism (and blind consumerism) is probably not really likely.

In the first week after the September 11 attacks, the cable operators and networks all did cover the same story—and for a moment the nation returned to something very much like the old three-network system.[49] Yet, the case of 9/11 also demonstrates that in the current media landscape, it is hard to sustain the fantasy of utopian collectivity that had been so central to previous media events. Comparing media coverage of 9/11 to the coverage of the Kennedy assassination, Fredric Jameson argues that back in 1963, a Utopian fantasy of collectivity was in part constructed through news reporters' "clumsiness [and] the technological naiveté in which they sought to rise to the occasion." But, he claims, the media are now so full of orchestrated spectacle and public violence on a daily basis that many people had a hard time seeing media coverage of 9/11 as documents of anything sincere, no less as any kind of inter-subjective, utopian communication. As Jameson puts it, despite the many claims that America lost its innocence on 9/11, it was "not America, but rather its media [that had] . . . definitively lost its innocence."[50]

Certainly, for industry executives who work in the competitive environment of narrowcasting, sentiments of national belonging and utopian collectivity quickly gave way to the "bottom line." In fact, even in the "good will" climate of September 2001, the industry was still widely aware of the competitive realities of the postnetwork marketplace. CNN, which then had an exclusive deal with the Al Jazeera network, tried to block other news outlets from broadcasting its satellite transmissions of bin Laden's video address.[51] Even the celebrity telethon was a source of industry dispute. Worried that cable telecasts would undercut audience shares for broadcasters, some network affiliates and network-owned-and-operated stations tried to stop a number of cable channels from simulcasting *America: A Tribute to Heroes.* According to *Variety,* upon hearing of possible cable competition, "some of the vocal managers at the Big Four stations . . . went bananas and threatened to cancel the telethon and schedule their own local programming."[52] So much for humanitarianism in the postnetwork age!

Given this competitive media marketplace, it comes as no surprise that industry insiders quickly revised their initial predictions about the fate of American popular culture. By October 4, the front page of the *New York Times* proclaimed, "In Little Time Pop Culture is Back to Normal," stating that the industry was backtracking on its initial predictions that the events of September 11 would completely change culture. David Kissinger, president of the USA Television Production Group, told the *Times* that the industry's initial reaction to the attacks may have been overstated and that because most industry people were "terror stricken" on September 11, "We shouldn't be held accountable for much of what we said that week."[53]

In fact, within a month, even irony was back in vogue, especially on late-night TV, but increasingly also on other entertainment programs. By mid-November, Comedy Central's *South Park*—a cartoon famous for its irreverence—ran an episode in which the *South Park* kids visit Afghanistan. Once there, Cartman (*South Park*'s leading bad boy) meets bin Laden, and the two engage in an extended homage to Warner Brothers' cartoons. Bin Laden takes the roles of the wacky Daffy Duck, the dull-headed Elmer Fudd, and even the lovesick Pepé Lé Pew (he is shown romancing a camel much as Pepé romances a cat that he thinks is a skunk). Meanwhile, Cartman plays the ever-obnoxious Bugs Bunny (like Bugs, he even does a drag performance as a harem girl wooing a love-sick bin Laden, whose eyes, in classic Tex Avery cartoon style, pop out of his head).

Although the episode was the usual "libertarian" hodgepodge of mixed political messages (some seemingly critical of U.S. air strikes, others entirely Orientalist), its blank ironic sensibility did at least provide for some unexpected TV moments. In one scene, when the *South Park* kids meet Afghan children in a war-torn village, American claims of childish innocence (promoted, for example, in *West Wing*'s fictional classroom) are opened up for comic interrogation. Dodging a U.S. bomb attack, the Afghan children tell the *South Park* kids, "Over a third of the world hates America." "But why?" ask the *South Park* kids, "Why does a third of the world hate us?" And the Afghan kids reply, "Because you don't realize that a third of the world hates you." While the episode ends with an over-the-top cartoon killing of bin Laden, and an American flag waving to the tune of "America the Beautiful," the program establishes such a high degree of pastiche, blank irony, and re-combinant images, that it would be difficult to say it encourages any particular "dominant" reading of the war. The laughter seems directed more at semiotic breakdowns, perhaps mimicking the way in which news coverage of the war seems to make people increasingly incapable of knowing what's going on—a point that one of the *South Park* characters underscores at the end of the show when he says, "I'm confused."

To be sure, programs like *South Park* and the niche cable channels on which they appear might not translate into the old enlightenment dream of "public service" TV with a moral imperative for its national public. Television Studies is, of course, riddled with debates over the question of whether these new forms of narrowcasting and multichannel media outlets will destroy what some critics call common culture. In response to the increasing commercialization and fragmentation of European electronic media, scholars like Jostein Gripsrud, Graham Murdock, and James Curran champion European public service broadcast models, and even while they do not advocate a simplistic return to paternalistic models of "cultivation" and taste, they seek a way to reformulate the ideal of an electronic democratic culture.[54] In the United States, the situation is somewhat different. The "public interest" policy rhetoric on which the national broadcast system was founded has been woefully underachieved; broadcasters did not engage a democratic culture of diverse interests, but rather for the most part catered to the cultural tastes of their target consumers (which for many years meant white middle-class audiences). Moreover, the networks often interpreted public service requirements within the context of public relations and the strengthening of their own oligopoly power.[55] Meanwhile, the underfunded Public Broadcasting System grew increasingly dependent on corporate funding. And, as Laurie Ouellette argues, by relying on paternalistic notions of "cultivation" and catering to narrowminded taste hierarchies, the network has alienated audiences.[56]

Still, I am not saying that the new multichannel and multiplatform system of niche culture is necessarily better. Instead, we need to ask exactly what the new fragmented niche networks, as well as the proliferation of Internet sites, provide. What do the new forms of multinational media outlets offer beyond the proliferation of products and styles? The question is even more complex when we consider the fact that cable and broadcast networks, Internet sites, search engines, television producers/distributors, movie studios, radio stations, newspapers, and publishing companies are increasingly part of global conglomerate media structures (Disney, Rupert Murdoch's News Corp., Viacom, Time-Warner, etc.)[57] As in other postindustrial modes of capitalism, in the media industries there is both fragmentation and centralization at the same time; any attempt to consider the political effects of the multiplication of channels (and fragmentation of audiences) still has to be considered within the overall patterns of consolidation at the level of ownership."[58]

Perhaps I am a bit overly optimistic, but I do want to end by suggesting some alternative possibilities within the highly consolidated, yet also fragmented, global mediasphere. As Daniel Dayan and Elihu Katz argue, although media events may be hegemonically sponsored and often function to restore consensual values, they always also "invite reexamination of the status quo." Following Victor Turner, Dayan and Katz claim that media events put audiences in a "liminal" context, outside the norms of the everyday. Even if media events do not institutionalize new norms, they do "provoke . . . mental appraisal of alternative possibilities.[59] In this sense, although I have focused primarily on media myths of reunification and nationalism, it is also true that 9/11 provoked counternarratives and political dialogues. In particular, 9/11 made people aware of new prospects for communication in a rapidly changing media environment.

Certainly, the Internet allowed for a collective interrogation of mainstream media and discussions among various marginalized groups. According to Bruce A. Williams, while "mainstream media reiterated themes of national unity, the chatrooms allowed different groups of Americans to debate what the impact of the attacks was for them specifically."[60] Internet sites like Salon.com—as well as access to a host of international news outlets—provided alternative views and global discussions. Convergence platforms opened up venues for expression. For example, after 9/11, the MTV chat room included criticisms of U.S. policy and the bombing of Afghanistan, while a chat room hosted by the Black Entertainment Television network included conversations on whether it was possible to reconcile black beliefs about racist police and fire departments with the heroic images of police and firefighters after 9/11. Resistance groups from around the globe used the Internet as a forum for antiwar e-mails, virtual marches, and group organizing. The Social Science Research Council's web site allowed scholars to weigh in on the events at Internet speed. The "low tech" medium of radio (especially National Public Radio) likewise provided alternative voices.

That said, my point here is not that "new" media or "alternative media" are categorically "better" than TV. Certainly, many Internet sites and talk radio stations were filled with right-wing war fever. As Williams suggests, because the Internet allows for insular conversations, some message boards (such as "Crosstar") discussed ways to draw clear ideological boundaries and to keep "dissident voices" (i.e., liberals) off the board.[61] In this respect, we should not embrace the Internet in some essentialist sense as a pure space of pluralism that is always already more democratic than "old" media. Instead, it seems more accurate to say that the presence of multiple media platforms holds out hopeful possibilities for increased expression, but what this will amount to in terms of democracy and citizenship remains a complex historical question.

In addition to the Net, the presence of the Al Jazeera news network had a desta-bilizing effect on the status of information itself. Al Jazeera officials defy the demo-cratic legacy of the "free press" that had been so crucial to U.S. Cold War politics. Whereas the United States used to claim that its so-called free press was a reigning example of "free world" democracy, Al Jazeera now has taken up that same public pose, claiming that it will present all sides of the story from a Middle Eastern van-tage point. In their book on Al Jazeera, Mohammed El-Nawawy and Adel Iskandar discuss how the network's post-9/11 coverage—especially its coverage of the U.S. bombings on Afghanistan and the circulation of bin Laden's videotapes—quickly became a public relations crisis for the Bush administration.[62] Troubled by the bad PR, the Bush administration formed a Hollywood Summit to discuss the role the industry might play in the war on terrorism. The military also met with Hollywood talent at the University of Southern California's Institute for Creative Technologies, a military/Hollywood alliance that Jonathan Burston aptly terms, "militainment."[63] By late November 2001, President Bush signed an initiative to start the Middle East Radio Network (which strives to counterbalance anti-Americanism in the Arab world and is aimed especially at youth audiences).[64] As such federally sponsored efforts suggest, the proliferation of news outlets, entertainment networks, and Internet sites, as well as the mounting synergy between Hollywood and the military, has changed the nature of semiotic warfare, and the United States is certainly keen to play by the new rules of the game.[65]

Back to Normal?

On the one hand, as I have suggested above, much of the TV landscape looks like a continuation of the same kinds of programs that aired prior to 9/11, and for this reason it is tempting to say that television's "return to normal" transcended the events of 9/11, and everything is as it was before. On the other hand, 9/11 haunts U.S. commercial television.[66] The memory of 9/11 now—in 2005—circulates in ways that disrupt the kind of historical narratives and nationalist logic that had been so central to the initial return to the normal TV schedule.

Since 2001 the history and memory of 9/11 has in fact become a national battleground—not only in the notorious fights over Ground Zero's reconstruction, but also on the electronic spaces of television. By March of 2002, major networks began to feature commemorative documentaries that told the story of 9/11.[67] By March of 2004, President Bush launched a presidential campaign with TV ads that showed historical footage of the firefighters, implicitly equating their heroism with his presidency. But whereas nationalist historical pedagogy initially served to solidify consent for the Bush administration, now the history and memory of 9/11 is not so simply marshaled. On March 5, 2004, just one day after the ads began to circulate, CNN interviewed a woman who had lost her husband on 9/11. Unlike the speechless pregnant widows on *Oprah* back in 2001, this woman had regained her voice and spoke quite articulately of her disgust for the president's use of 9/11 footage for political ends.

In the end, I suspect the current situation is ripe for new visions of apocalyptic techno-futures, with satellites, guided missiles, surveillance cameras, and communication media of all kinds at the core of an ongoing genre of techno-warfare criticism waged by the likes of Baudrillard, Virilio, and many others.[68] But, it seems to me that as forceful and perceptive as this kind of work has been, this is really just the easy way out. Instead of engaging in yet another stream of doom and gloom technological disaster criticism, it seems more useful to think about how cultural studies and media studies in particular might hold on to a politics of hope. What I have in mind is in no way the same as utopian claims to transcendence and unity (whether local, national, or global) through new media technologies. Rather, this politics of hope is situated in a confrontation with the actually existing historical divisions around us. This materialist politics of hope should embrace the new global media environment as an opportunity to listen to "the third of the world that hates us" rather than (to use Bush's formulation) clutter the globe with messages about "how good we are." The world has heard enough about America. Time now to tune in elsewhere.

NOTES

Lynn Spigel, "Entertainment Wars: Television Culture After 9/11," *American Quarterly* 56, no. 2 (2004): 235–270. © The American Studies Association. Reprinted with permission of The Johns Hopkins University Press.

Thank you to Marita Sturken, Jeffrey Sconce, Jan Olsson, Chris Berry, and four anonymous readers for their help with this essay.

1. "Disaster Programming," Variety.com, September 21, 2001,1. For more on TV network cancellations of violent movies see John Dempsey, "Cable Nets Nix Violent Pix in Wake of Tragedy," Variety.com, September 16, 2001, 1–2; Joe Flint and John Lippman, "Hollywood Revisits Terrorism-Related Projects," *Wall Street Journal,* September 13, 2001, B2; Joe Flint, "TV Programmers Avoid All Allusions to Attacks," *Wall Street Journal,* September 28, 2001, B6.

2. For speculations on the "end of irony" see Jeff Gordinier, "How We Saw It," *Entertainment Weekly,* September 28, 2001, 12; Peter Bart, "Where's the Snap & Crackle of Pop Culture?" Variety.com, September 30, 2001, 1–2. Note, however, that a counterdiscourse popped up immediately in venues like the *Onion* and Salon.com, which used irony early on. In an online essay, James Der Derian noted some of the inconsistencies in what he called the "protected zones of language" after 9/11. For example, Der Derian notes that irony was in some venues under attack; "President Bush was given room to joke in a morale-boosting visit to the CIA, saying he's 'spending a lot of quality time

lately' with George Tenet, the director of the CIA." Der Derian also took on *New York Times* reporter Edward Rothstein for taking an "opportunist shot at postmodernists and postcolonialists" by "claiming that their irony and relativism is 'ethnically perverse' and produces 'guilty passivity.'" See Der Derian's "9.11: Before, After, and In Between," in Social Science Research Council, After September 11 Archive, SSRC.org, 5. (The original posting date is no longer on the site.)

3. Jennifer Netherby, "Renters Flock to Video Stores," Videobusiness.com, September 21, 2001, 1–2. *Video On Line* reported; "Wall-mart stores asked the studios for a list of their titles that contain scenes of the World Trade Center, presumably to take some merchandising action on those movies." See VideoBusiness.com/news, September 13, 2001, 1.

4. "Domain Names Grow After Attacks," Variety.com, September 25, 2001, 1.

5. Even while cable outlets are not regulated by the Federal Communications Commission to the extent that the broadcast networks are, they are still widely perceived as "service" industries and arbiters of public safety in times of crisis (obviously, this is the platform of cable news outlets like CNN, which dramatically increased its viewership after 9/11).

6. I am borrowing Raymond Williams's term "a whole way of life," which he used to define culture. See his *Culture and Society: 1780–1950* (New York: Columbia University Press, 1958, 1983), 325.

7. More generally, 9/11 disrupted the familiar/consumer uses of a host of communication technologies from cell phones to television to satellites to video games, all of which now resonated in an uncanny sense with their militaristic/wartime uses for which their basic technology was developed.

8. Mary Anne Doane, "Information, Crisis, Catastrophe," in Patricia Mellencamp, ed., *Logics of Television: Essays in Cultural Criticism* (Bloomington: Indiana University Press, 1990), 222–239.

9. Vanessa O'Connell, "TV Networks Cut $320 Million of Ads in Crisis," *Wall Street Journal,* September 19, 2001, B5.

10. *Variety* reported that "commercial breaks were back across the board Monday [September 17]." Rick Kissell, "TV Getting Back to Biz and Blurbs," Variety .com, September 17, 2001, 1.

11. Jack Valenti, "Hollywood, and our Nation, Will Meet the Test," Variety.com, September 27, 2001, 1–2.

12. The president said this in a televised address he delivered at Chicago O'Hare Airport with the aim of convincing people to return to plane travel. Note, too, that in subsequent months, various advertisers linked their promotional discourses to 9/11 and the idea of patriotic consumption. (For example, ads for United and American airlines as well as financial corporations did this.)

13. For examples of literature on TV news, 9/11, and Afghanistan, see *Television and New Media* 3, no. 2 (May 2002); Daya Kishnan Thussu and Des Freedman,

eds., *War and the Media* (Thousand Oaks, Calif.: Sage, 2003); Stephen Hess and Marvin Kalb, eds., *The Media and the War on Terrorism* (Washington, D.C.: Brookings Institute, 2003); Barbie Zelizer and Stuart Allan, eds., *Journalism After September 11* (New York: Routledge, 2002).

14. As other scholars have argued, we should not accept at face value the information/entertainment binary that underpins the ideological logics of mainstream media systems. This binary—and the related binaries of important/trivial; private/public; masculine/feminine; and high/low—not only elides the fact that news is also narrative (and increasingly entertaining), but also fails to acknowledge that entertainment also serves to provide audiences with particular ways of knowing about and seeing the world. See, for example, Richard Dyer, *Only Entertainment* (New York: Routledge, 1992); John Fiske, "Popular News," in *Reading Popular Culture* (Boston: Unwyn and Hyman, 1989); James Freedman, ed., *Reality Squared: Televisual Discourse on the Real* (New Brunswick, N.J.: Rutgers University Press, 2002).

15. Der Derian, "9.11," 2.

16. For an interesting discussion of media references to Pearl Harbor and the rerelease of the film after 9/11, see Cynthia Weber, "The Media, The 'War on Terrorism' and the Circulation of Non-Knowledge," in Thussu and Freedman, *War and the Media,* 190–199.

17. This kind of coverage is, of course, symptomatic of the general rise of "infotainment" in the climate of media conglomeration and a ratings-driven commercial ethos. For speculation on the social/political effects of the news coverage of 9/11 in terms of "infotainment," see Daya Kishan Thussu, "Live TV and Bloodless Deaths: War, Infotainment and 24/7 News," in Thussu and Freedman, *War and the Media,* 117–132. There is much additional literature on issues of infotainment. See, for example, Leonard Downie Jr. and Robert G. Kaiser, *The News About the News: American Journalism in Peril* (New York: Knopf, 2002); and Pierre Bourdieu, *On Television,* trans. Priscilla Parkhurst Ferguson (New York: New Press, 1998). For analysis of the effect that 'round-the-clock coverage of "real time" wars has on foreign policy, see Piers Robinson, *The CNN Effect—The Myth of News, Foreign Policy and Intervention* (New York: Routledge, 2002).

18. Claude Brodesser, "Feds Seek H'wood Help," Variety.com, October 7, 2001; Michael Schneider, "Fox Salutes Request by Bush for 'Wanted' Spec," Variety.com, October 10, 2001.

19. Michel de Certeau, "History: Science and Fiction," in *Heterologies: Discourse on the Other,* trans. Brian Massumi (Minneapolis: University of Minnesota Press, 1986), 199–221.

20. Roland Barthes, *Mythologies,* trans. A. Lavers (London: Cape, 1972); Marita Sturken, *Tangled Memories: The Vietnam War, the AIDS Epidemic and the Politics of Remembering* (Berkeley: University of California Press, 1997). For more on the role of memory/nostalgia in film, television, and other

popular media, see for example, Cahiers du Cinéma interview with Michel Foucault, reprinted in *Edinburgh Magazine* 2 (1977): 19–25; Patrick Bommes and Richard Wright, "Charms of Residence," in Richard Johnson et al., eds., *Making Histories: Studies in History Writing and Politics* (London: Hutchinson, 1982); George Lipsitz, *Time Passages: Collective Memory and American Popular Culture* (Minneapolis: University of Minnesota Press, 1989); Robert Rosenstone, *Visions of the Past: The Challenge of Film to Our Idea of History* (New York: Belknap Press, 1996); Robert Rosenstone, *Revisioning History: Film and the Construction of a New Past* (Princeton, N.J.: Princeton University Press, 1994); Marcia Landy, ed., *The Historical Film: History and Memory in Media* (New Brunswick, N.J.: Rutgers University Press, 2000); "Special Debate," *Screen* 42, no. 2 (Summer 2001): 188–216 (this is a series of short essays on trauma and cinema); David Morely and Kevin Robins, "No Place Like Heimet: Images of Homeland," chapter 5 in Morely and Robins, *Spaces of Identity: Global Media, Electronic Landscapes and Cultural Boundaries* (London: Routledge, 1995), 85–104. Purnima Mankekar, *Screening Culture, Viewing Politics: An Ethnography of Television, Womanhood, and Nation in Postcolonial India* (Durham, N.C.: Duke University Press, 1999).

21. Louis Chunovic, "Will TV News—Or Its Audience—Finally Grow Up?" *TelevisionWeek,* September 24, 2001, 15. Note that news executives responded to such criticism. For example CBS's Mel Karmizan and Fox News Channel's Roger Ailes promised to upgrade news programs and to cover more international issues.

22. So, too, this ABC lineup followed the logic of what Daniel Dayan and Elihu Katz see as integral to media events more generally: namely, a "neo romantic desire for heroic action by great men followed by the spontaneity of mass action." See Dayan and Katz, *Media Events: The Live Broadcasting of History* (Cambridge, Mass.: Harvard University Press, 1992), 21.

23. Some people have told me that they found it a useful source of "modeling" for their own conversations with their children.

24. Several other series also created special episodes about the attacks or else planted references to 9/11 in preexisting episodes. NBC's *Third Watch* began its season on October 29 with a documentary in which real-life emergency workers recalled their experiences on 9/11. ABC's *NYPD Blue* added two scenes acknowledging the attack into its season opener on November 6. As *New York Times* critic Caryn James pointed out, "The creators of 'Third Watch' and 'N.Y.P.D. Blue' have said they felt a responsibility to deal with the events, but the decision was practical, too. Their supposedly realistic characters would have seemed utterly unbelievable if they had ignored such an all-consuming tragedy." See Caryn James, "Dramatic Events That Rewrite the Script," *New York Times,* October 29, 2001, E7.

25. Josh lists many of the same Taliban injustices that President Bush listed in his first televised speech to Congress after the attacks.

26. Edward W. Said, *Orientalism* (New York: Vintage Books, 1979), see especially 284–328.

27. Ibid., 291.

28. Lauren Berlant, *The Queen of America Goes to Washington City: Essays on Sex and Citizenship* (Durham, N.C.: Duke University Press, 1997).

29. As Slavoj Žižek wrote just days after the attacks, this sense of a pure "evil Outside" was the response of a public living in a fake Matrix-like existence, a public that had for so long considered itself immune to the suffering endured on a daily basis by other world populations, and in any case, in no way responsible for its own perpetuation of violence around the world. Slavoj Žižek, "Welcome to the Desert of the Real!" posted on Re: Constructions, mit.edu, September 24, 2001. The title is taken from a line in the film *The Matrix*. Žižek's short essay was later developed in a book. See his *Welcome to the Desert of the Real* (London: Verso, 2002). Der Derian, "9.11," 4–5, similarly evokes *The Matrix*.

30. Jack Lule, "Myth and Terror on the Editorial Page: The *New York Times* Responds to September 11, 2001," *Journalism and Mass Communication Quarterly* 29, no. 2 (2002): 275–293.

31. Yet, as Marita Sturken argues, this "end of innocence" theme is common to the stories spun around national disasters (for example, the same language was used after JFK's assassination). See Sturken, *Tangled Memories,* chap. 1.

32. Justin Lewis, "Speaking of Wars . . ." *Television and New Media* 3, no. 2 (May 2002): 170.

33. In this sense, it is interesting to note how television created a *continuous past,* particularly with regard to World War II and Vietnam. In place of the grave generational divides these wars had previously come to signify, television presented unifying narratives that bridged the gap between the self-sacrificing "Greatest Generation" and baby boomer draft dodgers. This was most vividly displayed when Vietnam POW/Senator John McCain met 1960s youth rebel Stephen Stills on the *Tonight Show,* reconciling their differences.

34. Jayne Rodgers, "Icons and Invisibility: Gender, Myth, and 9/11," in Thussu and Freedman, eds., *War and the Media,* 206, 207.

35. Linda Williams, *Playing the Race Card: Melodramas of Black and White: From Uncle Tom to O. J. Simpson* (Princeton, N.J.: Princeton University Press, 2001), 24.

36. One month after the attacks, *Variety* reported, "A rash of documentaries—some put together in a hurry—that aim to explain terrorism is a hot property." See Andrea R. Vaucher, "Arab, Terror Docus Heat Up the Market," Variety.com, October 10, 2001, 1.

37. U.S. and British air strikes on Afghanistan began on October 7, 2001, and American warplanes attacked the Taliban in the field on October 10, 2001.

38. Saira Shah cited in Janelle Brown, " 'Beneath the Veil' Redux," Salon.com, 1–2.

39. Rick Kissell, "Bush Speech, Telethon Both Draw Record Auds," Variety.com, September 23, 2001, 1–2.

40. As one of the readers for this article suggested, the telethon's aura of liveness might have also helped to stave off the fear that TV and commercial culture were themselves "dead." To be sure, live "call-in" donations to stars ensured that money was still circulating through the media wires (here, not through the crass commercialism of TV as usual, but through the exchange economies of charity).

41. He said this on the broadcast.

42. Gary Smith cited in Joseph Adalian, "Show Finally Goes On and TV Biz Takes Heart," Variety.com, November 4, 2001, 1.

43. Underscoring the show's global impact, later in the ceremony there is a video montage of leaders from around the globe offering their condolences to the American public.

44. Sigmund Freud, "The Uncanny," in *Studies in Parapsychology* (New York: Collier Books, 1919, 1963), 19–60. Freud discusses his lack of bibliographical references vis á vis the war in Europe on 20.

45. When I delivered this paper at a conference at the University of California, Berkeley, Ratiba Hadj-Moussa pointed out that this dynamic of national per-formance doesn't necessarily suggest that people don't in some way believe in the performance. I want to thank her for this observation. Clearly, through the act of national performance, it is possible to actually believe in the role you are playing—and even to believe in it more than ever!

46. Note, too, that "America the Beautiful" replaced the actual national anthem after 9/11 because no one seemed to be able to remember the words to the "Star Spangled Banner."

47. Even news is now a matter of taste and "branded" by networks in ways that appeal to consumer profiles. For example, the news on Fox (especially its mark-edly conservative talk-show hosts) attracts one of cable TV's most loyal pub-lics, but many on the left mock its pretense of "Fair and Balanced" reporting. Al Franken's bestseller *Lies and the Lying Liars Who Tell Them: A Fair and Balanced Look at the Right* (New York: E.P. Dutton, 2003), and the ensuing lawsuit with Fox, obviously drew on the more left-associated taste publics that define themselves in distinction—in Bourdieu's sense—not only to Fox News, but to the viewers who (they imagine) watch it. For his discussion of taste as social distinction, see Pierre Bourdieu, *Distinction: A Social Critique of the Judgement of Taste,* trans. Richard Nice (Cambridge, Mass.: Harvard University Press, 1984).

48. Even before the attacks, patriotic symbols were reemerging as a fashion fad. Corporations such as Tommy Hilfiger, Polo Ralph Lauren, and the Gap Inc.'s Old Navy sported the flag trend, while European haute couture designer Catherine Malandrino unveiled her flag-motif fall collection in the summer

of 2001 (which included a skirt that Madonna wore on her concert tour). See Teri Agins, "Flag Fashion's Surging Popularity Fits With Some Fall Collections," *Wall Street Journal,* September 19, 2001, B5. According to Agins, the post-9/11 flag fashions were an extension of this trend, not an invention of it.

49. In 1992 Dayan and Katz speculated on the fate of television, nationalism, and media events in what they saw to be an increasingly multichannel and segmented television system. They argued that while the old three-network or public broadcast systems "will disappear," television's previous functions of "national integration may devolve upon" media events. Their speculation now seems particularly apt. See Dayan and Katz, *Media Events,* 23. They also predicted that with new technologies and possible erosion of the nation-state, "media events may then create and integrate communities larger than nations," 23.

50. Fredric Jameson, "The Dialectics of Disaster," *South Atlantic Quarterly* 101, no. 2 (Spring 2002): 300.

51. According to *Variety,* news organizations were "furious that CNN wouldn't forego competition" and "rallied against exclusives, saying that they don't serve the public's interest during a time of national crisis." ABC News spokesperson Jeffrey Schneider disputed any exclusivity deal by arguing fair use. He said, "There was no question in anybody's mind that these images from Al-Jazeera were of compelling national interest," and "We felt we had a duty to broadcast them to the American people which far outweighed whatever commercial agenda CNN was attempting to pursue in this time of war." Meanwhile, Walter Isaacson, CEO of CNN News Group, told *Variety* that CNN had a "reciprocal affiliate deal" with Al-Jazeera and that "it's Al-Jazeera's material and we don't have a right to give it way." However, Isaacson did admit, "in a time of war, we won't make a big deal about this sort of thing." See Paul Bernstein and Pamela McClintock, "Newsies Fight over bin Laden Interview," Variety.com, October 7, 2001, 1–2.

52. John Dempsey, "Invite to Cablers to Join Telethon Irks Affils," Variety.com, September 20, 2001, 1. The underlying reasons for the broadcasters' concern had to do with issues of East Coast–West Coast transmission times. The big four networks—ABC, CBS, NBC, and Fox—aired the telethon at 9 P.M. Eastern time, and because they wanted to make it seem like a simultaneous nationwide event, they also showed it taped via a dual feed at 9 P.M. on the West Coast. Some single-feed cable networks such as TBS and the National Geographic Channel, however, planned to show the telethon live at 6 P.M. on the West Coast, and thereby preempt the 9 P.M. taped West Coast network broadcast. Some network affiliates and owned-and-operated stations were simply unhappy that any cable networks were airing the telethon, even if cablers showed it simultaneously (at 9 P.M.) with the Big Four.

53. David Kessinger cited in Rick Lynman with Bill Carter, "In Little Time Pop Culture Is Almost Back to Normal," *New York Times,* October 4, 2001, 1.

54. See, for example, Jostein Gripsrud, ed., *Television and Common Knowledge* (New York: Routledge, 1999), esp. Graham Murdock, "Rights and Representations," 7–17; James Curran, "Mass Media and Democracy Revisited," in James Curran and Michael Gurevitch, eds., *Mass Media and Society,* 2nd ed. (London: Arnold, 1996), 81–119.

55. See, for example, Vance Kepley, Jr., "The Weaver Years at NBC," *Wide Angle* 12, no. 2 (April 1990): 46–63, and "From 'Frontal Lobes' to the 'Bob-and-Bob Show': NBC Management and Programming Strategies, 1949–65," in Tino Balio, ed., *Hollywood in the Age of Television* (Boston: Unwin-Hyman, 1990), 41–62; Lynn Spigel, "The Making of a Television Literate Elite," in Christine Geraghty and David Lusted, eds., *The Television Studies Book* (London: Arnold, 1998), 63–85.

56. Laurie Ouellette, *Viewers Like You? How Public TV Failed the People* (New Brunswick, NJ: Rutgers University Press, 2002).

57. ABC is now owned by Disney (which owns, for example, the Disney theme parks, radio stations, cable networks like ESPN and Lifetime, retail outlets, feature film companies, newspapers, and magazines; the Multiple System Operator, Comcast, has recently bid for the now struggling Walt Disney Company; CBS is owned by Viacom (which also owns, for example, Paramount Studios as well as cable networks like MTV and Nickelodeon, theme parks, radio stations); NBC recently merged with Vivendi-Universal (GE owns 80 percent of NBC Universal; Vivendi owns 20 percent), it has a joint venture with Microsoft, and its holdings include, for example, cable channels like MSNBC and Bravo and film and television production houses; and Fox is owned by Rupert Murdoch's News Corp. (which owns, for example, Fox Broadcasting, Fox News Channel, Fox Sports Net, motion picture companies, magazines like *TV Guide, Elle* and *Seventeen,* book publishers, numerous newspapers, and delivers entertainment and information to at least 75 percent of the globe). Meanwhile, media conglomerate Time-Warner owns a large number of cable channels, production companies, home video, magazines, music companies, and book publishers (for example, HBO, Cinemax, TNT, Comedy Central, E! Entertainment, Black Entertainment Network, Time-Life Video, Warner Brothers Television, Book of the Month Club, and its notorious deal with AOL). With telephone and cable operators like Comsat acquiring and partnering with media corporations and moving into content, the synergy among these sectors is even more pronounced. These ownership structures make these media organizations more like vertically integrated movie studios of the classic period, as they have controlling stakes in all sectors of their industry—production, distribution, and exhibition—in addition to obvious benefits of owning multiple and related companies that reduces risk and increases opportunities for synergy between different companies in the umbrella corporation. Note, however, that the great instability of the technologies market (including, of course, the fate of AOL and the AOL–Time Warner merger) begs us to ask new questions regarding the future of media conglomeration and convergence.

58. Media conglomerates often say that consolidation of ownership leads to more choice (for example, some media conglomerates claim that consolidation of business holdings allows them to use income from their mainstream media outlets to launch minority channels). However, a variety of media activists, industry executives, media scholars, and government officials have sharply attacked conglomeration and questioned the degree to which freedom of speech and diversity of representation can exist in a deregulated media system in which just a few major corporations own most of the media sources. See, for example, Patricia Aufderheide, *Communications Policy and the Public Interest: The Telecommunications Act of 1996* (New York: Guilford Press, 1999); Patricia Aufderheide, ed., *Conglomerates and the Media* (New York: New Press, 1997); Robert McChesney, *Corporate Media and the Threat to Democracy* (New York: Seven Stories Press, 1997); Ben H. Bagdikian, *The Media Monopoly,* 6th edition (Beacon Press, 2000); Dean Alger, *Megamedia: How Giant Corporations Dominate Mass Media, Distort Competition, and Endanger Democracy* (New York: Rowman and Littlefield, 1998).

59. Dayan and Katz, *Media Events,* 20.

60. Bruce A. Williams, "The New Media Environment, Internet Chatrooms, and Public Discourse After 9/11," in Thussu and Freedman, *War and the Media,* 183. It should be noted that the Pew Research Center found that nine out of ten Americans were getting their news primarily from television after the 9/11 attacks. See "Troubled Times for Network Evening News," *Washington Post,* March 10, A1. However, citing an ABC News poll, Bruce A. Williams claims "almost half of all Americans now get news over the Internet, and over a third of them increased their reliance on online sources after September 11." See Williams, "The New Media Environment," 176.

61. Williams, "New Media Environment," 182. Although Williams cites various online attempts to draw ideological boundaries, he doesn't necessarily view this as a bad thing. While he admits that some such attempts were disturbing, he also argues that "insular conversations that are not easily accessible to the wider public play a positive role by allowing marginalized groups to clarify their distinct values in opposition to those of the society-at-large within the safety of a sympathetic and homogeneous group" (184). Despite his pointing to the insular nature of the web and the desire of some groups to draw ideological boundaries, Williams also argues that there was a general air of civility on the Net (188–189).

62. The administration viewed the presence of Al Jazeera's graphic war footage and bin Laden's videotapes (which were aired around the world) as a grave problem. On October 3, 2001 (a few days before the bombings began), Secretary of State Colin Powell asked the Qatari emir, Sheikh Hamad bin Khalifa, to "tone down" Al Jazeera's inflammatory rhetoric, and the Bush administration specifically requested that the tapes be taken off the network. The International Press Institute sent a letter to Colin Powell, stating Powell's tactics had "serious consequences for press freedom" (176–177). Al Jazeera journalists defended

their coverage of graphic images by stating that they were trying to cover the war objectively, from both sides (Mohammed El-Nawawy and Adel Iskandar, *Al-Jazeera: The Story of the Network That Is Rattling Governments and Redefining Modern Journalism,* updated ed. [Cambridge, Mass.: Westview Press, 2002], 176–81). See also El-Nawawy and Iskandar's discussion of Europe's and Al Jazeera's coverage of Afghanistan (ibid., 186–189).

63. Jonathan Burston, "War and the Entertainment Industries: New Research Priorities in an Era of Cyber-Patriotism," in Thussu and Freedman, *War and the Media,* 163–175. For more see James Der Derian, *Virtuous War: Mapping the Military-Industrial Media Entertainment Network* (Boulder, Colo.: Westview, 2001). At ICT, technologies—such as immersive simulation games—are being developed simultaneously as entertainment and military technologies.

64. A member of the Bush administration met with Hollywood studio chiefs and network executives in Beverly Hills on October 18 to discuss efforts to "enhance the perception of America around the world." See Peter Bart, "H'wood Enlists in War," Variety.com, October 17, 2001, 1–3. A few weeks later, they gathered in what was referred to as a "summit" to discuss more detailed plans for Hollywood's participation in the war effort. See Rick Lyman, "White House Sets Meeting with Film Executives to Discuss War on Terrorism," Variety.com, November 8, 2001, 1–3. See also Pamela McClintock, "Nets Rally Stars Around Flag," Variety.com, December 3, 2001, 1–2.

65. Meanwhile, in a connected fashion, Al Jazeera's presence also threatens the hegemony of Western global news sources. Driven by fierce competition for Arab audiences, in January 2002, CNN officially launched its Arabic web site, CNNArabic.com. See Noureddine Miladi, "Mapping the Al-Jazeera Phenomenon," in Thussu and Freedman, *War and the Media,* 159. Note that CNN launched the web site at the same time (January 2002) that Al Jazeera withdrew its exclusivity agreement with CNN because of the dispute over a tape CNN aired without Al Jazeera's approval.

66. In a provocative thesis, Bret Maxwell Dawson argues that while TV returned to much of its previous content, television's temporal and narrational forms were "traumatized" by 9/11. He argues that the effects of this trauma can be seen in the way that elements of catastrophe television (e.g., live broadcasts, an aura of authenticity, and an obsession with time) have appeared with increasing popularity in reality TV and programs like Fox's *24.* See his "TV Since 9/11," unpublished Master's Thesis, University of South Wales, Sydney, Australia, 2003. While I would not posit such deterministic notions of trauma, it does seem useful to think about how 9/11 relates to a particular historical conjuncture in aesthetic ideals of TV realism, and in particular TV's obsession with the reality genre and real time (which, as Dawson admits, began before 9/11).

67. This cycle of memorializing documentaries began with CBS's *9/11* (aired 3/10/02), which was followed by *Telling Nicholas* (HBO, 5/12/02), *In Memoriam: New York City, 9.11* (HBO, 5/26/02), and others. For a seminar I taught at UCLA, Sharon Sharp wrote a very interesting paper, "Remembering

9/11: Memory, History, and the American Family," which considers how these documentaries used sentimental images of the family in crisis to tell histories of 9/11.

68. Baudrillard and Virilio both have published monographs on 9/11. See Jean Baudrillard, *The Spirit of Terrorism: And Requiem for the Twin Towers,* trans. Chris Turner; Paul Virilio, *Ground Zero,* trans. Chris Turner (London: Verso, 2002).

Journal Topic

1. "Good taste" is a question of personal preference. Some people decry the use of footage of and references to the attacks on 9/11 in political advertisements as being in bad taste. Others feel the same way about the idea of TV shows or movies about the attacks. How do you feel about the "entertainment" and political uses of 9/11?

Questions for Critical Thought

1. Spigel points out that scholars "have analyzed the way in which history and memory serve to produce narratives of the nation." A narrative describes a sequence of real or unreal events, and it has one or more obvious or implied points of view adding layers of meaning. What do you think is meant by "narratives of the nation"? How do history and personal memory shape our "story" of our country?

2. After the 9/11 attacks, the charge that the terrorists responsible for the attacks were "cowards" was repeated frequently on TV and radio. Feeling that this was a simplistic response that did nothing to further our understanding of the motivations of the terrorists, Bill Maher, host of *Politically Correct,* said on his show, ". . . staying in the airplane when it hits the building, say what you want about it, it's not cowardly." This outraged many people, and ABC responded by canceling his show. Maher decried the attacks as terrible and unjustifiable. Why do you think people were so outraged by Maher saying that the terrorists weren't cowards? And how important are voices that offer dissident interpretations of highly emotional issues?

3. Spigel asserts that a "politics of hope" should cause us to listen to other points of view from around the world—including people who hate us—rather than concentrating on telling the world about how good America is. What do you think she means? What does this have to do with "hope"?

Suggestions for Personal Research

1. The day after the attacks, Ruth Propper, an Associate Professor of Psychology at Merrimack College in North Andover, Massachusetts, distributed a questionnaire to students in one of her courses who were keeping dream journals as a course requirement asking them to describe their activities on 9/11, including

how much TV they had watched, how much radio they had listened to, and how much time they had talked about the attacks with other people. Using the dream journals to measure levels of stress weeks later, the researchers led by Propper looked at the questionnaires, which indicated that the amount of TV exposure the students had increased their stress. In an article published in the journal *Psychological Science,* they concluded that "Repeated viewing of horrific images may result in increased levels of stress and trauma in the general population. . . . Insofar as watching television replaces talking with others about such events, these undesired consequences may be amplified. In light of these findings, news broadcasters might consider whether repetitious broadcasting of traumatic images is actually in keeping with their goal of serving the public." Look at this research and find other articles that report studies connecting stress in the population with the viewing of horrific images. Besides stress, what other factors might result? How do such images affect attitudes and beliefs?

2. Spigel refers to President Bush urging Americans to return to their normal lives by flying with their families to Disneyland as "bizarrely Baudrillardian." Jean Baudrillard (July 29, 1929–March 6, 2007) was a French cultural theorist, philosopher, and political commentator whose work is frequently associated with postmodernism and poststructuralism. Research his theories to find what Spigel means by her comment.

Multicultural Issues

1. Were you living in the United States or in another country on September 11, 2001? If you lived in another country, how did the attacks affect the way you looked at Americans and the United States? How did the actions and ideas expressed by people in the United States in the weeks, months, and years that followed the attacks affect your opinions?

2. If you are not American now or originally, do you think the attacks affected the way Americans look at you and your country of origin? Do you think that fictionalized depictions of the events of 9/11 or of other terrorist acts have much power to shape American attitudes and perceptions?

3. If you are American and have always lived in the United States, do you think the attacks affected the way that you look at people from other countries? Do you think that fictionalized depictions of the events of 9/11 or of other terrorist acts have shaped any of your own attitudes and perceptions?

Vocabulary Terms

rearticulated	jingoism
discursive	paucity
transcendence	fictive
framing	astute

mandates
heterology
pabulum
aberration
ethos
pedagogy
precepts
liberal Humanism
epitomize
vicarious
paroxysms

sentimental
pathos
trope
performative
niche
irony
parody
recombinant
paternalistic
hegemony
semiotic

Terms for Clarification

Orientalism   The term has negative connotations when used to mean archaic and prejudiced interpretations of Eastern cultures and people by Westerners. This is the sense popularized by Edward Said in his controversial book *Orientalism* (1978), and it is generally what critics mean when using the term.

Otherness   The concept of "the Other" has been used in philosophy, culture studies, and social studies to understand the processes by which societies and groups exclude "others" whom they want to subordinate or who do not fit into their group or society.

CHAPTER 16—TELEVISION ESSAY QUESTIONS

These questions are intended as potential essay topics for some of the themes suggested by the articles and related material in this chapter.

1. Literature has been described in many ways, including as "condensed life." Great literature is described in many ways, too, such as that which meets the test of time—a definition that is not very useful for recent examples. Present a clear set of criteria for what makes a work "literature" that can include less traditionally designated forms as television shows. Next, provide criteria for what makes "great literature." Choose a television series that you think meets the test for great literature, backing up your assertions with clear, concrete examples.

2. The range of television shows a viewer can choose from is huge. Crime shows, reality shows, family dramas, shows about young singles, and shows aimed at teens, tweens, and small children are just some of the general categories. Choose one or two television series to discuss that you think have the capacity to help people gain important insights into human nature and/or society. Back up your assertions with clear, concrete examples.

3. Discuss one or more negative aspects of television viewing, such as inappropriate content or the effects of too much television exposure for one or more groups, such as children, teenagers, and adults. For example, how does television affect family interaction? Peer interaction? Creativity? Eating habits? Self-image? As always, back up your assertions with clear, concrete examples.

4. In television's early days, there was very little minority representation, and what was there tended to be fairly stereotypical. Women have been represented from the beginning, but not proportionately, and their roles were very limited. Gay male and lesbian characters were once nonexistent. Write an essay discussing either stereotyping and/or the evolution in the way a particular group is treated on American television. You could focus on gender, race, ethnicity, sexual preference, or even combinations (for example, African American men or Latino women).

5. If you are familiar enough with foreign or foreign-language television programs, write an essay comparing and contrasting American and foreign or foreign-language versions of a genre or specific program. For example, the *telenovela,* a serial melodrama, is a very popular genre in Latin America. A Colombian telenovela, *Yo Soy Betty, la Fea,* was remade into the Mexican *La Fea Más Bella* (*The Prettiest Ugly Girl*) and later into ABC's *Ugly Betty.* The United States comedy *The Office* is based on a United Kingdom series by the same name. What do the differences and similarities say about the two cultures?

CHAPTER 17

Film

Fatima loves math, but she is a lot less comfortable with her literature class, and she's worried about writing a paper on that topic. She goes to the professor, who tells her she knows more than she may realize. She looks puzzled, and he asks her if she likes movies. Fatimah loves movies, but what do they have to do with

literature? Her professor explains that cinema is actually looked at by many critics as a form of "literature" itself. He explains that the disciplines of film studies and literature have an overlapping vocabulary. He asks her to describe a movie she likes, and to explain why. Shyly, she hesitates, then she mentions how she really enjoyed *Dreamgirls*. She talks about the happy and sad aspects of the film, about the people in it, about how it held her attention and made her think about what people do in difficult situations, and how others will do anything to get ahead.

When she's done, her professor tells her that in her description of the movie and of her response, she's touched on the basic building blocks of literature: plot, setting, tone, mood, motif, conflict, characterization, and theme—in particular, the enduring themes of betrayal, hope, and life's meaning. When she leaves his office, she feels a lot more encouraged about her ability to understand literature, and she also has an idea for her research paper for class. She thinks it would be both interesting and fun to write a paper that has something to do with movies. She isn't quite sure how to turn that into a research paper topic, but her professor in that class gives her the go ahead to do some preliminary research to see if she can come up with a topic that will allow her to generate an argumentative thesis. She has always found gender issues interesting, and she finds a lot of books and scholarly articles on the image of women in films. Confident that she will come up with the perfect topic, she starts to read.

In our media-dependent culture, developing a critical understanding and a historical knowledge of such a popular medium as film is important. Like Fatima first did, most people think of movies as simply entertainment—often cheerfully brainless entertainment—but films help to shape our attitudes toward and ideas about the world around us and our place in it. Information competency requires an understanding of at least basic aspects of film history, theory, vocabulary, and criticism, as well as film's social, political, economic, and cultural aspects. The study of film raises any number of questions. What underlying assumptions about race, ethnicities, gender, aesthetics, economics, politics, class, and other nationalities motivate the images, sounds, and narratives of the movies we consume? How do they reflect or shape our values and worldviews? How do they contribute to public conversations about important issues?

HISTORY OF FILM

Although cinema is a very current and technologically sophisticated form, it is also well over a century old. The world's first night at the movies occurred on November 1, 1895, in Berlin. Max and Emil Skladanowsky used their invention, the Bioskop, to entertain a music hall audience with a series of very short films (around six seconds each). The Bioskop, which was inspired by the magic-lantern projector—the candle-lit ancestor of the modern slide projector—used two loops of 54mm film, with one frame at a time projected alternately from each loop rapidly enough to create the illusion of movement. The Skladanowsky's show is the first recorded instance of "moving" photographed pictures being presented to a paying audience of more than a single person. (In 1893, Thomas Edison's Kinetoscope could show moving images, but to only one person at a time because an individual needed to peer through a little window into a cabinet that housed the machine's components.) Advertised as "the most interesting invention of the modern age," the Skladanowsky brothers' invention was rendered effectively obsolete by another pair of European brothers two months later.

On December 28, 1895, Auguste and Louis Lumière (whose last name, appropriately enough, means "light") showed a Parisian audience ten short films they had made (averaging two minutes apiece) on Louis's new invention, the Cinematograph, which combined the functions of camera, film processor, and projector. This was such an amazing innovation that a grainy image of a train approaching the camera as it pulled into a station reportedly had people screaming and heading for cover. Although other people had invented motion picture cameras around the same time, the three-in-one aspect of the Cinematograph was unique, as was its portability.

These early devices weren't even the first that used light to project images—the principles of the *camera obscura,* a darkened box (or even room) with an aperture for projecting the image of an external object onto a screen inside it, were recorded as far back as the fifth century BCE in China. But actually photographing and projecting moving images was a major breakthrough.

A lot has changed since the Lumière brothers (beating out the less successful and less famous Skladanowskys) were first credited as being the pioneers of motion picture development. Sound (which many predicted would be a quick-to-die novelty) was introduced in 1926, and color was introduced in 1936. These days, audiences are used to seeing people and objects morph into new shapes, fly through the air, or grow and shrink in size—all through the use of computer animation techniques. Rather ironically, we continue to call movies "films" and call their study "film studies," when, more and more, film itself as the literal medium is being replaced by newer technologies (in fact, George Lucas's last *Star Wars* films were created using purely digital mediums—no film at all).

FILM THEORY

Film theory itself is as varied as theory in other disciplines, such as philosophy, literature, and art. Many schools of thought and perspectives overlap different disciplines, such as formalism, neoformalism, postmodernism, Marxist criticism, psychoanalytic criticism, feminist criticism, queer theory, and, most recently, ecocriticism—just to name a few. Film is in some ways closely related to literature, as its creators and scholars are sometimes concerned with the same elements, such as plot, characterization, setting, tone, style, and theme. Some scholars consider film to simply be another literary genre, along with drama. The comparison to drama is an obvious one because direction, performance, and aural and visual elements are so important to both. Issues of artistic freedom and censorship are also historically relevant to both.

Film is also comparable to the visual arts. It shares the same compositional elements: form, line, volume, and mass. It uses color, light, shadow, and darkness. Different moods may be evoked in an audience by the use of black and white film versus color film. The camera can linger closely on a face or shift our point of view by moving rapidly back and forth between different characters. It can create a sense of isolation by filming lone figures at a distance. The possibilities for visual manipulation of images are virtually endless.

Nevertheless, film is also a very distinct medium, with unique characteristics and its own vocabulary, and some filmmakers have dispensed with narrative and characters entirely. An important fact that distinguishes film from literature is the incredible expense of creating and marketing a film. An author can write a poem, play, story, or novel with virtually no personal expense at all. The money needed to publish and market a work of literature is a fraction of what goes into making and advertising a movie. Without a tremendous amount of initial capital, most movie projects can't even start. Just as important, whereas a work of literature is usually created by a single author— sometimes two in collaboration—with an editor offering advice and suggestions, a legion of people are involved in creating a movie. These days, few directors have the status or clout to be able to successfully demand to be the controlling "author" of a movie, with all the important creative decisions firmly in their hands (film theorists call such a director an *auteur,* French for "author"). The creative decisions may be made by a team of people who are often at odds with each other—some concerned with the artistic integrity of the film and others worried about the financial return on the investment.

For example, when the Walt Disney Company "money men" financing the original *Pirates of the Caribbean* movie first saw rushes of Johnny Depp's eccentric portrayal of Captain Jack Sparrow, they hated his interpretation and wanted him fired. The director talked them out of it (and *Pirates* went on to be one of the most successful film franchises of all time), but, most of the time, the investors call the shots. Sometimes this happens after the fact; directors have finished movies only to find that some industry executive ordered the film cut down or even cut up and reassembled. Auteur Orson Welles's fifth—and last—American film, the 1958 *film noir* crime thriller classic *Touch of Evil,* was so altered by the studio that he disowned it. A final version of the film, re-edited based on Welles's original fifty-eight-page editing instructions, was finally released in 1998, thirteen years after Welles's death. We know as much as we know about this film's history because it became a classic (despite the studio's hatchet job) and because Orson Welles was a famously innovative and influential director. As something of an industry in-joke, many directors and actors use a fake name, "Alan Smithee," when they want to remove themselves from such a project. (You can find hundreds of Alan Smithees in film credits if you look for them.) Most of the time, though, when we see a movie in a theater or at home on TV or DVD, we have no way of knowing how far from its original ideas at inception a film may have been diverted. Films are sometimes art, sometimes merely entertainment, but always part of a huge industry. Even independent filmmakers have to find funding and distributors.

MOVIE MARKETING

The executives running the film industry are, quite understandably, in the business to make money for their studios. To do this, they must produce movies that make profits above their budget and marketing costs, which are growing increasingly sizable as audiences hunger for bigger and better special effects. Movies need to bring in as many ticket buyers as possible and as quickly as possible because the media will report on film grosses the first weekend a motion picture is released, which can itself amount to either positive or negative publicity, depending on audience size.

One tactic employed by studios is audience research. In the 1970s, studios began conducting market research to try to ensure that a movie would have a sizable audience before it was even made. Also, after a film had finished shooting and a rough cut was produced, it could be screened for a test audience. These practices are still in effect today. After a test screening, a studio evaluates audience responses and may alter the film considerably in response to what the audience didn't like and what they said they would prefer seeing. Sometimes this can be done through editing shots already available, but sometimes the studio will order whole sections of the film re-shot with new scripting.

One example is the 1987 movie *Fatal Attraction*. In that film, a seemingly normal and attractive woman has a one-night stand with a married man, but she turns out to be disturbed and begins stalking him when he rejects her. In the original version of the film, she becomes despondent enough to commit suicide—but she sets him up for her "murder" as a final act of revenge. Test audiences didn't like this ending, so it was rewritten to make her an increasingly crazy and dangerous character who goes after the man's wife and child and is ultimately killed by the wife. The new ending didn't, in the opinion of some critics, make it a better film, but it apparently made it a more profitable one.

When movies are transferred to DVD format, the DVDs may have sections of "deleted scenes" and "alternate endings." These can give you an idea of the director's original vision for the film. If you find a version of a film billed as the "director's cut," it probably contains the version of the film that wasn't altered due to pressure from the studio.

What concerns some filmmakers, critics, and audiences is the fear that creativity is being stifled by this sort of approach. There is a tension between the need to please the audience and make the highest possible profit and the desire to see a greater number of innovative movies made. People who want to see the latter occur have argued that mass audiences aren't being "stretched" and challenged enough, and that they are capable of enjoying more complex and creative films if they are given the chance. Others argue that it isn't the industry's job to try to educate the audience or shape their tastes. Still others argue that there is room for both points of view, and some studios are setting portions of their budgets aside to encourage the development of at least some innovative works. Part of the whole debate centers on how we look at cinema—as an art form to be analyzed or as entertainment to be experienced and forgotten. Can it be both?

WHY STUDY FILM?

Some people resist the idea that films should be studied and analyzed for much the same reasons that some don't think literature should be studied and analyzed—they argue that by breaking up a work into its component parts to scrutinize them to determine different levels of meaning that we are spoiling the beauty or the fun of simply appreciating the work without thinking too deeply about it. However, this point of view overlooks the different, deeper pleasures that can be obtained when our intellectual framework expands, and we can actually see more than we did before. When we develop our critical abilities, we can reach new depths of understanding that make our experience of good and great works even deeper. Apart from the aesthetic dimension, though, there are also the areas mentioned earlier: film's social, political, economic, and cultural aspects. Films are perhaps the most popular mass art form, and they say a lot about us—and to us.

If you decide to do some serious, scholarly research into films and film theory, you will need to understand the terms that film scholars use. (Note that many of these terms could be applied to research in television, as well.)

BASIC FILM VOCABULARY

Auteur   This term, French for "author," was originated by French film critics to indicate the figure, usually the director, directly responsible for the film's unique qualities, imbuing a film with his or her own "personality." This term is not used for any filmmaker responsible for the ultimate work; instead, it is used to refer to major creative figures—people who tend to be involved with every step of the process: originating the idea, writing or cowriting the script, directing the film, supervising the editing, and so on. Examples include Jean Renoir, Charlie Chaplin, Ingmar Bergman, Orson Welles, Alfred Hitchcock, Woody Allen, Quentin Tarantino, Francis Ford Coppola, Robert Altman, Spike Lee, and Martin Scorsese. A problem with auteur theory is that it can do a disservice to other people involved in the creation of a film. Hitchcock, for instance, regularly downplayed the importance of others, such as his screenwriters.

Cinema/film/movies/motion pictures/pictures   Synonymous terms used to describe motion pictures as a medium.

Classical cinema   A term usually taken to refer to mainstream American films from the mid-teens through the sixties, with strong story, production, and star values, and conventional structure with unambiguous conflicts, climaxes, and resolutions.

Convention   An artificial, unrealistic device required by a work and accepted by an audience. For example, when we see two lovers kiss, we don't wonder where the violin music suddenly came from, nor are we disturbed when one scene gives way to another scene that takes place hours, days, or even longer periods of time later. We don't worry where the characters "went" during that time.

Creative producer   This term is used for someone who supervises artistic choices so closely as to be the artistic director. Walt Disney is a famous example. An independent producer is one who is not associated with a large commercial firm or studio. Sometimes directors or stars become independent producers of their own films to maintain artistic control; this means they have to come up with their own financing, either from investors or sometimes from grants. Some countries have film boards to help with the financing of independent films. (See *producer*.)

Cross-cutting   When shots from different sequences are edited together to alternate, suggesting simultaneous actions.

Diegesis   This includes a film's events, objects, spaces, and characters, including objects, actions, and attitudes not explicitly presented in the film but that the film leads audiences to infer. This can be referred to as the world of the film's story. The audience is said to construct a diegetic world from the material presented. In the *Matrix* movie series, for example, the audience can imagine an entire complex world inhabiting physical, mental, and cyber space, complete with its own history, mythology, and philosophies.

Documentary   In contrast to films of fictional stories using actors and scripts (even if based on real events), a documentary purports to document reality by filming actual people and events. Obviously, directors of documentaries make choices not only about what they film, but about what they choose to leave out of a film and how the film is edited.

Fade-Out and **Fade-In**   In a fade-out, an image vanishes gradually into darkness. In a fade-in, darkness gradually gives way to an image. There is also the "dissolve," where one shot fades out not to darkness, but to another shot fading in.

Feature film   A feature film is a full-length movie made primarily for initial distribution in theaters.

Flashback and **flashforward**   A jump backward or forward in diegetic time. After its opening shots, the film *The Usual Suspects* is told entirely in flashback, with a policeman interviewing the apparent sole survivor of a massacre, and this man telling the story of how he and the dead men came to meet each other and form a criminal gang. Flashback time and current time join at the end when he finishes his story and leaves the police station.

Focus   The degree of sharpness of a film image. Focus can be deliberately softened, for example, to produce a dreamy or even eerie effect.

Frame   Either a single photograph from a film strip or the dividing line between the edges of the film screen and the darkness of the theater.

Genre   A category. Film has many of the same genres as literature—for example, science fiction, horror, fantasy, adventure, noir thriller, mystery, western, romance, and comedy.

Hollywood   The city of Hollywood became home to many filmmakers and studios in American cinema's early days. The term is now usually used as an adjective to describe films made by major studios along fairly formulaic lines.

Independent film   Sometimes referred to as an "indie film," this is a film initially produced without financing or promise of distribution from a major studio. These films have a reputation for being more creative and quirky than films financed by major studios, but the distinction is by no means absolute, especially because major movie studios started developing "indie studios" of their own in the late 1990s.

Mise en scène   The staging of the action—performance, setting, décor, lighting, costumes, and so on—and the way that it is photographed.

Off-screen space   Space that exists in the diegesis but is not visible in the frame. It is particularly important in thrillers and horror films.

Producer   The individual who secures essential elements to making a film (everything from the screenplay and funding to the film distributor and director). The producer may simply supply money and leave the creative choices up to the director, editor, and writer, but producers often want a much bigger say and may control the major decisions.

Rough cut   The first assembly of a film as it is prepared by the editor from selected takes, leaving the more precise points of editing to a later stage.

Scene   A segment of a narrative film composed of interrelated shots that usually takes place in a single time and place.

Shot   A single stream of images recorded continuously by the camera and uninterrupted by editing. Films are usually made up of a large number of shots edited together, with many often just seconds long. Hitchcock's 1948 film *Rope* is famous for being composed of relatively few shots, some of them as long as eight minutes, which was the length of a reel of film in those days. Hitchcock had wanted to do the entire film in one long shot, but that was not technically possible at the time. *City of Men* is a more recent film that consists of several very long and well-choreographed shots. There are many types of shots, including the following:

- A long shot shows action and characters from a distance that may roughly correspond to the distance between an audience in a theater and actors on a stage.
- A full shot shows the human body in full, with the head and feet near the top and the bottom of the frame, respectively.
- A medium shot shows actors relatively close up, such as from the knees or waist up; and a close-up focuses on a single element of the body, such as a face or hands.
- A point-of-view shot is one that is taken from the vantage point of a character.
- A master shot is an uninterrupted shot that is usually taken at a distance and contains an entire scene. The master shot is so-called because closer shots are usually filmed later, and the whole scene that the audience later sees is constructed by the editor.

Special effects   Any tricks of photography intended to create images on film that don't really exist. They range from animated clay models and tricks of camera and lighting to models shot to look larger than they really are and sophisticated (often robotic) masks and prosthetics for the actors. More recently, computer generated images (CGI) have become one of the standard. In CGI, images are generated on sophisticated computer software and later added to the film, often using green-screen technology. James Cameron's *Terminator 2* is famous for pioneering much of modern-day CGI, and George Lucas's Industrial Light and Magic has created industry-defining special effects for the past thirty years.

Story   Story is distinguished from plot in that a plot is the unfolding sequence of events, but the story is everything the audience infers about the events that occur, including emotional meaning.

Studio   The term once referred to the actual controlled environment for the making of a film, but it is now used to refer to any major film production and distribution company.

Theory   Film theory refers to the attempt to determine what the essential nature of film is. Film theorists study not only the works themselves, but also their creators and audiences. They are interested in exploring the social, political, and even philosophical implications of cinema, as well as what differentiates it from other art forms. In the United States, the focus has been more pragmatic than theoretical, with the French and the British dominating discussions and schools of theory. The French were particularly important in constructing the early schools of film theory—hence the common use of French terms like *auteur, mise-en-scène,* and *montage.*

IN THIS CHAPTER

This chapter focuses on the power of films. Many critics consider film to be as important to literature as novels, plays, or poems. Most of you have seen far more films than you have read books, so films take on a great importance in our culture. You should consider the following questions as you read about films:

- What is "art," and do films ever qualify?
- How do we define literature, and should films qualify?
- How have classic films in a variety of genres informed or even created our modern-day mythologies?
- How accurately and proportionately do films depict women and minorities?
- How do films help to establish and maintain our cultural values?
- How do films help define our gender roles?
- How do films influence our ideas of dating, romance, and marriage?
- What do films say about sexuality?

To Kill a Mockingbird

Mark Holcomb

Prereading Questions

1. Did you see the movie *To Kill a Mockingbird*? If you did, what values did it seem to promote? How did you feel about them?

2. Did you ever read the novel *To Kill a Mockingbird*? If you did, and you also saw the movie, how did the film adaptation compare to the original material?

3. Even if you have neither read the novel *To Kill a Mockingbird* nor seen the film adaptation, you have undoubtedly seen films that depicted racial injustice. Did any of them affect any of your own attitudes and beliefs?

By now, the iconic status of Robert Mulligan's *To Kill a Mockingbird* is as entrenched in popular culture as its story line is ingrained in the popular imagination. A few fans may compare it unfavorably with Harper Lee's more sharply observed 1960 Pulitzer Prize–winning source novel, but for most people the film is the more resonant work— inaugurating the movie myth about the wise lawyer who defends an innocent man knowing he'll lose the case because of the color of his client's skin. According to Gregory Peck, the star of *Mockingbird*, F. Lee Bailey once confided to him that he became a lawyer "because of Atticus Finch,"[1] and Peck himself went on to say of the role, "It was like climbing into a favorite suit of clothes. . . . I knew all about that man, those children and that small-town background." Another high-profile fan, director and screenwriter Cameron Crowe, became a virtual one-man cheering section for *Mockingbird* during the publicity blitz for *Almost Famous;* in addition to mentioning it in seemingly every interview he gave, he created opening titles for *Almost Famous* that pay homage to the celebrated title sequence in Mulligan's 1962 film, while its central, adolescent character is at one point urged to grow up to be "like Atticus Finch." Crowe also placed *Mockingbird* at number five on his list of "a dozen movie musts" and called it his "first favorite film."[2] In another movie list, the American Film Institute ranked *Mockingbird* 34th in its roster of the "100 best American films of all time" in 1998.

Worlds beyond the movie industry have also taken the film to heart: some law schools have structured whole ethics courses around the fictional Atticus, and Notre Dame Law School's Thomas Shaffer even wrote a 1981 law review article entitled "The Moral Theology of Atticus Finch." In a 1998 television interview on ABC's "20/20," independent counsel Kenneth Starr told Diane Sawyer, "I love the model of Atticus Finch of doing what he thought was right when everybody was saying, 'Why are you doing this? This is a terrible thing.' There is truth, and the truth demands respect."[3] (This was at the height of the Clinton-Lewinsky imbroglio, so Starr was either conveniently overlooking the outcome of *Mockingbird*'s case or flagrantly hedging his bets.) Perhaps writer Albert Murray—who, ironically enough, was honored as Alabama's most distinguished writer with the first-ever Harper Lee Award in 1998—put commentary on the film into 'its proper perspective when he graciously, ambiguously, referred to *Mockingbird* as a "Sunday school lesson."[4]

It has of course become more than that, and yet—accolades and misty-eyed, well-meaning hyperbole aside—*To Kill a Mockingbird* is actually not, in purely technical terms, a cinematic masterpiece. Robert Mulligan is best remembered for an indistinct directorial style: most of his films seem somehow beyond his control, as if they could career off course at any moment (*Inside Daisy Clover,* 1966) or coast to a halt from sheer apathy (1969's lugubrious *The Stalking Moon*). Screenwriter Horton Foote's sensitive adaptation of Lee's novel, composer Elmer Bernstein's delicately mournful score, and Peck's totemic central performance are, in large part, what make *Mockingbird* an exception among Mulligan's films.

The director's metier was mood, which *Mockingbird* has to spare. The bittersweet ambience of the Finch household and mysterious, Gothic milieu of fictional Maycomb, Alabama (especially in the nighttime sequences, which are shot in the style of Universal's horror programmers of the 1930s and 40s) are the stuff of childhood fancy, and Mulligan captures them with aplomb. (In this regard, the film diverges from Lee's novel, which unfolds with a distanced, mildly sardonic tone.) Little wonder that *Mockingbird* has such a strong hold on those of us who first saw it as children.

But aesthetic excellence, or the lack of it, isn't what gives movie myths their power, any more than fond recollections make a movie mythic. *To Kill a Mockingbird*'s hypercinematic charge derives instead from a convergence of powerful feelings of nostalgia and the movie's standing as what Peck called, in a 1997 documentary on its making, a "social problem" film. His dated terminology is revealing, for *Mockingbird* relies on a late-1950s liberal conception of race and class as its sociopolitical touchstone. Fair enough—the movie is 40 years old. But like a child forced to grow up too soon (or not allowed to grow up at all), it has since been pressed into service as a complacent, fanciful, bourgeois creed uninformed by the Civil Rights movement, scarcely altered by subsequent history, and wholeheartedly sanctioned by the mainstream media. As outmoded as its underlying principles are, they're upheld every time *To Kill a Mockingbird* is extolled as anything more than an entertaining and evocative populist relic. But in fact the film obscures the very questions of class and race that underlie its mythic reputation, relying on a portrait of America as a place in which racism and hatred are incidental to social and political inequality. As film scholar Linda Williams has noted, *Mockingbird* "neither radically changed national feeling about race nor innovated new forms of media."[5]

To be fair, *Mockingbird* encourages its skewed reputation by adopting a rigid, neatly implied internal hierarchy of race, class, and character, and a near-acrobatic ability to subvert those distinctions whenever convenient. The social structure of rural Maycomb is made plain almost from the film's opening scene, in which one of Atticus's clients, a white farmer named Walter Cunningham, delivers food to the Finch household as a payment against his "entailment." Cunningham is duly deferential to middle-class Atticus, and his hard-working decency is underscored by an awkward yet proud demeanor and neat, if frayed, appearance. Cunningham's homespun virtue is undermined only when he turns up with a mob intent on lynching the jailed black field hand Tom Robinson (who's guarded by Atticus), but is immediately redeemed once he convinces the other men to abandon the enterprise when Atticus's young daughter Scout recognizes him in the crowd. The incident goes unmentioned for the remainder of the film, but in Lee's novel it gives Atticus the opportunity to trot out *Mockingbird*'s pet metaphor. "You children last night made Walter Cunningham stand in my shoes for a minute,"⁶ he tells son Jem and Scout, temporarily disregarding the rather more vulnerable position of the man standing in Tom's.

Poor working-class whites like Cunningham comprise the visible majority of Maycomb, as Lee reveals in her description of Tom Robinson's jury: "Sunburned, lanky, they seemed to be all farmers. . . . One or two of the jury looked vaguely like dressed-up Cunninghams" (166–67). On the next level up are working townspeople such as Sheriff Tate and professionals like Atticus and Judge Taylor. Above them, evidently, are only the benevolent government of FDR, alluded to in an ironic bit of opening narration taken directly from Lee's novel ("It was a time of vague optimism for some of the people: Maycomb County had recently been told it had nothing to fear but fear itself" [10]), and God. Somewhere in the mix, one presumes, are Maycomb's blacks, but they remain a largely nebulous presence.

Maycomb's black community may be as invisible as its ruling elite, but its lowest-of-the-lower classes—the Ewells—are distinctly palpable. Lee describes the family and their habitat in nearly subhuman terms:

> No economic fluctuations changed their status—people like the Ewells lived as guests of the county in prosperity as well as in the depths of a depression. No truant officers could keep their numerous offspring in school; no public health officer could free them from congenital defects, various worms, and the diseases indigenous to filthy surroundings. . . . [T]he Ewells gave the dump a thorough gleaning every day, and the fruits of their industry (those that were not eaten) made the plot of land around [their] cabin look like the playhouse of an insane child. (172–73)

Lee's metaphor is taken to absurd lengths in the film, in which the repugnantly racist Bob Ewell and his daughter Mayella, Tom's purported rape victim, pitch their performances somewhere between pantomime and barely contained hysteria. The Ewells are thoroughly despicable creatures for whom we need feel no compassion, to the point that by the film's end there is a sense that the family has gotten precisely what it deserves. This may be understandable in the case of the predatory Bob, but one can't help wondering about Mayella and the seven other Ewell children mentioned repeatedly during the trial. Fatherless and with no means of support, what's to become of them? The movie never says.

It doesn't say much about race, either, although that's ostensibly the crux of its argument. There are essentially two speaking roles for African-American actors in *To Kill a Mockingbird*—Tom, and the Finches' servant, Calpurnia. As individuals they are solidly and humanely portrayed (Calpurnia disciplines the recalcitrant Scout with real authority), but neither provides the film with any sense of a unified black presence. We do see Tom's cabin and his wife Helen on the two occasions that Atticus visits on business, and while there are friends and family members gathered outside, we never hear their dialogue or glimpse an establishing shot of the surrounding neighborhood as a whole. And Calpurnia, who brings order to the Finch household, appears to exist in a complete vacuum: no husband or family are mentioned, and when Atticus demands that she stay overnight while he protects Tom from the lynch mob, she complies without hesitation. It's somewhat surprising to learn that she has a home to go to at all.

Graciously depicted though they may be, Tom and Cal fit snugly into familiar and distinct types in a genre that Linda Williams has dubbed the "melodrama of black and white." Tom is both the virtuous, suffering Uncle Tom-like black victim (something Harper Lee must surely have been aware of when she named her character) and the implicit, hypersexualized threat to white women, while Calpurnia is a nurturing, attentive mammy whose presence theoretically allows the Finches to "more fully exercise the privileges and authority granted by white skin."[7] *To Kill a Mockingbird* may function in part as a critique of the Southern desire for plantation-era "old days" and the "Tom/anti-Tom" dialectic Williams elucidates, but the presentation of its focal black characters fails to convincingly challenge the stereotypes that spawned them. Ultimately, Tom and Cal are as one-dimensionally good as the Ewells are broadly evil.

It's arguable that, for the purposes of the movie's narrative, black life in Maycomb is more than adequately represented by Tom, Calpurnia, and the spectators in the courthouse gallery. But if the blatantly fabricated charge against Tom and his disastrous trial are meant to be emblematic of a society that fails to protect blacks against such specious accusations—and worse, the cruel and unusual punishment (legally sanctioned or not) that follows—the lack of a viable black community or distinguishable black individuals in the film's Maycomb diminishes the scope of Tom's predicament. Moreover, the grotesque flamboyance of the Ewells gives the impression that ugly acts of racism are perpetrated only by the most degraded members of white society—Lee's "insane children," whose genesis, incidentally, goes unexplained.

To Kill a Mockingbird obscures the complexity of its subject matter not only with low-key warmth, comfortable stereotypes, and ossified good intentions, but also through an implicit desire for race and class to simply not matter. Or to matter, perhaps, only as indicators of personal aberration and failure—the failure of single individuals to "stand in the shoes" of others and deny them the right to sing innocuous mockingbird songs. The film's questions of systemic corruption and of our own complicity in or indifference to such systems fit into its conception of what a social problem is only insofar as we're led to identify with its while characters. All well and good, except that it's a foregone conclusion which ones we're likely to identify with.

Explicit in the film's view of race and class relations is the notion that social problems are best "solved" through the actions of official bodies, in this case the American judicial system. A good deal of *To Kill a Mockingbird's* second half is taken up by Tom's trial, which would appear to move the film squarely into the genre of courtroom drama, where it resides as legitimately as it does in the genre of black-and-white melodrama. Yet, as Carol J. Clover remarks, trial films "[position] us not as passive spectators, but as active ones, viewers with a job to do."[8] In one of its cleverer strokes, *Mockingbird* meets this criterion by making us act as the film's jury in place of the trial's jury, whom we see in only a handful of long and medium shots. Unfortunately, the predetermined outcome makes us as moot and inert as they are, and whatever outrage we may rightly feel is thus thwarted along with Tom's chance of a fair trial. Only Jem is moved to anger by the judicial travesty, but by then the film is too far along for him to assume the role of galvanizing key figure.

Jem's nascent activism is, in any event, subordinate to Boo Radley's climactic act of rescue, which provides the trial with its effective culmination. According to Kathy

Laster, "Courtroom films of all persuasions mostly manage to re-establish the legitimacy of the prevailing system or at least belief in the rule of law."[9] To its credit, *Mockingbird* is an equivocal exception to this rule. Boo may be the least socially and politically powerful white male in Maycomb, but he is white and male nonetheless, and as such is an agent of the prevailing system. Yet the fact remains that he is firmly outside that system, and Sheriff Tate and Atticus's ultimate reliance on his act of rough justice proves how impotent they and the system have become.

In his "Overture" to *The Raw and the Cooked,* Claude Lévi-Strauss asserts that "myths operate in men's minds without their being aware of the fact . . . as if the thinking process were taking place in the myths."[10] He was referring to the mythological systems of traditional, so-called primitive societies, but he could just as easily have been describing the way movies operate—or "think"—in ours. On a more pragmatic level, movies do little more than reinforce private mythologies or reflect the fragmentation of modern life. Even so, a few films, deserving or otherwise, live up to the phenomenon Lévi-Strauss describes. It *is* possible to enjoy and even champion *To Kill a Mockingbird* without turning a blind eye to its thematic flaws or overestimating its relevance. It daringly rejects the bland conformity of the not-so-recently-past (at the time of the film's original release) Eisenhower era by casting Atticus's futile challenge to the status quo in a heroic light. At the very least, it tells its story in the context of race and class, which precious few films have attempted to do even in the intervening four decades. Perhaps that's only a modest accomplishment for a film of such widely perceived importance, scaled more to preadolescent personal inspiration than all-encompassing cultural myth. I first saw *To Kill a Mockingbird* when I was five years old: the film was three. It kindled my love of "serious" movies and my sense of social justice as well. In some measure, the film's unique mixture of amiable sentimentality, atavistic dread, and warmed-over New Deal liberalism is responsible for who I am today. I have no doubt that I'm in good company. But if *To Kill a Mockingbird*'s true lasting strength is its ability to appeal to and inspire children to thoughts of equality and justice, it's probably best to remember that children, unlike myths, grow up to find themselves in a world decidedly more complicated than the one in Robert Mulligan's film.

NOTES

1. Eleanor Ringel, "Climbing into a Favorite Suit," *Y'all.com* (April 29, 1998).

2. Cameron Crowe, "Alan's Notes." *Film Comment* (September/October 2000), p. 64.

3. The interview aired on Wednesday, November 25, 1998.

4. Quoted in Roy Hoffman, "Long Lives the Mockingbird," *New York Times* (August 9, 1998), sec. 7, p. 31.

5. Linda Williams, *Playing the Race Card. Melodramas of Black and White from Uncle Tom to O.J. Simpson* (Princeton N.J.: Princeton University Press, 2001), p. 301.

6. Harper Lee, *To Kill a Mockingbird* (New York: J. B. Lippincott, 1960), p. 160.

7. Williams, *Playing the Race Card,* p. 203.

8. Carol J. Clover, "God Bless Juries!" *Refiguring American Film Genres: History and Theory,* ed. Nick Browne (Berkeley, CA: University of California Press, 1998), p. 256.

9. Kathy Laster with Krista Breckweg and John King, *The Drama of the Court-room* (Sydney: The Federation Press, 2000. p. 12.

10. Claude Lévi-Strauss, *The Raw and the Cooked* (New York: Harper & Row, 1969), p. 12.

Journal Topics

1. The article mentions a famous attorney who says that he went into law because of the film portrayal of Atticus Finch. Is there a movie that has had a big influence on your life? If so, what is it, and what has its impact been?

2. Do you have your own "dozen movie musts"? What, if anything, do they have in common? What are your own personal criteria for rating movies?

Questions for Critical Thought

1. Holcomb begins his article with the statement that ". . . the iconic status of . . . *To Kill a Mockingbird* is as entrenched in popular culture as its story line is ingrained in the popular imagination." Is he overstating its impact? Is everyone as familiar with the film and its storyline as he seems to think?

2. Holcomb claims that *To Kill a Mockingbird* "obscures the very questions of class and race that underlie its mythic reputation, relying on America as a place in which racism and hatred are incidental to social and political inequality." What does he mean by this? What are these "questions of class and race"? And how does the film "obscure" them?

3. The author quotes Linda Williams as calling certain types of films the "melo-drama of black and white." What does "melodrama" mean in this context? What other films—or television shows—do you think could be categorized as part of this "melodrama of black and white"?

Suggestions for Personal Research

1. Movies and television in the United States once depicted the lives of white Americans almost exclusively, and, when they depicted minorities at all, they generally depicted them in very stereotypical, even hostile, ways. Research the evolving depiction of one or more ethnic and racial minorities in film or television.

2. Research the genre of "courtroom films." Kathy Laster says that they "mostly manage to re-establish the legitimacy of the prevailing system or at least belief in the rule of law." Rent and watch some classics in the genre, such as *Twelve Angry Men, Inherit The Wind, Anatomy of a Murder, The Caine Mutiny, A Few Good Men,* and *The Verdict,* as well as some newer films, like *Class Action, A Cry in the Dark,* and *Amistad* (set in the days of slavery). Do you agree with Laster? Can you find some courtroom dramas that are more "subversive"?

3. Read what legal experts have to say about some of these films—do films give us an accurate image of how the judicial system really works?

Multicultural Issues

1. The article mentions the "melodrama of black and white." Do American films and television shows depict any other cross-cultural or cross-racial "melodramas"? If you are from another country, is there anything comparable?

Vocabulary

iconic	emblematic
comprise	specious
nebulous	implicit
elite	aberration
palpable	moot
pantomime	inert
ostensibly	travesty
crux	galvanizing
recalcitrant	nascent
dialectic	equivocal
elucidates	atavistic
blatantly	

Terms for Clarification

F. Lee Bailey   (June 10, 1933–   .) A controversial and extremely successful defense attorney.

Uncle Tom   A negative term for an African American who is seen as behaving subserviently and ingratiatingly toward white people. (The term comes from Harriet Beecher Stowe's novel *Uncle Tom's Cabin,* but many readers assert that the book's title character is not an "Uncle Tom" in the modern sense at all.)

Claude Lévi-Strauss   (November 28, 1908–   .) A French anthropologist whose works have had a large influence on contemporary thought, both inside and outside of the field of anthropology.

From Nerds to Napoleons

Jacqueline Bach

Prereading Questions

1. Did you identify with a particular group or type (nerd, geek, Goth, jock, etc.) when you were in high school—or even now that you are in college? What are the benefits and limitations of this identification? Do you think you could choose to become a member of a different group if you wanted to?

2. Were you ever stereotyped into one or more categories that you didn't feel expressed who you really are?

> *"And the number one sign that you're not the most popular guy in school?"*
> *"#1? How the heck would I know? I'm like the coolest kid in school. Gosh!"*
> —JON HEDER, APPEARING AS NAPOLEON DYNAMITE
> ON THE LATE SHOW WITH DAVID LETTERMAN

In the past twenty years of teenage angst movies, perhaps the most memorable message is delivered by the nerd archetype at the end of John Hughes's *The Breakfast Club*. Asked to write a 1000-word essay explaining what they have learned after spending a Saturday locked in a library for detention, the other students, the jock, the prom queen, the rebel, and the basketcase character, all convince the brain to write their essays for them. In his essay, he summarizes the rosy lesson each of them learned after the eight hours spent together, thereby emphasizing the function of social groups on identity formation in high school which not only determine who sits where but who can occupy what role in this space (the brain, incidentally, occupies the lowest level in this space). Twenty-four years later after numerous high school films depict the ability of the nerds to overcome their "geekiness" and become just like everybody else, the film *Napoleon Dynamite* challenges this notion and offers a new role model for the high school nerd. (1)

Napoleon's Story

Napoleon Dynamite opens with a brief nod to previous high school films, especially those by John Hughes, with the protagonist and a school bus. Napoleon, a tall, lanky, teenager with tight curly red hair and glasses, boards the telltale yellow bus and bee-lines for the coveted back seat typically reserved for the "cool kids." However, the only other "kids" on this bus are late elementary/early middle school students and Napoleon's claim to the popular space is unchallenged and unnoticed (perhaps because he is older than the other passengers). Napoleon maintains his confident aloofness, usually claimed by the rebellious teenagers (as in *Heathers, Some Kind of Wonderful,* etc.) throughout the remainder of the film. Napoleon lives with his rambunctious, fun-loving grandma and his unemployed, 32-year-old brother, Kip, who spends much of his time in an online chat room. At school, in between being bullied, Napoleon is a member of his school's Future Farmers of America organization and the Happy Hands Club, a group which performs sign language to pop music lyrics. His friends are the new Hispanic student, Pedro, and Deb, who tries to raise money for college by running a Glamour Shots type studio in her garage and selling woven key chains. When Napoleon's grandmother breaks her coccyx in an accident, his Uncle Rico moves in with him and Kip and proceeds to interfere in Napoleon's life. In the first half of the film, Napoleon and Pedro find dates for the upcoming school dance, and in the second half, the three friends work together to get Pedro elected as class president.

Napoleon Dynamite doesn't resist, reject, or oppose the traditional roles reserved for the nerdy teenager. Early in the movie, Napoleon and his brother visit the local dojo run by a sensei nearly as eccentric as they are. During the sales pitch for his eight-week course, Rex (of Rex Kwon Do) lays out his three-step plan to success: One, find a buddy; Two, discipline your image; and Three, possess self-respect. From this point on, Napoleon, albeit unconsciously, illustrates how he already lives by this mantra. In this way, Napoleon subverts what it means to be a nerd as he, Uncle Rico, Kip, and Pedro grapple within a cinematic world that offers only limited and prefabricated niches for each individual. *Napoleon Dynamite's* characters challenge the expectations the audience usually has for the outsiders in school films by continuing to remain in their self-designated and peer-designated roles. The message for those watching is multi-layered and multi-faceted, but obviously Jared Hess's film champions those who are able to negotiate high school without eternally questioning their "niche."

For the purposes of narrowing down the vast genre of teenage films, in order to examine the role of the nerd, I consider only those films which were filmed around the same time as or after *The Breakfast Club,* focus on teenagers in a school setting, and feature protagonists or supporting roles of those characters who represent "nerds." While this list includes only twenty films (see appendix A), I feel that it is possible to trace the evolving character of the nerd by noting how they are dressed, talk, treated by their peers, and behave at the conclusion of the film. Furthermore, I analyze the comments posted on the Sundance blog (postings begin November 2004 and still continue to the present time) to illustrate the ways in which those who view *Napoleon Dynamite* are moved by Hess's ability to capture the "realness" of high school life and offer their opinions as to what Napoleon and his friends mean to them. Finally, in order to gain a better idea of how nerds are categorized and described by those who study high schools, I examine sociological studies about adolescent behavior, more specifically social groups and identity formation, and the influence of film on adolescents in order to illustrate how not only the concept of the nerd has changed in film but how that change could translate or perhaps already has to "real life" nerds.

The Bloggers Versus the Experts?

When I began researching this topic on the web, I was intrigued by the conversations viewers of this film were posting to a website for bloggers who wanted to respond to films shown at the Sundance Film Festival. I was impressed by how many viewers identified with Napoleon, even to the point of using his language. According to Cameron McCarthy and Greg Dimitriadis, "television, film, radio, and the internet are now the most powerful sites for educating about difference and the production of resentment" (2000). I would suggest that although this notion is true, it's interesting to consider how blogs may or may not avoid perpetuating the "language of resentment" of which McCarthy and Dimitriadis write. Blogs (2) continue to affect and influence the public's opinion and reactions to politics, media, and commerce. According to the Pew Research Center, thirty-two million Americans read blogs in 2004. An editorial in *Technology Review* mentions the "great power" blogs have to "spread the ideas of individuals faster, farther, and more cheaply than anything seen before" (2005, p. 17). Because they are "reactive, unmediated, immediate opinion[s]" and a growing number of teenagers either have their own blog or subscribe to a blog site, these postings are becoming part of their identity and influencing their lives. The Sundance blog, which sponsors a site for bloggers to post opinions on the film *Napoleon Dynamite* and to read a review written by Jason Calacanis (2004), includes users under and over the age of 18 and offers a wide variety of responses. (3) Many also supply personal anecdotes about their families and their own adolescent experiences as nerds or involvement in situations similar to *Napoleon Dynamite*'s characters. Throughout the 196 postings, bloggers argue over whether or not this is a great film, whether or not Napoleon has special needs, and how the film surfaces in their schools, places of work, and relationships. Several bloggers conclude that those who post unfavorable reviews to the Sundance site probably identify with Summer, Trisha, and Ron, the popular students in *Napoleon Dynamite,* or prefer the more traditional sort of movie with a clear plot and slapstick humor.

Because several responses compared Napoleon to previous film nerds, I began to (re)view high school films in search of the roles nerds played/did not play in this genre. Rather than explore each film that falls into this broad description, I would rather explore the themes and roles that have been available to high school nerds in previous high school films. Frequently, the roles created for film nerds depict and rely on the negative side to being socially awkward, highly intelligent, and uninterested in mainstream extracurricular activities. Because of the need for someone to inhabit these characteristics, more often than not, nerds play background roles in films. As in *Heathers, Mean Girls,* and *Just One of the Guys,* they are victims of the popular crowd or serve as comic relief or are acknowledged by the protagonist who suddenly understands how he or she has underestimated this student or social group. The nerds also may undergo poignant transformations, either psychologically or physically or both, as the characters in *The Breakfast Club, Can't Buy Me Love,* and *She's All That* do, and either retain their popularity or reject it (as the protagonists in the latter two films do).

The stereotypes of schooling and education continue to be topics of conversations in education courses. Recent studies consider the positive influence films can have on preservice teachers, teachers, and students in shaping their notions of the peers and the world around them (Beyerbach, 2005; Dalton, 2004; Giroux, 1997; Shary, 2002). Critics also agree that much of what has been produced and mass marketed by Hollywood is, to use Mary Dalton's words, a "very limited construction of curriculum and radical teaching in popular culture" (2004, p. 137). Critics also agree on the role films have on identity formation and the need for media to portray positive adolescent experiences. In *The Cinema of Adolescence* (1985), David Considine writes:

> There is little doubt that motion pictures have the potential to influence adolescent audiences. . . . Caught in transition the young person is the stage of formulating a new identity.

> In this process film and the mass media in general have the opportunity to function as a valuable source of information. Excessive reliance upon stereotypes in the past has limited the honesty and the variety of the information imparted to the young. (pp. 273–4)

After discussing the ways in which these stereotypes also transform the way the public views institutions, Considine's generalization of most teenage movies still holds true today, although with films like *Napoleon Dynamite* (4), the face of teenage films might be changing: "In the cinema of adolescence, whites outnumber blacks, WASPs outnumber other racial and religious groups, big city stories depicting life in Los Angeles, New York, or Chicago by far outweigh images of small town or rural life, and stories about boys outnumber those about girls (1985, p. 274). These stereotypes are not just limited to students either. As Barbara Beyerbach (2005) notes: "More recent films tend to depict teachers even more negatively, as bumbling dullards who lack skills and are generally powerless, or who play adversarial roles toward students" (p. 270), a departure from the films like *To Sir with Love*. When a movie comes out that challenges these stereotypes, it's important for educators to take notice.

It's also important for educators and students to be aware of how the media shapes our idea of what it means to be cool or popular. As many researchers who point out the positive potential for films in creating new avenues for the marginalized, there seem to be twice as many researchers who remark on the dangers of the media in creating false mythologies or perpetuating stereotypes. In *Cool: The Signs and Meanings of Adolescents,* Marcel Danesi criticizes movies and television shows for "transform[ing] some ordinary happening into a momentous event"—one of the reasons for these media becoming "the maker of history and its documentor at the same time" and "conversely, television is also shaping history" (1994, p. 130, italics in original). He specifies their influence on identity formation in particular: "Teenagers seem to be continually following the lifestyle models that Hollywood and the television networks have intentionally scripted into their adolescent characters" (1994, xi). Both Quart and Milner accuse mass media marketers of not just exploiting the "popular kids" in high school by persuading them to buy certain items included in their films, but also spending an enormous amount of money observing and studying them to "anticipate" the next "hot item, the thing that must be purchased in order to be cool" (2004, Milner, p. 167). Giroux claims that the dominant media does not "demonize" our youth, instead they "either commodif[y] or construct [them] as consuming subjects" (1997, p. 2). Unfortunately, very few of these sources comment on independent films, other than to exclude them from the large Hollywood conglomerates.

The Nerd's Place in High School Films

The nerd, however, has not been excluded from films, both independent and mainstream. The prevalence of films which rely on the school nerd stereotype is why I wish to begin with *The Breakfast Club,* a film that explores traditional high school stereotypes. Because most high school films before this one tended to lump together teenagers into two groups: good kids and bad kids, the stories resulted in similar plot lines. In *The Breakfast Club,* however, each character represents a different social group and the hierarchy becomes quickly apparent. And who is at the bottom? Naturally, the others rely on the nerd to write the essay for the entire group. Here are his words that finish his opening remarks from the beginning of the film: (5)

> "We accept the fact that we had to sacrifice a whole Saturday in detention for whatever it is that we did wrong. But we think you're crazy to make us write an essay telling you who we think we are. You see us as you want to see us: in the simplest terms and the most convenient definitions. But what we found out is that each one of us is a brain . . ."
> Andrew, "and an athlete,"
> Allison, "and a basket case,"
> Claire, "a princess,"
> Bender, "and a criminal."
> Brian, "Does that answer your question?
> > —Sincerely yours, the Breakfast Club." (1985)

This letter reflects the two roles available to film nerds before *Napoleon Dynamite.* They can discover by the end of the film that they, like Brian, are actually like everyone else, and are accepted by their classmates (i.e., they get to join the "club." Think of *Sixteen Candles, Lucas,* or *Just One of the Guys,* a film in which a popular, pretty, but smart girl goes undercover as a geek and meets a geek, whom she transforms and ends up with at the conclusion of the film). Or film nerds undergo a complete transformation by exposing to their peers that underneath their veneers there exist teenagers just like themselves (as in *The Breakfast Club*). As Tim Shary (2002) puts it in his examination of nerds in films from the 1980s to the 1990s,

> The main emphasis in most nerd films of the '80s was on transformation or changing from someone who is smart and physically awkward to someone who is merely clever but popular and sophisticated, and this emphasis became more complicated in the '90s. Nerds are always "told" to transform, that their present image holds them back from being socially accepted and that social acceptance is indeed more valuable than idiosyncratic individuality, but nerds are usually portrayed as being smart enough to realize the fallacy of this expectation. (p. 40)

Napoleon, Pedro, and Deb fit neither of these portrayals. None of these characters exhibit the "intelligence" found in most film nerds (as in *Weird Science* and *Can't Buy Me Love,* a film which perfectly illustrates the nerd who undergoes a transformation, rejects it, and "wins" the girl, a typical path available to the onscreen nerd). If one were to argue that each nerd in *Napoleon Dynamite* undergoes a transformation, that transformation is so slight that it is negligible. "Popular" and "sophisticated" do not describe them by the end of the film. In the final scenes, Napoleon manages to add one person to his tetherball team (although the audience does like his dance), and Pedro celebrates his victory not with those who voted for him, but his family, acknowledging the importance of culture in identity formation, an often overlooked influence in high school films. And as for Shary's (2002) contention that "smart" film nerds are "smart" enough not to change, or to reject the "rewards" of changing (here Shary refers to the film *She's All That* to make his point), Napoleon, Deb, and Pedro seem oblivious to the fact that they are not socially accepted. They engage in activities such as running for class president, wearing their FFA medals, claiming to be a bowhunter, and asking girls out with little hesitation or emotion or differentiating among the different statuses associated with each activity. Instead, they approach each endeavor pragmatically as when Napoleon and Pedro discuss asking the most popular girls to the dance.

Is Napoleon and Pedro's unawareness of their place in the high school social hierarchy typical of today's "nerds"? Or does their portrayal offer a different model for nerds who are uncomfortable with their image? David Kinney (1998), in his study "From Nerds to Normals: The Recovery of Identity among Adolescents from Middle School to High School," identifies two paths for the "nerd" to become "normal," neither of which explain Napoleon and Pedro, but echo Shary's (2002) observation of the two paths available to the film nerd. The first alternative is to "embrac[e] behaviors and appearances that are respected by high-status peers, while the other path hinges on one's emancipation from popular peers' expectations and invidious comparisons" (p. 33). Clearly, Napoleon does not follow the first path and he never really worries about his peers' expectations as he continually experiences "the worst day of school ever" as he endures headlocks, smirks, and sarcastic remarks from his peers. However, the treatment Napoleon receives is not overly violent or humiliating when compared with how his nerd ancestors were tormented.

More recent studies point out the shifts in how nerds are viewed and treated by their peers. Another connection between sociological studies of nerds and the film nerd is the growing popularity of the character. In his study, *Freaks, Geeks, and Cool Kids,* Milner asks, "Why has the status of cheerleaders and football stars declined in many but not all schools?" (2004, p. 3). Shary (2002) answers this question from a cinematic point of view: "Out of the five character types available in most teenage films, the nerd, the delinquent, the rebel, the popular girl, and the athlete, it is the nerd who cannot only be endearing but also present a conflict that 'grants nerd characters a greater dramatic interest' when he or she can wrap his or her mind around what it means to be a popular" (pp. 35 & 40). Part of Napoleon's popularity is that he doesn't even consider himself a nerd. The Sundance bloggers find his hobbies and personality as being "endearing."

Rule One: Discipline (Not Makeover) Your Image

One of the reasons why studying teenage films helps illuminate the role the nerd plays in a school's hierarchy is the tie they share with their real counterparts—nearly all teenagers. "Above all else," according to psychologists Brown and Theobald (1998), "American adolescents are charged with the task of achieving a 'sense of identity'—crystallizing their self-concept, positioning themselves on a career path, and embracing a set of values and beliefs that will guide their choice of activities that will guide their interpersonal relationships (p. 126). According to Alissa Quart (2003), the media and marketing strategies by corporations affect much of that identity formation. But she contends the target audience of contemporary teen films tends to be the "in crowd" or those popular students, and the story line continues to be arrangements of the makeover scene from the end of *The Breakfast Club* when Ally Sheedy's (the basket case, or goth character as Quart calls her) character pulls her hair back, takes off her shirt, puts on makeup and proceeds to dazzle the athlete and the nerd. By beginning her discussion with *The Breakfast Club* and tracing the teen film to its state a couple of years before *Napoleon Dynamite,* Quart reminds the reader again and again of similar scenes in teenage films. Citing a recent one, *She's All That,* Quart contends that the purpose of the makeover movie is to "teach kids the importance of having fancy clothes and wearing good makeup" and these "fairy tale transformations don't happen by magic" (2002, p. 87). Although Napoleon rejects the act of reinventing himself or exposing his true self, does he undergo a "makeover"? If not, then does he fall under Quart's criticism of the films which "Creat[e] characters who can't change or become"? (p. 87). And if Napoleon doesn't undergo the coming of age theme Quart prefers, is that so bad?

One could argue that none of the main characters in the film plays a nerd; in fact, one of the commentators on the Sundance blog claims that Pedro is just misplaced and that he will be fine. Napoleon, on the other hand, is frequently called a "nerd" by movie reviewers (Burrow, 2005; Lally, 2004; Sterritt, 2004). However, once again the discussion on the Sundance blog and my own personal observation exposes something else. Kinney (1998) loosely defines a "nerd" as possibly possessing "superior academic performance . . . others as having low levels of social skills or . . . dressing out of fashion" (p. 27). Napoleon and his friends Pedro, the new Hispanic student, and Deb, the girl who is stuck in the 80's, represent a new kind of teenage character in this type of film. As one blogger explains, Napoleon is not the "chic geek" Max Anderson from *Rushmore,* but a "geek's geek" (Sundance Blog, Claudia, 2004). But overwhelmingly, the postings name Napoleon as a nerd—in positive terms.

Napoleon, however, doesn't consider himself a nerd or even seem to contemplate the superficial, yet real boundaries which separate him from his peers. But he recognizes others as sharing his space. For example, after seeing a student beat up another student who wears glasses and is awkwardly dressed, Napoleon approaches him and makes him an offer:

> Napoleon: "How's your neck?"
> Nerd: "Stings."
> Napoleon: "That's too bad. (pause) Pedro offers you his protection."

By this point in the film, Napoleon has already realized the importance of having a buddy—not changing one's image or behavior in order to avoid being beaten. After ditching the parachute pants and patriotic t-shirt, Napoleon moves on to the next step, finding a buddy.

Rule Two: Find a Buddy to "Get Your Back"

After demonstrating the need for disciplining one's image by referring to his stars and stripes "M.C. Hammer" pants and patriotic t-shirt, Rex advises his potential students that at "Rex Kwon Do, we use a buddy system, no more flying solo." Although Rex doesn't seem to have a "buddy," these words remain with Napoleon. Friends are undoubtedly important to adolescents and remain a complicated system within a school setting. Typically, the close circle of friends one makes in high school are what constitutes cliques (Brown & Theobald, 1998). According to Brown and Theobald (1998), cliques tend to be "the adolescent's primary source of peer companionship, support, and pressure or influence . . . and have dramatic impact on adolescents' experiences in schools" (1998, p. 127). Cliques in some circumstances have formal rules for membership. Some tend to be rather exclusive. A number of studies remark on the rigidity of these social groups and their purpose in the secondary school (McCarthy & Dimitriadis, 2000; Gressen, 2004; Steinburg & Kincheloe, 2004; Carlson & Dimitriadis, 2003).

Naturally, cliques and buddies are often the sources of conflict in high school films. In reviewing the films chosen for this study, I noticed that for the most part buddies tend to be of the same type, or if they are not then one must undergo a makeover to become like the other one or face rejection, humiliation, or bodily harm. The boy in *Pretty in Pink* rejects his friends and their elitist lifestyle for his girl; in *Clueless*, Cher and Dionne remake Tai into copies of themselves. These relationships are not give-and-take ones, rather they are attempts made by many teenagers, according to studies, to mold themselves into an identity rather than constructing their own based on their own interests. Researchers continue to cite peer influence as one of the most important factors in the development of a student's identity, but strong relationships in teenage films emphasize the power, both positive and negative, of influencing students to act.

As they sit on the school's bleachers (in perhaps an homage to *Grease*), Napoleon asks Pedro what kind of skills he has to convince Summer to go to the dance with him. "I don't know," Pedro answers, "I'll probably build her a cake." Later, Napoleon says to Pedro who asks him what kind of skills he has, "I don't have any cool skills like baking a cake or numchakus." Pedro notes, "You can draw, can't you?" And Napoleon proceeds to use his skill and draws a portrait of the popular girl he wishes to ask to the dance. It never occurs to either Pedro or Napoleon that these girls might be "out of their league" because they are "nerds" or "losers." Instead, they work together to find dates. (6)

Rule Three: Maintain an Attitude of Self-Respect

Rex closes his three-step system by crediting self-respect as the means of avoiding failure. Rex is vague on this step, but Napoleon seems to deduce that it has something to do with attitude. While he does not adopt Rex's harsh, commanding voice or seek a Starla-type girlfriend, he does pay attention to the abuse Rico is inflicting on his school image. Did Napoleon think he was popular before Trisha and Summer posted "Bust Must" flyers to his locker? It's possible. The almost cultish popularity of Napoleon Dynamite, not just the movie, but actor Jon Heder, mirrors Smith's contention in *Freaks, Geeks, and Cool Kids* about the shifting status of social groups in high school today (2004). Smith seeks to answer the question why cheerleaders and football players don't hold the same status they used to. This movie ventures a guess that it has something to do with Rex's attitude.

Throughout the film, Napoleon also exhibits a strong sense of self respect. After buying his suit for the school dance at a thrift store, the camera captures a shot of Napoleon confidently striding down the street as if he were John Travolta in *Saturday Night Fever*. His response to Pedro and Deb when they ask him where his date has gone during the dance (another homage to Hughes) also illustrates his awareness of the need to preserve some self-respect: "She probably went to the bathroom," he lies. Even when he delivers his outlandish current event report in front of his history class and someone snickers, he shoots them a look before continuing with his story. Napoleon understands the power of confidence and the effect it has on others.

Conclusions

Although *Napoleon Dynamite* thwarts the traditional roles of nerds in high school movies, it does little to dispel the usual depictions of cheerleaders as flighty and insensitive, jocks as bullies, and teachers and administrators as predictable, two-dimensional characters who are out of touch with today's youth. In fact, the principal quite possibly serves as the most unlikeable character in the film. After learning that Pedro used an effigy of Summer Wheatley, his opponent, as a pinata during his campaign, the principal calls Pedro into his office:

> Look Pedro. I don't know how they do things down in Juarez, but here in Idaho we have a little something called pride. Understand? Smashing in the face of a pinata that resembles Summer Wheatley is a disgrace to you, me, and the entire Gem State.

While this scene is comical on the surface, one wonders if Hess is commenting on the sorry state of administrators (Or is he using satire here?), setting Pedro's tactics in contrast to the traditional ones Summer employs, or just trying to make the audience laugh? Another critic might devise a post-colonial reading of Napoleon's rescuing Pedro's bid for student president as a representation of America rescuing the poor, third world nation from disaster (a la *The Magnificent Seven* or its parody, *The Three Amigos*). A feminist might wonder about Deb and her portrayal as a craft maker and pseudo-photographer (who only photographs males) and how she is easily passed from Pedro to Napoleon. A postmodernist reading might consider Hess's take on the lunch, dance, and bus scenes integral to high school films. But these readings are only possible if educators consider the growing influence of media on our students and continue their efforts in bringing media literacy to high school students.

Undoubtedly, many studies of teen films point out their influence on teenagers and their ensuing behavior and practices based on their viewing of the film. In addition to the many anecdotal stories of college and high school students speaking admiringly of *Napoleon Dynamite,* 39 out of the 196 Sundance bloggers admit to quoting lines from the movie.

> It is common to hear something like this in my school:
> "Matt, did you hand in the assignment yet?"
> "Heck yes I did!" (Sundance blog, Christian, 2005)

Napoleon Dynamite reminds viewers that it's okay to be who you are is perhaps most clearly demonstrated by his dance at the school's election ceremony. This unabashed display of creativity and abandonment essentially captures Pedro's victory (of course his promise that if "you vote for me all of your wildest dreams will come true" probably helped). As one blogger muses,

> The important message (in my OPINION) of this movie was about seeking happyness [sic] and about the sillyness [sic] of all highschool [sic] (not just the 'losers,' but also the

> cool kids, the dances, the jocks, etc.) I think it was about being who you are. Napolean [sic] just IS. He makes no apologies for his awkwardness. He finds his happiness in Pedro and Deb. And they have their own happy community. I think that they're much happier than Summer Wheatley or that mean spirited blond dude who scoffs at everything. (Sundance blog, Matt, 2005)

In typical teen movies, the characters must find that person, discover their identities, overcome their "problems" and become accepted by their communities. As educators, what if we viewed our positions not as companions or guardians, but illuminators? By bringing to our students' attention stereotyped characters and discussing studies like Kinney's and Milner's, students might consider what influence/d/ing their identities. Certainly, the simple three-step policy of Rex Kwon Do already surfaces in new programs designed to protect students from being bullied because they might be different. Napoleon Dynamite goes beyond the simple "I'm okay, you're okay" mantra.

But the real beauty of *Napoleon Dynamite* is its rejection of the feel-good messages of most teenage movies. Unlike his predecessor Brian, Napoleon is not a mixture of a princess, brain, criminal, jock, or basket case. He's not even a nerd; he's Napoleon. After his dance during the election ceremony, the camera pans to the audience, all of whom stand except for Summer and Don. And guess what? The audience looks like a bunch of Napoleons, Pedros, and Debs. They are just normal kids who may be in different social circles, who may be involved in extracurricular activities, and who may not be. The real message is that they are not labeled or as Quart (2004) points out branded by what they do, how they look, or whom they "hang with."

As *Napoleon Dynamite*'s newness fades, it will join the ranks of the other nerd films. But because Hess offers a third path for the high school nerd, whether he or she be real or fictional, he (and his wife who co-wrote the film) open up new discussions about teenagers and film portrayals. The growing popularity of blogs and the arrival of those "new" voices partnered with research on social groups and adolescent identity formation in high school provides another way of discussing films. Maybe Hess's message is "It's okay to be who you are." In fact, maybe nerds do not have to become "normal" as it seems educators, writers, peers, and even themselves wish them to be. As one blogger points out,

> Napoleon is proud of who he is and gets by in life with very little fanfare, oblivious to most things impacting him because he is too busy helping others. He obviously does not care what others think of him. . . . Not everyone can be a "cool" kid but you should still be proud of yourself and not look for outsider's acceptance. All that really matters is to be happy with yourself. (Sundance blog, AceM, 2004)

But Napoleon is aware of what's going on because at the end of each day, he exclaims "Geez, that was the worst day ever." Whether it's watching a bus load of elementary school children witnessing a cow shot in the head or having to tell a close friend that a girl turned him down, Napoleon always remains just as he is—an awkward role model for all of those "nerds" out there.

Appendix A

List of Nerd Films I do not claim this list to be the definitive list necessary for a discussion about film nerds. Instead, it is an arbitrary compilation of films that I have seen and considered when writing this essay:

10 Things I Hate About You (1999)

American Pie (1999)

Better off Dead (1985)

The Breakfast Club (1985)

Can't Buy Me Love (1987)

A Cinderella Story (2004)

Class Act (1991)

Clueless (1995)

Ghost World (2001)

Heathers (1989)

Just One of the Guys (1985)

Lucas (1986)

Mean Girls (2004)

Not Another Teen Movie (2001)

Pretty in Pink (1986)

The Princess Diaries (2001)

Rushmore (1998)

She's All That (1999)

Sixteen Candles (1984)

Some Kind of Wonderful (1987)

Welcome to the Dollhouse (1996)

REFERENCES

Beyerbach, B. (2005) The social foundations classroom: Themes in sixty years of teachers in films: *Fast Times, Dangerous Minds, Stand on Me. Educational Studies,* 37(3), 267–285.

Blogs Mix Up the Media. Encyclopaedia Britannica. Retrieved July 7, 2005, from Encyclopaedia Britannica Premium Service. <http://www.britannica.com/eb/article?tocId=9389625>.

Brown, B., & Theobald, W. (1998). Learning contexts beyond the classroom: Extracurricular activities, community organizations, and peer groups. In K. Borman & B. Schneider (Eds.), *The adolescent years: Social influences and educational challenges: Part 1*. Ninety-seventh yearbook of the National Society for the Study of Education (pp. 109–141). Chicago: University of Chicago Press.

Burrow, R. (2005). *Napoleon Dynamite. The Times* (UK). Features, p. 11.

Calacanis, J. (Jan. 19, 2004). Reviewed: *Napoleon Dynamite an instant classic*. bloggingsundance.com. Retrieved June 24, 2005, from http://sundance .weblogsinc.com/entry/3463694269313459.

Considine, D. M. (1985). *The cinema of adolescence*. Jefferson, NC: McFarland & Company Publishing.

Dalton, M. (2004). *The Hollywood curriculum: Teachers in the movies*. New York: Peter Lang.

Danesi, M. (1994). *Cool: The signs and meanings of adolescence*. Toronto, Ontario: University of Toronto Press.

Dimitriadis, G., & Carlson, D. (2003). Introduction. In G. Dimitriadis & D. Carlson, *Promises to keep: Cultural studies, democratic education, and public life*. New York and London: RoutledgeFalmer.

Giroux, H. (1997). *Channel surfing: Race talk and the destruction of today's youth*. New York: St. Martin's Press.

Hess, J. (Co-Writer/Director), & Hess, J. (Co-Writer). (2004). *Napoleon Dynamite* [Motion picture]. United States: Fox Searchlight.

Hughes, J. (Writer/Director). (1985). *The Breakfast Club* [Motion picture]. United States: Universal Studios.

Kinney, D. (1993). From nerds to normals: The recovery of identity among adolescents from middle school to high school. *Sociology of Education,* 66(1), 21–40.

Lally, K. (2004). *Napoleon Dynamite. Film Journal International,* 107(13), 1.

Letterman, D. (Producer). (2004, December 21). The Late Show with David Letterman [Television broadcast]. New York, CBS.

McCarthy, C., & Dimitriadis, G. (2000, June). Governmentality and the sociology of education: Media, educational policy and the politics of resentment. *British Journal of Sociology of Education,* 21(2), 169–185.

Mean media. (2005, April). *Technology Review,* 108(4), 17.

Milner, M., Jr. (2004). *Freaks, geeks, and cool kids: American teenagers, schools, and the culture of consumption*. New York: Routledge.

Quart, A. (2003). *Branded: The buying and selling of teenagers*. Cambridge, MA: Perseus Publishing.

Shary, T. (2002). *Generation multiplex: The image of youth in contemporary American cinema*. Austin, TX: University of Texas Press.

Sundance Blog. (Jan. 19, 2004). Reviewed: *Napoleon Dynamite* an instant classic: Readers' comments, bloggingsundance.com. Retrieved June 24, 2005, from http://sundance.weblogsinc.com/entry/3463694269313459.

Sterritt, D. (2004). Revenge of the (Idaho) nerd in *Napoleon Dynamite. Christian Science Monitor,* 96(138), 15.

Swanson, D., Spencer, M., & Petersen, A. (1998). Identity formation in adolescence. In K. Borman & B. Schneider (Eds.), *The adolescent years: Social influences and educational challenges: Part 1.* Ninety-seventh yearbook of the National Society for the Study of Education (pp. 18–41). Chicago: University of Chicago Press.

NOTES

1. Before I begin discussing any further the "nerds" role in films, I believe a working definition is needed. Although Napoleon does not display any of the "super-intelligence" indicative of other onscreen nerds, nearly all reviewers apply this nomenclature to him. Therefore, I am using the term nerd to describe a character who appears to be socially inept, is active in "non-mainstream" activities, and is ridiculed by most of his or her classmates not only for his or her appearance but also interactions with other members outside of his or her circle. This definition also seems to apply to "geeks, freaks, outcasts, and brains" but not the bumbling idiot role afforded to previous teenage films like *Bill and Ted's Excellent Adventure,* but to someone like Dawn from *Welcome to the Dollhouse* (1998), another character labeled as a nerd who lacks book smarts (2002, Shary, p. 38). This definition also resembles the one Kinney employs in his study of adolescent nerds.

2. A blog is an abbreviated form of the term "web log" or a sort of online journal, originating in the United States in 1997 (Britannica). Usually, a blog is created and updated by one user, but Calacanis, the creator of this particular blog, invites readers to respond to his review of *Napoleon Dynamite.*

3. According to the Sundance website, the only postings that are removed are the ones that are advertisements. The site suggests then that this process remains fairly unmediated.

4. Encouraged by the occasional teenage movie like *Save the Last Dance,* Shary suggests that the "American film industry would do well to produce many more images of youth like this" (2002, p. 262). I think that he and Considine would approve of much of the portrayals in *Napoleon Dynamite.*

5. It is interesting to note that Anthony Michael Hall, who plays Brian the "nerd" in *The Breakfast Club* played a similar role in the high school movie *Sixteen Candles.* In both films, he becomes accepted by the "popular" students. This acceptance is contrary to Napoleon's experience because he is never accepted by the "popular" students Summer Wheatley and Don.

6. A common plot in many teenage films like *10 Ways I Hate You,* but the first time it's been done without a thorough makeover or Cyrano de Bergerac type plot and certainly the first time a cake has been involved.

Journal Topics

1. Many adolescents try on a series of various "identities" to see how they fit. Did you explore a few or even several different role types? How did this process of changing roles feel to you?

2. If you were ever stereotyped into any categories that you didn't feel expressed who you really were, what did you do about this? Were you able to break free of the stereotyping? If not, were you able to overcome the emotions the stereotyping made you feel?

3. Did you ever avoid being friends with people that you basically liked just because of how they were stereotyped by your peers? How did that make you feel? How do you feel about it now, looking back? Conversely, did you ever defy the opinions of any people in your peer group and make friends with people that they didn't approve of? What happened?

4. Is there a movie that depicts a character or situation that you really identify with?

Questions for Critical Thought

1. "Identity" is the characteristic that defines each individual's sense of self. People feel a need to be unique, but they also create a social identity based on their memberships in various groups. In her article, Bach quotes Marcel Danesi, who states that "Teenagers seem to be continually following the lifestyle models that Hollywood and the television networks have intentionally scripted into their adolescent characters." How true is this statement? Is it an overgeneralization?

2. Bach states that the fictional Napoleon "exhibits a strong sense of self respect" and "understands the power of confidence and the affect it has on others." Do self-respect and confidence confer the ability to transcend the limitations of social roles?

Suggestions for Personal Research

1. Adolescence is often a period of identity crisis. Family, culture, peer groups, and media images are just some factors that influence teenagers' sense of personal identity. Research the primary influences on teenagers' identity formation.

2. Some people have argued that films have a predominantly negative influence over young people, but others have argued that they can have a positive influence. Both camps can offer evidence to support their assertions. Research whether films are more likely to have a positive influence, a negative influence, or negligible influence at all on children or teenagers.

3. Bach pointed out that a film like *Napoleon Dynamite* can get different kinds of "readings" depending on the perspective of the critic doing the analysis. She mentioned three theoretical perspectives as examples: postcolonialism, feminism, and postmodernism. There are numerous other approaches, including archetypal/myth criticism, psychoanalytic criticism, and Marxism. Research a critical theory and choose a film to analyze from its perspective.

Multicultural Issues

1. "Nerd" is a very American term for a person who is socially inept and unstylish, particularly someone devoted to intellectual or academic pursuits. What does it say about American culture that an interest in intellectual pursuits in itself is suspect and unstylish? Can you think of cultures where this is not the case at all? If you are from another culture, do similar stereotypes apply? What is your culture or native country's equivalent of a "nerd"?

Vocabulary Terms

angst
archetype
identity formation
lanky
aloofness
coccyx
dojo
sensei
mantra
niche
genre
unmediated
slapstick

anecdotes
poignant
curriculum
hierarchy
pragmatically
emancipation
superficial
cliques
effigy
postcolonial
postmodernism
unabashed

Sex and the Cinema: What *American Pie* Teaches the Young

Sharyn Pearce

Prereading Questions

1. In general, how do you think that young people are educated about sex and about sexual mores? How are they educated about gender roles?

2. Do you think that escapist films that appear on the surface to be mere entertainment can function not only to entertain, but also to transmit and reinforce social and moral values?

3. If you saw one or more of the *American Pie* films, what did you think of the characters and the type of "gross-out" humor that the films rely on? If you haven't seen the films, why would someone consider shocking or gross situations and images to be funny? Have you seen examples that you found funny, or are you simply turned off by gross humor?

Introduction

A couple of years ago I described the first *American Pie* (1999) movie as a new millennium sex manual geared for new age boys, cunningly using 1980s gross-out comedy (then as now the staple fare of adolescents) to teach them the new, egalitarian, touchy-feely mores of the twenty-first century, and most particularly to redefine masculinity so that desire is not dependent on oppression, and nor does it resort to aggression and misogyny to maintain its sense of coherence (Pearce, 2003). My point of view differed markedly from that of *Rolling Stone,* which, like virtually all the other commentators on that film, argued that the sweet, sloppy, sentimental parts were included as a cynical exercise so that the 'really important stuff', identified by *Rolling Stone* as 'the oral sex, the pie-screwing and so on', could be filmed (Hedegaard, 1999, p. 96). In fact these gross-out elements were deemed excessive even for teenage fare, and *American Pie* had some significant tussles with the US Ratings Board: according to its producer, Warren Zide, 'We went back 4 times before we got an R . . . we had to get rid of a few thrusts when he's having sex with the apple pie. The MPAA[1] was like "Can he thrust two times instead of four?"' (cited in Lewis, 2001, p. 31). But largely, I suspect, because of scenes like this, *American Pie* was an unexpectedly huge hit, going on to make over $100 million at the US Box Office, and it spawned two even more lucrative sequels.

In this paper I want to reappraise my earlier comments in the light of the franchise as a whole, while concentrating upon *American Pie 3—The Wedding.* (2003), and to discover whether what I described earlier as a revolutionary sex manual for remodelling and renegotiating masculinities is still reinforcing its subversive messages (by stealth, as it were) or whether it has—sadly—reverted to type. And I am treating sex education here not as an official programme, but I am using Kenneth Kidd's definition of 'a largely unexamined set of beliefs, practices and texts that tend to endorse a narrow vision of adolescence and maturation' (Kidd, 2004, p. 96), and I am concurring with Claudia Nelson and Michelle Martin's argument that 'sex education is not a stable identity, but something which responds quickly to national crises or to changes in social ethos. It reflects evolving ideas about gender, race, social class, and childhood, as well as about sexuality' (Nelson & Martin, 2004, p. 2). I am mindful too of Glyn Davis and Kay Dickinson's argument that most teen texts are created:

> to educate and inform while entertaining; to set certain agendas in this delicate time just prior to the onset of a more prominent citizenship; and/or to raise crucial issues (of *adult* choosing) in a "responsible manner" that is entirely hegemonically negotiated. (Davis & Dickinson, 2004, p. 3)

Commentators as diverse as Henry Giroux, Roger Simon and Peter McLaren (Giroux & Simon, 1989; Giroux & McLaren, 1994; Giroux, 1997, 2002), Cameron McCarthy (1998, 1999), and Anne Haas Dyson (2002), among many others, have contributed to the understanding of how popular cultural texts shape young people's identities, and how they exist as pedagogical sites where youth learn about the world. The respected ethnographer and cultural theorist Paul Willis, for example, argues that popular culture is a more significant, penetrating pedagogical force in young people's lives than schooling:

> The field of education . . . will be further marginalised in most young people's experience by common culture. In so far as educational practitioners are still predicated on traditional liberal humanist lines and on the assumed superiority of high art, they will become almost totally irrelevant to the real energies and interests of most young people and have no part in their identity formation. Common culture will, increasingly, undertake, in its own ways, the roles that education has vacated. (Willis, 1990, p. 147)

More recently Nadine Dolby has addressed the reasons why educators and educational researchers should pay particular attention to popular culture as a cultural practice that has its own power to create social change, 'to alter social conditions and the very foundations of people's lives' (Dolby, 2003, p. 259). Dolby claims that popular culture is not simply fluff that can be dismissed as irrelevant and insignificant; on the contrary, 'it has the capacity to intervene in the most critical issues and to shape public opinion' (Dolby, 2003, p. 259). What remains clear from this engaging and ongoing scholarly debate is that the popular is a site where youth are invested, where things happen, where identities are worked out, performed and negotiated, and where new futures are written, for better or for worse.

Films, Youth and the Pie *Franchise*

Critics generally agree upon the thoroughgoing juvenilisation of film content and film audiences. According to Thomas Doherty, 'In the nineteenth century young people had fuelled the Industrial Revolution with their labour; in the twentieth, they would fulfil a more enviable economic function as consumers whose leisure vicariously validated their parents' affluence' (Doherty, 2000, p. 91). Wheeler Winston Dixon declares that, because 'they are affluent, without responsibilities, and with plenty of time to kill', teens make up half the movie-going population, and 'teen presence' is essential in the enterprise of selling a motion picture (Dixon, 2000, pp. 126–127), while Graeme Turner declares that the film industry 'now depends upon pleasing the 12–24 age group' (Turner, 1999, p. 26). Meanwhile Wheeler Winston Dixon argues in *The End of Cinema as We Know It* that 'it doesn't matter which genre. All films are calculated to appeal to a teenage audience above and beyond any other considerations. Substance, depth and characterisation are ruthlessly stripped down in favour of a succession of instantly readable icons' (Dixon, 2001, p. 357). And so from its beginnings in the 1950s the teenpic, with its preoccupation with the rites of passage for white, college-bound boys, has become in many ways the operative reality of the film business. Given that they generally have lower production costs with less expensive stars, teen movies are ideal commodities for the marketplace—and a Hollywood teen movie demonstrably not only produces texts for mass consumption, but ideology for mass consumption as well. As Toby Miller notes in *Global Hollywood,* the cinema is a 'twentieth century cultural addition . . . that sits aside such traditional topics as territory, language, history and schooling' (Miller, 2001, p. 15), and it is 'an instrument of instruction and response that varies with place, time, genre and audience' (Miller, 2001, p. 177). Some experts, however, warn of the need to be careful about overt didacticism directed at the citizen/consumer; for example, Dixon cautions that young people generally 'want escapism without risk, and when it gets too close, they lose interest' (2000, p. 130). To express this in a slightly different way, messages need to be sugar-coated to become palatable—which is precisely my earlier argument about *American Pie 1* and its discourse on an alternative masculinity (Pearce, 2003).

It is generally accepted that from the beginning of the twentieth century the concept of adolescence has been entangled with concerns about and attempts to manage or at least regulate the sexuality of youth (Moran, 2000; Kidd, 2004). For example, in recent years the Religious Right in the United States has shifted from vehemently opposing all forms of sex education to strongly influencing the sex education students receive in schools and promoting 'abstinence education' (where no sex until marriage is presented as the only insurance against pregnancy and AIDS, and the only moral choice as well). Now while school programmes have had little impact upon adolescent sexuality, and researchers have found virtually no evidence that sex education causes students to change their behaviour in one direction or another (Moran, 2000, p. 219), mainstream films designed to appeal to mainstream audiences might just prove a more effective conduit for American youth than the classroom experience, especially given that teen film is the principal mass-mediated discourse of youth. After all, as Henry Giroux has observed, film is a compelling mode and form of public pedagogy, a visual technology that functions as a powerful teaching machine that intentionally tries to influence the production of meaning, subject positions, identities and experience. Because it offers a deeper pedagogical register for producing particular narratives, subject positions and ideologies than, for example, a popular song or television sitcom, it carries more pedagogical weight than other media. According to Giroux, it offers a uniquely powerful and persuasive "mobilisation of shared and public space", using spectatorial pleasure and symbolic meaning to shape young people's identities outside of school (Giroux, 2002, p. 6).

And now, more particularly, to the *American Pie* franchise. By the third movie, the formula is set—if somewhat over-tired by now. The squeaky-clean, wussy, boy protagonist, Jim, who spent the first two movies worrying about the inadequacy of his (pretty well non-existent) sexual performance, is now a new age man about to be married, and the gross-out comedy, used as always to cushion the moralising, here exceeds even the raunchy good spirits of the first movie. At first *American Pie 3* seems outrageous sexually; for example, the film opens with Jim about to propose marriage to Michelle in a crowded restaurant, but she misunderstands him and thinks he is asking her to fellate him under the table. Nonetheless, although the film is coated with a thick sheen of permissive sex gags and gross humour, in actual fact it heavily promotes traditional family values. For example, it endorses monogamy; Jim has always been a 'one-girl-guy' associated with male innocence and naivete, and Michelle is the only girl that he has ever really slept with. Moreover, although the film could never be called prim, there is a distinct lack of sex and sexiness generally; there are no soft-focus close-ups or sex scenes, and even the gay club scene is sanitised into wholesome, non-confrontational, inoffensive fun. There is little nudity, no penises and hardly any breasts (apart from the hookers at Jim's stag night, and I guess that that is par for the erotic course for the privileged heterosexual male gaze). In short, this film is not at all squeamish about grossness, but it is about sex. In its own way it is oddly reminiscent of the sex manuals of the 1950s (see, for example, Griffith, 1948; Kenny, 1957; Dorian, 1959), which pretty much avoided sex altogether. While these postwar sex booklets were preoccupied with dire warnings and cautionary advice instead of jokey grossness, in both instances actual information about sex is very murky indeed. More pertinently, perhaps, there is no sense in any of the *Pie* movies of sexual freedom, or sexual protest, which is surely something of a cliché in movies about young people. By the third film in the series, Jim has apparently found his sexual identity, and is happy with that. Instead this particular film appears to be about growing up, and in particular illustrating that after graduating and getting a good job, what a young man does is to settle down to marry and start a family of his own. While it does not exactly herald a return to the idealised values of the 1950s and its rigidly defined gender roles—like the earlier two *Pie* movies, men and women are on absolutely equal terms here—it certainly offers a noughties' reprising of those 1950s movies' accepted romantic paradigm of repartee, love and marriage. The only difference is that now the repartee has been replaced by poo jokes.

Indeed, in *American Pie 3—The Wedding,* the humour is even grosser than in the two previous films. For example, in keeping with the gratuitous over-abundance of bodily fluids and excessive ingestion and emission situations, Stifler, the reactionary dim-witted jock and the embodiment of crass crudity and boorishness who is the butt of all the jokes in the earlier two movies (and also incidentally a clear favourite with film audiences), finds a dog turd containing a lost wedding ring and has to pretend that it is a chocolate truffle and eat it, describing the flavour as he does so. Later he has sex in a dark linen cupboard with the bridegroom's grandmother in the belief that she is the bride's attractive younger sister. This results in the old woman being reconciled to her grandson's marriage to a Gentile, while Stifler comments defensively, 'Hey pussy's pussy, isn't it?' And so the movie recycles the same franchised formula of disgusting gags, but I would argue strongly that this additional grossness and humiliation now has to compensate for the increasingly reactionary 'take' on married life and neo-conservative values that the film seems to be espousing.

Teen Movies and Masculine Models

The standard teen movie convention is that the action takes place in a world pretty much uninhabited by parents. In keeping with Philip Larkin's comment that 'they fuck you up, your mum and dad/they may not mean to but they do', adults, according to Jonathan Bernstein in *Pretty in Pink: The Golden Age of Teenage Movies,* are customarily described as 'cringing, vindictive, foul-smelling, prehistoric, bewildered, spiritually undernourished and pathetic in their attempts to acclimatise themselves to the new age' (Bernstein, 1997, p. 53). Think, for example of teen classic films such as *Ferris Bueller's Day Off* (1986), where the adults are caricatures, played for laughs, or *The Breakfast Club*'s (1985) lament, 'When you grow up, your heart dies'. Familial relations are often treated only nominally in the teen movie genre because the real focus is of course the self-contained world of the teenager, where adults are sometimes inconvenient but more often peripheral. I am aware, however, that this last statement can seem rather too simplistic; and Kenneth Kidd makes the interesting point that the teen *film* assumes the role of surrogate parent (Kidd, 2004, p. 97) and that simply by not having parents there—or not as the protagonists—does not mean that adult authority is actually being usurped (it is often anything but). And as Jon Lewis argues elsewhere, in much the same vein, 'the films stand in with authoritative and authoritarian morality lessons of their own' (Lewis, 1992, p. 66), and 'the teen film presides over the eventual discovery of viable and often traditional forms of authority . . . the restoration of the adult world informed rather than radicalised by youth' (Lewis, 1992, p. 3).

It seems evident, too, that in some teen movies young men are not striving to escape parental authority, but to become just like Dad. This appears to be the case in this movie as it is clear that Jim does not rebel against the system, or more particularly the father, but rather evolves into him, becoming a repository of his values. Indeed, the father–son bond is an important element in all the *Pie* movies, particularly in terms of the ubiquitous father–son sex talks. Jim's father is always patient with and understanding about Jim's sexual debacles (his arrival consistently has a *coitus interruptus* effect upon his son's sex life, regardless of whether it is conducted with a handy warm apple pie or an obliging fellow freshman). Jim's Dad is never disciplinarian, and instead he dispenses excruciatingly embarrassing and totally unsolicited man-to-man talks about masturbation and sexual performance: 'Your uncle constantly slammed the salami—he was never into baked goods though', or 'Your mother, God bless her, can still make me squeal like a pig—and I mean that in the very best way'. As the series moves on, Jim seems to resemble more and more a chip off the old block, sharing the same bumbling, hapless ineptitude and goofiness but also the same endearing sweetness and decency. It is important to note too that the mother barely registers as a presence here; clearly she knows her place in the gendered generational scheme of things. The father, on the other hand, is on screen for a good deal of *American Pie 3* (amazingly, he even shares in the first fellatio scene with the two principals). And so, I would contend, the film guides boys to become like their heterosexual, middle-class fathers.

The *American Pie* series as a whole can consistently be 'read' as a contemporary sex education manual, where such manuals almost always inscribe and endorse the approved sexual conduct of the day. Traditionally, too, sex instruction manuals have been concerned at least as much with moral as with sexual education, and arguably that is the case here too. And *American Pie 1* is, in part, a deliberately tongue-in-cheek parody of man-to-man sex talks, of secret men's business generally. I have already mentioned Jim's father, whose well-meaning advice is a clever lampooning of the sitcom situation of a liberal father, and his wayward yet lovable son. Meanwhile Kevin, another of Jim's friends, is told by his brother of a book, an instructional 'Bible' of sex techniques handed down from one group of high school boys to the next (and this book is influential in enabling the naive Kevin to perform expert cunnilingus upon his clearly overjoyed partner). In keeping with Davis and Dickinson's earlier hypothesis, this scene is both very amusing and very instructive, reinforcing the message that female desire matters and that sex is not merely for personal gratification. Incidentally, sex in the *American Pie* movies is seen very much as a family affair (advice is given by fathers, brothers, etc.), not for the classroom (surely the Right would approve of that). In fact, the series is peppered with sexual advice and homilies, all of which is bandied around the focal group of needy boys, with some advisors more reliable than others (Stifler, for example, is always spectacularly wrong in his ruthless approach to sex and girls, whereas in *American Pie 2* (2001) Michelle more usefully instructs Jim not to be too uptight, and to be comfortable in every situation). Yet whereas in *American Pie 1* the film operates as one gigantic modern sex manual designed to subvert patriarchal domination via gross-out comedy, and offers advice about non-hegemonic masculinity and female desire, I would argue that by the end of the trilogy the sex manuals move from spoof to very serious indeed. Despite its spectacularly outrageous cinematic moments, the final *Pie* film is firmly rooted in the heteronormative institution of marriage, and hence family and responsibility chart its celluloid terrain.

This makeover, or sea change, is clearly seen in *American Pie 3* when, in a fit of extra-flabby moralising Stifler, that carnivalesque character hitherto associated with misrule, undergoes a redemption. Stifler proves what a good friend he is by actually saving the wedding when the flowers get ruined the night before, and he gets the girl in the end (and also the grandmother, but it is best not to go there). He sees that Jim really loves Michelle, and concludes that there might actually be something in it. Another wedding is a distinct possibility, and the movie seems to be saying that everyone grows up to be part of a heterosexual couple—there is just no escaping it. And as Kenneth Kidd has observed, adolescent male vulnerability-turned-triumph is the standard theme of teen films, where the horny, awkward boy stumbles through close encounters with the opposite sex (Kidd, 2004, p. 101). This 'heterosexual stumbling' (Kidd, 2004, p. 101) often gets ritualised as dancing (the most famous instance of this is surely Tom Cruise's ballet of unbridled liberation in *Risky Business* (1983)). Now in this movie dirty dancing is no longer a code for social rebellion, but instead dancing becomes a stately induction into the grown-up world where youthful excesses are left behind. Jim is taught to dance by Stifler, who also demonstrates his journeying into maturity, responsibility and cooperation at the same time as the movie scores sniggering laughs when the two men dance clumsily together; this is yet another instance, of course, of the conflation of pedagogy and entertainment, the coexistence of the gross humour and the serious intent. The mannered wedding waltz where Jim and Michelle enter the world of their parents appropriately ends the film—and this dance stands in eloquent contrast to the gloriously bizarre striptease of *American Pie 1,* where Jim 'performs' for the female gaze, the lovely Nadia, and also for the huge enjoyment of those watching on the Internet, spoofing, whether consciously or not, the popular notion that when male bodies are seen, the focus is on action (see Neale, 1983;

AJ Perez

Dyer, 1986). In that instance a space is constructed for resistance, opposition and change, and for an alternative audience positioning, but dancing is a serious business here, and subversive messages are seemingly no longer appropriate. It should be noted too that while the third movie focuses upon the hilarious things that go wrong in the lead-up to Jim's nuptials, the importance of that institution is never in doubt. While what we clearly see is a marriage of equals, described by one film critic as 'one big fat geek wedding' (Wilmington, 2003, p. 21), Jim also tries to ensure that Michelle has the marriage of her dreams with the most expensive trousseau, the mountains of flowers, the ceremony at the country club. The rites of passage that induct the American man into all-American family life now appear to involve a socialisation into consumer and corporate culture. So the movie does not just shape adolescent behaviour and consolidate teenage identity via the acquisition of romantic and sexual knowledge, but it presents marriage as a goal as well—interestingly at a time when large numbers of Americans and others do not marry at all, and there are exceptionally high divorce rates.

Conclusion

This paper has argued that the *American Pie* series, while by no means a programmatic sex education manual, plays an important part in providing lessons in sex and romance to young male audiences, and in shaping them as responsible, caring partners. It also contends that this series, with its boostering of what a man should be, serves to make kids wholesome, and to regulate sexual behaviour, similar to, for example, the 1950s guides. Like postwar sex manuals, movies such as these are concerned with the proper management of human sexuality, and about sexual morals. They provide a moral education by stressing the primacy of the family and the importance of marriage, and they also promote the *status quo*. Of course the 1950s emphasis upon celibacy, masturbation and homosexuality (usually associated with paedophilia) is missing (*American Pie* is an updated manual, after all), but the messages are, as I hope I have demonstrated, nonetheless highly traditional (they also include, for example, warnings about choosing the wrong sort of woman) and the series is overwhelmingly sanitised—like a traditional sex manual—with no drugs, and very little accurate information about sex.

And so finally, once more, to the notion of film and its role in channelling adolescent sexual behaviour into approved routes. According to Toby Miller (2001, p. 172), Hollywood films may be seen as potential forums for moral uplift, as vehicles for provoking social responsibility as audiences participate in probably the most global, communal and time-consuming practice of making meaning in world history. Meanwhile Henry Giroux is less sanguine, arguing that because movies are deeply imbricated within the material and symbolic relations of power, they tend to produce and incorporate ideologies that represent the outcomes of struggles marked by the historical realities of power and the deep anxieties of the times (Giroux, 2002, p. 30). Furthermore, according to Susan Jeffords, in the 1980s Reaganite cinema was a regeneration of the interests, values and projects of the patriarchy, embodying the renewed battle of the masculine to reconsolidate its control over the feminine and to recover the family order, restoring an idealised past, with authority vested in white, male, middle-class Americans (Jeffords, 1989). Judging by this analysis of the *American Pie* series it appears likely that a similar patriarchal response

Manners

is occurring in recent popular Hollywood movies of the twenty-first century (and if the Rambo superman of the 1980s can be seen as an embodiment of the gung-ho former President—who after all liked to be seen as the Father of the Nation—then it's perhaps wise not to go into the comparisons between Jim's father and George W. Bush).

Films undeniably fulfil an important function by narrativising and giving order to the otherwise chaotic and contradictory experience of youth by historicising, contextualising, re-presenting it. And according to Jeffrey Moran in *Teaching Sex*, twentieth-century sex education in America even at the beginning of the new millennium is about aiding youths in 'remaining chaste until the time of their monogamous, heterosexual marriage' (Moran, 2000, p. 197). Like the classroom sexual manuals, *American Pie 3* continues to idealise the heterosexual, nuclear family. According to Kidd, popular teen films teach adolescents about options in love and life, steering them towards sexual and cultural heterodoxy and emphasising the pleasure and profit of normative desire. What results is often a conservative film with a veneer of sexual radicalism (Kidd, 2004, p. 98). Such films have perhaps capitalised on and compensated for the failure of sex education programmes in schools. The men in the *American Pie* films might be SNAGS[2] (nominally at least), but they are certainly not rebels. And in the end, cinema might successfully propagandise what the school clearly cannot. By the end of the *American Pie* series there is no longer a reinforcement of subversive messages, and no more insubordinate performances of gender. Reluctantly, but to my mind undeniably, *American Pie* is best read *in toto* as an endorsement of a patriarchal social order rather than interpreted oppositionally as a subversive 'take' on gender dynamics and contemporary teen identity. As a sex manual, then, it is perfectly in keeping with the new conservatism on that side of the world.

NOTES

1. Motion Picture Association of America.
2. Sensitive new-age guys.

REFERENCES

American Pie (1999) Director: Paul Weitz (Los Angeles, CA, Universal).

American Pie 2 (2001) Director: J. B. Rogers (Los Angeles, CA, Universal).

American Pie 3—The Wedding (2003) Director: Jesse Dylan (Los Angeles, CA, Universal).

The Breakfast Club (1985) Director: John Hughes (Los Angeles, CA, Universal).

Bernstein, J. (1997) *Pretty in pink: the golden age of teenage movies* (New York, St Martin's Press).

Buckingham, D. (2003) *Media education: literacy, learning and contemporary culture* (Cambridge, Polity Press).

Davis, G., & Dickinson, K. (2004) *Teen TV: genre, consumption and identity.* (London, British Film Institute).

Dixon, W. W. (2000) Teen films of the 1990s, in: W. W. Dixon (Ed.), *Film genre 2000: new critical, essays* (Albany, NY, State University of New York Press), 125–141.

Dixon, W. W. (2001) 25 reasons why it's all over, in: J. Lewis (Ed.), *The end of cinema as we know it: American film in the nineties* (New York, New York University Press), 356–365.

Doherty, T. (2000) *Teenagers and teenpics: the juvenilization of American films in the 1950s* (Philadelphia, PA, Temple University Press).

Dolby, N. (2003) Popular culture and democratic practice, *Harvard Educational Review,* 73(3), 258–284.

Dorian, P. F. (1959) *Instructions for boys* (Melbourne, Polding).

Dyer, R. (1986) *Heavenly bodies* (New York, St Martin's Press).

Dyson, A. H. (2002) *The brothers and sisters learn to write: popular literacies in childhood and school cultures* (New York, Teachers College Press).

Ferris Bueller's Day Off (1986) Director: John Hughes (Los Angeles, CA, Paramount).

Giroux, H. (1997) *Channel surfing: race talk and the destruction of today's youth,* (Basingstoke, Macmillan).

Giroux, H. (2002) Breaking into the movies: film and the culture of politics (Maldon, Blackwell).

Giroux, H., & Simon, R. (Eds.) (1989) *Popular culture, schooling and everyday life* (Granby, MA, Bergin and Harvey).

Giroux, H., & McLaren, P. (1994) *Between borders: pedagogy and the politics of cultural studies* (New York, Routledge).

Griffith, E. (Ed.) (1948) *The road to maturity* (London, Gollancz).

Hedegaard, E. (1999) There's something about virgins, *Rolling Stone,* 19 August, pp. 94–100.

Jeffords, S. (1989) *The remasculinization of America: gender and the Vietnam war* (Bloomington, IN, Indiana University Press).

Kenny, P. (1957) *Guide to virile manhood: a reliable sex education book for young men* (Melbourne, Father and Son Movement).

Kidd, K. (2004) He's gotta have it: teen film as sex education, in: C. Nelson & M. Martin (Eds.), *Sexual pedagogies: sex education in Britain, Australia and America, 1879–2000* (New York, Palgrave), 95–112.

Lewis, J. (1992) *The road to romance and ruin: teen films and youth culture* (New York, Routledge).

Lewis, J. (2001) Those who disagree can kiss kick Jack Valenti's ass, in: J. Lewis (Ed.), *The end of cinema as we know it: American film in the nineties* (New York, New York University Press), 23–32.

McCarthy, C. (1998) *The uses of culture: education and the limits of ethnic affiliation* (New York, Routledge).

McCarthy, C. (Ed.) (1999) *Sound identities: popular music and the cultural politics of education* (New York, Peter Lang).

McLaren, P. (1995) *Rethinking media literacy: a critical pedagogy of representation* (New York, Peter Lang).

Miller, T. (2001) *Global Hollywood* (London, British Film Institute).

Moran, J. (2000) *Teaching sex: the shaping of adolescence in the twentieth century* (Cambridge, MA, Harvard University Press).

Neale, S. (1983) Masculinity as spectacle, *Screen, 24*(6), 2–16.

Nelson, C., & Martin, M. (2004) *Sexual pedagogies: sex education in Britain, Australia and America, 1897–2000* (New York, Palgrave).

Pearce, S. (2003) As wholesome as: American Pie as a new millennium sex manual, in: K. Mallan & S. Pearce (Eds.), *Youth cultures: texts, images and identities* (Westport, CT, Praeger), 69–80.

Risky Business (1983) Director: Paul Brickman (Los Angeles, CA, Warner).

Turner, G. (1999) *Film as social practice* (London, Routledge).

Willis, P. (1990) *Common Culture* (Buckingham, Open University Press).

Wilmington, M. (2003) *Chicago Tribune* 7 October, 21.

Journal Topics

1. Think about your own views of sex, courtship, and gender roles. What were the primary influences that shaped your beliefs? How do the guidelines and information explicitly provided by your parents and schools compare to what you picked up from popular culture, such as films, music, video games, and televisions shows?

2. How do you define "masculinity"? How do you define "femininity"? Do you have ideas about what is appropriate or inappropriate gender behavior?

Questions for Critical Thought

1. Think about the arguments and evidence presented in the article. How well do they support the definition of sex education provided by Kenneth Kidd as "a largely unexamined set of beliefs, practices and texts that tend to endorse a narrow vision of adolescence and maturation"?

2. Paul Willis states, ". . . so far as educational practitioners are still predicated on traditional liberal humanist lines and on the assumed superiority of high art, they will become almost totally irrelevant to the real energies and interests of most young people and have no part in their identity formation. Common culture will, increasingly, undertake, in its own ways, the roles that education has vacated." Does this quotation coincide with your own ideas of traditional education versus popular culture in their respective influences on how young people's identities are formed?

3. The *American Pie* films are known for their gross humor, yet the author says that they "inscribe and endorse the approved sexual conduct of the day." What is the "approved sexual conduct of the day"? Do these films (if you have seen them) serve to offer this sort of instruction? How about other films aimed at the target audience?

Suggestions for Personal Research

1. The author and the people she quotes see films in particular and popular culture in general as having a strong impact on the development of young people's identities. Do some research of your own to find what evidence there is that popular culture—including films, TV, music, and other aspects—really has a strong influence.

2. The author makes various references to gender roles, including some assertions about young American males. Research how gender roles develop. How big a part does biology play? How big are the parts that upbringing and culture play?

3. Compare and contrast gender roles in America with those in other cultures. What differences do you see? What accounts for the differences? Can gender roles have unhealthy consequences?

Multicultural Issues

1. Films tend to appeal to certain demographics, and the *American Pie* franchise is aimed primarily at the young white male audience. What "demographic" do you represent? What sort of movies do you think are designed to appeal to your demographic? Can you think of any recent examples? Is your demographic catered to or neglected by Hollywood?

2. This article was written by an Australian looking at American popular culture from the outside. How accurately do you think she assesses American trends and values?

Vocabulary

egalitarian
misogyny
lucrative
ethos
ethnographer
pedagogical
humanist
high art
vicariously
affluent
icon
overt

didacticism
discourse
pedagogy
prim
pertinently
nominally
ubiquitous
homilies
sanguine
patriarchy
heterodoxy

Terms for Clarification

Industrial Revolution   A period in the late eighteenth and early nineteenth centuries when major changes in manufacturing, agriculture, and transportation changed the socioeconomic and cultural conditions in Europe and North America and, eventually, most of the rest of the world.

Philip Larkin   (August 9, 1922–December 2, 1985.) An English poet, novelist, and critic. He is generally regarded as one of the greatest and best-loved English poets the of the latter half of the twentieth century.

Raising the Dead: Unearthing the Nonliterary Origins of Zombie Cinema

Kyle Bishop

Prereading Questions

1. How do you feel about horror films? If you like them, what is it about them that appeals to you? If you don't like them, what is it that turns you off?

2. Contemporary horror films are often based on brutal and shocking killing more than psychological horror. If you like horror movies, which type of horror do you prefer, and why?

3. What is most important to you when you watch a horror film—or, for that matter, any kind of thriller, action, or adventure film—graphic images and visual excitement or the plots and characters?

4. What does "nonliterary" mean? Why do you think the origins of zombie cinema might be of interest?

The year 2004 saw the theatrical release of three major zombie movies: *Resident Evil: Apocalypse,* a sequel to a movie based on a video game; *Dawn of the Dead,* a remake of a cult classic from the 1970s; and *Shaun of the Dead,* a sometimes funny, sometimes terrifying revisioning of an established genre. In addition, dozens of low-budget zombie movies were released directly to video or appeared as made-for-television movies. (1) Zombie cinema is clearly as popular today as it was fifty years ago, but is the genre socially relevant beyond being simply a successful entertainment venture? (2) Whereas many horror films may be easily dismissed as mindless entertainment or B-reel schlock, the zombie film retains its ability to make audiences think while they shriek. But to understand this much-maligned genre, one must consider its origins and the essential nature of its visual impact.

Although creatures such as vampires and reanimated corpses often have been realized by literary means, the traditional zombie story has no direct antecedent in novels or short fiction. In fact, zombies did not really see the light of day until filmmakers began to dig them out of their graves in the 1930s. The "classic" zombie horror film, which is the focus of this investigation, was pioneered by George A. Romero in the late 1960s and features a veritable plague of reanimated corpses that attack and slaughter the living. The established generic conventions of such movies are relatively simple and remarkably consistent: Ordinary characters in ordinary places are confronted with overwhelmingly extraordinary challenges, namely the unexpected appearance of an aggressive horde of flesh-eating ghouls. Zombie cinema is essentially a macabre romp—a live-action comic book brought to the big screen both to horrify and entertain.

Much has already been written concerning the more esoteric social commentary offered by zombie movies, but few critics have investigated the unusual origins of these monsters and their horrific stories. (3) Although the cinematic popularity of zombies has certainly made the move to video games and graphic novels, the zombie remains a primarily nonliterary phenomenon. (4) Establishing the folkloric origins of the zombie creature itself will explain this rather singular fact and illustrates its evolution into the more recognizable cinematic horror show developed by Romero. The zombie genre does not exist prior to the film age because of its essentially visual nature; zombies do not think or speak—they simply act, relying on purely physical manifestations of terror. This unique embodiment of horror recalls Sigmund Freud's concept of the uncanny, a phenomenon that finds itself better suited to filmic representations rather than prose renditions.

Preparing the Potion: Exhuming the Vodoun Zombie (5)

Most classic monsters—from ghosts to vampires to werewolves—have their origins in folklore, and the zombie is no exception. However, whereas those other creatures have cross-cultural mythologies, the zombie remains a purely American monster, born from Vodoun magic and religion. In addition, creatures such as Dracula passed through a literary tradition on their way to the silver screen, but the zombie did not. Zombie scholar Peter Dendle illustrates this point: Although possessing certain thematic characteristics that tie it to the traditions of classical horror, the zombie is "the only creature to pass directly from folklore to the screen, without first having an established literary tradition" (2–3). This singularity makes an investigation of the anthropological roots of the zombie an essential part of understanding the film genre.

According to anthropologist Wade Davis, the modern English word zombie most likely derives from the Kimbundu term nzumbe, which means "ghost" or "spirit of a dead person" (xii). This concept was brought from Africa to Haiti with the slave trade and was translated into the Creole zobi, which was modernized to zombie, a word with a number of accepted meanings, from a mindless automaton to an exotic mixed drink. As far as the traditional cinematic monster is concerned, however, the designation of zombie is reserved for the cannibalistic walking dead: people brought back to life either to serve or to devour the human race. This definition is tied to the Vodoun religion, a mystical practice that supposedly harbors the magic required to strike people down to a death-like state and revive them later from the grave to become virtually mindless servants—the most subordinate of slaves (Davis 42). But, in reality, zombification is the result of pharmacology, the careful administration of powerful neurotoxins.

Davis is the world's leading authority on the zombification ritual, and as a Harvard University ethnobotanist, he traveled to Haiti in 1985 in search of exotic new medicinal drugs. Davis recorded his weird experiences and botanical research in *The Serpent and the Rainbow*. (6) According to this primarily anthropological text, a limited number of powerful and unorthodox Vodoun priests, called bokors, possess a keen knowledge of natural drugs and sedatives and have created a "zombie powder"—called coup poudre—that renders its victims clinically dead (Davis 90). Davis's interest in the drug was purely scientific at first, but he soon realized that zombies are real creatures within the Vodoun religion. The method of creating such a dangerous substance is naturally a closely guarded secret, controlled by the secret societies of Haiti (Davis 260).

Those well versed in the administration of this powder could conceivably create the illusion of raising the dead and, thus, give the zombie legend credibility. The most potent poison included in the coup poudre comes from a specific kind of puffer fish, a nerve agent called tetradotoxin (Davis 134). This drug "induces a state of profound paralysis, marked by complete immobility during which time the border between life and death is not at all certain, even to trained physicians" (Davis 142). All major life functions are paralyzed for an extended period, and those suffering from the effects of the drug run the real risk of being buried alive. (7) If the powder is too strong or mixed incorrectly, the victim might die immediately—or suffocate slowly in the coffin (Davis 226). Unfortunately, even those victims lucky enough to be rescued from the grave inevitably suffer brain damage from the lack of oxygen; they are understandably sluggish and dimwitted (Davis 21).

These superstitious fears of the walking dead are not limited to Haiti, however; most cultures share a strong psychological response to the concept of death. Bodies of dead friends and family are burned, buried, walled up, or even eaten, but the result is the same: The corpses are hidden from sight and mind. Although statues, portraits, and photographs are treasured as valued reminders of those now dead, no one really wants to see the face of a loved one slowly rot or be reminded of the brutal realities of mortality; such a confrontation would be frightening, to say the least. In psychoanalytical terms, Freud identifies this fear of the once familiar as the unheimlich, a complex term that literally means "un-homely" or "un-homey" but is usually translated as "the uncanny." This concept is key to understanding the ability of the zombie to instill fear: Those who should be dead and safely laid to rest have bucked the natural order of things and have returned from the grave.

The anthropological origins of the zombie are important to recognize, but what makes zombie narratives unique to cinema are not the shambling foes themselves but rather the stories they tell. Zombie folklore and Vodoun traditions clearly set the stage for the zombie horror movie as it is known and recognized today; poisoning, premature burial, loss of cognition, slavery, the return of the dead, and death itself are all key features of zombie cinema. But the classic zombie movie owes its unique existence to George A. Romero, who Dendle calls the "Shakespeare of zombie cinema" (121). Romero took a rather insipid, two-dimensional creature, married it to an established apocalyptic storyline, and invented an entirely new genre.

Administering the Powder: Creating the Modern Zombie

Unlike the ancient traditions of the vampire and werewolf, the zombie did not enter Western consciousness until around the turn of the twentieth century. According to Dendle, most Americans were only vaguely aware of Haitian Voudo and zombie lore from nineteenth-century Caribbean travel literature (2). Civilized society probably dismissed such concepts as remote superstitions and pagan fantasies until the publication of William Seabrook's travel book *The Magic Island* in 1929, which brought the romantic exoticism—and possible reality—of the zombie to the attention of mainstream audiences (Dendle 2). Shortly thereafter in 1932, Kenneth Webb produced a play called *Zombie in New York City,* and "the creature fell irrevocably under the auspices of the entertainment industry" (Dendle 2).

Hollywood quickly recognized the marketability of the zombie, with the first true zombie movie arriving the same year as Webb's play: Victor Halperin's *White Zombie* (1932). Set in Haiti, Vodou is the central feature of the film, although the tone and style are obviously influenced by Tod Browning's *Dracula* (1931). As the white heroes travel across the countryside at night, their coach driver explains the mysterious figures they pass as "the living dead. Corpses taken from their graves and made to work in the sugar mills" (Halperin). These zombies are slow, dimwitted, and lumbering—but not completely mindless; they can follow commands and perform simple tasks. They are not monsters but rather hypnotized slaves who are still alive and can be saved with the death of the Vodoun priest who enslaved them. The true villain in *White Zombie* is Bela Lugosi's mad bokor Murder Legendre, not the pitiful zombies themselves.

A number of similar, if unremarkable, zombie films were made over the next few years—for example, *Revolt of the Zombies* (1936), *King of the Zombies* (1941), and *I Walked with a Zombie* (1943)—but their rather prosaic view of the undead would change gradually over the next few decades with the help of EC Comics. The 1940s and '50s saw a dramatic upswing in all horror media, most notably the publication of *Tales from the Crypt* in 1950. According to book columnist and comic aficionado Digby Diehl, "Horror comics of the 1950s appealed to teens and young adults who were trying to cope with the aftermath of even greater terrors—Nazi death camps and the explosion of the atomic bombs at Hiroshima and Nagasaki" (28). Terror had become a tangible part of daily life, and these early graphic novels brazenly presented images of rotting corpses, stumbling zombies, and gory violence. Film scholar Paul Wells claims the young Romero would have been directly influenced by such comics (82), for a predominately visual narrative format can be seen in his zombie movies, in which the action is presented through a series of carefully framed and largely silent images. Romero confirms this connection himself in a documentary by Roy Frumke, referring to the filming of *Dawn of the Dead* (1978) as "making a comic book."

Romero was likely influenced by popular horror films of the 1950s as well, especially those featuring end-of-the-world scenarios. According to Frumke, Romero's earliest film influence was Christian Nyby's *The Thing from Another World* (1951). This science fiction movie, based on the short story "Who Goes There?" by John W. Campbell, Jr., features a small group of isolated survivors who must fight off a mysterious foe that can take any form and exists only to kill.

Film scholar Robin Wood offers another connection, claiming the most obvious antecedent to Romero's zombies to be the pod-people in Don Siegel's *Invasion of the Body Snatchers* (1956), based on Jack Finney's 1955 novel (126). This unsettling story posits another view of the apocalypse, in which one's best friends and family members become threatening monsters. The film's ending departs from that of the novel, clearly illustrating the paranoia rampant in cold war America. Horror expert Stephen King writes how critics read Siegel's film as an allegory about "the witch-hunt atmosphere that accompanied the McCarthy hearings," although Siegel claimed it was really about the "Red Menace" itself (308). Either way, fear of the Other was clearly rampant on both sides of the political spectrum.

Romero established and codified the zombie horror genre in 1968 with *Night of the Living Dead*. The screenplay was based on Romero's own short story "Night of Anubis," a tale of isolation and supernatural peril that borrowed heavily from Richard Matheson's 1954 novella *I Am Legend* (Martin). Matheson's story features hordes of vampires who rampantly infect and replace the world's population. Richard Neville is essentially the last man on earth, and he must garrison himself inside his home each night to escape the hungry fangs of the vampiric infestation. During his struggle to survive. Neville must fortify his house, scavenge for food and supplies, and kill the monsters his friends and family have become. All of these fundamental plot elements are found in Romero's series of zombie movies and have become firm protocols of the genre.

The situation faced by Matheson's Neville is also seen in Alfred Hitchcock's *The Birds* (1963), based on the 1952 short story by Daphne du Maurier. Film scholar R. H. W. Dillard considers this film the artistic predecessor to Romero's *Night,* pointing out how "in both films, a group of people are besieged by an apparently harmless and ordinary world gone berserk, struggle to defend themselves against the danger, and struggle to maintain their rationality and their values at the same time" (26). *The Birds* explicitly presents the idea of the apocalypse; in fact, the Bodega Bay town drunk warns the protagonists that it is the "end of the world." The birds are an unstoppable collective, and the movie's heroes must board themselves up in a house against their relentless onslaught.

The essential motifs and tropes of the classic zombie movie have some thematic and stylistic roots in Haitian travel narratives and the zombie films of the 1930s and '40s, specifically the exoticism of Vodoun zombie folklore, and early horror and science fiction cinema, particularly the end-of-the-world scenario. In addition, the paranoia narratives of the cold war 1950s and '60s would have given Romero some core ideas about his general plot structure, but it was his own imagination and invention that united the zombie legend with these popular stories of the primal struggle for survival. Although such movies as *White Zombie* were first, Dendle points out that "Romero liberated the zombie from the shackles of a master, and invested his zombies not with a function . . . but rather a drive" (6). With the creation of *Night of the Living Dead,* Romero decisively established the structure of the classical zombie movie, and many directors have since followed his lead and conformed to the criteria of the new genre.

Performing the Ritual: Explaining Zombies' Cinematic Singularity

Zombies do not exist in a vacuum, nor did they spring forth fully grown from the head of Romero. In addition to being derived from mythology, legend, and the imagination, zombies also have close ties to other, more literary monsters. They belong to a diverse class of creatures that cross the metaphysical line between life and death, where a strong sense of the uncanny inspires unease and fear. But whereas ghosts, vampires, and golems have been a part of storytelling for thousands of years, the zombie is a relatively modern invention. Their lack of emotional depth, their inability to express or act on human desires, and their primarily visual nature make zombies ill suited for the written word; zombies thrive best on screen.

Freud defines the abstract concept of the uncanny as "that species of the frightening that goes back to what was once well known and had long been familiar" (124). He further points out how "this uncanny element is actually nothing new or strange, but something . . . estranged from [the psyche] only through being repressed" (147). The true manifestation of this fear occurs, therefore, when a repressed familiarity (such as death) returns in a disturbing, physical way (such as a corpse); the familiar (heimlich) becomes the unfamiliar or uncanny (unheimlich) (Freud 148). Of course, this concept applies to monsters other than zombies as well. As Dillard points out, "the idea of the dead's return to a kind of life is no new idea; it is present in all the ancient tales of vampires and ghouls and zombies, and it has been no stranger to films. . . . All of these tales and films spring from that ancient fear of the dead" (20–21). Dead bodies are not only a breeding ground for disease but also a reminder to the living of their own mortality. For such reasons, creatures that apparently have overcome the debilitating effects of the grave are treated with revulsion and fear—especially when said creatures are hostile, violent, and ambulatory.

Freud also claims that ". . . to many people the acme of the uncanny is represented by anything to do with death, dead bodies, revenants, spirits and ghosts" (148). There-fore, it is no surprise that those supernatural creatures able to defy the powers of death are usually at the heart of horror narratives and stories. Perhaps the oldest campfire tale is the ghost story: What is more uncanny than someone returning from the grave to wreak havoc on the living? Ghosts have a firmly established tradition, both orally and literarily, from Homer to Dante to Shakespeare to Dickens. But ghosts are merely spir-its, consciousnesses that lack physical form; zombies belong to a much more specific phylum: the corporeal monster. Such unnatural terrors include vampires (demons who constantly cheat death by preying on the living), golems (unnatural creatures reassem-bled and brought back to life through the means of science), and zombies (mindless automatons fueled by purely animalistic passions). (8)

However, when one considers the literary origins of these beasts (specifically in novels and short fiction), the zombie is virtually missing in action. Why are vampires and other supernatural creatures prevalent in horror stories and gothic literature but not the traditional zombie?

It is the essentially human behavior that explains the success of such fiends in nineteenth-century literature, and the vampire is the most prolific of these. Although un-dead, Bram Stoker's archetypical Count acts as though still alive, using his immortality to pursue rather carnal desires. Dracula is mysterious, cunning, and seductive, using his piercing stare and eloquent tongue to beguile young women and readers alike. He ap-pears both attractive and familiar by wearing the guise of youth and vitality, but Dracula is fundamentally an uncanny symbol of mortality. Not only is he decidedly inhuman—he lacks a reflection, which is regarded as a manifestation of the soul (Stoker 31)—he also represents the reality of death itself with his drinking of innocent blood, his propensity to murder women and small children, and his habit of sleeping in the grave.

Similarly, Victor Frankenstein's intriguing monster possesses essentially human qualities that make him such a complex literary character; he thinks and feels and speaks with great passion. Contrary to most screen adaptations, Frankenstein's crea-ture is not frightening by himself—he is in fact quite sympathetic and humane. His unnatural state makes him essentially uncanny: He is a collection of dead body parts and stitchery, a creature brought back to life through science, not the supernatural. However, although Dracula and Frankenstein's monster are both fine examples of the uncanny, neither of these classic monsters is technically a zombie; a vampire lives a conscious, basically human existence, and Frankenstein's creature is flesh made living and mortal once more.

In contrast to these monsters, the zombie is completely and thoroughly dead—it is essentially a walking corpse. (9) Zombies are not uncanny because of their humanistic qualities; they are uncanny because they are, in essence, a grotesque metaphor for humanity itself. Like the vampire, the zombie rises from the grave to feed off the living. Like the golem, the zombie has the form of someone familiar, yet monstrous. But the zombie is a much different creature from these established monsters: It does not think or act on reasonable motives—it is purely a creature of blind instinct. The zombie does not recognize individuals or discriminate in its quarry. Zombies have no speech or consciousness—they do not talk to their victims or speculate about their existence; they are essentially superficial, two-dimensional creatures. (10)

Because zombies do not speak, all of their intentions and activities are manifested solely through physical action. In other words, because of this sensual limitation, zombies must be watched. Their primary actions are visceral and violent: They claw, rend, smash, and gnaw. In addition, post-1960s zombie movies are most noteworthy not for violence or horror but for the gore (Dendle 6). Decapitations, disembowelings, and acts of cannibalism are particularly effective on the screen, especially if the audience does not have time to look away. Moreover, the recognition of former heroes as dangerous zombies realizes an uncanny effect, eliciting an instantaneous shock on the part of the film characters and the audience members alike.

Of course, shocking images can be conveyed quite effectively in writing as well. In Stoker's *Dracula,* the somewhat feckless Jonathan Harker methodically documents a horrific confrontation with the Count: "I raised the lid, and laid it back against the well; and then I saw something which filled my very soul with horror. There lay the Count, but looking as if his youth had been half renewed, for the white hair and moustache were changed to dark iron-grey; the cheeks were fuller, and the white skin seemed ruby-red underneath; the mouth was redder than ever, for on the lips were gouts of fresh blood, which trickled from the corners of the mouth and ran over the chin and neck. Even the deep, burning eyes seemed set amongst swollen flesh, for the lids and pouches underneath were bloated. It seemed as if the whole awful creature were simply gorged with blood; he lay like a filthy leech, exhausted with his repletion" (53). Stoker presents quite a visage, but the diachronic nature of prose forces him to describe one aspect of the Count at a time. This gradual, paratactic unfolding of visual detail must necessarily diminish the ultimate shock; it takes time for the audience to read it. Because humans process visual images synchronically, literary texts present an unrealistic form of perception. The cinematic representation is much closer to reality, showing the entire view simultaneously.

Aspects of the film zombie may be recognizable in other classic monsters, but no traditionally literary tale conforms to the genre as it has been so firmly established by Romero. Although they were once human, zombies have no real connection to humanity aside from their physical form; they are the ultimate foreign Other. They do not think, speak, or act on passionate or conscious desires as do the monsters found in novels or short fiction—a zombie's essentially silent and shallow nature makes it a fundamentally visual creature instead. The primitive characteristics of these ghouls make them ideal cinematic monsters.

Raising the Dead: Understanding the Romero Formula

The classic zombie story pioneered by Romero, and recognized in so many horror movies since, has a number of specific characteristics that distinguish it from other tales of the supernatural. Zombie movies are always set at the apparent end of the world, where devastating events have rendered the human race all but helpless. Yet, the primary details in Romero's films are in essence bland and ordinary, implying that such extraordinary events could happen to anyone, anywhere, at any time. Zombies confront audiences with stark horror and graphic violence, using the seemingly familiar to present the most unnatural and frightening. A detailed look at the prototypical zombie film—*Night of the Living Dead*—will best illustrate these defining cinematic features and help show the limitations of print.

Night of the Living Dead is presented on a very pessimistic stage: that of the apocalypse. A strange phenomenon overcomes society, resulting in a literal hell on earth where the dead walk and no one is safe. A space probe has returned from Venus, bearing some kind of unknown radiation. For some unexplained reason, this extraterrestrial fallout causes all recently dead humans to rise and attack the living—no Vodoun rituals here. The ghouls feed on human flesh in blatant disregard of society's cannibalism taboo, and those thus killed are infected as if by a blood-borne virus and soon rise themselves, assuming there is enough flesh remaining for the corpse to become mobile. The dead are mechanical juggernauts, and those left struggling to survive are forced to adopt a much more primordial stance—it is kill or be killed, and average folks are quickly transformed into desperate vigilantes.

Society's infrastructure begins to break down, especially those systems associated with the government and technology. Law enforcement is depicted as incompetent and backwater (the local sheriff is a stereotyped yokel with a "shoot first" attitude), so people must fend for themselves instead. The media do what they can, broadcasting tidbits of helpful information and advice by way of radio and television, but the outlook is fundamentally grim: Hide if you can, fight if you have to. In the end, the rigid structure of society proves little help; human survivors are left to their own devices with no real hope of rescue or support. Motley groups are forced into hiding, holing up in safe houses of some kind where they barricade themselves and wait in vain for the trouble to pass.

Of course, such a scenario is not necessarily limited to zombie movies: Slasher films and alien-invasion pics often have a similar modus operandi. However, whereas those movies feature either an unrealistic cast of vivacious eye candy, computer-savvy geniuses, or stylized superheroes, zombie cinema pursues the hapless adventures of bland, ordinary (heimlich) citizens. (11) As *Night* opens, a rather plain, average young woman and her equally pedestrian brother are traveling to visit the grave of their father in rural Pennsylvania. While they are paying their respects and praying at the gravesite, an innocuous gentleman can be seen shuffling across the background of the frame. Johnny begins to tease his sister about her childish fear of cemeteries, and he uses the passing stranger to feed the fire: "They're coming to get you, Barbara!" he taunts, forcing his sister's disgusted retreat. As Barbara embarrassingly approaches the man to apologize, the unthinkable happens—he is out to get her! Although the zombie looks like a normal human being (albeit a bit pasty), he attacks Barbara with wanton savagery and kills her ill-fated brother when Johnny tries to intervene.

In the grand tradition of most horror films, Barbara runs away, stumbling and tripping her way to the car. The zombie begins its methodical, if rather slow, pursuit, its every movement highlighted by lightning flashes and dramatic camera angles. Although she makes it to the car, Barbara is thwarted in her escape: The keys are still in Johnny's pocket. Another footrace ensues, and Barbara makes it to the relative safety of a farmhouse. Granted, the former occupants are already dead and partially eaten, but at least her friend from the cemetery is locked outside. Enter Ben, another survivor who has come to the farmhouse in search of refuge and hopefully some gasoline for his truck. At this point, the zombie film establishes another of its defining characteristics: hiding out.

The literal heimlich nature of the house quickly becomes something far more unheimlich. The farmhouse symbolizes the comforting idea that one's home is a place of security, but this place does not belong to either Barbara or Ben—it is a foreign, unfamiliar environment, and they are indeed strangers in a strange land. Barbara unsettlingly discovers the masticated corpses of the house's former occupants, and Ben must defend her from some zombies that have likewise broken in. Out of desperate necessity, Ben immediately begins a radical home renovation, quickly converting the farmhouse into a fortress. He incapacitates the zombies, tosses the bodies outside, and starts boarding up the doors and windows. Barbara can do little more than sit and stare, bemoaning the loss of her brother in a catatonic state. Although the home continues to possess its physical sense of security, it has lost its power to provide any psychological comfort.

That the seemingly harmless and ordinary would prove to be so life threatening is one of the fundamental precepts of the zombie formula. In addition to the slow-moving ghouls and the common farmhouse, the film's protagonists never become anything spectacular—Barbara is a simple girl, traumatized by the brutal slaying of her brother; Ben is a workaday "everyman"; and the Coopers, soon found hiding in the cellar, are an average middle-class family. This link to normalcy is emphasized by Dillard, who describes the essentially mundane nature of Night as "the story of everyday people in an ordinary landscape, played by everyday people who are, for the most part, from that ordinary locale" (20). In his afterword to the graphic novel *Miles Behind Us,* a zombie story told in another primarily visual medium, Simon Pegg points out that the protagonists of zombie movies are not superheroes or professional monster slayers such as Van Helsing—they are common, average folk forced to "step up" and defend themselves.

However, the ordinary by itself is not threatening—it also needs to be rendered as the fundamentally unfamiliar. In his introduction to *Horror Film Reader,* James Ursini writes, "Horror is based on recognizing in the unfamiliar something familiar, something attractive even as it is repulsive. . . . The best horror films are those that evoke that feeling of the uncanny in us most strongly" (5). Ursini refers here to Freud's sense of the uncanny as something that has been repressed (148). This makes the "familiar unfamiliar" (the heimlich unheimlich) even more terrifying, for the familiar and recognizable are wrought into the foreign and uncanny. This perspective on the monster is most apropos the zombie movie, in which the threat is not only manifested as a hostile undead human but likely a hostile undead human the victim recognizes as a former intimate.

The physical form of the zombie is its most striking and frightening aspect: It was once—quite recently—a living person. The one-time protagonists of the movie become its eventual antagonists; thus, the characters cannot fully trust each other. As Dillard points out, "The living people are dangerous to each other . . . because they are potentially living dead should they die" (22). Night introduces its audience to a number of diverse characters, but these so-called heroes, when infected, rapidly become the most savage and threatening of villains. This stark manifestation of the uncanny is chillingly illustrated when poor Johnny returns near the end of the picture as a zombie, "still wearing his driving gloves and clutching for his sister with the idiotic, implacable single-mindedness of the hungry dead" (King 134). His deceptive familiarity is what ultimately leads Barbara to her doom—she hesitates at the sight of her brother, failing to recognize the dangers of his zombification until it is too late.

This terrifying prospect is shown even more graphically when the young Karen Cooper feasts on her own parents. As the battle with the swarming zombies rages upstairs, Karen dies from a zombie bite and succumbs to the effects of the radiation. She then gnaws hungrily on her dead father's arm and brutally attacks her mother with a trowel. Helen Cooper does little more than allow herself to be butchered; shock at seeing her daughter turned into a zombie and a binding sense of love and compassion render her impotent. When Ben eventually retreats to the perceived safety of the cellar, he is forced to kill the zombie versions of the entire Cooper family. Such a visceral shock works so well in a cinematic medium because the audience instantly recognizes the former protagonists in their zombified forms and can intimately relate to the horrified reactions of the survivors.

Finally, the zombie monster is ultimately terrifying because in it one sees one's self. Pegg discusses the essential function of the zombie: "Metaphorically, this classic creature embodies a number of our greatest fears. Most obviously, it is our own death, personified. The physical manifestation of that thing we fear the most. More subtly, the zombie represents a number of our deeper insecurities. The fear that deep down, we may be little more than animals, concerned only with appetite." In a very real sense, *Night* is the story about humanity's struggle to retain its sense of humanity. Ben and the others fight the zombies just to stay alive, but they also clash among themselves. Although he remains uninfected by the zombie plague, Ben's civility suffers and crumbles under the stress of the siege: He strikes Barbara for being hysterical, beats Mr. Cooper for disagreeing with his plans, and eventually shoots and kills Mr. Cooper. Ben is almost as violent and irrational as the zombies themselves, although he is the closest thing the movie has to a real hero.

Because anyone can potentially become a zombie, these films deal unabashedly with human taboos, murder, and cannibalism, which Dillard proposes have much to do with the genre's success (15). The dead are not allowed to rest in peace: Barbara's attempt to honor the resting place of one relative turns into a nightmare in which she vainly combats the remains of another dead relative. Ben becomes a kind of avenging angel, bashing, chopping, and shooting people—he is not only forced to disrespect the sanctity of the dead, but he also becomes a type of mass murderer. The cannibalism taboo is the one broached most blatantly. After dying in an explosion, the bodies of Tom and Judy are mercilessly devoured by the gathered zombies, and Romero pulls no punches in showing charred flesh, ropy intestines, and closely gnawed bones. Karen's cannibalistic act even borders on incest, consuming the very flesh that originally gave her life.

Night, as with the zombie movies to follow, fulfills its generic promises with a great deal of gore and violence. This is a major reason film is so successful in telling the zombie story—blood, guts, and gore can be shown instantly with graphic detail. Humans have their intestines ripped out, zombies are cheerfully hunted and butchered, and mad doctors perform unspeakable acts on the reanimated corpses of their former associates. The synchronic nature of cinema allows these shocking images to be suddenly and thoroughly unleashed on the viewing public, resulting in the expected gleeful revulsion.

The horror of the zombie movie comes from recognizing the human in the monster; the terror of the zombie movie comes from knowing there is nothing to do about it but destroy what is left; the fun comes from watching the genre continue to develop. Although zombies are technically dead, their cinematic genre is a living, breathing entity that continues to grow and evolve. Zombie-themed video games have spawned such films as *Resident Evil* (2002), and the genre's popularity and longevity have resulted in remakes of both *Dawn of the Dead* and the forthcoming *Day of the Dead* (2006). But the genre is also constantly reinventing itself with revisionist films such as *Shaun of the Dead* and Romero's own *Land of the Dead* (2005). (12) Such overwhelming contemporary evidence firmly establishes zombie cinema as a valued member of genre studies.

NOTES

1. Some lesser-known 2004 titles include *Return of the Living Dead* 4 and 5, *Zombie Honeymoon, Dead and Breakfast, Zombie Planet, Hide and Creep,* and *Zombie Xtreme,* just to name a few of the more provocative titles.

2. According to the Internet Movie Database, *Resident Evil: Apocalypse* grossed $50 million domestically (with an estimated $50 million budget), *Dawn of the Dead* grossed $59 million (with a $28 million budget), and *Shaun of the Dead* grossed $13 million (with a $4 million budget). Like most horror films, zombie movies are considered safe commodities and are usually quite profitable.

3. Romero's zombie films are rife with symbolism and social commentary: *Night of the Living Dead* is often read as a metaphor for both the horrors of the Vietnam War and the civil inequality and unrest of the 1960s, *Dawn of the Dead* is seen as a critique of consumer culture, and *Day of the Dead* is viewed as a pessimistic look at the cold war. See Dillard's "Night of the Living Dead: It's Not Like Just a Wind That's Passing Through" and Wells's *The Horror Genre: From Beelzebub to Blair Witch* for discussions on the political and social statements in *Night of the Living Dead;* see Wood's "Neglected Nightmares" and Skal's *The Monster Show* for discussions on the role of consumerism in *Dawn of the Dead.*

4. Zombies are featured prominently in horror video games series such as *Doom, Resident Evil,* and *Silent Hill;* a number of popular zombie graphic novels also exist, particularly *The Walking Dead* series by Robert Kirkman, George A. Romero's *Dawn of the Dead* by Steve Niles, and *Remains,* also by Niles. It is curious to note that aside from some occasional cameos on Joss Whedon's *Buffy the Vampire Slayer* (1997–2003) and *Angel* (1999–2004), the "zombie story" has never been produced as a television series.

5. According to Wade Davis, although the term voodoo is more common and familiar to Westerners, Vodoun (also rendered Vodun or Voudou) is more accurately used by anthropologists when referring to the actual religion of Africa and Haiti (xi).

6. Davis's scientific text was quickly adapted by Wes Craven into a more mainstream horror movie in 1988. Although the first half of the film is somewhat loyal to Davis's actual experiences, Craven quickly departs from the anthropological sphere and presents a much more supernatural, violent, and spectacular version of Haiti.

7. Premature burial does have an established tradition in both fact and fiction. Edgar Allan Poe was particularly enamored with the subject, and Freud suggests that the idea of being buried alive would be the ultimate realization of the unheimlich (150)—a conscious confrontation with the inevitability of death.

8. The mummy might be considered a subclass of zombie; however, unlike its mindless cousins, a mummy is usually brought back to life by a curse, operates by itself, does not infect its victims or reproduce, single-mindedly pursues a specific task, shows some intelligence and possibly even speech, and eventually returns to its slumber.

9. It should be noted that many so-called zombie films fail to feature true zombies at all. Sam Raimi's *Evil Dead* films (1981 and 1987) deal with demonic possession, and the much-lauded *28 Days Later* (2002) from Danny Boyle is about living, breathing humans who have been infected by a deadly virus.

10. Zombie comedy movies (zombedies?) blatantly disregard Romero's model, attempting to negotiate the protocols of the genre to emphasize the corny over the uncanny. In such films as *Return of the Living Dead* (1985), *I Was a Teenage Zombie.* (1987), and *Braindead* (1992), the zombies speak with surprising loquaciousness and have clear memories of their former lives and relationships, and infected protagonists are eerily aware of their slow transition to the undead.

    Romero's *Day of the Dead* (1985) could also be considered somewhat problematic because of the introduction of a quasi-domesticated zombie named Bub. A crazed scientist attempts to train Bub like a caged animal, using a reward system to encourage good behavior. However, even though Bub seems to recall some of his former life—he can answer a phone, flash a salute, and even brandish a pistol—his actions never escalate beyond primitive imitation. Furthermore, Bub never regains the power of speech; like other zombies, he is limited to grunts and occasional roars of outrage. In the end, Bub's supply of "zombie treats" runs out, and he quickly joins the rampaging masses of his less-sympathetic kin. The experiment is a total failure, and Bub remains what he is: a mindless zombie.

11. Stephen Spielberg's 2005 version of *War of the Worlds* is a notable exception. Although it embraces the spectacular conventions of the alien-invasion picture, it tells the story in a decidedly mundane way, focusing on average citizens in rural locations—exactly like the classic zombie movie.

12. Romero departs completely from this established genre staple in his 2005 *Land of the Dead,* a revisionist film that is more an indication of Romero selling out than it is a milestone of the genre's development. He proposes the possible evolution of zombies over time, showing the development of rudimentary vocal communication (still grunts only, no speech), the ability to handle firearms, and a primitive form of compassion for their own kind. Unfortunately, a zombie's brain would actually get worse as it rots over time, so such cerebral evolution makes no sense, even in a fantastic horror film.

WORKS CITED

Davis, Wade. *The Serpent and the Rainbow*. New York: Werner, 1985. Print.

Dendle, Peter. *The Zombie Movie Encyclopedia*. Jefferson, NC: McFarland, 2001. Print.

Diehl, Digby. *Tales from the Crypt: The Official Archives*. New York: St. Martin's, 1996. Print.

Dillard, R. H. W. "*Night of the Living Dead:* It's Not Like Just a Wind That's Passing Through." *American Horrors*. Ed. Gregory A. Waller. Chicago: U of Illinois P, 1987. 14–29. Print.

Freud, Sigmund. *The Uncanny*. New York: Penguin, 2003. Print.

Frumke, Roy, dir. *Roy Frumke's Document of the Dead*. Synapse Films, 1989. DVD. Dawn of the Dead Ultimate Edition. Anchor Bay Entertainment, 2004.

Halperin, Victor, dir. *White Zombie*. Perf. Bela Lugosi. 1932. DVD. The Roan Group, 1999.

Hitchcock, Alfred, dir. *The Birds*. Universal City Studios, 1963. VHS. The Alfred Hitchcock Collection. MCA Universal Home Video, 1995.

King, Stephen. *Danse Macabre*. New York: Berkley, 1981.

Martin, Perry, dir. *The Dead Will Walk*. DVD. Dawn of the Dead Ultimate Edition. Anchor Bay Entertainment, 2004.

Matheson, Richard. *I Am Legend*. New York: Tom Doherty, 1995.

Nyby, Christian, dir. *The Thing from Another World*. Winchester Pictures Corporation, 1951. DVD. Warner Home Video, 2005.

Pegg, Simon. Afterword. *Miles Behind Us. The Walking Dead 2*. Image Comics, 2004. Print.

Romero, George A., dir. *Dawn of the Dead*. The MKR Group, 1978. DVD. Ultimate Edition. Anchor Bay Entertainment, 2004.

- - -, dir. *Day of the Dead*. United Film Distribution Company, 1985. DVD. Anchor Bay Entertainment, 2003.

- - -, dir. *Land of the Dead*. Universal Pictures, 2005.

- - -, dir. *Night of the Living Dead*. Image Ten, 1968. DVD. Millennium Edition. Elite Entertainment, 1994.

Siegel, Don, dir. *Invasion of the Body Snatchers*. Walter Wanger Productions, 1956. DVD. Republic Studios, 2002.

Skal, David J. *The Monster Show*. New York: Faber, 1993. Print.

Stoker, Bram. *Dracula*. 1897. Ed. Nina Auerbach and David J. Skal. Norton Critical Ed. New York: Norton, 1997. Print.

Ursini, James. Introduction. *Horror Film Reader*. Ed. Alain Silver and James Ursini. New York: Limelight, 2000. 3–7. Print.

Wells, Paul. The Horror Genre: From Beelzebub to Blair Witch. *Short Cuts: Introductions to Film Studies 1*. New York: Wallflower, 2002. Print.

Wood, Robin. "Neglected Nightmares." *Horror Film Reader*. Ed. Alain Silver and James Ursini. New York: Limelight, 2000. 111–27. Print.

Journal Topics

1. Horror writer Stephen King believes that horror films and fiction help us deal, cathartically, with the horrors of daily life—they help us let off steam. What has your experience been?

2. Do you have a favorite zombie movie? Do you have a favorite horror movie? What are your own criteria for judging such films? If you don't like any zombie or horror movies, what makes you dislike them all?

3. Some movies, like *Shaun of the Dead,* are as much or more about comedy than about horror. How well do you think the genres of comedy and horror mix? Can you think of some successful examples?

Questions for Critical Thought

1. Fictional horror is something that many human beings crave. Even before people created literary horror stories and novels, human beings told tales of ghosts and monsters. What is at the root of humanity's long fascination with the frightening, the grotesque, and the monstrous? What human need is fulfilled when we immerse ourselves in tales or images of fantastical horror?

2. Bishop writes that "The horror of the zombie movie comes from recognizing the human in the monster." This could be said of other types of horror film, as well. How much of a horror film's power comes from the notion that the fantasy elements of horror work as metaphors for real fears?

Suggestions for Personal Research

1. Kyle Bishop mentions Sigmund Freud's *The Uncanny,* which was written in 1925. Research what other psychologists and psychoanalysts since then have had to say about purposes and uses of horror fiction and films. What are the positive and negative attributes for mental health? What role does the age of the reader or viewer play? Should children be protected from horror? (It is worth

noting that many classic fairy tales, particularly those collected by the Brothers Grimm, are full of horrific elements like murder and cannibalism.)

2. The Cold War was a period of conflict that was political, economic, and ideological rather than directly military between the United States and the Soviet Union from the late 1940s to the early 1990s. It led to an atmosphere of fear in America that Communist agents could subvert the United States. Hundreds of people were accused of Communist sympathies and affiliations and called to testify before the House Committee on Un-American Activities (HUAC), which subjected them to hostile and threatening interrogations, a style adopted by Joseph McCarthy in his investigative hearings conducted in the 1950s. A number of horror films of the fifties and sixties were said to be allegories about either the threat of Communists or the threat of paranoid attacks on Americans' civil liberties. Research the impact of the Cold War on Hollywood during the 1950s and 1960s and its representation, both literal and metaphorical, in the movies of the time.

3. George A. Romero's *Night of the Living Dead,* made in 1968, was unusual in that the most important and significant character, Ben, is played by an African American actor, Duane Jones, without the race of the protagonist being relevant to the plot. This was at a time when an African American actor was routinely cast only if a role explicitly required an African American. Research the changing opportunities of African American actors and actors in other ethnic and racial minorities from early television and filmmaking to today.

4. Rent the 1968 *Night of the Living Dead* and director Tom Savini's 1990 remake of the same title. Savini also uses an African American actor, Tony Todd, as the main character, but he changes the ending somewhat and works in images of zombies being lynched by gleeful mobs. Furthermore, he considerably reimagines the character of Barbara. Compare and contrast the implications of casting and characterization in the two films, and look up film critics' analyses of these aspects.

Multicultural Issues

1. The horror film genre has been dominated by American movies for many years, but some noteworthy foreign films that can be categorized as horror films have been successful as well, such as the Mexican writer/director Guillermo del Toro's movies *Pan's Labyrinth* and *The Devil's Backbone,* French director Christopher Gans's *Brotherhood of the Wolf,* Japanese writer/director Takashi Shimizu's *The Grudge,* and Russian writer/director Timur Bekmambetov's *Nightwatch.* Rent and watch films from countries other than your own and compare them to what you are used to seeing. What are the differences and similarities? Are the films more or less graphic than what you are used to? How about tone and pace? Are the psychological elements more developed or less developed than what you are used to? What conclusions can you draw about the differences?

2. The term "Blaxploitation" (made by combining "black" with "exploitation") was coined in the early 1970s for a genre of inexpensively made movies targeting black audiences and featuring largely black casts. Some critics argue that some of the movies categorized as examples of Blaxploitation films have been unfairly labeled as such simply because they were made by black directors and starred black actors. *Blacula* is an example of a horror-comedy film that most critics feel deserves the "Blaxploitation" label, whereas *Ganja and Hess* has been described as an under-appreciated "art film" that used vampirism as a metaphor for obsession and addiction. Rent these movies to make up your own mind about their merits and to look at how filmmakers handled issues of black identity in movies that were not made for the white mainstream.

Vocabulary Terms

schlock
maligned
antecedent
generic
conventions
macabre
esoteric
graphic novels
unique
uncanny
Vodoun
Kimbundu
Creole
pharmacology
neurotoxins
ethnobotanist
insipid
auspices
prosaic
aficionado
graphic novels
rampant
Cold War
protocols
motifs

tropes
metaphysical
golems
debilitating
acme
revenants
automatons
visceral
feckless
diachronic
synchronically
Other
bland
prototypical
juggernauts
modus operandi
equally pedestrian
innocuous
wanton
catatonic
mundane
protagonists
apropos
implacable
metaphorically

CHAPTER 17—FILM ESSAY QUESTIONS

These questions are intended as potential essay topics for some of the themes suggested by the articles and related material in this chapter.

1. The term "genre film" is sometimes used dismissively to categorize films with certain subject matters and forms into categories outside "serious films," including films with artistic merit. These subgenres include Westerns, thrillers, horror, science fiction, and fantasy. Choose one or more films from one of these or other popular subgenres that you believe transcend the narrowness of their classification. Make sure that your criteria for what makes a film "serious" or "artistic" are clearly explained.

2. Zombie movies are classified as horror films, whereas movies like those in *The Matrix* series are classified as science fiction, though much of the "science" is far more like fantasy than actual science. Some horror films have strong science fiction or fantasy components. What are the differences between the subgenres of horror, science fiction, and fantasy? Come up with clear definitions and criteria, using a variety of movies as examples to clarify your assertions.

3. Question 1 mentioned some subgenres of films; these subgenres—even the Western—are also reflected in many foreign films. Some subgenres, however, are unique to some parts of the world, such as "Bollywood" films. Describe the conventions of one of these subgenres, using one or more films as examples.

4. Choose an American fiction film that has come out in the last decade or so that you think carries a strong political, social, or ideological message about some aspect of the United States. Discuss the ideas conveyed, how they are conveyed, and how effectively they are conveyed. Some possibilities—not that you need to limit yourself to films with "America" or "American" in the title—include the following: *American Beauty, American Dreamz, American Citizen X,* and even *American Pie.*

5. Choose a fiction film from another country that has come out in the last decade or so that you think carries a strong political, social, or ideological message. Discuss the ideas conveyed, how they are conveyed, and how effectively they are conveyed. Some possibilities include the following: *Pan's Labyrinth,* from Mexico (but set in Spain); *Osama,* from Afghanistan; *Life Is Beautiful,* from Italy; *Bend It Like Beckham,* from the United Kingdom; *The Magdalene Sisters,* from the United Kingdom and Ireland; *Rabbit-Proof Fence,* from Australia; and *The Death of Mister Lazarescu* and *4 Months, 3 Weeks and 2 Days,* from Romania.

18 CHAPTER

The Internet

A friend of yours has just finished her senior project to earn a degree in film and video production. Her project is a half-hour documentary film about some unsanitary and inhumane business practices employed by a meat-packing plant in your hometown that supplies beef and chicken to several major fast-food chains. With this little film, she's hoping to spread the word about what she discovered at the meat-packing plant, and she's also hoping that creating a buzz around her film will help her get funding to make a full-length film about the pitfalls of fast-food meat packing in general.

Your friend asks you to help her spread the word on her film. In recent years, the Web has seen a flourishing of self-publication and self-promotion, so you think that's your best venue. In no time, you have drawn up a plan. First, you'll launch a MySpace page that focuses on the film. If enough "Friends" sign up for your page, and you can link it to other "fast-food radicals" who post similar concerns on their own MySpace pages, you can hopefully generate some sort of an Internet buzz. Next, you decide to post several clips from the film on YouTube. You can link the YouTube clips to your MySpace page and get a little web ring started on this documentary.

As you dig deeper, though, ideas about how to share this information on the Web keep coming. You could start a blog about your thoughts on the film and get others to log on and share their own thoughts; similarly, you could find a popular blog that may address concerns about the meat-packing industry, fast food, or animal cruelty and post your own thoughts on this film, so others will learn about it and visit your other sites. You could create a podcast with clips of the film and an interview with your friend, the director, and people could download it onto their iPods and cell phones. You could go to Wikipedia and add some information about this film to some entries on meat packing. Finally, you could post information on a public online bulletin board for your campus or simply send an "all" email with information about this film and your new web campaign to every student on your campus.

The World Wide Web has gone from being a fledgling means to share information and spread corporate branding to a place for personal publication and social and political advocacy. Whether it is providing more traditional sources of information and research, offering entertainment, or giving budding pundits a chance to express their opinions about the state of the world through blogging, the Internet has become a very popular tool indeed. If you want to excel at information competency, you simply can't ignore the Internet. Following is a discussion of the history of the Internet as well as some major issues about the Web that have evolved over the years.

INTERNET BASICS

The infrastructure of the Internet is a series of millions of computers and computer servers linked together and communicating. There is not one body of people or one storehouse of computers that are the Internet. Nobody owns it, and, in democracies, nobody really governs it—yet.

Many futurists and theorists consider the birth of the modern Internet to be a bigger influence on the spread of human information than the printing press and even the development of written language were. The capability for people around the globe to communicate instantaneously is a profound notion that we've all come to take for granted. Just a hundred years ago, a few massive cables on the bottom of the ocean floor provided choppy and expensive transcontinental telegraph and telephone communication. A hundred years before that, people relied on letters carried by horses and ships and often waited months to hear from each. Now, however, someone with a modem and a phone or cable line can send a message from Sri Lanka to New York in a matter of nanoseconds.

Ordinary daily communication has been vastly improved by the Net, but perhaps the greatest gains made through use of the Internet have been by researchers and scientists. Traditionally, solitary scientists working to understand a particular biological process would spend years researching every element of the process. Perhaps at a few annual conferences, they could communicate in person with a few others doing similar research, and they could comb the journals to see what others were doing, but otherwise, they were on their own. Now, however, research that used to take years may take only months. Researchers can constantly share packets of information with other scientists worldwide. If someone else in the world is doing any research even remotely related to your own, you have the potential to know about it in "real-time." In fact, the idea of enhanced research was the driving force behind the origins of the Internet, once called the ARPAnet.

EVOLUTION OF THE NET

ARPANET

The Internet as we know it now began with a system known as the ARPAnet. The Advanced Research Projects Agency (ARPA) was formed in the late 1950s to help scientists develop research technologies in the space race against the Soviet Union. One of its many projects was a communications network that could continue operating even if one portion of it was damaged or eliminated (or, some speculate, if it was destroyed in a nuclear attack). The early ARPAnet was used by government agencies and the research institutions (such as UCLA and the Stanford Research Institute) that helped pioneer it. Unlike today's Internet, which consists of millions of connected nodes (computers), the original ARPAnet consisted of only four main computer systems, located at the University of California at Santa Barbara, the University of California at Los Angeles, the Stanford Research Institute, and the University of Utah, respectively. Though ARPA changed to DARPA (by adding the word Defense to its title), this early, private computer network grew through the 1970s and eventually reached coast to coast in America and even offshore to other nations. By the late 1980s, it had expanded to so many places that it was starting to resemble the Internet we know.

However, informational retrieval systems such as Gopher, WAIS, and the FTP Archive list weren't able to handle all the data types being used at the time. Hypertext technology (which was conceived in the 1960s by Ted Nelson) suggested solutions, and in 1991, Tim Berners-Lee developed a network-based implementation of the hypertext concept. The adoption of Berners-Lee's Hypertext Transfer Protocol (HTTP) enabled the success of Mosaic, a graphical browser developed in 1993 by a group led by Marc Andreessen (who was only in his early twenties) at the National Center for Supercomputing Applications at the University of Illinois at Urbana-Champaign. Funding came from a program initiated by then-Senator Al Gore's "High Performance Computing and Communication Act of 1991," also known as the "Gore Bill." Mosaic introduced the Net to a huge new audience of ordinary, nonspecialist users and marked the beginning of the Web that we know and use today.

DIAL-UP

After the adoption of Mosaic, the home Internet explosion began. At the time, technology was limited to relatively slow communication channels, such as standard phone lines to connect. Several **ISPs** (Internet Service Providers) pioneered the commercial Internet, such as Prodigy, Juno, and America Online. AOL is generally acknowledged as being the most successful and largest ISP.

With the growth of these service providers, the Internet boomed. Originally, it consisted of research and educational sites, but it was quickly coopted by corporations and entrepreneurs using it to make money through an incredible array of schemes, sales techniques, and even scams (see "E-Commerce," later in this chapter). This commercialism has helped the Net expand via constantly advancing software and hardware, with current modems running thousands of times faster than early models. Roughly half of American Internet users still use a dial-up connection to get to the Net, and many homes have a second phone line specifically for Net access.

BROADBAND

Currently, dial-up phone service for Net connection is being replaced by the exponentially faster **broadband** connections. Home broadband is typically DSL (Digital Subscriber Line) service provided through phone companies or cable service provided by cable and satellite providers. These types of connections are hundreds of times faster than those provided by regular phone lines, directly changing the nature of the Net. Although websites used to be largely text based, because "live" video and animation took too long to download with a dial-up connection, most sites now incorporate multimedia to visually stimulate the consumer's eye. These sites (and sites such as YouTube) would have been all but impossible with the slower machines of the mid-1990s.

WIRELESS

Another technological leap for the Net is **wireless** technology. Computers no longer need to be physically connected to a network at all, but can instead pick up wireless signals and communicate over the airwaves. Usually, you have to set up a wireless network in your own home and make sure your computers have the hardware to communicate with this local network. However, in larger cities, you can also find *open networks,* where people who dislike the corporate control over the once "free" Internet establish free **wi-fi hotspots,** where anyone with a laptop, Blackberry, iPhone, or similar device and wireless capability can log in at no charge. Similarly, some more progressive cities, such as San Francisco, California, and Sydney, Australia, are trying to create free, citywide wireless networks. They consider the infrastructure of the Net to be similar to roads and highways and believe access to the Net should be provided by the government, not owned by private companies. Finally, there are continuing advances in cellular wireless Internet access that allow us to get a Net connection anywhere in the world where we can connect to a cellular network.

SPECIALIZED PLATFORMS

The most recent evolution of the Net is a spread of the types of electronic devices that can access the Web. For the past few decades, only computers were designed to access the Web. This is changing rapidly, however, as more and more specialized platforms become affordable. These new web devices include sophisticated cellular phones, PDAs, cable and satellite boxes, and video game platforms. Systems such as the Xbox 360 and the Nintendo Wii have wireless Internet connection and their own, specialized type of web interface. They primarily exist to let gamers play with one another and download new games, but they also provide news, weather reports, email functions, and other types of information traditionally found only by logging on with a computer. Many speculators think that these types of devices may some day trump the "home computer Internet" and usher in a completely different type of Web.

E-COMMERCE

One feature of the Internet is handy shopping, and in many ways online stores and banking have truly revolutionized the global marketplace. At first using the Net for banking or shopping was a very scary proposition for most people. However, as encryption and security software have gotten better, huge numbers of people use it to shop for a broad spectrum of items.

Perhaps the biggest example of electronic commerce is eBay, one of the largest phenomena in the history of the Web. Started in the mid 1990s, eBay was mainly an auction house for collectibles and antiques. As its influence grew, however, it became a place that people could go to find virtually any used (or new) item they could imagine. To purchase something on eBay, you make a bid and check back in from time to time to see if you've been outbid. If you win the bid, you make the purchase through the PayPal banking system, one of the Net's largest banking entities, also owned by eBay. A Canadian man named Kyle MacDonald decided to use eBay to try "trading up." He wondered if he could start with an ordinary, used paper clip and trade it up for something worth more and keep doing so until he got a house. In a little less than a year, he was surprisingly successful and had acquired a house for the price of a red paper clip. MacDonald's story may be unusual—he ultimately received the house from a town that gave it to him in exchange for a role in a movie that they could auction off and use for publicity—but nonetheless, it illustrates the boundless potential to make money using the Internet.

Another large electronic storefront is Amazon.com. Initially, Amazon was simply a bookstore that tapped into the warehouse network that shipped books to traditional book chains like Barnes and Noble and Waldenbooks. Eventually, it expanded to include film and music, and now it is a juggernaut of online shopping, selling everything from groceries and computers to baby clothes and power tools. Writers now post blogs on the site to keep in touch with their fan bases and to promote new projects and ideas. Readers post lists of "best of" categories and influence other readers. Often new albums and books include summaries and messages written by the artists and authors themselves, and Amazon also contains a feature that lets you read portions of the books and listen to the albums you're considering.

Online shopping is not without controversy, though. Many people argue that Amazon.com's ability to beat virtually anyone's price on books has helped contribute to the death of local bookstores. Many such online stores are blamed for harming local economies because the scale they deal in allows them to undercut local prices. The Supreme Court has ruled that a state can't require a business to collect sales tax from online buyers unless it has an actual physical connection to that state, such as a store or warehouse, though Congress could enact legislation to change that. As a result of consumers doing more shopping online, states are losing tax money that they formerly collected through local commerce. As the economy evolves to include more electronic shopping, more issues such as these are sure to arise.

BLOGS

Blogs are websites that allow anyone to get content out on the Web. Blogs can be used to disseminate opinions to like-minded readers, or they can be personal diaries. In the early days of blogging, blogs were primarily individuals' hobbies. Now they are much, much more.

On December 5, 2002, Mississippi Senator Trent Lott spoke at a dinner honoring South Carolina Senator Strom Thurmond on his 100th birthday. In 1948, delegates from thirteen states had nominated Thurmond to run for President of the United States on a platform that included this statement: "We stand for the segregation of the races and the racial integrity of each race." In Lott's salute to Thurmond, he said, "I want to say this about my state: when Strom Thurmond ran for president, we voted for him. We're proud of it. And if the rest of the country had followed our lead, we wouldn't have had all these problems over all these years, either."

The next day, Josh Marshall's blog, TPM (talkingpointsmemo.com), called attention to U.S. Senator Lott's comments regarding Senator Thurmond and raised speculations about what Lott had meant by "all these problems." TPM noted the slowness of mainstream media to address the issue, pointing out that "On *Inside Politics* the John Kerry hair story made the cut, not the Trent Lott segregation story." The attention of political bloggers to Lott's remarks hastened the spread of comments and criticism on the Net and in mainstream media. Senator Lott soon resigned as Senate majority leader because of the controversy raised by his remarks.

On September 8, 2004, respected journalist Dan Rather reported on *60 Minutes* that scathing memos criticizing President George W. Bush's Texas Air National Guard service record had been discovered in the personal files of Bush's former commanding officer. In the days that followed, four blogs—Little Green Footballs, Power Line, Free Republic, and Allahpundit's (the pseudonym for an anonymous writer) blog—investigated the documents and announced that they were forgeries. The episode became known as "Rathergate," and six months later, Rather retired as the anchorman and managing editor of the *CBS Evening News* after twenty-four years as anchor—the longest period any individual had served as an anchor in TV history. The following year, he left his network, CBS, after forty-four years. The network's embarrassment over "Rathergate" is generally credited with causing Rather's departure from his positions as anchor and managing editor and from the network itself.

These and other high-profile incidents demonstrated that blogging had both the power to influence the mainstream and, in some cases, had become part of the mainstream itself. Today, mainstream news services sponsor their own blogs to reach wider audiences, and corporations, political and social commentators, political candidates, and office holders use them to discuss issues of local, national, and international importance in the hopes of reaching and influencing policymakers and public opinion.

YOU

In the past few years, the Web has become so popular for self-publication that *Time* magazine even named "You" as the person of the year in 2006, implying that art and entertainment on the Net doesn't depend on stars, producers, or corporate board rooms so much as it does on regular people—individuals like you who share, post, and wiki to create the new Web. The Net has long been a place for self-expression, but with recent technological advances (and the possibilities opened up through new high-speed connections), more and more means of expression have evolved. Sites such as MySpace and Facebook exist so that people have a place to publish and share information and art. Many famous musicians have MySpace pages that they manage themselves, and many up-and-coming acts have pages, hoping to get discovered. YouTube and the comedy storehouse Channel101.com are also available. These sites have helped several unknowns find success, such as *Saturday Night Live*'s Andy Samberg, who got a start by posting his now famous "Digital Shorts" on Channel 101.

Sites like YouTube and MySpace set the trends on the Internet, but other Web spaces are up and coming. One such site is Second Life. It is a world simulation, free to download and use—a fully user-created, 3D-rendered virtual reality, used by more than 3 million people who interact via avatars (computer-generated personas, often fashionable or downright bizarre). Second Life boasts several users who have made over a million dollars in real U.S. dollars selling virtual real estate. Nissan has a car dealership in the world where avatars can drive virtual cars, Sweden now has an official embassy in Second Life, and there are dozens of real colleges and universities with virtual Second Life campuses that hold actual online classes in virtual classrooms and help students enroll and register for their schools.

EXPRESS YOURSELF!

Here is a list of some possible ways to let your voice be heard on the Web:

blogs

podcasts

chat rooms

YouTube

Channel 101

MySpace

Facebook

a wiki meme

Second Life

.Mac home pages

NET MEMES/VIRAL VIDEOS

Biologist Richard Dawkins introduced the term **meme** in 1976 in his book *The Self-ish Gene,* combining the word "gene" with the word "mime" to name "a unit of cultural transmission, or a unit of imitation" that is carried throughout society by people repeating it. A meme may be insignificant, but it spreads rapidly and widely through a population. Net memes tend to be small videos, songs, or even emailed stories, jokes, urban legends, and chain letters that take on a life of their own. Typically, Net memes spread with no advertising or conscious effort on anyone's part to make them popular; something about them just catches on and helps them to spread all around the world.

Many memes are **viral videos;** this is a term for streaming or downloadable video clips that are so amusing, shocking, or sad that they spread in a matter of days through a naturally evolving spread of emails and Web links, as a virus would spread through a system. The creators are sometimes stunned (or, if the video was originally private, mortified) at the instant international fame they may gain. Many self-publishing sites, like YouTube, have created some Net memes (and even a few celebrities), and they will continue to do so. Following is a brief list of Net memes. Some you may recognize, and you can probably think of several that aren't on this list. Do a Web search for any of these, and you'll probably find them still posted out there; give them a chance, and you'll probably see why they caught the world's attention. As you'll see with this small list, the content, tone, and type of material here varies drastically.

THE EVOLUTION OF DANCE

In this lengthy video clip, comedian Judson Laipply dances to excerpts of popular songs, with artists ranging from Elvis Presley to Eminem, illustrating dance crazes and styles from the fifties through and past the nineties. By the end of 2007, the clip had been viewed over 68 million times, making it the most popular video on the site.

DANCING BABY

One of the earliest Net memes to really take off was the simple graphic of a three-dimensionally rendered dancing baby that made the rounds of the Web. It was picked up by the television show *Ally McBeal* and seen by millions of people.

THE HAMSTER DANCE

This innocent meme was simply a crudely animated GIF image of a hamster dancing to funny music. It was ridiculously addictive and sent to millions of people through email links. Eventually the song the hamster danced to was even remixed into a popular song played at dance clubs throughout the nation.

STAR WARS KID

An ordinary high school student filmed himself acting out the light saber battle scene from *Star Wars Episode 1: The Phantom Menace*. The film was allegedly found in a high school video camera and posted on the Net. Hundreds of users edited this original footage, adding *Star Wars* music, special effects, and aliens for the kid to battle. He was even featured as an unlockable "Easter Egg" in one of the Tony Hawk video games.

"ALL YOUR BASE ARE BELONG TO US"

A very high-concept Net meme, "All your Base," or simply AYBABTU, is a video of an incredibly poorly translated opening cut scene of a 1989 video game called Zero Wing. It's high melodrama and hysterical phrasing made "All your Base" a smash hit on the Net, with several edits and various user-created versions of the opening scene. In many high-tech circles, "All your Base" is part of the daily lexicon.

MENTOS FOUNTAINS

When Mentos are added to two-liter bottles of diet coke, an explosive fountain reaction occurs in the bottle, forcing a spout of soda several feet in the air. Videos of these experiments became viral on the Net, and any video Web search can yield dozens of these clips. Many of them are satirically artistic and set to music, evoking the complex fountain at the Bellagio hotel in Las Vegas, an intricate domino spread, or a "Rube Goldberg" device (Rube Goldberg was a twentieth-century political cartoonist best known for a series of cartoons depicting absurdly complex devices that performed simple tasks in hilariously elaborate and convoluted ways). Eventually, some of the pioneers of these videos made appearances on late-night talk shows, such as David Letterman's, and the television show *Myth Busters* experimented with this volatile chemical reaction.

LONELYGIRL15

Lonelygirl15 was a teenaged girl named Bree, who became one of YouTube's largest celebrities, releasing a regular video blog soap opera of her life. Bree was a home-schooled girl with strict religious parents, and she shared a video diary with YouTube. For four months, Bree's clips were regularly among the highest rated on YouTube, with around 100,000 subscribers and over 10 million all-time views of her videos as of this writing. Part of the fascination with "Bree," a beautiful girl who loved science and read complex authors like Richard P. Feynman and Jared Diamond, was whether she was a real diarist or part of a hoax. For some self-described techno-geeks, she seemed the perfect girl of their dreams—to others, she was just too perfect to be true. A lively debate ensued on both sides of the question. Tech-savvy fans, tracking clues on the Web and even engaging in an email "sting" operation, exposed the truth. Sixteen-year-old Bree turned out to be nineteen-year-old actress Jessica Rose, who had answered an ad posted on Craig's List by two would-be filmmakers. VH1 named Jessica fourth on its "Forty Greatest Internet Superstars" list.

COLBERT'S KEYNOTE

In 2006, comedian Stephen Colbert was invited to be the keynote speaker at the 2006 White House Correspondents' Association Dinner, an annual Washington tradition since the twenties. Colbert had become famous and popular as an over-the-top, radically conservative and enormously egotistical political talk show host. At this dinner, Colbert spoke in front of then-President George W. Bush and the First Lady, Laura Bush, as well as important members of Bush's cabinet and the journalists who are assigned to cover the White House. He appeared in the character of his television persona, lampooning the president and insulting the press and important people in attendance, and the video of the speech took on a life of its own as a viral video viewed and downloaded heavily on various websites. This particular meme also shows how widely Net coverage of an event can differ from that offered by the mainstream media. Much of the mainstream media ignored Colbert's part of the evening or dismissed him as unfunny, while viewers all over the Net gave it a great deal of attention, with a huge number of people finding his performance hilarious, not merely for satirizing the president, but for satirizing the White House correspondents themselves. *Time* magazine's James Poniewozik suggested that the performance may even have been intended more for the Web than the people in the room that night: "Colbert wasn't playing to the room, I suspect, but to the wide audience of people who would later watch on the Internet. If anything, he was playing against the room."

EMAIL

Many people who rarely access the Internet to browse, buy products, or post information are active emailers. In the business world, hundreds of thousands of memos are sent out on a daily basis, and countless businesses have gone "paperless." This means that instead of printing thousands of memos and using staff to deliver them throughout the work space, a simple email is sent to everyone.

Email is considered both a curse and a blessing by many educators. On the one hand, it gets young people to write and type and engage with each other through means other than cell phones and text messages. On the other hand, the language of most casual email isn't exactly grammatically correct standard English. Emoticons and Net abbreviations (such as LOL for "laughing out loud," AFK for "away from keyboard," and hundreds of others) have altered language. Often terms that should be used only in casual email now creep into emails to employers or professors and even into academic writing that students do for classes because some students think it is an acceptable way to communicate in any situation.

NET INTRUSIONS

Any phenomenon as widespread and important as the Internet is going to be used as a means to make money. Advertisers and public relations firms have dreamed up rather insidious means to spread their products over the Web. Forms of advertising like **spam, pop-up ads,** and **banners** are seen as intrusive and annoying by many people. Spam is any unsolicited advertisement that is sent to email boxes. Spam can be used to try to get you to visit pornographic websites or to buy anything from prescription drugs to real estate, and it sometimes comes to your box disguised with an email address belonging to someone you know or a subject heading that indicates a friend is sending you the email. Pop-up ads are advertisements that are programmed to pop up out of nowhere when you are visiting a Web page. They are typically animated and flashy, and usually you can't disable them; you just have to wait for the ad to finish and go away. Banner ads are the most innocent and prevalent form of advertising on the Web. Most commercial websites have a banner at the top or the side of the page advertising a new product, film, game, or web service. You merely click the banner and are taken to a site for more information.

All of this advertising may merely seem like a mild annoyance, but these ads actually cost American workplaces millions of dollars in lost revenue because of wasted work time, computer crashes, filled server space, and overburdened email boxes. (On the other hand, ads can also fund worthy sites run by people who are volunteers who want to provide educational websites to other people free of charge.)

The worst of all Internet intrusions, however, are the web scams. Scam artists take billions of dollars from unsuspecting Net users through "phishing," which is tricking someone into surrendering confidential information, like credit card numbers and account passwords. This typically leads to identity theft or just plain financial theft. Also, hackers can get onto computers and steal private information for later identity theft. Typically, though, hackers have a much larger goal than getting into your little computer. Either they tend to want to steal massive amounts of money from banks, corporations, and governments, or they tend to want to foster anarchy and damage the major channels of information on the Internet or harm corporations they consider to be too controlling over computer technologies.

NET NEUTRALITY

"Net neutrality" is the term used by people who argue that the Net needs to be a free source of information that is controlled by the users and publishers of the Internet, not by phone, cable, and entertainment corporations. These corporations spend millions of dollars lobbying the government to gain control of the major Internet hubs and server networks, often considered the "backbone" of the Internet. Part of this backbone consists of thousands of miles of "dark fiber" (fiber-optic cables that are in place and ready for Internet use, but are too costly to activate, so nobody uses them); communications corporations buy hundreds of miles of this dark fiber at a time. If this continues, they'll own a major portion of the physical infrastructure of the Net, and the face and nature of the Net will irrevocably change.

One thing that many corporations want is a "tiered" Internet system. This means that different sites would be given different levels of bandwidth (and faster or slower speeds) or that different users would have to pay more for access. For example, if you logged in using AT&T as an Internet service provider, AT&T could push any website owned by a rival corporation (such as AOL or Verizon) to a lower tier. This means that the websites maintained by their rivals would be slow, and you might end up avoiding those sites altogether if you get sick of slow access. Such tiers would be a very subtle and very effective way to manipulate the spread of information.

Some corporations also hope to control information through another important method. Currently, if you access data, it comes to you at a consistent rate, no matter where it comes from or what type of data it is. However, many corporations hope to one day control even this. Internet providers could make certain neighborhoods higher priority, ensuring some part of the city constant high-speed access but relegating other neighborhoods to perpetually slower access. This would lead to growth of "information ghettos," where the Web is slow and ineffective.

Many groups argue against these plans and advocate that the government should endorse and legally support a form of Net neutrality. They think the Net is a public space to which the public has a right, like the right to free airwaves, or the right to drive on American roads. And, like roads, they should be maintained and regulated by the government. No corporate entities should be allowed to dominate the flow of information through money-making schemes. These advocates argue that the Net is the greatest benefit to human communication in the history of the species, and that it should be illegal for anyone to control this access and therefore control the dissemination of much of the information in our world.

INTELLECTUAL PROPERTY

In the late 1990s, a phenomenon known as P2P or peer-to-peer communications exploded. P2P systems are ways to download data using a piece of shared software that lets one user explore, access, and download files from another user's computer. The most (in)famous of these P2P systems is Napster. At its height, Napster was a massive conduit for downloading music and movies. If you bought a new album and shared it with the peer-to-peer network, everyone else who used Napster could download the album from your computer for free. Although a lot of people loved suddenly being able to get all the music they wanted for free, the music industry lost billions of dollars over the years to P2P networks. This included not just the corporate executives and famous, wealthy artists, but smaller artists struggling to survive. Napster was shut down by the federal government in 2001, and it has now changed to become a legal place to purchase and download music, but other free P2P networks—such as KaZaA, Bit Torrent, LimeWire, and BearShare—continually pop up. (In fact, KaZaA itself was even hacked and rereleased by the hackers as "Zazaa++lite," which deleted the program's spyware and allowed users to break KaZaA's queue system and protocols.) Many people buy albums from record stores or download songs from a service such as iTunes or Rhapsody, but millions of people continue to illegally download music from each other for free.

This illegal downloading has sparked a very heated debate about intellectual property. Representatives of the music industry have sued random peer-to-peer users (many are college students, struggling to get by, and some are even young children who downloaded children's songs) as a way to get people to stop. Many musicians, such as members of the band Metallica, have testified before Congress and tried to convince the population that downloading free music is wrong. The artists wrote and recorded this music, and it is how they make a living. To download it without paying is stealing their intellectual property. Other artists, such as Prince and Radiohead, have intentionally released music as free downloads, and many view the peer-to-peer networks as a means for artists and customers to battle against the corporate music giants and their control over song ownership.

Since the early days of Napster, though, peer-to-peer downloads have expanded beyond music. People pirate movies (often before they are released), television shows (often before they are aired), and entire albums and pieces of software (often before they are legally for sale). While film studios are trying to make money selling DVD box sets of television seasons, many people are downloading them and burning them onto DVDs for free. Even YouTube.com is regularly under fire for copyright infringement. Users of YouTube will post their own recordings of popular shows (there are thousands of them, so the YouTube webmasters have a difficult task trying to police this). While the copyright owner of the video can complain, and YouTube can tell users to stop posting these clips and even delete these clips, other users can keep on posting them.

One trouble with enforcing intellectual property rights is that different countries have different laws about intellectual property. Some countries don't have laws against downloading entertainment data, such as music and movies. Thus, even if most countries crack down and ban the use of peer-to-peer and other types of downloads, it may always be legal in some country. This makes the issue very muddy. If it's illegal in America to download someone's music, is it still illegal if we download it from a country where it's perfectly legal to do so? Debates over intellectual property and peer-to-peer networking are just beginning, and, with billions of dollars on the line, the debates will continue.

IN THIS CHAPTER

These readings focus on the newest (and maybe already the most important) of the forms of mass media—the World Wide Web. These articles have been included to help you understand the major arguments and concerns surrounding the continuing evolution of the Internet. To become critical thinkers about the Net, you may ask yourself:

- What information on the Net can be trusted, and what is written by hoaxers, bigots, sloppy thinkers, lobbyists, or even crackpots?

■ How can you find and evaluate information on the Web that is worthy of including in academic writing?

■ How will the brief "fifteen minutes of fame" afforded by sites like YouTube and MySpace redefine the notion of celebrity?

■ Is Wikipedia, a user-created encyclopedia on everything under the sun, a good resource, or should it be avoided for serious research because of its open nature?

■ Should you have to pay for information on the Net, or should it be free to everyone?

■ Who—if anyone—should control and limit the "infrastructure" of the Net, an entity comprising millions of people, servers, and computers all over the globe?

■ Should corporations be able to control bandwidth and access to the Net, or should it be government regulated, like the airwaves are by the FCC?

Network Economics

Kevin Kelly

Prereading Question

1. How dependent are you on computers? How dependent are you on the Internet? Can you imagine going a month, a week, or even a day without logging on?

John Perry Barlow's exact mission in life is hard to pin down. He owns a ranch in Pinedale, Wyoming. He once made a bid for a Republican seat in that state's Senate. He often introduces himself to boomer types as the B-string lyricist for that perennial underground cult band, the Grateful Dead. It's a role he relishes, particularly for the cognitive dissonance it serves up: A Republican Deadhead?

At any one moment Barlow may be working on getting a whaleboat launched in Sri Lanka (so environmentalists can monitor gray whale migrations), or delivering an address to an electrical engineers association on the future of privacy and freedom of speech. He is as likely to be sitting in a Japanese hot spring in Hokkaido with Japanese industrialists, brainstorming on ways to unify the Pacific Rim, as he would be soaking in a sweat lodge with the last of the space visionaries planning to settle Mars. I know Barlow from an experimental computer meeting place, the WELL, a place where no one has a body. There, he plays the role of "hippie mystic."

On the WELL, Barlow and I met and worked together years before we ever met in the flesh. This is the usual way of friendships in the information age. Barlow has about ten phone numbers, several different towns where he parks his cellular phone, and more than one electronic address. I never know where he is, but I can almost always reach him in a couple of minutes. The guy flies on planes with a laptop computer plugged into an in-flight phone. The numbers I hit to contact him might take me anywhere in the world.

I get discombobulated by this disembodiment. When I connect, I am confused if I can't picture at least what part of the globe I'm connected to. He might not mind being placeless, but I mind. When I dial what I think is him in Now York City and I wind up with him over the Pacific, I feel flung.

"Barlow, where are you right now?" I demand impatiently during an intense phone call discussing some pretty hairy, nontrivial negotiations.

"Well, when you first called I was in a parking lot. Now I'm in a luggage store getting my luggage repaired."

"Gee," I said, "why don't you just get a receiver surgically wired into your brain? It'd be a lot more convenient. Free up your hands."

"That's the idea," he replies in total seriousness.

Barlow moved from the emptiness of Wyoming and is now homesteading in the vaster wilds of cyberspace, the frontier where our previous conversation technically took place. As originally envisioned by writer William Gibson, cyberspace encompasses the realm of large electronic networks which are invisibly spreading "underneath" the industrial world in a kind of virtual sprawl. In the near future, according to Gibson's science-fiction, cyberspace explorers would "jack in" to a borderless maze of electronic data banks and video-gamelike worlds. A cyberspace scout sits in a dark room and then plugs a modem directly into his brain. Thus jacked in, he cerebrally navigates the invisible world of abstracted information, as if he were racing through an infinite library. By all accounts, this version of cyberspace is already appearing in patches.

Cyberspace, as expanded by hippie mystic Barlow, is something yet broader. It includes not only the invisible matrix of databases and networks, and not only the three-dimensional games one can enter wearing computer-screen goggles, but also the entire realm of any disembodied presence and of all information in digital form. Cyberspace, says Barlow, is the place that you and a friend "are" when you are both talking on the phone.

"Nothing could be more disembodied than cyberspace. It's like having your everything amputated," Barlow once told a reporter. Cyberspace is the mall of network culture. It's that territory where the counterintuitive logic of distributed networks meets the odd behavior of human society. And it is expanding rapidly. Because of network economics, cyberspace is a resource that increases the more it is used. Barlow quips that it is "a peculiar kind of real estate which expands with development."

I bought my first computer to crunch a database of names for a mail order company I owned. But within several months of getting my first Apple II running, I hooked the machine up to a telephone and had a religious experience.

On the other side of the phone jack, an embryonic web stirred—the young Net. In that dawn I saw that the future of computers was not numbers but connections. Far more voltage crackled out of a million interconnected Apple IIs than within the most coddled million-dollar supercomputer standing alone. Roaming the Net I got a hit of network juice, and my head buzzed.

Computers, used as calculating machines, would, just as we all expected, whip up the next efficient edition of the world. But no one expected that once used as communication machines, networked computers would overturn the improved world onto an entirely different logic—the logic of the Net.

In the Me-Decades, the liberation of personal computers was just right. Personal computers were personal slaves. Loyal, bonded silicon brains, hired for cheap and at your command, even if you were only 13. It was plain as daylight that personal computers and their eventual high-powered offspring would reconfigure the world to our specifications: personal newspapers, video on demand, customized widgets. The focus was on you the individual. But in one of those quirks reality is famous for, the real power of the silicon chip lay not in its amazing ability to flip digits to think for us, but in its uncanny ability to use flipped switches to connect us. We shouldn't call them computers; we really should call them connectors.

By 1992 the fastest-growing segment of the computer industry was network technology. This reflects the light-speed rate at which every sector of business is electronically netting itself into a new shape. By 1993, both *Time* and *Newsweek* featured cover stories on the fast-approaching data superhighway that would connect television, telephones, and the Sixpack family. In a few years—no dream—you would pick up a gadget and get a "video dial-tone" which would enable you to send or receive a movie, a color photograph, an entire database, an album of music, some detailed blueprints, or a set of books—instantly—to or from anyone, anywhere, anytime.

Networking at that scale would truly revolutionize almost every business. It would alter:

- What we make
- How we make it
- How we decide what to make
- The nature of the economy we make it in.

There is hardly a single aspect of business not overhauled, either directly or indirectly, by the introduction of networking logic. Networks—not merely computers alone—enable companies to manufacture new kinds of innovative products, in faster and more flexible ways, in greater response to customers' needs, and all within a rapidly shifting environment where competitors can do the same. In response to these groundswell changes, laws and financing change, too, not to mention the incredible alterations in the economy due to global 24-hour networking of financial institutions. And not to mention the feverish cultural brew that will burst as "the Street" takes hold of this web and subverts it to its own uses.

Network logic has already shaped the products that are shaping business now. Instant cash, the product which is disgorged from ATM machines, could only be born in a network. Ditto for credit cards of any stripe. Fax machines, too. But also such things as the ubiquitous color printing in our lives. The high quality and low cost of modern four-color printing is made possible by a networked printing press which coordinates the hi-speed overlap of each color as it zips through the web of rollers. Biotech pharmaceuticals require networked intelligence to manage living soups as they flow by the barrelful from one vat to the next. Even processed snack foods are here to tempt us because the dispersed machines needed to cook them can be coordinated by a network.

Ordinary manufacturing becomes better when managed by netted intelligence. Networked equipment creates not only purer steel and glass, but its adaptive nature allows more varieties to be made with the same equipment. Small differences in composition can be maintained during manufacturing, in effect creating new kinds of precise materials where once there was only one fuzzy, imprecise material.

Networking will also inform the maintenance of products. Already, in 1993, some business equipment (Pitney Bowes's fax machines, Hewlett-Packard's minicomputers, General Electric's body scanners) can be diagnosed and repaired from a distance. By plugging a phone line into a machine, operators at the factory can peek inside its guts to see if it is working properly and often fix it if not. The technique of remote diagnostics was developed by satellite makers who had no choice but to do repairs at a distance. Now the methods are being used to fix a fax machine, to dissect a hard disk, or to speed repair of an X-ray machine thousands of miles away. Sometimes new software can be uploaded into the machine to create a fix; at the very least, the repairman can learn beforehand what parts and tools he'll need if he visits and thus speed up the on-site repair. In essence, these networked devices become nodes of a larger distributed machine. In time all machines will be wired into a net so that they warn repairmen when they are flaking out, and so that they can receive updated intelligence and thus improve while on the job.

The Japanese perfected the technique of combining well-educated human beings and networked computer intelligence into one seamless companywide network to ensure uncompromised quality. Intense coordination of critical information in Japanese manufacturing corporations gave the world palm-size camcorders and durable cars. While the rest of the industrialized sector frantically installs network-driven manufacturing machinery, the Japanese have moved on to the next frontier in network logic: flexible manufacturing and mass customization. For instance the National Bicycle Industrial Company in Kokubu, Japan, builds custom bicycles on an assembly line. You can order any one of 11 million variations of its models to suit your taste, at prices only 10 percent higher than mass-produced noncustomized models.

The challenge is simply stated: Extend the company's internal network outward to include all those with whom the company interacts in the marketplace. Spin a grand web to include employees, suppliers, regulators, and customers; they all become part of your company's collective being. *They* are the company.

Cases in both Japan and America where corporations have started building an extended distributed company demonstrate the immense power it releases. For example, Levi Strauss, makers of jeans for the whole world, has networked a large portion of its being. Continuous data flows from its headquarters, its 39 production plants, and its thousands of retailers into an economic superorganism. As stone-washed jeans are bought at the mall in, say, Buffalo, a message announcing those sales flies that night from the mall's cash register into Levi's net. The net consolidates the transaction with transactions from 3,500 other retail stores and within hours triggers the order for more stone-washed jeans from a factory in Belgium, or more dye from Germany, or more denim cloth from the cotton mills in North Carolina.

The same signal spurs the networked factory into action. Here bundles of cloth arrive from the mills decked in bar codes. As the stacks of cloth become pants, their bar-coded identity will be followed with hand-held laser readers, from fabric to trucker to store shelf. A reply is sent back to the mall store saying the restocking pants are on their way. And they will be, in a matter of days.

So tight is this loop of customer purchase/order materials/make, that other highly networked clothiers such as Benetton boast that they don't dye their sweaters until they are on their way out the door. When customers at the local chains start ringing up turquoise jumpers, in a few days Benetton's network will begin dyeing more jumpsuits in that color. Thus, the cash registers, not fashion mavens, choose the hues of the season. In this way, hip Benetton stays abreast of the unpredictable storms of fashion.

If you link computer-assisted design tools, and computer-assisted manufacturing, then not only can colors be nimbly manipulated but entire designs as well. A new outfit is quickly drawn up, made in low volume, distributed to stores, and then rapidly modified or multiplied if successful. The whole cycle is measured in days. Up until recently, the cycle of a far more limited choice was measured in seasons and years. Kao, a detergent and toiletry manufacturer in Japan, has developed a distribution system so tightly networked that it delivers even the smallest order within 24 hours.

Why not make cars or plastics this way? In fact, you can. A truly adaptable factory must be modular. Its tools and workflow can be quickly modified and reassembled to manufacture a different version of car or a different formula plastic. One day the assembly line is grinding out station wagons or Styrofoam, the next day jeeps or Plexiglas. Technicians call it flexible manufacturing. The assembly line adapts to fit the products needed. It's a hot field of research with immense potential. If you can alter the manufacturing process on the fly without stopping the flow, you then have the means to make stuff in batches of one.

But this flexibility demands tiptoe agility from multi-ton machines that are presently bolted to the floor. To get them to dance requires substituting a lot of mass with a lot of networked intelligence. Flexibility has to sink deep into the system to make flexible manufacturing work. The machine tools must themselves be adjustable, the schedules of material delivery must turn on a dime, the labor force must coordinate as a unit, the suppliers of packaging must be fluid, the trucking lines must be adaptable, the marketing must be in sync. That's all done with networks.

Today my factory needs 21 flatbed trucks, 73 tons of acetate resin, 2,000 kilowatts, and 576 man hours. The next day I may not need any of those. So if you are the acetate or electric company, you'll need to be as nimble as I am if we are to work together. We'll coordinate as a network, sharing information and control, decentralizing functions between us. It will be hard at times to tell who is working for whom.

Federal Express used to deliver key parts for IBM computers. Now they warehouse them too. By means of networks, Federal Express locates the just-finished part recently arrived in a FedEx warehouse from some remote overseas IBM supplier. When you order an item from an IBM catalog, FedEx brings it to you via their worldwide delivery service. An IBM employee may never touch the piece. So when the Federal Express man delivers the part to your door, who sent it, IBM or Federal Express? Schneider National, the first national trucking company to have all its trucks fully networked in real time by satellite, has some major customers who deposit their orders directly into Schneider's dispatching computers and who are billed by the same method. Who is in charge? Where does the company end and the supplier start?

Customers are being roped into the distributed company just as fast. Ubiquitous 800-numbers just about ring on the factory floor, as the feedback of users shape how and what the assembly line makes.

One can imagine the future shape of companies by stretching them until they are pure network. A company that was pure network would have the following traits: *distributed, decentralized, collaborative,* and *adaptive.*

Distributed. There is no single location for the business. It dwells among many places concurrently. The company might not even be headquartered in one place. Apple Computer, Inc., has numerous buildings spread thickly over two towns. Each one is a "headquarter" for a different function of the company. Even small businesses may be distributed within the same locality. Once networked, it hardly matters whether you are on the floor below, or across town.

Open Vision, based in Pleasanton, California, is an example of a rather ordinary, small software company, molded in the new pattern. "We are operating as a true distributed company," said CEO Michael Fields. Open Vision has clients and *employees* in most US cities, all served on computer networks, but "most of them don't even know where Pleasanton is," Fields told the *San Francisco Chronicle.*

Yet in this stretch toward ultimate networks, companies will not break down into a network of individuals working alone. The data collected so far, as well as my own experience, says that the natural resolution of a purely distributed company coalesces into teams of 8 to 12 people working in a space together. A very large global company in the pure network form could be viewed as a system of cells of a dozen people each, including minifactories manned by a dozen people, a "headquarters" staffed with a dozen, profit centers managed by eight and suppliers run by ten people.

Decentralized. How can any large-scale project ever get anything done with only ten people? For most of the industrial revolution, serious wealth was made by bringing processes under central control. Bigger was more efficient. The "robber barons" of yesteryear figured out that by controlling every vital and auxiliary aspect of their industry, they could make millions. Steel companies proceeded to control the ore deposits, mine their own coal, set up their own railways, make their own equipment, house their own workers, and strive for self-containment within the borders of a gigantic company. That worked magnificently when things moved slowly.

Now, when the economy shifts daily, owning the whole chain of production is a liability. It is efficient only while the last hours of its relevancy lasts. Once that moment of power recedes, control has to be traded in for speed and nimbleness. Peripheral functions, like supplying your own energy, are quickly passed on to another company.

Even supposedly essential functions are subcontracted out. For instance, Gallo Winery no longer grows the specialized grapes required for its wines; it farms that chore out to others and focuses on brewing and marketing. A car rental company subcontracts out the repair and maintenance of its fleet, and focuses on renting. One passenger airline subcontracted its cargo space on transcontinental flights (a vitally important profit center) to an independent freight company, figuring they would manage it better and earn the airline more than it could itself.

Detroit automobile manufacturers were once famous for doing everything themselves. Now they subcontract out about half of their functions, including the rather important job of building engines. General Motors even hired PPG Industries to handle the painting of auto bodies—a critical job in terms of sales—within GM's factories. In the business magazines this pervasive decentralization by means of subcontracting is called "outsourcing."

The coordination costs for large-scale outsourcing have been reduced to bearable amounts by electronic trading of massive amounts of technical and accounting information. In short, networks make outsourcing feasible, profitable, and competitive. The jobs one company passes off to another can be passed back several times until they rest upon the shoulders of a small, tightly knit group, who will complete the job with care and efficiency. That group will most likely be a separate company, or they may be an autonomous subsidiary.

Research shows that the transactional costs needed to maintain the quality of a task as it stretches across several companies *are* higher than if the job stayed within one company. However: (1) those costs are being lowered every day with network technology such as electronic data transfers (EDI) and video-conferencing, and (2) those costs are *already* lower in terms of the immense gains in adaptability—not having to manage jobs you no longer need, and being able to start jobs you will need—that centralized companies lack.

Extending outsourcing to its logical conclusion, a 100 percent networked company would consist solely of one office of professionals linked by network technology to other independent groups. Many invisible million-dollar businesses are being run from one office with two assistants. And some don't have an office at all. The large advertising firm of Chiat/Day is working on dismantling its physical headquarters. Project team members will rent hotel conference rooms for the duration of the project, working on portable computers and call-forwarding. They'll disband and regroup when the project is done. Some of those groups might be "owned" by the office; others would be separately controlled and financed.

Let's imagine the office of the future in a hypothetical Silicon Valley *automobile* manufacturer that I'll call Upstart Car, Inc. Upstart Car intends to compete with the big three Japanese automobile giants.

Here's Upstart's blueprint: A dozen people share a room in a sleek office building in Palo Alto, California. Some finance people, four engineers, a CEO, a coordinator, a lawyer, and a marketing guy. Across town in a former warehouse, crews assemble 120-mpg, nonpolluting cars made from poly-chain composite materials, ceramic engines, and electronic everything else. The hi-tech plastics come from a young company with whom Upstart has formed a joint venture. The engines are purchased in Singapore; other automobile parts arrive each day in bar-coded profusion from Mexico, Utah, and Detroit. The shipping companies deal with temporary storage of parts; only what is needed that day appears at the plant. Cars, each one customer-tailored, are ordered by a network of customers and shipped the minute they are done. Molds for the car's body are rapidly shaped by computer-guided lasers, and fed designs generated by customer response and targeted marketing. A flexible line of robots assemble the cars.

Robot repair and improvement is outsourced to a robot company. Acme Plant Maintenance Service keeps the factory sheds going. Phone reception is hired out to a small outfit physically located in San Mateo. The clerical work is handled by a national agency who services all the other groups in the company. Same with computer hardware. The marketing and legal guys each oversee (of course) the marketing and legal services which Upstart also hires out. Bookkeeping is pretty much entirely computerized, but an outside accounting firm, operating from remote terminals, tends to any accounting requests. In total about 100 workers are paid directly by Upstart, and they are organized into small groups with varying benefit plans and pay schedules. As Upstart's cars soar in popularity, it grows by helping its suppliers grow, negotiating alliances, and sometimes investing in their growth.

Pretty far out, huh? It's not so farfetched. Here's how a real pioneering Silicon Valley company was launched a decade ago. James Brian Quinn writes in the March-April 1990 *Harvard Business Review:*

> Apple bought microprocessors from Synertek, other chips from Hitachi, Texas Instruments, and Motorola, video monitors from Hitachi, power supplies from Astec, and printers from Tokyo Electric and Qume. Similarly, Apple kept its internal service activities and investments to a minimum by outsourcing application software development to Microsoft, promotion to Regis McKenna, product styling to Frogdesign, and distribution to ITT and ComputerLand.

Businesses aren't the only ones to tap the networked benefits of outsourcing. Municipalities and government agencies are rapidly following suit. As one example out of many, the city of Chicago hired EDS, the computer outsourcing company Ross Perot founded, to handle its public parking enforcement. EDS devised a system based on hand-held computers that print out tickets and link into a database of Chicago's 25,000 parking meters to increase fine collection. After EDS outsourced this service for the city, parking tickets that were paid off jumped from 10 percent to 47 percent, raising $60 million in badly needed income.

Collaborative. Networking internal jobs can make so much economic sense that sometimes vital functions are outsourced to competitors, to mutual benefit. Enterprises may be collaborators on one undertaking and competitors on another, at the same time.

Many major domestic airlines in the U.S. outsource their complex reservation and ticketing procedures to their competitor American Airlines. Both MasterCard and Visa credit card companies sometimes delegate their vital work of processing customer charges and transactions to arch-competitor American Express. "Strategic Alliances" is the buzz word for corporations in the 1990s. Everyone is looking for symbiotic partners, or even symbiotic competitors.

The borders between industries, between transportation, wholesaling, retailing, communications, marketing, public relations, manufacturing, warehousing all disappear into an indefinite web. Airlines run tours, sell junk by direct mail, arrange hotel reservations, while computer companies hardly even handle computer hardware.

It may get to the point that wholly autonomous companies become rare. The metaphor for corporations is shifting from the tightly coupled, tightly bounded organism to the loosely coupled, loosely bounded ecosystem. The metaphor of IBM as an organism needs overhauling. IBM is an ecosystem.

Adaptive. The shift from products to service is inevitable because automation keeps lowering the price of physical reproduction. The cost of copying a disk of software or a tape of music is a fraction of the cost of the product. And as things continue to get smaller, their cost of reproduction continues to shrink because less material is involved. The cost of manufacturing a capsule of drug is a fraction of the cost it sells for.

But in pharmaceutical, computer, and gradually all hi-tech industries, the cost of research, development, stylizing, licenses, patents, copyrights, marketing and customer support—the service component—are increasingly substantial. All are information and knowledge intensive.

Even a superior product is not enough to carry a company very long these days. Things churn so fast that innovative substitutions (wires built on light instead of electrons), reverse engineering, clones, third party add-ons that make a weak product boom, and quickly shifting standards (Sony lost badly on Beta VCRs but may yet prevail with 8-mm tapes) all conspire to bypass the usual routes to dominance. To make money in the new era, follow the flow of information.

A network is a factory for information. As the value of a product is increased by the amount of knowledge invested in it, the networks that engender the knowledge increase in value. A factory-made widget once followed a linear path from design to manufacturing and delivery. Now the biography of a flexibly processed widget becomes a net, distributed over many departments in many places simultaneously, and spilling out beyond the factory, so that it is difficult to say what happens first or where it happens.

The whole net happens at once. Marketing, design, manufacturing, suppliers, buyers are all involved in the creation of the successful product. Designing a product concurrently entails having marketing, legal, and engineering teams all design the product at once, instead of sequentially as in the past.

Retail products (cans of soda, socks) have communicated their movement at the cash register to the back office since the 1970s when the UPC bar code became popular in stores. However, in a full-bore network economy, the idea is to have these items communicate to the front office and customer as well by adding weak communication abilities. Manufacturing small items with active microchips instead of passive bar codes embedded into them means you now have hundreds of items with snail-minds sitting on a shelf in a discount store by the thousands. Why not turn them on? They are now smart packages. They can display their own prices, thank you, easily adjusting to sales. They can recalculate their prices if the store owner wants to sell them at a premium or if you the shopper are carrying a coupon or discount card of some sort. And a product would remember if you passed it over even after seeing the sale price, much to the interest of the store owner and manufacturer. At least you looked, boasts the product's ad agency. When shelf items acquire awareness of each other and themselves and interact with their consumers, they rapidly erupt into a different economy.

Despite my sunny forecast for the network economy, there is much about it that is worrisome. These are the same concerns that accompany other large, decentralized, self-making systems:

- You can't understand them.
- You have less control.
- They don't optimize well.

As companies become disembodied into some Barlowian cyberspace, they take on the character of software. Clean, massless, quick, useful, mobile, and interesting. But also complicated and probably full of bugs no one can find.

If the companies and products of the future become more like software of today, what does that promise? Televisions that crash? Cars that freeze up suddenly? Toasters that bomb?

Large software programs are about the most complex things humans can make right now. Microsoft's new operating system had 4 million lines of code. Naturally Bill Gates claims there will be no bugs in it after the 70,000 beta-test sites are done checking it.

Is it possible for us to manufacture extremely complex things without defects (or even with merely a few defects)? Will network economics help us to create complexity without any bugs, or just complexity with bugs?

Whether or not companies become more like software themselves, it is certain that more and more of what they make depends on more complex software, so the problems of creating complexity without defects becomes essential.

Journal Topic

1. As Kelly points out, extremely complex software has inherent instabilities. Are Americans becoming too dependent on computers and software? How about the world at large? What would be the consequences of a major software crash that affected the entire Internet or major government or financial system such as the stock market?

Question for Critical Thought

1. Kelly compares his first experience with connecting to the Internet to a "religious experience," and says that he realized that "the future of computers was not numbers but connections." What is your relationship to the Internet? How important is it to you in your personal life? In your school or professional life?

Suggestions for Personal Research

1. Kelly wrote the remarks we quoted in the question for critical thought before cell phone text messaging, BlackBerries, or the iPhone and other "smart phones" were developed. Research the development and evolution of personal communication devices like these and what their impact has been on the world.

2. Research how Internet connectivity has changed one or more aspects of the ways industries and companies do business in the past ten years. What trends emerge? What is the impact on employee satisfaction? What seems headed for obsolescence?

Vocabulary Terms

discombobulate

mystic

uncompromised

modular

collaborative

adaptive

ecosystem

Cyber-Bullying: Creating a Culture of Respect in a Cyber World

Susan Keith and Michelle Martin

Prereading Questions

1. Have you ever been bullied on or offline? How did it make you feel?
2. Have you ever bullied anyone on or offline? How did it make you feel? Did you think of the effects, both short term and long term, that this might have had on your targets?
3. What kinds of people are likely to bully others online? Are males or females more likely to be bullies?
4. How might online bullies be similar to or different from offline "real-world" bullies?

In the 1990s, many incidents revolved around student-on-student violence, usually involving guns. Schools implemented many programs to keep guns and gangs out of schools. In the 21st century, school violence is taking on a new and more insidious form. New technologies have made it easier for bullies to gain access to their victims. This form of bullying has become known as cyber-bullying. This article provides a window on this little known world and offers practical suggestions for dealing with this new challenge.

When we think about school violence, events like Columbine come to mind. Looking back at the incident, Andy Carvin for *The Digital Beat* reminds his readers that one of the killers, Eric Harris, had his own web site that contained "conspicuous threats against fellow students" (Carvin, 2000). It was brought to the attention of the police and led to both Harris and Klebold being questioned about the incident and was an early example of what is now called "cyber bullying."

Bill Belsey, a nationally recognized educator from Alberta, Canada, gives this definition:

> Cyber-bullying involves the use of information and communication technologies such as e-mail, cell phone and pager text messages, instant messaging (IM), defamatory personal Web sites, and defamatory online personal polling Web sites, to support deliberate, repeated, and hostile behavior by an individual or group, that is intended to harm others. (Belsey, 2004)

Cyber-bullying, while being similar in its intent to hurt others through power and control, is different due to the use of these new technologies. Nowadays, kids are always connected or wired, and communicate in ways that are often unknown by adults and away from their supervision. This can make it hard for parents and school administrators to both understand the nature of the problem and do something about it.

Several surveys have been taken to get a handle on the number of children across the country who have experienced cyber-bullying. It is estimated that 91% of kids 12 to 15 years old and almost all teens (99%) ages 16 to 18 use the Internet (UCLA Internet Report, 2003). Much of their time online is spent talking with other kids. i-SAFE America, an internet safety education foundation, conducted a nationwide survey of

1,566 students from grades four to eight to find out their experiences with bullying online (National i-Safe Survey, 2004).

The survey found:

- 57% of students said that someone had said hurtful or angry things to them online with 13% saying it happens "quite often"
- 53% of students admit saying mean or hurtful things to someone online and 7% admit to doing it "quite often"
- 35% of students have been threatened online with 5% saying it happens "quite often"
- 42% have been bullied online with 7% saying it happens "quite often"
- 20% have received mean or threatening e-mails
- 58% have not told their parents or another adult about their experiences online

Another survey conducted by the Crimes against Children Research Center at the University of New Hampshire (Wollack & Mitchell, 2000) found that along with sexual solicitations and approaches online (19% of children surveyed received unwanted sexual solicitation), six percent of the young people surveyed experienced harassing incidents, including threats, rumors, or other offensive behavior, and two percent reported episodes of distressing harassment that they described as making them feel very or extremely upset or afraid.

Most parents tend to think that this kind of bullying is uncommon and that their child would never do something this mean, Unfortunately not so, according to Alane Fagin, the executive director of Child Abuse Prevention Services (CAPS). On-line bullying has become very common and is particularly easy for girls to do. This is an example of relational aggression where girls use relationships as weapons. Imagine, she says, a group of girls sitting around a computer. The person being instant messaged thinks she is only talking to one person. Before she knows it, the "target" has said something negative about one of the group. The group then starts gossiping about her. "This leads to social isolation," says Fagin (cited in Wolfe, 2004).

In general, girls inflict virtual abuse more than boys through instant messaging, online conversations, and e-mails. A survey of girls ages 12 to 18 found that 74% of adolescent girls spend the majority of their time online in chat rooms or sending instant messages and e-mail (Migliore, 2003). Boys are more likely to make online threats and build websites targeting others. It can be much more difficult to identify bullies in cyberspace. Online screen names and e-mail addresses can hide a person's true identity. It is easier to bully someone you don't have to face. With no boundaries or tangible consequences, children are using technology to vent normal frustrations in ways that can become very destructive.

Traditionally, home was a place where a kid could go to escape his bully. With advances in technology, home is no longer a haven. Glenn Stutzky, a School Safety Violence Specialist at Michigan State University, said that today's bullies use technology to spread rumors and threats, making life miserable for their victims throughout the day and night. Today's kids have to deal with bullying in its newest forms: text messages, e-mail, websites, on-line voting booths, and blogs. They cannot escape their bully because he can now follow them home. This is the new reality.

In the past several years, parents have provided cell phones for their children in order to keep track of them and to keep them safe. The same cell phones that make parents feel more connected to their children have become tools of harassment. And the newest forms of cell phones include the ability to send text messages, pictures, and even live video. In the hands of bored teenagers, these additions can become weapons for bullies to spread rumors as well as pictures of unsuspecting kids in locker rooms. Stutzky provides examples of a middle school girl and a straight high school boy. The girl returned from vacation in Canada to find out that someone had spread rumors through text messages that she had contracted SARS. The boy was harassed by text messages implying he was gay. Stutzky states that "(children) are at a very vulnerable time in their development, and while these comments may seem silly to people who have matured, they are very devastating to the young people on the receiving end" (Wendland, 2003).

Websites can provide places where children can gain knowledge and communicate with others who share the same interests. This same benefit can also be used to do harm. Some children are now using Websites to mock, harass, and torment others. Bullies post slurs on Websites where kids congregate, or on personal on-line journals, called Web logs or Blogs. They can post pictures of students they don't like or create online voting booths. An example of the latter was set up by a group of Manhattan (New York) students who decided to create a Website to determine who was the biggest "ho" (Benfer, 2003). Called the Interschool Ho and posted on a free Website called freevote.com, this voting booth accumulated a list of 150 students along with their rank. It took a call by the Brooklyn district attorney to force freevote.com to shut down the site.

Alane Fagin (cited in Wolfe, 2004) also writes about Jay, who, along with some friends, created a "hit list" of kids from their middle school that they "just didn't like" and put it on the Internet. Jay describes a bunch of bored, 13-year-old kids who just started "fooling around." They wanted to change their image from being "clean-cut kids" to being "tough guys." On the site, he and his friends wrote about wanting to "weed out the people we didn't like. Anybody that we didn't hang out with was on the list. We titled it 'People We're Gonna Whack.'" When other students started visiting the site, one of the people on the list brought it to the attention of the principal. Initially, Jay and his friends only received a verbal reprimand by the school. Because their names were on the site, though, a parent brought it to the attention of the police. After four months, the police filed no charges. The consequence for the boys was the loss of trust from their parents, teachers, and peers.

An extreme case of Website bullying took place in Dallas (Benfer, 2003). A sophomore at a local high school was harassed about her weight. She was called a "fat cow MOO BITCH" on the school's message boards. Besides making fun of her weight, the anonymous writer also made fun of the fact that she suffered from multiple sclerosis, saying, "I guess I'll have to wait until you kill yourself which I hope is not long from now, or I'll have to wait until your disease [MS] kills you." This bullying escalated to action, with the student getting her car egged and a bottle of acid thrown at her front door, resulting in injury for her mother.

Part of the problem in combating cyber-bullying, say experts, is that parents and kids relate to technology very differently. Most adults approach computers as practical tools, while for kids the Internet is a lifeline to their peer group. "Cyber-bullying is practically subterranean because it lives in the world of young people," says Belsey

(2004). "Kids know there is a gap in the understanding of technology between themselves and their parents, and their fear is not only that the parents' response may make the bullying worse, but that the adults will take the technology away."

So what are some signs that your child or student is being cyber-bullied? The Australian Government (2004) lists the following signs as things to look for:

- Spending a lot of time on the computer;
- Having trouble sleeping or having nightmares;
- Feeling depressed or crying without reason;
- Mood swings;
- Feeling unwell;
- Becoming anti-social; and
- Falling behind in homework.

It is a fascinating time in history. Children have opportunities for learning that previously seemed like science fiction. Schools, parents and children gain much from these advances in technology, but at the same time, they create unique challenges. The primary thing that adults need to do is to be more knowledgeable regarding the use of current technology and the ways and means that children are using them. Many parents and teachers, who were not raised in a cyber world, do not feel comfortable with the tools children are using. By guiding children to use the technology in ways that promote respect, understanding, and responsibility, we can lessen the impact of this new form of bullying. (See below)

WHAT YOU CAN DO

Tips for Children

- Never share or give out personal information, PIN numbers, phone numbers, etc.
- Tell a trusted adult.
- Do not read messages by cyber bullies.
- Do not delete messages; they can be used to take action.
- Bullying through instant messaging and chat rooms can often be blocked.
- Do not open a message from someone you don't know.
- Do not reply to the person bullying or harassing you.

Tips for Parents

- Pay attention! Know how and when your children are using the Internet.
- Become more tech savvy.
- Install blocking or filtering software.
- Encourage your child to talk to you if they are being bullied.
- Limit your child's time using the Internet.
- Develop a family online agreement including:

(Continued)

Where kids can go online and what they can do there

How much time they can spend on the Internet

What to do if anything makes them uncomfortable

How to protect their personal information, stay safe in interactive environments and behave ethically and responsibly online.

Tips for Schools

- Develop school policies for acceptable Internet and cell phone use. Enforce them.
- Zero tolerance for bullying in any form.
- Ensure that children and young people are aware that all bullying concerns will be dealt with sensitively and effectively.
- Ensure that parents/guardians expressing bullying concerns have them taken seriously.

REFERENCES

Australian Government. (2004). *What are the signs that a child is being cyber bullied?* Retrieved August 1, 2004, from NetAlert Limited Web site: http://www.netalert.net .au/01154-What-are-the-signs-that-a-child-is-being-cyber-bullied.asp?qid=4047

Belsey, Bill. (2004). *Cyberbullying.ca.* Retrieved July 31, 2004, from Web site: www.cyberbullying.ca

Benfer, A. (2003, July 3). *Cyber slammed: Kids are getting arrested for raunchy online bullying. It's definitely offensive, but is it against the law?* Retrieved July 23, 2004, from Salon.com Web site: http://dir.salon.com/mwt/feature/ 2001/07/03/cyber_bullies/index.html?sid=1039555

Carvin, A. (2000, April 20). Student free speech rights on the Internet and the ghosts of Columbine. *The Digital Beat,* Vol. 2, No. 29. Retrieved July 31, 2004, from http://www.benton.org/publibrary/digitalbeat/db042000.html.

Migliore, D. (2003, March 18). *Bullies torment victims with technology.* Retrieved July 20, 2004, from http://www.azprevention.org/In_The_News/Newsletters/ Newsletters_March_2003_B.jsp

National i-SAFE Survey. (2004, June 28). *National i-SAFE survey finds over half of students are being harassed online.* Retrieved July 21, 2004, from www.isafe.org

UCLA Internet Report. (2003, February). *UCLA internet report: Surveying the digital future—year three.* Retrieved July 23, 2004, from http://www.polarityinc .com/Content/UCLA-Internet-Report-Year-Three.pdf

Wendland, M. (2003, November 17). Cyber-bullies make it tough for kids to leave playground. *Detroit Free Press.* Retrieved July 21, 2004, from http://www.freep .com/money/tech/mwend17_20031117.htm

Wolfe, M. (2004). *Cyber brats: Bullies who taunt their peers with the click of a mouse.* Retrieved July 20, 2004, from Long Island Parenting News Web site: http://longisland.parenthood.com/Articles.html?article_id=4334&segid=140

Wollack, J., & Mitchell, K. (2008, June). *Youth internet safety survey.* University of New Hampshire, Crimes against Children Research Center. Retrieved July 20, 2004, from www.unh.edu/ccrc/projects/internet_survey.html

Journal Topic

1. The stereotypical schoolyard bully is a boy, but the article indicates that cyber-bullying "through instant messaging, online conversations, and e-mails" is committed more often by girls than boys. Is this surprising to you? Why or why not?

Questions for Critical Thought

1. The article demonstrates that bullying is a lot easier on the Internet than it is off line because so much technology exists to support it and because bullies can be anonymous if they want. Could the very easiness of this kind of bullying be encouraging far more children to do it who might never have considered bullying anyone face-to-face, or does it simply make bullying easier for children who already have the tendency?

2. In what ways can parents protect their children from the damaging emotional effects of bullying without invading their privacy or restricting their freedom?

Suggestions for Personal Research

1. Does engaging in bullying of any kind carry over from childhood and adolescence into adulthood? Are young people who bully more likely to grow up to be mean, abusive adults? Research to see if studies show correlations.

2. Research the effects of being bullied in childhood and adolescence on adult mental health and self-esteem.

3. Research the efficacy of antibullying programs.

4. Research what makes people become bullies.

Multicultural Issues

1. Does the prevalence of bullying differ across cultures, subcultures, and nations? How might some cultures award compassion and empathy and others emphasize aggression and dominance? How does gender figure in this? Do some cultures encourage males to enhance their status by being bullies? Are there different rewards for female bullies?

Vocabulary Terms

implement	insidious
conspicuous	multiple sclerosis
defamatory	

YouTube: The Evolution of Media?

Christian Christensen

Prereading Questions

1. How often do you go to sites like YouTube? What do you look for?
2. Have you ever posted videos of yourself on the Web? How do you feel about hundreds, maybe thousands, of perfect strangers looking at you and making judgments about you?

In April 2006, a little-known U.S. comedian and motivational speaker, Judson Laipply, posted a six-minute video clip entitled 'The Evolution of Dance' on the YouTube website.[1] The clip shows a part of Laipply's performance in which he condenses fifty years of modern dance into a few minutes. Within a matter of months, the clip became an internet phenomenon, with individuals sending the link through blogs, chat rooms and email. As of February 2007, only ten months after the initial posting, the clip has been viewed over 42 million times, making it by far the most viewed item on YouTube.

YouTube.com, a 'video sharing' website, was the brainchild of three former employees (Chad Hurley, Steve Chen and Jawed Karim) of the PayPal online commerce company. Other websites that are classified as 'video sharing' include Google Video, MySpace and Revver. The YouTube.com domain name was activated in February 2005, and the first video to be uploaded onto the site was posted on 23 April 2005 by YouTube co-founder Jawed Karim.[2] The site was fully operational just before the end of 2005, and, within a matter of months, had become one of the fastest-growing websites in the world. To illustrate the point, by the summer of 2006 (just six months after launch of the site) 60–100 million clips were being viewed daily on YouTube, with 65,000 videos being uploaded onto the site every twenty-four hours.[3]

As of February 2007, YouTube.com is the fifth most-visited website in the world, behind only giants Yahoo.com, msn.com, Google.com and Baidu.com.[4] In November 2006, YouTube.com was purchased by Google for US$1.65 billion, netting founders Hurley (US$345 million), Chen (US$326 million) and Karim (US$64 million) enormous financial windfalls.

Judson Laipply's extraordinary rise to internet fame is an illustration—albeit a unique one—of the ways in which sites such as YouTube have created outlets for millions of non-professionals to distribute material that, only ten years ago, would most likely have not seen the light of day. As always, however, it is crucial that media students and scholars not fall into the trap of romanticizing 'new' technologies simply because they are new. Talk of 'technological revolutions' can be overblown, especially when we fail to address the fact that much of what we read, hear or see via the 'new media' are simply 'old media' products (such as films, music, newspapers and magazines) that have been re-packaged and re-distributed. With this idea in mind, I would like to address some important social, artistic and legal issues raised by the YouTube internet phenomenon, and ask if video-sharing sites such as YouTube and Google Video have fundamentally changed the media world.

Production, Distribution, Exhibition

I would like to begin with what I consider to be the most interesting aspect of the evolution of YouTube: the impact the site has had on re-adjusting our understanding of how media production, distribution and exhibition (discussed below) can work. Although I use the term 'our understanding' of media, it is worth pointing out that, as someone born in 1969, my perspectives on so-called 'new media' such as the Internet and mobile phones are undoubtedly different from those of people born, for example, in 1989 or 1999. I was brought up in a household with no computers, internet, mobile phones, digital video recorders, DVD players or VCRs, and so my relationship to digital technology is very much shaped by the fact that I have seen, in my relatively short lifetime, some rather large changes in the types of media people have access to, and how they might 'use' them.

While the issue of age and perspective is important to bear in mind, video sites such as YouTube and Google Video have forced us to re-think a number of fundamental assumptions about not only who can produce media material, but also who can distribute this material to a wider audience, and how that audience will be able to watch/listen/read it. This is what I mean when I write about media production, distribution and exhibition. While there is nothing new in 'regular' people producing media content—from making home videos and audio recordings, to writing poetry or books, to simply playing the piano—what the Internet and sites such as YouTube and Google Video have done is to open up huge new possibilities for these same 'regular' people to take their content and distribute it to a much wider audience. As media scholar David Croteau puts it:

> . . . the Internet is a different animal from other media. While 'independent,' 'alternative', and 'DIY' media have long existed in many forms, one key to the Internet's unique significance is that it provides the infrastructure necessary to facilitate the distribution of all forms of self-produced media to a potentially far-flung audience. Linked together via the Internet, scattered individuals and small groups with common interests can add up to a sizeable audience for self-produced media . . . Not only will users go deep into the catalog of existing commercial media providers, they will increasingly produce their own media products.[5]

The YouTube motto ('Broadcast Yourself') is indicative of the idea that the system is designed to allow members of the general public to engage in an activity ('broadcasting') that was traditionally the domain of large, powerful media corporations. The importance of distribution in the media process is often overlooked, yet it is perhaps almost as important as the actual media product itself. Consider the example of a hypothetical young film student shooting a film on her digital film camera. The work is truly original in every way: great script, great acting and great directing. It is a masterpiece. However, without *distribution*—getting the film from the producer out to movie theaters, television, DVD stores—the film will remain a hidden piece of art, never to be seen. The filmmaker needs to get her film out . . . but how? Traditionally, films have had to be picked up by distributors, who then had to find exhibitors (film theatres) willing to screen the film. This is a costly process, and particularly difficult when the filmmaker in question is an unknown with no track record. What YouTube and other video-sharing websites do is eliminate the need for attracting the interest of the narrow number of distribution companies from the media mix and allow media producers to self-distribute by simply uploading their films straight onto the web.

Copyright Who?

While allowing people to upload material on their own, and without oversight, could be seen as a more 'democratic' system of media distribution, it is also the case that a portion of the videos posted to sharing sites such as YouTube, Google Video and Revver infringe on copyright rules and regulations. With a global form of communication such as the Internet, a number of incredibly complex questions arise when considering questions of possible copyright infringement. For example, if a person in Argentina posts a video clip of a television program from Singapore on the US-based YouTube system, who has legal jurisdiction? Is the person who posted the video legally responsible? The owners of the website?

YouTube management claim that they follow the Digital Millennium Compliance Act: a particularly interesting piece of American legislation protecting not only copyright holders from technology that makes pirating easier, but that also protects Internet service providers from liability should their users be found guilty of copyright violation.[6] Basically, because YouTube cannot pre-screen the thousands of videos posted every day, they simply post a warning to users that the uploading of copyrighted material is a violation of law, thus leaving the responsibility for posting to the user.[7] Groups or individuals who feel that there has been a copyright violation or an unauthorized use of private video or audio material must notify YouTube before the material will be removed from the site.[8] Once YouTube obtains the request, and if they feel it has merit, only then will the material be removed.

The system, of course, is far from foolproof. YouTube has been accused by critics of being very slow in taking down certain material from their website. In addition, once illegal material is removed, if it is then re-posted by another user, those who consider their rights to have been violated must re-submit a request for removal. In other words, there must be one request for removal for every illegal video posted, making it virtually impossible for owners of popular material to stop unauthorized use.[9]

A particularly interesting case illustrating the complexities surrounding copyright violation involved the internationally popular US programs 24 and The Simpsons (copyright holder: News Corporation). In January of 2007, News Corp filed a subpoena in a U.S. court demanding that the identity of a YouTube user known only as 'ECOtotal' be revealed after the individual had illegally uploaded four episodes of 24 and twelve episodes of The Simpsons to the YouTube site. The videos were removed, but the name of the uploader was not immediately released.[10] In early February 2007, however, YouTube complied with the court order, and supplied the name of the individual, who, at the time of writing this article, faces the possibility of prosecution.

Internet Fame?

Of course, it is not only the already famous (such as Kiefer Sutherland from 24) who see themselves on the small YouTube screen. Nor are the majority of videos uploaded to the site violations of copyright. As noted earlier, the YouTube motto ('Broadcast Yourself') speaks to the real reason why the site has become such a phenomenon: it gives non-famous, non-wealthy, non-professional (and, in many cases, it would seem, non-talented) individuals the opportunity to distribute their own material to a waiting world.

YouTube has spawned a number of Internet celebrities, also known as 'viral video stars.' One of the most famous examples of online celebrity is that of 'lonely-girl15': a teenage video blogger (or 'vlogger') called Bree whose video clips about the problems and anguish of teenage life (under the channel 'lonelygirl15') attracted a collective total of over 37 million views on YouTube, making 'lonelygirl15' the fifth most viewed YouTube channel.[11] Lonelygirl15 seemed to capture the true spirit of YouTube: a young girl, with no media training, attracts millions of viewers with simple reflections on her daily life. All she needed was a digital webcam and an Internet connection. This story, while fascinating and amazing, was also a lie. It was revealed in late 2006 that the 'lonelygirl15' character was the creation of two Californian filmmakers, and that the character of Bree/lonelygirl was played by New Zealand-born actress Jessica Rose. Such was the popularity of the lonelygirl15 character that *Forbes* magazine ranked actress Jessica Rose the number one Internet star in their 'Web Celeb 25'.[12] The 'outing' of Rose as a fraud has done nothing to hurt the popularity of the lonelygirl15 character, and, in fact, Rose has landed a role in a film starring the US actress Lindsay Lohan.

The question that arises from the case of Jessica Rose (before her 'outing'), as well as that of Judson Laipply and his 'Evolution of Dance', is this: Has YouTube changed our conception of celebrity? Previously, the argument could be made that stardom was connected to a sense of distance from the audience: the film star on the big screen, the television actor, or the rock singer on stage in front of thousands of screaming fans. Distance, not in the sense of physical space (rock fans could be only a few metres away from the stage), but in the sense that these famous individuals were connected to a professional or artistic world beyond the reach of 'ordinary' people. Granted lonelygirl15 proved to be a fake, but many of the 'Most Viewed' videos on the YouTube website were shot and uploaded by ordinary members of the public, with content sometimes nothing more than a few minutes of a laughing baby in Sweden (viewed 10 million times),[13] or teenagers-lip-synching 'Hey' by the Pixies (13 million times).[14]

While we could say that YouTube is a far more 'democratic' system of media distribution than 'traditional' film or television, it should not be forgotten that, with 65,000 video uploads per day, YouTube is hardly likely to be the answer for struggling filmmakers, comedians, dancers, TV producers and actors. For every Judson Laipply and his 'Evolution of Dance', there are millions of individuals who have posted their materials, only to be drowned in a tidal wave of competition.

YouTube: New Media, Old Issues?

Despite the challenges, better understanding of the emerging crop of self-produced media offers interesting possibilities. It could provide a unique glimpse into an increasingly diverse society and an interconnected world. It could suggest new models for traditional media to adopt to facilitate civic engagement and participation. It could reveal a refreshingly broad range of self-expression and creativity, independent of market imperatives. It could—but then again it may not; we simply do not know until we study and better understand the new world of self-produced media. Some of the oldest questions in the field will continue to animate future media studies: Who owns and controls production *and* distribution? How is production structured? Who is creating content? What is being produced? Who is consuming? To what effect?[15]

—David Croteau

This quote is a good way to both conclude this piece and to consider how YouTube, along with other video-sharing sites, might change the way we look and think about media. There can be no doubt that YouTube challenges a number of basic ideas that have existed about the nature of the media business: as it being expensive, run by professionals, and usually outside of the control of 'ordinary citizens. Similarly, such sites open a number of doors for democratic participation, both in terms of entertainment production and political communication. Finally, YouTube allows for forms of expression to be distributed that might not otherwise be available to a broader audience. Some of these expressions might challenge certain notions of 'taste' or 'quality', but mainstream media, due to their need for advertising revenue, tend to favour entertainment that does not 'offend' or 'upset' (politically, socially, or otherwise) the general population.

While the benefits of YouTube are apparent, as noted at the start of this piece, we should be wary of over-celebrating a form of communication before we grasp fully how it works, who uses it, and how it might impact broader society (see the questions posed in the quote above). If the YouTube phenomenon spawns little more than millions of people watching laughing babies, vomiting teenagers or comedy dance routines, for example, we might well ask where to find the social benefit in such a development. There is evidence, however, that YouTube could become more than that. YouTube has started out as a fascinating example of how new technology can alter our conceptions about what media is, and can be. This, however, should not change the important questions—about ownership, control, financing and audiences—we ask about this new media kid.

ENDNOTES

1. http://www.youtube.com/watch?v=BlelWkK0t4s

2. http://www.youtube.com/watch?v=JNQXAC9IVRw

3. http://www.youtube.com/t/about; http://en.wikipedia.org/wiki/YouTube

4. Baidu.com is a Chinese-language search engine. For latest internet rankings, see: http://www.alexa.com/

5. David Croteau, 'The Growth of Self-Produced Media Content and the Challenge to Media Studies', *Critical Studies in Media Communication,* Vol. 23, No. 4, October 2006, pp. 340–344.

6. For the full text of the act, see: http://thomas.loc.gov/cgi-bin/query/z?c105; H.R.2281:

7. http://www.youtube.com/t/privacy

8. http://www.youtube.com/t/dmca_policy

9. http: //www.businessweek.com/magazine/content/06_32/b3996051.htm

10. http://www.businessweek.com/technology/content/jan2007/tc20070126_817521. htm

11. http://www.youtube.com/profile?user=lonelygirl15

12. http://www.forbes.com/2007/01/23/internet-fame-celebrity-tech-media-cx_de_ 06webceleb_0123land.html?partner=links

13. http://www.youtube.com/watch?v=5P6UU6m3cqk

14. http://www.youtube.com/watch?v=_CSo1gOd48

15. David Croteau, 'The Growth of Self-Produced Media Content and the Challenge to Media Studies', *Critical Studies in Media Communication,* Vol. 23, No. 4, October 2006, pp. 340–344.

Journal Topics

1. Some people who have posted videos of themselves on YouTube have come to deeply regret it. Even if they remove their own clips, others have copied them and disseminated them even more widely, such as people who posted résumés that they thought made them look impressive that actually made them famous laughingstocks. If you ever posted a video of yourself, did it occur to you that it could leave your control and have future ramifications?

2. If you have never looked at clips on YouTube or similar sites, visit, watch some clips, and record your impressions.

Questions for Critical Thought

1. Do you think that the ability to widely disseminate self-produced media will add to a greater understanding of and appreciation of diversity, as well as making the world more interconnected? Or will the glut of such media lead people to look at relatively narrow "niche" outlets?

2. Mainstream media, as the author points out, need to generate advertising revenue, so they tend to provide entertainment that won't be deemed offensive or upsetting—at least not to significant numbers of the population. Could edgier media disseminated through YouTube and similar sites, if they prove popular enough, encourage producers of mainstream entertainment programs to become more adventurous? Could such media even provoke a shift in what we consider "offensive"? Could it provoke a backlash?

Suggestions for Personal Research

1. Christensen wrote, "If the YouTube phenomenon spawns little more than millions of people watching laughing babies, vomiting teenagers or comedy dance routines . . . we might as well ask where to find the social benefit in such a development. There is evidence, however, that YouTube could become more than that." Christensen's article was published in April 2007. Three

months later, presidential candidates from both parties participated in debates where the questions came not from reporters, as was typical, but from YouTube videos. Do some research on the effectiveness of this and other political uses of YouTube and similar sites and how effective such activity is.

2. A number of companies are very unhappy about the copyright infringement that occurs when users post clips on the Net from TV shows or movies that the companies own—and in some cases, entire episodes or movies. Sites like YouTube assert no legal responsibility, saying that they are covered because they will, if requested, take clips off of individual sites—even though someone else may post the same clips later. Research copyright law and the legal arguments that are being made today on both sides of the issue. Try to make a prediction about how this issue will be resolved—or whether it will be resolved.

Multicultural Issues

1. YouTube and similar sites give us a chance to look at "home-made" media from around the world if we choose. But how interested are people in such explorations? Language issues certainly can pose a barrier. But what about images? Are there more similarities than differences?

Vocabulary Terms

facilitate	copyright
hypothetical	civic

The Amorality of Web 2.0

Nicholas Carr

Prereading Questions

1. How often do you use Wikipedia or other Internet sites to find information? Do you trust the information you find? Have you ever wondered who puts it there and whether it is regulated?

2. When you need to look up information, how do you rank order the following factors? Speed, ease of access, depth and detail of coverage, accuracy, and price.

From the start, the World Wide Web has been a vessel of quasi-religious longing. And why not? For those seeking to transcend the physical world, the Web presents a ready-made Promised Land. On the Internet, we're all bodiless, symbols speaking to symbols in symbols. The early texts of Web metaphysics, many written by thinkers associated with or influenced by the post-60s New Age movement, are rich with a sense of impending spiritual release; they describe the passage into the cyber world as a process of personal and communal unshackling, a journey that frees us from traditional constraints on our intelligence, our communities, our meager physical selves. We become free-floating netizens in a more enlightened, almost angelic, realm.

But as the Web matured during the late 1990s, the dreams of a digital awakening went unfulfilled. The Net turned out to be more about commerce than consciousness, more a mall than a commune. And when the new millennium arrived, it brought not a new age but a dispiritingly commonplace popping of a bubble of earthly greed. Somewhere along the way, the moneychangers had taken over the temple. The Internet had transformed many things, but it had not transformed us. We were the same as ever.

The New New Age

But the yearning for a higher consciousness didn't burst with the bubble. Web 1.0 may have turned out to be spiritual vaporware, but now we have the hyper-hyped upgrade: Web 2.0. In a profile of Internet savant Tim O'Reilly in the current issue of *Wired,* Steven Levy writes that "the idea of collective consciousness is becoming manifest in the Internet." He quotes O'Reilly: "The Internet today is so much an echo of what we were talking about at [New Age HQ] Esalen in the '70s— except we didn't know it would be technology-mediated." Levy then asks, "Could it be that the Internet—or what O'Reilly calls Web 2.0—is really the successor to the human potential movement?"

Levy's article appears in the afterglow of Kevin Kelly's sweeping "We Are the Web" in *Wired*'s August issue. Kelly, erstwhile prophet of the Long Boom, surveys the development of the World Wide Web, from the Netscape IPO ten years ago, and concludes that it has become a "magic window" that provides a "spookily godlike" perspective on existence. "I doubt angels have a better view of humanity," he writes.

But that's only the beginning. In the future, according to Kelly, the Web will grant us not only the vision of gods but also their power. The Web is becoming "the OS for a megacomputer that encompasses the Internet, all its services, all peripheral chips and affiliated devices from scanners to satellites, and the billions of human minds entangled in this global network. This gargantuan Machine already exists in a primitive form. In the coming decade, it will evolve into an integral extension not only of our senses and bodies but our minds. . . . We will live inside this thing."

The revelation continues:

There is only one time in the history of each planet when its inhabitants first wire up its innumerable parts to make one large Machine. Later that Machine may run faster, but there is only one time when it is born.

You and I are alive at this moment.

We should marvel, but people alive at such times usually don't. Every few centuries, the steady march of change meets a discontinuity, and history hinges on that moment. We look back on those pivotal eras and wonder what it would have been like to be alive then. Confucius, Zoroaster, Buddha, and the latter Jewish patriarchs lived in the same historical era, an inflection point known as the axial age of religion.

Few world religions were born after this time. Similarly, the great personalities converging upon the American Revolution and the geniuses who commingled during the invention of modern science in the 17th century mark additional axial phases in the short history of our civilization.

Three thousand years from now, when keen minds review the past, I believe that our ancient time, here at the cusp of the third millennium, will be seen as another such era. In the years roughly coincidental with the Netscape IPO, humans began animating inert objects with tiny slivers of intelligence, connecting them into a global field, and linking their own minds into a single thing. This will be recognized as the largest, most complex, and most surprising event on the planet. Weaving nerves out of glass and radio waves, our species began wiring up all regions, all processes, all facts and notions into a grand network. From this embryonic neural net was born a collaborative interface for our civilization, a sensing, cognitive device with power that exceeded any previous invention. The Machine provided a new way of thinking (perfect search, total recall) and a new mind for an old species. It was the Beginning.

This isn't the language of exposition. It's the language of rapture.

The Cult of the Amateur

Now, lest you dismiss me as a mere cynic, if not a fallen angel, let me make clear that I'm all for seeking transcendence, whether it's by going to church or living in a hut in the woods or sitting at the feet of the Maharishi or gazing into the glittering pixels of an LCD screen. One gathers one's manna where one finds it. And if there's a higher consciousness to be found, then by all means let's get elevated. My problem is this: When we view the Web in religious terms, when we imbue it with our personal yearning for transcendence, we can no longer see it objectively. By necessity, we have to look at the Internet as a moral force, not as a simple collection of inanimate hardware and software. No decent person wants to worship an amoral conglomeration of technology.

And so all the things that Web 2.0 represents—participation, collectivism, virtual communities, amateurism—become unarguably good things, things to be nurtured and applauded, emblems of progress toward a more enlightened state. But is it really so? Is there a counterargument to be made? Might, on balance, the practical effect of Web 2.0 on society and culture be bad, not good? To see Web 2.0 as a moral force is to turn a deaf ear to such questions.

Let me bring the discussion down to a brass tack. If you read anything about Web 2.0, you'll inevitably find praise heaped upon Wikipedia as a glorious manifestation of "the age of participation." Wikipedia is an open-source encyclopedia; anyone who wants to contribute can add an entry or edit an existing one. O'Reilly, in a new essay on Web 2.0, says that Wikipedia marks "a profound change in the dynamics of content creation"—a leap beyond the Web 1.0 model of Britannica Online. To Kevin Kelly, Wikipedia shows how the Web is allowing us to pool our individual brains into a great collective mind. It's a harbinger of the Machine.

In theory, Wikipedia is a beautiful thing—it has to be a beautiful thing if the Web is leading us to a higher consciousness. In reality, though, Wikipedia isn't very good at all. Certainly, it's useful—I regularly consult it to get a quick gloss on a subject. But at a factual level it's unreliable, and the writing is often appalling. I wouldn't depend on it as a source, and I certainly wouldn't recommend it to a student writing a research paper.

Take, for instance, this section from Wikipedia's biography of Bill Gates, excerpted verbatim:

> Gates married Melinda French on January 1, 1994. They have three children, Jennifer Katharine Gates (born April 26, 1996), Rory John Gates (born May 23, 1999) and Phoebe Adele Gates (born September 14, 2002).
>
> In 1994, Gates acquired the Codex Leicester, a collection of writings by Leonardo da Vinci; as of 2003 it was on display at the Seattle Art Museum.
>
> In 1997, Gates was the victim of a bizarre extortion plot by Chicago resident Adam Quinn Pletcher. Gates testified at the subsequent trial. Pletcher was convicted and sentenced in July 1998 to six years in prison. In February 1998 Gates was attacked by Noël Godin with a cream pie. In July 2005, he solicited the services of famed lawyer Hesham Foda.
>
> According to Forbes, Gates contributed money to the 2004 presidential campaign of George W. Bush. According to the Center for Responsive Politics, Gates is cited as having contributed at least $33,335 to over 50 political campaigns during the 2004 election cycle.

Excuse me for stating the obvious, but this is garbage, an incoherent hodge-podge of dubious factoids (who the heck is "famed lawyer Hesham Foda"?) that adds up to something far less than the sum of its parts.

Here's Wikipedia on Jane Fonda's life, again excerpted verbatim:

> Her nickname as a youth—Lady Jane—was one she reportedly disliked. She traveled to Communist Russia in 1964 and was impressed by the people, who welcomed her warmly as Henry's daughter. In the mid-1960s she bought a farm outside of Paris, had it renovated and personally started a garden. She visited Andy Warhol's Factory in 1966.

> About her 1971 Oscar win, her father Henry said: "How in hell would you like to have been in this business as long as I and have one of your kids win an Oscar before you do?" Jane was on the cover of Life magazine, March 29, 1968.
>
> While early she had grown both distant from and critical of her father for much of her young life, in 1980, she bought the play "On Golden Pond" for the purpose of acting alongside her father—hoping he might win the Oscar that had eluded him throughout his career. He won, and when she accepted the Oscar on his behalf, she said it was "the happiest night of my life." Director and first husband Roger Vadim once said about her: "Living with Jane was difficult in the beginning . . . she had so many, how do you say, 'bachelor habits.' Too much organization. Time is her enemy. She cannot relax. Always there is something to do." Vadim also said, "There is also in Jane a basic wish to carry things to the limit."

This is worse than bad, and it is, unfortunately, representative of the slipshod quality of much of Wikipedia. Remember, this emanation of collective intelligence is not just a couple of months old. It's been around for nearly five years and has been worked over by many thousands of diligent contributors. At this point, it seems fair to ask exactly when the intelligence in "collective intelligence" will begin to manifest itself. When will the great Wikipedia get good? Or is "good" an old-fashioned concept that doesn't apply to emergent phenomena like communal on-line encyclopedias?

The promoters of Web 2.0 venerate the amateur and distrust the professional. We see it in their unalloyed praise of Wikipedia, and we see it in their worship of open-source software and myriad other examples of democratic creativity. Perhaps nowhere, though, is their love of amateurism so apparent as in their promotion of blogging as an alternative to what they call "the mainstream media." Here's O'Reilly: "While mainstream media may see individual blogs as competitors, what is really unnerving is that the competition is with the blogosphere as a whole. This is not just a competition between sites, but a competition between business models. The world of Web 2.0 is also the world of what Dan Gillmor calls 'we, the media,' a world in which 'the former audience,' not a few people in a back room, decides what's important."

I'm all for blogs and blogging. (I'm writing this, ain't I?) But I'm not blind to the limitations and the flaws of the blogosphere—its superficiality, its emphasis on opinion over reporting, its echolalia, its tendency to reinforce rather than challenge ideological extremism and segregation. Now, all the same criticisms can (and should) be hurled at segments of the mainstream media. And yet, at its best, the mainstream media is able to do things that are different from—and, yes, more important than—what bloggers can do. Those despised "people in a back room" can fund in-depth reporting and research. They can underwrite projects that can take months or years to reach fruition—or that may fail altogether. They can hire and pay talented people who would not be able to survive as sole proprietors on the Internet. They can employ editors and proofreaders and other unsung protectors of quality work. They can place, with equal weight, opposing ideologies on the same page. Forced to choose between reading blogs and subscribing to, say, the *New York Times,* the *Financial Times,* the *Atlantic,* and the *Economist,* I will choose the latter. I will take the professionals over the amateurs.

But I don't want to be forced to make that choice.

Scary Economics

And so, having gone on for so long, I at long last come to my point. The Internet is changing the economics of creative work—or, to put it more broadly, the economics of culture—and it's doing it in a way that may well restrict rather than expand our choices. Wikipedia might be a pale shadow of the Britannica, but because it's created by amateurs rather than professionals, it's free. And free trumps quality all the time. So what happens to those poor saps who write encyclopedias for a living? They wither and die. The same thing happens when blogs and other free on-line content go up against old-fashioned newspapers and magazines. Of course the mainstream media sees the blogosphere as a competitor. It is a competitor. And, given the economics of the competition, it may well turn out to be a superior competitor. The layoffs we've recently seen at major newspapers may just be the beginning, and those layoffs should be cause not for self-satisfied snickering but for despair. Implicit in the ecstatic visions of Web 2.0 is the hegemony of the amateur. I for one can't imagine anything more frightening.

In "We Are the Web," Kelly writes that "because of the ease of creation and dissemination, online culture is the culture." I hope he's wrong, but I fear he's right—or will come to be right.

Like it or not, Web 2.0, like Web 1.0, is amoral. It's a set of technologies—a machine, not a Machine—that alters the forms and economics of production and consumption. It doesn't care whether its consequences are good or bad. It doesn't care whether it brings us to a higher consciousness or a lower one. It doesn't care whether it burnishes our culture or dulls it. It doesn't care whether it leads us into a golden age or a dark one. So let's can the millennialist rhetoric and see the thing for what it is, not what we wish it would be.

Journal Topic

1. Wikipedia, one of the most famous and used reference sites on the Web, has been found to be inaccurate in some instances. How important is the accuracy of information on the Net? Is the speed and ease worth maybe getting some details here and there wrong?

Questions for Critical Thought

1. What does "Web 2.0?" refer to? What does Carr mean when he writes, "From the start, the World Wide Web has been a vessel of quasi-religious longing." What point is he making? Can you think of examples to support his assertion?

2. Carr says Wikipedia can be useful, "But at a factual level it's unreliable, and the writing is often appalling. I wouldn't depend on it as a source, and I certainly wouldn't recommend it to a student writing a research paper." Should we judge Wikipedia as a reference source by its faults or by its strengths?

3. Carr writes that "The Internet is changing the economics of creative work—or, to put it more broadly, the economics of culture—and it's doing it in a way

that may well restrict rather than expand our choices . . . because it's created by amateurs rather than professionals, it's free. And free trumps quality all the time." Could Carr be right? Could publishers decide that quality print encyclopedias are too unprofitable to bother with?

Suggestion for Personal Research

1. Carr writes, "Of course the mainstream media sees the blogosphere as a competitor. It is a competitor. And, given the economics of the competition, it may well turn out to be a superior competitor. The layoffs we've recently seen at major newspapers may just be the beginning, and those layoffs should be cause not for self-satisfied snickering but for despair." Research the changing economics of newspaper production. Are major American newspapers known for decades of high-quality investigative journalism compromising their standards for economic survival? What are the ramifications?

Vocabulary Terms

metaphysics	echolalia
manna	fruition
diligent	amoral
emergent	wither
phenomena	hegemony

Educators Explore "Second Life" Online

Grace Wong

Prereading Question

1. Have you ever constructed an avatar and gone into a virtual world? Why or why not? If you have, how comfortable do you feel in that environment?

New York (CNN)—The classroom of the future isn't on a college campus. It's in the virtual world of "Second Life."

In "Second Life," virtual residents—cartoonish-looking characters controlled via keyboard and mouse—create anything their hearts desire.

Also known as avatars, the residents start up businesses, stage their own concerts, sell real estate and design fashion lines. Reuters news agency even has a correspondent based in the cyber community.

A growing number of educators are getting caught up in the wave. More than 60 schools and educational organizations have set up shop in the virtual world and are exploring ways it can be used to promote learning.

The three-dimensional virtual world makes it possible for students taking a distance course to develop a real sense of community, said Rebecca Nesson, who leads a class jointly offered by Harvard Law School and Harvard Extension School in the world of "Second Life."

"Students interact with each other and there's a regular sense of classroom interaction. It feels like a college campus," she said.

She holds class discussions in "Second Life" as well as office hours for extension students. Some class-related events are also open to the public—or basically anyone with a broadband connection.

Since opening in 2003, "Second Life" has experienced strong growth. Now some 1.3 million people around the world log on to live out their second lives.

The growing adoption of broadband Internet connection has helped drive that trend. Some 42 percent of Americans have a high-speed Internet connection at home, up from 30 percent last year, according to the Pew Internet & American Life Project.

Besides improving the quality of distance learning, educators are finding "Second Life" is a good way to introduce international perspectives. In Nesson's course, students as far away as Korea engage in the classroom discussion and work on team projects.

Flying Distractions

"Second Life" isn't without its drawbacks. It can be distracting to have people "flying" above you while you're trying to concentrate on a classroom discussion, said Brien Walton, 40, a master's degree student in educational technology at Harvard who is taking Nesson's course.

("Flying" and "teleporting" are two ways of navigating around the online digital world.)

Distractions aside, there's huge potential for the field of education in "Second Life," according to Walton, who in addition to being a student runs a company that develops distance courses for educational institutions and corporations.

Most people think online learning doesn't require participation or engagement with course material, he said. But in "Second Life" there's real-time interaction, which means students need to engage in the discussion—much as if they were sitting in a brick and mortar classroom.

John Lester, community and education manager at Linden Lab, the creator of "Second Life," echoed that view. "There is a real human being behind every avatar—the people are very real. It's just the medium is different," he said.

San Francisco, California-based Linden Lab develops the infrastructure for the online society, but it's up to its virtual residents to develop the content in the community.

That's one of the reasons some are skeptical about how much of an impact "Second Life" will have on the educational landscape.

"'Second Life' on its own doesn't force anyone to do anything," said Marc Prensky, a leading expert on education and learning. "It's a blank slate, and whether it develops into a useful tool depends on what sort of structures are created within it."

While it remains to be seen how much of an impact "Second Life" will have in the long run, there is immense interest within the educational community to find ways to harness its potential, said Mechthild Schmidt, a professor at NYU-McGhee, a division of the School of Continuing and Professional Studies.

Schmidt, who learned about "Second Life" from her teenage son, integrated the virtual world into a course she teaches on digital communication to give students a new avenue for collaboration.

Right now, it's the early adopters who are living second lives, said Elizabeth Edmonds, a trend researcher at future-focused marketing consultancy Faith Popcorn's BrainReserve.

But as broadband adoption goes more mainstream, she expects the site's popularity to grow—and not only with educators.

"Everyone will become involved in this," Edmonds said.

Journal Topics

1. Can you imagine yourself taking part in a virtual-world class? What do you think the advantages and limitations would be?

2. What would your reaction be to someone coming in to a virtual class wearing no clothes, displaying pornography, or wearing "garments" expressing offensive racist or terrorist propaganda?

Questions for Critical Thought

1. Classroom interactions can be a vital part of learning for various reasons. Can the virtual-world interactions that Rebecca Nesson refers to be as useful when people can never be sure of what other people look like or who they really are?

2. Do you see a big potential for schools operating in the world of virtual reality? Why or why not? What are the main advantages? What are the main disadvantages? How would professors guard against cheating?

Suggestion for Personal Research

1. Some people are exploring the educational potential of Second Life. For example, as mentioned in the article, Nesson teaches a Harvard-sponsored class, and The New Media Consortium purchased a "private island" in Second Life and built an entire campus there. Research the ways people are using Second Life to further education. What are some of the disciplines covered? How do the classes work? How well do people learn?

Multicultural Issues

1. In the real world, students are offered protections from harassment due to gender, culture, race, or place of national origin. In the virtual world, do the same protections exist? Because people can hide their identities, what safeguards can be enacted to ensure that everyone inside and outside a virtual class is treated with the respect that he or she can insist on in regular classes? Obviously, offensive students could be expelled from the class itself, but what about interactions outside the virtual classroom?

Vocabulary Terms

avatar   infrastructure

Second Life Just Like the First

Khue Pham

Prereading Question

1. The word "avatar" originally meant an incarnation of a deity or spirit in an Earthly body, but it now also means the graphical image a user creates for the Net. Have you ever visited a virtual world (such as Second Life or The Sims) and created an avatar? What does your avatar reflect about you? If you haven't, try imagining doing so. What kind of avatar do you think you would create? Would it be a lot like you, or would the fun come from creating someone very unlike you?

Jean Marie Le Pen is clearly unpopular among Porcupine residents. The far-right French presidential candidate's supporters from the Front National party are met with gunfire, explosions and angry protests outside their new office in the settlement of Porcupine, previously better known for its shops than its political institutions. But the fracas at the shopping paradise turned battlefield is different from the usual anti-Le Pen demonstrations—because Porcupine is not located in the real world but in the virtual one. Welcome to Second Life.

Le Pen may be politically conservative, but when it comes to technology he's clearly ahead of the game. He was the first politician to recognize that Second Life, the online game where users create avatar versions of themselves, could play a role in his campaign. Last November he gave his oui to his party's youth wing, the Young Front National (FNJ), to create a virtual branch to promote his presidential candidacy. "The media and the other parties laughed at us at first but then the Socialists and Conservatives quickly followed us into Second Life," FNJ vice director Nicolas Riac told SPIEGEL ONLINE. However, Le Pen turns out to be as controversial in the virtual world as in the real one, and his party's new Second Life offices were the scenes of violent virtual clashes between his far-right supporters and left-wing activists.

The latest member of the French political establishment to establish a virtual presence was interior minister Nicolas Sarkozy. "Sarkozy Island," a virtual island populated by avatar supporters of "Sarko"—as the presidential candidate is often nicknamed—opened last week. The virtual visitors' center is already proving more popular than Sarkozy's real Paris headquarters—organizers say it has had around 20,000 visitors since it opened, significantly more than at the real center, which only receives a couple of hundred visitors a day.

Goodbye cyberpunks, hello traditionalists. Four years after US company Linden Lab created Second Life, the virtual utopia is resembling the real world and its mechanisms more and more. And as the population booms—the number of registered avatars has risen 600 percent in the last six months to four million—the on- and offline worlds are beginning to wonder whether Second Life should be run by institutions of civil society rather than a benevolent corporate dictatorship.

Cash, Sex and Crime

For one thing, there is a lot of money to be made in Second Life—the game's currency, Linden Dollars, is convertible to real US dollars—and Second Life's smell of success has already lured big corporations like BMW, Gucci and AOL to set up virtual offices. Virtual entrepreneurs like Ailin Gräf, alias Anshe Chung, the game's first self-made US dollar millionaire, are taking over the property and clothing markets, while drug dealers and pimps compete with each other over the seedier side of business.

But money attracts trouble in the virtual world, too. In a postmodern version of David against Goliath, American lawyer Marc Bragg is suing Linden Lab over virtual property ownership at a federal court in Philadelphia. Bragg claims he was "dispossessed" when his Second Life account was cancelled because he wanted to sell a virtual estate which he had acquired by exploiting a system error.

Bragg says he lost several thousand US dollars which he had invested and made virtually, and is suing Linden Lab for breach of his property rights. The company, on the other hand, claims that Bragg breached their terms of service agreement. The case reflects a broader debate over the extent to which a company like Linden Lab should be allowed to have complete control over what, to many intents and purposes, is a virtual nation state.

Another problem is sex, which is rampant on Second Life—as are, inevitably, its perversions. While liberal-minded Internet denizens may not be too bothered by virtual swinger clubs or brothels, online pedophilia is more problematic. In Second Life, virtual rooms for sex between children and adult avatars exist. The Dutch Federal Court in The Hague is currently assessing, as part of a test case, if such activities constitute cases of sexual abuse or pedophilia. At the heart of the matter lies the question of whether watching virtual child pornography could lead to real-life copycat behavior, or whether virtual child abuse could be an offense in itself.

Acting Real

While the extent to which virtual behavior influences real behavior may be debatable, it seems that the real world has an indisputable influence on Second Life. A research team headed by Stanford University graduate student Nick Yee has found that avatars in Second Life behave just as humans do in real life, adhering to the same social rules. "We were surprised how many of the social norms transferred," Yee wrote in an email. "While we expected some of them to transfer, we didn't expect almost all of them to do so."

The researchers studied avatar gender roles and social interaction patterns and compared them to human behavior. They found that personal space matters even in the virtual world: Male and female avatars keep a physical distance from each other in the same way that men and women do. Pairs of male avatars tend to stay away from each other the furthest while female-female pairs stay physically closest to each other. Male-male pairs also exchange least eye contact while female avatar pairs look at each other most. That avatars act just like humans is not surprising to Yee: "It's hard to forget or ignore the norms that we have used every day in the physical world since we were born," he says. "These social norms help guide and sustain interaction."

This could be why the Second Life population models itself on real society. Behind every furry, flying or androgynous avatar is a player made of flesh and blood, whose preconceptions have been formed by his or her real life environment. Another Second Life expert, the French blogger Loic Le Mer, put it this way: "If you have a stupid player who creates an avatar, that avatar won't be smart just because it's a digital creature." In any case, the similarity in avatar and human behavior is likely to increase even further in the future. American company Vivox announced on Tuesday that it was developing a voice program for Second Life which will enable avatars to speak with each other—and even overhear other avatars' conversations.

Social Change Through Second Life?

Still, Loic Le Mer believes that the real world could change for the better because of Second Life. In his opinion, the online game is at the vanguard of globalization, "but globalization as an opportunity, not a threat." He predicts that more and more people from all over the world will earn a living through Second Life in the future. "The great thing about Second Life is that it brings together people from all countries, and everybody can make money by creating an object and selling it," he says, adding that an acquaintance of his makes €1,000 a month from selling virtual glasses to avatars.

Players from the developing world in particular can find ways of making money in Second Life, he says. The booming economy means that there is much demand for people who know how to create, for example, virtual buildings, which sell for around €50. "It may not be a lot of money to people living in the West, but for others it is," Le Mer says. However, he does agree that Second Life is not a place of total equal opportunity. "Of course, access, technology and skills vary between the developed and developing worlds," he admits.

But the link between Second Life and global capitalism could also herald another evolution: virtual terrorism. Second Life is already home to a group of self-proclaimed avatar revolutionaries, the Second Life Liberation Army. In order to fight what they call the "dictatorship of Linden Lab," the virtual freedom fighters have been setting off bombs at Second Life stores such as American Apparel and have put bounties on the heads of commercial contractors. So far, nobody has been injured by the code-toting anarchists. Fantasy and reality have not yet merged completely.

Journal Topics

1. Loic Le Mer thinks that the universe of Second Life can change the real world for the better. Do you think this is possible? If so, in what ways?

2. If you have experience in one or more virtual worlds, what are the pleasures and benefits that you find? Are there any downsides?

Questions for Critical Thought

1. Promoters of Second Life see it as a way for people to engage with other people in ways not possible before. Because it transcends geography, they have a point. On the other hand, critics argue that it is more likely to be used as an escape

from real life. Is the latter necessarily bad? Don't we read novels and watch TV and movies as a form of temporary escape?

2. What kind of ethical boundaries should exist in a virtual world like Second Life? If people decide to adopt avatars that are of different genders, races, or ages, should they disclose this with people they interact with? Or, in a world where you can choose to be a six-foot-tall flying green squirrel, are such concerns irrelevant?

3. If an adult adopts the avatar of a child and another adult has virtual online sex with that fake "child," is it child pornography even if no children or images of real children are involved?

Suggestions for Personal Research

1. Can a virtual world have a comparable psychological impact on its residents as activities in the real world? A group in London conducted a virtual recreation in Second Life of Stanley Milgram's obedience to authority experiment, in which subjects thought they were giving electric shocks of increasing intensity to other subjects when instructed by an authority figure to do so. In the virtual world, all participants knew that no one was getting shocked, but subjects were said to demonstrate similar stress and anxiety. Research the methodology and conclusions of this and other experiments conducted in Second Life.

2. In a virtual world, people can pretend to be anybody—they can alter all their characteristics and pass themselves off as being older, younger, richer, single, and so on. Sometimes they enter into personal relationships that have serious emotional ramifications. Research the legal and psychological issues that have arisen. Are there any dangers that originate in a virtual world that can carry over to the real one?

Multicultural Issues

1. How "equal" is the world of Second Life? Some nonwhite people have complained that it is difficult to find avatars that accurately reflect their own races and cultures—that they are limited to taking essentially white figures and altering their skin tones. What does this say about the "First Life"—the real world outside of virtual reality?

Vocabulary Terms

avatar	rampant
utopia	androgynous
currency	globalization
entrepreneur	anarchist

Harsh Words Die Hard on the Web

Ellen Nakashima

Prereading Questions

1. Do you have an account on a social networking site like MySpace or Facebook? If so, have you posted a photograph of yourself? Why or why not? If not, do you think it is innocent fun or possibly dangerous for others to post their pictures?

2. Have you ever been harassed or insulted on a website? If so, how did it make you feel at the time—and later?

3. Have you ever let off steam by posting negative remarks against someone? If so, how did it make you feel at the time—and later?

She graduated Phi Beta Kappa, has published in top legal journals and completed internships at leading institutions in her field. So when the Yale law student interviewed with 16 firms for a job this summer, she was concerned that she had only four callbacks. She was stunned when she had zero offers.

Though it is difficult to prove a direct link, the woman thinks she is a victim of a new form of reputation-maligning: online postings with offensive content and personal attacks that can be stored forever and are easily accessible through a Google search.

The woman and two others interviewed by *The Washington Post* learned from friends that they were the subject of derogatory chats on a widely read message board on AutoAdmit, run by a third-year law student at the University of Pennsylvania and a 23-year-old insurance agent. The women spoke on the condition of anonymity because they feared retribution online.

The law-school board, one of several message boards on AutoAdmit, bills itself as "the most prestigious law school admissions discussion board in the world." It contains many useful insights on schools and firms. But there are also hundreds of chats posted by anonymous users that feature derisive statements about women, gays, blacks, Asians and Jews. In scores of messages, the users disparage individuals by name or other personally identifying information. Some of the messages included false claims about sexual activity and diseases. To the targets' dismay, the comments bubble up through the Internet into the public domain via Google's powerful search engine.

The site's founder, Jarret Cohen, the insurance agent, said the site merely provides a forum for free speech. "I want it to be a place where people can express themselves freely, just as if they were to go to a town square and say whatever brilliant or foolish thoughts they have," Cohen said.

The students' tales reflect the pitfalls of popular social-networking sites and highlight how social and technological changes lead to new clashes between free speech and privacy. The chats are also a window into the character of a segment of students at leading law schools. Penn officials said they have known about the site and the complaints for two years but have no legal grounds to act against it. The site is not operated with school resources.

Nor is it the only forum for such discussions, but it may be the largest "and is certainly the highest profile," said David A. Hoffman, a Temple University law professor who has conducted research on AutoAdmit.

Employers, including law firms, frequently do Google searches as part of due diligence checks on prospective employees. According to a December survey by the Ponemon Institute, a privacy research organization, roughly half of U.S. hiring officials use the Internet in vetting job applications. About one-third of the searches yielded content used to deny a job, the survey said. The legal hiring market is very competitive. What could tip the balance is the appearance that a candidate is a lightning rod for controversy, said Mark Rasch, a Washington lawyer and consultant who specializes in Internet issues.

The trend has even spawned a new service, ReputationDefender, whose mission is to search for damaging content online and destroy it on behalf of clients. Generally, the law exempts site operators from liability for the content posted by others, though it does not prevent them from removing offensive items.

"For many people the Internet has become a scarlet letter, an albatross," said Michael Fertik, ReputationDefender's chief executive. The company is launching a campaign to get AutoAdmit to cleanse its site and encourage law schools to adopt a professional conduct code for students.

Kurt Opsahl, a staff attorney at the Electronic Frontier Foundation, a privacy and free speech advocacy group, said anonymous cyber-writers can be sued for defamation. A judge can require a Web site host or operator to disclose a user's identifying information. Also, he said, the Internet allows those who feel slandered to put forth their own point of view. "The cure to bad speech is more speech," he said.

The chats sometimes include photos taken from women's Facebook pages, and in the Yale student's case, one person threatened to sexually violate her. Another participant claimed to be the student, making it appear that she was taking part in the discussion.

"I didn't understand what I'd done to deserve it," said the student. "I also felt kind of scared because it was someone in my community who was threatening physical and sexual violence and I didn't know who."

The woman e-mailed the site's administrators and asked them to remove the material. She said she received no response. Then she tried contacting Google, which simply cited its policy that the Web site's administrator must remove the material to clear out the search results.

AutoAdmit.com, which also uses the domain name xoxohth.com and which hosts Google-served ads, was launched in 2004. Cohen and his partner, Anthony Ciolli, cite First Amendment ideals. "We are very strong believers in the freedom of expression and the marketplace of ideas . . . and almost never censor content, no matter how abhorrent it may be," they wrote in a posting on someone else's blog. The vast majority of chat threads, they wrote, are school-related. "The only time you'll see 20 or so racist threads on the site is if you proactively search for them."

They said the success of the site's message boards—they claim 800,000 to 1 million unique visitors a month—owes to its free, anonymous exchange of ideas. "In fact, one finds overall a much deeper and much more mature level of insight in a community where the ugliest depths of human opinion are confronted, rather than ignored," they wrote.

One chat thread included a sexual joke about a female Holocaust victim.

In another comment, a user said a particular woman had no right to ask that the threads be removed. "If we want to objectify, criticize and [expletive] on [expletive] like her, we should be able to."

In another posting, a participant rejected the idea that photos be removed on moral grounds: "We're lawyers and lawyers-in-training, dude. Of course we follow the law, not morals."

"I definitely don't agree with a lot of the conduct on the board," Ciolli said in an interview. But, he said, only Cohen, who created the message board, has authority to have the comments removed. Cohen, in a separate interview, said he will not "selectively remove" offensive comments, and that when he has attempted to do so, he was threatened with litigation for "perceived inconsistencies."

Another Yale law student learned a month ago that her photographs were posted in an AutoAdmit chat that included her name and graphic discussion about her breasts. She was also featured in a separate contest site—with links posted on AutoAdmit chats—to select the "hottest" female law student at "Top 14" law schools, which nearly crashed because of heavy traffic. Eventually her photos and comments about her and other contestants were posted on more than a dozen chat threads, many of which were accessible through Google searches.

"I felt completely objectified," that woman said. It was, she said, "as if they're stealing part of my character from me." The woman, a Fulbright scholar who graduated summa cum laude, said she now fears going to the gym because people on the site encouraged classmates to take cellphone pictures of her.

Ciolli persuaded the contest site owner to let him shut down the "Top 14" for privacy concerns, Cohen said. "I think we deserve a golden star for what we did," Cohen said.

The two men said that some of the women who complain of being ridiculed on AutoAdmit invite attention by, for example, posting their photographs on other social networking sites, such as Facebook or MySpace.

Cohen said he no longer keeps identifying information on users because he does not want to encourage lawsuits and drive traffic away. Asked why posters could not use their real names, he said, "People would not have as much fun, frankly, if they had to worry about employers pulling up information on them."

One woman e-mailed the University of Pennsylvania Law School associate dean, Gary Clinton, in February to ask for his help in persuading Ciolli remove the offensive threads. Clinton told her that since he became aware of AutoAdmit two years ago, he has had "numerous conversations about it" with Penn officials. "I've learned that there appears to be little legal recourse that we have as an institution," he wrote. He said he has had several conversations with Ciolli and has "pointed out time and again how hurtful these ad hominem attacks can be to individuals, and have asked him to delete threads." The effort, he noted, "has been largely unsuccessful."

In a telephone interview, Clinton said the university's position has not changed. "We believe we don't have grounds under the university's code of conduct to proceed," he said.

Journal Topics

1. Jarret Cohen and his partner, Anthony Ciolli, say some of the women who have been ridiculed on their site invited the harassment by, among things, putting their photographs on sites like Facebook or MySpace. Do you think their assertion is fair?

2. Do you have a site on a social networking site with your photograph on it? If so, does reading this article give you second thoughts?

3. A man on AutoAdmit argued against using moral grounds to remove photographs of women that were posted without their consent, saying, "We're lawyers and lawyers-in-training, dude. Of course we follow the law, not morals." What is your reaction to this?

Questions for Critical Thought

1. Like Keith and Martin's article on cyber-bullying among children and teens, this article demonstrates that reputation-maligning, racist speech, and sexual harassment are a lot easier on the Internet than offline because so much technology exists to support this behavior and because harassers can be anonymous. Could the very easiness of this kind of harassment be encouraging more men to sexually harass women and more people in general to malign others, or does it simply make this behavior easier for people who already have the tendency?

2. Cohen and Ciolli bill AutoAdmit as "the most prestigious law school admissions discussion board in the world." Nonetheless, they allow and even defend the posting of harassing, disparaging, and false accusations, saying, "We are very strong believers in the freedom of expression and the marketplace of ideas." What is generally meant by the expression "the marketplace of ideas"? How do the examples raised in the article fit this?

3. Cohen commented, when asked why posters shouldn't have to use their real names, that "People would not have as much fun, frankly, if they had to worry about employers pulling up information on them." Does this in any way undercut any of the other assertions that he makes?

4. As the article points out, "Generally, the law exempts site operators from liability for the content posted by others," yet the article raises the possibility that attacks on various people, particularly women, may have actually cost some people potential jobs. Should owners of sites like this face damages in civil courts if defamed targets of abuse on their sites can prove that they have suffered financial damages?

5. Many people post photographs of themselves on their personal websites. These can be easily copied by others, as the article shows, and be posted on other sites on the Web with any captions or remarks the posters desire to add. Cohen and Ciolli think women who have posted their photos have, in effect, asked for such treatment. Should this standard apply to similar offline situations? What about people at work or school who let their pictures be put on bulletin boards after

different events? How about people whose pictures appear in school yearbooks? It is easy to turn a nondigital photograph into a digital photograph and post it on the Internet, too. Is there an ethical difference? Why or why not?

Suggestions for Personal Research

1. Laws exist to protect people against slander, stalking, and sexual harassment. How far should such protections apply to people in cyberspace? Research the legal limits and responsibilities governing behavior on the Internet and compare and contrast the legal limits and responsibilities imposed in other settings, such as school and the workplace.

2. Research laws governing the advocacy of illegal acts on Internet sites. Do site owners have any legal responsibilities if anonymous posters advocate illegal acts and even provide information that would help other people commit illegal acts?

3. What are the legal responsibilities of sites maintained for the apparent purpose of exposing certain people to intimidation, harassment, or even violence and murder by enabling and applauding this behavior? Without explicitly advocating any illegal acts, an antiabortion website posted abortion providers' names, photographs, and addresses, and put a strike mark through the name of each provider who was killed. Doctors whose personal information was posted sued the site, and the owners of the site used a First Amendment defense. The same defense has been used by sites that post photographs of women going into abortion clinics. Research such cases and their outcome and the ramifications for other types of Internet sites.

Vocabulary Terms

retribution	slander
malign	expletive
liability	ad hominem attack

Terms for Clarification

Scarlet letter   In Nathaniel Hawthorne's 1850 book *The Scarlet Letter,* the heroine was forced to wear a scarlet-colored "A"as punishment for adultery. The term is now used to mean a public symbol of shame or a crime.

Albatross   In Samuel Taylor Coleridge's poem "The Rime of the Ancient Mariner," a character who shot an albatross, a symbol of good luck, is made to carry the corpse of the bird hung around his neck. The term "albatross" or the expression "an albatross around [someone's] neck" now also refers to a public and very unpleasant public symbol of shame or a crime, particularly one that the victim must live with for a very long time.

Phi Beta Kappa   A member of an honorary society of college and university students to which members are elected on the basis of high academic achievement.

CHAPTER 18—THE INTERNET ESSAY QUESTIONS

These questions are intended as potential essay topics for some of the themes suggested by the articles and related material in this chapter.

1. Write an essay explaining the Communications Decency Act (CDA), which is designed to regulate material on the Internet. The Act was Title V of the Telecommunications Act of 1996. In 1997, in *ACLU v. Reno,* the U.S. Supreme Court partially overturned the law. Title V was designed to regulate indecency and obscenity, and it declared that operators of Internet services were not to be considered publishers, freeing them from legal liability for the words of third parties using their services. Issues to discuss include effectiveness, civil liberties concerns, and the ethical responsibilities of the owners of Internet sites.

2. Discuss the ways in which the Internet benefits society and individuals in unique ways. Contrast these benefits with any problems and dangers. Back up your assertions with clear, concrete examples. What recommendations can you make to users? To parents?

3. Choose just one benefit or problem to discuss at length, making suggestions on how to enhance benefits or protect ourselves from dangers. On the positive side, the Internet's benefits include social networking across vast distances, ease of information gathering, and exposure to international points of view. Negative aspects include addiction, sexual predation, hate-mongering, and the proliferation of misinformation.

4. Scams and urban legends existed long before the Internet, but email has multiplied their spread exponentially. Discuss the proliferation of either or both and how people can protect themselves.

5. Sites that involve self-publication have thrived in recent years, making the Internet a place for homemade celebrity. Also, many small sites such as YouTube and MySpace have evolved rapidly and sold for hundreds of millions of dollars, making people multimillionaires. A few years ago, however, during a phase called the "dot bomb," many websites went bankrupt, making many newly made Web millionaires go bankrupt with them. Write an essay about the spread of Internet-based celebrity and/or Internet wealth. You could consider comparing "real world" celebrity and wealth to the Internet equivalents. You may also look at previous Internet celebrities, trends, or millionaires and see how they have held up over the years.

19 CHAPTER

Advertising

If you cruise your campus for one hour with a notepad and a pen, counting advertisements and brand logos, you may be surprised at what you find. First, you'll notice the obvious: snack and soda machines—dozens of them, all emblazoned with logos and designs, enticing you to deposit your money and satisfy yourself. Second, you'll probably see the actual advertisements that surround you. Ads for your bookstore are

surely there, inviting you to shop within your campus community instead of online. You'll probably also notice ads on any city bus benches on campus (or on the buses themselves as they pick up and drop off diligent students such as yourself). If you walk around the parking lot, you will see logo after logo on the cars and trucks parked there, and you can probably see billboards from where you stand.

Next, you may notice the corporate logos people are wearing: Gap, Nike, Reebok, Tommy Hilfiger, Ralph Lauren, Abercrombie and Fitch, Dickies, Aeropostal, and an endless, ever-renewing host of others. Many of us, in displaying these corporate logos on our clothes, pay money to wear what is ultimately an advertisement for a corporation. In fact, people will pay five times more for a t-shirt with a logo on it than they will for an identical t-shirt without a logo. Many of your fellow students are logo lemmings, following the hottest trends and paying good money to do so.

You can probably even find advertisements for student credit cards, summer jobs, and cheap spring break vacations posted right there in your classroom (more than likely without proper approval by campus officials). If there is a television or a computer in the classroom, its Sony, Zenith, or Hewlett Packard logo subtly advertises its corporate parent.

These incidental forms of advertisement are all around us. They make up what the American novelist Don DeLillo calls our cultural "white noise." But you also encounter more obvious kinds of advertisements every day, such as television commercials, which typically take up sixteen minutes of every hour of TV time, and radio ads, which play in the background where you work or as you drive around town. There is also the cyber side of things, such as spam in your email in box and pop-up ads and banners on your favorite websites. Advertising is endless.

Traditionally, if you were a businessperson with a product for sale, you would advertise in some fashion either to let potential customers know you exist or to boast that your product is the best on the market. You might use anything from a man walking the city streets in a sandwich board to a slick corporate logo and phone number painted on the side of your company car. Recently, however, there has been a shift in advertising strategy. Many corporations are now interested in selling an image of themselves and imposing their own brand name on the audience's consciousness instead of selling an actual product that they manufacture. Of course, the ultimate goal of advertising is for the corporation to eventually sell more products, but these newer commercials often sell an idea or an image instead of an actual product or service.

For example, when is the last time you saw a Nike ad that actually sold you a specific product? It has probably been several years. Nike's advertising challenges you to "do it." The message used to be "Just do it," but even the word *just* muddied the straightforward nature of such an appeal. Do it. You may wonder what "it" is, exactly, but that's the beauty of their advertising campaign. They show suggestively attractive male and female athletes sweating in their ads. "Do it" could mean that you should work out as hard as these professionals do in order to become as good as they are, but it could also mean that you should improve your sex appeal by wearing the most sought-after brand in athletic clothes and getting a partner as attractive as some of the people in the ad. The idea of selling a thought or desire rather than a product may seem strange, but it's very effective. Nike sells the idea that you'll be cooler in Nike than in anything else when you work out, and this approach has proven to be very successful. Nike no longer advertises a specific shoe or an individual article of clothing, just the corporation itself and all it is meant to symbolize in the American mediascape: health, success, ambition, and sex appeal.

Countless other corporations have altered our culture by programming us to flock to brands and images instead of products and quality. Though the products may be comparable in quality to those sold from high-end stores, many people are embarrassed to wear generic athletic clothing from a discount store. They want the other people at the gym to know that they buy high-end gear instead of shopping at some bargain-conscious big-box store. What many consumers don't know is that most brand-name products are built or made in the same factories as the off-brand items. The only difference is prestige, not performance. Most of us would rather spend more money on a fashionable, high-status item that we could get for less if some other company made it. The reason we do this is successful advertising.

Advertising is perhaps the most common form of information that any of us encounter. We witness or listen to hundreds of ads, logos, and jingles every day; however, the study of advertisements largely goes ignored. This omnipresent form of information should be critically approached, and that is where information competency comes in. You should understand the techniques and devices advertising agencies use to get you to purchase their products. You should become a master of the language of advertising. As you begin to understand how advertisements manipulate you, you will have an easier time resisting the urge to make a purchase on a whim.

Following is a list of many of the psychological appeals, logical fallacies, and propaganda devices used by advertisers to sell us their products. (Experts in the discipline of logic have traditionally pointed out a number of errors in reasoning based on unfair psychological appeals and logical fallacies. These and other devices are also discussed in Chapter 5.) Note that these dubious techniques can be used in virtually any medium in which advertising appears (print ads, billboards, television and radio commercials, Internet ads, spam, and so on).

PSYCHOLOGICAL APPEALS

All humans have certain basic needs, such as the need for food, companionship, sex, and security. Advertisers study and exploit these needs to appeal to our most basic desires to make us want to consume. Following is a list of several drives and impulses that advertising agencies regularly appeal to. The job of the advertisement is to convince us that buying a specific product will satiate these constant human needs.

Appeal to Sex

Sex is one of the most obvious drives exploited in advertising. A huge number of ads are driven on some level by sex. Sexy music, sexy cars, and images of beautiful or handsome models wearing very little clothing are provocative and memorable. Sex sells, and it's everywhere. Either explicit or implicit, sex sells products. Appeal to sex may be the most common ad technique in use.

Appeal to Safety

In the post-9/11 era, many of us feel far less safe than we did before. Even before 9/11, however, advertisers knew how to play on our fears. Think of how advertisements boast that this SUV or that set of tires will protect your family or argue that a home alarm will save you from burglaries or home invasions and even banish fear itself. By first making us feel unsafe, advertisers can then sell the illusion of safety.

Appeal to Sustenance

We must eat regularly, of course, or we'll perish. This seems pretty straightforward; however, when we're hungry, our bodies need only a certain ratio of protein, carbohydrates, fats, and sugar. When we're thirsty, our bodies need water. But, apart from the need for nourishment, food provides a sense of pleasure and comfort, as well as immediate gratification when we are feeling bored or depressed. Advertisers have helped to condition us: now, when we're hungry, we want a hamburger or burrito from a fast-food restaurant; when we're thirsty, we want our favorite brand of soda. We often flip past luscious photos of delicious food in a magazine and salivate at ads for home-delivered pizza late at night when we aren't even hungry. After we see this food (looking far better in the advertising than it will when we purchase it), we want to eat it, and it's easy to phone for a pizza, drive over to the nearest fast-food place, or simply raid the cupboards and refrigerators that we have filled with unhealthy snack foods.

Appeal to Belonging

Human beings desire to belong to a larger social group; we all want acceptance. Ads appealing to this need usually show large families or groups of friends coming together to show off clothes, drink beer, have a soda, or celebrate a new purchase. We often see happy, smiling people gathering at clubs, barbeques, parties, or other fun social outings. The ultimate idea behind these ads is that if we buy this product, we'll belong to a larger social network and never be lonely.

Appeal to Escape

We sometimes feel the need to escape it all and head out of town. Our lives get far too hectic or start to seem boring, and we yearn for something different and dream of exciting or glamorous locales. When we see people and products in exotic locations, we briefly picture ourselves in those places, and we want the item and the lifestyle that the item evokes—or we want to travel to that beach on the advertised cruise ship or fly to that glittering city on the advertised airline.

Appeal to Love and Romance

To quote the Blues Brothers, "everybody needs somebody to love." Advertisers know this and take pains to show that love can be associated with a particular product—whether it's cologne, flowers, romantic getaways, or jewelry—by always placing it near a happy couple. Though the practice of exchanging engagement rings is many centuries old, diamonds became a symbol of true love and commitment as a result of what many have called the twentieth century's most successful ad campaign, launched by the DeBeers company in the 1940s. Diamond sales in the United States had been declining for many years until DeBeers came up with the slogan "A diamond is forever." Today, the term "engagement ring" is synonymous with "diamond engagement ring," and most weddings do not occur without one. How many men would dare to suggest that they buy their beloved a beautiful garnet or amethyst instead of a diamond?

Appeal to Status and Power

Human beings are often motivated by ideas of success. Most Americans want to make a lot of money, drive an expensive car, wear a designer watch, have the most cutting-edge computer, and live in a large house with the latest high-tech television sets and stereo equipment. Advertisers constantly appeal to this desire for success, especially if they are selling expensive cars or luxury items.

If we feel that a product is a status symbol, we'll pay more and work harder for it. By appealing to our desire for status, ads give an item an exclusive quality that makes us yearn for it—after all, if we possess that item, we must have higher status as well, right? Notice the classy music and regal settings that surround the owners of luxury cars, diamond jewelry, $10,000 watches, and high-end brands of vodka, whisky, and gin.

Appeal to Feeling Attractive and Healthy

Americans' poor eating habits have made us fatter. Though we compose only 5% of the world's population, we are responsible for 33% of total global sugar consumption annually. According to the World Health Organization, more than half of Americans are overweight. Approximately a third qualify as obese, and obesity rates in children have risen 50% in recent years. We also consume products that are filled with saturated fats, hydrogenated trans fats, and high-fructose corn syrup. While one part of the advertising world works at making us fatter, another part plays on our justifiable fear of obesity by appealing to our desire to become fit—but only if we can do it the fast and easy way. Subway ads show Jared and how much weight he lost eating low-fat submarine sandwiches every day, and various diet products and exercise machines are offered to us with the promise that—quickly and easily—our pounds will simply melt away.

Appeals to Nostalgia and Shared Memories

Many of us have a psychological desire to return to a simpler time. Ads that appeal to this desire incorporate nostalgic sounds and images, such as songs from earlier eras that take the audience members back to what they believe were less complex and stressful times. Sometimes advertisers will incorporate television characters from a target group's childhood or bring back older ad campaigns. Classic Christmas tunes and Norman Rockwell-inspired depictions of families are always a hit during the holidays and remind us of wonderful moments—and presents—from our past.

PROPAGANDA DEVICES

Psychological appeals aren't the only way for advertising agencies to reach their clients' potential customers, as the governments of most nations learned during the two world wars of the twentieth century. **Propaganda devices** were all honed during the past century; most were used during World War I and perfected during World War II by both the Axis and the Allied powers. Ads use some of the same propaganda devices to sell products. These devices are effective in motivating populations and demoralizing enemies, and they can be just as effective at getting us to buy a certain brand of burger or a two-dollar bottle of water that may very well have come from a municipal water supply—in other words, tap water.

Slogans and Jingles

We can all think of dozens of songs and slogans. One of the most famous and enduring originated during World War I: Uncle Sam's well-known command, "I want YOU…" More recently, slogans and jingles like "A Diamond Is Forever," from the forties; the Oscar Meyer Weiner song, from the sixties; and "Where's the beef?" and "Just do it," from the eighties, are designed to insert a company's product or service into your memory. This technique helps foster brand recognition and brand loyalty, but it also fosters desires for certain types of products, as well. Many, many years from now, while you lie on your death bed, you'll probably still be able to sing a jingle that advertised a cereal you ate every Saturday morning when you were a child.

Name Calling

One of the most effective ways to sell a product can be to criticize the competition. Some attacks are subtle; some are obvious, but most are dependent on faulty evidence or reasoning. They don't prove how good a product is; they simply claim another product is not as good. This technique is never seen more often—nor used more brutally–than during a typical election season, where the other "product," the candidate's political rival, is often portrayed not only as not as inferior to the candidate, but as a bad human being, perhaps even a threat to the populace. As the campaigns heat up, "smear ads" demonize rivals, often playing very cynically with the facts, taking information out of context and ignoring inconvenient evidence.

Glittering Generalities and Faulty Logic

In commercials and on product packaging, we frequently see generalities that are offered as if they were concrete proof: "Better Formula," "New," or "Improved." Claims like these are empty of any real information. What is the formula better than? What did the manufacturer change to make this product new? What exactly has been improved? These vague statements can make us feel that a product is better than its competitors or has been improved in a measurable way. The boast that a laundry detergent is "Better at fighting harsh stains" is an incomplete comparison. What is it better than? Is it better than it used to be? Is it better than all the rival detergents? Or is it simply better than using nothing but water? If the advertisers never clarify the comparison, they can always truthfully make this kind of claim.

Transfer

Some ads try to transfer a value, a person, or an idea onto a product in an attempt to give it more value. This transfer enhances the value by taking something we covet or long for and trying to make us associate it with a product or a corporate name. Following are the three most common kinds of transfer—celebrity, sex, and patriotism.

CELEBRITY

Many ads use a celebrity who is very popular to try to subconsciously associate the hip and attractive nature of the celebrity with the product. Also, we may assume that if a company can afford to pay famous and glamorous spokespeople, the corporation must be very successful. Sometimes the advertiser will get tricky and simply have a celebrity do voice-over work, lending his or her voice to the ad but never actually appearing in it. As you watch the ad, you feel comfortable with a voice that you somehow recognize, although you may not consciously realize why you like hearing it. Advertisers will also hire actors that sound like celebrities who evoke positive feelings in groups (and sometimes get sued by the real celebrities for doing so). Whether we see the celebrity or only hear a familiar voice, advertisers hope that we will transfer the qualities about the celebrity that we admire onto the product in question.

SEX

The transfer of sex makes us think that using a certain product will help us have sex with beautiful people, or at least help us seem more attractive to them. Often, transfers involving sex are found in print ads for clothes, liquor, or cigarettes. We transfer notions of sexiness and sexual success onto a product and want to buy it that much more for what we unconsciously believe it will do for us. If someone asked you if you thought that a particular body spray, pair of jeans, or brand of liquor would make you sexier to other people, you'd think the question ridiculous, but the primary impact of these ads isn't really on our conscious minds.

PATRIOTISM

Whether we see a photo of the Statue of Liberty next to a bottle of vodka, an American flag waving behind a news program's logo, or a popular patriotic song playing in the background of a car commercial, we associate the product with being American. Most people love their country, especially in our post-9/11 lives, when standing together makes us feel more secure. When we transfer that love of country to a particular product, we may feel that using the product is a patriotic act. Many items proudly display a "Made in America" sticker as a way to make consumers feel that support of this product is support of the United States itself. Driving down the streets of your own town or city, you can probably find dozens of businesses with American flags flying in front of them or flag designs and patriotic slogans painted on their windows. We're left to wonder how much of this is really inspired by patriotism and how much by a desire to attract people to these businesses. And what do such displays have to do with the actual products or services?

Mascots and Icons

The original American icon is the red-white-and-blue-suited Uncle Sam. He wants YOU to join the armed forces. Soon after this image's debut in 1917, the Coca-Cola company created a red-suited, fat Santa Claus and used him to sell its cola with holiday warmth in freezing months historically low on sales of cold soft drinks. St. Nicholas existed before Coke, but not as the jolly, red-suited, corpulent man we know today. Even Rudolph the Red-Nosed Reindeer was invented as a mascot for the Montgomery Ward catalog company during the Christmas selling season. But now we've expanded the icon and mascot concept. Whether it's the Taco Bell Chihuahua or the Geico gecko, people love a memorable character. The AFLAC duck makes us think of a product— disability insurance—we might not ever think of otherwise. Even a substance as undesirable as toenail fungus medicine now has cute animated mascots. During the twentieth century, top icons included Ronald McDonald, the Energizer Bunny, Tony the Tiger, and the Marlboro Man (ironically, two of the men who played this character died of cancers that began in their lungs).

Humor

Most people remember funny commercials more than any other type of ad. If an ad is humorous, it stands out from the others during the endless hours of boring ads we are subjected to every week. If you think back and recall a favorite ad, you probably enjoyed it because it made you laugh. Funny ad campaigns include the Geico cavemen ads, with actors playing cavemen somehow resurrected into the modern world and hypersensitive to slights about their kind; the famous "Got Milk?" ads that show minor tragedies unfolding for characters who can't get their hands on a glass of milk; and the Jack-in-the-Box ads, with "Jack," sporting a head that looks like a painted ping-pong ball, behaving—and being treated—like a successful CEO.

Eye Candy

An ad needs to be visually appealing to grab your attention. Sexy supermodels, bright colors, and interesting lettering appear in print ads. Quick film cuts, animation, and text that moves across the screen on TV and the Net all grab our attention and keep it fixed on an ad long enough for the advertiser to pitch the product or service. If we are drawn to an unusual ad, we take it in and remember it. The average magazine or hour of television programming contains numerous ads competing with each other, and the goal of many advertisers is to design an ad that is so strange, beautiful, flashy, or surprising that you're drawn to look at it instead of flipping a page or walking out of the room for a break during a commercial. If an ad can grab your eye or ear for just a second, it has succeeded in pitching its product.

Testimonials

Some ads use testimonials—statements of people attesting to the effectiveness of products or services. Sometimes the people are real; other times they are actors portraying experts like doctors, lawyers, scientists, or even chefs. Nine out of ten dentists recommend a particular toothpaste, so it must be good, right? Whether these people are real professionals or are actors, one thing is consistent—they are all being paid for their testimonies.

Bandwagon Effect

Like the testimonial, advertisers use the bandwagon technique to try to convince us that huge numbers of people are using their product or service, so said product or service must be the best of its kind. In nineteenth- and early-twentieth-century America, a wagon carrying a musical band was used to lead parades and create excitement at political rallies. Sometimes audience members would get so enthusiastic that they would clamber on to the wagons, so the expression "to jump on the bandwagon" came to be used for anyone following excitement and a crowd on an issue instead of being motivated by reason or conviction. For example, infomercials often show an audience of eager consumers who could be your next-door neighbors. Diet ads show normal people who used a product and lost weight—if they can do it, so can you. Other common types of bandwagon ads are beverage commercials that show happy people relaxing at pool parties and enjoying themselves in nightclubs. A lot of people who use a certain product have friends and fun, so you can use it and have fun, too.

DEMOGRAPHICS

Advertisers carefully focus their appeals by using **demographics,** statistical data that are used to categorize populations and particular subgroups within them by age, gender, race, religion, sexual persuasion, income level, family size, and so on. The primary demographic group purchasing a hot new cell phone or MP3 player is probably composed of males between the ages of eighteen and thirty. The company that produces this phone will advertise during football games and action dramas. Advertisers try to learn as much about their audiences as possible, so they can match their product to the likeliest groups of consumers.

Think about a series of commercials for a fast-food restaurant, for example. At 3:00 in the afternoon, during a cartoon show, you'll see commercials that are pitching children's meals, complete with toys and happy mascots. During the 5:00 news, you'll see ads for the same restaurant, but these may feature harassed mothers or fathers trying to get food for their families during a rush-hour commute. Later in the evening, you may watch a rerun of a vintage sitcom and notice that an ad for the same restaurant is catering to the nostalgia of the older crowd that is presumably watching this old show. Finally, during the 11:00 news, you'll see ads for the restaurant pitching breakfast items, anticipating a hungry, impatient commuter crowd the next morning.

IN THIS CHAPTER

Advertising is anything produced to help someone sell something. Advertising includes television and radio commercials; print ads in periodicals; roadside billboards; pop-ups, banner ads, and spam on the Net; and even the packaging of products at the grocery store. This chapter looks at the techniques behind typical types of ads. To understand how you are being manipulated by advertising agencies, you should consider the following:

- What techniques do advertisers use to get our attention and money, and how effective are they?
- Why did some corporations stop advertising only specific products and instead start advertising the corporations themselves?
- What different groups do different ads appeal to?
- Should corporations be legally allowed to target young children who still don't have the cognitive capacity to see through the ads' appeals?
- How can a parent combat the power of a billion-dollar ad industry?
- How do ads shape appetites and desires and ultimately affect our health?
- How does advertising successfully define certain products as luxury items that we feel we must possess to maintain or raise our status?

The following readings have been included to give you an opportunity to explore different kinds of advertising and to give you a better understanding of the history, techniques, and possibly the future of advertising. As media technology rapidly changes, so does the nature of advertising. These articles address some of the current issues about commercials, marketing, and public relations. As you read through them, apply your powers of critical thinking to their content.

New Branded World, from *No Logo*

Naomi Klein

Prereading Questions

1. What other work could the title "New Branded World" allude to? (*Allude* means to suggest or refer to something outside indirectly; for example, the title of one work can resemble or refer to the title of a more famous work.) "New Branded World" sounds like the title of Aldous Huxley's book *Brave New World,* which depicts a deeply flawed future society. Knowing this, what do you think will be the tone of Klein's piece?

2. What does the term *branded* suggest? How many meanings can you think of for the word *brand*? What are the emotional associations?

> As a private person, I have a passion for landscape, and I have never seen one improved by a billboard. Where every prospect pleases, man is at his vilest when he erects a billboard. When I retire from Madison Avenue, I am going to start a secret society of masked vigilantes who will travel around the world on silent motor bicycles, chopping down posters at the dark of the moon. How many juries will convict us when we are caught in these acts of beneficent citizenship?
>
> —DAVID OGILVY, FOUNDER OF THE OGILVY & MATHER ADVERTISING AGENCY, IN CONFESSIONS OF AN ADVERTISING MAN, *1963*

The astronomical growth in the wealth and cultural influence of multinational corporations over the last fifteen years can arguably be traced back to a single, seemingly innocuous idea developed by management theorists in the mid-1980s: that successful corporations must primarily produce brands, as opposed to products.

Until that time, although it was understood in the corporate world that bolstering one's brand name was important, the primary concern of every solid manufacturer was the production of goods. This idea was the very gospel of the machine age. An editorial that appeared in *Fortune* magazine in 1938, for instance, argued that the reason the American economy had yet to recover from the Depression was that America had lost sight of the importance of making *things:*

> This is the proposition that the basic and irreversible function of an industrial economy is *the making of things;* that the more things it makes the bigger will be the income, whether dollar or real; and hence that the key to those lost recuperative powers lies . . . in the factory where the lathes and the drills and the fires and the hammers are. It is in the factory and on the land and under the land that purchasing power *originates* [italics theirs].

And for the longest time, the making of things remained, at least in principle, the heart of all industrialized economies. But by the eighties, pushed along by that decade's recession, some of the most powerful manufacturers in the world had begun to falter.

A consensus emerged that corporations were bloated, oversized; they owned too much, employed too many people, and were weighed down with *too many things*. The very process of producing—running one's own factories, being responsible for tens of thousands of full-time, permanent employees—began to look less like the route to success and more like a clunky liability.

At around this same time a new kind of corporation began to rival the traditional all-American manufacturers for market share; these were the Nikes and Microsofts, and later, the Tommy Hilfigers and Intels. These pioneers made the bold claim that producing goods was only an incidental part of their operations, and that thanks to recent victories in trade liberalization and labor-law reform, they were able to have their products made for them by contractors, many of them overseas. What these companies produced primarily were not things, they said, but *images* of their brands. Their real work lay not in manufacturing but in marketing. This formula, needless to say, has proved enormously profitable, and its success has companies competing in a race toward weightlessness: whoever owns the least, has the fewest employees on the payroll and produces the most powerful images, as opposed to products, wins the race.

And so the wave of mergers in the corporate world over the last few years is a deceptive phenomenon: it only *looks* as if the giants, by joining forces, are getting bigger and bigger. The true key to understanding these shifts is to realize that in several crucial ways—not their profits, of course—these merged companies are actually shrinking. Their apparent bigness is simply the most effective route toward their real goal: divestment of the world of things.

Since many of today's best-known manufacturers no longer produce products and advertise them, but rather buy products and "brand" them, these companies are forever on the prowl for creative new ways to build and strengthen their brand images. Manufacturing products may require drills, furnaces, hammers and the like, but creating a brand calls for a completely different set of tools and materials. It requires an endless parade of brand extensions, continuously renewed imagery for marketing and, most of all, fresh new spaces to disseminate the brand's idea of itself. In this section of the book, I'll look at how, in ways both insidious and overt, this corporate obsession with brand identity is waging a war on public and individual space: on public institutions such as schools, on youthful identities, on the concept of nationality and on the possibilities for unmarketed space.

The Beginning of the Brand

It's helpful to go back briefly and look at where the idea of branding first began. Though the words are often used interchangeably, branding and advertising are not the same process. Advertising any given product is only one part of branding's grand plan, as are sponsorship and logo licensing. Think of the brand as the core meaning of the modern corporation, and of the advertisement as one vehicle used to convey that meaning to the world.

The first mass-marketing campaigns, starting in the second half of the nineteenth century, had more to do with advertising than with branding as we understand it today. Faced with a range of recently invented products—the radio, phonograph, car, light bulb and so on—advertisers had more pressing tasks than creating a brand identity for any given corporation; first, they had to change the way people lived their lives. Ads had to inform consumers about the existence of some new invention, then convince them that their lives would be better if they used, for example, cars instead of wagons, telephones instead of mail and electric light instead of oil lamps. Many of these new products bore brand names—some of which are still around today—but these were almost incidental. These products were themselves news; that was almost advertisement enough.

The first brand-based products appeared at around the same time as the invention-based ads, largely because of another relatively recent innovation: the factory. When goods began to be produced in factories, not only were entirely new products being introduced but old products—even basic staples—were appearing in strikingly new forms. What made early branding effort different from more straightforward salesmanship was that the market was now being flooded with uniform mass-produced products that were virtually indistinguishable from one another. Competitive branding became a necessity of the machine age—within a context of manufactured sameness, image based difference had to be manufactured along with the product.

So the role of advertising changed from delivering product news bulletins to building an image around a particular brand-name version of a product. The first task of branding was to bestow proper names on generic goods such as sugar, flour, soap and cereal, which had previously been scooped out of barrels by local shopkeepers. In the 1880s, corporate logos were introduced to mass-produced products like Campbell's Soup, H.J. Heinz pickles and Quaker Oats cereal. As design historians and theorists Ellen Lupton and J. Abbott Miller note, logos were tailored to evoke familiarity and folksiness, in an effort to counteract the new and unsettling anonymity of packaged goods. "Familiar personalities such as Dr. Brown, Uncle Ben, Aunt Jemima, and Old Grand-Dad came to replace the shopkeeper, who was traditionally responsible for measuring bulk foods for customers and acting as an advocate for products . . . a nationwide vocabulary of brand names replaced the small local shopkeeper as the interface between consumer and product." After the product names and characters had been established, advertising gave them a venue to speak directly to would-be consumers. The corporate "personality," uniquely named, packaged and advertised, had arrived.

For the most part, the ad campaigns at the end of the nineteenth century and the start of the twentieth used a set of rigid, pseudoscientific formulae: rivals were never mentioned, ad copy used declarative statements only and headlines had to be large, with lots of white space—according to one turn-of-the-century adman, "an advertisement should be big enough to make an impression but not any bigger than the thing advertised."

But there were those in the industry who understood that advertising wasn't just scientific; it was also spiritual. Brands could conjure a feeling—think of Aunt Jemima's comforting presence—but not only that, entire corporations could themselves embody a meaning of their own. In the early twenties, legendary adman Bruce Barton turned General Motors into a metaphor for the American family, "something personal, warm and human," while GE was not so much the name of the faceless General Electric Company as, in Barton's words, "the initials of a friend." In 1923 Barton said that the role of advertising was to help corporations find their soul. The son of a preacher, he drew on his religious upbringing for uplifting messages: "I like to think of advertising as something big, something splendid, something which goes deep down into an institution and gets hold of the soul of it. . . . Institutions have souls, just as men and nations have souls," he told GM president Pierre du Pont. General Motors ads began to tell stories about the people who drove its cars—the preacher, the pharmacist or the country doctor who, thanks to his trusty GM, arrived "at the bedside of a dying child" just in time "to bring it back to life."

By the end of the 1940s, there was a burgeoning awareness that a brand wasn't just a mascot or a catchphrase or a picture printed on the label of a company's product; the company as a whole could have a brand identity or a "corporate consciousness," as this ephemeral quality was termed at the time. As this idea evolved, the adman ceased to see himself as a pitchman and instead saw himself as "the philosopher-king of commercial culture," in the words of ad critic Randall Rothberg. The search for the true meaning of brands—or the "brand essence," as it is often called—gradually took the agencies away from individual products and their attributes and toward a psychological/anthropological examination of what brands mean to the culture and to people's lives. This was seen to be of crucial importance, since corporations may manufacture products, but what consumers buy are brands.

It took several decades for the manufacturing world to adjust to this shift. It clung to the idea that its core business was still production and that branding was an important add-on. Then came the brand equity mania of the eighties, the defining moment of which arrived in 1988 when Philip Morris purchased Kraft for $12.6 billion—six times what the company was worth on paper. The price difference, apparently, was the cost of the word "Kraft." Of course Wall Street was aware that decades of marketing and brand bolstering added value to a company over and above its assets and total annual sales. But with the Kraft purchase, a huge dollar value had been assigned to something that had previously been abstract and unquantifiable—a brand name. This was spectacular news for the ad world, which was now able to make the claim that advertising spending was more than just a sales strategy: it was an investment in cold hard equity. The more you spend, the more your company is worth. Not surprisingly, this led to a considerable increase in spending on advertising. More important, it sparked a renewed interest in puffing up brand identities, a project that involved far more than a few billboards and TV spots. It was about pushing the envelope in sponsorship deals, dreaming up new areas in which to "extend" the brand, as well as perpetually probing the zeitgeist to ensure that the "essence" selected for one's brand would resonate karmically with its target market. For reasons that will be explored in the rest of this chapter, this radical shift in corporate philosophy has sent manufacturers on a cultural feeding frenzy as they seize upon every corner of unmarketed landscape in search of the oxygen needed to inflate their brands. In the process, virtually nothing has been left unbranded. That's quite an impressive feat, considering that as recently as 1993 Wall Street had pronounced the brand dead, or as good as dead.

The Brand's Death (Rumors of Which Had Been Greatly Exaggerated)

The evolution of the brand had one scary episode when it seemed to face extinction. To understand this brush with death, we must first come to terms with advertising's own special law of gravity, which holds that if you aren't rocketing upward you will soon come crashing down.

The marketing world is always reaching a new zenith, breaking through last year's world record and planning to do it again next year with increasing numbers of ads and aggressive new formulae for reaching consumers. The advertising industry's astronomical rate of growth is neatly reflected in year-to-year figures measuring total ad spending in the U.S. (see Table 1), which have gone up so steadily that by 1998 the figure was set to reach $196.5 billion, while global ad spending is estimated at $435 billion. According to the 1998 United Nations Human Development Report, the growth in global ad spending "now outpaces the growth of the world economy by one-third."

This pattern is a by-product of the firmly held belief that brands need continuous and constantly increasing advertising in order to stay in the same place. According to this law

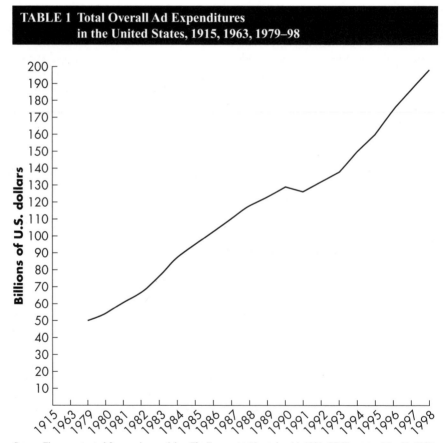

TABLE 1 Total Overall Ad Expenditures in the United States, 1915, 1963, 1979–98

Source: Figures extracted from various articles: *The Economist,* November 14, 1981; *PR Newswire,* May 23, 1983; *Business Week,* August 15, 1983; *Advertising Age,* July 23, 1984; *Ad Age,* May 6, 1985; *Ad Age,* December 16, 1985; *The Record,* January 25, 1986; *Ad Age,* May 12, 1986; *Ad Age,* June 30, 1986; *Ad Age,* August 17, 1987; *Ad Age,* December 14, 1987; *Ad Age,* May 15, 1989; *Marketing,* June 30, 1997; *Ad Age,* December 15, 1997; figures for 1979, 1981 and 1982 are estimates; 1998 figure is a projection based on *Ad Age,* December 15, 1997; all amounts include total of measured and unmeasured ad expenditures in the U.S.

of diminishing returns, the more advertising there is out there (and there always is more, because of this law), the more aggressively brands must market to stand out. And of course, no one is more keenly aware of advertising's ubiquity than the advertisers themselves, who view commercial inundation as a clear and persuasive call for more—and more intrusive—advertising. With so much competition, the agencies argue, clients must spend more than ever to make sure their pitch screeches so loud it can be heard over all the others. David Lubars, a senior ad executive in the Omnicom Group, explains the industry's guiding principle with more candor than most. Consumers, he says, "are like roaches—you spray them and spray them and they get immune after a while."

So, if consumers are like roaches, then marketers must forever be dreaming up new concoctions for industrial-strength Raid. And nineties marketers, being on a more advanced rung of the sponsorship spiral, have dutifully come up with clever and intrusive new selling techniques to do just that. Recent highlights include these innovations: Gordon's gin experimented with filling British movie theaters with the scent of juniper berries; Calvin Klein stuck "CK Be" perfume strips on the backs of Ticketmaster concert envelopes; and in some Scandinavian countries you can get "free" long-distance calls with ads cutting into your telephone conversations. And there's plenty more, stretching across ever more expansive surfaces and cramming into the smallest of crevices: sticker ads on pieces of fruit promoting ABC sitcoms, Levi's ads in public washrooms, corporate logos on boxes of Girl Guide cookies, ads for pop albums on takeout food containers, and ads for Batman movies projected on sidewalks or into the night sky. There are already ads on benches in national parks as well as on library cards in public libraries, and in December 1998 NASA announced plans to solicit ads on its space stations. Pepsi's ongoing threat to project its logo onto the moon's surface hasn't yet materialized, but Mattel did paint an entire street in Salford, England, "a shriekingly bright bubblegum hue" of pink—houses, porches, trees, road, sidewalk, dogs and cars were all accessories in the televised celebrations of Barbie Pink Month. Barbie is but one small part of the ballooning $30 billion "experiential communication" industry, the phrase now used to encompass the staging of such branded pieces of corporate performance art and other "happenings."

That we live a sponsored life is now a truism and it's a pretty safe bet that as spending on advertising continues to rise, we roaches will be treated to even more of these ingenious gimmicks, making it ever more difficult and more seemingly pointless to muster even an ounce of outrage.

But as mentioned earlier, there was a time when the new frontiers facing the advertising industry weren't looking quite so promising. On April 2, 1993, advertising itself was called into question by the very brands the industry had been building, in some cases, for over two centuries. That day is known in marketing circles as "Marlboro Friday," and it refers to a sudden announcement from Philip Morris that it would slash the price of Marlboro cigarettes by 20 percent in an attempt to compete with bargain brands that were eating into its market. The pundits went nuts, announcing in frenzied unison that not only was Marlboro dead, all brand names were dead. The reasoning was that if a "prestige" brand like Marlboro, whose image had been carefully groomed, preened and enhanced with more than a billion advertising dollars, was desperate enough to compete with no-names, then clearly the whole concept of branding had lost its currency. The public had seen the advertising, and the public didn't care. The Marlboro Man, after all, was not any old campaign; launched in 1954, it was the longest-running ad campaign in history. It was a legend. If the Marlboro Man had crashed, well, then, brand equity had crashed as well. The implication that Americans were suddenly thinking for themselves en masse reverberated through Wall Street. The same day Philip Morris announced its price cut, stock prices nose-dived for all the household brands: Heinz, Quaker Oats, Coca-Cola, PepsiCo, Procter and Gamble and RJR Nabisco. Philip Morris's own stock took the worst beating.

Bob Stanojev, national director of consumer products marketing for Ernst and Young, explained the logic behind Wall Street's panic: "If one or two powerhouse consumer products companies start to cut prices for good, there's going to be an avalanche. Welcome to the value generation."

Yes, it was one of those moments of overstated instant consensus, but it was not entirely without cause. Marlboro had always sold itself on the strength of its iconic image marketing, not on anything so prosaic as its price. As we now know, the Marlboro Man survived the price wars without sustaining too much damage. At the time, however, Wall Street saw Philip Morris's decision as symbolic of a sea change. The price cut was an admission that Marlboro's name was no longer sufficient to sustain the flagship position, which in a context where image is equity meant that Marlboro had blinked. And when Marlboro—one of the quintessential global brands—blinks, it raises questions about branding that reach beyond Wall Street, and way beyond Philip Morris.

The panic of Marlboro Friday was not a reaction to a single incident. Rather, it was the culmination of years of escalating anxiety in the face of some rather dramatic shifts in consumer habits that were seen to be eroding the market share of household-name brands, from Tide to Kraft. Bargain-conscious shoppers, hit hard by the recession, were starting to pay more attention to price than to the prestige bestowed on their products by the yuppie ad campaigns of the 1980s. The public was suffering from a bad case of what is known in the industry as "brand blindness."

Study after study showed that baby boomers, blind to the alluring images of advertising and deaf to the empty promises of celebrity spokespersons, were breaking their lifelong brand loyalties and choosing to feed their families with private-label brands from the supermarket—claiming, heretically, that they couldn't tell the difference. From the beginning of the recession to 1993, Loblaw's President's Choice line, Wal-Mart's Great Value and Marks and Spencer's St. Michael prepared foods had nearly doubled their market share in North America and Europe." The computer market, meanwhile, was flooded by inexpensive clones, causing IBM to slash its prices and otherwise impale itself. It appeared to be a return to the proverbial shopkeeper dishing out generic goods from the barrel in a prebranded era.

The bargain craze of the early nineties shook the name brands to their core. Suddenly it seemed smarter to put resources into price reductions and other incentives than into fabulously expensive ad campaigns. This ambivalence began to be reflected in the amounts companies were willing to pay for so-called brand-enhancing advertising. Then, in 1991, it happened: overall advertising spending actually went down by 5.5 percent for the top 100 brands. It was the first interruption in the steady increase of U.S. ad expenditures since a tiny dip of 0.6 percent in 1970, and the largest drop in four decades.

It's not that top corporations weren't flogging their products, it's just that to attract those suddenly fickle customers, many decided to put their money into promotions such as giveaways, contests, in-store displays and (like Marlboro) price reductions. In 1983, American brands spent 70 percent of their total marketing budgets on advertising, and 30 percent on these other forms of promotion. By 1993, the ratio had flipped: only 25 percent went to ads, with the remaining 75 percent going to promotions.

Predictably, the ad agencies panicked when they saw their prestige clients abandoning them for the bargain bins and they did what they could to convince big spenders like Procter and Gamble and Philip Morris that the proper route out of the brand crisis wasn't less brand marketing but more. At the annual meeting of the U.S. Association of National Advertisers in 1988 Graham H. Phillips, the U.S. chairman of Ogilvy & Mather, berated the assembled executives for stooping to participate in "a commodity marketplace rather than an image-based one. "I doubt that many of you would welcome a commodity marketplace in which one competed solely on price, promotion and trade deals, all of which can easily be duplicated by competition, leading to ever-decreasing profits, decay and eventual bankruptcy." Others spoke of the importance of maintaining "conceptual value-added," which in effect means adding nothing but marketing. Stooping to compete on the basis of real value, the agencies ominously warned, would spell not just the death of the brand, but corporate death as well.

Around the same time as Marlboro Friday, the ad industry felt so under siege that market researcher Jack Myers published *Adbashing: Surviving the Attacks on Advertising,* a book-length call to arms against everyone from supermarket cashiers handing out coupons for canned peas to legislators contemplating a new tax on ads. "We, as an industry, must recognize that adbashing is a threat to capitalism, to a free press, to our basic forms of entertainment, and to the future of our children," he wrote.

Despite these fighting words, most market watchers remained convinced that the heyday of the value-added brand had come and gone. The eighties had gone in for brands and hoity-toity designer labels, reasoned David Scotland, European director of Hiram Walker. The nineties would clearly be all about value. "A few years ago," he observed, "it might have been considered smart to wear a shirt with a designer's logo embroidered on the pocket; frankly, it now seems a bit naff."

And from the other side of the Atlantic, Cincinnati journalist Shelly Reese came to the same conclusion about our no-name future, writing that "Americans with Calvin Klein splashed across their hip pocket aren't pushing grocery carts full of Perrier down the aisles anymore. Instead they're sporting togs with labels like Kmart's Jaclyn Smith and maneuvering carts full of Kroger Co.'s Big K soda. Welcome to the private label decade."

Scotland and Reese, if they remember their bold pronouncements, are probably feeling just a little bit silly right now. Their embroidered "pocket" logos sound positively subdued by today's logomaniacal standards, and sales of name-brand bottled water have been increasing at an annual rate of 9 percent, turning it into a $3.4 billion industry by 1997. From today's logo-quilted perch, it's almost unfathomable that a mere six years ago, death sentences for the brand seemed not only plausible but self-evident.

So just how did we get from obituaries for Tide to today's battalions of volunteer billboards for Tommy Hilfiger, Nike and Calvin Klein? Who slipped the steroids into the brand's comeback?

The Brands Bounce Back

There were some brands that were watching from the sidelines as Wall Street declared the death of the brand. Funny, they must have thought, we don't feel dead.

Just as the admen had predicted at the beginning of the recession, the companies that exited the downturn running were the ones who opted for marketing over value every time: Nike, Apple, the Body Shop, Calvin Klein, Disney, Levi's and Starbucks. Not only were these brands doing just fine, thank you very much, but the act of branding was becoming a larger and larger focus of their businesses. For these companies, the ostensible product was mere filler for the real production: the brand. They integrated the idea of branding into the very fabric of their companies. Their corporate cultures were so tight and cloistered that to outsiders they appeared to be a cross between fraternity house, religious cult and sanitarium. Everything was an ad for the brand: bizarre lexicons for describing employees (partners, baristas, team players, crew members), company chants, superstar CEOs, fanatical attention to design consistency, a propensity for monument-building, and New Age mission statements. Unlike classic household brand names, such as Tide and Marlboro, these logos weren't losing their currency, they were in the midst of breaking every barrier in the marketing world—becoming cultural accessories and lifestyle philosophers. These companies didn't wear their image like a cheap shirt—their image was so integrated with their business that other people wore it as *their* shirt. And when the brands crashed, these companies didn't even notice—they were branded to the bone.

So the real legacy of Marlboro Friday is that it simultaneously brought the two most significant developments in nineties marketing and consumerism into sharp focus: the deeply unhip big-box bargain stores that provide the essentials of life and monopolize a disproportionate share of the market (Wal-Mart *et al.*) and the extra-premium "attitude" brands that provide the essentials of lifestyle and monopolize ever-expanding stretches of cultural space (Nike *et al.*). The way these two tiers of consumerism developed would have a profound impact on the economy in the years to come. When overall ad expenditures took a nosedive in 1991, Nike and Reebok were busy playing advertising chicken, with each company increasing its budget to outspend the other. In 1991 alone, Reebok upped its ad spending by 71.9 percent, while Nike pumped an extra 24.6 percent into its already soaring ad budget, bringing the company's total spending on marketing to a staggering $250 million annually. Far from worrying about competing on price, the sneaker pimps were designing ever more intricate and pseudoscientific air pockets, and driving up prices by signing star athletes to colossal sponsorship deals. The fetish strategy seemed to be working fine: in the six years prior to 1993, Nike had gone from a $750 million company to a $4 billion one and Phil Knight's Beaverton, Oregon, company emerged from the recession with profits 900 percent higher than when it began.

Benetton and Calvin Klein, meanwhile, were also upping their spending on lifestyle marketing, using ads to associate their lines with risque art and progressive politics. Clothes barely appeared in these high-concept advertisements, let alone prices. Even more abstract was Absolut Vodka, which for some years now had been developing a marketing strategy in which its product disappeared and its brand was nothing but a blank bottle-shaped space that could be filled with whatever content a particular audience most wanted from its brands: intellectual in *Harper's,* futuristic in *Wired,* alternative in *Spin,* loud and proud in *Out* and "Absolut Centerfold" in *Playboy.* The brand reinvented itself as a cultural sponge, soaking up and morphing to its surroundings.

Saturn, too, came out of nowhere in October 1990 when GM launched a car built not out of steel and rubber but out of New Age spirituality and seventies feminism. After the car had been on the market a few years, the company held a "homecoming" weekend for Saturn owners, during which they could visit the auto plant and have a cookout with the people who made their cars. As the Saturn ads boasted at the time, "44,000 people spent their vacations with us, at a car plant." It was as if Aunt Jemima had come to life and invited you over to her house for dinner.

In 1993, the year the Marlboro Man was temporarily hobbled by "brand-blind"' consumers, Microsoft made its striking debut on *Advertising Age*'s list of the top 200 ad spenders—the very same year that Apple computer increased its marketing budget by 30 percent after already making branding history with its Orwellian takeoff ad launch during the 1984 Super Bowl. Like Saturn, both companies were selling a hip new relationship to the machine that left Big Blue IBM looking as clunky and menacing as the now-dead Cold War.

And then there were the companies that had always understood that they were selling brands before product. Coke, Pepsi, McDonald's, Burger King and Disney weren't fazed by the brand crisis, opting instead to escalate the brand war, especially since they had their eyes firmly fixed on global expansion. They were joined in this project by a wave of sophisticated producer/retailers who hit full stride in the late eighties and early nineties. The Gap, Ikea and the Body Shop were spreading like wildfire during this period, masterfully transforming the generic into the brand-specific, largely through bold, carefully branded packaging and the promotion of an "experiential" shopping environment. The Body Shop had been a presence in Britain since the seventies, but it wasn't until 1988 that it began sprouting like a green weed on every street corner in the U.S. Even during the darkest years of the recession, the company opened between forty and fifty American stores a year. Most baffling of all to Wall Street, it pulled off the expansion without spending a dime on advertising. Who needed billboards and magazine ads when retail outlets were three-dimensional advertisements for an ethical and ecological approach to cosmetics? The Body Shop was all brand.

The Starbucks coffee chain, meanwhile, was also expanding during this period without laying out much in advertising; instead, it was spinning off its name into a wide range of branded projects: Starbucks airline coffee, office coffee, coffee ice cream, coffee beer. Starbucks seemed to understand brand names at a level even deeper than Madison Avenue, incorporating marketing into every fiber of its corporate concept—from the chain's strategic association with books, blues and jazz to its Euro-latte lingo. What the success of both the Body Shop and Starbucks showed was how far the branding project had come in moving beyond splashing one's logo on a billboard. Here were two companies that had fostered powerful identities by making their brand concept into a virus and sending it out into the culture via a variety of channels: cultural sponsorship, political controversy, the consumer experience and brand extensions. Direct advertising, in this context, was viewed as a rather clumsy intrusion into a much more organic approach to image building.

Scott Bedbury, Starbucks' vice president of marketing, openly recognized that "consumers don't truly believe there's a huge difference between products," which is why brands must "establish emotional ties" with their customers through "the Starbucks Experience." The people who line up for Starbucks, writes CEO Howard Shultz, aren't just there for the coffee. "It's the romance of the coffee experience, the feeling of warmth and community people get in Starbucks stores."

Interestingly, before moving to Starbucks, Bedbury was head of marketing at Nike, where he oversaw the launch of the "Just Do It!" slogan, among other watershed branding moments. In the following passage, he explains the common techniques used to infuse the two very different brands with meaning:

> Nike, for example, is leveraging the deep emotional connection that people have with sports and fitness. With Starbucks, we see how coffee has woven itself into the fabric of people's lives, and that's our opportunity for emotional leverage. . . . A great brand raises the bar—it adds a greater sense of purpose to the experience, whether it's the challenge to do your best in sports and fitness or the affirmation that the cup of coffee you're drinking really matters.

This was the secret, it seemed, of all the success stories of the late eighties and early nineties. The lesson of Marlboro Friday was that there never really was a brand crisis—only brands that had crises of confidence. The brands would be okay, Wall Street concluded, so long as they believed fervently in the principles of branding and never, ever blinked. Overnight, "Brands, not products!" became the rallying cry for a marketing renaissance led by a new breed of companies that saw themselves as "meaning brokers" instead of product producers. What was changing was the idea of what—in both advertising and branding—was being sold. The old paradigm had it that all marketing was selling a product. In the new model, however, the product always takes a back seat to the real product, the brand, and the selling of the brand acquired an extra component that can only be described as spiritual. Advertising is about hawking product. Branding, in its truest and most advanced incarnations, is about corporate transcendence.

It may sound flaky, but that's precisely the point. On Marlboro Friday, a line was drawn in the sand between the lowly price slashers and the high-concept brand builders. The brand builders conquered and a new consensus was born: the products that will flourish in the future will be the ones presented not as "commodities" but as concepts: the brand as experience, as lifestyle.

Ever since, a select group of corporations has been attempting to free itself from the corporeal world of commodities, manufacturing and products to exist on another plane. Anyone can manufacture a product, they reason (and as the success of private-label brands during the recession proved, anyone did). Such menial tasks, therefore, can and should be farmed out to contractors and subcontractors whose only concern is filling the order on time and under budget (ideally in the Third World, where labor is dirt cheap, laws are lax and tax breaks come by the bushel). Headquarters, meanwhile, is free to focus on the real business at hand—creating a corporate mythology powerful enough to infuse meaning into these raw objects just by signing its name.

The corporate world has always had a deep New Age streak, fed—it has become clear—by a profound need that could not be met simply by trading widgets for cash. But when branding captured the corporate imagination, New Age vision quests took center stage. As Nike CEO Phil Knight explains, "For years we thought of ourselves as a production-oriented company, meaning we put all our emphasis on designing and manufacturing the product. But now we understand that the most important thing we do is market the product. We've come around to saying that Nike is a marketing-oriented company, and the product is our most important marketing tool." This project has since been taken to an even more advanced level with the emergence of on-line corporate giants such as Amazon.com. It is on-line that the purest brands are being built: liberated from the real-world burdens of stores and product manufacturing, these brands are free to soar, less as the disseminators of goods or services than as collective hallucinations.

Tom Peters, who has long coddled the inner flake in many a hard-nosed CEO, latched on to the branding craze as the secret to financial success, separating the transcendental logos and the earthbound products into two distinct categories of companies. "The top half—Coca-Cola, Microsoft, Disney, and so on—are pure 'players' in brainware. The bottom half [Ford and GM] are still lumpy-object purveyors, though automobiles are much 'smarter' than they used to be," Peters writes in *The Circle of Innovation* (1997), an ode to the power of marketing over production:

When Levi's began to lose market share in the late nineties, the trend was widely attributed to the company's failure—despite lavish ad spending—to transcend its products and become a free-standing meaning. "Maybe one of Levi's problems is that it has no Cola," speculated Jennifer Steinhauer in *The New York Times*. "It has no denim-toned house paint. Levi makes what is essentially a commodity: blue jeans. Its ads may evoke rugged outdoorsmanship, but Levi hasn't promoted any particular life style to sell other products."

In this high-stakes new context, the cutting-edge ad agencies no longer sold companies on individual campaigns but on their ability to act as "brand stewards": identifying, articulating and protecting the corporate soul. Not surprisingly, this spelled good news for the U.S. advertising industry, which in 1994 saw a spending increase of 8.6 percent over the previous year. In one year, the ad industry went from a near crisis to another "best year yet." And that was only the beginning of triumphs to come. By 1997, corporate advertising, defined as "ads that position a corporation, its values, its personality and character" were up 18 percent from the year before.

With this wave of brand mania has come a new breed of businessman, one who will proudly inform you that Brand X is not a product but a way of life, an attitude, a set of values, a look, an idea. And it sounds really great—way better than that Brand X is a screwdriver, or a hamburger chain, or a pair of jeans, or even a very successful line of running shoes. Nike, Phil Knight announced in the late eighties, is "a sports company"; its mission is not to sell shoes but to "enhance people's lives through sports and fitness" and to keep "the magic of sports alive." Company president-cum-sneaker-shaman Tom Clark explains that "the inspiration of sports allows us to rebirth ourselves constantly."

Journal Topics

1. Are you "loyal" to any brand names (such as Coke over Pepsi, Chevy over Ford, or iPod over other MP3 players)? Why or why not?

2. To you, what is the difference between *branding* and *advertising*?

3. Many people want to own only expensive, brand-name clothing. Do you prefer clothing that is branded or generic? Explain.

4. Would you want a phone service that gave free long-distance calls but got interrupted every few minutes to play an advertisement?

Question for Critical Thought

1. Scott Bedbury, the vice president of marketing at Starbucks, argues that "consumers don't truly believe there's a huge difference between products, which is why brands must 'establish emotional ties' with their customers." What types of emotions do certain brands carry with them? Discuss several brands and what their companies try to make the consumer feel by purchasing them. To do this, consider your own feelings when you see an ad, make a purchase, or take your first taste of a product.

Suggestion for Personal Research

1. Select a major brand name (such as Nike, Wal-Mart, Starbucks, etc.). Conduct a field survey on your campus to determine consumers' emotional reactions to the brand in question. Pay attention to demographics (age, gender, etc.) to see if any differences emerge.

Multicultural Issues

1. If you came here from someplace else, did brands in your country seem to matter as much as they do in the U.S.? Compare and contrast the two countries in regard to branding.

2. Were there any American brands that were very popular or even dominated the market in your country? What accounts for their popularity? How much of it is because they summoned up dreams about what America itself could offer?

3. Are there any massive brand names that were very popular in your country that are very small or nonexistent in America? Discuss.

Vocabulary Terms

divestment	ubiquity
disseminate	inundation
overt	truism
burgeoning	prosaic
ephemeral	baby boomers
bolstering	ostensible
zenith	corporeal

But First, a Word from Our Sponsors

James B. Twitchell

Prereading Questions

1. How important are material goods and shopping to you? Do you *have* to have the newest gadget? Do you think shopping is a great way to escape stress or boredom?

2. Do you ever worry that you shop too much? If you get a rush from buying new clothes and products, how do you tend to feel about these purchases after you have had them for a little while?

3. Do you ever get the feeling that American culture is getting "dumbed down"?

Whenever a member of my paunchy fiftysomething set pulls me aside and complains of the dumbing down of American culture, I tell him that if he doesn't like it, he should quit moaning and go buy a lot of Fast-Moving Consumer Goods. And every time he buys soap, toothpaste, beer, gasoline, bread, aspirin, and the like, he should make it a point to buy a different brand. He should implore his friends to do likewise. At the same time, he should quit giving so much money to his kids. That, I'm sorry to say, is his only hope.

Here's why. The culture we live in is carried on the back of advertising. Now I mean that literally. If you cannot find commercial support for what you have to say, it will not be transported. Much of what we share, and what we know, and even what we treasure, is carried to us each second in a plasma of electrons, pixels, and ink, underwritten by multinational advertising agencies dedicated to attracting our attention for entirely nonaltruistic reasons. These agencies, gathered up inside worldwide conglomerates with weird, sci-fi names like WPP, Omnicom, Saatchi & Saatchi, Dentsu, and Euro RSCG, are usually collections of established shops linked together to provide "full service" to their global clients. Their service is not moving information or creating entertainment, but buying space and inserting advertising. They essentially rent our concentration to other companies—sponsors—for the dubious purpose of informing us of something that we've longed for all our lives even though we've never heard of it before. Modern selling is not about trading information, as it was in the 19th century, as much as about creating an infotainment culture with sufficient allure to enable other messages—commercials—to get through. In the spirit of the enterprise, I call this new culture Adcult.

Adcult is there when we blink, it's there when we listen, it's there when we touch, it's even there to be smelled in scent strips when we open a magazine. There is barely a space in our culture not already carrying commercial messages. Look anywhere: in schools there is Channel One; in movies there is product placement; ads are in urinals, played on telephone hold, in alphanumeric displays in taxis, sent unannounced to fax machines, inside catalogs, on the video in front of the Stairmaster at the gym, on T-shirts, at the doctor's office, on grocery carts, on parking meters, on tees at golf holes, on inner-city basketball backboards, piped in along with Muzak . . . ad nauseam (and yes, even on airline vomit bags). We have to shake magazines like rag dolls to free up their pages from the "blow-in" inserts and then wrestle out the stapled- or glued-in ones before reading can begin. We now have to fast-forward through some five minutes of advertising that opens rental videotapes. President Bill Clinton's inaugural parade featured a Budweiser float. At the Smithsonian, the Orkin Pest Control Company sponsored an exhibit on exactly what it advertises it kills: insects. No venue is safe. Is there a blockbuster museum show not decorated with corporate logos? The Public Broadcasting Service is littered with "underwriting announcements" that look and sound almost exactly like what PBS claims they are not: commercials.

Okay, you get the point. Commercial speech is so powerful that it drowns out all other sounds. But sounds are always conveyed in a medium. The media of modern culture are these: print, sound, pictures, or some combination of each. Invariably, conversations about dumbing down focus on the supposed corruption of these media, as demonstrated by the sophomoric quality of most movies, the fall from the golden age of television, the mindlessness of most bestsellers, and the tarting-up of the news, be it in or on *USA Today, Time,* ABC, or *Inside Edition.* The media make especially convenient whipping boys because they are now all conglomerated into huge worldwide organizations such as Time Warner, General Electric, Viacom, Bertelsmann, and Sony. But, alas, as much fun as it is to blame the media, they have very little to do with the explanation for whatever dumbing down has occurred.

The explanation is, I think, more fundamental, more economic in nature. These media are delivered for a price. We have to pay for them, either by spending money or by spending time. Given a choice, we prefer to spend time. We spend our time paying attention to ads, and in exchange we are given infotainment. This trade is central to Adcult. Economists call this "cost externalization." If you want to see it at work, go to McDonald's. You order. You carry your food to the table. You clean up. You pay less. Want to see it elsewhere? Buy gas. Just as the "work" you do at the self-service gas station lowers the price of gas, so consuming ads is the "work" you do that lowers the price of delivering the infotainment. In Adcult, the trade is more complex. True, you are entertained at lower cost, but you are also encultured in the process.

So far, so good. The quid pro quo of modern infotainment culture is that if you want it, you'll get it—no matter what it is—as long as there are enough of you who (1) are willing to spend some energy along the way hearing "a word from our sponsor" and (2) have sufficient disposable income possibly to buy some of the advertised goods. In Adcult you pay twice: once with the ad and once with the product. So let's look back a step to examine these products because—strange as it may seem—they are at the center of the dumbing down of American culture.

Before all else, we must realize that modern advertising is tied primarily to things, and only secondarily to services. Manufacturing both things and their meanings is what American culture is all about. If Greece gave the world philosophy, Britain drama, Austria music, Germany politics, and Italy art, then America gave mass-produced objects. "We bring good things to life" is no offhand claim. Most of these "good things" are machine made and hence interchangeable. Such objects, called parity items, constitute most of the stuff that surrounds us, from bottled water to toothpaste to beer to cars. There is really no great difference between Evian and Mountain Spring, Colgate and Crest, Miller and Budweiser, Ford and Chevrolet. Often, the only difference is in the advertising. Advertising is how we talk about these fungible things, how we know their supposed differences, how we recognize them. We don't consume the products as much as we consume the advertising.

For some reason, we like it this way. Logically, we should all read *Consumer Reports* and then all buy the most sensible product. But we don't. So why do we waste our energy (and billions of dollars) entertaining fraudulent choice? I don't know. Perhaps just as we drink the advertising, not the beer, we prefer the illusion of choice to the reality of decision. How else to explain the appearance of so much superfluous choice? A decade ago, grocery stores carried about 9,000 items; they now stock about 24,000. Revlon makes 158 shades of lipstick. Crest toothpaste comes in 36 sizes and shapes and flavors. We are even eager to be offered choice where there is none to speak of. AT&T offers "the right choice"; Wendy's asserts that "there is no better choice"; Pepsi is "the choice of a new generation"; Taster's Choice is "the choice for taste." Even advertisers don't understand the phenomenon. Is there a relationship between the number of soft drinks and television channels—about 27? What's going to happen when the information pipe carries 500?

I have no idea. But I do know this: human beings like things. We buy things. We like to exchange things. We steal things. We donate things. We live through things. We call these things "goods," as in "goods and services." We do not call them "bads." This sounds simplistic, but it is crucial to understanding the power of Adcult. The still-going-strong Industrial Revolution produces more and more things, not because production is what machines do, and not because nasty capitalists twist their handlebar mustaches and mutter, "More slop for the pigs," but because we are powerfully attracted to the world of things. Advertising, when it's lucky, supercharges some of this attraction.

This attraction to the inanimate happens all over the world. Berlin Walls fall because people want things, and they want the culture created by things. China opens its doors not so much because it wants to get out, but because it wants to get things in. We were not suddenly transformed from customers to consumers by wily manufacturers eager to unload a surplus of products. We have created a surfeit of things because we enjoy the process of "getting and spending." The consumption ethic may have started in the early 1900s, but the desire is ancient. Kings and princes once thought they could solve problems by amassing things. We now join them.

The Marxist balderdash of cloistered academics aside, human beings did not suddenly become materialistic. We have always been desirous of things. We have just not had many of them until quite recently, and, in a few generations, we may return to having fewer and fewer. Still, while they last, we enjoy shopping for things and see both the humor and the truth reflected in the aphoristic "born to shop," "shop til you drop," and "when the going gets tough, the tough go shopping." Department store windows, whether on the city street or inside a mall, did not appear by magic. We enjoy looking through them to another world. It is voyeurism for capitalists. Our love of things is the cause of the Industrial Revolution, not the consequence. We are not only homo sapiens, or homo ludens, or homo faber, but also homo emptor.

Mid-20th-century American culture is often criticized for being too materialistic. Ironically, we are not too materialistic. We are not materialistic enough. If we craved objects and knew what they meant, there would be no need to add meaning through advertising. We would gather, use, toss out, or hoard based on some inner sense of value.

But we don't. We don't know what to gather, we like to trade what we have gathered, and we need to know how to evaluate objects of little practical use. What is clear is that most things in and of themselves simply do not mean enough. In fact, what we crave may not be objects at all but their meaning. For whatever else advertising "does," one thing is certain: by adding value to material, by adding meaning to objects, by branding things, advertising performs a role historically associated with religion. The Great Chain of Being, which for centuries located value above the horizon in the world Beyond, has been reforged to settle value into the objects of the Here and Now.

I wax a little impatient here because most of the literature on modern culture is downright supercilious about consumption. What do you expect? Most of it comes from a culture professionally hostile to materialism, albeit secretly envious. From Thorstein Veblen on there has been a palpable sense of disapproval as the hubbub of commerce is viewed from the groves of academe. The current hand-wringing over dumbing down is not new. It used to be Bread and Circuses. Modern concepts of bandwagon consumption, conspicuous consumption, keeping-up-with-the-Joneses, the culture of narcissism, and all the other barely veiled reproofs have limited our serious consideration of Adcult to such relatively minor issues as manipulation and exploitation. People surely can't want, ugh!, things. Or, if they really do want them, they must want them for all the wrong reasons. The idea that advertising creates artificial desires rests on a profound ignorance of human nature, on the hazy feeling that there existed some halcyon era of noble savages with purely natural needs, on romantic claptrap first promulgated by Rousseau and kept alive in institutions well isolated from the marketplace.

We are now closing in on why the dumbing down of American culture has occurred with such startling suddenness in the last 30 years. We are also closing in on why the big complainers about dumbing down are me and my paunchy pals. The people who want things the most and have the best chance to acquire them are the young. They are also the ones who have not yet decided which brands of objects they wish to consume. In addition, they have a surplus of two commodities: time and money, especially the former. If you can make a sale to these twentysomethings, if you can "brand" them with your product, you may have them for life. But to do this you have to be able to speak to them, and to do that you have to go to where you will be heard.

The history of mass media can be summarized in a few words: if it can't carry advertising, it won't survive.

Books are the exception that almost proves the rule. Books used to carry ads. Initially, publishing and advertising were joined at the press. Book publishers, from William Caxton to modern university presses, have advertised forthcoming titles on their flyleaves and dust jackets. No doubt publishers would have been willing to bind other material into their products if only there had been a demand. While we may have been startled when Christopher Whittle marketed his Larger Agenda series of books ("big ideas, great writers, short books") by inserting advertising into what was essentially a long magazine article bound in hardcover, he was actually behaving like a traditional book publisher. When Whittle published William Greider's *Trouble with Money*—94 pages of text and 18 pages of Federal Express ads—book reviewers turned away, aghast. But when Bradbury & Evans published Charles Dickens's *Little Dorrit* in 1857, no reviewer or reader blanched at seeing the bound-in ad section touting Persian parasols, smelling salts, portable India-rubber boots, and the usual array of patent medicines.

The reason why books were not an advertising medium is simple: there wasn't much to advertise, and once there was a surplus of machine-made parity items, there was a cheaper medium—the magazine. The death knell of book advertising is still being rung not by publishers but by the postal service. Put an ad in a book and it no longer travels at fourth-class book rate but at third-class commercial rate. A prediction: advertising will return to books. UPS, Federal Express, and the other commercial carriers make no such distinction about content, only about weight and size. In addition, since Dr. Spock fought Pocket Books to have cigarette ads removed from his baby-care book in the late 1940s, the Authors' Guild has advised writers to have a no-advertising clause inserted in the boilerplate of their contracts with publishers. What would it take to reverse this? Not much, I suspect. Put a few ads in, drop the price 10 percent, and most people would accept it. Of course, the real reason books are currently ad free is that the prime audience for advertisers, namely the young, is functionally illiterate.

Here is the history of magazine and newspaper publishing on a thumbnail. All the innovations in these media were forced on them by advertisers. You name it: the appearance of ads throughout the pages, the "jump" or continuation of a story from page to page, the rise of sectionalization (as with news, cartoons, sports, financial, living, real estate), common page size, halftone images, process engraving, the use of black-and-white photography, then color, sweepstakes, and finally discounted subscriptions were all forced on publishers by advertisers hoping to find target audiences.

From the publishers' point of view, the only way to increase revenues without upping the price, or adding advertising space, is to increase circulation. First-copy costs in magazine and newspaper publishing are stupendous. Ironically, the economies of scale are such that to increase the "reach" of this medium and lower your last-copy cost, you must also run the risk of alienating core readership. This is not advertising-friendly. What amounts to a Hobson's choice for the publisher has proved a godsend for the advertiser. It means that papers and magazines will tend to self-censor in order to provide a bland and unobtrusive plasma as they, on their own, seek to maximize their profits. They dumb down automatically. Look at the *New York Times* and you can see this operating in slow motion. The increase of infotainment and the presence of movie ads, the jazzy "Style" section of Sunday, and, of course, the use of color, to say nothing of the appearance on the front page of stories that used to be deemed tabloidlike and were therefore relegated to the back sections—were attempts to find the "proper" readership, not to find all that is "Fit to Print." If newspapers want to survive, they will have to think of themselves not as delivering news or entertainment to readers but delivering readers to advertisers.

One might even see newspapers and magazines, in the current bafflegab, as members of a "victim" class. They are remnants of a print culture in which selling was secondary to informing. To survive, they had to replace their interest in their reader as reader with the more modern view of the reader as commodity. Still, print media might have maintained their cultural standards, had not radio and television elbowed them aside. Ironically, print had to conglomerate, to fit itself into huge oligopolies such as Scripps-Howard, the Tribune Company, the New York Times Company, Gannett, the Washington Post Company, Times Mirror, Meredith, and the rest, in order to sell advertising space profitably. As advertising will flow to that medium which finds the target audience cheapest, the demographic specialization of print is a direct result of the rise of Adcult.

This struggle to find targeted audiences has led to two interesting extremes. On one extreme are magazines that are pure advertising, such as *Colors from Benetton, Le Magazine de Chanel,* and *Sony Style,* which erase the line between advertising and content so that you cannot tell what is text and what is hype. At the other extreme are magazines such as the reincarnated *Ms.* or *Consumer Reports,* which remain ad free for political or economic reasons. Meanwhile, the rest of magazine culture aspires to the condition of women's magazines, in which the ratio of advertising space to print space is about 10 to 1, and to the editorial condition of newspapers, which is as bland as vanilla.

The electronic media have turned the screws on print, have made it play a perpetual game of catch-up, have forced it into niches so that only a few national magazines and newspapers have survived. Broadcasting has forced print to narrow-cast. Television is usually blamed, but the real culprit is radio. Radio started with such high hopes. It has achieved such low reality. Rush Limbaugh and Howard Stern are not stars of this medium by accident.

After World War I, Westinghouse found itself with a surplus of tubes, amplifiers, transmitters, and crystal receivers. So in November 1920, it started KDKA in Pittsburgh on the Field of Dreams principle ("If you build it, they will come"). It worked. Once transmitters were built, Westinghouse receiving apparatuses could be unloaded. You could make them at home. All you needed was a spool of wire, a crystal, an aerial, and earphones—all produced by Westinghouse. Patience and a cylindrical oatmeal box were supplied by the hobbyist. By July 1922, some 400 stations had sprung up.

Rather like users of the Internet today, no one then seemed to care "what" was on as long as they were hearing something. When stereophonic sound was introduced in the 1950s, at first the most popular records were of the ordinary sounds of locomotives and cars passing from speaker to speaker. People used to marvel at the test patterns of early television as no doubt monks stood in awe before the first printed letters. However, in the 1920s, great plans were being hatched for radio. Universities would take advantage of this new way to dispense their respective cultures by building transmitters. The government would see to this by allocating special licenses just for universities. This medium would never dumb down, it would uplift.

The problem was that everyone was broadcasting on the same wavelength. When transmitters were placed too close together, the signals became mixed and garbled. AT&T suggested a solution. It would link stations together using its existing lines, and soon everyone would hear clearly. AT&T envisioned tying some 38 stations together in a system it called "toll broadcasting." The word "toll" was the tip-off. Someone was going to have to pay. The phone company suggested that time could be sold to private interests, and it called this subsidy "ether advertising." The suggestion was not an immediate success. Secretary of Commerce Herbert Hoover, considered a presidential possibility, warned that it was "inconceivable that we should allow so great a possibility for service . . . to be drowned in advertising chatter," and that if presidential messages ever "became the meat in a sandwich of two patent medicine advertisements it would destroy broadcasting." Such Cassandras were uniformly ignored. This would never happen. The universities would see to it by their responsible use of the medium.

In 1922, AT&T started WEAF (for wind, earth, air, fire) in New York. The station tried all kinds of innovative things, even broadcasting live from a football stadium. It tried letting companies buy time to talk about their products. Such talk was always in good taste: no mention of where the products were available, no samples offered, no store locations, no comparisons, no price information—just a few words about what it is that you offer. At 5 P.M. on August 28, the station manager even let a Mr. Blackwell step up to the microphone and say his piece about a housing development. He spoke only once. This is what he said, and it is every bit as important as "Mr. Watson, come here, I want you," only a bit longer. It was to be the Mayday distress call of high culture:

It is 58 years since Nathaniel Hawthorne, the greatest of American fictionists, passed away. To honor his memory the Queensboro Corporation has named its latest group of high-grade dwellings "Hawthorne Court." I wish to thank those within sound of my voice for the broadcasting opportunity afforded me to urge this vast radio audience to seek the recreation and the daily comfort of the home removed from the congested part of the city, right at the boundaries of God's great outdoors, and within a few miles by subway from the business section of Manhattan. This sort of residential environment strongly influenced Hawthorne, America's greatest writer of fiction. He analyzed with charming keenness the social spirit of those who had thus happily selected their homes, and he painted the people inhabiting those homes with good-natured relish. . . . Let me enjoin upon you as you value your health and your hopes and your home happiness, get away from the solid masses of brick, where the meager opening admitting a slant of sunlight is mockingly called a light shaft, and where children grow up starved for a run over a patch of grass and the sight of a tree. Apartments in congested parts of the city have proved failures. The word "neighbor" is an expression of peculiar irony—a daily joke. . . . Let me close by urging that you hurry to the apartment home near the green fields and the neighborly atmosphere right on the subway without the expense and trouble of a commuter, where health and community happiness beckon—the community life and the friendly environment that Hawthome advocated.

Three weeks later, the Queensboro Corporation had sold all its property in Hawthorne Court (named for "America's greatest writer of fiction," who clearly had never been read by Mr. Blackwell) in Jackson Heights, Queens. The genie was out of the bottle.

Giving the public what it wants had its price. Like television today, the messenger was soon being blamed for the message. Commercial radio broadcasting was "dumbing down" American culture with its incessant repetition of mindless humor, maudlin sentimentality, exaggerated action, and frivolous entertainment. Proving yet again the power of Gresham's Law when applied to culture, radio programming by the 1930s was selling out to the lowest common denominator. Typical of highcult outrage was James Rorty, erstwhile advertising copywriter turned snitch for such leftward-leaning periodicals as the *New Republic:*

American culture is like a skyscraper: The gargoyle's mouth is a loudspeaker [the radio], powered by the vested interest of a two-billion-dollar industry, and back of that the vested interests of business as a whole, of industry, of finance. It is never silent, it drowns out all other voices, and it suffers no rebuke, for is it not the voice of America? That is this claim and to some extent it is a just claim. . . . Is it any wonder that the American population tends increasingly to speak, think, feel in terms of this jabberwocky? That the stimuli of art, science, religion are progressively expelled to the periphery of American life to become marginal values, cultivated by marginal people on marginal time?

But wait! What about those universities? Weren't they supposed to make sure the airwaves would be full of "the best that had been thought and said"? While there were more than 90 educational stations (of a total 732) in 1927, by the mid-1930s there were only a handful. What happened? Surely, the universities would never participate in any dumbing down. Alas, the universities had sold their radio licenses to the burgeoning networks—called "nets" or, better yet, "webs"—emanating from Manhattan. In one of the few attempts to recapture cultural control from commercial exploitation, the National Education Association (NEA) lobbied Senators Robert Wagner of New York and Henry Hatfield of West Virginia to reshuffle the stations and restore a quarter of them to university hands. These stations would forever be advertisement-free, making "sweetness and light" available to all. The lobbying power of the NEA met the clout of Madison Avenue. No contest. The Wagner-Hatfield bill died aborning, defeated by a margin of almost two to one.

One of the reasons the Wagner-Hatfield bill floundered so quickly was the emergence of a new cultural phenomenon, the countrywide hit show. Never before had an entertainment been developed that an entire nation—by 1937 more than three-quarters of American homes had at least one radio—could experience at the same time. "Amos 'n' Andy" at NBC had shown what a hit show could do. NBC thought a "hit" was the way to sell its RCA receivers, and the network was partially right—more than 100,000 sets were sold just so people could hear the minstrel antics of "The Mystic Knights of the Sea." But CBS knew better. Hits could make millions of dollars in advertising revenue. Although they were not yet called "blockbusters" (that would come with the high-explosive bombs of World War II), the effect of hits was already acknowledged as concussive. One could support hundreds of programming failures.

In truth, CBS or not, television never had a chance to be anything other than the consummate selling machine. It took 25 years for radio to evolve out of wireless; it took much less time for television to emerge. And while it took a decade and an economic depression for advertisers to dominate the radio spectrum, it took only a few years and economic expansion for them to do the same with television. Advertisers had rested during the war. They had no product to sell. No surplus = no advertising.

Even though radio not only survived but prospered during the war, the new kid on the block was too tough to beat. From the first narrow broadcast, television was going commercial. The prophetic Philo T. Farnsworth presented a dollar sign for 60 seconds in the first public demonstration of his television system in 1927. Once Hazel Bishop became a million-dollar company in the early 1950s based on television advertising, the direction of the medium was set. It would follow radio. Certain systemic changes in both broadcast media did occur, the most important being the networks' recapture of programming from the agencies. Although this shift away from agency control took scandals to accomplish (notably, the scandals involving quiz shows rigged under pressure from ad agencies), it would have happened anyway. Simple economics made it cheaper to sell time by the ounce than by the pound. The "nets" could make more by selling minutes than by selling half- or full hours. Magazines maximized ad revenues by selling space by the partial page; why not television? The motto of this new medium became, "Programs are the scheduled interruptions of marketing bulletins." How could it be otherwise?

We need not be reminded of what is currently happening to television to realize the direction of the future. MTV, the infomercial, and the home-shopping channels are not flukes but the predictable continuation of this medium. Thanks to the remote-control wand and the coaxial (soon to be fiber-optic) cable, commercials will disappear. They will become the programming. Remember, the first rule of Adcult is this: given the choice between paying money or paying attention, we prefer to pay attention.

What all this means is that if you think things are bad now, just wait. There are few gate-keepers left. Most of them reside on Madison Avenue. Just as the carnival barker doesn't care what is behind the tent flap, only how long the line is in front, the poobahs of Adcult care only about who's looking, not what they are looking at. The best-seller lists, the box office, the Nielsens, the various circulation figures for newspapers and magazines, are the meters. They decide what gets through. Little wonder that so much of our popular culture is derivative of itself, that prequels and sequels and spin-offs are the order of the day, that celebrity is central, and that innovation is the cross to the vampire. Adcult is recombinant culture. This is how it has to be if advertisers are to be able to direct their spiels at the appropriate audiences for their products. It's simply too expensive to be any other way.

Will Adcult continue? Will there be some new culture to "afflict the comfortable and comfort the afflicted"? Will advertising, in its own terms, lose it? Who knows? Certainly, signs of stress are showing. Here are a few: (1) The kids are passing through "prime-branding time" like a rabbit in the python, and as they get older things may settle down. The supposedly ad-proof Generation X may be impossible to reach and advertisers will turn to older audiences by default. (2) The media are so clogged and cluttered that companies may move to other promotional highways, such as direct mail, point-of-purchase displays, and couponing, leaving the traditional avenues targeted at us older folks. (3) Branding, the heart of advertising, may become problematic if generics or store brands become as popular in this country as they have in Europe. After all, the much-vaunted brand extension whereby Coke becomes Diet Coke which becomes Diet Cherry Coke does not always work, as Kodak Floppy Disks, Milky Way Ice Cream, Arm & Hammer antiperspirant, Life Saver Gum, and even EuroDisney have all shown. And (4)—the unthinkable—mass consumption may become too expensive. Advertising can flourish only in times of surplus, and no one can guarantee that our society will always have more than it needs.

But by no means am I predicting Adcult's imminent demise. As long as goods are interchangeable and in surplus quantities, as long as producers are willing to pay for short-term advantages (especially for new products), and as long as consumers have plenty of disposable time and money so that they can consume both the ad and the product, Adcult will remain the dominant meaning-making system of modern life. I don't think you can roll this tape backwards. Adcult is the application of capitalism to culture: dollars voting. And so I say to my melancholy friends who bemoan the passing of a culture once concerned with the arts and the humanities that the only way they can change this situation is if they buy more Fast-Moving Consumer Goods, change brands capriciously, and cut the kids' allowances. Good luck.

Journal Topic

1. The article talks about what it calls "Adcult." How would you define "Adcult" in your own words? How would you relate this concept to your own life?

Questions for Critical Thought

1. Twitchell suggests that "what we crave may not be objects at all but their meaning . . . by adding value to material, by adding meaning to objects, by branding things, advertising performs a role historically associated with religion." Discuss what he could mean by this. Does consumerism and the obsession with material objects and the status that they confer fulfill some role once associated only with religion?

2. One of Twitchell's main arguments is that the mass media is "'dumbing down' American culture with its incessant repetition of mindless humor, maudlin sentimentality, exaggerated action, and frivolous entertainment." Do you agree with Twitchell when he says that the media plays to the "lowest common denominator" in our society?

Suggestions for Personal Research

1. Twitchell says that American grocery stores went from typically having 9,000 items in stock to carrying over 24,000 items. Pick a major brand, and then research to see how many varieties it has. You may want to pick a soda, snack chip, frozen food line, or a cleaning product because they tend to have the most brand offshoots. You will probably want to visit your own cupboards, several grocery stores, and the corporation's web page to get the most information. Because brands cancel varieties regularly, you may even want to ask other people if there are items that have been cancelled that were once part of the product line.

2. Look to see how many brands are made and sold by the same parent companies. Do many companies make brands that actually compete with each other? Why would they do this? Are there any benefits or extra costs to consumers because of this practice?

Multicultural Issues

1. Twitchell claims that consumerism and material goods are the driving force in the U.S. economy. Do you think this to be the case in other countries as well? If you are from a different country, how does it compare to the United States in this regard?

2. Has the consumer mindset of America bled into other countries and changed the way they think? Think about your country of origin if it isn't the United States and compare the two.

Vocabulary Terms

implore	surfeit
nonaltruisitc	cloistered
conglomerates	aphoristic
sophomoric	voyeurism
quid pro quo	supercilious
fungible	maudlin
fraudulent	jabberwocky
superfluous	recombinant

Term for Clarification

Nathaniel Hawthorne   (July 4, 1804–May 19, 1864.) A major American novelist and short story writer, most famous for his masterpiece *The Scarlet Letter*. He was involved with life at Brook Farm, an experimental cooperative farm founded and run in the 1840s in Massachusetts.

Stealth TV: Channel One Delivers News and Advertising to the Classroom

Channel One—and Lots of Advertising—Seeps into America's Schools

Russ Baker and Kimberly Smith

Prereading Question

1. Did you have Channel One in your high school? If so, how did you feel about being forced to watch advertisements as part of your "education" every day while in school? (If you didn't have Channel One, how do you think you would feel about having to watch a twelve-minute TV news program that had two out of the twelve minutes devoted to advertising?)

At Clifton High School, a mostly white, working-class institution in suburban New Jersey, it's time for second period—and for Channel One, a public-affairs TV broadcast available exclusively for school viewing. Mounted high in a corner of every classroom—as omnipresent an icon as the American flag—is a large-screen television set, provided by Channel One. The face on the screen is that of school principal William Cannici. Speaking into a microphone, he tries a few jokes, then announces student vocational-award winners. In Mrs. Rossi's Spanish class, restless students begin talking among themselves. Suddenly, the teacher shushes her charges: It's show time.

The hip-hop music starts. Heads bounce to the beat. Cut to two young, fashionably dressed anchorwomen, one white and one black. First up in the news is a tough sell to almost any viewership: the census. Point: Without an accurate count, schools can't get their rightful aid. The census form flashes on the screen. "Hey, I got that!" remarks a student. Channel One's reporter interviews a census spokesperson, a sexually ambiguous-looking woman with her hair pulled back in a ponytail. "What the heck is that?" a student in the back of the room asks with a chortle.

Time for a commercial break. Teens snowboard and dirt-bike their way through the Mountain Dew life (170 calories, 46 grams of sugar per can): "Do the Dew!" Then a Twinkies spot (150 calories, 14 grams of sugar per two-pack).

Back to the news. As a story airs about the pope's ground-breaking mea culpa over the Catholic Church's transgressions toward the Jews, much of the class is deep in chitchat; the teacher tries, without success, to silence the talk. Other students appear to be doing their homework. Two young women are checking their makeup, and four are resting their heads on their desks. Not one person has a comment about the story, described by *The New York Times* as "the most sweeping papal apology ever."

Another commercial break. As the first frames roll, a student shrieks, "Pokemon!" Declares another: "I need to get that." Next ad: Join the Marines. One viewer chimes along with the script: "The Few. The Proud. . . ."

For 10 years now, the folks behind Channel One have been able to offer advertisers a dream demographic: a captive audience composed of nearly half of all American teenagers. (And they truly are captive, as Carlotta and D.J. Maurer, two students at Perrysburg Junior High School in Ohio, can attest. Their refusal to watch Channel One in school bought them a day in the Wood County Juvenile Detention Center.) On the condition that all teachers will air and all students will watch its daily satellite-broadcast programs, Channel One lends television sets and other equipment to schools. The company, which claims to reach a teen market 50 times larger than MTV's, profits by selling two of every 12 program minutes for commercials coupled with call-in contests and cool banter.

As noxious as these school-sanctioned ads are, Channel One's success is part of a larger trend toward in-school marketing: Textbook manufacturers insert proprietary brand names into math equations, corporations provide book covers emblazoned with their logos, soda companies entice school officials into signing deals for on-campus product exclusivity, and companies donate computers that have the ability, in some cases, to track the online behavior of individual students. A whole new industry of consultants has sprung up to help corporate clients position their products in schools.

Even in today's thoroughly commercialized environment, there is something especially insidious about school-endorsed product pushing. For one thing, schools are supposed to offer a haven from the worst the world has to offer. We authorize metal detectors and locker sweeps to prevent deadly violence on campus. But there are other dangers to impressionable minds. Channel One's hyperkinetic blend of "current-affairs broadcasting" and carefully targeted commercials blurs the line between fact and fiction, between reporting that at least tries to be objective and the self-serving rhetoric of the advertising business. Unquestionably, young people lack the media "literacy" skills necessary to understand fully what they are dealing with: A recent study cited in Education Week shows that ninth-graders who watched ads in which professional athletes endorsed products thought the athletes had themselves paid for the ads.

Channel What?

Few American adults have ever heard of Channel One—a remarkable fact, considering that one in four middle and high schools now broadcasts it and an estimated 40 percent of all high school students are compelled to watch its programming every single school day. Perhaps parents do not know about Channel One because their kids (some eight million of them, in 12,000 schools) do not tell them about it. As for the key American institutions—governmental, educational—that might be expected to raise an alarm, they have mostly been looking the other way.

Last fall the first-ever government study of commercialization in the schools was published. The General Accounting Office (GAO) report, requested by two Democrats—Representative George Miller of California and Senator Christopher Dodd of Connecticut—notes that in-school marketing is dramatically on the rise and that deals between schools and companies are being made on a district-by-district basis. Local educators are not equipped to negotiate with crafty marketers bearing freebies, much less to address the larger educational issues. While the GAO study was being circulated, the Federal Trade Commission released a report specifically condemning the marketing of violent content to underage children.

In some ways, the "new" political interest in protecting our children from the on-slaught of the marketers harks back to 1989, when Channel One was launched by entrepreneur Chris Whittle (later, in 1994, he sold the company to K-III Communications, now called Primedia). Initially, the service faced heavy criticism from liberal groups and from educational powerhouses such as the national Parent-Teacher Association, the American Federation of Teachers (AFT), the National Education Association (NEA), and various principals' associations; even the American Academy of Pediatrics frowned upon for-profit classroom television. But the well-financed company won over school system after school system, and effective opposition dried up.

Of late, none of the major teachers' or school administrators' organizations has seemed willing to mount a serious challenge to Channel One. Two years ago, NEA officials told Channel One critics that while the association remains opposed to the service, removing it from America's classrooms was not a priority. The AFT offered a similar line. And the National Association of School Principals rebuffed Channel One opponents several times when they requested a meeting. As a result, the battle against Channel One is being waged by several tiny public-interest groups and through scattered, small-scale parent uprisings. The educational establishment apparently believes that the issue lacks urgency.

Governmental bodies tend to accept the claim that the free equipment and the "news value" of Channel One more than make up for any downside; besides, the argument goes, local governments can address the matter if they so choose. Even the GAO report declares that it is impossible to differentiate the effects of bombardment by Channel One from those of the commercial messages directed at young people outside school hours. Although the GAO researchers were undoubtedly well-meaning, such a claim is a cop-out: Many in-school marketers specially design ads, promotions, contests, and the like to track the impact of their sales pitches.

Can anyone doubt that the ads on Channel One are grossly out of place in an academic environment? Mark Crispin Miller, a professor of media and culture at New York University who studied Channel One's content in 1997, concluded that its commercial messages reinforced bad body image, emphasized the importance of buying things, and glamorized boorish and loutish behavior. To ensure "stickiness," the ad campaigns often feature interactive components. One that I saw urged students to watch a film called *Never Been Kissed,* then to call in and answer questions about the movie's content in order to qualify for a chance to win a $500 shopping spree and a watch.

Rather than defend the indefensible, Channel One insists that the ads are not what matters. At the company's Madison Avenue headquarters, sleek, gunmetal-silver placards fit for the starship Enterprise proclaim "Education" and "Our Missions: To Inform and Empower Young People." These displays imply that the ads are a necessary evil that makes possible a bounty of fresh educational content and free equipment. Indeed, in a meeting with me last year, Channel One officials sought repeatedly to focus attention on the educational merits of their product. The company has been able to orchestrate favorable publicity ranging from a laudatory *New York Times* op-ed by a Catholic priest who is also a principal in a Channel One school to supportive statements from the ordinarily populist Senator Paul Wellstone of Minnesota.

Company executives claim that the broadcasts hold students' interest because they deliver important information in an appealing manner. (The students appear to identify with the youthful newscasters as stars; indeed, one of them, Lisa Ling, has moved on to anchoring a commercial-network morning show.) The solution to disaffection among youths, say executives, is to deliver a product that shows them how world affairs are relevant to them and their families. "We go to Kosovo and talk to kids who are their age," said Susan Tick, an outside PR representative for Channel One. "You don't connect with them otherwise."

Even by these standards, the compilation tape Channel One gave me was not impressive: It included a segment summarizing the Bill Clinton impeachment situation, delivered at a rapid-fire pace that seemed harder for an average teen to follow than a conventional news broadcast. The commentary is often self-promotional, with Channel One correspondents and anchors gushing about how they've gotten to travel to exotic places, and with interviewed students identified as attendees of "a Channel One school."

If we are to accept Channel One's request that it be judged on its news content, we have to face the fact that there just isn't much there. Of the 10 minutes of "news," only two to three minutes is breaking news, according to William Hoynes, a Vassar College sociologist who studies the intersection of media and education. The remainder is a hodgepodge of contests, self-promotion, light features and profiles, music intros, and pop quizzes. And Hoynes concludes that even those paltry hard-news minutes frame the issues in rigid terms that do not promote original thought or critical thinking.

Not surprisingly, Channel One doesn't offer any statistics to prove that its programs benefit students. "We have attitudinal studies showing that teachers believe it to be productive," said Jeffrey Ballabon, a Channel One executive vice president. "They know kids don't read newspapers. They also don't watch the evening news." Perhaps the citation of "attitudinal" evidence is necessitated by the findings of one study the company did commission: A 1994 University of Michigan analysis found that students performed just 5 percent better in high schools that aired the programs and 8 percent better in participating middle schools—and then only in an "exemplary" (read: highly atypical) environment in which the teacher actively sought to incorporate the broadcast content into the class and made sure the students were paying attention. There was no measurable increase in discussion of news outside the school or in efforts to seek out additional information from outside news sources.

Nevertheless, most administrators and teachers seem to love their Channel One. With good reason: The company provides TV sets and a broadcast system that the schools use for their own purposes, including the principal's morning addresses. "Our district is not a real wealthy district," explains Lawrence Westerfield, principal of Mt. Healthy South Middle School in Cincinnati, Ohio, which airs Channel One. If you want the technology, says Westerfield, "you have to count on advertisers to pay."

Yet there is evidence that the schools aren't getting a very good deal. A 1998 study co-authored by Alex Molnar, an education professor at the University of Wisconsin–Milwaukee, concluded that broadcasting Channel One takes up six or seven days of instruction over the school year and costs American taxpayers $1.8 billion annually. Molnar, who heads the Center for Education Research, Analysis, and Innovation, compared the average cost of 12 daily minutes of a secondary school's time, or about $158,000 a year, with the total value of Channel One's equipment ($17,000) and the annual rental value of the equipment ($4,000). Even the value of the time spent watching the two minutes of commercials ($26,000) exceeded the value of the equipment. And those Channel One minutes add up. A child who views the shows from sixth grade to graduation will lose seven weeks of school time.

Ad Nauseam

Despite Channel One's self-proclaimed educational mission, the company offers a different story to advertisers. As Channel One's then-president bragged to a youth marketing conference in 1994, "The biggest selling point to advertisers [is that] . . . we are forcing kids to watch two minutes of commercials. . . . The advertiser gets a group of kids who cannot go to the bathroom, who cannot change the station, who cannot listen to their mother yell in the background, who cannot be playing Nintendo, who cannot have their headsets on." Channel One continually conducts surveys about the spending patterns of teens; and its Web site, heavily touted on the shows themselves, provides an ideal means of obtaining direct feedback from the students.

Channel One also makes much of its public-service announcements, including those warning students to resist peer pressure to take drugs. Meanwhile, it airs ads stressing ways to be cool and brags to advertisers that controlled viewing in the classroom is the ideal way to play on teens' insecurity and desire to fit in.

Channel One makes a lot of money—$346 million in 1999 ad revenues—for its financially troubled parent company, Primedia, which reported a net loss of $120 million that year. With an estimated $200,000 price per 30-second ad (a rate comparable to the major networks'), Channel One is a crucial element in the company's future strategy. In its 1999 stockholder report, Primedia declared: "Our products serve highly specialized niches and capitalize on the growing trend toward targeted rather than mass information distribution. Many of the company's products, such as . . . CHANNEL ONE NEWS, . . . afford advertisers with an opportunity to directly reach niche market audiences. CHANNEL ONE NEWS has no direct competition in the schools [my emphasis] but does compete for advertising dollars with other media aimed at teenagers."

With so vast a market at stake, Channel One has not been reluctant to spend in order to protect its franchise. When Republican Senator Richard Shelby of Alabama, an ally of the ragtag band of Channel One opponents, initiated Senate hearings in 1999, Channel One dumped almost $1 million into a lobbying effort led by former Christian Coalition Director Ralph Reed and the powerful law firm of Preston, Gates, and Ellis—and effectively kept a lid on further action or hearings. Last spring a Shelby-sponsored sense-of-the-Senate resolution opposing commercialization of the schools was blocked by Republican Senator Sam Brownback of Kansas and heavy lobbying by Reed and former New York Senator Alfonse D'Amato. The company has other means of winning support: Channel One's Ballabon insisted on faxing me a mound of positive letters; several from students mentioned free trips to Channel One's Los Angeles production studios.

Lined up against Channel One's PR juggernaut is a spirited and diverse coalition that includes Professor Molnar's group; Ralph Nader's D.C.-based Commercial Alert; the Center for Commercial-Free Public Education, located in Oakland, California; and

Obligation, Inc., a group from Birmingham, Alabama, headed by Republican businessman Jim Metrock. When Metrock found out that his children were watching Channel One, he did his own study; he's been a committed opponent ever since. He has helped recruit a number of socially conservative groups—like Phyllis Schlafly's Eagle Forum and James Dobson's Focus on the Family—some of which are more concerned with what they perceive as risque content than with commercialism per se. In addition, Channel One's critics convinced the 15.8-million-member Southern Baptist Convention to pass a resolution in 1999 opposing the enterprise.

That's about it on a national scale. Channel One likes to keep the battleground local, where school officials often lack the training and policy sophistication to ask tough questions about content control and educational philosophy. Thus far, only one state, New York, has banned Channel One from the public schools.

Still, a few small districts have voted to bar Channel One, and Metrock says that some teachers in schools contractually obligated to show the programs are nevertheless switching them off. The company has apparently responded by warning errant schools that it will yank its equipment. And Channel One has now retained Nielsen Media Research to measure student viewing in 1,500 schools.

Sooner or later, it seems, educational advocates are going to have to make Channel One and its ilk a priority. If we are really on the brink of a top-to-bottom reconstitution of American education, then surely the intrusion of corporate products must be addressed. And enthusiasm for these new methods of "improving" the educational experience bears scrutiny if the letters of support from teachers and principals that Channel One's Ballabon forwarded to me are any evidence. Many contained the sorts of appalling errors—in spelling, grammar, syntax, and exposition—that these educators are supposed to be helping students avoid.

Were the topic ever to reach the national agenda, many vexing questions about education itself would be raised. For example, Channel One advocates contend that the broadcasts make it easier to teach young people about the news because the young hosts know how to speak kids' language. This, of course, suggests that adult educators (and parents, for that matter) are incapable of discussing the ways of the world in a compelling manner—a sentiment not everyone shares. And anyway, in an America awash in exhortations to buy and consume, shouldn't institutions of learning and discussion be free from the constant pressures toward superficiality and conformity?

Meanwhile, Primedia has announced a merger with the Internet company About. com, which has intricate business partnerships with pornography purveyors. Conservatives are upset by that, as they are with Senator Brownback, who is a leader in denouncing violence in the media yet enthusiastically backs Channel One, with its advertising for violent movies.

This year opponents are likely to concentrate on challenging the federal government's role as a major Channel One benefactor through its paid advertising for the armed services and the Office of National Drug Control Policy. But if there's strong, broad, untapped sentiment against the juggernaut, it probably needs to coalesce fairly soon: Channel One officials told me the company looks forward to rolling out the programs in thousands of additional schools.

Related Article: Pop Quiz

Kathleen Ryan, a history teacher at Clifton High in New Jersey, believes that Channel One is a helpful supplement to her lesson plans. "Although the kids are like sitting ducks for the commercials," she says, "sometimes I see Channel One seeping through when they talk about the news."

Several anecdotal studies by groups critical of Channel One found that students retained virtually none of the news material when quizzed the following day but did remember most of the commercial content. (Channel One, sensitive to the criticism, has begun to offer schools additional, commercial-free programming on topics such as science, drug prevention, and sports.) Immediately after Clifton students viewed a Channel One news program, we conducted our own quiz on the broadcast and on general knowledge of current events. Here's what the students said.

Two females, ages 14 and 15 (interviewed together):

Q: For what is the pope apologizing?

A: He didn't say nothing about the Jews.

Q: What is the importance of the census?

A: I don't know why it is important. But it may help to know if someone needs help bathing.

Q: Can you recall the commercials?

A: [They can name all except for the Marines' spot.]

Q: Why were there riots in Seattle a few months ago?

A: Don't know.

Q: What does WTO stand for?

A: Isn't that wrestling?

Q: What is your favorite commercial on Channel One?

A: The Twinkle one where the raccoon gets hit by the truck.

Male, age 16:

Q: What do you think about the verdict in the Diallo case?

A: Those four cops were not charged with nothing, and they should be.

Q: What do you know about Bob Jones University?

A: Nothing.

Q: Why were there riots in Seattle a few months ago?

A: Something to do with jobs.

Female, age 14:

Q: What is the importance of the census?

A: So you know how many people are in the world.

Q: For what is the pope apologizing?

A: I don't know. He went to the Holy Land.

Q: What is your favorite commercial on Channel One?

A: I wasn't paying attention.

Q: What do you think about the verdict in the Diallo case?

A: The cops should go to jail.

Q: Name two Democratic presidential candidates.

A: Bush and Gore.

Male, age 14:

Q: What is the importance of the census?

A: To find out population. Something to do with the economy and Congress.

Q: For what is the pope apologizing?

A: Pope John Paul let all the Jews die.

Q: Name two Democratic presidential candidates.

A: Dole, McCain.

Q: What is your favorite commercial on Channel One?

A: The Nike one with the guy running.

Female, age 16:

Q: Why do you like Channel One?

A: I get to do my homework in class.

Female, age 15:

Q: What do you know about Bob Jones University?

A: Interracial dating. George Bush just spoke there.

Q: Where did you learn about this?

A: Mr. Grohl, my English teacher. He always talks about it.

Q: Name two Democratic presidential candidates.

A: I do not know.

Female, age 16:

Q: What is your favorite commercial on Channel One?

A: I like the sticky-film one. All the kids in my class always sing along together.

Q: Why were there riots in Seattle a few months ago?

A: No idea.

Q: What does WTO stand for?

A: No idea.

Female, age 18:

Q: What is your favorite commercial on Channel One?

A: The antidrug one. It's funny. People laugh at it.

Q: Why were there riots in Seattle a few months ago?

A: Don't know.

Q: Name two Democratic presidential candidates.

A: Gore, Bush. Don't know their first names. I am into politics but I can't remember.

Q: For what is the pope apologizing?

A: Pope Pius never stood up and did nothing. That is what the pope is apologizing for.

Q: How did you learn about this?

A: I'm Catholic. I just did a research paper on it.

Male, age 17:

Q: For what is the pope apologizing?

A: People don't believe in what he believes. Something like that.

Q: Name two Democratic presidential candidates.

A: McCain and Bradley.

Q: Why were there riots in Seattle a few months ago?

A: Trade organization or something. Workers.

Q: How do you know about this?

A: I saw it on the news at home.

Q: What is your favorite commercial on Channel One?

A: The guy running around with the boom box. Nike.

Journal Topic

1. Who should have the right to decide if Channel One is offered in a school? School administrators? Parents? The students themselves?

Questions for Critical Thought

1. According to the article, two students in a junior high school in Ohio refused to watch Channel One. "Their refusal to watch Channel One in school bought them a day in the Wood County Juvenile Detention Center." Is it wrong that these students ended up in a juvenile detention center for refusing to watch TV, or were educators simply exercising their rights to kick students out of school for noncompliance?

2. Baker and Smith argue that "schools are supposed to offer a haven from the worst the world has to offer. We authorize metal detectors and locker sweeps to prevent

deadly violence on campus. But there are other dangers to impressionable minds." What dangers do you think Channel One poses to the minds of youth?

Suggestion for Personal Research

1. How much of an influence do advertisements have on children and teenagers? Research this issue and decide for yourself. Based on the information you obtain, discuss whether Channel One is a good idea or not.

Multicultural Issues

1. Do you know of anything like Channel One in your native country? If not, do you think it would be helpful or popular?

Vocabulary Terms

omnipresent   laudatory
ambiguous   *ad nauseum*
mea culpa   PR (Public Relations)
transgressions   errant
noxious   exhortations
proprietary   benefactor
insidious   juggernaut

Term for Clarification

Madison Avenue   A famous street in New York City that is home to several of the top advertising firms in the world. If people refer to "Madison Avenue," they are typically talking about the American advertising industry in general.

Group Wants Shrek off Anti-Obesity Campaign

David Crary

and

Fighting Obesity but Fronting for Junk Food

Barbara F. Meltz

These two articles are short companion pieces, meant to be read together.

Prereading Questions

1. When you were a child, were you convinced through the marketing of any of your favorite fictional characters that you wanted a certain product? Have you recently seen any children become convinced by the use of characters they love?

2. If you have children in your life, do you find that advertisements using popular characters make them demand certain products? How do you deal with this? Does it create problems for you?

Group Wants Shrek off Anti-Obesity Campaign

NEW YORK—A children's advocacy group wants the Department of Health and Human Services to oust Shrek, the animated ogre, from his role as spokesman for an anti-obesity drive.

The Campaign for a Commercial-Free Childhood says the soon-to-open *Shrek the Third* has too many promotional ties with unhealthy foods to justify using Shrek as a health advocate.

"There is an inherent conflict of interest between marketing junk food and promoting public health," Susan Linn, the group's director, wrote in a letter sent Wednesday to Health and Human Services Secretary Michael Leavitt.

"Surely Health and Human Services can find a better spokesperson for healthy living than a character who is a walking advertisement for McDonald's, sugary cereals, cookies and candy," said Linn, an instructor in psychiatry at Harvard Medical School.

Health and Human Services spokesman Bill Hall said the department had no intention of halting the public service ads, which were launched in February.

The ad campaign—which seeks to curtail childhood obesity—is a joint project of the Health and Human Services Department, the Ad Council's Coalition for Healthy Children and DreamWorks Animation SKG, creator of the three Shrek movies. It features ads in which Shrek, a stout and often clumsy ogre, and his fellow characters urge children to exercise at least an hour a day.

"Shrek is a very well known character in the target population of this campaign," Hall said. "We have always promoted a balanced, healthy diet, which does not necessarily exclude the occasional treat."

Linn's organization—a nationwide coalition that monitors marketing aimed at children—said *Shrek the Third,* which opens May 18, has promotional deals with dozens of food products, including Mars Inc.'s Snickers and M&M's candy; PepsiCo Inc.'s Sierra Mist drink; and Kellogg Co.'s Fruit Loops, Frosted Flakes, Pop-Tarts, Cheez-Its and Keebler cookies.

Penelope Royall, the Health and Human Services deputy assistant secretary for disease prevention and health promotion, stressed that the public services ads were using Shrek to promote exercise, not foods.

"Shrek is a good model, especially for children who can benefit from more exercise," Royall said. "He doesn't have a perfect physique; he's not a great athlete. . . . We hope children will understand that being physically fit doesn't require being a great athlete."

Fighting Obesity but Fronting for Junk Food

Wanting to avoid the appearance of a government agency seeming to endorse a Hollywood movie, the US Department of Health and Human Services has temporarily halted its public service ad campaign in which the animated movie character Shrek urges children to exercise. *Shrek the Third,* released by DreamWorks, opened Friday.

But, says HHS spokesman Bill Hall, "We'll pop them right back up there as soon as the hype for the movie dies down, in six weeks or so."

Who knew that conflicts of interest come with expiration dates?

If that's not bizarre enough, there's also this: HHS sees no problem using Shrek as a frontman in the fight against childhood obesity at the very same time Shrek's image is also licensed for use on more than 75 fast-food products including M&Ms, Pop-Tarts, and McDonald's Happy Meals.

"I'd call that naive, disingenuous, or hypocritical—take your pick," says psychologist Susan Linn, co founder of the Campaign for a Commercial-Free Childhood, based at the Judge Baker Children's Center in Boston.

Last month CCFC called for HHS Secretary Mike Leavitt to "fire" Shrek, saying there is an inherent conflict of interest for a government agency that is mandated to protect the health and well-being of children to tie itself to a character that is also tied to energy-dense, low-nutrient foods. Hall's counter is that the public service ads are not about diet.

"Shrek is conveying the message that, 'Hey, I'm overweight, I'm out of shape, and I eat a lot of snacks. I'm adding physical activity to my lifestyle so I can be healthier. You should, too,'" Hall says. "If we were to pull the Shrek campaign completely, what kids would be left with is Shrek promoting only food products. That would be a very one sided message."

That thinking dumbfounds people such as child psychologist David Walsh. As it is, he says, children are only getting one message.

"When two messages undercut each other as these do, the one that is more prominent is the one that gets through," says Walsh, president of the National Institute on Media and the Family in Minneapolis. Not everyone blames HHS for wanting to stick with Shrek.

"He's a character kids are powerfully drawn to," says Kathy Merlock Jackson, a children's media and culture specialist at Virginia Wesleyan College. "They identify with him. He's kind, caring, funny, and he's not perfect. They like that. They admire that. Just think how wonderful it would be if all of Shrek's appeal were focused on one message: promoting children's exercise."

Jackson says the responsibility lies with DreamWorks. "I call on them to withdraw the licensing for the [fast-food] venues and do the right thing for kids: Let Shrek be a spokesperson only for exercise."

Not a bad idea, says Walsh, especially considering that the Centers for Disease Control has labeled childhood obesity a public health emergency.

In a telephone interview Saturday, DreamWorks spokesperson Bob Feldman defended the choice of Shrek for both HHS and food products, noting that DreamWorks paid attention to the products Shrek appeared on.

"We made a conscious, thought-out effort to [license] the healthier choices of the fast food that is out there. Since when did candy become evil? People know candy is a treat, and parents know to dole it out carefully."

What's more, he noted, DreamWorks initiated the collaboration with HHS and the Ad Council.

"We want to be socially responsible. We support balanced diet and regular exercise," Feldman said. "DreamWorks Animation is committed to responsible marketing and we are proud of our relationship with HHS, McDonald's, and other companies."

Journal Topics

1. If you have ever had weight problems, or have them now, what do you think are the biggest reasons for this?

2. If you have always had a healthy weight, what do you think makes you different from people who struggle with weight?

Questions for Critical Thought

1. Susan Linn from the Harvard Medical School argues that "[s]urely Health and Human Services can find a better spokesperson for healthy living than a character who is a walking advertisement for McDonald's, sugary cereals, cookies and candy." Do you think this is true? Will a handful of ads in which Shrek suggests children exercise be enough to counter the hundreds of commercials, cereal boxes, and fast-food billboards that they were exposed to when the movie was released?

2. Bob Feldman, a spokesperson for DreamWorks—the studio that makes the *Shrek* franchise—argues that they "made a conscious, thought-out effort to [license] the healthier choices of the fast food that is out there. Since when did candy become evil? People know candy is a treat, and parents know to dole it out carefully." Is the solution this simple? Will parents be able to counteract the advertising and keep children from eating candy and drinking sodas, or could the influence of beloved characters like Shrek condition children to like these foods even if parents fight to avoid them?

Suggestions for Personal Research

1. The article claims that the "Centers for Disease Control has labeled childhood obesity a public health emergency." Investigate childhood obesity. What are the causes? What are the resulting health problems later in life? What could be done to stop this emergency?

2. Do some research to answer the following questions: How prevalent is junk food consumption among children and adults in other countries? Is it increasing? If so, why? How strong and prevalent is the presence of McDonald's and other corporate fast-food giants outside the United States? What are health advocates in other countries doing about this?

Multicultural Issues

1. As implied in the second research suggestion, American habits of consumption and American companies may be affecting eating habits and obesity rates around the world. If you are from another country, do you see any changes in your own culture that may be related to American influence? Did you face any "culture shock" when you came to the United States?

Vocabulary Terms

spokesman
advocate
inherent
curtail
stout
physique

conflict of interest
naive
disingenuous
hypocritical
licensing

CHAPTER 19—ADVERTISING ESSAY QUESTIONS

These questions are intended as potential essay or research paper topics suggested by the ideas raised in the articles in this chapter.

1. More and more, schools are being economically forced or seduced into signing contracts with major corporations. These corporations offer goods and services to the schools in exchange for a chance to get brand loyalty out of the schools and their students. Research and explore the continuing trend of advertising in schools. Consider answering some of the following questions: Are there levels of education where this should be allowed and levels where it shouldn't? Could a corporation with a school contract start to dictate who attends the school or what is taught by the curriculum? Are there other, more pedagogically sound, ways for the schools to make supplemental income? Should public American education be funded privately by corporations, or should we allow only the government to do so?

2. The introduction for this chapter discusses several advertising techniques that help to make an ad effective. Find a print ad from a major national magazine and critique it. Study the visual rhetoric of the ad: the layout, the print, the graphics, the pictures, the models, the size and presence of the item being advertised, and anything that catches your eye. What techniques are used in it? Do they effectively convey an emotion to you or make you curious about the product? Do you ultimately consider this advertising to be a success or a failure?

3. Advertising has grown more and more pervasive. We used to simply get ads on TV and radio, in print, and on roadside billboards. Now, however, it is every-where, from the ads on the floor of grocery stores to logo-covered trash cans. There are also guerilla marketing techniques and product placement that keep brands in our consciousness all the time. How much is too much? Should our entire public space be open to advertisers, or should there be limits?

4. More and more critics argue that we should enact legislation that prevents corporations from bombarding our youth with advertising. Ads for junk food, fast food, and sodas encourage poor eating habits, and some people argue that ads for TV, film, and video games encourage violence and laziness, adding even further to America's obesity problem. Some even argue that constant exposure to fashion models encourages eating disorders in young women and girls who feel they aren't attractive unless they are as skinny as the models. Should advertising directed at children and teenagers be limited by government regulations?

CHAPTER 20

Media Multinationals

Every few years, you're expected to go out and vote on everything from who sits on your local school board to who will be our next president. This year, you may have decided to be a model citizen and start taking American politics seriously. For the next important election, you make up your mind that instead of just voting for the person your parents and friends tell you to, you will do some serious fact finding. You swear that you'll vote for the one candidate who has your best interests at heart and who feels the same way that you do about major issues. You have one candidate in mind already, but you're hungry to learn more about this person.

You decide that you're going to be sure you check various sources. You plan to watch both local and national satellite news feeds, listen to radio talk shows, read newspapers from your area and other cities, and do some Net surfing to top it all off. The easiest first step for you is to start watching television news. You don't watch much news, but you know that there are several major cable news networks, and you pick one to start watching. That night, you watch a news show that has two political experts arguing about who is the best candidate. The wittier expert supports the candidate you're leaning toward, and so does the host of the show. Later, you tune in to some local news at 11:00 that night, and you see a story that speaks well of your candidate's education plans, but is largely negative about the other person who is running. About a week later, you tune in to a talk radio program on your way to campus. It's a nationally syndicated show that plays from coast to coast, and a political scientist from an Ivy League school is talking with the host. They both seem in favor of the budget proposal your candidate supports. You look up more details about the budget plans in your local newspaper, and it comes to the same conclusions that the radio show host and you have come to.

As the election draws near, you do some research online and read magazine articles about your candidate. By election day, you've consulted dozens of independent sources from every type of mass media you could get your hands on (even some cartoons and articles in your favorite magazines helped in some minor way to inform your decision). You go to the polls the morning of the election, and you vote for the candidate who is best for the office. You know this is the case because you dug so deep getting impartial information. Or did you?

If you did some research, you'd probably learn that the TV networks, radio stations, newspapers, magazines, and even the Internet service you turned to are all owned by just a few larger umbrella corporations. Although you thought you were getting impartial information from dozens of different sources, these sources could all be owned and controlled by one large board of directors. Over the past decade, several multinational media corporations have started to purchase virtually every aspect of electronic communication. If the board of directors from such a corporation ever desired to push a particular agenda, they would be able to reach the American (and global) audience through hundreds of angles and avenues of information. We have faith that they don't abuse their power like this, but they definitely have the power to do so. Every time you search for a new, fresh source of information on a political candidate, however, you may just be getting the same perspective from a different arm of one colossal parent corporation.

DEREGULATION

Until about a decade ago, all aspects of the media were highly regulated by the government's Federal Communications Commission (FCC). The FCC was formed as part of the Communications Act of 1934. Its official function is to regulate and monitor all electronic communications in America—radio, television, cable, print, satellite, the Internet, and even phones. World War II occurred in the FCC's infancy, and many of the horrors of that war were encouraged by fascist propaganda. This propaganda was unavoidable in Axis countries because the fascist governments controlled every aspect of the media. There were no dissenting voices, no debates about the pending war—simply one side of an argument everywhere the citizens turned. This type of continual media pressure helped to support these regimes and keep them in power. When the war ended, the Germans enacted strict laws to keep media from ever being concentrated in one group's hands. Similarly, the FCC monitored media in America to protect us from our information being controlled by only a few people or corporations, lest we face the same kind of monopoly that allowed fascist propaganda to thrive in WWII Axis nations.

Times and technology changed, however, and in 1996, the Telecommunications Act was passed, updating the FCC's charter for the first time in more than sixty years. The goal of this act was to lessen the regulations regarding media ownership. For example, prior to the act, a company was restricted in the amount of radio stations it could own at one time. The act lifted all bans, so corporations could now buy hundreds of small stations and own a majority of all the airwaves in America. The Telecommunications Act allowed corporations to start owning multiple communications venues in order to "promote competition in the marketplace," effectively reducing competition. The ultmate effect of the act is overwhelming ownership of many media outlets by just a few corporations. The new mergers that were allowed under the act of 1996 were said to be a boon for several reasons, discussed below.

Financial Gain

One of the largest of these media outlets, Disney, employs a staggering 130,000 people worldwide and thus aids in the economy of certain areas around the world. Disney and other media multinational corporations can make billions of dollars every year through their film, television, advertising, video games, and media infrastructure. This money and these employees certainly aid America's economy.

Synergy

Corporations can now experience something called **synergy.** Synergy allows a corporation to push one product or film through all its different arms. For example, when a movie studio releases an animated summer children's movie, the umbrella corporation that owns the studio does far more than release just the movie. It also releases a wave of media and products surrounding this film. This wave will include a line of toys through a toy company it owns or has a partnership with. The movie may spawn a video game from a gaming company that is also owned by the corporation. Most importantly, the corporation will engage in a cross-promotion campaign. There will be contests on its cable stations, give-aways on the local news channel it owns, popcorn buckets advertising the film at its movie chains, and sneak previews on its networks' TV shows and DVD releases. Information and products about this film will become inescapable, maximizing the size of the audience and corporate profits.

Bigger Budgets

Media mergers also create bigger budgets for some movies and television programs. As the corporations get bigger, there is more money backing films and shows as they are produced. Such big-budget films as the *Lord of the Rings* trilogy or the *Pirates of the Caribbean* series might never have been produced under the older model of Hollywood financing because of their huge price tags. With hundreds of millions of dollars to support such projects, we have a chance for even bigger, more technologically enhanced films.

These benefits exist primarily as a means for these corporations to make more money and spread their reach, and that is the primary goal of any corporation. However, critics say that these corporate benefits of media mergers are far outweighed by the negative effects on U.S. citizens. The corporations reap the rewards and profits, but the average consumer has to pay the price in a loss of media diversity. Following are some of the negative aspects of these ongoing media mergers.

Loss of Unique Voices

Although the size of the major media corporations may create a bigger filming budget, many in Hollywood (including representatives of the Screen Actors Guild and Directors Guild of America who testified at a public hearing about media consolidation in 2005) think these corporations are actually harming film and television. Instead of independent minds willing to break out of molds and take true creative risks, most entertainment created in Hollywood is churned out formulaically. Some fans and makers of independent films, or "indies" (small, original films that are not distributed by the major distribution companies), argue that the big companies have a stranglehold on the movie business, keeping intelligent, often quirky, small-budget films out of movie theaters and edging independent filmmakers out of the business. Once there were dozens of independent studios making film and television shows, and now there are a mere handful. And even these independent studios are controlled directly by the boards of directors of these overarching media conglomerates. Independent websites are also gobbled up by the media giants (such as MySpace.com's sale to Rupert Murdoch's NewsCorp for $580 million).

Concentration of Power

Another criticism aimed at these media multinationals is that there is a dangerous concentration of power over all avenues of information. A few dozen men and women (the boards of directors and CEOs of these companies) control most information in the modern world. They own vast portions of the Internet, radio, television, communications satellites, and the printed press. They have the power to highlight or bury any news story that occurs, and the populace has precious little resources left by which to verify the mainstream information fed to us by a potentially manipulated media. Citizens hope that these corporations are not distorting the news in a meaningful way, but we would all be hard pressed to find out if they were, because they own most of the means we'd use to verify information.

Loss of Free Press

In the United States Bill of Rights, citizens are guaranteed freedom of the press. In its usual interpretation, this means that the government has no power to stop people from saying, printing, or broadcasting their own opinions. A free press must be free from more than just the government, however, and this is what critics of the recent media mergers worry about. Ideally, the news media must have the interests of the populace in mind, not only the interests of sponsors and investors. A hard-hitting news story can offend people, and if a major corporation is also offended, it can pull its ads, costing millions of dollars to the news network. A board of directors can kill a story because of pressure from a major advertiser. Owners of news outlets can pressure their editors and reporters to soft pedal or ignore news that might upset people with whom they have profitable business connections. This is a serious form of information control. According to the critics, some stories of sweatshops, pollution, injuries and diseases caused by various products, global warming, and even corporate crime aren't given the breadth of coverage they deserve because the media conglomerates are afraid of losing sponsors and, therefore, revenue.

Danger to Democracy

The cornerstone of any democracy is the ability of anyone to run for office and for all citizens to have access to the truth regarding elections. However, the current media system is said by many to deny us this. Democratic elections are won and lost on the battlegrounds of advertising campaigns. These cost millions of dollars, and whichever candidate has the most money can hire the best directors and writers and pay for the most air time—and such air time helps candidates win elections, which some critics say leaves us with a government by finance, not a government by educated voters. Whoever can generate the most campaign funding, run the deepest smear campaign, or saturate the mass media the most has a distinct advantage. Without a free flow of reliable information, the notion of a truly free and democratic people vanishes.

BIG FOUR

Four corporations own the bulk of American media outlets, thus owning our access to information. They are **Time Warner** (previously America Online Time Warner), Rupert Murdoch's **News Corporation** (the parent company of the Fox networks), Sumner Redstone's **Viacom,** and the iconic **Disney Corporation.** Who owns what may not seem important, but when so few people own so much of the media, the possibility of free voices, unique perspectives, and fresh art diminishes in the wake of corporate profit. Even sites where ordinary people can publish themselves on the Internet, such as YouTube.com and MySpace.com, are now owned by these giants.

Following is a list of some of the holdings of the "Big Four" multinational media corporations. Represented here are various companies, television stations, cable networks, newspapers, magazines, radio stations, and even amusement parks and sports teams that these multinationals own or owned until recently (entire corporations are bought and sold with such frequency that some of these corporations may have bought each other out by the time you read this).

INFORMATION COMPETENCY

No look at information competency can be complete without a study of these corporations and their holdings. Knowing who owns these aspects of the media is a critical part of information competency. Many people don't understand where our knowledge comes from and fail to have an understanding of the power of the media. However, these media giants can make or break presidential elections and inform us on everything from foreign policy to what clothes we should wear this season. Understanding how and what the corporations communicate to us is a crucial part to being competent with information.

Time Warner

Time Warner is arguably the world's most influential media conglomerate. It has more than 85,000 employees, is in the top fifty of the Fortune 500, and it saw over $43 billion in revenue in 2005. In a way, Time Warner set the stage for the business model of expanding media corporations. Although *Time* magazine and Warner Brothers Films Studios both date back to the 1920s, they remained independent corporate entities until the 1990s, when they merged and were quickly bought by America Online, creating the largest and wealthiest media corporation in the world.

Following is a list of Time-Warner's holdings.

TELEVISION AND CABLE

CNN, HBO, CNN Headline News, Court TV, TBS Superstation, Turner Network Television (TNT), Cartoon Network, In-Demand Pay-Per-View, fifty percent of CW Network, and fifty percent of Comedy Central.

STUDIOS AND INTELLECTUAL PROPERTIES

Warner Bros. Studios, WB Network, Hanna-Barbera Cartoons, Looney Tunes, DC Comics, Castle Rock Entertainment, Telepictures Productions, *The Sopranos, Entourage, True Blood,* Batman, Superman, The Justice League, Wonder Woman, Bugs Bunny, and Space Ghost.

PRINT

Time Life Books; Sunset Books; Warner Books; Little, Brown and Company; more than sixty magazines, including *Time, People, Life, Sports Illustrated, Entertainment Weekly, Popular Science, Fortune, In Style, Field and Stream, People en Español, Teen People,* and *Mad Magazine.*

MISCELLANEOUS

America Online Internet Service, Warner Music Group (more than forty recording labels, including Elektra, Atlantic, Asylum, and Reprise), Warner Brothers Recreational Enterprises (including Six Flags Amusement Parks), Warner Bros. International Theaters (which owns and runs movie theaters in several countries), Road Runner Cable Network, Bright House High Speed Internet, AOL Instant Messenger, Netscape, Moviephone, and the Atlanta Braves and Atlanta Hawks.

News Corporation

The News Corporation is unique compared to the other big four media conglomerates because it was built and owned by one man: Rupert Murdoch. Murdoch started out with two Australian newspapers and has turned that into a global corporation with more than 47,000 employees and revenues of $25 billion in 2006. With his salary and bonuses, Rupert Murdoch typically makes around $25 million a year for his work as CEO of The News Corporation, and he has even parodied himself on *The Simpsons* (a show his corporation owns).

Following is a list of News Corporation's holdings.

TELEVISION AND CABLE

Fox Broadcasting Company, FX, Speed Network, Fox News, Fox Spots, Fox Kids, and more than 200 Fox Television Stations in major American markets.

STUDIOS AND INTELLECTUAL PROPERTIES

Twentieth Century Fox Studios and Fox Searchlight studios. *X-Files, The Simpsons, King of the Hill, Family Guy, 24, Prison Break, That '70s Show*, and *American Idol*.

PRINT

More than twenty publishing houses, including Harper Collins, Morrow/Avon, Perennial, and Harper Collins UK. It also owns sixteen magazines and more than thirty newspapers in over ten countries, including the extremely influential *Wall Street Journal*.

MISCELLANEOUS

Myspace.com, DirecTV, and Sky Global Satellite Network.

Viacom/CBS

The Viacom Corporation is one of the largest media conglomerates, and this is evidenced by the fact that it owned the massive CBS network until relatively recently when it split into two separate corporations. This move helped streamline both corporations, but in a very real way, they are still the same entity, using their synergy and infrastructure to ensure each other's success. The real connection keeping these two corporations tied together is the Redstone family. Sumner Redstone and his wife, Shari Redstone, are the CEO and Vice Chairman, respectively, of both CBS and Viacom, running them as one corporate entity. Under this new structure, Viacom had revenues of $9.6 billion in 2005, and CBS had $14 billion in the same time span. With Sumner Redstone acting as both heads of this corporate hydra, CBS rose to the number one rated network in America. The holdings that follow represent both CBS and Viacom collectively.

Following is a list of Viacom/CBS's holdings.

TELEVISION AND CABLE

CBS Network, MTV, MTV2, VH1, Nickelodeon, TV Land, Nick at Night, BET, Spike TV, Showtime, The Movie Channel, Country Music Television, Sundance Channel, fifty percent of CW Network, and fifty percent of Comedy Central.

STUDIOS AND INTELLECTUAL PROPERTIES

Paramount Pictures, Kingworld, *CSI, Survivor,* the *Star Trek* franchise, *Sponge Bob Square Pants, The Hills, The Real World, Road Rules, My Super Sweet Sixteen, Jackass, Total Request Live* (*TRL*), and partial ownership of DreamWorks SKG.

PRINT

Simon and Schuster, Scribner, Pocket Books, and The Free Press.

MISCELLANEOUS

More than 100 radio stations nationwide, CBS Outdoor and Viacom Outdoor (roadside billboard advertising).

Disney

Disney is the second largest of the media multinationals ($34 billion in revenue and more than 130,000 employees), and it is undeniably the most famous and endearing. Disney aims to create brands that people will love from infancy through adulthood, ranging from Mickey Mouse to *The Little Mermaid* and *Toy Story.* Disney is unique in that it owns not only its own cruise line, but its own city: Celebration, Florida.

Following is a list of Disney's holdings.

TELEVISION AND CABLE

ABC, ESPN, Disney Channel, ABC Family, Toon Disney, SOAPnet, and partial ownership of the following: E!, A&E, The History Channel, The Biography Channel, and Lifetime.

FILM STUDIOS AND INTELLECTUAL PROPERTIES

Walt Disney Pictures, Touchstone Pictures, Miramax Films, Buena Vista, Pixar, Mickey Mouse, Donald Duck, *Pirates of the Caribbean, The Little Mermaid, The Lion King, Toy Story, Lost, Desperate Housewives, Grey's Anatomy,* and *Boston Legal.*

PRINT

Hyperion Books, Disney Publishing, *Discover Magazine, Disney Magazine,* partial ownership of *Biography Magazine,* and *US Weekly.*

MISCELLANEOUS

Disneyland Resorts, Walt Disney World, Disney Cruiselines, Disneyland Paris/Hong Kong/Tokyo, nearly fifty radio stations in major markets, ESPN radio, Buena Vista Music, Walt Disney Records, Hollywood Records, Disney Store retail chain, and Celebration, Florida.

Secondary Media Conglomerates

Other corporations own large portions of the American mediascape, but not at the scale of the big four listed previously. Corporations such as Clear Channel own hundreds of radio and television stations coast to coast. Entities such as the Bertelsmann group own dozens of major American publishing houses. Following is a brief list of some other corporations that also own major stakes in our information domain. Look them up and learn more about them to help make sure that you are information competent.

Bertelsmann

Clear Channel

Comcast

Cox Enterprises

Gannett

GE/NBC

Hearst Corporation

Sony

Tribune Company

Vivendi/Universal

Note: All corporate holding information came from Hoover's Company Records and *Columbia Journalism Review's* "Who Owns What" website found at http://www.cjr .org/tools/owners/.

IN THIS CHAPTER

The following readings have been included to give you a better understanding of the major multinational media corporations and the power they wield. They are included to help foster an understanding of who owns the sources and controls the flow of the information we consume. This chapter focuses on corporations that own most of the forms of the mass media. They own virtually every major newspaper, TV station, radio station, major Internet service, magazine, and record company on Earth, and this should prompt you to ask the following questions:

- Why is there a trend to relax the laws regulating these corporations (such as the Telecom Act of 1995), and what effect does this have on the information we receive?

- Have these media corporations become a threat to American democracy?

- Are these multinational corporations becoming monopolies?

- How can a single corporation, with all of its print, TV, and media power, shape our opinions without our even being aware of it?

- Who are Rupert Murdoch and Sumner Redstone?

- Why was it once illegal for these corporations to own multiple types of media outlets (for example, a cable network, local network, movie studio, and local TV station) all at once?

- What problems with "information control" might surface in coming decades?

From Corporate Media and the Threat to Democracy

Robert McChesney

Prereading Questions

1. What do you think of news coverage in general? Is it thorough enough for you?
2. Do you think the media is inherently biased? If so, in what direction? Or does it depend on the source?
3. What is most important for a democracy to be successful?

Participatory self-government, or democracy, works best when at least three criteria are met. First, it helps when there are not significant disparities in economic wealth and property ownership across the society. Such disparities undermine the ability of citizens to act as equals. Second, it helps when there is a sense of community and a notion that an individual's well-being is determined to no small extent by the community's well-being. This provides democratic political culture with a substance that cannot exist if everyone is simply out to advance narrowly defined self-interests, even if those interests might be harmful to the community as a whole. Third, democracy requires that there be an effective system of political communication, broadly construed, that informs and engages the citizenry, drawing people meaningfully into the polity. This becomes especially important as societies grow larger and more complex, but has been true for all societies dedicated toward self-government. While democracies by definition must respect individual freedoms, these freedoms can be exercised in a meaningful sense only when the citizenry is informed, engaged, and participating. Moreover, without this, political debate can scarcely address the central issues of power and resource allocation that must be at the heart of public deliberation in a democracy. As James Madison noted, "A popular government without popular information, or the means of acquiring it, is but a prologue to a farce or a tragedy, or perhaps both."[1]

These three criteria are related. In non-democratic societies those in power invariably dominate the communication systems to maintain their rule. In democratic societies the manner by which the media system is structured, controlled and subsidized is of central political importance. Control over the means of communication is an integral aspect of political and economic power. In many nations, to their credit, media policy debates have been and are important political issues. In the United States, to the contrary, private commercial control over communication is often regarded as innately democratic and benevolent, and therefore not subject to political discussion. Government involvement with media or communication is almost universally denigrated in the U.S. as a direct invitation to tyranny, no matter how well intended. The preponderance of U.S. mass communication is controlled by less than two dozen enormous profit-maximizing corporations, which receive much of their income from advertising placed largely by other huge corporations. But the extent of this media ownership and control goes generally unremarked in the media and intellectual culture, and there appears to be little sense of concern about its dimensions among the citizenry as a whole.

In my view, private control over media and communication is not a neutral or necessarily a benevolent proposition. The commercial basis of U.S. media has negative implications for the exercise of political democracy: it encourages a weak political culture that makes depoliticization, apathy and selfishness rational choices for the citizenry, and it permits the business and commercial interests that actually rule U.S. society to have inordinate influence over media content. In short, the nature of the U.S. media system undermines all three of the meaningful criteria necessary for self-government. Accordingly, for those committed to democracy, it is imperative to reform the media system. This is not going to be an easy task, for there is no small amount of confusion over what would be a superior democratic alternative to the status quo. The political obstacles seem even more daunting because the terrain is no longer local or even national. Media politics are becoming global in scope, as the commercial media market assumes global proportions and as it is closely linked to the globalizing market economy. The immensity of the task of changing and democratizing media is sobering, but it is a job that must be done.

Media corporations also make unusually powerful adversaries for proponents of media reform. They not only enjoy significant political and economic power, but, of course, they also control the media that must provide much of the information citizens need to evaluate media conduct. Moreover, the corporate media system is also protected by several powerful myths, that in combination make it nearly impossible to broach the subject of media reform in U.S. political culture. These myths include: that an advertising-supported, profit-driven media system was ordained by the Founding Fathers and the First Amendment; that professionalism in journalism will protect the public interest from private media control; that the Internet and new digital technologies with their billions of potential channels eliminate any reason to be concerned about corporate domination of media; that the market is the best possible organization for a media system because it forces media firms to "give the people what they want"; that a commercial media system was selected historically in public debate as the best possible system for a democracy, and the matter has therefore been determined for all time; and that the media are not dominated by corporate interests but, instead, have a liberal or left-wing anti-business bias.

The first task for changing the media system is to put control of the media on the political agenda—exactly where it belongs in a democratic society. The purpose of this essay is to assist in that process, by providing an analysis of the contours and trajectory of the contemporary media system. In particular, I sketch out ownership and subsidy patterns of the commercial media system and argue that these present a direct threat to the ability of the United States to have a viable democratic media culture. I also debunk—or at least qualify—the ideological myths that shield corporate control of the media from public scrutiny. I conclude by specifically discussing what is being done and what needs to be done to construct a democratic media.

The Problem of Journalism

Media systems provide many types of content, including numerous varieties of entertainment and journalism. Although entertainment and cultural fare can and do provide vital social and political commentary and information, this is a direct responsibility of journalism. A healthy political culture requires that to some extent each of these forms of communication be politicized—open to public questioning and discussion. In the absence of a viable democratic journalism, art and entertainment may fill some of the breach, but they will likely accommodate themselves to the depoliticized or repressive political culture. Indeed, the burden upon journalism to provide political information is increased in the modern media marketplace, where commercial values tend to discourage the "politicization" of entertainment and cultural material beyond a fairly narrow and safe range.

How best to provide a democratic journalism, broadly construed to include public affairs as well as "news," is a difficult problem for any democracy. To the extent that journalism deals with politics, it will always be a source of some controversy. Moreover, journalism requires institutional support and subsidy of some kind, and it reflects the conscious decisions of editors and reporters, not to mention those that hire and fire them. In short, journalism can never be an entirely neutral enterprise. And, if one de-emphasizes the goal of neutrality, attempting to make it accurately reflect the range of perspectives in a society, especially in an inegalitarian society, is no easy task. With this in mind, and in view of the complex nature of modern societies, it seems likely that there is no one "solution" to the problem of journalism.

In recent years the work of Jurgen Habermas and others has pointed toward a way of conceptualizing a democratic media.[2] According to Habermas, a critical factor that led to the rise and success of democratic revolutions and societies in the 18th and 19th centuries was the emergence—for the first time in modern history—of a "public sphere" for democratic discourse. This public sphere was a "space" independent of both state and business control which permitted citizens to interact, study and debate on the public issues of the day without fear of immediate reprisal from the political and economic powers that be. The media existed in the public sphere, but they were only part of it.

Although Habermas's model is idealized, the notion of the public sphere provides a useful framework for democratic media activists. In Habermas's view, the public sphere loses its democratic capacities as it is taken over by either the state or business or some combination of the two. In the United States, clearly, business and commercial values have come to dominate the media as perhaps nowhere else in the world. To reassert the "public sphere" notion of a media system would require a major commitment to nonprofit and noncommercial media, at the very least, and perhaps a good deal else. But the public sphere framework only points in the direction of solutions; there are probably any number of workable alternatives. The immediate objective for media activists is to get this long neglected subject on the political agenda and to encourage public participation.

Even if the "public sphere" is based on an idealized interpretation of western media history, it contradicts the prevailing mythology of a "free press," which is widely cherished in the United States. Indeed, the power of the corporate media rests to no small extent upon the myth that only a commercial capitalist media system that produces "unbiased" journalism can be truly democratic, and that this was the express purpose of the Founding Fathers as they crafted the First Amendment to the U.S. Constitution. In fact, U.S. history reveals a media culture that is unrecognizable by the standards of the myth. The Founding Fathers, to the extent we can generalize, envisioned a press that above all else would stimulate public involvement—what media historian John Nerone has termed the "town meeting" metaphor of the press. In the first 50 or 60 years of the republic, journalism moved away from that ideal and became highly partisan. It was not especially profitable and was often subsidized directly or indirectly by government printing contracts, political parties or factions. Advertising played a minor and unimportant role, and did not exist in the modern sense of the term. The press was closely linked to the political culture of the day; any given city might have several newspapers providing very different interpretations of public issues. Some modern scholars term this era the "Dark Ages of American Journalism," the assumption being that these partisan newspapers operated as propaganda sheets, not unlike the Stalinist or Nazi media. The key ingredient of Nazi and Stalinist journals was that opposing viewpoints were banned. In a democratic system, where differing perspectives are protected by the constitution, a diverse partisan press tends to produce a highly informed and engaged citizenry. Hence the Jacksonian era (1820s and 1830s), the last great period of partisan journalism, is sometimes characterized as the "Golden Age of American Politics," for its high level of political interest and participation.

All of this began to change around the 1840s when entrepreneurs began to realize that they could make lots of money publishing newspapers. By the end of the Civil War, the partisan system had been displaced by a dynamic and vibrant commercial newspaper system. "America is the classic soil of newspapers; everybody is reading," an English writer observed in 1871. "No political party, or religious sect, no theological school, no literary or benevolent association, is without its particular organ; there is a universality of print."[3] Throughout the balance of the 19th century, the newspaper industry was highly competitive. Many newspapers served every major market. Newspapers developed enormous circulations and penetrated every niche of society. The press tended to remain partisan by contemporary standards, but its fundamental reason for being was now profit, not political influence, and this contributed to fundamentally altering the way editors, publishers, and, eventually, the public thought about journalism.[4]

Two critical developments crystallized by the beginning of the 20th century, just when the political economy was becoming dominated by large corporations. First, newspapers grew bigger and bigger and their markets grew increasingly concentrated. The largest newspaper in a market might now reach 40 to 60 percent of the population, rather than 10 percent, as had been the case in 1875. Second, with the rise of corporate capitalism, advertising emerged as the dominant source of income for the press. This had enormous consequences. Most advertisers sought out newspapers with the highest circulations, which drove most other papers in a market out of business. In this context, highly partisan journalism tended to be bad business. Wanting the largest possible circulation to dangle before advertisers, publishers did not want to upset any significant part of their potential readership. Moreover, as the control of newspapers in each market became concentrated among one or two or three owners, and as ownership concentrated nationally in the form of chains, journalism came to reflect the partisan interests of owners and advertisers, rather than diverse interests in any given community.

This was the context for the emergence of professional journalism schools, which were nonexistent at the turn of the century but were training a significant percentage of the nation's reporters by 1920. The core idea behind professional journalism was that news should not be influenced by the political agendas of the owners and advertisers, or by the editors and journalists themselves. At its crudest, this doctrine is characterized as "objectivity," whereby trained professionals develop "neutral" news values so that accounts of public affairs are the same regardless of who the reporter is, or which medium carries the report. Professional journalism's mission was to make a capitalist, advertising-supported media system seem—at least superficially—to be an objective source of news to many citizens.

The newly emergent professional journalism was a very different animal from its partisan ancestor. It was hardly neutral. On one hand, the commercial requirements for media content to satisfy media owners and advertisers were built implicitly into the professional ideology; were that not the case, owners and advertisers would have been far more hostile to the rise of professional journalism than they were. On the other hand, corporate activities and the affairs of the wealthy were not subject to the same degree of scrutiny as government practices; the professional codes deemed the affairs of powerful economic actors vastly less newsworthy than the activities of politicians. In this manner "objective" journalism effectively internalized corporate capitalism as the natural order for a democracy. Thus, as Ben Bagdikian puts it, journalists became oblivious to the compromises with authority they constantly make.[5]

Moreover, in its pursuit of "objectivity," professional journalism proved a lifeless enterprise. In order to avoid the controversy associated with determining which news stories to emphasize and which to deemphasize, it came to accept official sources (government, big business) as appropriate generators of legitimate news. It also looked for news "events" or "hooks" to justify story selection. This gave the news a very "establishment" orientation, since anything government officials or prominent business people said was seen as newsworthy by definition. It was a safe course of action for journalists and a fairly inexpensive way for publishers to fill the news hole. This practice was soon exploited by politicians and public figures, who learned how to take advantage of their roles as legitimate news sources by carefully manipulating their coverage. More importantly, the emergence of professional journalism was quickly followed by the establishment of public relations as an industry whose primary function it was to generate favorable coverage in the press without public awareness of its activities. By many surveys, press releases and PR-generated material today account for between 40 and 70 percent of the news in today's media.[6]

The new professional journalism is of course not solely responsible for the depoliticization of American society. This is a broad, complex historical phenomenon with many factors. It is worth noting that, as the market expands its influence and commercialism undermines and replaces the role of traditional nonprofit organizations in bringing people and communities together, the "public sphere" where individuals become citizens is reduced and corrupted.[7] Moreover, the rise of corporate-dominated capitalism in the 20th century has seen a shift such that core political decisions concerning resource allocation and affairs of state tend to be made by elites outside of public purview, and the political culture concentrates upon tangential or symbolic issues.[8]

The range of debate between the dominant U.S. parties tends to closely resemble the range of debate within the business class. This is a context that makes depoliticization a rational choice for much of the citizenry, especially the dispossessed whose fate appears to be affected only marginally by changes in power. "Free market" conservatives like Milton Friedman are unapologetic about this turn of events; in their view the market (i.e. business) should rule and the political system should logically deal with how best to protect private property and not much else. It is counterproductive for citizens to apply much attention or energy to public life, except to chastise those who criticize business.[9] As Noam Chomsky has observed, when traditionally apathetic sectors of the population became politically active and demanded a say in basic political issues in the 1960s and 1970s, elite business and intellectual figures characterized this as a "crisis of democracy," and with no sense of irony.[10]

Yet no institution is more important to the public sphere than the media, so as journalism became "professionalized" it played a major role in assisting the depoliticization of U.S. society. By defining the news as being based on specific events or on the activities of official sources, the news media neglect coverage of long-term social issues that dominate society. Moreover, by sanitizing coverage and seemingly depriving it of ideological content, the news made public affairs increasingly obtuse, confusing and boring. The excitement once associated with politics was now to be found only in coverage of crime, sports and celebrities. This depoliticization has been marked by a general decline in political knowledge, by lower voter turnouts, and by a narrowing range of legitimate political debate.

To be sure, professionalism did bring a certain degree of autonomy to the newsroom and permit journalists to pursue stories with far more freedom than would have been the case in the 19th century. On certain types of issues that clear the professional criteria for selection, commercial journalism has been and is first-rate. Moreover, there have been countless outstanding U.S. journalists throughout the 20th century—and there still are—thoroughly committed to the democratic and progressive aspects of the professional journalistic ideology. Even so, the dominant institutional factors have pressed for a decontextualized, depoliticized and conservative journalism. By the early 1980s, these characteristics had been observed and chronicled widely by numerous scholars including Gaye Tuchman, Herbert Gans, Mark Fishman, and W. Lance Bennett.[11] Edward S. Herman and Noam Chomsky have demonstrated how, on the fundamental political issues of the day, journalism tends to conform to elite interests, and to avoid antagonizing the powers-that-be.[12] Indeed, in what stands as perhaps the most damning statement one could make about the news media, some studies have suggested that the more a person consumes commercial news, the less capable that person is of understanding politics or public affairs.[13]

Corporate Media Consolidation

The journalism that emerged in the 20th century is a product well suited to the needs of the dominant media firms and advertisers that profited from the status quo. Yet the system was far from stable. On the one hand, new technologies like radio and television emerged and changed many aspects of media and journalism. On the other hand, the market moved inexorably toward becoming an integrated oligopoly, with a handful of firms dominating all forms of U.S. media, from radio, television, music and film to newspapers, magazines, and book publishing. In the early 1980s, Ben Bagdikian's *The Media Monopoly* concluded that less than 50 firms had come to dominate the entirety of the U.S. media, with the result that journalism was increasingly losing its ability to address the role and nature of corporate power in the U.S. political economy. As Bagdikian put it, the range of debate in U.S. journalism concerning capitalism and corporate power was roughly equivalent to the range of debate in the Soviet media concerning the nature of communism and the activities of the Communist Party. In the decade following the publication of *The Media Monopoly,* as traditional ownership regulations were relaxed, the market continued to consolidate at an even faster rate. By the time of the fourth edition of *The Media Monopoly,* in 1992, Bagdikian calculated that mergers and acquisitions had reduced the number of dominant media firms to two dozen.

Since 1992 there has been an unprecedented wave of mergers and acquisitions among media giants, highlighted by the Time Warner purchase of Turner and the Disney acquisition of Cap Cities/ABC. Fewer than ten colossal vertically integrated media conglomerates now dominate U.S. media. The five largest firms—with annual sales in the $10–25 billion range—are News Corporation, Time Warner, Disney, Viacom, and TCI. These firms are major producers of entertainment and media software and have distribution networks like television networks, cable channels and retail stores. Time Warner, for example, owns music recording studios, film and television production studios, several cable television channels, cable broadcasting systems, amusement parks, the WB television network, book publishing houses, magazine publishing interests, retail stores, motion picture theaters, and much else. In most of the above categories, Time Warner ranks among the top five firms in the world. The next three media firms include NBC (owned by General Electric), Universal (formerly MCA, owned by Seagram), and Sony. All three of these firms are conglomerates with non-media interests, with Sony and GE being huge electronics concerns that at least double the annual sales of any other media firm.

Below this first group there are another dozen or so quite large media firms—usually conglomerates—with annual sales generally in the $2–5 billion range.[14] This list includes Westinghouse (owner of CBS), Gannett, Cox Enterprises, The New York Times, Advance Communications, Comcast, Hearst, Tribune Co., The Washington Post Co., Knight-Ridder, Times-Mirror, DirecTV (owned by General Motors and AT&T), Dow Jones, Reader's Digest, and McGraw-Hill. By the year 2000 it is probable that some of these firms will make deals to get larger or be acquired by other firms seeking to get larger.

The most striking development in the 1990s has been the emergence of a global commercial media market, utilizing new technologies and the global trend toward de-regulation. A global oligopolistic market that covers the spectrum of media is now crystallizing with very high barriers to entry. National markets remain, and they are indispensable for understanding any particular national situation, but they are becoming secondary in importance. The U.S.-based firms just named dominate the global media market along with a handful of European-based firms and a few Latin American and Asian operations. By all accounts they will do so for a long time to come.[15] Firms like Disney and Time Warner have seen their non-U.S. revenues climb from around 15 percent in 1990 to 30 percent in 1996. Sometime in the next decade both firms expect to earn a majority of their income outside of the United States. What stimulates much of the creation of a global media market is the growth in commercial advertising worldwide, especially by transnational firms. Advertising tends to be conducted by large firms operating in oligopolistic markets. With the increasing globalization of the world economy, advertising has come to play a crucial role for the few hundred firms that dominate it. From this vantage point it becomes clear, also, how closely linked the U.S. and global media systems are to the market economy.[16]

Media firms have great incentive to merge, acquire, and globalize. It is when the effects of sheer size, conglomeration, and globalization are combined that a sense of the profit potential emerges. When Disney produces a film, for example, it can also guarantee the film showings on pay cable television and commercial network television, it can produce and sell soundtracks based on the film, it can create spin-off television series, it can produce related amusement park rides, CD-roms, books, comics, and merchandise to be sold in Disney retail stores. Moreover, Disney can promote the film and related material incessantly across all its media properties. In this climate, even films that do poorly at the box office can become profitable. Disney's *Hunchback of Notre Dame* (1996) generated a disappointing $99 million at the North American box office. However, according to *Adweek* magazine, it is expected to generate $500 million in profit (not just revenues), after the other revenue streams are taken into account. And films that are hits can become spectacularly successful. Disney's *The Lion King* (1994) earned several hundred million at the box office, yet generated over $1 billion in profit for Disney.[17] Moreover, media conglomerates can and do use the full force of their various media holdings to promote their other holdings. They do so incessantly. In sum, the profit whole for the vertically integrated firm can be significantly greater than the profit potential of the individual parts in isolation. Firms without this cross-selling and cross-promotional potential are simply incapable of competing in the global marketplace.

In establishing new ventures, media firms are likely to participate in joint ventures, whereby they link up—usually through shared ownership—with one or more other media firms on specific media projects. Joint ventures are attractive because they reduce the capital requirements and risk on individual firms and permit the firms to spread their resources more widely. Each of the eight largest U.S. media firms has, on average, joint ventures with four of the other seven giants. They each also have even more ventures with smaller media firms. Beyond joint ventures, there is also overlapping direct ownership of these firms. Seagram, owner of MCA, for example, owns 15 percent of Time Warner and has other media equity holdings.[18] TCI is a major shareholder in Time Warner and has holdings in numerous other media firms.[19] The Capital Group Companies mutual fund, valued at $250 billion, is among the very largest shareholders in TCI, News Corporation, Seagram, Time Warner, Viacom, Disney, Westinghouse, and several other smaller media firms.[20]

Even without joint ventures and cross-ownership, competition in oligopolistic media markets is hardly "competitive" in the economic sense of the term. Reigning oligopolistic markets are dominated by a handful of firms that compete—often quite feruciously within the oligopolistic framework—on a non-price basis and are protected by severe barriers to entry. The "synergies" of recent mergers rest on and enhance monopoly power. No start-up studio, for example, has successfully joined the Hollywood oligopoly in 60 years.[21] Rupert Murdoch of News Corporation poses the rational issue for an oligopolistic firm when pondering how to proceed in the media market: "We can join forces now, or we can kill each other and then join forces."[22]

When one lays the map of joint ventures over the global media marketplace, even the traditional levels of competition associated with oligopolistic markets may be exaggerated. "Nobody can really afford to get mad with their competitors," says TCI chairman John Malone, "because they are partners in one area and competitors in another."[23] *The Wall Street Journal* observes that media "competitors wind up switching between the roles of adversaries, prized customers and key partners."[24] In this sense the U.S. and global media and communication market exhibits tendencies not only of an oligopoly, but of a cartel or at least a "gentleman's club."

ENDNOTES

1. Quotation from Edward S. Herman, *Beyond Hypocrisy* (Boston: South End Press, 1992), p. 2.

2. Jurgen Habermas, *The Structural Transformation of the Public Sphere,* Thomas Burger with Frederick Lawrence, translators (Cambridge, Mass.: MIT Press, 1989). Originally published in German in 1962.

3. Cited in Frank Luther Mott, *American Journalism* (New York: The Macmillan Company, 1941), p. 405.

4. See Gerald J. Baldasty, *The Commercialization of the News* (Madison: University of Wisconsin Press, 1992).

5. Ben H. Bagdikian, *The Media Monopoly,* fourth edition (Boston: Beacon Press, 1992).

6. See Alex Carey, *Taking the Risk Out of Democracy* (Champaign: University of Illinois Press, 1996).

7. See C. Wright Mills, *The Power Elite* (New York: Oxford University Press, 1956).

8. See C. B. Macpherson, *The Life and Times of Liberal Democracy* (New York: Oxford University Press, 1977).

9. Milton Friedman, *Capitalism and Freedom* (Chicago: University of Chicago Press, 1962), ch. 2; see also, David Kelley and Roger Downey, "Liberalism and Free Speech," in Judith Lichtenberg, editor, *Democracy and the Mass Media* (Cambridge and New York: Cambridge University Press, 1990), pp. 66–101.

10. See Noam Chomsky, *On Power and Ideology: The Managua Lectures* (Boston: South End Press, 1987).

11. See Gaye Tuchman, *Making News* (New York: Basic Books, 1978); Mark Fishman, *Manufacturing the News* (Austin: University of Texas Press, 1980); Herbert Gans, *Deciding What's News* (New York: Pantheon, 1979).

12. Edward S. Herman and Noam Chomsky, *Manufacturing Consent: The Political Economy of the Mass Media* (New York: Pantheon, 1988).

13. See W. Lance Bennett, *News: The Politics of Illusion* (New York: Longman, 1983); Robert Entman, *Democracy Without Citizens* (New York: Oxford University Press, 1989); Michael Morgan, Justin Lewis and Sut Jhally, "More Viewing, Less Knowing," in Hamid Mowlana, George Gerbner and Herbert I. Schiller, editors, *Triumph of the Image* (Boulder, Col.: Westview Press, 1992).

14. Diane Mermigas, "Still to come: Smaller media alliances," *Electronic Media,* February 5, 1996, p. 38.

15. Doug Wilson, *Strategies of the Media Giants* (London: Pearson Professional Ltd., 1996), p. 5.

16. See Edward S. Herman and Robert W. McChesney, *The Global Media: The New Missionaries of Global Capitalism* (London: Cassell, 1997).

17. Maria Matzer, "Contented Kingdoms," *Superbrands '97,* supplement to *Adweek,* October 7, 1996, pp. 30, 33.

18. Bernard Simon, "Seagram to hold on to 15% stake in Time Warner," *The Financial Times,* June 1, 1995, p. 18.

19. Raymond Snoddy, "Master of bits at home in the hub," *Financial Times,* May 28, 1996, p. 17.

20. Catherine E. Celebrezze, "The Man Who Bought the Media," *Extra!,* Vol. 9, No. 2, March-April 1996, pp. 21–22.

21. Ronald Grover, "Plenty of Dreams, Not Enough Work?" *Business Week,* July 22, 1996, p. 65.

22. Paula Dwyer, "Can Rupert Conquer Europe?" *Business Week,* March 25, 1996, p. 169.

23. Raymond Snoddy, "Master of bits at home in the hub," *Financial Times,* May 28, 1996, p. 17.

24. Elizabeth Jensen and Eben Shapiro, "Time Warner's Fight With News Corp. Belies Mutual Dependence," *The Wall Street Journal,* October 28, 1996, p. Al.

Journal Topic

1. What are your thoughts on Madison's famous quote: "A popular government without popular information, or the means of acquiring it, is but a prologue to a farce or a tragedy, or perhaps both."

Questions for Critical Thought

1. McChesney argues that democracy needs three criteria to be successful. Consider his three criteria listed in this article. Do you think these are the keys to participatory self-government? If so, why? If not, name three things that you think democracy depends upon.

2. According to the article, media conglomerates "control the media that must provide much of the information citizens need to evaluate media conduct." If the companies themselves own the media that would be needed to successfully complain widely and publicly about those same companies, can citizens ever make this issue a major national subject of debate? How much dissent do you think is stifled because so many outlets are owned by these major media corporations?

Suggestion for Personal Research

1. Pick a type of mass communication (newspapers, television, radio, the Net, etc.). Research and create a detailed timeline of major events, laws, technological innovations, regulations, and deregulations surrounding this medium and its technology.

Multicultural Issues

1. Consider the three things McChesney says democracy needs in order to thrive. If you are from a different country, do you think these three things were important to governance there? How does the United States compare in these three areas to that country?

Vocabulary Terms

disparities	reprisal
polity	partisan
benevolent	chronicled
denigrated	oligopoly
preponderance	incessantly
inegalitarian	

Term for Clarification

James Madison   (March 16, 1751–June 28, 1836.) An American founding father and the fourth President of the United States, Madison was often called the "Father of the Constitution" (though he denied sole authorship himself). Madison was also known for having a major part in the development of the Bill of Rights and was a coauthor of the *Federalist* essays.

Big Media Is Ravenous

Bill Moyers

Prereading Questions

1. What do you think about the widening gap between the rich and the poor in America? How about the widening gap between the rich and the middle class? Have you seen any effects in your own life or the life of your family?

2. Where do you get most of your news—from print sources such as newspapers, magazines, and journals, or from nonprint sources, such as the TV, radio, and the Net? How do these sources compare to each other?

3. Do you think that Americans in general constitute a fully informed public that understands the major national and international issues affecting all our lives? If your answer is "Yes," why do you think this? If your answer is "No," what do you think the problem is? Is the fault the public's, or are media to blame?

Benjamin Franklin once said, "Democracy is two wolves and a lamb voting on what to have for dinner."

"Liberty," he said, "is a well-armed lamb, contesting the vote."

My fellow lambs—it's good to be in Memphis and find you well-armed with passion for democracy, readiness for action, and courage for the next round in the fight for a free and independent press in America. I salute the conviction that brought you here. I cherish the spirit that fills this hall, and the camaraderie that we share here.

All too often, the greatest obstacle to reform is the reform movement itself. Factions rise, fences are erected, jealousies mount, and the cause all of us believe in is lost in the shattered fragments of what once was a clear and compelling vision.

Reformers, in fact, often remind me of Baptists. I speak as a Baptist. I know whereof I speak. One of my favorite stories is of the fellow who was about to jump off a bridge, when another fellow ran up to him crying, "Stop, stop, don't do it."

The man on the bridge looks down and asks, "Why not?"

"Well, there's much to live for."

"What for?"

"Well, your faith. Your religion."

"Yes?"

"Are you religious?"

"Yes."

"Me, too. Christian or Buddhist?"

"Christian."

"Me, too. Are you Catholic or Protestant?"

"Protestant."

"Me, too. Methodist, Baptist or Presbyterian?"

"Baptist."

"Me, too. Are you Baptist Church of God or Baptist Church of the Savior?"

"Baptist Church of God."

"Me, too. Are you Original Baptist Church of God or Reformed Baptist Church of God?"

"Reformed Baptist Church of God."

"Me, too. Are you Reformed Baptist Church of God Reformation of 1879, or Reform Baptist Church of God Reformation of 1917?"

"1917."

Whereupon, the second fellow turned red in the face and yelled, "Die, you heretic scum," and pushed him off the bridge.

Doesn't that sound like a reform movement? But by avoiding contentious factionalism, you have created a strong movement. And I will confess to you that I was skeptical when Bob McChesney and John Nichols first raised with me the issue of media consolidation a few years ago. I was sympathetic but skeptical. The challenge of actually doing something about this issue beyond simply bemoaning its impact on democracy was daunting. How could we hope to come up with an effective response to any measurable force? It seemed inexorable, because all over the previous decades, a series of mega-media mergers have swept the country, each deal bigger than the last. The lobby representing the broadcast, cable, and newspaper industries was extremely powerful, with an iron grip on lawmakers and regulators alike.

Both parties bowed to their will when the Republican Congress passed and President Clinton signed the Telecommunications Act of 1996. That monstrous assault on democracy, with malignant consequences for journalism, was nothing but a welfare giveaway to the largest, richest, and most powerful media conglomerations in the world. Goliaths, whose handful of owners controlled, commodified, and monetized everyone and everything in sight. Call it "the plantation mentality."

That's what struck me as I flew into Memphis for this gathering. Even in 1968, the civil rights movement was still battling the plantation mentality, based on race, gender and power, which permeated Southern culture long before, and even after, the groundbreaking legislation of the 1960s.

When Dr. Martin Luther King Jr. came to Memphis to join the strike of garbage workers in 1968, the cry from every striker's heart—"I am a man"—voiced the long-suppressed outrage of people whose rights were still being trampled by an ownership class that had arranged the world for its own benefit. The plantation mentality is a phenomenon deeply insinuated in the American experience early on, and it has permeated and corrupted our course as a nation.

The journalist of the American Revolution, Thomas Paine, envisioned the new republic as a community of occupations, prospering by the aid with which each receives from the other and from the whole. But that vision was repeatedly betrayed, so that less than a century after Thomas Paine's death, Theodore Roosevelt, bolting a Republican Party whose bosses had stolen the nomination from him, declared: "It is not to be wondered at, that our opponents have been very bitter, for the line-up in this crisis is one that cuts deep to the foundations of democracy."

"Our democracy," he said, "is now put to a vital test, for the conflict is between human rights on the one side, and on the other, special privilege asserted as property rights. The parting of the ways has come."

Today, a hundred years after Teddy Roosevelt's death, those words ring just as true. America is socially divided and politically benighted. Inequality and poverty grow steadily along with risk and debt. Too many working families cannot make ends meet with two people working, let alone if one stays home to care for children or aging parents. Young people without privilege and wealth struggle to get a footing. Seniors enjoy less security for a lifetime's work. We are racially segregated today in every meaningful sense, except for the letter of the law. And the survivors of segregation and immigration toil for pennies on the dollar, compared to those they serve.

None of this is accidental. Nobel laureate economist Robert Solow, not known for extreme political statements, characterizes what is happening as "nothing less than elite plunder"—the redistribution of wealth in favor of the wealthy, and the power in favor of the powerful. In fact, nearly all the wealth America created over the past 25 years has been captured by the top 20 percent of households, and most of the gains went to the wealthiest. The top 1 percent of households captured more than 50 percent of all the gains in financial wealth, and these households now hold more than twice the share their predecessors held on the eve of the American Revolution.

The anti-Federalist warning that government naturally works to fortify the conspiracies of the rich proved prophetic. It's the truth today, and America confronts a choice between two fundamentally different economic visions. As Norton Garfinkle writes in his marvelous new book, *The American Dream vs. the Gospel of Wealth,* the historic vision of the American dream is that continuing economic growth and political stability can be achieved by supporting income growth and economic security of middle-class families, without restricting the ability of successful business men to gain wealth.

The counter-belief is that providing maximum financial rewards to the most successful is the way to maintain high economic growth. The choice cannot be avoided. What kind of economy do we seek, and what kind of nation do we wish to be? Do we want to be a country in which the rich get richer and the poor get poorer, or do we want a country committed to an economy that provides for the common good, offers upward mobility, supports a middle-class standard of living, and provides generous opportunities for all?

"When the richest nation in the world has to borrow hundreds of billions of dollars to pay its bill," Garfinkle says in his book, "when its middle class citizens sit on a mountain of debt to maintain their living standards, when the nation's economy has difficulty producing secure jobs, or enough jobs of any kind, something is amiss."

You bet something is amiss, and it goes to the core of why we are here in Memphis. For this conference is about a force, the media, that cuts deep to the foundation of democracy. When Teddy Roosevelt dissected what he called "the real masters of the reactionary forces" in his time, he concluded that, indirectly or directly, "they control the majority of the great newspapers that are against us." Those newspapers, the dominant media of the day, choked "the channels of the information ordinary people needed to understand what was being done to them."

And today, two basic pillars of American society, shared economic prosperity and a public sector capable of serving the common good, are crumbling. The third pillar of American democracy, an independent press, is under sustained attack, and the channels of information are choked. A few huge corporations now dominate the media landscape in America. Almost all the networks carried by most cable systems are owned by one of the major media common conglomerates. Two-thirds of today's newspapers are monopolies.

As ownership gets more and more concentrated, fewer and fewer independent sources of information have survived in the marketplace; and those few significant alternatives that do survive, such as PBS and NPR, are undergoing financial and political pressure to reduce critical news content and to shift their focus in a mainstream direction, which means being more attentive to establishment views than to the bleak realities of powerlessness that shape the lives of ordinary people.

What does today's media system mean for the notion of an informed public cherished by democratic theory? Quite literally, it means that virtually everything the average person sees or hears, outside of her own personal communications, is determined by the interests of private, unaccountable executives and investors whose primary goal is increasing profits and raising the share prices. More insidiously, this small group of elites determines what ordinary people do not see or hear. In-depth coverage of anything, let alone the problems real people face day-to-day, is as scarce as sex, violence and voyeurism are pervasive.

Successful business model or not, by democratic standards this is censorship of knowledge by monopolization of the means of information. In its current form, which Barry Diller happily describes as "oligopoly," media growth has one clear consequence. There is more information and easier access to it, but it's more narrow and homogenous in content and perspective. What we see from the couch is overwhelmingly a view from the top. The pioneering communications scholar Murray Edelman wrote that opinions about public policy do not spring immaculately or automatically into people's minds. They are always placed there by the interpretations of those who most consistently get their claims and manufactured cues publicized widely.

For years, the media marketplace for opinions about public policy has been dominated by a highly disciplined, thoroughly networked, ideological "noise machine," to use David Brock's term. Permeated with slogans concocted by big corporations, their lobbyists, and their think tank subsidiaries, public discourse has effectively changed the meaning of American values. Day after day, the ideals of fairness and liberty and mutual responsibility have been stripped of their essential dignity and meaning in people's lives. Day after day, the egalitarian creed of our Declaration of Independence is trampled underfoot by hired experts and sloganeers, who speak of the "death tax," "the ownership society," "the culture of life," "the liberal assault on God and family," "compassionate conservatism," "weak on terrorism," "the end of history," "the clash of civilizations," "no child left behind." They have even managed to turn the escalation of a failed war into a "surge," as if it were a current of electricity through a wire, instead of blood spurting from the ruptured vein of a soldier.

The Orwellian filigree of a public sphere in which language conceals reality, and the pursuit of personal gain and partisan power, is wrapped in rhetoric that turns truth to lies and lies to truth. So it is that limited government has little to do with the Constitution or local economy anymore. Now it means corporate domination and the shifting of risk from government and business to struggling families and workers. Family values now mean imposing a sectarian definition of the family on everyone else. Religious freedom now means majoritarianism and public benefits for organized religion without any public burdens. And patriotism has come to mean blind support for failed leaders.

It's what happens when an interlocking media system filters through commercial values or ideology, the information and moral viewpoints people consume in their daily lives. And by no stretch of the imagination can we say today that the dominant institutions of our media are guardians of democracy.

Despite the profusion of new information platforms on cable, on the Internet, on radio, blogs, podcasts, YouTube and MySpace, among others, the resources for solid, original journalistic work, both investigative and interpretative, are contracting, rather than expanding.

I'm old-fashioned. I'm a fogey at this, I guess, a hangover from my days as a cub reporter and a newspaper publisher. But I agree with Michael Schudson, one of the leading scholars of communication in America, who writes in the current *Columbia Journalism Review* that while all media matter, some matter more than others. And for the sake of democracy, print still counts most—especially print that devotes resources to gathering news.

Network TV matters, he said. Cable TV matters, he said. But when it comes to original investigation and reporting, newspapers are overwhelmingly the most important media. But newspapers are purposely dumbing-down, "driven down," says Schudson, by Wall Street, whose collective devotion to an informed citizenry is nil and seems determined to eviscerate those papers.

Worrying about the loss of real news is not a romantic cliché of journalism. It's been verified by history. From the days of royal absolutism to the present, the control of information and knowledge had been the first line of defense for failed regimes facing democratic unrest. The suppression of parliamentary dissent during Charles I's 11 years of tyranny in England rested largely on government censorship, operating through strict licensing laws for the publication of books.

The Federalist's infamous Sedition Act of 1798 in this country, likewise, sought to quell republican insurgency by making it a crime to publish false, scandalous and malicious writing about the government or its officials. In those days, our governing bodies tried to squelch journalistic information with the blunt instruments of the law: padlocks for the presses and jail cells for outspoken editors and writers. Over time, with spectacular wartime exceptions, the courts and the Constitution have struck those weapons out of their hand.

But now they have found new methods in the name of national security and even broader claims of executive privilege. The number of documents stamped "Top Secret," "Secret," or "Confidential" has accelerated dramatically since 2001, including many formerly accessible documents that are now reclassified as "Secret." Vice President Cheney's office refuses to disclose, in fact, what it is classifying. Even their secrecy is being kept a secret.

Beyond what is officially labeled "Secret" or "privileged" information, there hovers on the plantation a culture of selective official news implementation, working through favored media insiders to advance political agendas by leak and innuendo and spin, by outright propaganda mechanisms, such as the misnamed public information offices that churn out blizzards of factually selective releases on a daily basis, and even by directly paying pundits and journalists to write on subjects of mutual interest.

They needn't have wasted the money. As we saw in the run-up to the invasion of Iraq, the plantation mentality that governs Washington turned the press corps into sitting ducks for the war party, for government, and neoconservative propaganda and manipulation. There were notable exceptions—Knight Ridder's bureau, for example—but on the whole, all high-ranking officials had to do was say it, and the press repeated it until it became gospel. The height of myopia came with the admission (or was it bragging?) by one of the Beltway's most prominent anchors that his responsibility is to provide officials a forum to be heard, what they say more newsworthy than what they do.

The watchdog group FAIR found that during the three weeks leading up to the invasion, only 3 percent of U.S. sources on the evening news of ABC, CBS, NBC, CNN, Fox and PBS expressed skeptical opinions of the impending war, even though a quarter of the American people were against it. Not surprisingly, two years after 9/11, almost 70 percent of the public still thought it likely that Saddam Hussein was personally involved in the terrorist attacks of that day.

One Indiana schoolteacher told the *Washington Post:* "From what we've heard from the media, it seems what they feel is that Saddam and the whole Al-Qaeda thing are connected." Much to the advantage of the Bush administration, a large majority of the public shared this erroneous view during the build-up to the war, a propaganda feat that Saddam himself would have envied. It is absolutely stunning, frightening how the major media organizations were willing, even solicitous, hand puppets of a state propaganda campaign, cheered on by the partisan, ideological press to go to war.

But there are many other ways the plantation mentality keeps the American people from confronting reality. Take the staggering growth of money in politics. Compared to the magnitude of the problem, what the average person knows about how money determines policy is negligible. In fact, in the abstract, the polls tell us, most people generally assume that money controls our political system. But people will rarely act on something they understand only in the abstract. It took a constant stream of images—water hoses, and dogs and churches ablaze—for the public at large finally to understand what was happening to black people in the South. It took repeated scenes of destruction in Vietnam before the majority of Americans saw how we were destroying the country in order to save it. And it took repeated crime-scene images to maintain public support for many policing and sentencing policies.

Likewise, people have to see how money and politics actually work and concretely grasp the consequences for their pocketbooks and their lives before they will act. But while media organizations supply a lot of news and commentary, they tell us almost nothing about who really wags the system and how. When I watch one of those faux debates on a Washington public affairs show, with one politician saying, "This is a bad bill," and the other politician saying, "This is a good bill," I yearn to see the smiling, nodding, Beltway anchor suddenly interrupt and insist, "Good bill or bad bill, this is a bought bill. Now, let's cut to the chase. Whose financial interests are you advancing with this bill?"

Then there's the social cost of free trade. For over a decade, free trade has hovered over the political system like a biblical commandment striking down anything—trade unions, the environment, indigenous rights, even the constitutional standing of our own laws passed by our elected representatives—that gets in the way of unbridled greed. The broader negative consequences of this agenda, increasingly well-documented by scholars, get virtually no attention in the dominant media. Instead of reality, we get optimistic, multicultural scenarios of coordinated global growth. And instead of substantive debate, we get a stark formulated choice between free trade to help the world and gloomy-sounding protectionism that will set everyone back.

The degree to which this has become a purely ideological debate, devoid of any factual basis that people can weigh the gains and losses is reflected in Thomas Friedman's astonishing claim, stated not long ago in a television interview, that he endorsed the Central American Free Trade Agreement (CAFTA) without even reading it. That is simply because it stood for "free trade." We have reached the stage when the Poo-Bahs of punditry have only to declare that "the world is flat," for everyone to agree it is, without going to the edge and looking over themselves.

I think what's happened is not indifference or laziness or incompetence, but the fact that most journalists on the plantation have so internalized conventional wisdom that they simply accept that the system is working as it should. I'm doing a documentary this spring called "Buying the War," and I can't tell you again how many reporters have told me that it just never occurred to them that high officials would manipulate intelligence in order to go to war. Hello?

Similarly, the question of whether or not our economic system is truly just is off the table for investigation and discussion, so that alternative ideas, alternative critiques, alternative visions never get a hearing. And these are but a few of the realities that are obscured. What about this growing inequality? What about the re-segregation of our public schools? What about the devastating onward march of environmental deregulation? All of these are examples of what happens when independent sources of knowledge and analysis are so few and far between on the plantation.

So if we need to know what is happening, and Big Media won't tell us; if we need to know why it matters, and Big Media won't tell us; if we need to know what to do about it, and Big Media won't tell us, it's clear what we have to do. We have to tell the story ourselves.

And this is what the plantation owners feared most of all. Over all those decades here in the South, when they used human beings as chattel, and quoted scripture to justify it, property rights over human rights was God's way, they secretly lived in fear that one day—instead of saying, "Yes, Massa"—those gaunt, weary, sweat-soaked field hands, bending low over the cotton under the burning sun, would suddenly stand up straight, look around, see their sweltering and stooping kin and say, "This ain't the product of intelligent design. The boss man in the big house has been lying to me. Something is wrong with this system."

This is the moment freedom begins, the moment you realize someone else has been writing your story, and it's time you took the pen from his hand and started writing it yourself.

When the garbage workers struck here in 1968, and the walls of these buildings echoed with the cry, "I am a man," they were writing this story. Martin Luther King came here to help them tell it, only to be shot dead on the balcony of the Lorraine

Motel. The bullet killed him, but it couldn't kill the story, because once the people start telling their story, you can't kill it anymore.

So I'm back where I started with you, and where this movement is headed. The greatest challenge to the plantation mentality of the media giants is the innovation and expression made possible by the digital revolution. I may still prefer the newspaper for its investigative journalism and in-depth analysis, but we now have it in our means to tell a different story from Big Media, our story.

The other story of America that says, free speech is not just corporate speech. That news is not just what officials tell us. And we are not just chattel in the fields living the boss man's story. This is the great gift of the digital revolution, and you must never, never let them take it away from you. The Internet, cell phones and digital cameras that can transmit images over the Internet makes possible a nation of story tellers, every citizen a Tom Paine.

Let the man in the big house on Pennsylvania Avenue think that over, and the woman of the House on Capitol Hill. And the media moguls in their chalets at Sun Valley, gathered to review the plantation's assets and multiply them, nail it to their door. They no longer own the copyright to America's story. It's not a top-down story anymore. Other folks are going to write this story from the ground up. And the truth will be out that the media plantation, like the cotton plantation of old, is not divinely sanctioned. It's not the product of natural forces. The media system we have been living under for a long time now was created behind closed doors where the power-brokers met to divvy up the spoils.

Bob McChesney has eloquently reminded us through the years how each medium—radio, television and cable—was hailed as a technology that would give us greater diversity of voices, serious news, local programs, and lots of public service for the community. In each case, the advertisers took over.

Despite what I teasingly told you the last time we were together in St. Louis, the star that shines so brightly in the firmament the year I was born, 1934, did not, I regret to say, appear over that little house in Hugo, Oklahoma. It appeared over Washington when Congress enacted the 1934 Communications Act. One hundred times in that cornerstone of our communications policy, you will read the phrase "public interests, convenience, and necessity."

I can tell you reading about those days that educators, union officials, religious leaders and parents were galvanized by the promise of radio as a classroom for the air, serving the life of the country and the life of the mind—until the government cut a deal with the industry to make sure nothing would threaten the already vested interests of powerful radio networks and the advertising industry. And soon, the public largely forgot about radio's promise, as we accepted the entertainment produced and controlled by Jell-O, Maxwell House and Camel cigarettes.

What happened to radio, happened to television, and then it happened to cable; and, if we are not diligent, it will happen to the Internet. Powerful forces are at work now, determined to create our media future for the benefit of the plantation: investors, advertisers, owners and the parasites that depend on their indulgence, including many in the governing class.

Old media acquire new media and vice versa. Rupert Murdoch, forever savvy about the next key outlet that will attract eyeballs, purchased MySpace, spending nearly

$600 million, so he could, in the language of Wall Street, monetize those eyeballs. Google became a partner in Time Warner, investing $1 billion in its AOL online service. And now Google has bought YouTube, so it would have a better vehicle for delivering interactive ads for Madison Avenue. Viacom, Microsoft, large ad agencies, and others have been buying up key media properties, many of them the leading online sites, with a result that will be a thoroughly commercialized environment, a media plantation for the 21st century, dominated by the same corporate and ideological forces that have produced the system we have lived under the last 50 years.

So what do we do? Well, you've shown us what we have to do. And twice now, you have shown us what we can do. Four years ago, when FCC Commissioner Michael Powell and his ideological sidekicks decided it was ok for a single corporation to own a community's major newspapers, three of its TV stations, eight radio stations, its cable TV system, and its major broadband Internet provider, you said, enough's enough!

Free Press, Common Cause, Consumer's Union, Media Access Project, the National Association of Hispanic Journalists, and others working closely with commissioners Adelstein and Copps, two of the most public, spirited members of that commission ever to sit there, organized public hearings across the country where people spoke deeply felt opinions about how poorly the media were serving their towns. You flooded Congress with petitions, and you never let up. And when the court said Powell had to back off, the decision cited the importance of involving the public in these media decisions.

Incidentally, Powell not only backed off, he backed out. He left the commission to become senior adviser at a private investment firm specializing in equity investments in media companies around the world. And that firm, by the way, made a bid to take over both Tribune and Clear Channel, two media companies that just a short time ago were under the corporate-friendly purview of—you guessed it—Michael Powell. That whooshing sound you hear is Washington's perpetually revolving door through which they come to serve the public and through which they leave to join the plantation.

You made a difference. You showed that the public cares about media and democracy. You turned a little publicized vote—little publicized because Big Media didn't want the people to know—a little publicized and seemingly arcane regulation into a big political fight and a public debate.

Now it's true, as commissioner Copps has reminded us, that since that battle three years ago, there have been more than 3,300 TV and radio stations that have had their assignment and transfer grants approved, so that even under the old rules, consolidation grows, localism suffers, and diversity dwindles. It's also true that even as we speak, Michael Powell's successor, Kevin Martin, put there by George W. Bush, is ready to take up where Powell left off and give the green light to more conglomeration. Get ready to fight.

But then you did it again more recently. You lit a fire under the people to put Washington on notice that it had to guarantee the Internet's First Amendment protection in the $85 billion merger of AT&T and BellSouth. Because of you, the so-called Net Neutrality, I much prefer to call it the "equal-access provision of the Internet"—neutrality makes me think of Switzerland—the equal-access provision became a public issue that once again reminded the powers-that-be that people want the media to foster democracy, not to quench it.

This is crucial. This is crucial, because in a few years, virtually all media will be delivered by high-speed broadband. And without equality of access, the Net can become just like cable television where the provider decides what you see and what you pay. After all, the Bush Department of Justice had blessed the deal last October without a single condition or statement of concern. But they hadn't reckoned with Michael Copps and Jonathan Adelstein, and they hadn't reckoned with this movement. Free Press and SavetheInternet.com orchestrated 800 organizations, a million and a half petitions, countless local events, legions of homemade videos, smart collaboration with allies and industry, and a top shelf communications campaign. Who would have imagined that sitting together in the same democratic broadband pew would be the Christian Coalition, Gun Owners of America, Common Cause, and Moveon.org? Who would have imagined that these would link arms with some of the powerful new media companies to fight for the Internet's First Amendment?

We owe a tip of the hat, of course, to Republican Commissioner Robert McDowell. Despite what must have been a great deal of pressure from his side, he did the honorable thing and recused himself from the proceedings because of a conflict of interest. He might well have heard the roar of the public that you helped to create. So AT&T had to cry "uncle" to Copps and Adelstein, with a "voluntary commitment to honor equal access for at least two years." The agreement marks the first time that the federal government has imposed true neutrality—oops, equality—on an Internet access provider since the debate erupted almost two years ago.

I believe you changed the terms of the debate. It is no longer about whether equality of access will govern the future of the Internet. It's about when and how. It also signals a change from defense to offense for the backers of an open net. Arguably the biggest, most effective online organizing campaign ever conducted on a media issue can now turn to passing good laws, rather than always having to fight to block bad ones. Just this week, Sen. Byron Dorgan, a Democrat, and Sen. Olympia Snow, a Republican, introduced the Internet Freedom Preservation Act of 2007 to require fair and equitable access to all content. And over in the House, that champion of the public interest, Rep. Ed Markey, is once again standing there waiting to press the battle.

A caveat here. Those other folks don't give up so easy. Remember, this agreement is only for two years, and they will be back with all the lobbyists money can hire. As the *Washington Post* follows George Bush into the black hole of Baghdad, the press in Washington won't be covering many stories like this because of priorities.

A further caveat. Consider what AT&T got in the bargain. For giving up on Net Neutrality, it got the green light from government to dominate over 67 million phone lines in 22 states, almost 12 million broadband users, and total control over Cingular Wireless, the country's largest mobile phone company with 58 million cell phone users. It's as if China swallowed India.

I bring this up for a reason. Big Media is ravenous. It never gets enough, always wants more. And it will stop at nothing to get it. These conglomerates are an empire, and they are imperial.

Last week on his Web site, MediaChannel.org, Danny Schechter recalled how some years ago he marched with a band of media activists to the headquarters of all the big media companies concentrated in the Times Square area. Their formidable buildings strutted with logos and limos, and guarded by rent-a-cops, projected their power and prestige. Danny and his cohorts chanted and held up signs calling for honest news and an end to exploited programming. They called for diversity and access for more perspectives. "It felt good," Danny said, "but it seemed like a fool's errand. We were ignored, patronized and marginalized. We couldn't shake their edifices or influence their holy business models. We seemed to many like that lonely and forlorn nut in a *New Yorker* cartoon carrying an 'End of the World is Near' placard."

Well, yes, my friends, that is exactly how they want you to feel. As if media and democracy is a fool's errand. To his credit, Danny didn't give up. He's never given up. Neither have the early pioneers of this movement: Andy Schwartzman, Don Hazen, Jeff Chester. I confess that I came very close not to making this speech today, in favor of just getting up here and reading from this book, *Digital Destiny,* by my friend and co-conspirator, Jeff Chester. Take my word for it. Make this your bible, until McChesney's new book comes out. As Don Hazen writes in his review in AlterNet this week, it's a terrific book, "a respectful loving, fresh, intimate comprehensive history of the struggles for a 'democratic' media—the lost fights, the opportunities missed, and the small victories that have kept the corporate media system from having complete *carte blanche* over the communication channels."

It's also a terrifying book, because Jeff describes how we are being shadowed online by a slew of software digital gumshoes working for Madison Avenue. Our movements in cyberspace are closely tracked and analyzed, and interactive advertising infiltrates our consciousness to promote the brand-washing of America. Jeff asks the hard questions: Do we really want television sets that monitor what we watch? Or an Internet that knows what sites we visit and reports back to advertising companies? Do we really want a media system designed mainly for Madison Avenue?

But this is a hopeful book. "After scaring the bejeezus out of us," as one reviewer wrote, Jeff offers a policy agenda for the broadband era. Here is a man who practices what the Italian philosopher Gramsci called the "pessimism of the intellect and the optimism of the will." He sees the world as it is, without rose-colored glasses and tries to change it, despite what he knows.

So you'll find here the core of the movement's mission. You'll agree with much and disagree with some. But that's what a reform movement is about. Media reform—yes. But the Project in Excellence concluded in its "State of the Media Report" for 2006, "At many old media companies, though not in all, the decades-long battle at the top between idealists and accountants is now over. The idealists have lost." The commercial networks are lost, too, lost to silliness, farce, cowardice and ideology. Not much hope there. You can't raise the dead.

Policy reform, yes. But, says Jeff, we will likely see more consolidation of ownership with newspapers, TV stations, and major online properties in fewer hands. So, he says, we have to find other ways to ensure the public has access to diverse, independent, and credible sources of information.

That means going to the market to find support for stronger independent media. Michael Moore and others have proven that progressivism doesn't have to equal penury. It means helping protect news-gathering from predatory forces. It means fighting for more participatory media, hospitable to a full range of expression. It means building on Lawrence Lessig's notion of the "creative commons" and Brewster Kahle's Internet Archives, with his philosophy of universal access to all knowledge.

It means bringing broadband service to those many millions of Americans too poor to participate so far in the digital revolution. It means ownership and participation for people of color and women. And let me tell you, it means reclaiming public broadcasting and restoring it to its original feisty, robust, fearless mission as an alternative to the dominant media, offering journalism you can afford and can trust, public affairs of which you are a part, and a wide range of civic and cultural discourse that leaves no one out.

You can have an impact here. For one thing, we need to remind people that the federal commitment to public broadcasting in this country is about $1.50 per capita, compared to $28 to $85 per capita in other democracies.

But there is something else I want you to think about. Something else you can do. And I'm going to let you in here on one of my fantasies. Keep it to yourself, if you will, because fantasies are private matters, and mine involves Amy Goodman. But I'll just ask C-SPAN to bleep this out. Oh, shucks, what's the use. Here it is. In moments of revelry, I imagine all of you returning home to organize a campaign to persuade your local public television station to start airing *Democracy Now!*

I can't think of a single act more likely to remind people of what public broadcasting should be, or that this media reform conference really means business. We've got to get alternative content out there to people, or this country is going to die of too many lies. And the opening rundown of news on Amy's daily show is like nothing else on any television, corporate or public. It's as if you opened the window in the morning and a fresh breeze rolls over you from the ocean. Amy doesn't practice trickle-down journalism. She goes where the silence is, and she breaks the sound barrier. She doesn't buy the Washington protocol that says the truth lies somewhere in the spectrum of opinion between the Democrats and the Republicans.

On *Democracy Now!* the truth lies where the facts are hidden, and Amy digs for them. And above all, she believes the media should be a sanctuary for dissent, the Underground Railroad tunneling beneath the plantation. So go home and think about it. After all, you are the public in public broadcasting and not just during pledge breaks. You live there, and you can get the boss man at the big house to pay attention.

Meanwhile, be vigilant about the congressional rewrite of the Telecommunications Act that is beginning as we speak. Track it day by day and post what you learn far and wide, because the decisions made in this session of Congress will affect the future of all media, corporate and noncommercial. If we lose the future now, we'll never get it back.

So you have your work cut out for you. I'm glad you're all younger than me and up to it. I'm glad so many funders are here, because while an army may move on its stomach, this movement requires hard, cold cash to compete with big media in getting the attention of Congress and the people.

I'll try to do my part. Last time we were together, I said to you that I should put my detractors on notice. They might just compel me out of the rocking chair and back into the anchor chair. Well, in April, I will be back with a new weekly series called *Bill Moyer's Journal,* thanks to some of the funders in this room. We'll take no money from public broadcasting because it compromises you even when you don't intend it to—or they don't intend it to. I hope to complement the fine work of colleagues like David Brancaccio of *NOW* and David Fanning of *Frontline,* who also go for the truth behind the news.

But I don't want to tease you. I'm not coming back because of detractors. I wouldn't torture them that way. I'll leave that to Dick Cheney. I'm coming back, because it's what I do best. Because I believe television can still signify, and I don't want you to feel so alone. I'll keep an eye on your work. You are to America what the abolition movement was, and the suffragette movement, and the civil rights movement. You touch the soul of democracy. It's not assured you will succeed in this fight. The armies of the Lord are up against mighty hosts. But as the spiritual sojourner Thomas Merton wrote to an activist grown weary and discouraged protesting the Vietnam War, "Do not depend on the hope of results. Concentrate on the value and the truth of the work itself."

And in case you do get lonely, I'll leave you with this. As my plane was circling Memphis the other day, I looked out across those vast miles of fertile soil that once were plantations, watered by the Mississippi River, and the sweat from the brow of countless men and women who had been forced to live somebody else's story. I thought about how in time, with a lot of martyrs, they rose up, one here, then two, then many, forging a great movement that awakened America's conscience and brought us closer to the elusive but beautiful promise of the Declaration of Independence. As we made our last approach, the words of a Marge Piercy poem began to form in my head, and I remembered all over again why I was coming and why you were here:

> *What can they do*
> *to you? Whatever they want.*
> *They can set you up, they can*
> *bust you, they can break*
> *your fingers, they can*
> *burn your brain with electricity,*
> *blur you with drugs till you*
> *can't walk, can't remember, they can*
> *take your child, wall up*
> *your lover. They can do anything*
> *you can't blame them*
> *from doing. How can you stop*
> *them? Alone, you can fight,*
> *you can refuse, you can*
> *take what revenge you can*
> *but they roll over you.*
>
> *But two people fighting*
> *back to back can cut through*
> *a mob, a snake-dancing file*
> *can break a cordon, an army*
> *can meet an army.*

Two people can keep each other
sane, can give support, conviction,
love, massage, hope, sex.
Three people are a delegation,
a committee, a wedge. With four
you can play bridge and start
an organization. With six
you can rent a whole house,
eat pie for dinner with no
seconds, and hold a fundraising party.
A dozen make a demonstration.
A hundred fill a hall.
A thousand have solidarity and your own newsletter;
ten thousand, power and your own paper;
a hundred thousand, your own media;
ten million, your own country.

It goes on one at a time,
it starts when you care
to act, it starts when you do
it again after they said no,
it starts when you say We
and know who you mean, and each
day you mean one more.

Journal Topics

1. The article quotes Benjamin Franklin as saying, "Democracy is two wolves and a lamb voting on what to have for dinner. Liberty is a well-armed lamb, contesting the vote." In light of Moyers' arguments in this article, how could this quotation apply to modern-day life?

2. Do you think the increasing gap between rich and poor in America is just a natural extension of capitalism that should be tolerated and expected, or is it an inequity in the system that should be corrected?

3. What are your thoughts on the Marge Piercy poem at the end of the article? Who are the "They" that the poem refers to? How can you fight "Them" according to Piercy? What does this poem have to do with Moyers' speech on "Big Media"?

Questions for Critical Thought

1. During the American Revolutionary War, early journalist Thomas Paine said, "Our democracy is now put to a vital test, for the conflict is between human rights on the one side, and on the other, special privilege asserted as property

rights. The parting of the ways has come." How well does this apply to today? Do we still have a conflict between human rights and "special privilege asserted as property rights"? What are the implications for our democracy?

2. Moyers argues that "today, two basic pillars of American society, shared economic prosperity and a public sector capable of serving the common good, are crumbling. The third pillar of American democracy, an independent press, is under sustained attack, and the channels of information are choked." Discuss these three pillars of American society. Why would these three things "crumbling" harm America and democracy?

3. Moyers states that "The watchdog group FAIR found that during the three weeks leading up to the [Iraq] invasion, only 3 percent of U.S. sources on the evening news of ABC, CBS, NBC, CNN, Fox and PBS expressed skeptical opinions of the impending war, even though a quarter of the American people were against it. Not surprisingly, two years after 9/11, almost 70 percent of the public still thought it likely that Saddam Hussein was personally involved in the terrorist attacks of that day." What do you think has changed since Moyers made these remarks? Do sources in the evening news seem more responsible these days? The same? Less? What about other news sources?

4. Moyers says, "But there are many other ways the plantation mentality keeps the American people from confronting reality." What does he mean by a "plantation mentality"? Do you agree that the American people aren't confronting reality? And what are the "other ways" that he speaks of?

Suggestions for Personal Research

1. What does Moyers mean when he calls the reappropriation of language "Orwellian"? Who was Orwell? What did he predict and write, and how accurate are his predictions now? (A good place to start would be to read his essay "Politics and the English Language.")

2. Investigate one of the groups that actively campaigns against "Big Media." Some mentioned in the article are Free Press, Common Cause, Consumer's Union, Media Access Project, the National Association of Hispanic Journalists, and MediaChannel.org. Who are these people, what do they fight for, and how do they fight?

Multicultural Issues

1. One point made in this article is that the divide between rich and poor keeps getting wider. If you are from a different country, how wide do you think the gap is between rich and poor in your country? Is there more inequity, or less, than there is in America?

Vocabulary Terms

bemoan
malignant
insinuated
permeated
monopoly
immaculately

Orwellian
pundit
erroneous
free trade
ideological

Terms for Clarification

Telecommunications Act of 1996   An act of the Federal Communications Commission that drastically weakened the laws preventing media conglomeration and monopolies. Since this act, most stations and broadcasters have been purchased by massive multinational media corporations.

Thomas Paine   (January 29, 1737–June 8, 1809) An American revolutionary. He wrote several important pamphlets, such as *Common Sense*. His writings called for revolution against Great Britain. He was perhaps most famous for the line "These are times that try men's souls."

Grand Theft: The Conglomeratization of Media and the Degradation of Culture

25 Years of Monitoring the Multinationals

Ben Bagdikian

Prereading Questions

1. How important is television in your life? How many hours a week do you watch?

2. Do you know who owns the media outlets where you live? Do you know who owns the major media outlets? Why would it be important to know who owns what?

3. What do the words "Grand Theft" in the title suggest to you? How about the phrase "the Degradation of Culture"? What do you expect to be the main points the author will make?

For 25 years, a handful of large corporations that specialize in every mass medium of any consequence has dominated what the majority of people in the United States see about the world beyond their personal experience. These giant media firms, unlike any in the past, thanks to the hands-off attitude of the Federal Communications Commission (FCC) majority, are unhampered by laws and regulation. In the process, they have been major agents of change in the social values and politics of the United States.

They have, in my opinion, damaged our democracy. Given that the majority of Americans say they get their news, commentary and daily entertainment from this handful of conglomerates, the conglomerates fail the needs of democracy every day.

Our modern democracy depends not just on laws and the Constitution, but a vision of the real nature of the United States and its people. It is only humane philosophy that holds together the country's extraordinary diversity of ethnicity, race, vastly varied geography and a wide range of cultures. There are imperfections within every individual and community. But underneath it, we expect the generality of our population to retain a basic sense of decency and kindness in real life.

We also depend on our voters to approach each election with some knowledge of the variety of ideas and proposals at stake. This variety and richness of issues and ideas were once reflected by competing newspapers whose news and editorial principles covered the entire political spectrum. Every city of any size was exposed to the early Hearst and E. W. Scripps newspapers that were the champions of working people and critics of the rich who exploited workers and used their power to evade taxes. There were middle-of-the-road papers, and a sizeable number of pro-business papers (like the old *New York Sun*). They were, of course, a mixed bag. Not a few tabloids screamed daily headlines of blood and guts.

With all of that, the major papers represented the needs and demands of the mass of ordinary people and kept badgering politicians who ignored them.

Today, there is no such broad political spectrum and little or no competition among media. There is only a handful of exceptions to the rule of one daily paper per city. On radio and television, Americans see limited ideas and the largest media groups spreading ever-more extreme right-wing politics, and nightly use of violence and sex that tell parents and their children that they live in a cruel country. They have made sex a crude commodity as an inexpensive attention getter. They have made sex, of all things, boring.

Instead of newsboys earlier in the nineteenth century hawking a variety of papers to the people leaving their downtown factories and offices for home, we have cars commuting between suburbs with radio turned to news of traffic and crime. At home, TV is the major home appliance. What it displays day and night is controlled by a handful of giant media conglomerates, heavily tilted to the political right. And all of them have substantial control of every medium—newspapers, magazines, books, radio, television and movies.

The giant conglomerates with this kind of control are Time Warner, the largest media company in the world; Rupert Murdoch's News Corporation, which owns the Fox networks, a steady source of conservative commentary; Viacom, the old CBS with similarly heavy holdings in all the other important media; Bertelsmann, the German company with masses of U.S. publications, book houses, and partnerships with the other giant media companies; Disney, which has come a long way from concentrating on Mickey Mouse and now, in the pattern of its fellow giants, owns 164 separate media properties from radio and TV stations to magazines and a multitude of other outlets in print and motion picture companies; and General Electric, owner of NBC and its multiple subsidiaries.

One radio firm, ClearChannel, the sponsor of Rush Limbaugh and other exclusively right-wing commentators, owns 2,400 stations, dwarfing all other radio outlets in size and audience.

In their control of most of our newspapers, the great majority of our radio and television, of our most widely distributed books, magazines and motion pictures, these conglomerates have cheapened what once was a civilized mix of programming.

We have large cadres of talented screen writers who periodically complain that they have exciting and touching material that the networks reject in favor of repetitious junk. These writers do it for the money and could quit, as some of them have. But they once got paid for writing original dramas like those of Paddy Chayevsky and other playwrights whose work was heard in earlier days of television.

Programs appealing to the variety of our national tastes and variations in politics are so rare they approach extinction. The choices for the majority of Americans are the prime-time network shows that range from the relatively harmless petty jokes and dating games typified by "Seinfeld" to the unrelieved sex and violence of Murdoch's Fox network and "reality" shows in which "real people"—that is, non-professional amateurs—are willingly subjected to contests in sexual seduction, deceit and violation of friendships. Most TV drama is an avalanche of violence.

This is not an appeal for broadcasting devoted solely to the nostalgia of *Andy Hardy* and *Little House on the Prairie*. Nor is this an appeal for solely serious classics designed for elite audiences (though surely more of such programs would be good). It is an appeal for a richer variety to meet the range of tastes, regional interests, ethnic documentaries and dramas for the millions of Americans who embrace memories of "the old country," as well as other appeals, like of soap operas, popular music and classical music, lectures.

Here and there, at later hours of the evening, there are occasional book-and-author, actors-and-producers interviews, as well as talented performers of the contemporary pop forms. But they are rare gems glimpsed through the masses of stereotyped nightly trash.

A basic root of the problem is two-fold. One is the domination of our broadcasting by a handful of giant media conglomerates whose performance is measured not just by Nielsen or Arbitron ratings, but what these create on the stock market, whose major investors' standards are, "I don't care how you do it, but if your program doesn't raise your stock market prices, your president and CEO will be out of their jobs."

The other is a Federal Communications Commission which, for the last 30 years, has forgotten its mandated task of making certain that broadcasters serve "the public interest." Instead, the present majority members believe that, contrary to broadcast law, the free market of maximized profits is what constitutes the standard for what is in "the public interest."

More than 40 years ago, a Commission member, Newt Minow, electrified the industry and most of the listening and viewing public by describing television programming as a "vast wasteland." It was a measure of the standards of that day. It is a measure of today's standard that this would be ignored as the whining of a crank; and defense of today's far more bleak "wasteland" lets the broadcast industry sneer all the way to the bank.

The media giants argue that they are only giving people what they want. But that lost much of its democratic gloss when the two Democratic minority members of the FCC at the start of the decade held hearings in major cities across the country to hear what citizens felt about current broadcasting. The hearings were packed with people who testified with seriously documented complaints that they are not getting what they want, and that more concentration would only make the problem worse.

Behind these country-wide complaints is the bitter knowledge that, in effect, "The media giants have stolen our property."

It is Grand Theft.

"Stolen our property" is not just a figure of speech. Communications law established that the American people are the owners of the radio and television frequencies, not the commercial broadcasters.

The theft is not just of the electromagnetic frequencies on which the giants broadcast. The theft is also of the inherent and varied needs and wants of the country's real families and individuals, citizens in the real country.

That loss tells us that we are in danger of losing some part of what we call "America."

Journal Topics

1. Some people call television a "vast wasteland." Do you think television is mainly a waste of time, or are a significant number of shows worth watching?

2. In America, the airwaves belong to the people (in contrast to many nations where the government owns the airwaves). Do you think *your* airwaves are being used properly?

Questions for Critical Thought

1. Bagdikian argues that the owners of contemporary media outlets are heavily "tilted to the political right." However, many media critics argue that the news

is dominated by left-wing leanings. Do you think the media is tilted toward one political leaning over another? If so, is this good, bad, or largely irrelevant?

2. According to Bagdikian, television fails to appeal to the "range of tastes, regional interests, ethnic documentaries and dramas" that the varied population of America needs. Do you think all genders, ethnicities, religions, sexual persuasions and social backgrounds are met by prime-time television programming? Should they be equitably and proportionately represented?

3. What is the connection between the title of the article, "Grand Theft," and the content of the article? What has been stolen on a grand scale? How has culture been degraded?

Suggestion for Personal Research

1. The article references early media magnates, such as William Randolph Hearst and E. W. Scripps. Research the background of one of these people and his organization. How did he help to define the mass media as we know it today? What differences do you see between the newspapers of these two individuals and the media conglomerates that dominate the media environment of today?

Multicultural Issues

1. If you are not American, do you see much of a difference between American television and the programming in your native country? Does U.S. television have more of a political leaning or more sex or violence? Discuss.

Vocabulary Terms

conglomerates   subsidiary
diversity   cadres
political spectrum   mandated

Terms for Clarification

William Randolph Hearst   (April 29, 1863–August 14, 1951.) A controversial American millionaire and newspaper magnate. One of his papers, the *New York Morning Journal,* became especially known for sensationalist writing and for its support for the Spanish-American War. The term "yellow journalism," meaning journalism focusing on scandal-mongering, sensationalism, and jingoism, was coined from the *Journal*'s color comic strip, *The Yellow Kid*.

Nielson Ratings   A system developed by Nielsen Media Research to determine the audience size and composition of television programming. It measures the number of viewers or households tuned to a television program in a particular time period during a week.

Rupert Murdoch's Cool New Thing (MySpace.com)

Edie G. Lush

Prereading Question

1. Many people have MySpace.com accounts and love the social network that it lets them tap into. Do you have a MySpace or Facebook account? Why or why not? What could explain the vast popularity of these websites?

Rupert Murdoch is probably the last person in the world who would use an online social networking service, but he may be the first to make serious money out of the concept. MySpace, which he bought for $580 million in 2005, is one such service, and it may or may not be the coolest thing on the Internet. It has about 70 million users, but is already being squeezed by an upstart website called Bebo which is attracting a greater share of UK visitors. Nevertheless, Murdochwatchers see MySpace as the next big weapon in his relentless battle to maintain global media dominance.

But what exactly is an online social networking service? It is a website which allows anyone to build a homepage for free. You can list your likes and hates, top films, favourite books, sexual orientation and relationship status, and communicate with "friends"—people you meet both online and off. You can upload photos and videos, communicate via instant messenger, and blog to your heart's content.

It's easy to see why the 16–34-year-old crowd targeted by MySpace are liable to flee as soon as something cooler comes along.

Competition in the social networking arena is fierce—Buzznet, Facebook, Xanga, TagWorld, and Friendsorenemies are just a few of the challengers. Many users have homepages on two or three websites and flit between them all. But arguing about which is the hippest site on the web is rather missing the point. MySpace is one of a handful of companies now redefining the way we communicate. Look at who else is sucked into its vortex—more than a million bands have pages on the site. Users can hear and download songs from both signed and unsigned bands and check out forthcoming gigs. The Arctic Monkeys' rapid rise from unknown to number one in the charts is well documented. They owe much to fans on MySpace sharing Arctic Monkey songs by providing links on their homepages, and sending those links to their friends.

Murdoch used MySpace recently to market the product of another arm of his group NewsCorp, Twentieth Century Fox. To publicise its film *X-Men: The Last Stand,* Fox launched an *X-Men* page on MySpace, allowing users to host the *X-Men* trailer on their own website and list a favourite X-Man as a 'friend' on their pages. Nearly a million MySpace users had a link to the *X-Men* page on their own profile page, and the hype thus created helped *X-Men* to breaking box-office records. It was the biggest holiday weekend movie release ever, banking $123 million in its first four days.

All this is creating new optimism in the media industry. In a world in which we spend increasing amounts of time surfing the internet, often downloading illegal video content, media moguls have been worried that their staple box-office and television advertising revenues were draining away. Fox's clever marketing of *X-Men* proves that this is not necessarily the case.

You don't have to look far to spot other potential synergies for Fox and MySpace.

ITV's [pounds sterling] 175 million purchase of Friends Reunited—the hugely successful website through which users trace old school friends—has given birth to a television show on the digital channel ITV Play where friends brought together via the website answer trivia questions about a year when they were together at school. Interestingly, it is the first ITV channel not to be funded by advertising, but instead by revenue from phone and text charges.

NBC Universal's $600 million purchase of iVillage Inc, the top US women's community website, offers similar possibilities. NBC is examining the idea of "recycling" news and entertainment programming from top-rated daytime shows such as *Today* onto iVillage's site—and providing alternative endings to popular shows and pairing these items with specific advertising.

So it is no surprise that Fox is launching a new television station that will be closely linked with MySpace. My Network TV will be the first new US terrestrial television service in more than a decade. Its accompanying website will allow users to send clips of programmes to each other via mobile phones and email, and will host a "casting call" section for budding actors. MySpace will play a major role in promoting the new channel.

Advertising also plays a big part in the MySpace strategy. In the next few months a deal is expected to be signed with either Google or Microsoft to supply Internet searches on MySpace pages, alongside advertisements tied to the search results. Such deals involve advertising revenue being split between the two sides, with the company providing the audience for the ads usually gaining most of the revenue.

It isn't a huge leap to imagine a world in which ads will be targeted specifically at you, based on your listening and viewing profile. In fact, it's already happening. MySpace and other sites can track what music listeners select, and suggest other bands they might enjoy. Whole websites such as Pandora and Last. fm are designed specifically for this purpose. Some of these sites allow you to link up with people who enjoy similar music and listen to the music they like via personalised radio stations. All the while the website providers are building up a profile of your likes, dislikes and moods at different times of the day. They can use this data to deliver highly targeted advertising direct to you, charging a significant premium to the advertiser.

Six years ago, the web claimed only 1 per cent of the British advertising market. WPP estimates that by the end of this year, it will account for more than 13 per cent of the [pounds sterling] 12 billion market, overtaking national newspapers. WPP also notes that spending on television advertising is at its lowest since 2001.

Faster and cheaper broadband deals mean that 40 per cent of British homes are now connected at high speed to the Internet, surfing more and watching television less. Where television ads often miss their mark, web advertising is highly targeted and has measurable results. Rupert Murdoch bought MySpace to ensure that he has revenue in this growth sector of the market, protecting himself against any corresponding decline in NewsCorp's television and newspaper earnings.

Does it matter if MySpace is not the newest, coolest thing? No. NewsCorp is already adept at linking parts of its vast empire to exploit the Internet's "viral" promotion abilities. So while Murdoch himself is lampooned on numerous fake MySpace sites as an "evil billionaire tyrant" and "The Dear Leader of the Kim Jong-Il Fan Club," he is—as so often—laughing all the way to the bank. He may not be interested in making online "friends" but he has always been remarkably good at understanding what people want and selling it to them, and through MySpace he has found a valuable new audience ripe for exploitation. If anyone can do it, Rupert Murdoch can.

Journal Topic

1. What do you think is the appeal behind sites like MySpace.com? More people have popular websites now than ever before; how does the social interaction of sites like MySpace help feed that? And how "real" is the social interaction? Do some people bask in the illusion of a huge social network when they really have dozens, even hundreds, of "friends" that they hardly know?

Question for Critical Thought

1. Would knowing that the News Corporation is using your personal MySpace page to promote its own movies and shows make you think less of MySpace or even migrate to another similar website instead? Would you care that your own web page can be covered in ads that you can't edit, control, or delete?

Suggestion for Personal Research

1. Lush claims that more than one million bands have created MySpace pages. Many major and local bands use this site as a means of free promotion. Search through MySpace.com and find both local and major bands that have sites here. Are the sites what you expected? Are there more or fewer enjoyable bands than you had expected? Now find a band that has an official website that isn't part of MySpace. Compare them. Is the official website easier to navigate and perhaps more aesthetically pleasing, or do you prefer this MySpace format?

Multicultural Issues

1. Sites such as MySpace.com are incredibly popular in the United States. If you are from a different country, were social network sites like this popular there? If you're not sure, feel free to do some web searches and investigation to generate your answer.

Vocabulary Terms

social networking service	budding
vortex	revenue
synergies	broadband

Term for Clarification

Rupert Murdoch   The CEO and founder of the News Corporation and one of the most powerful men in the world of mass media. Leading the charge when it came to consolidating and purchasing different media outlets, his company owns Fox, Fox News, and the rights to many popular franchises such as *American Idol, The Simpsons,* and the *X-Files.*

CHAPTER 20—MEDIA MULTINATIONALS ESSAY QUESTIONS

These questions are intended as potential essay or research paper topics suggested by the ideas raised in the articles.

1. The Telecommunications Act of 1996 made groundbreaking changes in the rules, laws, and regulations surrounding media ownership. Prior to 1996, major media corporations such as the News Corporation and Viacom were severely limited in what they could own. The government watched such mergers and acquisitions, trying to avoid both monopolies and information control. Proponents of the Act claim that it allows for the marketplace to regulate itself and that the public is better off since the changes in the laws. Opponents claim that we've allowed a handful of corporations to dominate what we're allowed to watch and what information we do and do not get. What do you think about these changes? Did the Telecommunications Act change things for the better or worse? And what changes have taken place since?

2. Several major corporations dominate the modern American mediascape. The biggest four (as of this writing) are Viacom, Disney, Time Warner, and the News Corporation. Pick one of these corporations and research its history and current holdings and infrastructure. Who owns and controls the corporation you've selected? What media outlets does this corporation own? When did it start to grow in size?

3. One criticism of media ownership being concentrated in just a few hands is that there is a lack of representative minority voices. The majority of the ownership is in the hands of white males, and many minority groups feel this marginalizes the needs and concerns of the diverse American population. How strong is the presence of minorities and women in the mainstream media today? Are minorities and women proportionately and accurately represented? Would a system that encourages diversity in media ownership make any difference?

4. Many of the articles in this section discuss key components to a successful democracy. Most of the articles suggest that a vibrant, free press with the interests of the population at heart (instead of primarily a corporate profit motive) is key to healthy self-governance. Some questions you may want to answer include the following: How important are strong, reliable sources of news to American democracy? How did this help the founding fathers win the revolutionary war? Why did they consider it to be so important to the birth of America? How has the press changed from early America to the present? What do media critics think await us in our future?

CHAPTER 21

News Media

Television is a circus, a carnival, a traveling troupe of acrobats and storytellers, singers and dancers, jugglers, side-show freaks, lion-tamers and football players. We're in the boredom-killing business! If you want truth, go to God, go to your guru, go to yourself because that's the only place you'll ever find any real truth! But, man, you're never going to get any truth from us. We'll tell you anything you want to hear. We lie like hell! . . . And no matter how much trouble the hero is in, don't worry: just look at your watch—at the end of the hour, he's going to win. We'll tell you any shit you want to hear! We deal in illusion, man! None of it's true! But you people sit there—all of you—day after day, night after night, all ages, colors, creeds—we're all you know. You're beginning to believe this illusion we're spinning here.
—*Howard Beale,* Network, *1977.*

Your favorite celebrity couple is due to have a baby any day now, and out of innocent curiosity, you want to find out some details about the birth. Up until a few decades ago, you would have to rely on the news to keep up on this event, and the news itself was limited to just a few options: (1) You could wait until the 5:00 evening news on television or radio and see if they happened to mention it among the day's headlines during an entertainment portion of the broadcast. (2) You could wait for shows like *Entertainment Tonight* or *Extra!* to come on after the news and give you information. (3) You could read the morning paper and see if the baby was born yet.

In recent years, however, these options have expanded dramatically. In the 1980s, communication satellite technology experienced rapid growth, and, as a result, an explosion of satellite news networks and international stations began reporting global news twenty-four hours a day. In the past ten years, though, even cable news was trumped by the birth of Internet news. Now, you can log on for a nearly instantaneous look at current events—with most stories being updated every minute, not every day. You can go to a major news source, like the *New York Times* website, or stick with a major news network, such as MSNBC.com's main web page. Either of these will allow you to search for details of that celebrity birth or whatever other news you're after. If it hasn't happened yet, check back in a few minutes. The information is refreshed constantly, so there's no need to wait for a traditional news broadcast; you have instant access (even for something as trivial as a celebrity birth).

For example, if you decide to visit Google's news service (http://news.google.com), you may think you're just looking at a snapshot of the day's headlines and not give it a second thought. However, what you're really looking at is a true revolution in the spread of information and news. The biggest stories here are mentioned at the top of the page, but you can scroll down to see a multitude of other categories: world news, U.S. news, entertainment, weather, health, business, science/technology, sports, and any number of others. The stories come from a variety of sources, including the *New York Times,* the *Boston Globe,* Reuters, Bloomberg, and other sources. These dozens of stories are listed with their time of posting (some will be only a few minutes old). In fact, Google's website itself boasts 4,500 sources updated continuously.

With this much news at everyone's fingertips every second of every day, being proficient in the management of information is one of the most important skills of our age.

The people and the corporations (for more on media multinationals and corporations, see Chapters 20 and 22) who own the news outlets often think of news as entertainment and spectacle more than as a disseminator of important facts. The expression "If it bleeds, it leads" is often an accurate description of the way decisions about programming are made. Celebrities always seem to command attention, especially if the stories are squalid. As you are watching a genuinely important story on a news network, you may notice a banner at the bottom reporting for the hundredth time that some starlet is pregnant or bumped into someone else's car. A politician caught in some kind of sex scandal is pure gold to the news media, and stories like this may circulate before anyone has carefully checked the facts. As the news transforms, our world transforms with it. Following is a discussion of several of the factors in the evolving presentation of the news.

Instant Access

Gone are the days of solemn reports covering the day's events at the same times every weekday and weeknight. Historically, the news would air in the early morning while people got ready for work, at noon, and during the news "prime time" of 5:00, 6:00, and 11:00 p.m. The newspapers in most cities are issued only early in the morning. If your preferred form of news gathering is reading the paper, you have to wait until first thing the next morning to read about any major events happening the previous day.

Now, however, technology has given us dozens of alternatives. We can turn to any number of cable news networks that will recirculate stories a few times an hour. The proliferation of DVRs (digital video recorders such as TiVo) allows us to record daily news and watch it when we please. We can also turn to the Internet for a number of sources: your local newspaper's website, which will update far more frequently than the print edition does; other city newspapers; Yahoo News, Google News, or some other Internet news "storehouse" site that contains major articles from all over the Web. And the technologies keep coming. We can now get the news on our cellular phones and other portable devices no matter where we are. We can download them onto our iPods to listen to a broadcast while on the go, and we can subscribe to a news blog or a listserv that will email us with automatic news updates. As communication technology continues to advance, the need to sit on the couch at prescribed times to watch a specific show or to read the paper continues to be replaced with fresh options.

Ratings

Several years ago, the three major television networks (NBC, ABC, and CBS) maintained news divisions that often lost money or had poor ratings. The public service of broadcasting the news was considered more important to these networks than the mere pursuit of profit. One of the reasons we have the freedom of the press in our Constitution is that the Founding Fathers understood the need for reliable news and information about our world. For centuries in the United States, the news was considered a very important part of public life and democracy, and, as such, the truth was what supposedly mattered in news, not ratings or advertising revenue. Now, though, as more news sources are bought out by bigger media conglomerates, the bottom line of profits is perhaps the most important factor behind a news broadcast, and this is far more obvious than it was in the past, as we see news about celebrities—meltdowns, romantic tiffs, drug and alcohol rehabilitation, and paternity mysteries—pushing out news about war casualties, election scandals, or genocide in foreign countries.

Now that the news is largely a televised business, news shows are prey to the same pressure facing any other TV programs—pressure from a board of directors to maximize profits by maintaining higher ratings than competing news programs. The result is a focus on spectacle. Weather, sports, and entertainment news used to be side notes in the daily broadcasts, taking up only a few minutes' time, but these categories now typically make up half of a thirty-minute local news broadcast. Scattered throughout the broadcast are also "personal interest" pieces ranging from "stowaway" cats sailing to France to burglars stuck in chimneys. These stories have no social, cultural, or political significance, yet they are allowed to replace more serious stories and reduce the depth of the coverage of serious stories that they don't supplant. Why? Because network executives believe that the largest segment of the viewing population is more interested in entertainment—light-hearted fluff pieces and personal-interest stories—than in-depth coverage of stories that are often complex and troubling.

Many media critics worry that the hunt for ratings is hurting us all. Instead of unbiased accounts of important matters, many reporters are put to work chasing odd stories and focusing on violent crimes, often related by attractive news anchors whose looks may have been more important factors in their hiring than their experience, acumen, or journalistic integrity. Global news is practically nonexistent in America, and many media watchdogs argue that in recent years serious coverage of national issues has also deteriorated, with news programs increasingly content to simply report politicians' and other newsmakers' assertions, accusations, and counterattacks instead of taking the time to pursue investigative reporting.

With news so easily come by on the Net, TV, and radio, newspapers also have to worry about shrinking audiences, and boards of directors at newspapers around the country are cutting costs by laying off reporters. For example, the newsroom staff of the *Los Angeles Times,* one of the United States' largest and most influential papers, declined from 1,200 to 940 over five years between 2001 and 2006, and in 2006 executives decided to cut news staff to around 800. The *Times*' editor, Dean Baquet—under whose leadership the paper won fourteen Pulitzer Prizes for investigative reporting—refused to make the cuts his corporate bosses demanded because he believed they would severely reduce the paper's ability to continue quality investigative reporting; he was fired, and the cuts were made.

Spin/No Spin

Serious journalists used to pride themselves on their **journalistic integrity:** truthfulness, accuracy, objectivity, and public accountability. This doesn't mean that all journalists were truthful, accurate, objective, or concerned about accountability—but the standards were high and the motivation to appear above suspicion was strong. Now, however, there is a steadily growing audience for news sources—primarily found on cable news—that are purposefully biased. It is now possible to choose news coverage according to your favorite "flavor" and get your news perpetually slanted in the direction that you prefer (be it to the left or to the right), with predigested, opinionated selections of news stories that may omit details that could make you uncomfortable or challenge your prevailing worldview. These shows draw large ratings, and this is worrisome to media critics who fear that growing segments of the population are consuming distorted views of reality.

Are Americans increasingly looking for news sources that support what they already think, rather than looking for objective journalism? Many viewers watch only one source for their daily news, and they may be unaware of how partial and slanted the coverage actually is. For such viewers, daily events are being manipulated by news personalities looking for ratings or supporting favored cultural and political agendas. After time, these news consumers begin to believe the spin and live in a world that is largely fiction, one or more steps removed from the complete, unvarnished facts. Stephen Colbert, a comedian whose show satirizes this type of programming, summed up the problem when his news-anchor persona promised "truthiness"—ideas that look like the truth if you choose to believe them.

This happens with the Internet news media as well. Many popular websites have user blogs posted under the stories, and people log in to open a dialogue. These blogs may be highly biased, and if someone isn't savvy enough to know the difference, spun news can be taken for straight news. Trusting slanted journalism is about as far from information competency as we can get. Instead, we all must actively search out the truth behind stories by exploring as many viewpoints, articles, websites, and stories as we can and confirm information before we trust it.

Personalized News

The bias and spin in news broadcasts are two factors that hurt information competency by limiting the types of news we receive. As technologies allow us to personalize our news sources more and more, we start to get a progressively more limited view of the world around us. For example, many people use Yahoo or Google's news website as their home pages in their Internet browsers. Millions of people also use America Online. These sites can be personalized to show only what interests the viewer. If politics bores you and wars and genocide depress you, then you can avoid boredom and stress by limiting the headlines you see and logging on to more entertaining news about sports and celebrities.

When you log on next time, the headlines you didn't care for don't even appear, and instead you get only the news that you selected. There are obvious emotional benefits to getting news like this; ultimately, it is much more relaxing for the viewer. This makes your time spent online more entertaining to you, but it seriously limits your knowledge of the world.

Satire

In the first episode of *Saturday Night Live* in 1975, America was introduced to "Weekend Update," a short parody of the nightly news full of witty and often insightful looks at the week's events. This regular feature has been one of the major draws of *Saturday Night Live,* and it is still popular today. Comedians sometimes provide genuine insight and pointed criticism, and satires of the news have been popular for years because of this. Though "Weekend Update" has gone through a variety of hosts, it continues to be a popular spoof of the world around us and the personalities who report the news.

The satirical news format has grown through different media, however, and has taken on a new importance. In the mid-1990s, a small Wisconsin-based satirical newspaper called *The Onion* started posting its news parodies on the Web. *The Onion* went much further than "Weekend Update," creating fake news instead of merely providing witty remarks on real events, and it was an instant underground hit among college students. The fictional editor Howard T. Zweibel (German for "Onion") even helped to put a hit book together called *Our Dumb Century,* which took a poke at the past 100 years of news by printing headlines from a fictional history of this fake newspaper. Over the years, *The Onion* went from a local news spoof to a national resource (and even a feature film). It is now published out of New York and has an increasingly large circulation in both print subscriptions and a very popular website. In 2002, a Chinese journalist made a mistake that sounded like the kind of story the satirists at *The Onion* delight in making up: he plagiarized one of *The Onion*'s fake news stories, mistaking it for a real one, and turned it in to his editor, who published it. The *Beijing Evening News* ran a story that asserted that Congress was threatening to move out of Washington unless a luxurious new Capitol building was constructed. That the story appeared in the same issue that included stories with the titles "Sexual Tension Between Arafat, Sharon Reaches Breaking Point" and "Man Blames Hangover on Everything But How Much He Drank" didn't raise the reporter's suspicions that he had stumbled across a parody site.

Similarly, in 2000, the *Ironic Times* appeared on the Web. This satirical newspaper takes a different approach than that of *The Onion*—every one of its headlines are true; it's just the explanatory sentences following that are made up, but in a way that packs a punch, such as these two from the December 24, 2007 edition: "FCC Relaxes Media Ownership Rules"—"According to only remaining news source" and "Copy of Magna Carta Sold For $21.3 Million"—"Includes King John's signing statement."

No news satire, however, can boast more popularity or importance than Jon Stewart's *The Daily Show* and Stephen Colbert's *The Colbert Report.* Comedian Jon Stewart took over *The Daily Show* in 1999, and it has ironically become one of the most important news shows on television. Every Monday through Thursday night, Stewart interviews a guest, ranging from major Hollywood actors and directors to major authors, thinkers, and politicians. One such, John Edwards, even used this show instead of a "genuine" news program to announce his campaign for president of the United States. Many of these politicians claim they love the show and watch it regularly and enjoy the freedom that the show's comic bent lends them while they're interviewed.

The Daily Show's hit spinoff, *The Colbert Report,* was such an immediate success that its host, Stephen Colbert, was invited to be the keynote speaker at the 2006 White House Correspondents' Association Dinner, an event that was attended by President George W. Bush and other high-ranking officials. Colbert and Stewart interview some of the most important politicians, activists, authors, and intellectuals around and are considered an indispensable source of news by some in the American media-scape. Though this "news" is tongue-in-cheek, the two hosts are indispensable in the media environment because of their uncompromising ability to cut through any spin. Ironically, because their primary role is entertainment, a significant number of people choose them as news sources over real news shows. But sharp as their satirical vision may be, the shows are based on the pleasure people get out of seeing the pompous skewered and the foolish made fun of—they don't really report the news, they just make the audience laugh, and an argument can be made that the news shouldn't be primarily a laughing matter. However, the fact that so many people choose to get their news from sources such as Stewart and Colbert proves that the news isn't about fact finding anymore; it's about entertainment and spectacle.

IN THIS CHAPTER

This chapter focuses on current issues about the news media (local and national TV news, cable news, radio, newspapers, and the Net). As the media multinationals have grown in power, they have dramatically changed the face of the news media. To be fully proficient in understanding the news, you should be able to answer the following questions:

- Why did television networks in the past broadcast some news programs even when they actually lost money and had relatively poor ratings?
- When did ratings become more important than reporting scrupulous, in-depth journalism?
- What proportion of information broadcast on cable news networks is actually news, what proportion is opinion, and how much are the two blended?
- Why are some news stories never aired?
- How are minorities and women depicted in local and national news?
- Why do some murder cases become national news, whereas others get only one or two days of local air time—if that?
- Why do many people consider parodies of the news media, such as television's *The Daily Show* with Jon Stewart and *The Colbert Report* and the Internet "newspapers" *The Onion* and the *Ironic Times,* to be more valuable than serious news programs on the major networks?

War Takes Up Less Time on Fox News

David Bauder

Prereading Questions

1. Where do you get most of your news? Have you ever wondered how trustworthy or thorough your favorite sources are? How important do you think a diversification of news sources is?

2. Do you think of the news media in general as being biased? Why or why not?

3. Do you enjoy hearing and reading about celebrities' lives as much as you enjoy "hard" news? Why or why not?

On a winter day when bomb blasts at an Iraqi university killed dozens and the United Nations estimated that 34,000 civilians in Iraq had died in 2006, MSNBC spent nearly nine minutes on the stories during the 1 p.m. hour. A CNN correspondent in Iraq did a three-minute report about the bombings.

Neither story merited a mention on Fox News Channel that hour.

That wasn't unusual. Fox spent half as much time covering the Iraq war than MSNBC during the first three months of the year, and considerably less than CNN, according to the Project for Excellence in Journalism.

The difference was more stark during daytime news hours than in prime-time opinion shows. The Iraq war occupied 20 percent of CNN's daytime news hole and 18 percent of MSNBC's. On Fox, the war was talked about only 6 percent of the time.

The independent think tank's report freshens a debate over whether ideology drives news agendas, and it comes at a delicate time for Fox. Top Democratic presidential candidates have refused to appear at debates sponsored by Fox. Liberals find attacking Fox is a way to fire up their base.

"It illustrates the danger of cheerleading for one particular point or another because they were obviously cheerleaders for the war," said Jon Klein, CNN U.S. president. "When the war went badly they had to dial back coverage because it didn't fit their preconceived story lines."

Fox wouldn't respond to repeated requests to make an executive available to talk about its war coverage.

So how to explain the divergent priorities? Different opinions on what is newsworthy? A business decision?

A mere coincidence?

Fox News Channel viewers argue that their favorite network is simply the most fair. Fox has long objected to suggestions that its newscasts go through a conservative filter. Surveys have shown its audience is dominated by Republicans.

There are no similar differences in priorities among the broadcast evening-news programs, where Iraq was the top story between January and the end of March. NBC's "Nightly News" spent 269 minutes on Iraq, ABC had 251 and CBS 238, according to news consultant Andrew Tyndall.

Another story that has reflected poorly on the Bush administration, the controversy over U.S. attorney firings, also received more attention on MSNBC (8 percent of the news hole) and CNN (4 percent) than on Fox (2 percent), the Project for Excellence in Journalism found.

Tim Graham of the conservative Media Research Center said Fox has always claimed to report from an American perspective and to not follow the pack. While Graham said he may have questions about the PEJ's methodology, he doesn't dispute the results.

His group published its own study last year about the content of coverage. Fox didn't have its head in the sand; there were more negative stories about what was happening in Iraq than positive. But his group's view was that Fox was more balanced while CNN and MSNBC were relentlessly pessimistic. Between May 15 and July 21 of last year, Fox aired nearly twice as many stories about successes in Iraq as CNN and MSNBC combined, he said.

Most coverage of Iraq focuses on what gets blown up, he said.

"The problem we have with the media elite is that they clearly see Fox as pandering to an audience and they don't see CNN as pandering to an audience," Graham said. "That's where I think the double standard sets in."

While polls say its size is diminishing, there's clearly an audience that resists the general tenor of war coverage. GOP presidential candidate Rudolph Giuliani was applauded during last week's debate when he wondered aloud what would happen if the American war effort succeeds over the next few months. "Are we going to report that with the same amount of attention that we would report the negative news?" he said.

Klein disputed the idea that CNN doesn't give a complete picture of what is happening in Iraq.

"Certain folks don't want to see any bad news," he said. "It's our job to report all of the news."

The project's findings surprised MSNBC chief executive Dan Abrams, who has been pushing his network to concentrate on politics and inside-the-Beltway issues lately.

"I'm not going to get on a high horse and judge our competition based on the numbers," he said. "We are looking for the right balance."

Fox's business interests may depend on less negative news about Iraq.

If Fox's audience is dominated by Republicans who are disgusted about hearing bad news on Iraq, it would stand to reason that you'd want to feed them less of it. Bill O'Reilly touched upon that idea on the air one night last December, telling viewers that the lowest-rated segment of his show the previous night was when Iraq was discussed. Ratings jumped at talk about Britney Spears, he said.

The danger is whether those concerns eat away at journalistic credibility.

"They're a news network," said CNN's Klein, "so it is surprising that they're not covering the biggest story in the country and the world."

The Project for Excellence in Journalism steered clear of questions about what its findings proved. "We just wanted to tell people that it does make a difference where you go for the news," said the group's Mark Jurkowitz.

So with less on-air attention being paid to Iraq during the first few months of the year, what filled the void for Fox? PEJ's report said the network gave the death of Anna Nicole Smith significantly more air time than its rivals.

Journal Topics

1. Should news networks devote less coverage to celebrity gossip when there are major world events, including wars, that could be given more coverage? Or do you think major events are getting enough coverage?

2. What are some reasons you can think of that Fox News (at least up to the time the article was written) did not show as much coverage as other news networks of the war in Iraq?

Questions for Critical Thought

1. According to the article, Fox News showed much less war coverage on its network than the other news networks. Conversely, it showed more positive stories about the Iraq War. What do you make of this difference between time of coverage and type of coverage? Which would better serve the American public?

2. Bauder says that "If Fox's audience is dominated by Republicans who are disgusted about hearing bad news on Iraq, it would stand to reason that you'd want to feed them less of it." Should a news organization filter out news content to get higher ratings, or does it have a journalistic obligation to report the most important news without worrying about ratings? Or, like other businesses, should it focus on giving its consumers what they want?

Suggestions for Personal Research

1. The Project for Excellence in Journalism and the Media Research Center both provide statistical findings included in this article. Do some research to find out more about them. What are their mission statements? What are their political leanings? Who provides their funding?

2. Do your own field research on the types of stories different news networks air. Watch at least two different twenty-four-hour cable news broadcasts at a designated time every day for a week or more. See which stories get the attention of each network and which ones don't.

Multicultural Issues

1. If you are from a different country, how much did the press cover any wars that were occurring around the world? If you were still there after 9/11, how did your country's media treat America's "War on Terror"?

Vocabulary Terms

stark	preconceived
prime-time	divergent
ideology	pandering

AP: We Ignored Paris

Associated Press

and

U.S. Weekly Blacks Out Hilton Coverage

John Rogers

These two short articles are meant to be read together.

Prereading Questions

1. Do you like the typical coverage of celebrities, or do you think the media spends too much time talking about people who have no real political, cultural, social, or economic importance?

2. What would be a good balance of "entertainment news" and "real news"?

3. Do you find yourself hungry for information about particular celebrities? What is the source of your interest?

AP: We Ignored Paris

NEW YORK (AP)—So you may have heard: Paris Hilton was ticketed the other day for driving with a suspended license.

Not huge news, even by celebrity-gossip standards. Here at the Associated Press, we put out an initial item of some 300 words. But it actually meant more to us than that.

It meant the end of our experimental blackout on news about Paris Hilton.

It was only meant to be a weeklong ban—not the boldest of journalistic initiatives, and one, we realized, that might seem hypocritical once it ended. And it wasn't based on a view of what the public should be focusing on—the war in Iraq, for example, or the upcoming election of the next leader of the free world, as opposed to the doings of a partygoing celebrity heiress/reality TV star most famous for a grainy sex video.

No, editors just wanted to see what would happen if we didn't cover this media phenomenon, this creature of the Internet gossip age, for a full week. After that, we'd take it day by day. Would anyone care? Would anyone notice? And would that tell us something interesting?

It turned out that people noticed plenty—but not in the way that might have been expected. None of the thousands of media outlets that depend on AP called in asking for a Paris Hilton story. No one felt a newsworthy event had been ignored. (To be fair, nothing too out-of-the-ordinary happened in the Hilton universe.)

The reaction was to the idea of the ban, not the effects of it. There was some internal hand-wringing. Some felt we were tinkering dangerously with the news. Whom, they asked, would we ban next? Others loved the idea. "I vote we do the same for North Korea," one AP writer said facetiously.

The experiment began on February 19. A few days before, the AP had written from Austria about Hilton's appearance at the Vienna Opera ball, just ahead of her 26th birthday. We didn't cover her weekend birthday bash in Las Vegas.

During "blackout week," the AP didn't mention Hilton's second birthday party at a Beverly Hills restaurant, at which a drunken friend reportedly was ejected by security after insulting Paula Abdul and Courtney Love. And editors asked our Puerto Rico bureau not to write about her visit there to hawk her fragrance. However, her name did slip into copy unintentionally three times, as background: in stories about Britney Spears, Nicole Richie, and even in the lead of a story about Democrats in Las Vegas.

Then Hilton was arrested on February 27 for driving with a suspended license—an offense that could conceivably lead to jail time because she may have violated conditions of a previous sentence. By that time, our blackout was over anyway, so reporting the development was an easy call. (On the flip side, we never got to see what repercussions there would have been if we hadn't.)

Also by then, an internal AP memo about the ban had found its way to the outside world. The *New York Observer* quoted it on Wednesday, and the Gawker.com gossip site linked to it. Howard Stern was heard mentioning the ban on his radio show, and calls came in from various news outlets asking us about it. On *Editor and Publisher* magazine's website, a reader wrote: "This is INCREDIBLE, finally a news organization that can see through this evil woman." And another: "You guys are my heroes!"

We felt a little sheepish that the ban was over, and braced ourselves for the comments that would come when people realized it wasn't permanent.

We also learned that Lloyd Grove, former columnist for the *New York Daily News,* had attempted a much longer Paris Hilton blackout. He began it a year into his "Lowdown" column and stuck to it, he says, for two years until the column was discontinued last October—except for a blind item (no names) about Hilton crashing a pre-Oscar party.

So was Grove attempting to raise the level of discourse in our society by focusing on truly newsworthy subjects?

Well, not really. "The blackout was a really heartfelt attempt on my part," he says, "to get publicity for myself."

A trait that Hilton, it must be said, has turned into an art. Grove thinks the so-called "celebutante" achieved her unique brand of fame because she boasts an irresistible set of traits: wealth, a big name, beauty with a "downmarket" appeal, and a tendency to seem . . . oversexed. "This is what mainstream society celebrates," he says. "She is, in the worst sense, the best expression of the maxim that no bad deed goes unrewarded in our pop culture."

One measure of Hilton's fame: She was No. 5 last year on the Yahoo Buzz Index, a list of overall top searches on the Web site (her ever-so-brief buddy Spears is a perennial No. 1).

Another is that *US Weekly* has at least a mention or a photo in just about every issue. "People now come to expect to see pictures of her," says Caroline Schaefer, deputy editor of the celebrity magazine. "They're intrigued by her unshakable self-esteem. People are fascinated by that."

Jeff Jarvis, who teaches journalism at the City University of New York, decries the "one-size-fits-all disease" afflicting media outlets, who feel that "everybody's covering it, so we must, too." Even the *New York Times,* he noted, had substantial coverage of a hearing concerning where Anna Nicole Smith—perhaps the one person who rivaled Hilton in terms of fame for fame's sake—would be buried.

"That disease leads to the Paris Hilton virus spreading through the news industry," says Jarvis, who puts out the BuzzMachine blog.

So what have we learned from the ban? "It's hard to tell what this really changes, since we didn't have to make any hard decisions," says Jesse Washington, AP's entertainment editor. "So we'll continue to use our news judgment on each item, individually."

Which means that for the immediate future, if not always, we'll still have Paris.

U.S. Weekly Blacks Out Hilton Coverage

Paris Hilton gets out of jail on Tuesday and she won't be on the cover of *US Weekly* on Friday? How, short of the Apocalypse, is this possible?

"When it came down to it, the staff and I felt what I believe a lot of people in America are feeling. Which is just enormous Paris fatigue," *US Weekly* Editor Janice Min told The Associated Press on Tuesday.

As a result, Hilton not only won't be on the cover, there won't even be a mention of her in the magazine.

"I don't think," Min joked, "we even mention the city of Paris."

That was no easy task, she said, adding *US Weekly* editors had to comb carefully through every beauty story and every fashion item to make sure there wasn't an off-hand mention of the hotel heiress somewhere.

The Associated Press put in place a similar Hilton moratorium for a week earlier this year, just to see what would happen.

As it turned out, the celebutante didn't do much that was of interest to anyone that week. Certainly she didn't get out of jail and get chased across town by a pack of Hilton-hungry photographers.

Still, Min expects her magazine will do just fine without her. Hilton, she said, has become such a mainstream media staple "that in many ways her time with *US Weekly* has moved on."

So look instead for an *US Weekly* cover photo Friday of Tom Cruise's baby and, inside the magazine, a dozen pages of other Hollywood babies.

Which raises the question, what would *US Weekly* do if Paris Hilton had a baby?

"That will elevate her, probably, back onto the cover," Min said with a laugh.

Journal Topics

1. What does the need to constantly cover even the trivial exploits of celebrities in the news say about American culture? Should we care about the daily lives of celebrities? What emotional needs are filled by an interest in—or even an obsession with—the lives of famous people?

2. Would you enjoy newspapers, magazines, and radio and news shows that never mentioned celebrities unless the story was actually important? Think about

what you normally read, watch, and listen to; what changes do you think would happen if there were a dramatic reduction in the coverage of celebrities like Paris Hilton?

Questions for Critical Thought

1. Jeff Jarvis, a journalism instructor at the City University of New York, says of news outlets that cover Paris Hilton that "everybody's covering it, so we must, too." He even calls this copycat behavior a "disease." Do news outlets do their duties when they all cover stories just because other outlets covered the story, or should they be more discriminating in what they consider news?

Suggestions for Personal Research

1. Search the Web and see how many news stories you can find about a celebrity who seems constantly to be in the news. Make sure each article was published the day of your search. How many did you find? Was it more or less than you expected?

2. Choose a major story in the last year about a celebrity's exploits, such as a DUI, being caught making scandalous remarks, a love affair or marriage breaking up, etc. Now choose a major story occurring in the same week that consisted of hard news. Compare coverage of both, noting depth and frequency of coverage.

Multicultural Issues

1. If you are from a different country, are there any celebrities whom the nation seems obsessed with? Who are they, what do they do, and why do you think people love to know about their lives?

2. If you are from a different country, were any big American celebrities also big there? If so, who were they? What traits do you think they possess that make them appealing to the citizens of multiple countries?

Vocabulary Terms

initiative	repercussions
hypocritical	fatigue
facetiously	"celebutante"

Rediscovering the World

Thomas Ginsberg

Prereading Questions

1. How much do you pay attention to news and opinion from outside the United States? Can you think of any criticisms that have been leveled against the United States from people in other countries? If so, what are your reactions? Do you automatically reject any assertions that aren't flattering to Americans in general or to American foreign policies in particular?

2. Off the top of your head, how many heads of foreign countries can you name? Ten? Five? Fewer? Whatever your answer, what are your feelings about this? Is it important to know much about what is going on politically outside your own nation?

In April 1992, on a warm spring evening in Kabul, I picked up the handset of a trunk-sized satellite telephone and carefully dialed New York. Sunlight was fading over the capital. The night sky soon would be filled with tracer bullets fired by mujaheddin—"muj" fighters to reporters—still celebrating the fall of the Soviet-installed government a few days earlier. Nobody yet had counted the bodies or fathomed the meaning of the warfare just beginning in the country. Nobody ever would count the people maimed or killed that night by spent bullets hurling silently back to earth.

After hearing clicks and buzzes, and pausing for the long satellite connection, I caught a voice through the receiver saying, "AP Foreign Desk." The conversation went something like this:

TG: "Hi, this is Ginsberg in Kabul. I have to dictate, can somebody take it?"

AP: "Hi. Sure, but you should keep it short. It probably won't make the budget."

TG: "Why? We've got the muj trying to form a government."

AP: "There's a big riot in Los Angeles. Not sure anybody will have room for Afghanistan."

The rioting over the beating of Rodney King was a huge story, justifiably trumping Afghanistan. But something else was going on. And it eventually became clear. From the early 1990s until September 11, 2001, the U.S. news media had subtly turned foreign news into a niche subject. No longer feeling seriously threatened after the Cold War, many Americans didn't seem to care as much about the world; at least that was the common wisdom. And many U.S. editors, producers and news executives, their own eyes glazing over, had abetted Americans' retreat into a cocoon.

Today, a price is being paid for that retreat. More foreign news coverage certainly would not have prevented the September 11 attacks. But perhaps closer attention to the world would have given Americans a clearer warning sign or two. Keeping more correspondents abroad might have meant better reporting today and without a doubt, more resonant and compelling foreign coverage would have shortened the distance the nation now has to travel to understand why it was attacked.

I was a foreign correspondent for the AP from 1990 to 1996, covering upheaval from Moscow to Kabul to Sarajevo. I later reported from Southeast Asia and Panama for the

Philadelphia Inquirer. Seeing U.S. networks, newspapers and magazines scramble in September to send reporters overseas, I found myself recalling the words of the AP's legendary sometimes irascible foreign editor, the late Nate Polowetzky.

One day in 1988, we were walking out of the AP newsroom in New York. It was a year before the end of the Cold War and long before anybody could imagine the United States going to battle against terrorism on its own soil. I muttered something to the effect that I would never really be a foreign correspondent until I had covered a war. Polowetzky squawked:

"Ha. You think covering war is hard? Try covering peace."

I had no idea how right he was. Covering war, I found out, taxes your stamina, emotional fortitude, resourcefulness, guts and—most of all—luck. For a long time I figured Polowetzky had meant covering peace is harder because it demands more brains and creativity to spot truly vital, meaningful stories without the blatant drama of war. (And after a few scares, I believed I had more luck than brains.)

But as the years went on, I learned the hardest part is often something else entirely. It is grabbing and holding Americans' attention to some faraway place when they don't feel directly threatened or affected by it. That particularly includes American editors, producers and news executives. With their attention, even the nastiest war can be covered. Without it, covering any foreign event is exasperatingly difficult.

Many correspondents kept trying anyway (which probably says something about us, good and bad). At the wires and organizations like CNN International and Newsweek International, foreign stories increasingly got more attention abroad than in the United States. While I was still reporting overseas—I'm now based in Philadelphia—I often found myself agonizing over how to make my stories compelling to Americans, too. I wondered whether their disinterest was my fault, or theirs, or both.

Finding answers is important now, because the media's interest in the world will wane again, perhaps sooner than we expect. Before then, journalists, just as they scrutinize U.S. government actions against terrorists, should examine their own culpability in Americans' ignorance about the world. John Owen, director of the recently shuttered London office of the Freedom Forum, put it bluntly during the scramble to explain September 11: "I think these are the chickens coming home to roost. I don't think American readers and viewers have any context for what happened," he told me. "The networks and news managers are guilty as charged."

In late 1993, I was back in the United States after covering a half-dozen conflicts across the former Soviet Union. I happened to flip on a local TV newscast just as the cheery anchorman was wrapping up a local story. Then he said: "Now for 'The World in a Minute!'" "A game-show-style clock popped up beside him as he raced through sundry war stories, before handing off to the weather reporter. I was speechless—it seemed like a rerun of *Saturday Night Live.* No wonder Americans weren't taking the world seriously.

The United States has a long history of turning inward in peacetime. Television coverage just illustrates the latest trend. In 1991, the percentage of network stories about foreign affairs aired by CBS, ABC and NBC peaked at 51 percent, almost half of it concerning the Persian Gulf War. By 1997 the share fell to 20 percent and stabilized there until September 11, according to the Center for Media and Public Affairs. Airtime devoted to foreign and diplomatic news fell by more than half between 1990 and 2000, according to the *Tyndall Report,* which monitors the networks' nightly news.

Newspapers aren't in a position to gloat. A Newspaper Advertising Bureau survey in 1971 put the percentage of news inches dedicated to foreign news at about 10 percent. By the late 1990s, it had fallen to 2 percent, according to the American Society of Newspaper Editors.

Foreign news also vanished from the covers of the U.S. editions of the newsweeklies. In 1977, a third of the covers of *Time* and *Newsweek* featured a political or international figure. In 1997, only about a tenth did, according to the Committee of Concerned Journalists.

Reader interest in foreign news is difficult to measure. In a variety of polls in the 1990s, readers put international news in fifth place among most-interesting topics, usually below local news but above sports, according to an ASNE review in 1998. But what readers say isn't necessarily what they mean. The Pew Research Center For The People & The Press found that the only foreign stories most respondents follow closely involve U.S. military actions.

Meanwhile, news organizations hacked their rosters of foreign correspondents. ABC News closed 10 of its 17 bureaus between the mid-1980s and 2000. *Time* magazine pulled back nine of 33 foreign correspondents it deployed in 1989. Knight Ridder reduced its lineup of correspondents from 21 to 15 over two decades.

By the end of the '90s, with cable TV and the Internet splintering audiences, and media conglomerates demanding news divisions make more money, broadcasters and some publications gradually changed formats to cover more scandal, lifestyle, personalities. There simply were fewer shows and pages where hard news, much less foreign news, could find a home.

There were holdouts, including TV programs like *Nightline* and *60 Minutes* and the large national and regional dailies, led by the *New York Times,* the *Wall Street Journal,* the *Washington Post* and the *Los Angeles Time*s. Bloomberg Business News became a new source of foreign news. AP created a global video service called APTN (which enabled U.S. networks to close bureaus) and Reuters expanded its video service.

The Internet also created a medium for delivering international news and background information, perhaps mitigating some of the loss of traditional foreign coverage. And U.S. cable TV brought new sources such as BBC News, foreign-language news shows, even National Geographic TV.

But for the most part those outlets reached specialized audiences. The world faded away for the vast majority of U.S. readers and viewers.

Mark Bauman, a former ABC producer based in Moscow, recalls that he was sent to Rwanda in the mid-1990s "when the movement of Tutsis was so large it was seen by satellite. While I was there, they asked me to tell the South African [crew] that basically ABC was going to close the bureau and put them all on retainer. . . . I remember it was really, really depressing. You're in a grim place, looking at churches piled floor-to-ceiling with human skeletons, telling the African crews that their continent isn't important enough for the evening news broadcast, isn't economically viable for the evening news, to keep the bureau open."

Joseph Angotti, an NBC News vice president in the early 1990s and now a journalism professor at Northwestern University, says that the closing of TV's foreign bureaus "was a pure issue of reducing the budget and reducing the head count. . . . We just kind of made a decision that we would be protected visually at least by these video organizations. . . . It's not like we sat around and said foreign news wasn't important anymore. But we did say, do we close Paris or Chicago? That was the decision-making process. It wasn't a disinterest in international news or a feeling that the public was becoming disinterested."

But media people ought to know: The best way to kill the message is to kill the messenger. Any story pushed by a staff correspondent and editor has a better chance of getting attention at a news meeting and seeing the light of day. Still, the closing and downsizing of bureaus was a symptom as much as a cause of dwindling media interest in the world.

Tom Nagorski, foreign editor at ABC's "World News Tonight" since the early 1990s, says before September 11, a foreign story had to be very good indeed to earn significant airtime. "We would keep reading the surveys and studies about more people traveling abroad and studying abroad," he recalls. Nevertheless, he adds, "we had to fight for every story."

Given the realities of the media business today, a turnaround in coverage may hinge not just on bureaus but on parachutists, an admittedly daunting proposition in situations where experience and preparation may count above all.

Andrea Mitchell, NBC's chief foreign affairs correspondent, who has traveled extensively overseas from her base in Washington, told me she cut back on official State Department trips in the 1990s because the network could get more bang for the buck on assignments of its own design. "Inevitably, we missed some stories by not traveling with the secretary of state, but I think we did better by trying to do original reporting outside the official trip. . . . It was a more efficient use of money, with an admittedly limited budget. . . . When you're there with the secretary of state, there's no time to do interviews and develop sources on the ground."

David Zucchino, a Pulitzer-winning foreign correspondent and former foreign editor at the *Philadelphia Inquirer,* compares the 1990s with earlier periods. "What changed was that you had to know, you had to be pretty assured, before you went somewhere, that you were going to get what you were going after," says Zucchino, now reporting for the *Los Angeles Times.* "You had to hone and refine the story and take fewer chances. . . . It did save money, but it also meant there's less of a chance that you go over and come up with a truly good story."

I asked Leslie H. Gelb, president of the Council on Foreign Relations, what big foreign stories the media had missed, and he answered without hesitation.

"About a year-and-a-half ago, [then-Defense Secretary William] Cohen wrote an op-ed in the *Washington Post,* and the last line said there's going to be a serious terrorist attack in the United States. I turned on the network news that night and nobody mentioned it. Nobody, not even the *Washington Post* the next day which had printed the piece. Imagine that! The secretary of defense saying there was going to be a whole bunch of attacks and nobody even asked him, 'What are you going to do about it?' . . . It was the trees falling in the foreign-policy forest, and the press not caring."

David Remnick, editor of *The New Yorker* and a former *Washington Post* Moscow correspondent, says "it goes without saying that people are less informed than they would've been. . . . You're seeing a lot of hustling now to understand everything from fundamentalism and terrorism to blowback and Islamic history."

But far from the foreign-policy elite, some take a different view. Douglas C. Clifton, former editor of the *Miami Herald* and now editor of Cleveland's *Plain Dealer,* is a proponent of occasional packages to spotlight a faraway region in addition to daily foreign stories. He describes the reams of stories about Yugoslavia in the 1990s as "white noise." Says Clifton, "My sense is that people are as shocked and stunned about the [September 11 attacks] in Great Britain as they are here, and in Britain they get as robust a foreign report as anyone."

He adds: "My view is that foreign coverage in the majority of American newspapers is not very good. We don't present it in much abundance or in much insight. . . . All of that said, I think people, readers in general, don't get interested in a subject until they have a need to know. The cliché about Afghanistan is sadly true. Not until we think about scrambling jets do people pay attention."

Those people would include editors and producers. So what have they learned from September 11? Walter Isaacson, the chairman of CNN, told the *New York Times* two weeks after the attacks: "I think this has been a wake-up call to the public and to all of us in the news business that there are certain things that really matter more than the latest trivial thing that can cause a ratings boost."

Martin Baron, editor of the *Boston Globe,* told the *Los Angeles Times:* "I think most Americans are clueless when it comes to the politics and ideology and religion in the [Muslim] world and, in that sense, I think we do bear some responsibility."

During the 1990s, journalists struggled to find ways to combat the marginalization of world news, beyond citing why-we-should-care statistics about globalization. One recipe for increasing foreign coverage was leveraging attention focused on a major event by pumping out as much background as possible; such was the case with India and Pakistan's nuclear standoff in the late 1990s. The drawback is that by waiting for a crisis, the context comes too late.

Another popular prescription was "localizing" the world, which came to mean giving people explicit reasons why they should care about a place by pegging the story directly to the local economy, local business, local culture, local immigrants. This has been a particularly effective way for regional and local print and broadcast news organizations to flesh out angles relevant to their readers, by sending their own staffers overseas. (This is good for building expertise and staff morale as well.) There have been many excellent stories from staffers both overseas and at home, from the *Richmond Times-Dispatch*'s report on competition from Brazilian tobacco farmers to Knight Ridder's investigation of slave labor in African cocoa production for U.S. chocolate companies.

This tactic has pitfalls, though. There are important, compelling foreign stories that have no obvious local or domestic pegs. For example, this approach probably would not have produced much more coverage of Osama bin Laden for much of the decade. And there's a risk attached to trying to hang foreign news on a domestic link: It could feed easily into the media's established tendency to follow the White House's lead on foreign affairs.

Some editors advocate replacing a steady stream of incremental foreign news stories, particularly the standard coups-and-earthquakes coverage, with less frequent but more detailed takeouts explaining why a far-off place is relevant, interesting or important. And some strive to find the emotional hooks, the universal curiosities, that make a story compelling whether it's from Iowa or Indonesia, such as coverage of China's mass relocation of people to make way for its Three Gorges Dam, or the *Detroit Free Press* reporting on the rising belief in witchcraft in Zimbabwe. The downside is that those angles may be few and far between, and the stories are tough to pull off consistently.

For television, some have hoped that new technology will make foreign reporting easier and more affordable. One breakthrough is the small videophones now being used in Pakistan and Afghanistan. Small digital video cameras and satellite phones might make TV reporting almost as easy, and cheap, as print reporting. But it's important to keep the promise in perspective: The dwindling coverage of the 1990s came amid a dramatic improvement in communications technology. In fact, new gadgets may have made it easier to justify downsizing foreign bureaus.

Some have opted to veer from commercial broadcasting altogether. ABC has negotiated a deal with the BBC to rebroadcast reports from its correspondents. NPR and PBS stood out during the past decade with their foreign coverage on programs like *The NewsHour with Jim Lehrer* and *Frontline*. Public broadcasting, however, will not unseat the dominant commercial broadcasters.

So that left some people, including prominent journalists, to make raw appeals to publishers and networks to look beyond profits and put more foreign headlines on front pages and covers, and more foreign stories in prime time. "It's time the cost-cutters, the money-managers and the advertisers . . . gave us room to operate in a way that's meaningful," said CNN chief international correspondent Christiane Amanpour last year in a speech to the Radio-Television News Directors Association. "Otherwise, we will soon be folding our tents and slinking off into the sunset."

Neither, likely, will happen. The financial pressures of the news business and the adventurous zeal of aspiring correspondents both may be sharpened by the current crisis.

Ultimately it will take some combination of all approaches. When this war subsides and Americans' interest in foreign news inevitably wanes, the lessons of September 11 should be clear. For media executives who think all news is local, it should force them once and for all to broaden their definition of local. For journalists who believe in foreign coverage, it proves the need for compelling and relevant coverage that spells out why Americans should care.

With any luck, Americans might stay a little better informed about the world. It will not be easy. After all, covering peace is harder than covering war.

Journal Topic

1. How do you feel when people argue that Americans haven't paid enough attention to foreign dissatisfactions and suggest that Americans don't really understand or care about the rest of the world? Is this how you see yourself or anyone that you know? Is this how you see Americans in general?

Questions for Critical Thought

1. Is Ginsberg correct that a sharper international press in the United States would have mentally prepared us for foreign dissatisfaction toward our country and therefore the horrors of 9/11?

2. Ginsberg ends the article by recalling advice given to him some years ago: "covering peace is harder than covering war." What does he mean by this? Why would this be true?

3. Martin Baron, editor of the *Boston Globe,* argues, "I think most Americans are clueless when it comes to the politics and ideology and religion in the [Muslim] world and, in that sense, I think we do bear some responsibility." Is he correct? Does the average American's ignorance of the Muslim world place any amount of responsibility for the terrorist actions on our shoulders?

Suggestions for Personal Research

1. Pick a weekly newsmagazine (such as *Time, Newsweek,* or *Weekly News and World Report*). Research to find articles from today, ten years ago, and twenty years ago. Compare the types of stories running over these three decades. Is there more international news coverage in the older magazines? If so, what are those stories replaced with in more contemporary magazines?

2. Complete the task listed in the previous research question, but this time with your local newspaper or a major newspaper such as the *New York Times*.

3. Look at news coverage of an international event, such as an armed conflict, and in your local newspaper, in a major national newspaper, in a weekly newsmagazine, and one or more foreign news sources, such as the BBC Online, and compare the slant of and depth of the coverage.

Multicultural Issues

1. If you are from a different country, how do you feel about the international press from that country? How does it compare to America's press coverage of international news? Are foreign stories covered more or less frequently there than they are here? If so, why do you think that may be?

2. If you are from a different country, do you believe that most Americans don't really understand or care about the rest of the world?

3. If you are an American, try asking people you know who come from or have lived in other countries how those countries tend to see Americans' interest in foreign news. Would they describe Americans as insular? As naïve?

Vocabulary Terms

niche   Cold War
abetted   fundamentalism
resonant

Terms for Clarification

Mujaheddin   A Muslim fundamentalist warrior who engages in a jihad.

The Associated Press (AP) and Reuters   The two major "wire" news services. They write stories and send them over the wire and the Internet to various news organizations around the world. They are regularly printed in almost every major newspaper in the world, and many of the lead stories on nightly news broadcasts were first covered by them. Often, no author is listed in such a news story, simply the wire service itself.

What the Mainstream Media Can Learn from Jon Stewart

Rachel Smolkin

Prereading Question

1. Do you watch *The Daily Show, The Colbert Report,* or any shows that may be similar? If so, how much truth do you see in the satire? Is the appeal for you based on how accurately you think the writers satirize real news and point out the foibles, dishonesty, mistakes, or manipulations of those in power, or simply on the comedy? Are these shows simply entertainment for you, or do you feel you get something more out of them?

When Hub Brown's students first told him they loved "The Daily Show with Jon Stewart" and sometimes even relied on it for news, he was, as any responsible journalism professor would be, appalled.

Now he's a *Daily Show* convert.

"There are days when I watch *The Daily Show,* and I kind of chuckle. There are days when I laugh out loud. There are days when I stand up and point to the TV and say, You're damn right!'" says Brown, chair of the communications department at Syracuse University's S.I. Newhouse School of Public Communications and an associate professor of broadcast journalism.

Brown, who had dismissed the faux news show as silly riffing, got hooked during the early days of the war in Iraq, when he felt most of the mainstream media were swallowing the administration's spin rather than challenging it. Not *The Daily Show,* which had no qualms about second-guessing the nation's leaders. "The stock-in-trade of *The Daily Show* is hypocrisy, exposing hypocrisy. And nobody else has the guts to do it," Brown says. "They really know how to crystallize an issue on all sides, see the silliness everywhere."

Whether lampooning President Bush's disastrous Iraq policies or mocking "real" reporters for their credulity, Stewart and his team often seem to steer closer to the truth than traditional journalists. *The Daily Show* satirizes spin, punctures pretense and belittles bombast. When a video clip reveals a politician's backpedaling, verbal contortions or mindless prattle, Stewart can state the obvious—ridiculing such blather as it deserves to be ridiculed—or remain silent but speak volumes merely by arching an eyebrow.

Stewart and his fake correspondents are freed from the media's preoccupation with balance, the fixation with fairness. They have no obligation to deliver the day's most important news, if that news is too depressing, too complicated or too boring. Their sole allegiance is to comedy.

Or, as *The Daily Show's* Web site puts it: "One anchor, five correspondents, zero credibility. If you're tired of the stodginess of the evening newscasts, if you can't bear to sit through the spinmeisters and shills on the 24-hour cable news networks, don't miss *The Daily Show with Jon Stewart,* a nightly half-hour series unburdened by objectivity, journalistic integrity or even accuracy."

That's funny. And obvious. But does that simple, facetious statement capture a larger truth—one that may contain some lessons for newspapers and networks struggling to hold on to fleeing readers, viewers and advertisers in a tumultuous era of transition for old media?

Has our slavish devotion to journalism fundamentals—particularly our obsession with "objectivity"—so restricted news organizations that a comedian can tell the public what's going on more effectively than a reporter? Has Stewart, whose mission is to be funny, sliced through the daily obfuscation more effectively than his media counterparts, whose mission is to inform?

This is, perhaps, a strange premise for a journalism review to explore. *AJR's* (*American Journalism Review*) mission is to encourage rigorous ethical and professional standards, particularly at a time when fake news of the non Jon Stewart variety has become all too prevalent. Stewart's faux news is parody, a sharp, humorous take on the actual events of the day, not to be confused with fake news of the Jayson Blair, Jack Kelley, National Guard memos or even WMD variety, based only loosely on actual events yet presented as real news.

As I posed my question about lessons of *The Daily Show* to various journalism ethicists and professionals, some carefully explained why mainstream news organizations should refrain from engaging in such whimsy.

Ed Fouhy, who worked for all three broadcast networks in his 22-year career as a producer and network executive before retiring in 2004, is a regular "Daily Show" watcher. "Sometimes conventional journalism makes it difficult for a journalist to say what he or she really thinks about an incident. Sometimes you can cut closer to the bone with another form, another creative form, like a novel or a satire on television," Fouhy says. "I think what we're seeing is just a daily dose of it. You think back to 'Saturday Night Live,' and they've satirized the news for a long time with their 'Weekend Update.' 'That Was the Week That Was' was an early television satire on the news."

But Fouhy cringes at the idea that real journalists should model themselves after such a show. When readers pick up a newspaper or viewers turn on a news broadcast, they're looking for serious information, and they should be able to find it. "When you begin to blur the line . . . to attract more viewers and younger viewers, I think that's a lousy idea," he says.

Adds Robert Thompson, director of the Bleier Center for Television and Popular Culture at Syracuse University, "Journalists have a really inconvenient thing they've got to go through: a process of trying to get [the story] right. . . . I don't think journalists should try to be more hip. Journalists have to learn the one lesson which is important, which is to try to get it right."

Fouhy and Thompson are correct, of course. But Thompson's colleague Hub Brown and some others interviewed for this piece believe the lesson of *The Daily Show* is not that reporters should try to be funny, but that they should try to be honest.

"Stop being so doggone scared of everything," Brown advises journalists. "I think there is much less courageousness than there needs to be. There are people out there who stick out because of their fearlessness. Somebody like Lara Logan at CBS," the network's chief foreign correspondent who has reported extensively from Iraq and Afghanistan, "is a great example who is fearless about saying the truth."

In the hours and days following Hurricane Katrina, state and federal officials dithered while New Orleanians suffered inside the filth and chaos of the Louisiana Superdome. Many journalists, notably CNN's Anderson Cooper, jettisoned their usual care in handling all sides equally. They were bewildered, appalled and furious, and it showed.

"We saw a lot of that during Hurricane Katrina, but it shouldn't take a Hurricane Katrina to get journalists to say the truth, to call it as they see it," Brown says. "The thing that makes *The Daily Show* stick out is they sometimes seem to understand that better than the networks do." He adds: "I think it's valuable because when the emperor has no clothes, we get to say the emperor has no clothes. And we have to do that more often here. . . . The truth itself doesn't respect point of view. The truth is never balanced. . . . We have to not give in to an atmosphere that's become so partisan that we're afraid of what we say every single time we say something."

Venise Wagner, associate chair of the journalism department at San Francisco State University, argues with her students over whether *The Daily Show* is real journalism. They think it is; she tells them it isn't, explaining that journalism involves not just conveying information but also following a set of standards that includes verification, accuracy and balance.

But she says *The Daily Show* does manage to make information relevant in a way that traditional news organizations often do not, and freedom from "balance" shapes its success. "*The Daily Show* doesn't have to worry about balance. They don't have to worry about accuracy, even. They can just sort of get at the essence of something, so it gives them much more latitude to play around with the information, to make it more engaging," Wagner says. "Straight news sometimes places itself in a box where it doesn't allow itself—it doesn't give itself permission to question as much as it probably should question." Instead, the exercise becomes one of: "I'm just going to take the news down and give it to you straight."

But what exactly is straight news, and what is balance? Is balance a process of giving equal weight to both sides, or of giving more weight to the side with more evidence? Does accuracy mean spelling everybody's name right and quoting them correctly, or does it also mean slicing to the heart of an issue? "Nowhere is the comedy show balanced," says Wagner, "but it allows them more balance in showing what is really going on."

As journalists, by contrast, "We've presented a balanced picture to the public. But is it accurate? Is it authentic?" She cites coverage of the global warming debate, which, until recently, often was presented as an equal argument between scientists who said global warming was occurring and scientists who denied it. "That reality was not authentic. There were very few scientists who refuted the body of evidence" supporting global warming, Wagner says, yet the coverage did not always reflect that.

Martin Kaplan, associate dean of the University of Southern California's Annenberg School for Communication, dislikes journalists' modern perception of balance. "Straight news is not what it used to be," he says. "It has fallen into a bizarre notion that substitutes something called 'balance' for what used to be called 'accuracy' or 'truth' or 'objectivity.' That may be because of a general postmodern malaise in society at large in which the notion of a truth doesn't have the same reputation it used to, but, as a consequence, straight journalists both in print and in broadcast can be played like a piccolo by people who know how to exploit that weakness.

"Every issue can be portrayed as a controversy between two opposite sides, and the journalist is fearful of saying that one side has it right, and the other side does not. It leaves the reader or viewer in the position of having to weigh competing truth claims, often without enough information to decide that one side is manifestly right, and the other side is trying to muddy the water with propaganda."

Kaplan directs USC's Norman Lear Center, which studies how journalism and politics have become branches of entertainment, and he has worked in all three worlds: former editor and columnist for the now-defunct *Washington Star;* chief speech-writer for Vice President Walter Mondale; deputy presidential campaign manager for Mondale; Disney studio executive and motion picture and television producer.

He borrows Eric Alterman's phrase "working the ref" to illustrate his point about balance. Instead of "reading a story and finding out that black is black, you now read a story and it says, 'Some say black is black, and some say black is white.' . . . So whether it's climate change or evolution or the impact on war policy of various proposals, it's all being framed as 'on the one hand, on the other hand,' as though the two sides had equal claims on accuracy."

Therein lies *The Daily Show's* appeal, he says. "So-called fake news makes fun of that concept of balance. It's not afraid to have a bullshit meter and to call people spinners or liars when they deserve it. I think as a consequence some viewers find that helpful and refreshing and hilarious."

In addition to the user-generated satire on YouTube, Kaplan thinks the Web is bursting with commentators, including Alterman and Salon's Glenn Greenwald, who brilliantly penetrate the fog—sometimes angrily, sometimes amusingly, sometimes a bit of both.

Broadcasters have tackled this least successfully, he says, citing CBS' ill-fated "Free Speech" segment. Launched on and then discarded from *The CBS Evening News with Katie Couric,* the segment gave personalities such as Rush Limbaugh uninterrupted airtime to trumpet their views. And "the challenge for the great national papers," Kaplan adds, "is to escape from this straightjacket in which they're unable to say that official A was telling the truth, and official B was not."

Part of *The Daily Show's* charm comes from its dexterity in letting public figures from Bush to House Speaker Nancy Pelosi (D-Calif.) speak for—and contradict—themselves, allowing the truth to emanate from a politician's entanglement over his or her own two feet. It's one way to hold government officials accountable for their words and deeds. Some might even call it fact-checking.

Brooks Jackson directs FactCheck.org, a project of the Annenberg Public Policy Center of the University of Pennsylvania, which monitors the accuracy of prominent politicians' statements in TV ads, debates, speeches, interviews and press releases. Jackson himself is a former reporter for the Associated Press, Wall Street Journal and CNN who pioneered "ad watch" coverage at the cable network during the '92 presidential race.

"I'm totally buying it," he told me after I stumbled through my fake-news-gets-at-the-truth-better premise. "I am in awe of the ability of Stewart and however many people he has working for him to cull through the vast wasteland of cable TV and pick out the political actors at their most absurd. They just have an unerring eye for that moment when people parody themselves. And I guess while the cable news hosts are obliged to take those moments of idiocy seriously, Jon Stewart can give us that Jack Benny stare—Does anybody remember Jack Benny?—give us that Jon Stewart stare and let the hilarity of the moment sink in, often without saying a word."

Does this qualify as fact-checking? Not exactly, Jackson replies, but "one thing he does do that is fact-checking: If somebody says, 'I never said that,' and next thing you know, there's a clip of the same guy three months ago saying exactly that, that's great fact-checking," and a great lesson for journalists. Jackson thinks NBC's Tim Russert is the master of that art in the mainstream media, confronting his subjects as he puts their quotes on-screen and reading them verbatim. "Stewart does it for laughs, and Russert does it for good journalistic reasons, and we all can learn from the two of them."

The form has its limits as a fact-checking technique. Jackson doesn't envision Stewart giving a State of the Union address rigorous ad-watch-type treatment, complete with statistical analysis of the president's proposed budget. Why would he? He'd put his audience to sleep. "Not every misleading statement can be debunked out of the person's own mouth," notes Jackson. "That's a particular kind of debunking that's very effective as comedy. . . . There's plenty that needs debunking that isn't funny."

Asked about Stewart's influence on mainstream reporters, Jackson says: "Jon's been holding up the mirror to them for quite a while without any particular effect. The forces that are making the news more trivial and less relevant are frankly much more powerful than a show like Jon Stewart's can change."

Much of the allure of Stewart's show lies in its brutal satire of the media. He and his correspondents mimic the stylized performance of network anchors and correspondents. He exposes their gullibility. He derides their contrivances.

On March 28, the broadcast media elite partied with their government sources at the annual Radio and Television Correspondents' Association dinner. The disquieting spectacle of White House adviser Karl Rove rapping in front of a howling audience of journalists quickly appeared on YouTube. Quipped Stewart, only too accurately, the next night: "The media gets a chance to, for one night, put aside its cozy relationship with the government for one that is, instead, nauseatingly sycophantic."

His 2004 textbook satire, *America (The Book): A Citizen's Guide to Democracy Inaction,* devotes a section to media in the throes of transformation and punctures this transition far more concisely, and probably more memorably, than the millions of words AJR has devoted to the subject:

"Newspapers abound, and though they have endured decades of decline in readership and influence, they can still form impressive piles if no one takes them out to the trash. . . . Television continues to thrive. One fifteen-minute nightly newscast, barely visible through the smoky haze of its cigarette company benefactor, has evolved into a multi-channel, twenty-four-hour-a-day infotastic clusterfuck of factish-like material. The 1990s brought the advent of a dynamic new medium for news, the Internet, a magnificent new technology combining the credibility of anonymous hearsay with the excitement of typing."

Phil Rosenthal, the *Chicago Tribune*'s media columnist, thinks part of the reason *The Daily Show* and its spinoff, *The Colbert Report,* resonate is that they parody not only news but also how journalists get news. "It's actually kind of a surefire way to appeal to people because if the news itself isn't entertaining, then the way it's covered, the breathless conventions of TV news, are always bankable," Rosenthal says. "You can always find something amusing there."

He adds that "so much of the news these days involves managing the news, so a show like Stewart's that takes the larger view of not just what's going on, but how it's being manipulated, is really effective. I think there's a general skepticism about the process that this plays into. . . . The wink isn't so much we know what's really going on. The wink is also we know you know what we're doing here. It's down to the way the correspondents stand [in front of] the green screen, offering commentary and intoning even when their commentary may not be important."

Irony-deficient journalists have rewarded Stewart over the last five years by devoting more than 150 newspaper articles alone to his show and to studies about his show. Most have discussed the program's popularity. (*The Daily Show* attracted an average 1.5 million viewers nightly from January 1 through April 19, according to Nielsen Media Research. Couric's beleaguered CBS newscast, by contrast, netted an average 7.2 million viewers nightly during the same period.)

Many stories have pondered whether *The Daily Show* has substance and credibility; mourned young people's alleged propensity to rely on such lighthearted fare for news; brooded over what this reliance says about the state of the news media; and grieved that the show poisons young people's outlook on government, leaving them cynical and jaded. Stewart, who declined to be interviewed for this article, has patiently explained that his show is supposed to be funny.

That hasn't stopped the onslaught of serious discourse and research about *The Daily Show*. A 2004 survey by the Pew Research Center for the People and the Press found that 21 percent of people age 18 to 29 cited comedy shows such as *The Daily Show* and *Saturday Night Live* as places where they regularly learned presidential campaign news, nearly equal to the 23 percent who regularly learned something from the nightly network news or from daily newspapers.

Even if they did learn from his show, a more recent study indicates Stewart's viewers are well-informed. An April 15 Pew survey gauging Americans' knowledge of national and international affairs found that 54 percent of regular viewers of *The Daily Show* and *Colbert Report* scored in the high-knowledge category, tying with regular readers of newspaper Web sites and edging regular watchers of *The NewsHour with Jim Lehrer*. Overall, 35 percent of people surveyed scored in the high-knowledge category.

In October, Julia R. Fox, who teaches telecommunications at Indiana University, and two graduate students announced the results of the first scholarly attempt to compare Stewart's show with traditional TV news as a political information source. Their study, which will be published this summer by the *Journal of Broadcasting & Electronic Media,* examined substantive political coverage in 2004 of the first presidential debate and political conventions on *The Daily Show* and the broadcast television networks' nightly newscasts. Fox concluded Stewart's show is just as substantive as network news.

Fox says she wasn't surprised by the study results, but she was surprised by the general lack of surprise. "People have e-mailed me and said, 'I think you're absolutely wrong. I think *The Daily Show* is more substantive.'"

Beyond the debate over whether Stewart's show is a quality source of information or whether wayward young fans have lost their minds, the media have treated him with admiration bordering on reverence. In early 2005, press reports handicapped his chances of landing on the *CBS Evening News,* which, like Comedy Central, was then owned by Viacom. After Dan Rather had announced his abrupt retirement following revelations that alleged memos about President Bush's National Guard Service had not been authenticated, CBS chief Leslie Moonves said he wanted to reinvent the evening news to make it more relevant, "something that younger people can relate to." Asked at a news conference whether he'd rule out a role for Stewart, Moonves took a pass, fueling more speculation.

In 2004, the Television Critics Association bestowed the outstanding achievement in news and information award not on ABC's *Nightline* or PBS' *Frontline,* but on *The Daily Show.* Stewart, who had won for outstanding achievement in comedy the previous year, seemed bemused by the honor. Instead of accepting in person, he sent a tape of himself sitting at *The Daily Show* anchor desk. "We're fake," he informed the TV critics. "See this desk? . . . It folds up at the end of the day, and I take it home in my purse."

But Melanie McFarland, the critic who presented Stewart's award, calls him a "truth teller" who speaks plainly about the news and offers a "spoonful of sugar that helps the medicine, the news, go down."

That sugar is not just delightful; it's provocative. "Any comedian can do sort of a *Saturday Night Live* presentation and just do the punch line," says McFarland, who writes for the *Seattle Post-Intelligencer.* "He actually gives you some stuff to consider in addition to the punch line. He and his staff show an awareness of the issues and [are] able to take a longer view than a 24-hour news cycle can, which is funny because it's also a daily show." Other news programs and journalists, including *Frontline* and Bill Moyers, do this also, she says, but not as often. "So much of the news is not digestion but regurgitation. He's sort of looking at the raw material and making a commonsense assessment of what it means."

McFarland says Stewart's mockery of the media should galvanize journalists to perform better. "If there's a guy who's making great headway in giving people information by showing people what you're not doing in giving them information, let's try to do our jobs."

For serious news organizations, change is easier advised than enacted. Take Stewart's imitation of the stylized anchor persona, which—with precious little exaggeration—makes TV personalities look silly and stilted. Altering that persona is no easy task, as Katie Couric discovered when she tried to make the nightly news chattier.

"While Jon Stewart is a guy in a suit pretending to be a newscaster, and he acts like a guy in a suit pretending to be a newscaster, there's a certain formality and rigidity we've come to expect from our news, so much so that when Katie Couric opens the news with 'Hi,' or now I think it's 'Hello,' this is thought of as some kind of breakdown in the proper etiquette of newscasting," says the *Chicago Tribune*'s Rosenthal. He thinks perhaps the time has come to abandon the old formality of newscasting but says such a process will be evolutionary.

In other broadcast formats, incorporating a more sardonic tone can work well. Rosenthal cites MSNBC's *Countdown with Keith Olbermann* as one news program that does a pretty good job incorporating the same sorts of elements that make *The Daily Show* successful. "Keith Olbermann gets a lot of attention for his editorializing, but the meat of that show is this hybrid blend of the news you need to know, the news that's entertaining, with a little bit of perspective [in] taking a step back from what the news is and what the newsmakers want it to be," he says.

Rosenthal thinks ABC's quirky overnight show, *World News Now,* also has achieved a more detached, looser tone, and says it's no accident that the program has been "such a fertile breeding ground for unorthodox newspeople," including Anderson Cooper and Aaron Brown.

Public radio, known for its sober (and sometimes stodgy) programming, is experimenting with a more freewheeling search for truth as well. In January, Public Radio International launched "Fair Game from PRI with Faith Salie," a one-hour satirical news and entertainment show that airs on weeknights. The *Sacramento Bee*'s Sam McManis likened the new show to "the quirky love child of *The Daily Show With Jon Stewart* and 'All Things Considered.' It's smart enough to slake the traditional public-radio fans' thirst for intellectual programming but satiric enough to catch the attention of the prematurely cynical Gen X and Gen Y sets."

Salie is a comedian and a Rhodes Scholar with a bachelor's degree from Harvard and a master of philosophy from Oxford in modern English literature. "I'm not a journalist, and I don't have to pretend to be one," she says, describing herself as her listeners' proxy. When she interviews newsmakers—topics have included the Taliban, Hillary Clinton and the Dixie Chicks—"I don't feel like I have to mask my incredulousness. I can say, 'For real? Are you kidding me?' That leads to spontaneity."

Sometimes humor results from a certain framing of the news. Each Monday, the show revisits metaphors from the Sunday morning news shows. On *Fox News Sunday* on April 8, Juan Williams first compared Republican presidential hopeful John McCain to a "deflated balloon," then declared the Arizona senator was on the "wrong path" with his Iraq policy and concluded that he shouldn't be "tying his tail" to such an albatross. On NBC's *Meet the Press,* Judy Woodruff in January described the administration's Iraq policy as akin to "putting a fist in a sink full of water, leaving it there for a few minutes and taking it out."

Salie says *The Daily Show* has demonstrated that young people are savvier than many elders believe, and the mainstream media should learn from that. Young people "are aware of the news and can recognize the preposterousness of some of it." But don't try too hard to be funny, she cautions. "I don't think real news shows should try the scripted, cutesy, pithy banter. It gives me the heebie-jeebies. It makes me feel sad for them, and it feels pathetic."

For an informal, satirical or even humorous take on the news to work in a mainstream newspaper, the format must be exactly right. Gene Weingarten, the *Washington Post* humor writer, thinks the media would do their jobs better if they had more fun, and he cringes whenever editors insist on labeling his pieces as satire. "Nothing could be worse for satire than labeling it satire," he laments.

But he concedes his editors may have a point. In August, Paul Farhi, a reporter for the *Post*'s Style section (and an AJR contributor), reviewed the debut of colleague Tony Kornheiser on ESPN's *Monday Night Football.* The critique was not flattering, and an apoplectic Kornheiser retaliated by publicly trashing Farhi as "a two-bit weasel slug," whom he would "gladly run over with a Mack truck."

The smackdown drew national attention, and Weingarten decided he wanted a piece of the action. So he skewered Kornheiser's second show with an outrageous, over-the-top rant on the front of Style about the "failed Kornheiser stewardship" taking "yet another bumbling misstep toward its inevitable humiliating collapse."

"It was patently unfair," Weingarten says of his tongue-in-cheek diatribe, which was not labeled as satire. "A child would have understood this piece. No one could have misunderstood this."

And yet they did. Weingarten got hundreds, possibly thousands, of complaints from sports lovers pummeling him for attacking Kornheiser unfairly. (Kornheiser himself called Weingarten, unsure how to interpret the piece.) "The mail I got was just absolutely hilarious," Weingarten says. "There is a problem of applying irony, humorous satire, in a newspaper when readers are not accustomed to seeing it there."

Did he learn from the experience? "No," he replies. "Because my reaction was, 'These people are idiots.'"

Perhaps the hardest lesson to take away from *The Daily Show* is the most important one. How can journalists in today's polarized political climate pierce the truth, Edward R. Murrow-style, without a) being ideological, or b) appearing ideological?

Olbermann's show, cited in several interviews as a serious news program that excels in revealing hypocrisy, is unabashedly liberal, and *The Daily Show* itself is frequently tagged with that label. In February, Fox News Channel debuted *The 1/2 Hour News Hour,* billed as the conservative riposte to Stewart's liberal bent; after two pilot shows, the network has agreed to pick up 13 additional episodes.

"Unfortunately, people are heading for news that sort of reinforces their own beliefs," says *Washington Post* reporter Dana Milbank. "That may be Jon Stewart on the left, or that may be Rush Limbaugh on the right. . . . Limbaugh isn't funny, but he's starting with something that has a kernel of truth and distorting it to the point of fakery as well, so I think they are parallel."

Milbank is the author of Washington Sketch, an experiment at slashing through the hazy words and deeds of federal power players. Milbank pitched the idea, based on British newspapers' parliamentary sketches, and argued for a few years before getting the green light in early 2005. "There was a lot of sort of figuring out the place, and first it really floated in the news section," he says. "I think we fixed that problem [by] putting it consistently on page two, and it's labeled more clearly."

Occasionally, Washington Sketch has appeared on page one, as it did March 6 when Milbank tartly contrasted the style of two generals who testified before Congress on the deplorable conditions at Walter Reed Army Medical Center. Then and at other times, Milbank's acerbic take has proved more enlightening than the longer, more traditional accompanying news story.

The column lacks a consistent ideology. Milbank says his goal is a "pox on both their houses sort of thing," and adds, "I'm not trying to be 50-50, particularly. The goal is to pick on all of them. . . . It's observational as opposed to argumentative." Too often, he says, "We seem to make the mistake of thinking that if you're not being ideological, you therefore have to be boring, and all sort of 50-50 down the middle and follow the inverted pyramid."

Jeff Jarvis, the blogger behind BuzzMachine.com, says journalists should engage in more open, honest conversations with readers. "I think what Stewart et al. do is remind us of what our mission and voice used to be and should be," says Jarvis, who also is a media consultant and head of the interactive journalism program at the City University of New York Graduate School of Journalism. He notes that Stewart is "very much a part of the conversation. He's joking about things we're talking about. And then the next day, we're talking about him talking about it."

Jarvis wants journalists to unleash their inner Stewart. "After enough drinks, reporters talk like Stewart: 'You won't BELIEVE what the mayor said today!' Why don't we talk to our readers that way?" he asks, and then acknowledges: "OK There's a lot of arguments: The mayor won't talk to us again.' 'It's biased.' 'We don't want to turn everything into blogs.'"

Jarvis doesn't mean that every story should become a first-person diatribe, and obviously the mainstream media can't fall back on Stewart's I'm-just-joking excuse after they've infuriated a thin-skinned politician. But there are instances when a little unorthodoxy may be appropriate, and speaking frankly may enhance credibility.

Eric Deggans, the TV and media critic for the *St. Petersburg Times,* also wants to see a little more pluck. "*The Daily Show* is pushing us to be less traditional about how we deliver people information," Deggans says. "Are we going to turn around and turn into the *Onion*?" (The cult publication parodies news in print and online; its facetious Onion News Network debuted on March 27.) "Of course not. But if you've got a long-time state capitol bureau chief, and they see something go down in the capitol, and they have a great, acerbic take on it, why not let them go at it in a column?"

Or, he suggests, experiment just a bit with the sacred space on page one. "Sometimes editors have really rigid ideas about what can go on the front page," he says. "If somebody has a really good column on [Don] Imus, why wouldn't you put it on the front page, as long as you label it clearly as opinion? There are some editors who would say your first next-day story about Don Imus has to be traditional. Why? Why does it have to be traditional? As long as the reader isn't fooled, why do you let yourself be handcuffed like that?"

Deggans is quick to add some caveats, including the importance of fairness. "You always have to be careful because there's a good reason why we had those rules," Deggans says. "But we have to challenge ourselves to subvert them more often. You have to be subversive in a way that maintains your credibility. When you have smart, capable people who want to write in a different way, let them try it."

The mainstream media can not, should not and never will be *The Daily Show.* The major news of our time is grimly serious, and only real news organizations will provide the time, commitment and professionalism necessary to ferret out stories such as the *Washington Post*'s exposé of neglected veterans at Walter Reed or the *New York Times*' disclosures of secret, warrantless wiretapping by the federal government.

But in the midst of a transition, our industry is flailing. Our credibility suffers mightily. The public thinks we're biased despite our reluctance to speak plainly. Our daily newspapers often seem stale. Perhaps *The Daily Show* can teach us little, but remind us of a lot: Don't underestimate your audience. Be relevant. And be bold.

Says Deggans: "In a lot of news organizations, it's the fourth quarter. It's fourth down, man. It's time to show a little pizzazz. It's time to reinvent what's going on, so people get engaged."

Journal Topics

1. Should we turn to satirical news shows like *The Daily Show, The Colbert Report,* or *Saturday Night Live*'s "Weekend Update," or the Internet's *Ironic Times* and *The Onion* to inform ourselves, or should they be used only for entertainment purposes?

2. Pick a story that is in the news right now and write a satirical treatment. You could write this in a format meant to be read aloud by a fake news anchor or TV reporter, or as an article that pokes fun at newspaper stories, such as the material you find in the *Ironic Times* or *The Onion*.

Questions for Critical Thought

1. Martin Kaplan, Associate Dean of the Annenberg School for Communication, says news "has fallen into a bizarre notion that substitutes something called 'balance' for what used to be called 'accuracy' or 'truth' or 'objectivity.'" What does he mean? In the news, what do you consider the difference between balance and accuracy? How might one be more important to the accurate presentation of the news than the other?

2. In the article, Smolkin argues that *The Daily Show*'s practice of juxtaposing old clips of politicians' assertions to more recent statements they've made allows "the truth to emanate from a politician's entanglement over his or her own two feet. It's one way to hold government officials accountable for their words and deeds." Do mainstream news media do as good a job at holding politicians accountable?

Personal Research

1. Compare *The Daily Show*'s take on a major national news story with a national evening news broadcast or a cable news station's broadcast. After watching both broadcasts, which one seems to have informed you more? Which one was more hard hitting? Which was more informative? Did either appear biased to a particular political side?

2. Factcheck.org, a project of the Annenberg Public Policy Center of the University of Pennsylvania, is "a nonpartisan, nonprofit, 'consumer advocate' for voters that aims to reduce the level of deception and confusion in U.S. politics." It monitors the "factual accuracy of what is said by major U.S. political players in the form of TV ads, debates, speeches, interviews, and news releases." Select some articles, preferably about different political parties, and read Factcheck's analyses. How many inaccuracies do they uncover? How deliberate do the inaccuracies appear to be?

Multicultural Issues

1. If you are not originally from the United States, think about what place ironic or humorous news has in your native country. Are there any shows satirizing the news on the air there? How prevalent is political humor? Are there any limits on how far shows and comics can go when poking fun at political institutions and people in power? Did *The Daily Show* or any American shows of this nature air there? If so, how are such shows received?

2. If you are from the United States, you may be interested in investigating how popular political satire is in other countries and whether it is regulated in any manner. A simple way is to talk to friends and classmates from other countries. Do they see greater freedom here? Or is it about the same?

Vocabulary Terms

hypocrisy
credulity
bombast
facetious
obfuscation
partisan

contrivances
sycophantic
green screen
galvanize
incredulousness

CHAPTER 21—NEWS MEDIA ESSAY QUESTIONS

These questions are intended as potential essay topics for the themes and evidence presented in the articles in this chapter.

1. Thomas Ginsberg states, "More foreign news coverage certainly would not have prevented the September 11 attacks. But perhaps closer attention to the world would have given Americans a clearer warning sign or two. Keeping more correspondents abroad might have meant better reporting today and without a doubt, more resonant and compelling foreign coverage would have shortened the distance the nation now has to travel to understand why it was attacked."

   Is he correct that a lack of accurate reporting has somehow made us fail to see the way the world really is? Do Americans need to know more about the issues that concern people in other nations? Will the animosity and violence aimed toward us get worse? How much power do news media have to bring us more understanding of the rest of the world? How much of a problem is the interest level of the public? Would more news about the rest of the world serve to make us take a greater interest?

2. Television news programs, just like any television shows, can survive only if they have good ratings and wealthy corporations sponsoring them. In years past, television networks would often find a loss of money from a news show acceptable because it served a crucial public interest of accurate information through journalism. After several waves of mergers, however, many critics suggest that the profit of such shows has become the most important thing.

   Do you think the news should focus on the most important stories of the day, or should a responsibility to ratings and getting advertisers outweigh the news? Should the news be based on a business model or strive to serve our democracy?

3. Many people get their news from a wider and wider variety of sources these days. Whereas news used to be found just on radio and in print, more and more people are getting it through broadcast television, cable television, magazines, satirical news shows, the Net, and even podcasts.

   What are the different benefits and drawbacks of news as it is presented in these different media? How much accuracy and depth is lost when the focus is on entertainment? The best way to compare different types of media may be tracking one story through as many different types of source as possible.

CHAPTER 22

Corporate America

O n your way home from campus, a good friend text messages you. He loves a good joke, and he often watches clips that a local improvisational comedy troupe posts on its MySpace site and YouTube. He tells you that he just sent a link to the funniest video he's ever seen to your email account. When you get home, you eagerly boot up and jack in to see what exactly is sitting in your inbox. You type in the familiar username and password, as automatic as breathing these days, but there is a strange message waiting for you. It comes from the Internet itself. It says,

"I have decided that viewing video clips does not help the efficiency of the Net. Please stop wasting MY bandwidth. Do something more productive with your email, and keep me happy. Sincerely, the Internet."

This would, of course, never happen. The Net itself cannot contact you because it isn't a person; it's a conglomerate of millions of people using an infrastructure to pass information back and forth. There is not a "Net" in the real world, no person who represents it, simply the disparate people, computers, and servers who make it up. This email, thankfully, would never come to your inbox. You can watch as many silly videos as you like.

In a sense, this fictional version of the Internet is like what a corporation is. Technically, a corporation is an entity having its own rights and privileges that exist outside of its members and stockholders. It is, in fact, a legal entity, one that possesses no physical form (though thousands of people are stockholders or employees). Yet it has just as much say about what happens in the world as we do. In fact, the vast amount of wealth owned by a corporation allows it even more power than any but the wealthiest, most powerful individual citizens have.

You probably know people who were fired or laid off from a corporation so that the corporation could save money. Perhaps their jobs were shipped overseas where a cheaper labor forces lives. These people now face one of the toughest challenges of their lives—starting over again in a hostile job market. Even worse, we've all heard of health insurance companies and HMOs refusing to allow expensive, life-saving surgery. Why? Because the surgery may make one person live longer, but the rest of the shareholders would gain nothing from this costly operation. In fact, they would lose profits, so the operation is refused. A human being dies, but the corporation saves money. Many people, offended at the growing power of corporations, wonder how we let them have this much control over our lives. After all, didn't we create them? Aren't they, simply, us?

If you looked back several centuries through history, you'd see that two institutions called all the shots and made all the rules: religion and monarchies. All jobs, all land, all chances at bettering yourself in life were based on your working for or with these two groups. Today in most of the world, the dominant institution is the multinational mega corporation.

Currently, a handful of multinational corporations largely define the world we live in. For example, Microsoft controls most software used on personal computers; a handful of media conglomerates such as Viacom, Disney, and the News Corporation own our daily flow of televised news; and you probably have no choice but to get your daily water or power from one corporation that dominates your area. Our environment is filled with corporate messages, corporate branding, and corporate plans, all of which are forms of information. This information, however important and pervasive it may be, is the information most of us are least adept at understanding.

Although the corporations we focus on in this chapter do not immediately generate the mass media, it is still crucial to practice information competency while interacting with and scrutinizing them. Because their common agenda is simply to make more money for their shareholders, often with little attention paid to the consequences of their actions, we cannot blindly trust their intentions or motives. The readings in this section will help you peel back some layers of corporate propaganda and see that a lot of the "information" given to us by corporations is untrue.

CORPORATE CRITICISM

Currently, many cultural critics look at the modern corporation with disdain. An assortment of films, such as *The Corporation,* and books, such as *Affluenza: The All-Consuming Epidemic* and *Culture Jam,* give voice to some of these critics. In their work, they make some serious claims against corporations and their actions. Many of these criticisms are discussed in this chapter.

Criticism #1: Corporations Too Often Abuse the Power and Trust We Give Them

Because we as citizens grant these corporate giants their corporate charter, and thus their very right to exist, many critics argue that corporations should do more to keep us happy and healthy. Whether we are stockholders and employers or merely customers, corporations owe us and our culture the decency of being honest and responsible.

In the past several years, however, there have been dozens of corporate scandals, costing citizens billions of dollars. One of the most infamous scandals concerned the energy giant Enron. The people who controlled Enron faked its profits to make its stock appear to be worth more money than it really was, and they manipulated the California energy market, causing rolling blackouts that affected millions of people for months during the summer of 2001. This almost doubled the price of energy in some areas, not because there was a genuine shortage of energy, but because Enron wanted higher profits. The poor and the elderly in particular suffered greatly from this dishonest manipulation.

Since the Enron scandal, however, the public has discovered that several other corporations have lied about their worth to make their stock prices rise and their boards of directors richer. There were plenty of corporations doctoring books and fleecing ordinary Americans. Some you might recognize include Adelphia Communications, AOL Time Warner, Bristol-Myers Squibb, Halliburton, Kmart, Merck, Tyco, Xerox, and World Com. Even the massive oil companies that control our flow of gasoline have come under fire. As our gas prices reach an all-time high, the oil company profits also reach an all-time high, implying that these high prices may in part be due to corporate greed, not supply and demand.

Where does information competency come in? When you invest in stock for any of these companies, you may be getting conned. You may think the corporation is worth $7 billion because they lied and inflated figures from the actual $2 billion they're worth. Or, when you hear in the news that there isn't enough power to keep your heater turned on, you may have been lied to so that members of the board of directors can buy extra summer homes. You may be told that damaged pipe lines or hurricanes are causing spikes in gas prices even though these problems may be responsible for only a few cents more per gallon compared to the dollar spike that you were hit with.

Criticism #2: Corporations Use Sweatshop Labor

Because of scandals like the Kathy Lee Gifford/Wal-Mart scandal some years back, more and more people are becoming aware that many of their favorite clothes and goods are being manufactured in sweatshops in other countries. Business trade agreements like NAFTA allow corporations to export work to other countries, and these countries often have very lax laws about working conditions and no labor unions to regulate corporate behavior. That backpack you bought in a back-to-school sale at your favorite big-box store was probably made at such a sweatshop, a factory where both adult and child workers routinely face slave wages, inhumane conditions, disfiguration, permanent injuries, diseases, and death.

Corporations can make billions of dollars in profits from this behavior. Pay a fifteen-year-old worker three cents an hour to make a sneaker in an overheated, dangerous factory, and turn around and sell it to Americans for nearly two hundred dollars. Even after shipping and the price of materials, that type of profit makes corporate managers starry-eyed. As soon as safety regulations are enforced, however, the price of manufacturing may go as high as, say, thirty dollars. Throw in a labor union to help fight for worker's rights, and it goes up to, say, fifty dollars to manufacture the shoe. Move the worker to America where the world is just more pricey (and we have to have every new gadget), and the worker needs ten dollars an hour plus overtime, the price for health insurance and retirement gets added into the equation, and there goes the corporate profit margin. If that shoe is produced in America, with all these added costs, the profits will be cut in half; thus, many corporations (making everything from cell phones to stuffed animals) will do anything they can to lessen the cost of production, including benefiting from the miserable conditions that workers in impoverished countries are forced to endure to survive.

Information competency comes from knowing the true history of the products you buy. Did the jeans you're wearing get made by someone working fourteen-hour-a-day shifts and trying to survive on wages that amount to three dollars a day? Did the drive-through latte you're drinking come from beans covered in so many unregulated pesticides that a twelve-year-old farm worker is permanently disfigured from chemical burns she got while picking them? In America, we assume that corporations take good care of their workers. Often, they don't. But it's up to us to know who does and who doesn't. And you can make a difference. For example, United Students Against Sweatshops, an international student movement fighting to end sweatshop labor conditions and protect workers' rights, has fought to ensure that various colleges and universities adopt strong codes of ethical and legal conduct, including full public disclosure of company information and independent verification systems to ensure that their institutions aren't buying products from companies that exploit sweatshops. They have been successful in getting corporations to take notice.

Criticism #3: Corporations Are a Threat to Democracy

Corporations have many of the same legal rights as any individual in the United States. They can sue, apply for patents, own land, and buy other corporations. They can't vote, but they have something most citizens aren't likely to ever have: billions of dollars to use for advertising and lobbying.

It is nothing new that the wealthy can influence politics with the use of money. Money funds political campaigns, gets candidates known, and even determines many of the issues that political debates center upon. Without money, nobody could ever become a governor, mayor, senator, or president. Corporations have the money, and they often use it to support candidates who will help them out later. Regulations are in place to limit such donations and gifts, in order to try to keep the playing field even, but with the power of a corporation behind an idea, opinions can easily spread through the minds of the citizens. For example, advocacy groups funded by corporate interests air commercials that make one side seem foolish or one candidate seem brave. There are also political organizations that can be formed to drum up grassroots support. Advocacy groups like these tend to give themselves misleading names so that they appear to be ordinary people in support of a cause. One example is the American Council on Science and Health, which was funded by major fast-food, soda, and chemical companies to present evidence that supported claims about the health benefits of their products.

Another disturbing trend is related to the growing cost of entering politics, with political campaigns now costing millions of dollars. Increasingly, only the wealthy can afford to run for political office. Some critics charge that when ex-CEOs and other people connected to industries and corporations gain power, they help to empower the corporation or industry that they were once a part of (and may be part of again, after their term in office is over). Critics of the Bush Administration's energy policies charged that representatives of the energy industry were given preferential access to the National Energy Policy Development Group, headed by Vice President Dick Cheney (and sometimes referred to as the Cheney Energy Task Force), while representatives of environmental groups and consumer advocates were virtually shut out. As of this writing, the administration refused to disclose to the public information about the membership of the National Energy Policy Development Group. Dick Cheney was the CEO of Halliburton from 1995 to 2000 and also had close ties to former Enron CEO Kenneth Lay. At this level, some people start to see the modern corporation as indistinguishable from the government.

American corporations also impede the progress toward democracy in other countries. Human Rights Watch published a report in 2006 called "Race to the Bottom: Corporate Complicity in Chinese Internet Censorship," documenting how Western Internet companies help Chinese authorities by censoring political material, sometimes without informing users. Yahoo! released the identity of private users to the Chinese authorities, enabling them to imprison four Chinese citizens who had posted comments online that criticized their government. To keep the Chinese government happy, Google created a version of its search engine, called www.google.cn, that censored searches. Microsoft censored words like "democracy" and "freedom" in the titles of Chinese blogs, but, bowing to public outcries, it modified its policy and decided to remove access to blog content only if the content violates MSN's terms of use or if it receives a legally binding notice from the Chinese government indicating that the material is in violation of the law. Because of pressure coming from ordinary consumers, corporations are being forced to reconsider the way they do business with countries that violate human rights.

SOCIAL RESPONSIBILITY

Many critics assert that the corporation has a social responsibility to not only make money, but to give something back to consumers, employees, and the Earth itself. Although the criticisms previously listed are pretty harsh claims that target many corporate entities, other corporations go out of their way to make a positive impact on the planet. Following are some actions that more socially conscious corporations are engaging in.

Quality of Life Improvements

Many corporations try to make a positive impact on the quality of life of their employees and customers. Although some corporations pay the smallest amount they can to their workers, many pay high wages and improve the life of their employees with great health benefits and friendly workplaces. Similarly, many corporations make life easier on the consumer, providing us with better cell phones, hybrid cars, time-saving household gadgets, and high-quality clothing—these things improve our daily lives in a myriad of ways, and most of them are brought to us by corporations. If you can find a corporation that tries to do the least amount of damage to the environment and the local community where it manufactures its products, then even better.

For example, Interface Incorporated, one of the world's largest carpet and flooring corporations, has decided to become fully "sustainable" by 2020. **Sustainability** means a corporation can create its products without having any negative impact on the environment or economy anywhere on Earth. Many corporations consider profit to be the most important factor in their business practices, so it is an admirable goal for any corporation to attempt sustainability, especially if it will cost them money.

Fair Trade

Coffee and cocoa farms are largely found in Central and South America, and these business are notorious for horrible labor practices, ridiculously low pay, and the use of types of pesticides that can permanently harm the pickers. Many corporations, however, are actively trying to avoid these unethical business practices by buying more and more "Fair Trade coffee," which ensures farmers a better standard of living and a guaranteed minimum fair price for their crops, and "shade grown coffee," which protects migratory bird habitats and reduces clear-cutting in tropical rainforests. Starbucks, for example, imports over twenty percent of all Fair Trade coffee purchased in America, and it pledges to buy more each year. Many critics claim Starbucks doesn't do enough, but it still leads the pack in its Fair Trade practices, and they hope that other coffee giants, such as Folgers and Maxwell House, follow its lead.

Meat and Fur

Most of the major American fast-food chains use meat and poultry that come from a handful of massive slaughterhouses across the nation. Critics claim that these slaughterhouses often fail to kill the animals humanely, so some are still alive while being butchered. As we write, the Humane Society of the United States is suing the Secretary of Agriculture because the United States Department of Agriculture (USDA) has been excluding chickens, turkeys, and other species of poultry, which account for approximately ninety-five percent of all animals killed for food in the U.S., from the Humane Methods of Slaughter Act of 1958. According to this law, animals should be stunned into unconsciousness prior to their slaughter so that they have a quick and relatively painless death and that they are dead before being butchered. The Humane Society suit alleges numerous problems, including that live poultry entering scalding tanks of water defecate and then inhale feces from the water, potentially contaminating the meat. Chickens are also forced against each other in little pens, their sensitive beaks cut off to prevent them from pecking at each other, a behavior fostered by the overcrowding.

Many farms, restaurants, and stores aren't waiting for the long, slow process of lawsuits to reach a conclusion before taking action themselves. They refuse to use this type of meat. They use organic farming practices, grain-fed beef, and chickens who are "free range" instead of penned. There is no overcrowding or unnatural feed, so the animals don't need antibiotics or other drugs, and this is intended not only to treat the animals more ethically, but to lead to healthier meats for consumers.

Also, that jacket you may have from a major American coat company with a label saying that its collar is "faux fur" may actually be sporting fur from a cat or dog slowly strangled or drowned or even skinned alive in China for its pelt. Congress passed the Dog and Cat Protection Act of 2000, prohibiting the importation of dog or cat fur, when consumers expressed outrage that Chinese suppliers were killing cats and dogs in terrible ways, then marketing the products as "fake fur." Recently, major clothing companies have been found to have been buying the Chinese pelts and mislabeling the clothing and accessories made from them.

You can't safely assume that any given corporation is behaving ethically or unethically. Explore the practices and histories of the corporations selling your favorite clothing brands, dairy products, foods, electronics, and cars, as well as other consumer items. You may find that the clothing store where you shop supports sweatshops and your favorite dairy uses bovine growth hormones, which leads to pus-infected milk and dairy products, or, conversely, that the coffee you drink is actually Fair Trade, and the car company you like is the industry leader on alternative fuels. One of the best ways to influence a corporation is by letting it know how you plan to spend your money. If a corporate entity endorses bad practices, and people like you find out and stop supporting it, the corporation will feel it. A small corporation doing the right thing can become an overnight success and lead the industry toward improvement, however, if you buy more of its products and get friends and families to do the same.

IN THIS CHAPTER

The following readings have been included to give you a better understanding of the nature and composition of corporations and the power and influence they wield. If you find some of the content of these articles to be shocking, do what we suggest in every chapter: conduct your own investigations. To understand these powerful forces better, you may consider the following:

- What is the history of the American corporation, and how did it get to become as powerful as it is today?
- What does it take to become incorporated?
- Why did we let corporations gain some of the same legal rights as human beings (for example, they can own land, sue people, and buy stock), and what impact does this have on our lives?
- What harm and what good do corporations do to the environment or the economy?
- Are corporations such as Microsoft, Chevron/Texaco/Caltex, General Motors, or Monsanto too powerful?

The Chain Never Stops

American Slaughterhouses Are Grinding Out Meat Faster Than Ever—and The Production Line Keeps Moving, Even When The Workers Are Maimed by The Machinery

Eric Schlosser

Prereading Question

1. How protected do you think workers in American companies are against hazardous conditions? What kinds of regulations do we have in force? If companies don't comply and their practices cause injury, what sorts of penalties do you imagine they face? What sorts of penalties do you think they should face?

In the beginning he had been fresh and strong, and he had gotten a job the first day; but now he was second-hand, a damaged article, so to speak, and they did not want him . . . they had worn him out, with their speeding-up and their carelessness, and now they had thrown him away!

—*Upton Sinclair,* The Jungle *(1906)*

Kenny Dobbins was hired by the Monfort Beef Company in 1979. He was 24 years old, and 6 foot 5, and had no fear of the hard work in a slaughterhouse. He seemed invincible. Over the next two decades he suffered injuries working for Monfort that would have crippled or killed lesser men. He was struck by a falling 90-pound box of meat and pinned against the steel lip of a conveyor belt. He blew out a disc and had back surgery. He inhaled too much chlorine while cleaning some blood tanks and spent a month in the hospital, his lungs burned, his body covered in blisters. He damaged the rotator cuff in his left shoulder when a 10,000-pound hammer-mill cover dropped too quickly and pulled his arm straight backward. He broke a leg after stepping into a hole in the slaughterhouse's concrete floor. He got hit by a slow-moving train behind the plant, got bloodied and knocked right out of his boots, spent two weeks in the hospital, then returned to work. He shattered an ankle and had it mended with four steel pins. He got more bruises and cuts, muscle pulls and strains than he could remember.

Despite all the injuries and the pain, the frequent trips to the hospital and the metal brace that now supported one leg, Dobbins felt intensely loyal to Monfort and Con-Agra, its parent company. He'd left home at the age of 13 and never learned to read; Monfort had given him a steady job, and he was willing to do whatever the company asked. He moved from Grand Island, Nebraska, to Greeley, Colorado, to help Monfort reopen its slaughterhouse there without a union. He became an outspoken member of a group formed to keep union organizers out. He saved the life of a fellow worker—and was given a framed certificate of appreciation. And then, in December 1995, Dobbins felt a sharp pain in his chest while working in the plant. He thought it was a heart attack. According to Dobbins, the company nurse told him it was a muscle pull and sent him home. It was a heart attack, and Dobbins nearly died. While awaiting compensation for his injuries, he was fired. The company later agreed to pay him a settlement of $35,000.

Today Kenny Dobbins is disabled, with a bad heart and scarred lungs. He lives entirely off Social Security payments. He has no pension and no health insurance. His recent shoulder surgery—stemming from an old injury at the plant and costing more than $10,000—was paid by Medicare. He now feels angry beyond words at ConAgra, misused, betrayed. He's embarrassed to be receiving public assistance. "I've never had to ask for help before in my life," Dobbins says. "I've always worked. I've worked since I was 14 years old." In addition to the physical pain, the financial uncertainty, and the stress of finding enough money just to pay the rent each month, he feels humiliated.

What happened to Kenny Dobbins is now being repeated, in various forms, at slaughterhouses throughout the United States. According to the Bureau of Labor Statistics, meatpacking is the nation's most dangerous occupation. In 1999, more than one-quarter of America's nearly 150,000 meatpacking workers suffered a job-related injury or illness. The meatpacking industry not only has the highest injury rate, but also has by far the highest rate of serious injury—more than five times the national average, as measured in lost workdays. If you accept the official figures, about 40,000 meatpacking workers are injured on the job every year. But the actual number is most likely higher. The meatpacking industry has a well-documented history of discouraging injury reports, falsifying injury data, and putting injured workers back on the job quickly to minimize the reporting of lost workdays. Over the past four years, I've met scores of meatpacking workers in Nebraska, Colorado, and Texas who tell stories of being injured and then discarded by their employers. Like Kenny Dobbins, many now rely on public assistance for their food, shelter, and medical care. Each new year throws more injured workers on the dole, forcing taxpayers to subsidize the meatpacking industry's poor safety record. No government statistics can measure the true amount of pain and suffering in the nation's meatpacking communities today.

A list of accident reports filed by the Occupational Safety and Health Administration gives a sense of the dangers that workers now confront in the nation's meatpacking plants. The titles of these OSHA reports sound more like lurid tabloid headlines than the headings of sober government documents: Employee Severely Burned After Fuel From His Saw Is Ignited. Employee Hospitalized for Neck Laceration From Flying Blade. Employee's Finger Amputated in Sausage Extruder. Employee's Finger Amputated in Chitlin Machine. Employee's Eye Injured When Struck by Hanging Hook. Employee's Arm Amputated in Meat Auger. Employee's Arm Amputated When Caught in Meat Tenderizer. Employee Burned in Tallow Fire. Employee Burned by Hot Solution in Tank. One Employee Killed, Eight Injured by Ammonia Spill. Employee Killed When Arm Caught in Meat Grinder. Employee Decapitated by Chain of Hide Puller Machine. Employee Killed When Head Crushed by Conveyor. Employee Killed When Head Crushed in Hide Fleshing Machine. Employee Killed by Stun Gun. Caught and Killed by Gut-Cooker Machine.

The most dangerous plants are the ones where cattle are slaughtered. Poultry slaughterhouses are somewhat safer because they are more highly mechanized; chickens have been bred to reach a uniform size at maturity. Cattle, however, vary enormously in size, shape, and weight when they arrive at a slaughterhouse. As a result, most of the work at a modern beef plant is still performed by hand. In the age of the space station and the microchip, the most important slaughterhouse tool is a well-sharpened knife.

Thirty years ago, meatpacking was one of the highest-paid industrial jobs in the United States, with one of the lowest turnover rates. In the decades that followed the 1906 publication of *The Jungle,* labor unions had slowly gained power in the industry, winning their members good benefits, decent working conditions, and a voice in the workplace. Meatpacking jobs were dangerous and unpleasant, but provided enough income for a solid, middle-class life. There were sometimes waiting lists for these jobs. And then, starting in the early 1960s, a company called Iowa Beef Packers (IBP) began to revolutionize the industry, opening plants in rural areas far from union strongholds, recruiting immigrant workers from Mexico, introducing a new division of labor that eliminated the need for skilled butchers, and ruthlessly battling unions. By the late 1970s, meatpacking companies that wanted to compete with IBP had to adopt its business methods—or go out of business. Wages in the meatpacking industry soon fell by as much as 50 percent. Today meatpacking is one of the nation's lowest-paid industrial jobs, with one of the highest turnover rates. The typical plant now hires an entirely new workforce every year or so. There are no waiting lists at these slaughterhouses today. Staff shortages have become an industrywide problem, making the work even more dangerous.

In a relatively brief period of time, the meatpacking industry also became highly centralized and concentrated, giving enormous power to a few large agribusiness firms. In 1970, the top four meatpackers controlled just 21 percent of the beef market. Today the top four—IBP, ConAgra, Excel (a subsidiary of Cargill), and National Beef—control about 85 percent of the market. While the meatpackers have grown more powerful, the unions have grown much weaker. Only half of IBP's workers belong to a union, allowing that company to set the industry standard for low wages and harsh working conditions. Given the industry's high turnover rates, it is a challenge for a union simply to remain in a meatpacking plant, since every year it must gain the allegiance of a whole new set of workers.

In some American slaughterhouses, more than three-quarters of the workers are not native English speakers; many can't read any language, and many are illegal immigrants. A new migrant industrial workforce now circulates through the meatpacking towns of the High Plains. A wage of $9.50 an hour seems incredible to men and women who come from rural areas in Mexico where the wages are $7 a day. These manual laborers, long accustomed to toiling in the fields, are good workers. They're also unlikely to complain or challenge authority, to file lawsuits, organize unions, fight for their legal rights. They tend to be poor, vulnerable, and fearful. From the industry's point of view, they are ideal workers: cheap, largely interchangeable, and disposable.

One of the crucial determinants of a slaughterhouse's profitability is also responsible for many of its greatest dangers: the speed of the production line. Once a plant is fully staffed and running, the more head of cattle slaughtered per hour, the less it costs to process each one. If the production line stops, for any reason, costs go up. Faster means cheaper—and more profitable. The typical line speed in an American slaughterhouse 25 years ago was about 175 cattle per hour. Some line speeds now approach 400 cattle per hour. Technological advances are responsible for part of the increase; the powerlessness of meatpacking workers explains the rest. Faster also means more dangerous. When hundreds of workers stand closely together, down a single line, wielding sharp knives, terrible things can happen when people feel rushed. The most common slaughterhouse injury is a laceration. Workers stab themselves or stab someone nearby. They struggle to keep up with the pace as carcasses rapidly swing toward them, hung on hooks from a moving, overhead chain. All sorts of accidents—involving power tools, saws, knives, conveyor belts, slippery floors, falling carcasses—become more likely when the chain moves too fast. One slaughterhouse nurse told me she could always tell the line speed by the number of people visiting her office.

The golden rule in meatpacking plants is "The Chain Will Not Stop." USDA inspectors can shut down the line to ensure food safety, but the meatpacking firms do everything possible to keep it moving at top speed. Nothing stands in the way of production, not mechanical failures, breakdowns, accidents. Forklifts crash, saws overheat, workers drop knives, workers get cut, workers collapse and lie unconscious on the floor, as dripping carcasses sway past them, and the chain keeps going. "The chain never stops," Rita Beltran, a former IBP worker told me. "I've seen bleeders, and they're gushing because they got hit right in the vein, and I mean they're almost passing out, and here comes the supply guy again, with the bleach, to clean the blood off the floor, but the chain never stops. It never stops."

Albertina Rios was a housewife in Mexico before coming to America nearly 20 years ago and going to work for IBP in Lexington, Nebraska. While bagging intestines, over and over, for eight hours a day, Rios soon injured her right shoulder. She was briefly placed on light duty, but asked to be assigned to a higher-paying position trimming heads, an even more difficult job that required moving heavy baskets of meat all day. When she complained about the pain to her supervisor, she recalls, he accused her of being lazy. Rios eventually underwent surgery on the shoulder, as well as two operations on her hands for carpal tunnel syndrome, a painful and commonplace injury caused by hours of repetitive motion.

Some of the most debilitating injuries in the meatpacking industry are also the least visible. Properly sutured, even a deep laceration will heal. The cumulative trauma injuries that meatpacking workers routinely suffer, however, may cause lifelong impairments. The strict regimentation and division of labor in slaughterhouses means that workers must repeat the same motions again and again throughout their shift. Making the same knife cut 10,000 times a day or lifting the same weight every few seconds can cause serious injuries to a person's back, shoulders, or hands. Aside from a 15-minute rest break or two and a brief lunch, the work is unrelenting. Even the repetition of a seemingly harmless task can lead to pain. "If you lightly tap your finger on a desk a few times, it doesn't hurt," an attorney for injured workers told me. "Now try tapping it for eight hours straight, and see how that feels."

The rate of cumulative trauma injuries in meatpacking is the highest of any American industry. It is about 33 times higher than the national average. According to federal statistics, nearly 1 out of every 10 meatpacking workers suffers a cumulative trauma injury every year. In fact, it's very hard to find a meatpacking worker who's not suffering from some kind of recurring pain. For unskilled, unschooled manual laborers, cumulative trauma injuries such as disc problems, tendonitis, and "trigger finger" (a syndrome in which a finger becomes stuck in a curled position) can permanently limit the ability to earn a decent income. Much of this damage will never be healed.

After interviews with many slaughterhouse workers who have cumulative trauma injuries, there's one image that stays with me. It's the sight of pale white scars on dark skin. Ana Ramos came from El Salvador and went to work at the same IBP plant as Albertina Rios, trimming hair from the meat with scissors. Her fingers began to lock up; her hands began to swell; she developed shoulder problems from carrying 30- to 60-pound boxes. She recalls going to see the company doctor and describing the pain, only to be told the problem was in her mind. She would leave the appointments crying. In January 1999, Ramos had three operations on the same day—one on her shoulder, another on her elbow, another on her hand. A week later, the doctor sent her back to work. Dora Sanchez, who worked at a different IBP plant, complained for months about soreness in her hands. She says the company ignored her. Sanchez later had surgery on both hands. She now has a "spinal cord stimulator," an elaborate pain-reduction system implanted in her body, controlled from a small box under the skin on her hip. She will need surgery to replace the batteries every six or seven years.

Cumulative trauma injuries may take months or even years to develop; other slaughterhouse injuries can happen in an instant. Lives are forever changed by a simple error, a wrong move, a faulty machine. Raul Lopez worked as a carpenter in Mexico, making tables, chairs, and headboards, before coming to the United States in 1995 to do construction work in Santa Fe, New Mexico. He was 20 years old at the time, and after laying concrete foundations for two years, he moved to Greeley and got a job at the Monfort Beef plant, where the pay was higher. He trimmed hides after they came up from the kill floor, cutting off the legs and heads, lifting them up with mechanical assistance, and placing the hides on a hook. It was one of the most difficult jobs in the plant. Each hide weighed about 180 pounds, and he lifted more than 300 of them every hour. He was good at his job and became a "floater," used by his supervisor to fill in for absent workers. Lopez's hands and shoulders were sore at the end of the day, but for two years and two months he suffered no injuries.

At about seven in the morning on November 22, 1999, Lopez was substituting for an absent worker, standing on a four-foot-high platform, pulling hides from a tank of water that was washing blood and dirt off them. The hides were suspended on hooks from a moving chain. The room was cold and foggy, and it was difficult to see clearly. There were problems somewhere up ahead on the line, but the chain kept moving, and Lopez felt pressure to keep up. One of his steel-mesh gloves suddenly got snagged in the chain, and it dragged him down the line toward bloody, filthy water that was three feet deep. Lopez grabbed the chain with his free hand and screamed for help. Someone ran to another room and took an extraordinary step: He shut down the line. The arm caught in the chain, Lopez's left one, was partially crushed. He lost more than three pints of blood and almost bled to death. He was rushed to a hospital in Denver, endured the first of many operations, and survived. Five months later, Lopez was still in enormous pain and heavily medicated. Nevertheless, he says, a company doctor ordered him back to work. His previous supervisor no longer worked at the plant. Lopez was told that the man had simply walked off the job and quit one day, feeling upset about the accident.

I recently visited Lopez on a lovely spring afternoon. His modest apartment is just a quarter mile down the road from the slaughterhouse. The living room is meticulously neat and clean, filled with children's toys and a large glass display case of Native American curios. Lopez now works in the nurse's office at the plant, handling files. Every day he sees how injured workers are treated—given some Tylenol and then sent back to the line—and worries that ConAgra is now planning to get rid of him. His left arm hangs shriveled and lifeless in a sling. It is a deadweight that causes severe pain in his neck and back. Lopez wants the company to pay for an experimental operation that might restore some movement to the arm. The alternative could be amputation. ConAgra will say only that it is weighing the various medical options. Lopez is 26 years old and believes his arm will work again. "Every night, I pray for this operation," he says, maintaining a polite and dignified facade. A number of times during our conversation, he suddenly gets up and leaves the room. His wife, Silvia, stays behind, sitting across from me on the couch, holding their one-year-old son in her arms. Their three-year-old daughter happily wanders in and out to the porch. Every time the front door swings open for her, a light breeze from the north brings the smell of death into the room.

The meatpacking companies refuse to comment on the cases of individual employees like Raul Lopez, but insist they have a sincere interest in the well-being of their workers. Health and safety, they maintain, are the primary concerns of every supervisor, foreman, nurse, medical claims examiner, and company-approved doctor. "It is in our best interest to take care of our workers and ensure that they are protected and able to work every day," says Janet M. Riley, a vice president of the American Meat Institute, the industry's trade association. "We are very concerned about improving worker safety. It is absolutely to our benefit."

The validity of such claims is measured best in Texas, where the big meatpackers have the most freedom to do as they please. In many ways, the true heart of the industry lies in Texas. About one-quarter of the cattle slaughtered every year in the United States—roughly 9 million animals—are processed in Texas meatpacking plants. One of the state's U.S. senators, Phil Gramm, is the industry's most powerful ally in Congress. His wife, Wendy Lee, sits on the board of IBP. The state courts and the legislature have also been friendly to the industry. Indeed, many injured meatpacking workers in Texas now face a system that has been devised not only to prevent any independent scrutiny of their medical needs, but also to prevent them from suing for on-the-job injuries.

In the early years of the 20th century, public outrage over the misfortune of industrial workers hurt on the job prompted legislatures throughout the United States to enact workers' compensation laws. Workers' comp was intended to be a form of mandatory, no-fault insurance. In return for surrendering the legal right to sue their employer for damages, injured workers were guaranteed immediate access to medical care, steady income while they recuperated, and disability payments. All 50 states eventually passed workers' comp legislation of one sort or another, creating systems in which employers generally obtained private insurance and any disputes were resolved by publicly appointed officials.

Recent efforts by business groups to "reform" workers' comp have made it more difficult for injured employees to obtain payments. In Colorado, the first "workers' comp reform" bill was sponsored in 1990 by Tom Norton, a conservative state senator from Greeley. His wife, Kay, was a vice president at ConAgra Red Meat at the time. Under Colorado's new law, which places limits on compensation, the maximum payment for losing an arm is $37,738. Losing a digit brings you anywhere from $2,400 to $9,312, depending on whether it's a middle finger, a pinkie, or a thumb.

The meatpacking companies have a vested interest in keeping workers' comp payments as low as possible. IBP, Excel, and ConAgra are all self-insured. Every dime spent on injured workers in such programs is one less dime in profits. Slaughterhouse supervisors and foremen, whose annual bonuses are usually tied to the injury rate of their workers, often discourage people from reporting injuries or seeking first aid. The packinghouse culture encourages keeping quiet and laboring in pain. Assignments to "light duty" frequently punish an injured worker by cutting the hourly wage and forbidding overtime. When an injury is visible and impossible to deny—an amputation, a severe laceration, a chemical burn—companies generally don't contest a worker's claim or try to avoid medical payments. But when injuries are less obvious or workers seem uncooperative, companies often block every attempt to seek benefits. It can take injured workers as long as three years to get their medical bills paid. From a purely financial point of view, the company has a strong incentive to delay every payment in order to encourage a less-expensive settlement. Getting someone to quit is even more profitable—an injured worker who walks away from the job is no longer eligible for any benefits. It is not uncommon to find injured workers assigned to meaningless or unpleasant tasks as a form of retaliation, a clear message to leave. They are forced to sit all day watching an emergency exit or to stare at gauges amid the stench in rendering.

In Texas, meatpacking firms don't have to manipulate the workers' comp system—they don't even have to participate in it. The Texas Workers Compensation Reform Act of 1989 allowed private companies to drop out of the state's workers' comp system. Although the law gave injured workers the right to sue employers that had left the system, that provision was later rendered moot. When a worker is injured at an IBP plant in Texas, for example, he or she is immediately presented with a waiver. It reads: "I have been injured at work and want to apply for the payments offered by IBP to me under its Workplace Injury Settlement Program. To qualify, I must accept the rules of the Program. I have been given a copy of the Program summary. I accept the Program."

Signing the waiver means forever surrendering your right—and the right of your family and heirs—to sue IBP on any grounds. Workers who sign the waiver may receive immediate medical care under IBP's program. Or they may not. Once they sign, IBP and its company-approved doctors have control over the worker's job-related medical treatment—for life. Under the program's terms, seeking treatment from an independent physician can be grounds for losing all medical benefits. If the worker objects to any decision, the dispute can be submitted to an IBP-approved arbitrator. The company has said the waivers are designed "to more effectively ensure quality medical care for employees injured on the job." Workers who refuse to sign the IBP waiver not only risk getting no medical care from the company, but also risk being fired on the spot. In February 1998, the Texas Supreme Court ruled that companies operating outside the state's workers' comp system can fire workers simply because they're injured.

Today, an IBP worker who gets hurt on the job in Texas faces a tough dilemma: Sign the waiver, perhaps receive immediate medical attention, and remain beholden, forever, to IBP. Or refuse to sign, risk losing your job, receive no help with your medical bills, file a lawsuit, and hope to win a big judgment against the company someday. Injured workers almost always sign the waiver. The pressure to do so is immense. An IBP medical case manager will literally bring the waiver to a hospital emergency room in order to obtain an injured worker's signature. Karen Olsson, in a fine investigative piece for the *Texas Observer,* described the lengths to which Terry Zimmerman, one of IBP's managers, will go to get a signed waiver. When Lonita Leal's right hand was mangled by a hamburger grinder at the IBP plant in Amarillo, Zimmerman talked her into signing the waiver with her left hand, as she waited in the hospital for surgery. When Duane Mullin had both hands crushed in a hammer mill at the same plant, Zimmerman persuaded him to sign the waiver with a pen held in his mouth.

Unlike IBP, Excel does not need to get a signed waiver after an injury in Texas. Its waiver is included in the union contract that many workers unwittingly sign upon being hired. Once they're injured, these workers often feel as much anger toward the union as they do toward their employer. In March, the Texas Supreme Court upheld the legality of such waivers, declaring that the "freedom of contract" gave Americans the ability to sign away their common-law rights. Before the waiver became part of the standard contract, Excel was held accountable, every so often, for its behavior.

Hector Reyes is one of the few who has managed to do something productive with his sense of betrayal. For 25 years, his father was a maintenance worker at the Excel plant in Friona, Texas, a couple of hours southwest of Amarillo. As a teen-ager, Reyes liked to work in the plant's warehouse, doing inventory. He'd grown up around the slaughterhouse. He later became a Golden Gloves champion boxer and went to work for Excel in 1997, at the age of 25, to earn money while he trained. One day he was asked to clean some grease from the blowers in the trolley room. Reyes did as he was told, climbing a ladder in the loud, steam-filled room and wiping the overhead blowers clean. But one of the blowers lacked a proper cover—and in an instant the blade shredded four of the fingers on Reyes' left hand. He climbed down the ladder and yelled for help, but nobody would come near him, as blood flew from the hand. So Reyes got himself to the nurse's office, where he was immediately asked to provide a urine sample. In shock and in pain, he couldn't understand why they needed his urine so badly. Try as he might, he couldn't produce any. The nurse called an ambulance, but said he wouldn't receive any painkillers until he peed in a cup. Reyes later realized that if he'd failed the urine test, Excel would not have been obligated to pay any of his medical bills. This demand for urine truly added insult to injury: Reyes was in training and never took drugs. He finally managed to urinate and received some medication. The drug test later came back negative.

On his fourth night in a Lubbock hospital, Reyes was awakened around midnight and told to report for work the next morning in Friona, two hours away. His wife would have to drive, but she was three months pregnant. Reyes refused to leave the hospital until the following day. For the next three months, he simply sat in a room at the Excel plant with other injured workers or filed papers for eight hours a day, then drove to Lubbock for an hour of physical therapy and an hour of wound cleaning before heading home. "You've already cost the company too much money," he recalls one supervisor telling him. Reyes desperately wanted to quit but knew he'd lose all his medical benefits if he did. He became suicidal, despondent about the end of his boxing career and his disfigurement. Since the union had not yet included a waiver in its Excel contract, Reyes was able to sue the company for failing to train him properly and for disregarding OSHA safety guidelines. In 1999, he won a rare legal victory: $879,312.25 in actual damages and $1 million in punitive damages. Under the current Excel contract, that sort of victory is impossible to achieve.

Federal safety laws were intended to protect workers from harm, regardless of the vagaries of state laws like those in Texas. OSHA is unlikely, however, to do anything for meatpacking workers in the near future. The agency has fewer than 1,200 inspectors to examine the safety risks at the nation's roughly 7 million workplaces. The maximum OSHA fine for the death of a worker due to an employer's willful negligence is $70,000—an amount that hardly strikes fear in the hearts of agribusiness executives whose companies have annual revenues that are measured in the tens of billions. One of President George W. Bush's first acts in office was to rescind an OSHA ergonomics standard on repetitive-motion injuries that the agency had been developing for nearly a decade. His move was applauded by IBP and the American Meat Institute.

The new chairman of the House Subcommittee on Workforce Protections, which oversees all legislation pertaining to OSHA, is Rep. Charles Norwood, a Republican from Georgia. Norwood was an outspoken supporter of the OSHA Reform Act of 1997—a bill that would have effectively abolished the agency. Norwood, a former dentist, became politically active in the early 1990s out of a sense of outrage that OSHA regulations designed to halt the spread of AIDS were forcing him to wear fresh rubber gloves for each new patient. He has publicly suggested that many workers get repetitive-stress injuries not from their jobs, but from skiing and playing too much tennis.

For Kevin Glasheen, one of the few Texas attorneys willing to battle IBP, the plight of America's meatpacking workers is "a fundamental failure of capitalism." By failing to pay the medical bills of injured workers, he says, large meatpackers are routinely imposing their business costs on the rest of society, much as utilities polluted the air a generation ago without much regard to the consequences for those who breathed it. Rod Rehm, an attorney who defends many Latino meatpacking workers in Nebraska, believes that two key changes could restore the effectiveness of most workers' comp plans. Allowing every worker to select his or her own physician would liberate medical care from the dictates of the meatpacking companies and the medical staff they control. More important, Rehm argues, these companies should not be permitted to insure themselves. If independent underwriters had to insure the meatpackers, the threat of higher insurance premiums would quickly get the attention of the meatpacking industry—and force it to take safety issues seriously.

Until fundamental changes are made, the same old stories will unfold. Michael Glover is still awaiting payment from IBP, his employer for more than two decades. For 16 of those years, Glover worked as a splitter in the company's Amarillo plant. Every 20 to 30 seconds, a carcass would swing toward him on a chain. He would take "one heavy heavy power saw" and cut upward, slicing the animal in half before it went into the cooler. The job took strength, agility, and good aim. The carcasses had to be sliced exactly through the middle. One after another they came at him, about a thousand pounds each, all through the day.

On the morning of September 30, 1996, after splitting his first carcass, Glover noticed vibrations in the steel platform beneath him. A maintenance man checked the platform and found a bolt missing, but told Glover it was safe to keep working until it was replaced. Moments later, the platform collapsed as Glover was splitting a carcass. He dropped about seven feet and shattered his right knee. While he lay on the ground and workers tried to find help, the chain kept going as two other splitters picked up the slack. Glover was taken in a wheelchair to the nurse's station, where he went into shock in the hallway and fell unconscious. He sat in that hall for almost four hours before being driven to an outpatient clinic. A full seven hours after the accident, Glover was finally admitted to a hospital. He spent the next six days there. His knee was too badly shattered to be repaired; no screws would hold; the bone was broken into too many pieces.

An artificial knee was later inserted. Glover suffered through enormous pain and a series of complications: blood clots, ulcers, phlebitis. Nevertheless, he says, IBP pressured him to return to work in a wheelchair during the middle of winter. On snowy days, several men had to carry him into the plant. Once it became clear that his injury would never fully heal, Glover thinks IBP decided to get rid of him. But he refused to quit and lose all his medical benefits. He was given a series of humiliating jobs. For a month, Glover sat in the men's room at the plant for eight hours a day, ordered by his supervisor to make sure no dirty towels or toilet paper remained on the floor.

"Michael Glover played by IBP's rules," says his attorney, James H. Woods, a fierce critic of the Texas workers' comp system. The day of his accident, Glover had signed the waiver, surrendering any right to sue the company. Instead, he filed for arbitration under IBP's Workplace Injury Settlement Program. Last year, on November 3, Glover was fired by IBP. Twelve days later, his arbitration hearing convened. The arbitrator, an Amarillo lawyer named Tad Fowler, was selected by IBP. Glover sought money for his pain and suffering, as well as lifetime payments from the company. He'd always been a hardworking and loyal employee. Now he had no medical insurance. His only income was $250 a week in unemployment. He'd fallen behind in his rent and worried that his family would be evicted from their home.

On December 20, Fowler issued his decision. He granted Glover no lifetime payments but awarded him $350,000 for pain and suffering. Glover was elated, briefly. Even though its workplace-injury settlement program clearly states that "the arbitrator's decision is final and binding," the company so far has refused to pay him. IBP claims that by signing the waiver, Glover forfeited any right to compensation for "physical pain, mental anguish, disfigurement, or loss of enjoyment of life." IBP has even refused to pay its own arbitrator for his services, and Fowler is now suing the company to get his fee. He has been informed that IBP will never hire him again for an arbitration.

Glover's case is now in federal court. He is a proud man with a strong philosophical streak. He faces the possibility of another knee replacement or of amputation. "How can this company fire me after 23-and-one-half years of service," he asks, "after an accident due to no fault of my own, and requiring so much radical surgery, months and months of pain and suffering, and nothing to look forward to but more pain and suffering, and refuse to pay me an award accrued through its own program?"

There is no good answer to his question. The simple answer is that IBP can do it because the laws allow them to do it. Michael Glover is just one of thousands of meat-packing workers who've been mistreated and then discarded. There is nothing random or inscrutable about their misery; it is the logical outcome of the industry's practices. A lack of public awareness, a lack of outrage, have allowed these abuses to continue, one after another, with a machine-like efficiency. This chain must be stopped.

Journal Topics

1. How does Schlosser's description of a cattle slaughterhouse compare to your assumptions of what such a place would be like?

2. How do you think workers at major meatpacking companies such as these can get more rights and safety?

3. What are your thoughts on the treatment of Kenny Dobbins, Raul Lopez, or Michael Glover?

Questions for Critical Thought

1. OSHA's job is to safeguard workers against hazardous work environments. In fact, Schlosser claims that OSHA's "federal safety laws were intended to protect workers from harm, regardless of the vagaries of state laws like those in Texas." However, recently the agency has drastically cut factory inspectors (only 1,200 for nearly 7 million American workplaces) and eliminated laws that protect workers. Do you think our work places are still safe? Is OSHA just responding to a new world, or does it need to re-examine how it operates?

2. Schlosser cites loss of limbs, mutilation, beheadings, head crushing, and suffocation due to toxic gasses in these meatpacking plants. These companies are under immense pressure to speed up the line, making it more hazardous to the employees. Increasing speed increases profits. What is the proper balance between limiting potentially dangerous operations and maximizing profitability? How far should governmental regulations go?

Suggestion for Personal Research

1. Look into the meat industry. Based on your research, is all of it as bad as the corporations discussed in this article, or are these just the extreme examples Schlosser uses to make his point? Consider investigating organic, kosher, free range, or "sustainable" meatpackers and ranches as well as the big corporations, such as ConAgra, IBP, and Excel.

Multicultural Issues

1. Most of the mistreated workers in the meatpacking plants are immigrants, many of them illegally in this country. Does this give corporations more of a right to abuse and mistreat them? Some people argue that they are being given a chance to make money that they otherwise would not be able to earn. Discuss.

2. If you are from another country, can you relate to the plight of the workers discussed in this article? Is living in America or making higher wages worth the danger and punishment faced by these employees?

3. If you are from another country, what were conditions for workers, including child workers, like there? How do they compare with conditions here, and how do they affect your opinion of conditions here?

Vocabulary Terms

decapitation	cumulative
vulnerable	mandatory
determinants	recuperated
laceration	waiver
carpal tunnel syndrome	despondent

Terms for Clarification

OSHA   The Occupational Safety and Health Administration is an agency of the U.S. government. Its mission is "to assure the safety and health of America's workers by setting and enforcing standards; providing training, outreach, and education; establishing partnerships; and encouraging continual improvement in workplace safety and health."

The Jungle   This is Upton Sinclair's famous novel from 1906, which provides brutal details about Chicago's slaughterhouses of 100 years ago. This book was so popular and influential it helped change safety laws and established labor unions in America.

The Unofficial History of America, from *Culture Jam*

Kalle Lasn

Prereading Question

1. In the United States, "persons" have a number of rights, such as the right against self-incrimination and the right to privacy. What legal differences do you think should exist between the rights that "persons" who are actual people should have versus "persons" that are businesses?

The history of America is the one story every kid knows. It's a story of fierce individualism and heroic personal sacrifice in the service of a dream. A story of early settlers, hungry and cold, carving a home out of the wilderness. Of visionary leaders fighting for democracy and justice, and never wavering. Of a populace prepared to defend those ideals to the death. It's the story of a revolution (an American art form as endemic as baseball or jazz) beating back British imperialism and launching a new colony into the industrial age on its own terms.

It's a story of America triumphant. A story of its rise after World War II to become the richest and most powerful country in the history of the world, "the land of the free and home of the brave," an inspiring model for the whole world to emulate.

That's the official history, the one that is taught in school and the one our media and culture reinforce in myriad ways every day.

The unofficial history of the United States is quite different. It begins the same way—in the revolutionary cauldron of colonial America—but then it takes a turn. A bit player in the official history becomes critically important to the way the unofficial history unfolds. This player turns out to be not only the provocateur of the revolution, but in the end its saboteur. This player lies at the heart of America's defining theme: the difference between a country that pretends to be free and a country that truly is free.

That player is the corporation.

The United States of America was born of a revolt not just against British monarchs and the British parliament but against British corporations.

We tend to think of corporations as fairly recent phenomena, the legacy of the Rockefellers and Carnegies. In fact, the corporate presence in prerevolutionary America was almost as conspicuous as it is today. There were far fewer corporations then, but they were enormously powerful: the Massachusetts Bay Company, the Hudson's Bay Company, the British East India Company. Colonials feared these chartered entities. They recognized the way British kings and their cronies used them as robotic arms to control the affairs of the colonies, to pinch staples from remote breadbaskets and bring them home to the motherland.

The colonials resisted. When the British East India Company imposed duties on its incoming tea (telling the locals they could buy the tea or lump it, because the company had a virtual monopoly on tea distribution in the colonies), radical patriots demonstrated. Colonial merchants agreed not to sell East India Company tea. Many East

India Company ships were turned back at port. And, on one fateful day in Boston, 342 chests of tea ended up in the salt chuck.

The Boston Tea Party was one of young America's finest hours. It sparked enormous revolutionary excitement. The people were beginning to understand their own strength, and to see their own self-determination not just as possible but inevitable.

The Declaration of Independence, in 1776, freed Americans not only from Britain but also from the tyranny of British corporations, and for a hundred years after the document's signing, Americans remained deeply suspicious of corporate power. They were careful about the way they granted corporate charters, and about the powers granted therein.

Early American charters were created literally by the people, for the people as a legal convenience. Corporations were "artificial, invisible, intangible," mere financial tools. They were chartered by individual states, not the federal government, which meant they could be kept under close local scrutiny. They were automatically dissolved if they engaged in activities that violated their charter. Limits were placed on how big and powerful companies could become. Even railroad magnate J. P. Morgan, the consummate capitalist, understood that corporations must never become so big that they "inhibit freedom to the point where efficiency [is] endangered."

The two hundred or so corporations that were operating in the U.S. by the year 1800 were each kept on a fairly short leash. They weren't allowed to participate in the political process. They couldn't buy stock in other corporations. And if one of them acted improperly, the consequences were severe. In 1832, President Andrew Jackson vetoed a motion to extend the charter of the corrupt and tyrannical Second Bank of the United States, and was widely applauded for doing so. That same year the state of Pennsylvania revoked the charters of ten banks for operating contrary to the public interest. Even the enormous industry trusts, formed to protect member corporations from external competitors and provide barriers to entry, eventually proved no match for the state. By the mid-1800s, antitrust legislation was widely in place.

In the early history of America, the corporation played an important but subordinate role. The people—not the corporations—were in control. So what happened? How did corporations gain power and eventually start exercising more control than the individuals who created them?

The shift began in the last third of the nineteenth century—the start of a great period of struggle between corporations and civil society. The turning point was the Civil War. Corporations made huge profits from procurement contracts and took advantage of the disorder and corruption of the times to buy legislatures, judges and even presidents. Corporations became the masters and keepers of business. President Abraham Lincoln foresaw terrible trouble. Shortly before his death, he warned, "Corporations have been enthroned. . . . An era of corruption in high places will follow and the money power will endeavor to prolong its reign by working on the prejudices of the people . . . until wealth is aggregated in a few hands . . . and the republic is destroyed."

President Lincoln's warning went unheeded. Corporations continued to gain power and influence. They had the laws governing their creation amended. State charters could no longer be revoked. Corporate profits could no longer be limited. Corporate economic activity could be restrained only by the courts, and in hundreds of cases judges granted corporations minor legal victories, conceding rights and privileges they did not have before.

Then came a legal event that would not be understood for decades (and remains baffling even today), an event that would change the course of American history. In *Santa Clara County v. Southern Pacific Railroad,* a dispute over a railbed route, the U.S. Supreme Court deemed that a private corporation was a "natural person" under the U.S. Constitution and therefore entitled to protection under the Bill of Rights. Suddenly, corporations enjoyed all the rights and sovereignty previously enjoyed only by the people, including the right to free speech.

This 1886 decision ostensibly gave corporations the same powers as private citizens. But considering their vast financial resources, corporations thereafter actually had far *more* power than any private citizen. They could defend and exploit their rights and freedoms more vigorously than any individual and therefore they were *more free.* In a single legal stroke, the whole intent of the American Constitution—that all citizens have one vote, and exercise an equal voice in public debates—had been undermined. Sixty years after it was inked, Supreme Court Justice William O. Douglas concluded of *Santa Clara* that it "could not be supported by history, logic or reason." One of the great legal blunders of the nineteenth century changed the whole idea of democratic government.

Post–*Santa Clara* America became a very different place. By 1919, corporations employed more than 80 percent of the workforce and produced most of America's wealth. Corporate trusts had become too powerful to legally challenge. The courts consistently favored their interests. Employees found themselves without recourse if, for example, they were injured on the job (if you worked for a corporation, you voluntarily assumed the risk, was the courts' position). Railroad and mining companies were enabled to annex vast tracts of land at minimal expense.

Gradually, many of the original ideals of the American Revolution were simply quashed. Both during and after the Civil War, America was increasingly being ruled by a coalition of government and business interests. The shift amounted to a kind of coup d'état—not a sudden military takeover but a gradual subversion and takeover of the institutions of state power. Except for a temporary setback during Franklin Roosevelt's New Deal (the 1930s), the U.S. has since been governed as a corporate state.

In the post–World War II era, corporations continued to gain power. They merged, consolidated, restructured and metamorphosed into ever larger and more complex units of resource extraction, production, distribution and marketing, to the point where many of them became economically more powerful than many countries. In 1997, fifty-one of the world's hundred largest economies were corporations, not countries. The top five hundred corporations controlled 42 percent of the world's wealth. Today, corporations freely buy each other's stocks and shares. They lobby legislators and bankroll elections. They manage our broadcast airwaves, set our industrial, economic and cultural agendas, and grow as big and powerful as they damn well please.

Every day, scenes that would have seemed surreal, impossible, undemocratic twenty years ago play out with nary a squeak of dissent from a stunned and inured populace.

At Morain Valley Community College in Palos Hills, Illinois, a student named Jennifer Beatty stages a protest against corporate sponsorship in her school by locking herself to the metal mesh curtains of the multimillion-dollar "McDonald's Student Center" that serves as the physical and nutritional focal point of her college. She is arrested and expelled.

At Greenbrier High School in Evans, Georgia, a student named Mike Cameron wears a Pepsi T-shirt on the day—dubbed "Coke Day"—when corporate flacks from Coca-Cola jet in from Atlanta to visit the school their company has sponsored and subsidized. Mike Cameron is suspended for his insolence.

In suburban shopping malls across North America, moms and dads push shopping carts down the aisle of Toys "R" Us. Trailing them and imitating their gestures, their kids push pint-size carts of their own. The carts say, "Toys 'R' Us Shopper in Training."

In St. Louis, Missouri, chemical giant Monsanto sics its legal team on anyone even considering spreading dirty lies—or dirty truths—about the company. A Fox TV affiliate that has prepared a major investigative story on the use and misuse of synthetic bovine growth hormone (a Monsanto product) pulls the piece after Monsanto attorneys threaten the network with "dire consequences" if the story airs. Later, a planned book on the dangers of genetic agricultural technologies is temporarily shelved after the publisher, fearing a lawsuit from Monsanto, gets cold feet.

In boardrooms in all the major global capitals, CEOs of the world's biggest corporations imagine a world where they are protected by what is effectively their own global charter of rights and freedoms—the Multinational Agreement on Investment (MAI). They are supported in this vision by the World Trade Organization (WTO), the World Bank, the International Monetary Fund (IMF), the International Chamber of Commerce (ICC), the European Round Table of Industrialists (ERT), the Organization for Economic Co-operation and Development (OECD) and other organizations representing twenty-nine of the world's richest economies. The MAI would effectively create a single global economy allowing corporations the unrestricted right to buy, sell and move their businesses, resources and other assets wherever and whenever they want. It's a corporate bill of rights designed to override all "nonconforming" local, state and national laws and regulations and allow them to sue cities, states and national governments for alleged noncompliance. Sold to the world's citizens as inevitable and necessary in an age of free trade, those MAI negotiations met with considerable grassroots opposition and were temporarily suspended in April 1998. Nevertheless, no one believes this initiative will remain suspended for long.

We, the people, have lost control. Corporations, these legal fictions that we ourselves created two centuries ago, now have more rights, freedoms and powers than we do. And we accept this as the normal state of affairs. We go to corporations on our knees. *Please* do the right thing, we plead. *Please* don't cut down any more ancient forests. *Please* don't pollute any more lakes and rivers (but please don't move your factories and jobs offshore either). *Please* don't use pornographic images to sell fashion to my kids. *Please* don't play governments off against each other to get a better deal. We've spent so much time bowed down in deference, we've forgotten how to stand up straight.

The unofficial history of America™, which continues to be written, is not a story of rugged individualism and heroic personal sacrifice in the pursuit of a dream. It is a story of democracy derailed, of a revolutionary spirit suppressed, and of a once-proud people reduced to servitude.

Journal Topics

1. Lasn claims the American Revolution was "born of a revolt not just against British monarchs and the British parliament but against British corporations." How does this change your perception of the Revolutionary War? Would it be possible to "revolt" against modern-day corporations?

2. Are you surprised by the difference between how corporations used to be treated and watched versus their rights currently?

Questions for Critical Thought

1. The court case *Santa Clara County v. Southern Pacific Railroad* redefined corporate entities and gave them the same legal rights as human beings. Should this be allowed? Is there something wrong with a system that allows billion-dollar industries the same rights as actual people, or is this just a natural extension of capitalism?

2. Abraham Lincoln warned shortly before his death that "[c]orporations have been enthroned. . . . An era of corruption in high places will follow and the money power will endeavor to prolong its reign by working on the prejudices of the people . . . until wealth is aggregated in a few hands . . . and the republic is destroyed." Discuss this warning. Has any of what Lincoln warned of come true?

3. Lasn ends his piece saying the story of America is "a story of democracy derailed, or a revolutionary spirit suppressed, and of a once-proud people reduced to servitude." Does he exaggerate, or have corporations really done this to us?

Suggestion for Personal Research

1. Lasn mentions several schools that have made strong alliances with corporations (even expelling students for challenging their corporate friends). Research and find several other instances of public places (sporting arenas, for example) and schools (including colleges and universities) which make deals and sell public space to corporations. Start in your own home town, and see what you find.

Multicultural Issues

1. If you are from another country, do some research and investigate the history of corporations in that country. How much power do they have? When did they get this level of power? How much influence do they have on laws and governance?

2. Research the influence of corporations on other countries. If you are an American, what foreign corporations hold a great deal of influence in the United States? If you are from another country, what American and other foreign corporations have an impact on the quality of life in your native land?

Vocabulary Terms

individualism

populace

imperialism

industrial age

provocateur

saboteur

intangible

magnate

aggregated

ostensibly

annex

coup d'état

metamorphosed

inured

grassroots

servitude

Term for Clarification

Rockefellers and Carnegies Two extremely wealthy and influential families in American history.

Business As Usual, from *The Corporation*

Joel Bakan

Prereading Question

1. Do you think corporations should try to clean up the neighborhoods in which their factories and headquarters are located? Do they owe anything to their communities?

Business leaders today say their companies care about more than profit and loss, that they feel responsible to society as a whole, not just to their shareholders. Corporate social responsibility is their new creed, a self-conscious corrective to earlier greed-inspired visions of the corporation. Despite this shift, the corporation itself has not changed. It remains, as it was at the time of its origins as a modern business institution in the middle of the nineteenth century, a legally designated "person" designed to valorize self-interest and invalidate moral concern. Most people would find its "personality" abhorrent, even psychopathic, in a human being, yet curiously we accept it in society's most powerful institution. The troubles on Wall Street today, beginning with Enron's spectacular crash, can be blamed in part on the corporation's flawed institutional character, but the company was not unique for having that character. Indeed, all publicly traded corporations have it, even the most respected and socially responsible among them, such as Pfizer Inc.

In 1849, Charles Pfizer and his cousin Charles Erhart established a small chemical firm in Williamsburg, then a rural section of Brooklyn accessible from Manhattan only by boat. Over the last century and a half the firm, Pfizer Inc., has prospered and become the world's largest pharmaceutical company. Williamsburg, now linked to Manhattan by bridges and tunnels, also prospered, then declined, and now, at least in part because of Pfizer, it has enjoyed something of a revival.

On a recent summer afternoon, Tom Kline, a senior vice president at Pfizer, took a documentary film crew on a walkabout tour of the inner-city neighborhood that now surrounds his company's original plant in Williamsburg. A tall white man in late middle age, dressed in neat blue slacks and a matching wrinkle-free short-sleeved shirt, Kline looked conspicuous in this predominantly low-income neighborhood, but he clearly felt at home here. (During the tour he greeted strangers on the street as if they were old friends, promising one woman that "working with you and Pfizer and our other partnerships, we'll make this a better place" and saying "Love you" to another person after a brief conversation.) The tour commenced at the Flushing Avenue subway station, whose stairwell entrance lies just across the street from the entrance to Pfizer's plant. Kline explained how he had almost been mugged on the subway station's platform one evening in the early 1980s as he waited for a train to take him home from the plant, where he then worked as plant manager. He had fled from the would-be muggers, made it safely to the far side of the tracks, and hid there terrified but oddly inspired by his plight to do something about the spiral of crime and drugs that was ruining the neighborhood. He had decided, at that perilous moment, to scuttle Pfizer's recently devised plan to close the plant and instead work "to make a change to make this community better."

Today the plant is still open, and thanks to Kline and Pfizer, the subway station is safer. Kline showed the film crew a yellow box attached to the wall of a designated waiting area on the subway platform. The box is connected to a sophisticated security system, financed and maintained by Pfizer, which allows threatened subway patrons to summon help from Pfizer security guards at the nearby plant. Down the block from the station, at Pfizer's original corporate headquarters, there is a children's school, developed by Kline, and partly funded by the company. Though the school is officially part of the New York City public school system, principal Sonia Gerrardo explained that the "children really have an ongoing relationship with the company" through Pfizer mentors and volunteers. There is also a middle-income housing development in the neighborhood, spearheaded by the company's Redevelopment Program and administered jointly with the city.

Kline believes that "if we really want to improve the conditions of American cities, we business people . . . have to take responsibility," and his actions show that these are not empty words. As Hank McKinnell, chairman and CEO of Pfizer, said, Kline is "the driving force behind the rejuvenation of a very devastated inner city area."

McKinnell, however, wants Pfizer to do more than just save cities. "Pfizer can be the company which does more good for more people than any other company on the planet," he said. Every year his company donates hundreds of millions of dollars' worth of products and cash around the globe, making it, it claims, "one of America's most generous companies." McKinnell is especially proud of the company's work to end trachoma, an infection that blinds eight to ten million people every year. Pfizer produces Zithromax, a drug that prevents trachoma with just a single dose per year, and donates it to African countries. McKinnell claims that the drug has cut the infection rate in Africa in half and could eliminate the disease altogether by the year 2020. "We at Pfizer never stop looking for innovative solutions to society's problems," the company proclaims on its Web site. "Whether it's donating medicine to people in need or lending employees to local schools [or] rebuilding our first neighborhood . . . we are dedicated to our company purpose: helping people around the world live healthier, more productive lives."

Corporations have always been philanthropic. They have donated to charities, sponsored Little League teams, and helped to build theaters. Traditionally, such generosity was quietly practiced and peripheral to their main goal of making money. Now, however, large corporations such as Pfizer have put corporate good deeds at the core of their business plans. A sense of responsibility to society, not just to a company's shareholders, has come to define the very nature of the corporation, what it is supposed to be and what it must and cannot do. Corporations are now often expected to deliver the good, not just the goods; to pursue values, not just value; and to help make the world a better place.

During the 1980s, testosterone-fueled corporate slashers such as Sunbeam's "Chainsaw" Al Dunlap, who once posed on a magazine cover wielding a machine gun to symbolize his take-no-prisoners approach to management, were cheered as heroes and fearless knights of the bottom line. These men now seem like barbarians, uncouth and uncool, as ridiculous as their red suspenders. Today's leading CEOs cultivate compassion and seem genuinely concerned about how their corporations' actions affect social and environmental interests, not just their stockholders'; they say they are obliged to meet social and environmental bottom lines, not just the financial one. As Goodyear Tire's Samir Gibara explained, today "the corporation is much broader than just its shareholders. . . . The corporation has many more constituencies and needs to address all these needs." Its obligations are no longer limited to making money for investors but, according to William Ford, Jr., chairman of the Ford Motor Company and great-grandson of corporate social responsibility pioneer Henry Ford, "corporations could be and should be a major force for resolving environmental and social concerns in the twenty-first century."

Former Harvard business scholar Ira Jackson believes that such attitudes herald the start of an entirely new stage of capitalism, what he calls "capitalism with a conscience." There is much evidence to support his view. Corporations now boast about social and environmental initiatives on their Web sites and in their annual reports. Entire departments and executive positions are devoted to these initiatives. The business press runs numerous features on social responsibility and ranks corporations on how good they are at it. Business schools launch new courses on social responsibility, and universities create centers devoted to its study (at the University of Nottingham, tobacco giant ABT donated $7 million to create an International Centre for Corporate Social Responsibility). Social responsibility is on the agenda wherever business leaders meet—at the World Economic Forum in Davos, Switzerland, WTO ministerial meetings, industry conferences, and international trade and investment summits—and corporations compete against one another for ever higher moral ground.

Pious social responsibility themes now vie with sex for top billing in corporate advertising, whether on television or in the pages of glossy magazines and newspapers. A recent television advertisement by Shell is typical. It shows self-styled "romantic" environmentalist Frances Abbots-Guardiola flying around beautiful mountains and lakes in a helicopter and talking to aboriginal people in grass-roofed huts. She eyes skeptically a convoy of heavy dump trucks lumbering across the pristine landscape. "This woman is trying to protect a fragile environment from being destroyed by oil and gas," a lyrical Scottish-accented narrator tells us (she must be one of those anticorporate Greenpeace types, we think). "Despite that, she's not at war with the oil company. She *is* the oil company"—a Shell geologist, we learn.

The message is clear, as is that of legions of similar advertisements: corporations care about the environment and communities, not just the soulless pursuit of profit; they are part of the solution to world ills, not the cause; they are allies of governments and nongovernmental organizations, not enemies.

Just a few years ago, says Jackson, "you'd have been laughed out of the office, if not escorted out by an armed guard" for suggesting to a CEO that his corporation should abide by the UN Universal Declaration of Human Rights. Yet recently in New York, a hundred CEOs from the world's largest corporations met with their counterparts from NGOs such as Greenpeace and Amnesty International, along with national ambassadors, to sign a promise to adhere to the general principles of the Universal Declaration of Human Rights. This is just one example, says Jackson, of the new corporate order of conscience. He, along with many other business pundits, applauds big-business leaders who embrace the values of corporate social responsibility and predicts failure for those who do not:

Even President Bush now says that corporate responsibility is a fundamental business value, indeed a patriotic duty. "America is ushering in a responsibility era, a culture regaining a sense of personal responsibility," he told a group of top business leaders in a speech addressing Enron's collapse, "and this new culture must include a renewed sense of corporate responsibility. . . . Business relationships, like all human relationships, are built on a foundation of integrity and trust."

Not everyone, however, is convinced of corporate social responsibility's virtue. Milton Friedman, for one, a Nobel laureate and one of the world's most eminent economists, believes the new moralism in business is in fact immoral.

When Friedman granted me an interview, his secretary warned that he would get up and walk out of the room if he found my questions dull. So I was apprehensive as I waited for him in the lobby of his building. This must be how Dorothy felt, I thought, just before Toto pulled back the curtain to reveal the real Wizard of Oz. Friedman is an intellectual giant, revered and feared, deified and vilified, larger than life. So I felt some relief when he entered the room smiling, a charming little man who, like the wizard himself, barely broke five feet. Friedman surveyed the lobby, now a chaotic makeshift television studio (the interview was for a government-funded TV documentary). Lights and cameras cluttered the room, tangles of wire covered the floor. Two crew members stood ready, cotton balls in hand, to remove the shine on the great man's nose. Bemused, Friedman curmudgeonized, "ABC came in here the other day with two guys and one camera. Here we see government fat and waste at its worst."

Friedman thinks that corporations are good for society (and that too much government is bad). He recoils, however, at the idea that corporations should try to *do* good for society. "A corporation is the property of its stockholders," he told me. "Its interests are the interests of its stockholders. Now, beyond that should it spend the stockholders' money for purposes which it regards as socially responsible but which it cannot connect to its bottom line? The answer I would say is no." There is but one "social responsibility" for corporate executives, Friedman believes: they must make as much money as possible for their shareholders. This is a moral imperative. Executives who choose social and environmental goals over profits—who try to act morally—are, in fact, immoral.

There is, however, one instance when corporate social responsibility can be tolerated, according to Friedman—when it is insincere. The executive who treats social and environmental values as means to maximize shareholders' wealth—not as ends in themselves—commits no wrong. It's like "putting a good-looking girl in front of an automobile to sell an automobile," he told me. "That's not in order to promote pulchritude. That's in order to sell cars." Good intentions, like good-looking girls, can sell goods. It's true, Friedman acknowledges, that this purely strategic view of social responsibility reduces lofty ideals to "hypocritical window dressing." But hypocrisy is virtuous when it serves the bottom line. Moral virtue is immoral when it does not.

Though Friedman's views are rejected by many sophisticated businesspeople, who think his brand of cynicism is old-fashioned, mean-spirited, and out of touch with reality, his suspicion of corporate social responsibility attracts some weighty support. William Niskanen, a former Ford economist and now chairman of the Cato Institute, said he "would not invest in a firm that pioneered in corporate social responsibility."

"I think Ford Motor Company still makes fine cars and trucks," he continued, "but I think the [socially responsible] actions by the new Mr. Ford are likely to undermine the value of the corporation to the owners." Peter Drucker, the guru of all business gurus, who believes that Friedman is "probably our greatest living economist," echoes his view that corporate social responsibility is a dangerous distortion of business principles. "If you find an executive who wants to take on social responsibilities," Drucker said, "fire him. Fast." Harvard Business School professor Debora Spar insisted that corporations "are not institutions that are set up to be moral entities. . . . They are institutions which have really only one mission, and that is to increase shareholder value." And Noam Chomsky—Friedman's intellectual and ideological nemesis—shares his view that corporations must "be concerned only for their stockholders and . . . not the community or the workforce or whatever."

Corporations are created by law and imbued with purpose by law. Law dictates what their directors and managers can do, what they cannot do, and what they must do. And, at least in the United States and other industrialized countries, the corporation, as created by law, most closely resembles Milton Friedman's ideal model of the institution: it compels executives to prioritize the interests of their companies and shareholders above all others and forbids them from being socially responsible—at least genuinely so.

In 1916, Henry Ford learned this legal lesson the hard way and unwittingly helped entrench the law's intolerance of corporate social responsibility.

Ford believed that his Ford Motor Company could be more than just a profit machine. He paid his workers substantially more than the going rate at the time and rewarded customers with yearly price cuts on his Model T cars (their original price of more than $900 was slashed to $440 by 1916). "I do not believe that we should make such awful profits on our cars," he is reported to have said. "A reasonable profit is right, but not too much."

John and Horace Dodge had helped Ford establish his company in 1906 with a $10,500 investment. They were major shareholders, and John Dodge became a director of the company. The brothers had also pledged that their Chicago machine shop would make parts exclusively for Ford, having turned down overtures from the more established Oldsmobile company. By 1916, however, the Dodge brothers had larger ambitions. John Dodge quit the Ford board and devised a plan with his brother to build their own car company. They hoped to finance the venture with the quarterly dividends from their Ford shares but were stopped by Ford's decision to cancel the dividend and divert the money to customers in the form of further price reductions on Model T automobiles. The Dodge brothers took Ford to court. Profits belong to shareholders, they argued, and Ford had no right to give their money away to customers, however good his intentions. The judge agreed. He reinstated the dividend and rebuked Ford—who had said in open court that "business is a service, not a bonanza" and that corporations should be run only "incidentally to make money"—for forgetting that "a business corporation is organized and carried on primarily for the profit of the stockholders"; it could not be run "for the merely incidental benefit of shareholders and for the primary purpose of benefiting others."

Dodge v. Ford still stands for the legal principle that managers and directors have a legal duty to put shareholders' interests above all others and no legal authority to serve any other interests—what has come to be known as "the best interests of the corporation" principle. That principle provided a legal fix to a flaw in the corporate form that had famously worried Adam Smith 140 years before *Dodge v. Ford* was decided. Smith, in his 1776 classic, *The Wealth of Nations,* said he was troubled by the fact that corporations' owners, their shareholders, did not run their own businesses but delegated that task to professional managers. The latter could not be trusted to apply the same "anxious vigilance" to manage "other people's money" as they would their own, he wrote, and "negligence and profusion therefore must prevail, more or less, in the management of such a company."

The "best interests of the corporation" principle, now a fixture in the corporate laws of most countries, addresses Smith's concern by compelling corporate decision makers always to act in the best interests of the corporation, and hence its owners. The law forbids any other motivation for their actions, whether to assist workers, improve the environment, or help consumers save money. They can do these things with their own money, as private citizens. As corporate officials, however, stewards of other people's money, they have no legal authority to pursue such goals as ends in themselves—only as means to serve the corporation's own interests, which generally means to maximize the wealth of its shareholders.

Corporate social responsibility is thus illegal—at least when it is genuine.

Corporate lawyer Robert Hinkley quit his job at international legal powerhouse Skadden, Arps when he realized, after twenty-three years in practice, "that the law, in its current form, actually inhibits executives and corporations from being socially responsible." As he puts it:

> [T]he corporate design contained in hundreds of corporate laws throughout the world is nearly identical . . . the people who run corporations have a legal duty to shareholders, and that duty is to make money. Failing this duty can leave directors and officers open to being sued by shareholders. [The law] dedicates the corporation to the pursuit of its own self-interest (and equates corporate self-interest with shareholder self-interest). No mention is made of responsibility to the public interest. . . . Corporate law thus casts ethical and social concerns as irrelevant, or as stumbling blocks to the corporation's fundamental mandate.

Does this mean that the big corporations that now embrace social responsibility— Pfizer, Ford, Goodyear, BP, to name just a few—are outlaws? Not exactly. Recall Milton Friedman's belief that social responsibility can be tolerated when in the service of corporate self-interest. On this point, the law again agrees with him.

Hutton v. West Cork Railway Company, a case from nineteenth-century England, established the relevant principle. One company, Bandon, had bought another, West Cork Railway. When West Cork announced a bonus of several thousand pounds to its soon-to-be redundant directors, Bandon's shareholders took the railway to court. The money from which the bonus would be drawn now belonged to them, they argued, and it could not be used to benefit others, i.e., the West Cork directors. Lord Bowen, one of the judges who heard the case, agreed with their claim, but he also insisted that corporate generosity was, in some cases, permissible under the law. "Take this sort of instance," he wrote. "A railway company, or the directors of the company, might send down all the porters at a railway station to have tea in the country at the expense of the company. Why should they not?" After all, Lord Bowen observed, the company might itself derive considerable benefit from such generosity in light of the fact that "a company which always treated its employees with Draconian severity, and never allowed them a single inch more than the strict letter of the bond, would soon find itself deserted." Hence, Lord Bowen concluded.

> The law does not say that there are to be no cakes and ale, but there are to be no cakes and ale except such as are required for the benefit of the company . . . charity has no business to sit at boards of directors *qua* charity. There is, however, a kind of charitable dealing which is for the interest of those who practise it, and to that extent and in that garb (I admit not a very philanthropic garb) charity may sit at the board, but for no other purpose.

Today the law remains the same: charitable dealing must be in the interest of those who practice it—the corporation and its shareholders. "While allowing directors to give consideration to the interests of others," states the American Bar Association, "[the law] compel[s] them to find some reasonable relationship to the long-term interests of shareholders when so doing." The rule is now thoroughly entrenched within the corporation's culture, so it is a rare case when shareholders must resort to the courts to enforce it, as the Dodge brothers had to do in 1916. As Burson-Marsteller head Chris Komisarjevsky put it, "The expectations of investors, whether they're institutional or individual, will always make sure that the driving force is to make sure that we produce the profits, we produce the returns and therefore give back to the investors. So there's rarely going to be a situation where philanthropy or corporate giving will undermine the corporate performance from a financial perspective."

The rule that corporations exist solely to maximize returns to their shareholders is "the law of the land," to quote business journalist Marjorie Kelly, "universally accepted as a kind of divine, unchallengeable truth." And, today, even the most inspired leaders of the corporate social responsibility movement obey it.

Journal Topic

1. If several of the world's largest corporations decided to spend money and time trying to clean up the environment, solve world hunger, or help cure AIDS, how much good do you think they could do?

Questions for Critical Thought

1. Bakan argues that a corporation's main reason for existing is simply to make money for the stockholders, not to care about the environment, workers, or people living near their factories. In fact, businessman Peter Drucker says, "If you find a executive who wants to take on social responsibility, fire him. Fast." Should corporations worry about the world in which they exist, or should they simply worry about making more money?

2. The Pfizer Corporation built a school near its corporate headquarters, provided security for a dangerous subway route, and helped spearhead a housing development in the neighborhood. However, it may have done this only as a public relations move, not out of any true compassion for the people involved. Do these good deeds, if motivated by selfish objectives (such as public relations or the profit motive), remain "good"?

Suggestions for Personal Research

1. Develop a set of criteria that you think consumers can use to evaluate the objectivity and honesty of sources operating as spokespeople, experts, etc. Find biographical information on some of the businesspeople and professors that Bakan quotes: Tom Kline (Pfizer), Al Dunlap (Sunbeam), Samir Bigara (Goodyear), Ira Jackson (Harvard), Milton Friedman (Nobel laureate), Peter Drucker (business "guru"), William Niskanen (Ford/Cato Institute), Debora Spar (Harvard), and Noam Chomsky (MIT). Using the criteria that you have devised, evaluate the relative trustworthiness of these people.

2. In 1989, after an oil tanker called the *Exxon Valdez* hit a reef, 11 million gallons of crude oil were released and spread over 13,000 miles of coastline in Alaska's Prince William Sound. Commercial fisheries were closed, and thousands of marine mammals and hundreds of thousands of seabirds were killed. In 2007, the plaintiffs in the legal case initiated after the oil spill—more than 30,000 individuals, including fishermen, Alaska natives, property owners, and others who suffered harm—asked the U.S. Supreme Court to reinstate the full $5 billion punitive fine initially imposed on Exxon (now ExxonMobil) in 1994. The fine was cut in half by the 9th Circuit Court of Appeals, and ExxonMobil filed a petition asking to drop the remaining punitive fine. Attorneys for the plaintiffs have accused the company of mounting a series of legal challenges to the original verdict simply to prolong the case and potentially have it dropped even though record earnings made the company quite able to pay the entire fine. Research this case and the legal arguments made on both sides. Where is the case now? What did the Supreme Court decide?

3. In 1984, more than forty tons of toxic chemicals leaked from Union Carbide's pesticide factory in a poor neighborhood in Bhopal, India, exposing half a million people and killing thousands. It is still considered the worst industrial disaster in history. Ten years later, an estimated 50,000 people were still partially or totally disabled. Union Carbide's lawyers successfully shifted the lawsuits from American courts, where they felt that juries would be more likely to award large punitive damages, to Indian courts. The Indian Government initially asked Union Carbide for $3 billion, but it eventually settled for $470 million in 1989 when it was trying to improve relations with foreign investors. Union Carbide claims the plant was sabotaged, but cost-cutting measures that increased profits disabled safety procedures essential to prevent or alert employees of disasters. The battle over liability is still being fought in courts. Where is the fight now?

What suits did the plaintiffs win? What suits did the company win? Who owns the company now?

4. In 1985, a year after the Bhopal disaster, another Union Carbide plant leaked clouds of toxic gas. This leak, which affected four communities and caused the hospitalization of more than 100 people, happened in West Virginia. This accident and the one at Bhopal caused enough concern to lead to the Emergency Planning and Community Right to Know Act, passed by the U.S. Congress in 1986. Research this act. What rights does it give to communities and individuals? How successful has it been? What practices have been changed since its passage?

Multicultural Issues

1. If you are from another country, can you think of any corporations that have helped to clean up neighborhoods or the environment there? If so, who was it, and what has it done to help?

2. If you are from another country, can you think of any corporations that have harmed or abused the environment, workers, or the neighborhoods their factories are in? If so, who were they, and what did they do?

Vocabulary Terms

valorize

invalidate

abhorrent

predominantly

perilous

scuttle

philanthropic

uncouth

constituencies

herald

pious

legions

pundits

deified

vilified

bemused

pulchritude

shareholder/stockholder

draconian

Industrial Diarrhea, *from* Affluenza

John DeGraaf, David Wann, and Thomas H. Naylor

Prereading Questions

1. In their article, DeGraaf, Wann, and Naylor say that we all grew up with the Green Giant, Joe Camel, the Marlboro Man, the Energizer Bunny, and Ronald McDonald, assuming an American audience—and one of a certain age range. What are the advertising icons of your youth? What characters do you best remember, and why? Did they inspire loyalty to particular brands and products?

2. Do you worry about buying products that might contain chemicals that are bad for your health? Do you ever read labels to see just what's in the products you consume?

DDT is good for me!

—1950s JINGLE

The chemical age has created products, institutions and cultural attitudes that require synthetic chemicals to sustain them.

—THEO COLBURN ET AL., OUR STOLEN FUTURE

Imagine spotting them through binoculars at a baseball game—the all-stars of advertising, sitting together in front row seats behind home plate. There's the Marlboro Man and Joe Camel, signing autographs and passing out smokes to the kids. The Energizer Bunny flings handfuls of potentially toxic batteries into the crowd like Tootsie Rolls, while Ronald McDonald argues defensively with an environmentalist about hormones, antibiotics, and pesticide residues now being detected in the Big Mac. The Green Giant looks down on the game from the parking lot, ho-hoing every time the home team scores. No one messes with a guy that size, even though chunks of pesticide slough off his green body like gigantic flakes of dry skin. (Look out, here comes another one!)

They all seem so innocent, don't they—so American? We grew up with these guys, and we love their optimism, their goofiness, and their cool. Our demand for their products keeps the U.S. economy cranking at a feverishly giddy pace, and it can't be denied that America's dazzling products make life seem bright, shiny, and convenient. But with a steady diet of this stuff, we risk serious damage to our environment and to our health. Many of die goods we buy contain toxic "bads" such as dangerous chemicals hidden from plain view, but for some reason, we don't want to believe that.

The Generation of Surprises

We don't want to believe that cigarettes now kill more than 430,000 Americans annually, wiping out *five million years of potential life each year*. That radiation from nuclear power—once thought to be "too cheap to meter"—really does destroy DNA and cause cancer, and has obliterated a handful of bioregions, effectively forever. That one tiny particle of dioxin transmitted to a fetus at the wrong time could permanently disrupt the unborn child's reproductive system. That between 1940 and 1995 the production of synthetic chemicals increased 600 times—we now produce 1,600 pounds a year per capita. And that two out of every five Americans will contract cancer at some point in their lives, including increasing percentages of children.[1]

"Americans have a tradition of trusting manufacturers," said Dr. Suzanne Wuerthele, a toxicologist in EPA's Denver office. "Ever since the days of the flour mill, the small leather-tanning company, and the blacksmith, products have been assumed innocent until proven guilty—just the opposite of the way it should be. We've worked within an 'acceptable risk' strategy. Industry's stance is, 'Show me the dead bodies, or else let me make my product the way I want to.' When a disaster happens, industry begins to respond, and sometimes not even then."

As Wuerthele points out, the track record for synthetic chemicals is laced with unpleasant surprises. From nuclear radiation and CFCs to the various chlorinated hydrocarbon pesticides, we're always playing catch up, finding out about health and ecological effects after it's too late. The most recent surprise is that genetically engineered organisms can migrate into the environment, even when they're engineered into the cells of plants. For example, pollen from genetically engineered corn plants migrates to plants like milkweed, where it has been shown to kill the "Bambis" of the insect world—Monarch butterflies. That shouldn't have caught the corporate and government scientists by surprise—with hundreds of thousands of acres of genetically engineered corn already planted—but it did."[2]

We typically assume that somebody else is minding the shop, making sure all these chemicals are safe. Yet the truth is that out of 75,000 chemicals now in common commercial use, only about 1,200 to 1,500 have been tested for carcinogenicity. Dr. Sandra Steingraber writes in her book *Living Downstream,* "The vast majority of commercially used chemicals were brought to market before 1979, when federal legislation mandated the review of new chemicals. Thus many carcinogenic environmental contaminants likely remain unidentified, unmonitored, and unregulated."[3]

Steingraber, herself a victim of bladder cancer, recalls the advertising blitz for DDT, a product that returned home victorious from World War II after protecting American soldiers from malaria and other diseases overseas. "In one ad," writes Steingraber, "children splash in a swimming pool while DDT is sprayed above the water. In another, an aproned housewife in stiletto heels and a pith helmet aims a spray gun at two giant cockroaches standing on her kitchen counter. They raise their front legs in surrender. The caption reads, 'Super Ammunition for the Continued Battle on the Home Front."[4]

DDT was seen as a harmless pal, despite the fact that by the time those ads appeared, biologists had already documented that the chemical killed birds and fish, disrupted the reproductive systems of laboratory animals, created population explosions of pests with newly evolved resistance, and showed strong signs of causing cancer. By 1951, DDT had become a contaminant of human breast milk and was known to pass from mother to child.

Yet DDT continued to be seen as an "elixir" until Rachel Carson's book *Silent Spring* put the spotlight on birds with convulsions, twitching to death under the elm tree. Since the time of those DDT ads, cancer has become an epidemic in slow motion.

Cancers of the brain, liver, breast, kidney, prostate, esophagus, skin, bone marrow, and lymph have all escalated in the past fifty years, while the incidence of cancer increased by more than fifty percent.

The use of chemicals like DDT seemed justified at first. After all, the use of other pesticides has played a role in the low prices Americans pay for food. (As a percentage of income, we have the world's cheapest food.) But what hidden costs do we pay?

Accidental Concoctions

Ever since the days of alchemy, the field of chemistry has suffered from a tragic flaw: its isolation from the field of biology. Humans were deploying technology long before they understood what causes disease, or how living things interrelate. Sir Isaac Newton may have discovered gravity, but he didn't seem to have a clue that the heavy metals he experimented with could kill him. In a 1692 letter to colleague John Locke, he blamed insomnia, depression, poor digestion, amnesia, and paranoia on "sleeping too often by my fire." We found out otherwise 300 years later, when scientists analyzed a lock of his hair, passed along as a family heirloom. The hair was a repository of lead, arsenic, antimony, and mercury molecules from his alchemy experiments. Carefully recorded in his logs were descriptions of the *taste* of each chemical. Little did he know the gravity of his actions.

Even when a toxic cause-and-effect connection was made, our ancestors often adopted a policy of "acceptable risk." Mercury was mined in Spain as far back as 400 B.C., despite severe health effects like chronically bleeding gums, dementia, and eventual death. In that case, the risks were deemed acceptable because convicts and slaves did the mining.

While the benefits accrue only to those who sell or use the products, the risks are often spread among the whole population. Chemicals, if profitable, are deemed innocent until alarming evidence proves otherwise. For example, workers in a pesticide factory didn't realize that their exposure to Kepone was sterilizing them until they sat around the lunch table talking about a common inability to start a family.

Better Living Through Chemistry?

As America's economy grew at rates never seen in human history, millions of chemical compounds were brought into the world. Most did not find immediate uses, but a century's worth of tinkering created an alphabet soup of persistent molecules that hang around in our world like uninvited guests. Many of these ingredients are incorporated into familiar products like detergents, varnishes, plastics, fingernail polish, bug spray, and pharmaceuticals, as well as behind-the-scenes industrial products like degreasers and plasticizers.

A new chemical substance is discovered every nine seconds of the working day, as the "invisible hand of the market" continues to call forth legions of them, like a throng of marching broomsticks straight out of "The Sorcerer's Apprentice." It's become impossible to call them off and, as a consequence, we're living in a sea of our own waste products. Scientists call them PBTs—Persistant Bioaccumulative Toxins. We're exposed to chemicals in consumer products and in the workplace. We're also bombarded by invisible particles that escape into our water, the air in our houses, and the living tissue in our bodies. There is no place on Earth that does not contain runaway molecules. "Tree bark sampled from more than ninety sites around the world found that DDT, chlordane and dieldrin were present no matter how remote the area," writes Ann Platt McGinn in *State of the World 2000.*[5]

If we had microscopic vision, we might get outdoors a bit more—where the air is cleaner—because the horrors we'd see in our own houses would send us running. We'd see microscopic bits of plastics, carpet fibers, and pesticides disappear into the nostrils of family members, and never come back out! Because of all the chemicals contained in our everyday products, indoor pollution levels can be two to 100 times higher than those found outdoors, especially now that homes are more tightly sealed for energy efficiency and air-conditioning.

Nowhere to Run

David and Mary Pinkerton were trusting souls. They were buying a "dream house" in Missouri, and they liked to walk through the construction site after work, to see the house taking shape. On one visit just before moving in, David noticed a health warning printed on the sub-flooring that had been put in their new house. Irritation of the eyes and upper respiratory system could result from exposure to the chemicals in the plywood. But David trusted the builder. "He makes a living building houses. He wouldn't put anything in there that would hurt anybody."

"Within a month," write the authors of *Toxic Deception,* "the three girls and their parents had grown quite ill. David would sit in an old overstuffed chair until supper was ready; after dinner he would usually go right to bed. . . . One night Mary tried to make dinner and David found her leaning against the wall with the skillet in her hand. . . . All five had bouts of vomiting and diarrhea that would wake them up, almost nightly. Brenda no longer wanted to go to dance classes, even though ballet had been 'her big thing in life,' Mary later recalled."[6]

After the family was forced to evacuate the house within six months of moving in, a state environmental inspector found ten parts per million of formaldehyde in the house, many times higher than the standard.

As many as forty million Americans may be allergic to their own homes, according to the American Lung Association. Fifteen million of us have become allergic just in the last five years, bombarded by chemicals in paint fumes, cleaning products, particleboard, plastics, glues, wallpaper, cosmetics, and a hundred other standard products of the twenty-first century.

Dead Zones

Scientists *do* have microscopic vision, and with new-millennium equipment they are now finding toxic chemicals wherever they look. The average American hosts up to 500 different chemicals in his or her body. Among the most exotic of the chemicals now being found in waterways are refugees from the American lifestyle: trace amounts of pain relievers, antibiotics, birth control pills, perfumes, codeine, antacids, cholesterol-lowering agents, antidepressants, estrogen replacement drugs, chemotherapy agents, sunscreen lotions, and hormones from animal feed lots. These compounds survive the assault of sewage treatment's microbes, aeration, and chlorination, and eventually show up unannounced in drinking water.

With reports of pesticide, lead, and other industrial compounds gracing the front pages of newspapers across the country, it's no wonder per-capita consumption of bottled water increased by a whopping 900 percent between 1977 and 1997. Yet the Natural Resources Defense Council advises that bottled water, at up to 1,000 times the cost of tap water, is not only expensive but somewhat suspicious. At least a third of the bottled water on the market is just packaged tap water, and another twenty-five percent contains traces of chemical contaminants.

"In the past we looked for the really toxic actors that have immediate effects like death or cancer," said Edward Furlong, a chemist with the U.S. Geological Survey.[7] "Now we're starting to look more closely at compounds whose effects are more subtle and less easily identified." To his surprise, Furlong discovered what he calls "The Starbucks Effect," an indicator that caffeine may be giving aquatic life an unsolicited buzz. In addition to being a basic fuel of the American lifestyle (twenty-four gallons a year per capita), caffeine is a very persistent and detectable compound. Just as it often persists in our bloodstreams when we try to sleep, it also lingers in our rivers and streams. These findings are only the most recent in a series of aquatic conundrums presented by our affluent, often oblivious civilization. How long can an economy boom without adequate supplies of drinking water?

A decade or so ago, fishermen began reporting a "dead zone" in the Gulf of Mexico, where their nets always come up empty and their lines never record a strike. By the time the Mississippi River reaches the Gulf of Mexico, it contains enough pesticides, wasted nutrients (from eroded farm soil), and petrochemicals to poison a body of water the size of New Jersey. Luxury cruise ships in the Gulf add insult to critical injury by dumping raw sewage and other wastes into open waters. Because of regulatory loopholes, cruise ships can legally discharge "graywater" (used water that doesn't contain human wastes) anywhere, and can dump human waste and ground-up food when they're more than three miles from shore. On a weeklong voyage a typical Carnival or Royal Caribbean cruise ship with 3,000 passengers and crew members generates eight tons of garbage, one million gallons of gray water, 25,000 gallons of oil-contaminated water, and 200,000 gallons of sewage.[8] Scuba diving, anyone?

Deadly Mimicry

The surprises just keep coming, some of them involving other dead zones, in the Great Lakes, the Arctic, and, potentially, even the human womb. Like evidence in a gruesome criminal case, the mounting data tells us more than we really want to know. Scientist and author Theo Colburn compiled thousands of data sets spanning three decades. The data report chaos and dysfunction in the natural world: male alligators with stunted sex organs; roosters that didn't crow; eagles that didn't build nests to take care of their young; "gay" female seagulls that nested together because males weren't interested; whales with both male and female sex organs; and other cases of "sexual confusion."

Though she knew that chemicals were central evidence in the case, Colburn couldn't deduce the mechanism until she began to look beyond cancer, the standard disease of toxicology. She and her colleagues traced persistent chemicals like PCBs, DDT, dioxin, and other pollutants into the human body, where they are stored in fatty tissue, passing from prey to predator, and from mother to breastfed baby. The key finding was that these persistent chemicals fake their way into the endocrine system, masquerading as hormones like estrogen and androgen. It's a deadly case of miscommunication. When hormones, our chemical messengers, are released or suppressed at the wrong time in the wrong amounts, life gets bent out of shape.

For example, ecotoxicologist Pierre Béland began finding dead whales washed up on the shores of the St. Lawrence River in the early '90s, sometimes too toxic to be disposed of as hazardous waste. His autopsies typically reveal a devil's brew of breast tumors, stomach tumors, and cysts—all indicators of industrial production gone haywire.

It would be distressing enough if endocrine disruption was taking a toll on the planet's wildlife, but not on humans. However, research is now revealing what some scientists have suspected for years: Humans are by no means immune, since endocrine systems function similarly throughout the animal kingdom. One experiment studied the health of children whose mothers had eaten PCB-contaminated fish during pregnancy. As compared with a control population, the 200 exposed children, on average, were born sooner, weighed less, and had lower IQs.[9]

Let Them Eat Viagra

Other research demonstrated that barely detectable molecules of a certain plastic unexpectedly leached off laboratory beakers, mimicked estrogen, and initiated cancerous growth in lab experiments with human breast cells. Perhaps most startling of all is the 1992 study involving 15,000 men in twenty countries, indicating up to a fifty-percent decline in human sperm production since 1938. "Consider what it might mean for our society if synthetic chemicals are undermining human intelligence in the same way they have apparently undermined human male sperm count," write the authors of *Our Stolen Futures,*[10] who also speculate on possible connections between chemicals and increased incidence of hyperactivity, aggression, and depression—all behaviors regulated by hormones.

The products that cause industrial diarrhea are innocent enough on the surface: plastic packaging, toys, cars, and computer circuit boards. But when we track hazardous chemicals to their sources and endpoints, we slosh through muck every step of the way. Even the familiar bacon on our plates literally results in industrial diarrhea, as writer Webster Donovan describes:

> Raising hogs used to be a family business, until one enterprising North Carolina farmer made it big business. But this booming national industry is churning out at least one unwelcome by-product—millions of gallons of pig waste that soil the water and foul the air.
>
> The smell is what hits you first. Like a hammer, it clamps against the nerve endings of your nose, then works its way inside your head and rattles your brain. Imagine a filthy

dog run on a humid day; a long-unwashed diaper in a sealed plastic bag; a puffed road-kill beneath the hottest summer sun. This is that smell; equal parts outhouse and musk, with a jaw-tightening jolt of ammonia tossed in.

In recent years, this potent mix of acrid ammonia, rotting-meat ketones, and spoiled-egg hydrogen sulfide has invaded tens of thousands of houses—and millions of acres—across rural America. The vapor billows invisibly, occasionally lifting off and disappearing for hours or weeks, only to return while the neighbors are raking leaves, scraping the ice off their windshield, or setting the table for a family cookout.[11]

Isn't it time to say good-bye to the Industrial Revolution—plagued from the start with diarrhea—and bring in a new Era of Ecological Design and Caution?

NOTES

1. Theo Colburn, Diane Dumanoski, and John Peterson Myers, *Our Stolen Future: Are We Threatening Our Fertility, Intelligence, and Survival? A Scientific Detective Story,* p. 137.
2. Personal interview, March 2000.
3. *Living Downstream: An Ecologist Looks at Cancer and the Environment,* p. 99.
4. Ibid., pp. 6–7.
5. "Phasing Out Persistent Organic Pollutants," *State of the World 2000,* p. 85.
6. Dan Fagin, Marianne Lavelle, Center for Public Integrity, *Toxic Deception: How the Chemical Industry Manipulates Science, Bends the Law, and Endangers Your Health,* p. 43.
7. Chris Bowman, "Medicines, Chemicals Taint Water: Contaminants Pass Through Sewage Plants," *Sacramento Bee,* March 28, 2000, online.
8. Douglas Frantz, "E.P.A. Asked to Crack Down on Discharges of Cruise Ships," *American* online, March 20, 2000.
9. Colburn, op. cit., p. 24.
10. Colburn, op. cit., p. 236.
11. Webster Donovan, "The Stink About Pork," *George,* April 1999, p. 94.

Journal Topics

1. Do you agree that Americans just don't want to believe that we are buying products full of "toxic 'bads' like dangerous chemicals"? Why would anyone want to avoid knowing about toxic chemicals in the products they buy?
2. The authors write, "out of 75,000 chemicals now in common commercial use, only about 1,200 to 1,500 have been tested for carcinogenicity." What is your reaction to this? How many chemical products do you routinely use in your home? Do you ever consciously seek out safer, "greener" products? Having read this article, do you think you will modify your own purchasing habits?

Question for Critical Thought

1. DeGraaf, Wann, and Naylor discuss some pretty frightening problems and potential problems from our use of and exposure to massive amounts of chemicals. Many people get sick and even die because of them, and we are causing environmental damage that may not be repairable. What are the psychological reasons that cause us to keep doing business as usual?

Suggestions for Personal Research

1. The authors state, "two out of every five Americans will contract cancer at some point in their lives, including increasing percentages of children." Research these figures. Are they accurate? What are the percentages for children? Compare the figures of percentages of cancers in different age groups today with figures for past decades, going as far back as you can go. What do experts have to say about the increasing ratios of cancers? How many have environmental factors involved? How many have factors of personal choice, such as tobacco and alcohol use and prolonged exposure to the sun?

2. Research the economic impact in America today of avoidable cancers. How much does this cost taxpayers? What impact does it have on insurance costs to consumers?

3. Research the pros and cons of genetically engineered organisms. Do the benefits outweigh the problems caused? What are those problems? What are some possible long-term ramifications?

4. Research the marketing campaign for DDT and the efforts of industry to fight allegations that it was dangerous. How prolonged and expensive was the fight to ban DDT? How many people are estimated to have become ill or even to have died because of the effects of DDT during this time?

5. Research another product, such as the drug thalidomide, which was marketed to women as a treatment for morning sickness in the late 1950s and early 1960s, and which resulted in more than 10,000 children being born with severe deformities, or the Dalkon Shield, a birth control device on the market for four years in the 1970s that caused the deaths of at least 200 women, injured approximately 235,000 other women, and resulted in spontaneous septic abortions and some children being born with severe deformities. What sorts of tests did the companies perform before putting the products on the market? What did they do when evidence came in that their products were dangerous? How long did it take the federal government to act? How many suits were filed against the companies, and how long did the legal battles drag on? What strategies were employed? Were the companies able to continue to profit on dangerous products by delaying recalls or by making interest on the money that they delayed paying out in damages?

6. Research the prevalence of people becoming "allergic to their own homes." How widespread a problem is it? Alternatively, choose another health problem that DeGraaf et al. expose in their article.

7. Conduct your own survey of people's attitudes toward different dangers. Interview as many people as you can, asking them to name what they consider the three biggest threats to American lives. Tabulate them, and see how people's fears correspond to reality.

Multicultural Issues

1. Americans as a group have somewhat different views on issues of health and the environment than people in other countries. Find people from different countries and ask them to contrast views of health and the environment in their country of origin (you may include yourself if you are not American or not originally American) with common views of people in the United States.

2. Sometimes American standards are stricter than those in other countries (at least after a product is proven unsafe). The Dalkon Shield, for example, was proven to be a very harmful contraceptive device with side effects that included sterility, spontaneous abortions, and infant deformities. When the company marketing it, A. H. Robins, could no longer sell it in the United States, it continued to profit from the device by marketing it to women in other countries without adequately warning them of the potential dangers. If you are from another country, have you seen examples of American-made products that turn out not to be safe enough to be legally sold in the United States? If you are from the United States, what do you think about such practices? What message do they send about Americans and about how they view people of other nationalities?

Vocabulary Terms

giddy

carcinogenicity

CFCs

mandated

mimicry

ecotoxicology

hyperactivity

acrid

How Ronald McDonald Became a Health Ambassador, and Other Stories

Michelle Simon

Prereading Question

1. How much junk food do you eat? Have you ever decided that you need to cut back on your consumption of fast food, sodas, and other junk foods? How successful were you?

Any parent who goes grocery shopping with young children in tow will tell you it can be quite a challenge, enduring endless battles over fat- and sugar-laden food products adorned with the latest Disney movie character. But what used to be mainly a private matter has now become a full-blown public debate over the role the food industry plays in children's health.

Major food companies and fast food chains are coming under increasing public scrutiny in the wake of a growing childhood obesity epidemic. Not taking the finger-pointing lying down, Big Food has set its PR machine into overdrive; companies are tripping over each other trying to position themselves as caring about children's health.

But national experts and grassroots activists alike are skeptical. Behind the mainstream media hype, they say, is a trail of deception, lobbying and utter hypocrisy.

The New Greenwashing

To demonstrate its commitment to children, McDonald's has introduced "Happy Meal Choices" so that parents can replace high-fat French fries with "Apple Dippers" (sliced apples and caramel dipping sauce); and instead of a Coke, kids can now have apple juice or milk. There is, however, no substitute for the hamburger, cheeseburger or Chicken McNuggets.

In addition to promoting its food as nutritious, the fast food giant is also attempting to deflect attention from its unhealthy products by promoting physical activity as the "real" answer to the obesity problem. In January, McDonald's announced that it was sending its mascot, Ronald McDonald, into elementary schools to promote fitness among children. Dubbed the company's new "chief happiness officer," Ronald has become an "ambassador for an active, balanced lifestyle," McDonald's Chief Creative Officer Marlena Peleo-Lazar told a government panel studying food advertising.

Nutritionist Melinda Hemmelgarn, a food and society policy fellow with the Thomas Jefferson Agricultural Institute in Missouri, is unimpressed. "Their goal in going into schools is, in a word, branding. If Ronald was truly an ambassador of health, he would promote organic, sustainably produced foods, preferably from local producers to support local economies and protect the environment," she says.

Susan Linn, a psychologist at Harvard's Judge Baker Children's Center and author of *Consuming Kids: The Hostile Takeover of Childhood,* agrees that McDonald's has no place in school. "This is just another marketing ploy. The notion that children need Ronald McDonald to get them to enjoy exercise is bogus. Given the opportunity, kids naturally like to be active," she says.

Another company seeking to teach children about exercise is PepsiCo, the world's fifth-largest food and beverage company. Last fall, PepsiCo reached 3 million students by sending educational materials on fitness to elementary schools. In March, the company targeted all 15,000 middle schools in the United States with its get-fit message. Ironically, PepsiCo already has a strong marketing presence in public schools. Exclusive contracting with school districts allows the company to sell highly sweetened beverages and Frito-Lay–branded junk food, much to the dismay of nutrition advocates.

To deflect critics, PepsiCo has created a Web site (www.healthispower.net) devoted to making the case that it cares about children's health. The site claims that "kid-friendly" school snacks such as Doritos and Pepsi are "part of a balanced diet."

"If companies like McDonald's and Pepsi really cared about children's health, they would stop hawking their wares in schools," says Linn.

The food and beverage giant also recently introduced the "Smart Spot" symbol, a small green circle with the message "Smart Choices Made Easy" that appears on such "healthy products" as Diet Pepsi, Gatorade and Baked Lays. But labeling a food healthy does not make it so. Hemmelgarn thinks the labels can be misleading. "Gatorade is simply sugar and water; it's not a healthy product," she says. Gatorade is often marketed in schools as a healthy alternative to soda.

Nutrition consultant Fern Gale Estrow is concerned about the more insidious nature of the Smart Spot. She says it's a way of marketing to kids because children respond to symbols. She also notes that the Smart Spot symbol contains a check mark that looks very similar to the VeriSign—the symbol that means certain Internet sites are secure. "That's a positive message. A check mark means something is ok; so I have real concerns about the marketing and media messaging," she says.

Another company jumping on the "good for you" bandwagon is General Mills. A leader in children's cereals with annual sales of more than $1 billion, the corporation markets products in more than 100 countries. In January, General Mills reformulated its cereals sold in the United States to contain whole grains, the company says, in response to the federal government's recommendations to eat more whole grains.

But what about all those high-sugar cereals aimed at kids? Marybeth Thorsgaard, a General Mills spokesperson, says, "Even with pre-sweetened cereals, there really is no better breakfast your child could eat in the morning. Pre-sweetened cereals account for less than 5 percent of your sugar for the entire day, but because it's fortified and nutritionally dense for the amount of calories, there really is no better breakfast that your child could eat."

Marion Nestle, Paulette Goddard Professor of Nutrition, Food Studies and Public Health at New York University and author of *Food Politics,* has heard this argument before. "It's hard not to react sarcastically to such statements from cereal makers. I have heard them say the reason sugary cereals are good for kids is because of the milk that's added. That, I suppose, would also be the rationale for giving kids cookies for breakfast. This is a marketing ploy to make people think that whole grain Cocoa Puffs are healthy. Sugar is still the first ingredient," she says.

Estrow is also skeptical about the General Mills move and is concerned that parents might be duped by the new labels. "The level of confusion in nutrition is already massive. Now we have whole grain Lucky Charms. I think it's totally bogus. The dietary guidelines were changed to make a stronger statement about fiber, and this product has less than one gram of fiber per serving. That's just not sufficient," she says.

Nutrition experts say that these health claims boil down to nothing more than marketing gimmicks. Melinda Hemmelgarn says the goal is not to actually promote health, but rather simply "to increase sales by health-conscious parents."

Marion Nestle is more blunt: "Food companies are desperate for sales and growth and if they can use 'health' to sell junk food, they will," she says.

Fighting for the Right to Advertise

The issue of excessive food marketing to kids is fast becoming a hotly debated topic. Many experts, including nutritionist Hemmelgarn, think that marketing to children under age eight is unethical because young children don't have the critical thinking skills to evaluate media messages.

In January, the Institutes of Medicine (IOM, a Congressionally chartered independent advisory body to the federal government) hosted a "Workshop on Marketing Strategies that Foster Healthy Food and Beverage Choices in Children and Youth." Featured speakers included executives from Kraft, PepsiCo and McDonald's, as well as television and advertising representatives. Health advocates had almost no representation.

In its remarks, the mega food conglomerate Kraft Foods (owned by Altria, the company formerly known as Philip Morris) was especially eager to portray itself as doing right by children. Lance Freidmann, senior vice president of global health and wellness, promised that Kraft's R&D team was "hard at work creating new products for kids" that meet the company's self-defined healthy criteria. He also stressed the importance of self-regulation, concluding that industry and government should develop "responsible self-regulatory practices for marketing to kids while permitting companies to compete vigorously in the growing market for healthier foods."

Also in January, Kraft promised to scale back junk food ads to children, a move that earned the company much free positive media. But the potential impact of Kraft's promises isn't entirely clear. For example, only certain products, including regular Kool-Aid, Oreo cookies, several Post children's cereals and some varieties of Lunchables, will no longer be advertised to children under age 11. However, according to a press release, "products that the company will continue to advertise in media aimed specifically at the 6–11 age group include: Sugar-Free Kool-Aid, Half the Sugar Fruity Pebbles cereal, and Chicken Dunks Lunchables Fun Pack." Why are these products fair game? Kraft claims that they offer 'beneficial nutrients or a functional benefit.'"

Less than two weeks later, Kraft turned right around to join with other major food companies and ad agencies to create a new lobbying group, the Alliance for American Advertising. Together, Kraft and fellow members General Mills (which refused to comment on its involvement for this story) and Kellogg comprise the top three advertisers of packaged food to kids. Their combined annual spending on kids' ads is close to $380 million in the United States alone.

Other alliance founders include the American Association of Advertising Agencies and the Grocery Manufacturers of America, two powerful trade associations in their own right. The alliance's stated purpose is to defend the industry's purported First Amendment rights to advertise to children and to promote self-regulation as an alternative to government restrictions.

Susan Linn is appalled at this marketing campaign to defend the right to advertise. "Food companies and the advertising industry should be thinking about their responsibilities to children, not about their 'right' to exploit them. Whether we rely on research or common sense, we know that children are more vulnerable to marketing than adults and that they should be protected because of their vulnerabilities," she says.

Commercial-Free Childhood

Public health advocates are increasingly insisting that parents have the right to raise their children without being undermined by corporate marketersrs, and that the government should restrict commercial access to children.

Those sentiments were expressed in a public statement signed by dozens of leading educators and health advocates, and organized by a public health coalition with which Linn works called the Campaign for Commercial-Free Childhood, stating that children have the fight to grow up in a safe and healthy environment.

This health perspective is beginning to make inroads in the corridors of power. In March, Senator Tom Harkin, D-Iowa, announced plans to introduce a bill to give the Federal Trade Commission (FTC) the authority to regulate advertising to children. Congress stripped the agency of the authority to regulate unfair advertising to kids in 1980, when the commission was on the verge of restraining ads targeting children. As a result, the commission now has greater authority over advertising aimed at adults than at children.

At a press conference surrounded by toys used to promote junk food to kids, Harkin criticized the food industry for contributing to childhood obesity by spending as much as $15 billion last year on marketing to children. Harkin singled out General Mills' Shrek cereal as being particularly egregious. The product consists of sweetened corn puffs with marshmallow pieces and contains 14 grams of sugar per serving. "Kids just see that it's Shrek," Harkin said.

Also in March, the chair of the FTC, Deborah Majoras, announced a workshop to be held this summer on food marketing to children. In the same breath, she also asserted that the agency did not intend to regulate industry. "Let me make this clear, this is not the first step toward new government regulations to ban or restrict children's food advertising and marketing. The FTC tried that approach in the 1970s and it failed," Majoras said at a Consumer Federation of America conference.

The food industry relies on a self-regulatory body called the Children's Advertising Review Unit (CARU) to police its advertising policies.

"We support CARU, a self-regulatory mechanism that reviews all ads directed to children and ensures that they are appropriate for them and takes into account where children are developmentally," says Stephanie Childs, a spokesperson for the Grocery Manufacturers of America, a trade association whose 140 members enjoy annual sales of more than $500 billion in the United States alone, and consists of major food corporations such as Kraft, Nestle and PepsiCo.

She also asserts that "CARU has not hesitated once to let companies know when they think an ad is inappropriate and if the company does not make changes, CARU takes the complaint directly to the FTC." She is unable to point to any examples of CARU doing so, however.

Many experts question CARU's effectiveness. Attorney Ellen Fried teaches food law at New York University and has filed complaints with CARU to challenge food industry ads. "As with all self-regulatory bodies, CARU is hampered by its being a creature of, and supported by, industry." She adds that few people even know CARU exists. "Most of their activity is self-initiated because consumers—as opposed to industry competitors—don't even know where, or to whom, to complain."

Senator Harkin says that self-regulation has been a complete failure. "The current industry efforts are woefully inadequate," he says.

"I sincerely hope that the industry will develop tough and effective marketing guidelines, but when private interests work against the public good like this, government is obliged to act."

When it comes to undermining children's health, many advocates would place Coca-Cola among the worst offenders. The top soda company has spent years becoming firmly entrenched in public schools by forming lucrative, long-term contracts that contain various marketing devices.

Amidst growing health concerns, state legislatures and school districts all over the United States are now attempting to rid schools of unhealthy beverages. Determined not to go down without a fight, Coca-Cola has responded with heavy-hitting lobbying and PR tactics reminiscent of Big Tobacco's response to public health demands.

Veteran dietician Carolyn Dennis, chair of the Kentucky Action for Healthy Kids Taskforce, has been battling Coca-Cola lobbyists for four years. In March, the Kentucky state legislature finally passed a compromise bill that gets rid of soda in elementary schools. Allowing soft drink companies to continue to sell soda in middle and high schools was the only way the bill could possibly pass. Even that wasn't enough for Coke. The bill's original language called for "healthy beverages" to replace soda, but Coca-Cola balked, worried about the implications for its flagship product's reputation. Dennis explains: "The Coke lobbyist wanted the language 'school-day appropriate beverages.' We debated it for hours, and finally my colleagues said, 'Look, if this will get them off our backs, let's do it.' So we compromised on 'school-day approved.'"

Fellow Kentucky schools health advocate Martin Solomon, a retired economics professor, says "numerous studies show conclusively that the significant calorie content of sweetened beverages is a serious threat to children's health. And yet the soda industry continues to say that it's a lack of exercise—not excess calories—that's responsible."

In March, at a conference on childhood obesity at Harvard University, Dr. Maxime Buyckx, Coca-Cola's director of nutrition and health sciences, denied any scientific connection between soda and obesity, despite a Harvard study concluding that each additional soda a child drinks a day increases their risk of obesity by 60 percent.

Professor Richard Daynard, of Northeastern University School of Law and the Public Health Advocacy Institute, challenged Buyckx at the meeting: "Does your company feel any responsibility for creating this situation?" he asked.

In response, Buyckx claimed that the study in question was methodologically flawed and should merely be treated as "hypothesis-generating."

Later, Daynard, a long-time tobacco control advocate, said: "Buyckx's response eerily echoed claims that the tobacco companies made about the numerous studies showing that smoking causes lung cancer—they were all just 'hypothesis-generating.' The tobacco industry is currently defending a racketeering suit brought by the U.S. Department of Justice based on its decades-long campaign of scientific denial and disinformation. Will Coke be next?"

Journal Topic

1. Do you think fast-food restaurants should be held liable in court for "causing obesity"? Should people blame the restaurants and claim that their multibillion-dollar ad campaigns strip of us of any real choice, or do people always have a choice? Or is the truth somewhere in between?

Questions for Critical Thought

1. "Greenwashing" is a term used to describe the dissemination of misleading pro-environmental claims by companies trying to conceal their abuses of the environment while presenting positive public images. Pro-health, pro-environment activists charge that companies like PepsiCo and McDonald's, which send mascots and educational materials about exercise and healthy eating into schools, are engaged not only in greenwashing, but in "branding" as well. Are schools that accept materials and visits from mascots promoting health in the names of their companies actually helping these companies to sell their products? If so, is this ethical?

2. Companies are, as they point out, in business to make profits. They are not responsible for the foods that children eat, they argue—parents are. The government passes laws and regulations to protect the public health, and companies must obey them. Also, companies argue, they have First Amendment rights to advertise. Do they have any ethical responsibilities beyond obeying the law?

3. How far should government go to impose restrictions that might improve children's health? Should the government "restrict commercial access to children"? Or is industry self-regulation enough?

Suggestions for Personal Research

1. Find studies that explore the impact of advertising that promotes fast-food restaurants, junk food, and soda consumption on childhood obesity. What are their conclusions?

2. Compare childhood obesity in America to that in other industrialized nations. What differences do you find? What are the reasons for the differences? Are there any countries whose profiles are becoming closer to America's?

3. Research whether a correlation exists between childhood consumption of junk food and parents' educational backgrounds and income levels.

Multicultural Issues

1. Studies show that childhood obesity is increasing around the world, and some activists say that it is because corporations have successfully exported a desire for the American lifestyle and attitude toward food. Are American food habits replacing healthier modes of food consumption around the world? If so, why?

Vocabulary Terms

scrutiny   compromise
organic   methodology
ploy   disinformation
exploit

CHAPTER 22—CORPORATE AMERICA ESSAY QUESTIONS

These questions are intended as potential essay or research paper topics suggested by the ideas raised in the articles.

1. Many corporations are said to put profit above anything else—the environment, the law, even the health and lives of employees. Other corporations, however, have positive reputations for helping the world through foundation donations, helping the poor, and even going "green." Select one major international corporation and find out about its business practices. Is this a corporation you would want to buy products from or work for, or is it one you will now stay away from?

2. Choose two corporations to compare and contrast—one that seems to take seriously the idea of ethical and altruistic challenges, and one that considers anything other than raising profits (within the boundaries set by laws) to be irrelevant or undesirable. What are the major differences in these corporations' treatments of their employees, worker satisfaction, community satisfaction, and even profitability? (If you have more time, you might want to look at several corporations in each of the two categories.)

3. Corporations get more and more powerful and more and more wealthy thanks to globalization and changes in laws that benefit them. Some critics wonder if the most powerful corporations can be successfully held accountable for the damages that they may do. If the population wanted to force a corporation to make some changes, how could it still do so?

4. Research famous cases addressing corporate accountability, such as the Bhopal toxic gas leak in India, the *Exxon Valdez* oil spill in Alaska, or the Ford Pinto case, in which executives at Ford used a cost-benefit analysis approach when faced with the issue of a fuel system that burst into flames at low impact. Ford had a new design that would have decreased the likelihood of the car exploding, and it would have cost only $11 per car. Ford's analysis showed that the new design would result in 180 fewer deaths. Ford multiplied the $11 by 12.5 million vehicles, putting the cost to the company at $137 million. It set a cost of $200,000 for a human life and $67,000 for injuries and estimated the number of accidents that could be expected. The cost to the company in this scenario, with the gas tank problem left unfixed, was only $49.5 million. Executives decided to save $87.5 million and deal with the lawsuits from the expected deaths and injuries.

APPENDIX I

Commonly Confused Words and Phrases

a, an, and *And* is a coordinating conjunction that links words, clauses, or sentences: *I like movies and concerts. A* and *an* are indefinite articles; they introduce something nonspecific. Use *a* in front of words beginning with consonant sounds: *a book, a house.* Use *an* in front of words that begin with vowel sounds: *an actor, an hour.*

accept, except *Accept* is a verb that means "to receive willingly": *I accept responsibility. Except* is a preposition meaning "but; not including": *You can borrow any book except the one that I am reading.*

adapt, adopt, adept *Adapt* is a verb that means "to make suitable for a new purpose": *She adapted her car to run on electricity;* "to become accustomed to": *We adapted to the mountain's higher altitude;* or "to alter a text into another form, such as a film or play": *The movie was adapted from a bestselling novel. Adopt* is a verb that means "to take on or assume as one's own": *We adopted the practice of using cloth shopping bags. Adept* is an adjective meaning "very skilled at something": *He is adept at calming people down.*

adolescents, adolescence *Adolescence* is a noun referring to the teenage years: *Adolescence is a period of great emotional change and growth. Adolescents* is the plural of adolescent, which means "a person in his or her adolescence": *Adolescents need more sleep than adults.*

advice, advise *Advice* is a noun that means "guidance or recommendations": *She was happier to give advice than to take it. Advise* is a verb that means "to offer advice": *I advise you to start looking for good sources for your paper as early as possible.*

affect, effect Each of these words can be a verb or a noun, but only *effect,* when it means "a result or consequence of an action or other cause," is common as a noun: *An important effect of frequent and vigorous exercise is a lowered risk of heart disease.* The noun *affect* is a psychological term for "an observable expression of emotion": *Psychological disorders can cause people to display variations in their affect. Effect* as a verb means "to bring about": *Therapy and exercise helped to effect a cure for his depression. Affect* as a verb usually means "to produce an effect on, to influence": *Physical ailments can affect mental health.* It can also mean "to pretend to feel an

715

emotional state or to have a particular trait": *She affected nonchalance even though she was rather worried.*

agree to, agree on, agree with *Agree to* means "to consent to do something that has been suggested by another person": *He got an A in the class, and he has agreed to tutor us. Agree on* means to reach agreement about an issue or a situation: *They agreed on a price for the used car after negotiating for half an hour. Agree with* means "to be consistent with": *Her behavior did not agree with the values she claimed to believe in.*

allot, a lot *Allot* means "to give or apportion something to someone as a share or task" or "to distribute something": *We were each allotted ten minutes for our class presentations. He was willing to allot blame for his failure to everyone but himself.* "A lot" means "a large amount of something": *The child ate a lot of candy Halloween night and became quite sick.* Also, remember that "a lot" is two words.

all ready, already *All ready* means "completely ready": *I am all ready to go to the play. Already* is an adverb that means "before now" or "before a certain time": *I've already bought the tickets to the play.*

all right, alright *All right* is an adjective meaning "acceptable": *The play wasn't wonderful, but it was all right. Alright* is a variant spelling of *all right* that is generally considered nonstandard and to be avoided in formal written English.

all together, altogether *All together* means "all at once" or "all in one place: *They recited the pledge all together. Altogether* is an adverb meaning "completely; totally": *I find your attitude altogether refreshing.*

allude, elude *Allude* is a verb that means to suggest or call attention to something indirectly or in a disguised way: *She alluded to our earlier difficulties without naming them. Elude* means to escape from something, or, referring to ideas or achievements, to fail to be attained: *The fox eluded the hounds. Your logic eludes me.*

allusion, illusion *Allusion* is a noun referring to an indirect or passing reference in speech or writing, or, in a work of art or literature, an idea or image that indirectly refers to something outside itself, such as a cultural or literary reference: *The title of Chinua Achebe's novel* Things Fall Apart *is an allusion to a line in a poem by William Butler Yeats.* An "illusion" is a false belief or a false sensory perception: *The artist made a pavement drawing in chalk that gave the illusion of great depth.*

altar, alter An *altar* is a table or other raised structure that is a focal point for a ritual: *They were married before an altar. Alter* is a verb that means to change or cause to change: *When you paraphrase, be careful not to alter the meaning of the original passage.*

among, between *Among* is a preposition meaning surrounded by; in the company of; being a member or members of a group; involving the members of a group; and it is used with more than two items: *Don't worry—you're among friends; an argument broke out among the rivals. Between,* a preposition indicating a separating interval or a relationship between people or things, is generally used with two items, except in some collective relationships: *What I am about to tell you is just between you and me. A fight broke out between the two brothers. In 1940, a pact was formed between Germany, Italy, and Japan.*

amount, number *Amount* is a "non count noun" (nouns that refer to items that can't be counted because they are thought of as wholes), and it means a quantity of something: *I'd love to have a larger amount of spare time; Only a small amount of air leaked out of the tire; I'll have a small amount of penne pasta with my eggplant parmesan* (individual pieces of the pasta could be counted, but we think of the food as a whole, not as a countable collection of components). *Number* is a noun referring to "count nouns" (nouns that can be individually counted): *I have a small number of hours free next week. He shared a number of theories with me.*

anyone, any one *Anyone* is a pronoun meaning any person at all; it is a singular pronoun: *Would anyone like to share a cab with me? Any one* means any single person or thing: *Any one of you would be a fine chairperson.*

are, our, hour *Are* is the second person singular present and the first, second, and third person plural present of the verb *be: I am glad that you are here. I am glad that all of us are here. Our* is a possessive adjective: *We finally finished our group project. Hour* is the period of time composed of sixty minutes.

as, like *As* is a conjunction used to indicate through a comparison the way that something happens or is: *He's as mean as a junkyard dog. Like* is a preposition that means similar to; having the same characteristics or qualities as something else; in a way appropriate to: *That dog looks suspiciously like a wolf. She treated me like a member of the family.*

assure, ensure, insure *Assure* means "to make someone confident of something": *I assure you that I will get to my morning class on time. Ensure* means "to make certain that something will happen": *To ensure that I will get to class on time, I will set my alarm clock earlier than usual. Insure* means "to issue an insurance policy": *I think you should insure your house against earthquake damage.*

aural, oral, verbal *Aural* means "relating to the ear or to hearing": *Musicians need good aural skills to identify chords, intervals, and other elements of music. Oral* means "related to the mouth" or transmitted by word of mouth rather than writing: *The earliest literature was orally transmitted. Verbal* means "relating to words," and it can refer to written as well as spoken speech: *His verbal skills made her both a good writer and public speaker.*

award, reward The verb *award* means to give something as a prize or payment: *She was awarded a medal for her bravery.* The noun *award* refers to a prize or honor given in recognition of an achievement or money given as payment or compensation: *He won an award for his performance. The original award of compensatory damages was reversed on appeal, but the punitive damages award was upheld.* The noun *reward* means something given in recognition of effort or achievement or the offer of money or something else of value for returning lost property, finding a criminal, or providing valuable information: *She offered a reward to anyone who found her lost kitten.* The verb *reward* means to receive what someone deserves or to make a gift of something in recognition of achievement or services: *We were rewarded with good grades after all of our hard work in school.*

awhile, a while *A while* is a noun phrase; *a* is an article, and *while* is a noun meaning "a short period of time." *Awhile* is an adverb meaning "for a while." You can correctly say the following: *I will stay awhile, I will stay a while,* and *I will stay for a while,* but you cannot correctly say, *I will stay for awhile* because the meaning would literally be *I will stay for for a while.* To be safe, the phrase *a while* is more often likely to be correct.

bad, badly *Bad* is an adjective, so it should be used with nouns and pronouns: *No! Bad dog! Badly* is an adverb, so it should be used with adjectives, verbs, and other adverbs: *The car performed badly in the tests* (*badly* is describing the verb *performed*). You can correctly say, *I feel bad,* if you are describing your state of mind, but *I feel badly* would mean that you are not very competent at feeling—the adverb *badly* modifies *feel,* which is a verb, not *I,* which is a pronoun.

bear, bare The verb *bear* means "to carry": *Beware of Greeks bearing gifts—especially if the gift is a really, really big wooden horse.* It also means "to support," "to endure," or "to give birth to a child." The noun *bear* refers to the animal: *Polar bears are facing extinction due to global warming.* The adjective *bare* means *"unclothed," "uncovered," "without addition,"* or "very small; just sufficient": *The candidate won by a bare majority.*

been, being *Been* is the past tense of *be: I have never been this embarrassed before. Being* is the present participle of *be,* which means the form of the verb used in continuous tenses, such as *I am being as careful as I can be.* It is also a noun meaning "existence" or "a real or imaginary creature; an entity": *Many cultures have elaborate myths about how the world came into being. J. R. R. Tolkien's books are full of many strange and fascinating beings.*

beside, besides *Beside* is a preposition meaning "next to": *You can sit beside me. Besides* is a preposition meaning "in addition to" or "apart from": *Who besides me are you inviting to dinner?* It is also an adverb meaning "furthermore": *His essay was turned in late; besides, it was handwritten, not typed.*

book, novel, story, play A *book* is any full-length, bound prose (nonverse) work. A *novel,* however, is a book-length work of prose fiction. Any novel can be a book, but most books aren't novels. Also, don't call a novel or a play a *story;* when referring to works of literature, the terms are not interchangeable. The technical term for a short piece of fiction is *short story: Last week I read* Anansi Boys, *a novel by Neil Gaiman, and two of his short stories: "Troll Ridge" and "Don't Ask Jack."*

brake, break A *brake* is a device for stopping a vehicle: *I think you'd better get your brakes fixed . Break* is a verb that means "to interrupt": *I don't want to break my concentration.* It also means "to cause to separate into pieces," "or to sustain a fracture": *If you break my computer, I will break every bone in your body.* As a noun, it means "an interval or gap": *I can't wait till spring break.*

breath, breathe, breadth *Breath* is a noun meaning "an inhalation or exhalation of air": *Take a deep breath. Breathe* is a verb meaning "to take in then expel breath": *Calm down, and breathe deeply and slowly. Breadth* means "width" or "a wide extent or range": *His breadth of experience made him a wise mentor.*

bring, take *Bring* means "to bear here"; *take* means "to bear there": *After you bring me the cash, you can take the bicycle.*

by, bye, buy *By* means "beside": *I think your keys are over there by your wallet. Bye* is short for "goodbye." *Buy* means "to purchase": *You aren't going to be able to buy anything if you forget your wallet.*

can, may *Can* indicates ability to do something: *I am sure I can get an A in the class if I work hard enough. May* indicates permission or possibility: *Yes, you may leave early. It may snow, so you should put snow tires on your car.*

cannot, can not Technically, both *cannot* and *can not* are acceptable, but *cannot* is the safest choice in most instances because it is far more common, and *can not* is treated in some style manuals as an error—unless the word *not* is supposed to be emphasized, as in *I can **not** emphasize this too much.*

can't hardly *Can't hardly* is nonstandard and should be avoided in formal writing.

canvas, canvass *Canvas* is a noun meaning a type of strong, coarse cloth: *She bought canvas to stretch for her oil painting class. Canvass* is a verb meaning "to solicit votes from," "to try to obtain," or "to ascertain opinion by questioning or polling": *They canvassed potential voters on the propositions.*

capital, capitol The noun *capital* refers to the city that contains the seat of government of a country, state, or region; it also refers to wealth, particularly that used to invest or start up a business: *He put all his capital into the company he started.* The adjective *capital* applied to a crime means one that can result in the death penalty: *First-degree murder is a capital crime in some states.*

censor, censure To *censor* means "to examine a work, like a book, film, song, or letter, and suppress any parts deemed unacceptable": *The Hays Office was formed to censor Hollywood movies.* The noun *censor* refers to a person doing the censoring. To *censure* means "to express severe disapproval of," typically in a formal statement: *The National Council on Public Polls recently censured a pollster for mischaracterizing data.*

choice, choose, chose *Choice* is a noun meaning "the act of selecting or making a decision" or "a course of action, person, or object that is selected": *You need to make a choice. She was their choice for class president. Choose* is a verb meaning "to select," and *chose* is the past tense of *choose: They chose her to be class president.*

cite, site, sight To *cite* is "to give credit to a source used in research": *Don't forget to cite the sources of all the information that you use, including ideas that you do not directly quote.* A *site* is the location on which something is constructed or where human activities occurred and left material evidence: *Cahokia is the site of an ancient Native American city in Illinois. Sight* is the faculty of seeing.

clothe, cloth *Clothe* is a verb meaning "to dress; to put clothes on": *The bridesmaids were clothed in lavender gowns.*

clothes, cloths *Clothes* are what we wear: *You have great taste in clothes. Cloths* is the plural of *cloth: I always keep some cloths near the TV to clean DVDs.*

coarse, course *Coarse* is an adjective that means "rough" or "crude": *Coarse speech can be offensive. Course* is a noun that means "a route or direction": *The boat changed course,* or a "series of lectures and lessons": *We took a course in anatomy,* or "one of successive parts of a meal": *We cooked a five-course dinner for our parents' anniversary party.*

compare, contrast *Compare* is a verb meaning "to examine two or more items for the purpose of noting similarities and differences": *I compared three schools before making my final choice. Contrast* is a verb meaning "to present a difference": *His soft voice* *contrasted with his blunt comments. Contrast* can also be a noun meaning "a state of being markedly different": *The contrast between your first draft and your final version is striking and shows your hard work.*

compare to, compare with   When you are stressing similarities, use *compare to: She complimented him by comparing his cooking to that of a gourmet chef.* When you are emphasizing both differences and similarities, use *compare with: I compared the car Elian recommended with the one Lynnda recommended, but I still couldn't make up my mind.*

complement, compliment   *Complement* means "to make complete": *The wine was a perfect complement to the dinner.* It can also refer to a number or quantity of something required to complete a group: *They didn't have the full complement of workers.* A *compliment* is an expression in praise of something: *She paid him a compliment on his cooking.*

continual, continuous   *Continual* means "frequently recurring; repeating at intervals": *The continual phone calls from telemarketers destroyed her concentration. Continuous* means "going on without interruption": *After continuous criticism, he stormed out.*

could have, could of   *Could* is the past tense of *can,* and if we want to refer to the past and make a statement about actions that did not happen, we follow it with *have: If I had started my paper earlier, I could have finished it in time. Could of* is just a slurred version of *could have,* and it should not be used in your writing.

council, counsel, consul   A *council* is "an advisory or legislative body of people formally constituted to offer guidance or to manage the affairs of a school, city, county, or other entity." To *counsel* is "to give advice." A *consul* is an official appointed by a government to live in a foreign city to promote the government's interests there.

criteria, criterion   A *criterion* is a standard by which something can be evaluated; *criteria* is the plural: *What are your criteria for rating movies?*

data, datum   *Data* are facts and statistics gathered for analysis; *datum* is the singular form. *He collected a lot of good data for his research paper.*

decent, descent, dissent   *Decent* means "morally respectable," "appropriate," or "of an acceptable standard": *She made a decent offer on the house. Descent* refers to the action of moving downward: *We watched the descent of the hot air balloon. Dissent* as a verb means "to express opinions that vary from those that are commonly, officially, or previously expressed"; as a noun, it refers to the expression of such opinions: *A few delegates dissented from the majority; their dissent caused some concern.*

desert, dessert   The verb *desert* means "to treacherously abandon": *The soldier who deserted was court martialed.* The noun *desert* refers to dry, barren areas of land. A *dessert* is a sweet course served at the close of a meal: *You cannot have your dessert until you finish your Brussels sprouts.*

device, devise   A *device* is an item made for a specific purpose: *Rube Goldberg was a cartoonist best known for drawing bizarre and humorous imaginary devices that performed simple tasks in ridiculously convoluted ways.* It is also an element in an artistic work designed to achieve a particular effect: *As plot devices go, I think the evil twin* *sister has been overused.* The verb *devise* means "to invent or plan through careful thought": *The evil twin sister devised a diabolical plan to murder her good twin and take her place; however, since she was a fraternal twin, it really didn't work out.*

different from, different than *Different from* is a preposition that precedes a noun phrase: *Yogi is different from your average bear. Different than* is a preposition that precedes a noun clause: *He is looking different than he used to look.*

discreet, discrete To be *discreet* is to be "careful and unobtrusive in speech and actions; prudent; circumspect": *She made a discreet inquiry. Discrete* means "separate and distinct": *The teacher divided the class into two discrete groups before the spelling bee.*

disinterested, uninterested *Disinterested* originally meant "impartial; not influenced by any personal interest or considerations of advantage," and it retains that meaning: *The competition requires a disinterested judge.* The word became confused with *uninterested,* which means "unconcerned" or "not interested in something," and is sometimes used that way, especially by people unaware of the original meaning of *disinterested.*

e.g., i.e., etc. *E.g.* means "for example"; it is the abbreviation for the Latin phrase *exempli gratia* ("for the sake of an example"). *I.e.* means "that is to say"; it is the abbreviation of the Latin phrase *id est* ("that is"). *Etc.* (note that it is not spelled "ect.") means "and so on"; it is the abbreviation of the Latin phrase *et cetera* ("and the rest").

elicit, illicit *Elicit* is a verb meaning "to draw out information or a reaction by one's questions or actions," and *illicit* is an adjective that means "prohibited by law, moral standards, rules, or customs": *His accusations of illicit behavior elicited an angry response.*

emigrate, immigrate To *emigrate* means "to leave one country to settle in another": *My parents emigrated here from overseas.* To *immigrate* means "to come to live in a new country": *She wants to immigrate to England.*

enervate, energize The *ener* of *enervate* causes many people to assume that it means the same thing as *energize,* but they are actually opposites. The verb *enervate* means "to cause someone to feel weakened or drained of energy," and the adjective means "lacking energy or vitality": *Enervated by the 110-degree heat, the dog napped in the shade.*

everybody, every body *Everybody* means "every individual; all persons"; however, it is a singular pronoun: *Everybody here agrees with the plan. Every body* means each individual body: *After the vampire fled the morgue, every body was carefully inspected for tell-tale marks.*

everyone, every one *Everyone* means "every individual; all persons"; it is also a singular pronoun: *Everyone wants to be treated fairly and equally. Every one* means "each one": *Every one of us was satisfied with our treatment.*

explicit, implicit *Explicit* means "expressly and clearly stated": *Her instructions are explicit, so there is no room for doubt. Implicit* means "implied but only indirectly expressed": *The song's implicit message was controversial.* It can also mean "with no qualification or question": *He had an implicit faith in basic human decency.*

faint, feint A *faint* sight, sound, or smell is one that is barely detectable: *We heard the coyotes faint howl in the distance. Faint* can also mean "weak and dizzy": *The heat made me feel faint.* To *faint* means "to lose consciousness": *The shock caused him to* *faint*. A *feint* is a "deceptive or pretended blow" or a "mock attack": *The boxer's feint fooled his opponent.* The verb form of *feint* means to make such a movement: *The boxer feinted left before delivering a blow on the right.*

farther, further *Farther* refers to physical distance: *Portland is farther north than San Francisco. Further* refers to an extent of time or degree: *My paper requires further research.*

fewer, less Use *fewer* with things that can be individually counted: *I always read labels to see which snacks have fewer calories.* Use *less* with abstract qualities or quantities that cannot be individually counted: *After I finished my paper, I felt a lot less stress about the class.*

forth, fourth To move *forth* is "to move out from a starting point," "to move into view," or "to move forward": *The witness was hesitant to come forth.* To be *fourth* is to be number four in a sequence.

good, well *Good* is an adjective: *What a good dog! Well,* except when it means "healthy," is an adverb: *You performed very well on the exam. I hope you are well soon.* (Avoid using *well* as a filler word at the beginning of sentences—it tends to add nothing to the meaning and is a distraction.)

hear, here *Hear* means to use the ear to perceive sounds: *We could hear the crickets chirping. Here* means "in, at, or to this place or position": *Why don't you come over here?*

heroine, heroin *Heroine* is a female hero (although the term *hero* is increasingly used without reference to gender); *heroin* is a drug: *The heroine of the film stopped the drug dealers from releasing tainted heroin on the streets.*

hole, whole A *hole* is a hollow place, aperture, or cavity in an object: *I lost some money because I had a hole in my pocket. Whole* means all of something or "in an unbroken state": *I cannot believe you ate a whole pizza.*

immanent, imminent, eminent *Immanent* refers to qualities that are spread throughout something; inherent: *She believed that altruism was immanent in human nature. Imminent* means "about to happen": *His arrival is imminent. Eminent* means "famous and respected": *The speakers they invited were eminent in their fields.*

immoral, amoral *Immoral* means going against standards of morality: *Most people consider theft to be immoral. Amoral* means something outside of the scope of moral standards or someone with no understanding or moral standards: *Infants are amoral beings.*

imply, infer To *imply* is to suggest something without expressly stating it: *Are you implying that I made a mistake?* To *infer* is to conclude information from evidence and reasoning instead of from direct statements: *She inferred from his manner that he was having second thoughts.*

incidence, incidents *Incidence* is the occurrence, frequency, or rate of something: *People who live near toxic waste disposal sites may have a higher incidence of cancer than the rest of the population.* An *incident* is an event or occurrence: *I think we should just forget that unfortunate incident and move on.*

incite, insight To *incite* means "to urge, encourage, or stir up," especially when referring to violent or unlawful behavior: *They were accused of inciting rebellion. Insight* means "the capacity to gain a deep and accurate understanding of a person or thing" or an example of such an understanding: *She has a lot of insight; let me share some of my insights with you.*

incredible, incredulous *Incredible* means "extraordinary" or "impossible to believe": *His story was too incredible for anyone to take seriously. Incredulous* means "unable to believe something": *When he told me his story, I was incredulous.*

instance, instants An *instance* is an "example or single occurrence of something": *Can you think of a single instance when you were on time?* An *instant* is a "brief, precise moment of time"; *instants* is the plural form.

intents and purposes, intensive purposes *For all intents and purposes* is a commonly used expression meaning "in all practical respects." Do not write "for all intensive purposes," which would mean purposes that were intensive in some way. *He left his iPod sitting on the park bench when he went to shoot some hoops, which, for all intents and purposes, was an invitation to grab it and run away.*

its, it's *Its* is the possessive form of *it.* Remember that possessive pronouns are already possessive in form, so you should not add an apostrophe to make a pronoun possessive. (After all, we say, *his,* not *hi's.*) *It's* is the contraction of *it is.*

knew, new *Knew* is the past tense of *know. New* means "not used; in the original condition; of recent origin or arrival": *I knew that I should get some new clothes before going out on job interviews.*

know, no To *know* is "to be aware of something through observation or information": *Did you know all the answers on the exam? No* means "not any" or is an exclamation used to give a negative response: *No, I am afraid I got some of them wrong.*

later, latter *Later* is the comparative form of *late,* which means "taking place near the end of a particular time or taking place after the usual or expected time": *We finished work later than we had hoped. Latter* means "indicating the second or second mentioned of two people or things": *I could have bought either a desktop or a laptop computer, and I chose the latter.*

lay, lie To *lie* is an intransitive verb, which means that it doesn't take a direct object: *I want to lie down.* (*Down* is an adverb, not an object.) To *lay* is a transitive verb, which means it needs a direct object; we use it when we are doing something to something: *Every evening I lay out the clothes I plan to wear the next day.*

lead, led The noun *lead* is a kind of metal. The verb *lead* means "culminate in" or "to show the way to a destination by going in front of" or "to be in charge of": *Who is going to lead the committee? Led* is the past tense of *lead: I led the committee last time.*

leave, let The verb *leave* means "to depart or to go away from," "to cause to remain behind," or "to cut off a relationship from someone": *I didn't mean to leave my keys in the car when I locked it.* The noun *leave* refers to a period of time when a person has permission to be absent from work or from the armed forces. The verb *let* means "to allow" or "to permit": *Will you let me help you?*

literally, figuratively *Literally* means "exactly"; use it only for something that is actually true: *When I told him to go jump in a lake, I never thought that he would take it literally and actually jump in a lake. Figuratively* is the term to use when an expression is metaphorical (departing from a literal use of words): *When I said I was hungry enough to eat a horse, I meant it figuratively, not literally; I could not possibly eat a horse—not even a small pony.*

loose, lose *Loose* is an adjective meaning "not tight": *Since I lost weight, my clothes feel too loose. Lose* is a verb meaning "to misplace" or "to be defeated": *Be careful, or you will lose your money.*

media, medium A *medium* is a singular form of a noun meaning "a means by which something is communicated or expressed: *Text messaging was her preferred medium of communication.* It also refers more specifically to a print or electronic form of communicating news and information: *Television is a more popular medium than radio. Media* is the plural form: *Television and radio have become more popular than print media.*

might have, might of *Might* is the past tense of *may,* and if we want to refer to the past and make a statement about actions that did not happen, we follow it with *have: I might have done a better job if I had started earlier. Might of* is just a slurred version of *might have,* and it should not be used in your writing.

miner, minor A *miner* works in a mine. A *minor* is a person who is not legally adult. *Minor* is also an adjective that means "not serious" or "unimportant": *It was just a minor infraction.*

moral, morale *Moral* is an adjective meaning "concerned with the standards and principles of right and wrong": *It is our moral obligation to try to make sure that future generations inherit an Earth that can sustain them.* It is also a noun meaning "a lesson, especially one concerned with what is right": *The moral of the story was to treat others with kindness. Morale* refers to how a person or members of a group feel about themselves and their abilities: *The team's morale was high after winning six games in a row.*

nowadays, now a days, now and days *Nowadays* means "at the present time," but it is very informal English and should be avoided in formal writing. *Now a days, now and days,* and other similar phrases are misspelled versions of *nowadays.*

passed, past *Passed* is the past tense of *pass: We passed them on the way here. Past* refers to an earlier time or times: *Historians study the past.*

peace, piece *Peace* means "freedom from war or disturbance": *We hope to see peace in the world during our lifetimes.* A *piece* is a portion of an object or material: *I would like another piece of pie, please.*

percent, percentage *Percent* is specific and should be used with a number: *You should tip the server fifteen percent. Percentage* is not specific and should not be used with a number: *Do you know how to convert decimals and fractions into percentages?*

plain, plane *Plain* means "easy to understand" or "not elaborate or decorated": *Just tell me the plain truth.* A *plane* is "a flat or level surface" or "a level of existence or thought"; *plane* is also short for *airplane.*

ponder, wonder, wander To *ponder* means "to carefully think about something before making a decision or reaching a conclusion": *She pondered whether to buy a desktop computer or a laptop.* (Note that *ponder* isn't followed with *about* because it already means "to think about.") To *wonder* means "to be curious to know something": *I wonder what I will get for my birthday.* (Note that "I wonder" expresses curiosity—it doesn't ask a question, so you should not use a question mark unless you combine it with an actual question.) To *wander* is "to walk in an aimless way": *We wandered around the city just enjoying the sights.*

poor, pore, pour *Poor* means "lacking sufficient money or material goods": *The gap between the wealthiest Americans and the poorest keeps getting bigger every year.* To *pore* means "to be deeply absorbed in the reading or study of something," and it requires a word like "over" after it: *She pored over the letters she received.* To *pour* is "to flow rapidly and steadily" or to cause something to do so: *The rain poured down. I poured my feelings out.*

practical, practicable *Practical* means "concerned with actual use or practice rather than mere theory": *I try to be practical when I devise a budget.* *Practicable* means "workable or feasible; able to be put into practice successfully": *We need to come up with a practicable solution to our problem.*

pray, prey To *pray* is "to express thanks to or make a request of a deity or an object of worship": *He prayed that he would get a good grade on the test.* The noun *prey* refers to "a person or animal that is hunted" or "a person who is taken advantage of or who is vulnerable to harmful emotions or beliefs": *Superstitious people are easy prey for con artists. Prey* is also a verb meaning "to hunt, take advantage of, or exploit": *Many con artists prey on the elderly.*

precede, proceed To *precede* is to "come before": *A comma should precede a coordinating conjunction when it connects two independent clauses.* To *proceed* is to "begin or continue a course of action; to move forward": *The detectives proceeded with their investigation.*

precedence, precedent *Precedence* refers to "status established in order of urgency or importance": *Necessities take precedence over luxuries.* A *precedent* is "an earlier event or action that is used to justify similar occurrences at a later time": *I am not going to make an exception to the rules because I do not want to establish a precedent.*

presence, presents *Presence* is "the state of being present; current existence," and *presents* are gifts: *The presence of tape, colorful paper, and ribbon suggested that there were presents to be wrapped.*

principal, principle A *principal* is the head of a school. A *principle* is a fundamental truth or proposition upon which something is founded: *Freedom of speech is one of the most important principles of a democracy.*

quiet, quit, quite To be *quiet* means "to make little or no noise": *She gave a quiet laugh.* To *quit* means "to resign": *He quit his job when his boss refused to give him a raise,* or "to stop": *You would live longer if you quit smoking;* or "to leave, usually permanently": *"You are too much for me, Ennis. . . . I wish I knew how to quit you." Quite* means "absolutely; completely" or "to a fairly significant extent": *I am quite sure. It is quite hot today.*

quote, quotation *Quote* is a verb meaning "to use the exact words": *When you quote a passage, be sure to attribute it to its source.* A *quotation* is "a group of words repeated by someone other than the original source": *A clever quotation can be a great way to begin an essay.* The word *quote* can also be used to mean a quotation, but some style manuals advise avoiding this usage.

rain, reign, rein The noun *rain* refers to falling drops of water in the atmosphere; the verb *rain* means "to pour down": *We had a lot of rain this year; after a small tornado, it rained toads in the town of Villa Angel Flores.* The noun *reign* refers to the period of a sovereign's rule; the verb *reign* means "to rule": *Queen Elizabeth I's reign is referred to as the Elizabethan Era, and Elizabeth reigned for forty-five years.* A *rein* is "a long, narrow strap used to control a horse"; it can also be used as a verb meaning "to bring under control; restrain": *I think we should try to rein in our spending.*

raise, rise To *raise* something is "to lift or move up"; it is also a noun referring to an increase in wages. *Rise* means "to move from a lower position to a higher one." Use the verb *raise* if you are talking about performing an action with something: *I think we should raise the hem just a little.* Use *rise* if you are or someone else is moving upward: *Please rise from your seats.*

real, really *Real* means "not artificial" or "actually existing": *Pinocchio wanted to be a real boy. I'm sorry to tell you this, but Santa isn't real.* *Really* is an adverb, so use it only with adjectives, verbs, and other adverbs. It means "in actual fact" or "very, thoroughly": *Did we really win? The game was really close.*

sea, see A *sea* is a division of an ocean; to *see* means "to perceive with the eyes": *Did you see how blue the sea was?*

should have, should of *Should* is used to give advice, to talk about duty, or to indicate what is probable. If we want to refer to the past and make a statement about actions that did not happen, we follow it with *have: I now realize that I should have started working on my paper earlier.* *Should of* is just a slurred version of *should have,* and it should not be used in your writing.

simple, simplistic *Simple* means "uncomplicated; not complex" or "easily understood or accomplished": *She had a simple plan, and it was simple to carry it out.* *Simplistic* means "treating complex issues as if they were much simpler than they really are": *Politicians often treat serious problems simplistically.*

sit, set To *sit* is an intransitive verb, which means that it doesn't take a direct object: *Would you like to sit?* To *set* is a transitive verb, which means it needs a direct object; we use it when we are doing something to something: *Would you like to help me set the table?*

stationary, stationery *Stationary* means not moving: *The flying saucer was stationary in the sky over Washington.* *Stationery* refers to writing paper and envelopes: *He wrote all his letters on monogrammed stationery.*

than, then *Than* is used to indicate the second item in a comparison and in expressions introducing contrast: *Her dog is smaller than her cat.* *Then* means "at that time"; "after that; next"; and "in that case": *If you study hard, then you should pass the test.*

they're, their, there *They're* is the contraction of *they are.* *Their* is the possessive adjective: *They're both glad that they passed their classes.* *There* means "in, at, or to this place or position": *You can put your coat over there on the coat rack.* (Think about the word *here,* which also means "in, at, or to this place or position"; when you see *here* in *where* or *there,* you know that these words also refer to place.)

threw, through *Threw* is the past tense of *throw; through* means "moving in one side and out the other" or "up to and including" or "by means of": *I threw the book at Dave. After seeing the look on his face, I ran through the house as quickly as I could to escape.*

to, too, two *To* is a preposition or part of the infinitive form of a verb. *Too* means "also" or "to a higher degree than desired": *Are you too tired to go to the dance, too? Two* is the number.

unique, very unique, quite unique *Unique* is an adjective that refers to someone or something that is the only one of its kind; therefore, "very unique" and "quite unique" are not logical expressions and should be avoided.

vain, vane, vein The adjective *vain* can mean "conceited; having an excessively high opinion of one's own worth": *Cinderella's two sisters were extremely vain.* It can also mean "producing no result": *They took the herbal supplements in the vain hope of losing weight without having to diet or exercise.* A *vane* is a broad blade on a rotating axis, as found on windmills and weathervanes. A *vein* carries blood toward the heart.

waist, waste The *waist* is the part of the body above the hips and below the ribs. *Waste* is a verb meaning "to use carelessly; to throw away; to squander": *He didn't want to waste his money on expensive designer clothes.*

weak, week *Weak* means lacking physical strength or energy; a *week* is seven days.

wear, were, where The verb *wear* means "to have on one's body as clothes or accessories": *I like to wear a hat on sunny days. Were* is the past tense of *are: We were at the theater last night.* It is also used to indicate the *subjunctive mood*—meaning that we can use it for something that is contrary to actual fact: *If I were you, I'd be more careful. Where* means "in, at, or to this place or position": *Where did you go?* (Think about the word *here,* which also means "in, at, or to this place or position"; when you see *here* in *where* or *there,* you know that these words also refer to place.)

weather, whether, rather *Weather* refers to the state of the atmosphere at a place; *whether* expresses doubt or choice between alternatives: *Whether we go to the beach depends on how nice the weather is. Rather* is used to indicate preference: *I'd rather go to the beach than to the mountains.* It can also mean "on the contrary," "to a certain degree," or "instead of."

which, witch, that Many grammar experts advise using *which* to introduce nonrestrictive information and *that* to set off restrictive information: *My car, which is currently at the garage, ran into the tree that was blocking the road.* A *witch* is a person thought to have magical powers, typically evil: *Dorothy was pursued by the Wicked Witch of the West.*

who, whom *Who* forms the subjective case of the pronoun: *Who is going to wash the dishes? I wonder who will volunteer. Whom* forms the objective case of the pronoun: *Do not ask for whom the bell tolls.* Increasingly in modern English, *whom* is vanishing, especially when speaking, but in formal writing, it is usually best to adhere to the grammatical rules.

whose, who's *Whose* is an interrogative possessive pronoun and adjective: *Whose car is parked in my space?* *Who's* is the contraction of *who is: Who's going to wash the dishes?*

would have, would of *Would* is the past tense of *will,* and if we want to refer to the past and make a statement about actions that did not happen, we follow it with *have: If I had known it was your birthday, I would have gotten you a gift. Would of* is just a slurred version of *would have,* and it should not be used in your writing.

your, you're *Your* is a possessive adjective: *Your pizza is ready. You're* is the contraction of *you are: You're welcome to drop by anytime.*

A P P E N D I X | II

Common Correction Marks

Symbol or Abbreviation	Meaning
abbr	faulty abbreviation
add	add missing word
adj	misuse of adjective
adv	misuse of adverb
agr	faulty agreement
apos	problem with apostrophe use (incorrect or missing)
appr	inappropriate language
art	an article is misused or missing
awk	awkward phrase or sentence
cap or three lines under letter	capitalize
case	error in pronoun case
coh	problem in coherence
coord	faulty coordination
cs	comma splice
dev	needs more development
dict	faulty diction
dm or dng or dang	dangling modifier
-ed	error in –ed ending
ESL	second-language problem
exact	language needs to be more exact
frag	sentence fragment
fs	fused sentence
hyph	hyphen error
idiom	idiom
inc	incomplete construction
irreg	irregular verb error
ital	italicize or underline
jarg	jargon
lc or / through letter	make lowercase
mix	mixed construction
mm	misplaced modifier
mood	error in mood
nonst	nonstandard usage
num	error in use of numbers

om	omitted word
P	There is a punctuation error here—figure out what it is.
pass	passive voice
pn agr	error in pronoun agreement
pron	pronoun problem of some kind
proof	proofread this carefully
ref	it is not clear what the pronoun refers to
rep	unnecessary repetition; redundancy
run-on or r-o	run-on sentence
-s or -es	error in -s ending
sexist	sexist language
shift	shift in voice, tense, person, etc.
sl	slang
sp	spelling error
STET	Oooops—my bad—ignore my editing mark here. I goofed.
sub	faulty subordination
sv agr	error in subject-verb agreement
t	error in verb tense
trans	transition needed
usage	error in usage
v	voice
var	sentence variety
vb	error in verb form
w or wdy	wordy
ww	wrong word
//	faulty parallelism
^ or upside-down carat	insert something here
# or / between letters	insert space
⌣	close up space
¶	start new paragraph here
No ¶	this should not be the start of a new paragraph
ℐ	delete this
∽	transpose these
X	There is a problem here somewhere—find it.

CREDITS

Photos/Art

Text

CHAPTER SIXTEEN

CHAPTER SEVENTEEN

CHAPTER EIGHTEEN

CHAPTER NINETEEN

"New Branded World" by Naomi Klein from *No Logo: Taking Aim at the Brand Bullies*. Copyright © 2000 by the author and reprinted by permission of St. Martin's Press, LLC.

"But First a Word from our Sponsors" by James B. Twitchell from *Wilson Quarterly*, Summer 1996, p. 68. Reprinted by permission of the author.

"Stealth TV: Channel One Delivers News and Advertising to the Classroom" reprinted with permission from Russ Baker, from *The American Prospect*, Volume 12, Number 3: February 12, 2001. The American Prospect, 2000 L Street NW, Suite 717, Washington, DC 20036. All rights reserved.

"Group wants Shrek off anti-obesity campaign" by David Crary reprinted with permission of The Associated Press.

"Child Caring: Fighting Obesity, But Fronting for Junk Food" by Barbara Meltz reprinted with permission of *The Boston Globe*.

CHAPTER TWENTY

"From: *Corporate Media and the Thread to Democracy*" by Robert McChesney, excerpted from pp. 5–22. Copyright © 1997. Reprinted with the permission of Seven Stories Press, www.sevenstories.com.

"Address to the Third National Conference on Media Reform" by Bill Moyers. Reprinted by Creative Commons license from democracynow.org.

"Grand Theft: The Conglomeratization of Media and the Degradation of Culture" by Ben Bagdikian reprinted with the permission of the author and originally appeared in Multinational Monitor.

"Ruper Murdoch's Cool New Thing" by Edie G. Lush. Reprinted with permission.

CHAPTER TWENTY ONE

"War Takes Up Less Time at Fox News" by David Bauder reprinted with permission of The Associated Press.

"US Weekly Blacks Out Hilton Coverage" by John Rodgers reprinted with permission of The Associated Press.

"We Ignored Paris Hilton" reprinted with permission of The Associated Press.

"Rediscovering the World" by Thomas Ginsberg. Reprinted from *American Journalism Review*, January/February 2002. Reprinted with permission

"What the Mainstream Media Can Learn from Jon Stewart" by Rachel Smolkin. Reprinted with permission from *American Journalism Review*.

CHAPTER TWENTY TWO

"The Chain Never Stops" by Erich Schlosser reprinted with permission of *Mother Jones*. © 2001, Foundation for National Progress.

"The Unofficial History of America™" by Kalle Lasn from pp. 65–71 of *Culture Jam: The Uncooling of America* by Kalle Lasn. Copyright © 1997 by Kalle Lasn. Reprinted by permission of HarperCollins Publishers.

"Business as Usual" by Joel Bakan reprinted with the permission of The Free Press, a Division of Simon & Schuster Adult Publishing Group, from *THE CORPORATION: The Pathological Pursuit of Profit and Power* by Joel Bakan. Copyright © 2004 by Joel Bakan. All rights reserved.

"Industrial Diarrhea" by John DeGraff, David Wann, and Thomas Naylor. Reprinted with permission of the publisher. From *Affluenza*, copyright © 2006 by DeGraff, Winn, Naylor. Berrett-Koehler Publishers, Inc., San Francisco, CA. All rights reserved. www.bkconnection.com

"Junk Food's Health Crusade: How Ronald McDonald Became a Health Ambassador, and Other Stories" by Michelle Simon reprinted with the permission of the author and originally appeared in Multinational Monitor.

Websites

Yahoo! search page reproduced with permission of Yahoo! Inc. © 2010 by Yahoo! Inc.

Google pages reproduced with permission of Google Inc. © 2010 by Google.

INDEX

A

abbreviations, 218, 490
abstracts
  in APA-style papers,
    317–318
  in research
    prospectus, 130
  in scientific papers, 153
  use of, 73
abusive ad hominem
  fallacy, 103
abusive argument against the
  person fallacy, 102, 107
accident, fallacy of, 100
accidental plagiarism, 187
acronyms, 218
action verbs, 207
active reading, 78–80
  annotating a text, 81–84,
    122–123
  double-column note
    taking, 85–86
  finding and noting main
    ideas, 80–81
  outlining material, 81. *See
    also* outlines
  previewing, 79–80
  reviewing notes, 81
  rhetorical précis, 87
  SASE method, 84–85
active voice, 239–240
ad hoc hypothesis, 100, 110
ad hominem fallacy, 103
adverbs
  conjunctive, 208–209, 210
  parallel structure in, 240
advertising, 536–584
  "But First, a Word
    from Our Sponsors"
    (Twitchell), 559–569
  citations for
    advertisements, 296

demographics and, 544
"Fighting Obesity but
  Fronting for Junk
  Food" (Meltz), 580–583
"Group Wants Shrek
  off Anti-Obesity
  Campaign" (Crary),
  580–583
Net intrusions, 486
"New Branded World"
  from *No Logo* (Klein),
  546–558
propaganda devices in,
  541–544
psychological appeals in,
  538–540
"Stealth TV: Channel
  One Delivers News
  and Advertising to the
  Classroom" (Baker and
  Smith), 570–579
alignment, 249, 315
Allmusic database, 53
"All Your Base Are Belong to
  Us" video clip, 488
alphabetization of
  reference entries, 281,
  284, 317
Amazon.com, 481
American Psychological
  Association (APA), 314,
  320. *See also* APA style
"The Amorality of Web 2.0"
  (Carr), 517–522
AND operator, 29
Andreessen, Marc, 483
anecdotal evidence
  fallacy, 101
animal studies, 318
annotated bibliographies,
  311–313
Annotated List of Works
  Cited, 311–313

Annotated List of Works
  Consulted, 308–310
annotating a text, 81–84,
  122–123
antecedents, 230
anthologies
  citing multiple selections
    from, 293–294
  parenthetical citations of
    works from, 280
  scholarly articles in, 68
  works-cited entry for
    entire, 288, 322
  works-cited entry for work
    from, 283, 288–289, 290
"AP: We Ignored Paris"
  (Associated Press),
  639–642
APA (American
  Psychological
  Association), 311, 315
APA style. *See also*
  References, APA-style
  abstracts, 314–315
  annotated sample paper
    in, 327–342
  corrections and
    insertions, 316
  first page of the body, 318
  footnotes, 316
  format of authors'
    names, 320, 324
  general appearance,
    315–316
  headers, 316
  in-text parenthetical
    citations, 327–329
  references page, 320
  running head, 316
  sections and subsections,
    318–319
  title and byline, 316
  title page, 316